A Machine-Gunner in France

A Machine-Gunner in France

The Memoirs of Ward Schrantz, 35th Division, 1917–1919

By Ward Schrantz
Edited by Jeffrey L. Patrick

Number 16 in the North Texas Military Biography and Memoir Series

University of North Texas Press
Denton, Texas

Printed in the United States of America.

10 9 8 7 6 5 4 3 2 1

Permissions:
University of North Texas Press
1155 Union Circle #311336
Denton, TX 76203-5017

The paper used in this book meets the minimum requirements of the American National Standard for Permanence of Paper for Printed Library Materials, z39.48.1984. Binding materials have been chosen for durability.

Library of Congress Cataloging-in-Publication Data
Schrantz, Ward L., 1890–1958, author. | Patrick, Jeffrey L., 1963– editor.
A machine-gunner in France : the memoirs of Ward Schrantz, 35th Division, 1917–1919 / by Ward Schrantz ; edited by Jeffrey L. Patrick.
pages cm.
Includes bibliographical references and index.
ISBN-13 978-1-57441-753-1 (cloth : alk. paper)
ISBN-13 978-1-57441-761-6 (ebook)
1. LCSH: Schrantz, Ward L., 1890–1958. 2. United States. Army. Division, 35th—History. 3. Soldiers—United States—20th century—Biography. 4. World War, 1914–1918—Personal narratives, American. 5. Argonne, Battle of the, France, 1918. 6. World War, 1914–1918—Campaigns—France. 7. World War, 1914–1918—Regimental histories—United States. I. Title.

D570.3 35th . S37 2019
DDC 940.4/1273092 [B] –dc23
2018052342

A Machine-Gunner in France: The Memoirs of Ward Schrantz, 35th Division, 1917–1919 is Number 16 in the North Texas Military Biography and Memoir Series

The electronic edition of this book was made possible by the support of the Vick Family Foundation. Typeset by vPrompt eServices.

Contents

Acknowledgments

In *Guarding the Border*, Ward Schrantz's 1912–1917 memoirs published in 2009, I paid tribute to his family and friends who initially preserved his unique archival legacy of manuscripts, photographs, and ephemera. This second volume only increases my admiration for them. His family recognized the historical value of his reminiscences and photographs, and gave the archive to Schrantz's fellow journalist, Jasper County (Missouri) historian Marvin VanGilder. VanGilder, in turn, generously donated the materials to the Jasper County Records Center and made them available to researchers.

Retired Jasper County Archivist Steve Weldon, the former custodian of the Schrantz materials, along with Records Center volunteers Marjorie Bull and Doris Wardlow, were likewise dedicated to the preservation and accessibility of an enormous number of primary source documents relating to the rich history of Jasper County. All three continued to answer my many questions, locate and copy important materials, and provide support and encouragement.

Special thanks are due to my good friends Kip Lindberg and Brian Grubbs, who read the manuscript and made numerous helpful suggestions. Fred Pitts and Reverend Tim Coppinger, friends and fellow scholars of the 35th Division, also freely shared their own research and urged me to complete this work.

Drs. Richard S. Faulkner and Mitchell Yockelson, acknowledged experts on the American Expeditionary Forces, offered valuable advice and strongly endorsed the manuscript. Ronald Chrisman, editor of the University of North Texas Press, was an advocate for this project from the beginning and skillfully guided me through the publishing process.

Renee Glass, local history librarian at the Springfield-Greene County (Missouri) Public Library, cheerfully responded to reference questions and searched for newspaper microfilm. Christopher Wiseman, director of the Joplin History and Mineral Museum, helpfully located and provided scans of photographs of the 128th Machine Gun Battalion's parade in Joplin in 1919.

And finally, I would be remiss if I did not thank my family for their patience and understanding. Although they have not come to know Ward Schrantz as well as I have, they have learned that he was an American hero, and have agreed to allow me at least one more foray into his world.

Introduction

On February 27, 2011, Missouri-native Frank Buckles, the last United States veteran of World War I, died at the age of 110. With the passing of Corporal Buckles, Americans lost their final living link to the "doughboys" of 1917–18. Now, only the diaries, letters, memoirs, photographs, and memorials the veterans left behind keep alive the memory of what has become a forgotten war—a conflict lost in the popular imagination between the "brother against brother" romanticism of the Civil War and the admiration for the "greatest generation" that defeated fascism in World War II.

We are fortunate, then, that men like Ward Loren Schrantz of Carthage, Missouri, not only led troops in combat during World War I, but also compiled an extensive record of both his experiences and those of his fellow Carthaginians during their odyssey to "make the world safe for democracy" by defeating the forces of Imperial Germany.

Schrantz, a newspaperman, author, and historian, faithfully served his country as a soldier for nearly half a century. His service took him from the fields of Missouri, to Texas in the turbulent days of the Mexican Revolution, to the trenches of France with their machine guns, barbed wire, and mud in 1918, and to the perilous Mediterranean Sea in 1943. He began his unusual military career in the Missouri National Guard in 1909, then joined the Regular Army three years later. Discharged in 1914 after serving on the Mexican border, he returned to the Missouri National Guard, and went back to the border during General John J. Pershing's "Punitive Expedition" in pursuit of Pancho Villa from 1916 to 1917. During World War I, Schrantz led troops in combat as a captain in command of Company A, 128th Machine Gun Battalion, 35th Division. As a reserve infantry officer, he continued his military education in the 1920s and 30s and prepared for a future war, and after Pearl Harbor he contributed to the liberation of Europe by commanding a troop transport on numerous trips overseas. He finally retired from the Army Reserve in 1950 with the rank of colonel.

Throughout it all, the highly literate Schrantz recognized the unique nature of his army service, and at various times he recorded his experiences while in uniform. He assembled the typed reminiscences of his travels in the United States and throughout the world in several large notebooks, preserving an important record of the American armed services in transition.

In a continuation of my earlier study of Ward Schrantz, this volume reproduces that portion of his memoirs that document his service in a federalized National Guard unit from 1917–19. Although numerous published reminiscences by American soldiers who served in the "Great War" are readily available, few veterans of the Missouri-Kansas 35th Division left behind extensive memoirs of their service.[1] Ward Schrantz, on the other hand, filled dozens of pages with his recollections of what it was like to be an officer in the Missouri National Guard and a company commander in the A.E.F. (American Expeditionary Forces). He enjoyed a "front row seat" for the European war, avoiding a quiet, stateside training assignment by leading his men to France, where he experienced life in the trenches and an intense period of combat in the largest battle in American military history to that time.

1. Examples include two University of Missouri Press titles, both edited by Robert H. Ferrell. William S. Triplet's *A Youth in the Meuse-Argonne: A Memoir, 1917–1918* was published in 2000, while *The Autobiography of Harry S. Truman* (containing a relatively brief chapter on his World War I service) appeared in 2002. Triplet was a non-commissioned officer in one of the division's infantry regiments, while Truman served as an officer in one of the 35th's artillery regiments.

His is not simply a stereotypical story of trench warfare, poison gas, and mass slaughter, however. In fact, Schrantz extensively documented a wide range of experiences in the United States and Europe, including recruiting citizen-soldiers for his company, preparing his men for service "over there" in an Oklahoma training camp, braving the U-boat-infested Atlantic, facing his German foes for the first time while manning frontline trenches in France's Vosges Mountains, and returning home to the adulation of his fellow Missourians.

Ward Schrantz's writings are significant for a number of other reasons. Although he was not a professional writer, Schrantz's education and small-town newspaper experience allowed him to craft a well-written and entertaining narrative. Because he doesn't seem to have prepared his memoir for publication, the Missourian wrote in an honest, unpretentious, and unassuming style, with extensive detail, vivid descriptions, and occasional humor. Although he did not hesitate to criticize civilians, his fellow officers, and even his superiors, Schrantz's recollections also include a number of self-deprecating remarks and anecdotes.

For historians of social history and military material culture, Schrantz recorded important aspects of soldier life during this period. He described in detail the daily life of a soldier, including living conditions, relations between officers and enlisted men, their training, and the horrific experience of combat. Information about army rations, weapons, and equipment was deemed worthy of inclusion as well. He painted literary portraits of the varied collection of officers and enlisted men who populated the A.E.F., from career soldiers to new recruits, from shirkers to determined professional warriors. Schrantz also recalled the colorful civilians he encountered, including French and English women and children who had become accustomed to the grueling existence experienced by non-combatants in a war zone.

Any reader of Ward Schrantz's account will quickly realize that his is not a romantic, whitewashed account of the war, celebrating an American victory won by heroic doughboys. His gritty, realistic memoir records how soldiers behaved and how World War I was actually fought. For instance, Schrantz confessed that one of his officers went outside official "channels" to scrounge badly needed parts for their vehicles; he reported that some of his comrades were accidentally killed in their training camp and at the front, and finally, once the Missourians plunged into the Meuse-Argonne Offensive, he noted that physical exhaustion, confusion, command blunders, and incredible heroism all played a role in the fighting.

In addition, Schrantz did not serve in a famous A.E.F. division, such as the 1st ("Big Red One"), General Douglas MacArthur's 42nd ("Rainbow"), or Sergeant Alvin York's 82nd ("All American"), but in a less celebrated division with an interesting but troubled history. Composed largely of National Guardsmen from Kansas and Missouri, the 35th "Santa Fe" Division spent time in the trenches in a quiet sector at the front in the summer of 1918 and was held in reserve during the first great American offensive of the war at St. Mihiel. The Midwesterners were finally bloodied during the Meuse-Argonne operation that September. The 35th did not perform well for a number of reasons and made only moderate gains against stiff German opposition. After five days, Schrantz and his comrades were replaced by fresh American troops. Although Schrantz did not try to justify his division's lack of success, his memoir provides a valuable "common soldier's" view of why the "Santa Fe" men failed to live up to the expectations of the American high command.

Finally, because he served in a federalized National Guard unit, Schrantz provides a fascinating look at the trials and tribulations of citizen-soldiers in the war's opening months, including their contentious relationship with Regular Army officers. Schrantz not only had difficulties recruiting his company to "war strength" in the spring of 1917, but thanks to decisions in Washington, his regiment lost its long-established and cherished identity and the services of a number of respected career National Guard officers.

The young soldier who found himself caught up in the "war to end all wars" began with a modest upbringing in a small Midwestern town. Born in Stark County, Ohio, on November 13, 1890, Ward Loren Schrantz moved with his parents to Carthage, Missouri, a short time later. Located about 150 miles south of Kansas City, in southwest Missouri, Carthage was founded in the 1840s and had experienced great unrest and devastation during the Civil War, but following the war impressive commercial growth and the arrival of railroads had made it one of the most important towns in that part of the state. By the 1890s, Carthage was known for rich deposits of zinc, lead, and building stone. In 1900, the town's population stood at more than 9,000.[2]

Tragedy struck the Schrantz family not long after their arrival in Carthage. Thirty-four-year-old Henry Schrantz died in late January 1893, leaving behind a thirty-two-year-old pregnant wife and five children. Although it must have been quite difficult for her to keep the family together, by 1910 Catherine (Kate) Schrantz had remarried and all but one of her children were employed, including her son Ward, who had joined the business department of the *Carthage Evening Press* (one of the town's two newspapers) the year before.[3] Schrantz actually began his career as a carrier boy with the *Carthage Democrat*, then went to work for the *Press*, becoming a "printer's devil" (apprentice) in 1908, then a reporter, and finally circulation manager.[4] Rather than continue working for the newspaper, or in one of the other prosperous commercial enterprises in Carthage, young Schrantz was soon convinced that he needed to make soldiering his profession.

Such a desire must have been relatively common in the town of Carthage. During the Civil War, Carthage and Jasper County were bitterly divided between Unionists and Secessionists, and units from both sides found recruits in the area. In addition to being the scene of a major battle on July 5, 1861, Carthage was devastated twice by Confederate forces before peace returned in 1865. After the conflict, the fertile soil and numerous business opportunities in southwest Missouri made the region an attractive one for

2. One publication described Carthage as "the most beautiful city of its size in America," featuring "surpassing natural attractiveness, handsome residences, stately business blocks, shady avenues, magnificent court house, pretty lawns, and enchanting park." Walter Williams, *The State of Missouri: An Autobiography* (Columbia, MO: E.W. Stephens, 1904), 309–10. An extensive profile of the town at the turn of the century may be found in Howard L. Conard, ed., *Encyclopedia of the History of Missouri*, 6 vols. (New York: The Southern History Company, 1901), I: 508–15.

3. Twelfth Census of the United States, 1900, Population Schedule for Carthage, Marion Township, Jasper County, Missouri, T623, Roll 866; Thirteenth Census of the United States, 1910, Population Schedule for Carthage, Marion Township, Jasper County, Missouri, T624, Roll 791. Henry Schrantz married Catherine Ream on February 19, 1878. Homer Schrantz, their first child, was born in 1879 but died the following year. The remaining children included Henry H., born in 1881; Lottie, born in 1883; Rachel V., born in 1886; Michael Roy, born in 1888; Ward, born in 1890; and Katie, born in March 1893. Reverend George Witwer and Ananias Clime Witwer, *Witwer Genealogy of America* (No place: No publisher, 1909), n.p.

4. *Carthage* (MO) *Evening Press*, December 11, 1950.

settlement by Union veterans. A local Grand Army of the Republic post flourished, and young Schrantz had frequent contact with veterans from both sides of the conflict. "Veterans of the great civil war were all about in my home town at that time," he recalled, "and many of them willing enough to tell their experiences to an interested small boy."[5] Despite the often unromantic and vicious nature of the guerrilla war in southwest Missouri from 1861–1865, veterans who had served in various campaigns could still recount tales of glory, honor, and heroism for impressionable youths. As one historian explained it, veterans "remained powerful arbiters of popular values," who urged the young to treat "war as an adventurous and romantic undertaking, a liberating release from the stultifying conventions of civilized society."[6]

Even if the Civil War had not affected Carthage, young men could look to the events of 1898 for inspiration. Company A of the 2nd Missouri Infantry, known locally as the "Carthage Light Guard," had enthusiastically marched off when the United States went to war with Spain. Schrantz himself was part of the crowd that gathered to see the volunteers leave the local train station. "In memory, looking back at them," he noted many years later, "they still seem huge," with their blue uniforms, knapsacks, and breech-loading rifles.

Although the company remained stateside, that very fact probably reinforced the belief in the glorious nature of war. The city's citizens did not have to hear of the horrific combat deaths of local sons or the other hideous aspects of battle, and it is quite likely that few members of Company A returned to Carthage deeply scarred or disillusioned by their military experience. Instead, the one notable casualty from the town was Charles P. Wood, the unofficial "soldier-correspondent" for one of the local newspapers, who kept readers abreast of the company's activities. Wood did not suffer terribly from a battlefield wound, but died of disease at a training camp in Georgia. He was returned to lie in state in the rotunda of the local courthouse, a shining example of heroic

5. In fact, a Civil War veteran lived in Schrantz's household. His widowed mother married Dr. Wilson D. Monnett, a veteran of the 55th, 115th, 132nd, and 148th Indiana Infantry regiments, in 1900. *Carthage* (MO) *Evening Press*, December 13, 1918.

6. David M. Kennedy, *Over Here: The First World War and American Society* (New York: Oxford University Press, 1980), 178. Kennedy includes a brief but valuable examination of the heroic legacy of the Civil War and views of war in the early 1900s.

sacrifice by a promising young resident of the city. Later in 1898, another volunteer infantry company left Carthage for the war, and a third served in the Philippine-American War. All these units returned from the "glorious adventure" to the cheers and praise of the local citizenry, having maintained the proud tradition of volunteer service.

Schrantz's decision to pursue a military career was apparently not a sudden one—he had always been enamored with the military. "Nature, kindly or otherwise, endowed me with an innate interest in military subjects and in military history and my boyhood in Carthage, Mo. was filled with thoughts along that line," he wrote years later. Schrantz played "war" with his schoolmates (one friend recalled he was always a leader). The *Carthage Evening Press* explained that "in younger years, it is said that he actually cried because he had not lived in the time of the civil war [*sic*] and had missed an opportunity to obtain actual war experience."[7] The same newspaper praised Schrantz when he enlisted in the Regular Army, noting that he was "an enthusiastic militiaman and anxious to enter the service of Uncle Sam," well-informed regarding army duties, and one whose friends predicted would advance rapidly in the military. "Young Schrantz is well deserving of success," the *Press* article continued. "He is an industrious worker, is thoroughly dependable, has no bad habits and does everything thoroughly which he undertakes. The PRESS and his many friends wish him success in his new undertaking."[8] With the encouragement of family and friends, at the age of twenty-one Ward Schrantz resigned his newspaper job and set off on a military odyssey that was to last, with some interruptions, for nearly fifty years and through two world wars.

After a few weeks of instruction at Jefferson Barracks outside St. Louis, Schrantz joined Company F, 22nd U.S. Infantry in the Texas border town of El Paso on December 7, 1912. Company F was charged with patrolling the border to prevent armed parties from entering or leaving Mexico, keeping arms or ammunition from being taken into that country, and protecting American property. Over the next few weeks, Schrantz and his fellow Regulars did exactly that, without incident.

7. *Carthage* (MO) *Evening Press*, November 13, 1918.

8. *Carthage* (MO) *Evening Press*, October 21, 1912.

In early 1913, with the murder of Mexico's president and a revolt against the government in that nation's capital, Schrantz and his comrades found themselves on a train to Texas City, Texas, to prepare for possible offensive operations south of the border. The young soldier was elated by the prospect of combat: "Off to the wars! Altogether I was in a most happy frame of mind—possibly because I had never yet seen war."

After the 22nd Infantry arrived in Texas City, "a vigorous training period" followed, according to Schrantz, so that the men were "toughened and in as good physical condition as it is possible for men to be." Although other troops sailed south to seize the Mexican port city of Veracruz in April 1914, Schrantz's regiment remained behind in Texas City. Finally, after nearly two years in the ranks, Schrantz became disillusioned with the Regular Army. It did not appear likely that more American troops would see action against the Mexicans. Unable to obtain an officer's commission, and with a lucrative job offer at home, Schrantz decided to leave the service. Taking advantage of a decades-old option available to enlisted men, Schrantz purchased his discharge and left the Regulars in November 1914, his career as a professional soldier at an end.

Back in Missouri, Schrantz rejoined Company A, 2nd Missouri Infantry, his old National Guard unit. The Guard labored under "many handicaps," Schrantz explained, but the new non-commissioned officer participated in regimental maneuvers and tried his best to make sure that Company A could furnish a framework of professional soldiers around which a larger wartime force could be assembled when needed. "I added my efforts to those of the others to build the unit up," he proudly recalled, knowing that "it was certain that it would be called if America needed more troops."

Schrantz got his wish in March 1916. That month, Mexican revolutionary Pancho Villa and his followers slipped across the border and launched a surprise attack on the town of Columbus, New Mexico. Two months later, President Woodrow Wilson ordered the National Guards of Texas, New Mexico, and Arizona to the border to protect against bandit incursions while Regular Army forces under General John J. Pershing tried to capture the elusive Villa south of the border. In June, Wilson ordered the rest of the National Guard into service. Schrantz returned to the

Texas-Mexico border the following month, as Company A and the entire Missouri National Guard went into camp at Laredo. Weeks of inactivity sapped the morale of most of the Guardsmen. Schrantz's unit, however, remained optimistic: "In my own company, morale was good enough. . . . We made a point of pride in being punctiliously military with our officers, however well we had known them at home. We had, in fact, a very good opinion of ourselves."

By early 1917, the Missourians had participated in numerous drills, patrols, maneuvers and other training, but had not actually traded shots with Mexican regulars or bandits. With the border relatively safe, and relations deteriorating with Kaiser Wilhelm II's Germany, the National Guard troops came home. That January, Schrantz and the other members of the 2nd Missouri were mustered out of federal service.

On January 14, 1917, the National Guardsmen of Company A, 2nd Missouri Infantry returned to Carthage, Missouri, and soon settled back into their civilian jobs and former routine. The Missouri troops had gained valuable experience that would soon be put to good use, however, for, as Schrantz wrote, "within less than three months after the return of my own company to civil life, the United States was at war with Germany."

With congressional approval of a declaration of war against Germany on April 6, 1917, the Carthage guardsmen spent that spring and summer recruiting new soldiers for their company, but on August 17, 1917, "after a splendid send-off by the home town," they left for the war. Newly promoted Captain Schrantz led Company A to Camp Doniphan (Fort Sill) Oklahoma, where the Missourians were converted from infantrymen to machine gunners and prepared for duty in Europe.

Unlike during their recent stint on the Mexican border, the Missouri troops would experience a far more arduous and costly period of service in France. It fell to Captain Schrantz to lead his fellow townsmen into combat for the first time and endeavor to bring them safely home, while maintaining the reputation of Carthage and guaranteeing that the grim mission of defeating the enemy was accomplished. Company A, the "Light Guard," arrived in France in May 1918, two months after the Germans began a series of massive offensives in an attempt to break the stalemate of trench warfare before a significant number of American troops arrived on the Western Front. By the time the men of the "Light Guard" returned to the grateful citizens of Carthage in 1919, they had suffered from gas, cold, hunger, and sickness, watched comrades die, and battled tenacious and more experienced German soldiers ensconced in well-prepared defensive positions. The citizen-soldiers from Carthage, Missouri, were no doubt grateful, though, that conscientious, dedicated, and talented former Regular Army veterans like Ward Schrantz had led them through the hell of the Great War.

Editorial Method

Two of Ward Schrantz's memoirs of his service in World War I are preserved in the Marvin VanGilder Collection at the Jasper County Records Center in Carthage, Missouri. One untitled manuscript begins in early 1917 and ends in the summer of 1918. The other, entitled "Memoirs of a Machine Gun Captain" focuses on the period from the fall of 1917 through Schrantz's promotion to major in 1919. A third manuscript (actually the second part of the memoir held in the Jasper County Records Center) is in the collection of the Harry S. Truman Presidential Library and Museum in Independence, Missouri. References to the manuscript at the Harry S. Truman Presidential Library will be abbreviated "HST" in the notes. All three manuscripts have been combined here into a single narrative.

It is difficult if not impossible to determine precisely when he penned these recollections, as the manuscripts are undated. Because there are references to both World War II and the Korean War in the memoir, it is logical to assume that Schrantz composed the bulk of his recollections in the 1950s, only a few years before his death.[9]

9. On January 20, 1962, Schrantz's widow Delphia wrote a letter to the Truman Presidential Library and Museum in Independence, Missouri, offering to donate his manuscript, which she found to be "interestingly written." Apparently she donated only the second volume of his memoir. In July 1962, Milton F. Perry of the Truman Library wrote Mrs. Schrantz that he had read the manuscript "with considerable interest" and found it "remarkably well done," noting that Schrantz was a "good writer, with a fine eye for detail." Although he asked Delphia Schrantz to donate the first volume of her husband's memoir as well, she apparently did not. The first volume was eventually donated to the Jasper County Records Center. Ward Schrantz File, Box 11, Records of the Thirty-Fifth Division Association, Harry S. Truman Presidential Library and Museum, Independence, Missouri. (Hereafter HST.)

Schrantz also penned a serialized history of the Carthage Light Guard (Company A, 2nd Missouri Infantry) for the *Carthage* (MO) *Evening Press* that was published from October 1931 to June 1935. Understandably, this detailed narrative of the service of the company did not include most of the personal anecdotes found in his memoir. Excerpts from the *Evening Press* serialization have been integrated into this narrative to add detail to the events discussed in Schrantz's memoir.

Schrantz's recollections appear here largely as written. Minor changes in spelling have been made and additional words (indicated by brackets "[ ]") have been added for clarity's sake. Redundant words have been omitted. Ship and newspaper names have been italicized. Non-standard capitalization has been corrected. Brackets and a question mark [?] indicate unclear or unreadable words. The spelling of French place names has been standardized for consistency.

Chapter 1

Back from the Border

Early January 1917 found then-Sergeant Ward Schrantz and his comrades in Company A, 2nd Missouri Infantry, the old "Carthage Light Guard," in the cavalry barracks at Fort Riley, Kansas. The Missourians had just returned from several months in the Laredo, Texas, area, guarding the U.S.-Mexican border against potential attacks by Mexican bandits.

Mobilized in June 1916, the company arrived in Laredo on July 7 and established camp on the outskirts of the city. Practice marches, drills, parades, and guard duty kept the men occupied for several weeks, until Company A was ordered to leave the city to garrison a remote village in the Laredo District. On September 8, Schrantz and his fellow Guardsmen moved into the village of Ramireno, about fifty miles from Laredo on the Rio Grande, where they lived in a fortified camp until October 16. Following that pleasant, uneventful duty, the company returned to Laredo and participated in a four-day tactical exercise that pitted them against other National Guardsmen and U.S. Regulars. Their stint on the border finally at an end, the Missourians boarded a train to return north on December 28, 1916. Awaiting their official muster out at Fort Riley, "most of the guardsmen spent their spare time reading or wandering over the reservation," Schrantz recalled, "staring at the points of interest of that old post from whence cavalry in the old Indian days had sallied out as occasion warranted to restore peace to the plains." On January 13, 1917, the Carthage men received a month and thirteen days' pay and the cash due them for their clothing allowance, all in gold coins, and climbed aboard a train for home. At 9 a.m. the following day the train rumbled into the Carthage station. A large crowd of well-wishers, Spanish-American War veterans, and the local band waited to welcome the returning warriors. The company marched to their armory, where a few announcements were made before the men were dismissed and "broke ranks with a cheer," as their service on the Mexican border became "a closed episode."

Their respite from active duty would be short-lived, however. The United States moved inexorably toward involvement in the war in Europe, and as Schrantz recalled, "the fat was now in the fire and beginning to sizzle, and Carthage, like other communities, was buzzing with talk of impending conflict."

With the Mexican border service in the background but with a world war still in progress in Europe, it seemed to me that I had already served a somewhat overlong apprenticeship as an enlisted man and that if I ever was going to see service as an officer that it was high time that I do something about getting a commission.[1]

The National Defense Act of 1916 had provided that for the purpose of securing a reserve of officers available for service as temporary officers in the Regular Army or volunteers that the president might commission officers up to the grade of major, inclusive, for an "Officers Reserve Corps of the Regular Army." I felt sure that I could pass any examination likely to be given and that the recommendation for a commission received upon my discharge from the Regular Army would be of assistance. I accordingly made application, sending in the required number of character recommendations, etc. required. However I made this direct and not through National Guard channels and it came back with a notation that since I was a member of the National

1. The 2nd Missouri Infantry spent several months guarding the Texas-Mexico border while General John J. Pershing and his Regular Army "Punitive Expedition" pursued bandit Francisco "Pancho" Villa in northern Mexico. The regiment arrived at Laredo, Texas, on July 7, 1916, and was mustered out of service at Fort Riley, Kansas, on January 13, 1917. Schrantz and the other members of the Carthage company returned home the following day.

Guard I would need recommendations from my company, battalion and regimental commander.[2]

These were easily secured but my regimental commander suggested that I not be in any hurry about sending them in—that my company commander probably would soon be made a major and that it was quite likely that I would be made captain of my home town company. I took the suggestion of a captaincy with some mental reservations but a little delay could make no difference and if there was to be a vacancy in my company I might reasonably expect a lieutenancy. So I waited.

A rather amusing incident happened to me about this time which, with a different turn, might have rendered a commission of no use to me.

There had been a number of grocery store hold-ups recently and on going home one Saturday evening past a residence grocery I saw the little clump of loungers around the stove with their hands in the air, and one of them waved his hand at me. I passed on a few steps thinking it a joke, then wondered and turned to go back. Just then a young man ran from the store, thrust a dingy-appearing nickel-plated revolver close to my stomach and demanded in quavering voice that I put up my hands. My hands at the time were in my overcoat pockets and I felt reluctant to remove them, joke or not. I declined. The pistol was wavering in nervous circles but the muzzle was still on the target and I felt it wise to comply with the next order to come back into the store. The boy was scared and hence dangerous.

Inside an older man thrust another revolver at my anatomy and repeated the demand that I put up my hands. Hesitating still, I probably would have complied except for his next words: "Put up your hands, you so and so," he barked, "Or I'll knock the hell out of you." This was reassurance. All I was perturbed about at the moment was the possibility of getting shot and it seemed to me the pair would not start any shooting if they could avoid it. I again declined to take my hands out of my pockets.

2. The National Defense Act authorized the president to appoint and commission citizens who, after examination, were found "physically, mentally, and morally qualified" to serve in the Officers' Reserve Corps. U.S. Government, *The Statutes at Large of the United States of America from December, 1915, to March, 1917*, Vol. 39, Part I (Washington, D.C.: U.S. Government Printing Office, 1917), 189–90.

Continuing threats the pair backed into the street, requiring me at gun's point to accompany them. My courage was rising at having gone thus far unshot and I shouted at a passing car. "Don't yell at those cars," said the older man. I called to the next one. "Let's get out of this," said the younger man turning and running down the street. The older one cursed me and followed.

Stepping in the store I ascertained that the pair had robbed the till and were about to search those present when I appeared. The proprietor, in response to my question if he had a gun, took one from under the counter. Outside I could see nothing of the men. Knocking at a neighboring house in front of which a car stood I asked the owner, a young man calling on a girl there, if he would help me search for the pair. He agreed. As we were ready to start the girl came running out. "Can I go too?" she queried. We had no objection—it was an affair like a comic motion picture—so in the car we scoured that section of the town in the chance the men might have been on foot and still about, but of course never saw them, nor could the police notified by the storeowner do so.[3]

As I went home much later I reflected that perhaps I had not come out of the affair too badly. I at least had not lost the thirty or forty dollars I had on my own person and I had blundered along in time to save the men in the store being searched. My mother, when I narrated my adventures, commended me with some obvious reservations. It was not difficult to see that she felt a son of hers should have come out of the affair with a complete victory, leaving the bandits dead or in jail. That was really my own view of the matter, but I had not been able to figure out how to do it. But she probably was appreciative of my personal safety. When I told her my story I had tossed on the table a five and a ten-dollar gold piece, saying that I had nearly lost them and that she might have them. After her death some eight or nine years later I found that she had placed them in her safety deposit box at the bank and kept them.

3. The bandits robbed two stores on the night of January 20, 1917. Shortly after 9 p.m. they struck the W.H. Wilbur and Son store on the corner of Chestnut and Clinton Streets and nabbed about $40. About an hour later, they stole about $45.35 from the store of William French on the corner of Garrison and Pine Streets. Schrantz was carrying approximately $30 at the time of the robbery. As he implies, Schrantz borrowed a gun from the store to use against the robbers. *Carthage* (MO) *Evening Press*, January 22, 1917.

The newspapers gave my refusal to put up my hands some prominence, so it became a subject of some personal raillery. My friends gently suggested that my conduct showed a low order of intelligence or else that I had been too frightened to control my muscles. I secretly hoped that there might be those not so well acquainted with me who would misinterpret it as courage. What it really had been was a conviction gained from the men's demeanor that they did not want to shoot anyone. However when they were captured in nearby Webb City a few weeks later after a similar hold-up there was an exchange of shots in which a policeman was wounded in the leg. They went to the penitentiary for the Webb City incident and I was never called upon to testify against them.

In February, Germany started her unrestricted submarine warfare and the course of events steadily carried us toward war as American ships were armed and sent into the submarine zone and some sunk.[4]

The government lost no time in checking up on its troops. On February 5 Company A, home less than three weeks, was given what was termed its annual spring inspection—and did not show up so good. If the government had wanted the National Guard in good condition it should have kept it in federal service, for everywhere the return home had been marked by two principal disorganizing elements. First, there was the necessity of getting a new job to take the place of the old one lost when called to the border. Many men had wandered away in search of work. Secondly, there had been an epidemic of marriages, presence evidently making the heart grow fonder. This too had taken the thoughts of the newly returned guardsmen from matters military and when Capt. Raymond Sheldon, U.S. Army, scanned the ranks of soldiers lined up to greet him that night, he could count three officers and only

4. On January 9, 1917, Kaiser Wilhelm II authorized the German Navy to recommence unrestricted submarine warfare, effective February 1, 1917, indicating that American merchant or naval vessels traveling to Allied ports would be subject to attack without warning. American merchant ship losses from February 1–April 6, 1917, included the *Housatonic* (February 3, 1917), no casualties; the *Lyman M. Law* (February 12, 1917), no casualties; the *Algonquin* (March 12, 1917), no casualties; the *Vigilancia* (March 16, 1917), loss of 15 lives; the *City of Memphis* (March 17, 1917), no casualties; the *Illinois* (March 18, 1917), no casualties; the *Healdton* (March 21, 1917), loss of 20 lives; the *Aztec* (April 1, 1917), loss of 28 lives; the *Marguerite* (April 4, 1917), no casualties; and the *Missourian* (April 4, 1917), no casualties.

twenty-odd men.[5] Whereupon he smiled, for the summer before he had been the lieutenant colonel of the Second Illinois on the border and had seen that organization melt away after its return—and he understood. Perhaps he smiled too at what he sensed ahead of him, for Capt. Sheldon, as events later showed, was to be a lieutenant colonel again within six months and within a year after that was to be wearing the eagles of a colonel and a decoration awarded for valor on the battlefield.

The First and Third Missouri Infantry regiments, which had left the border early, were called into federal service [on] March 26 under the militia clause of the Constitution for a second time, this time to guard railways and bridges.

On the night of April 2 there was a great loyalty meeting—a war meeting—held in Carthage, presided over by Mayor C.B. Gammon and Judge Howard Gray and numerous speeches were made, urging a solid support of President Wilson.[6] The city had been aflutter with flags since early morning and the meeting solemnly resolved that "We unreservedly endorse the steps taken by the president to uphold the honor of the country and to protect the admitted rights of American citizens upon the high seas." It was time, too, for such support for the chief executive.

On April 6 the United States entered the war.[7]

As the regimental commander had predicted, Capt. E.B. Trowbridge, my company commander, had been elected major

5. Raymond Sheldon, born in New Jersey on April 19, 1876, was commissioned a second lieutenant of infantry in 1898. He was promoted to first lieutenant in 1899, and to captain in 1904. As Schrantz indicates, Sheldon was promoted to major in May 1917, lieutenant colonel (temporary) in August 1917, and to colonel (temporary) in June 1918. U.S. Adjutant General's Office, *Official Army Register, December 1, 1918* (Washington, D.C.: U.S. Government Printing Office, 1918), 595. Sheldon was awarded the Distinguished Service Cross in 1918 for his actions in combat with the 307th Infantry Regiment in October and November 1918. He died on October 1, 1930.

6. Charles Breckenridge Gammon was born on November 15, 1864, in Cadiz, Kentucky. He died on March 13, 1938, in Ontario, California. Howard Gray was born in Delaware County, Iowa, on June 5, 1861, and died in Carthage on September 5, 1939. He was buried in Park Cemetery in Carthage. He served as judge of the Circuit Court, 25th Judicial Circuit of Missouri from 1904–08, and judge of the Springfield Court of Appeals from 1909 to 1913. *Joplin* (MO) *Globe*, September 6, 1939.

7. The Senate voted for Wilson's declaration of war on April 4, 1917. The House of Representatives did likewise on April 6. A total of 455 members of Congress voted for war, while 56 opposed the measure. Ironically, Perl D. Decker, who represented Schrantz's district in the House of Representatives, was one of those who voted against the measure.

by the line officers of the regiment—promotion by election was required by Missouri law—and on April 9 a field officer of the regiment conducted an election in my own company to fill the vacancy.[8] In our unit it was deemed unmilitary to "campaign for office" and no one did so. I expected the first and second lieutenants to be moved up and that I would become the new second lieutenant. Each of the lieutenants were nominated for captain, however, and finally an older man who had just joined the company and who had once known my elder brother, nominated me. My friends looked around at me in surprise to see if I would decline. Normally I would have done so since it was a little unusual for a sergeant to be considered for a captaincy while two lieutenants were in the field. But I knew that the first lieutenant, a fine and conscientious officer, was in no physical condition to stand a campaign, and that the second lieutenant, one of the best drillmasters I have ever known, was in high disfavor at state headquarters because he was alleged to have borrowed money from enlisted men of the 9th U.S. Infantry at Laredo while he was attached to that regiment, and was unlikely to be commissioned if elected. Besides, the colonel had mentioned the captaincy to me, and I probably wanted to be a captain anyhow. So I gave no sign. I was elected on the fourth ballot. Due to some mistake in the handling of the election it was declared invalid the next day and another election held the night of April 13. This time I was elected by an overwhelming majority on the first ballot.[9]

8. Elmer Best Trowbridge was born in Springdale, Arkansas, on December 13, 1883, but moved with his parents to Carthage at the age of nine months. He joined Company A, Second Missouri Infantry in March 1902. Discharged, he reenlisted in 1905 and became a second lieutenant in 1908, a first lieutenant in 1909, and captain in 1912. Trowbridge commanded the company on the Mexican border from June 1916–January 1917. Adjutant General's Office, State of Missouri, *The Service of the Missouri National Guard on the Mexican Border* (Jefferson City, MO: Hugh Stephens Co., 1919), 21 (hereafter referred to as *The Service of the Missouri National Guard on the Mexican Border*). A major in the 2nd Missouri Infantry in 1917, Trowbridge commanded the 130th Machine Gun Battalion from October to December 1917 but did not go overseas. He died in Anderson, Missouri, on July 10, 1959, and was buried in Park Cemetery in Carthage, Missouri. *Carthage* (MO) *Evening Press*, July 10, 1959.

9. The first election was declared illegal when it was discovered that only a majority vote was needed, rather than two-thirds. Four ballots were taken, with Dettwiler receiving a majority with the first, but support shifted to Schrantz on the next ballot. At the second election, Schrantz was victorious over Louis Dettwiler by a vote of 35 to 8. Schrantz and Dettwiler were the only two members to be nominated. *Joplin* (MO) *Globe*, April 14, 1917.

Captain Ward Schrantz, c. 1917 (*Memorial Hall, Carthage, MO*)

The first lieutenant served under me loyally as such until given a medical discharge some eight or nine months later. He died soon after the end of the war. The second lieutenant was given a commission in the Regular Army a short time later as the result of an examination he had taken at Laredo and was a captain at the time of his death several years after the war.[10]

10. Louis Eoff Dettwiler, born in Jefferson County, Missouri, on December 20, 1889, enlisted in Company A, Second Missouri Infantry in 1908 and rose to the rank of

Though I still had an examination to take before I could be commissioned, I actually took charge of the company immediately and pushed the recruiting campaign, the first lieutenant signing all papers in the interim. There was a large group taking the examinations at Jefferson City and they were thorough ones. Since I was jumping the two lieutenant positions I had three sets of examination questions to answer. My commission dated from April 13—Friday the 13th—the day of the final election.

The elective system of choosing officers has been widely condemned though it was still to continue in Missouri for several decades. Since my first commission came through it, I naturally may be supposed to have some kindly feelings toward it. Since I could hardly have won any popularity contest I feel that I was chosen because I had somewhat more military experience than either of the two lieutenants or because of some other reason. I even hoped that it might be because they preferred to serve under me in war and in point of fact under the now defunct elective system I believe that those balloting on such occasions attempted to select officers on the basis of probable qualifications and efficiency insofar as they could judge such qualities. If mistakes were occasionally made, mistakes are also made occasionally under any system of selecting and appointing officers.

---

first lieutenant in 1913. He served in that capacity when the company went to the Mexican border in 1916. Transferred to the 128th Machine Gun Battalion in October 1917, Dettwiler was discharged in April 1918 due to disability, died of pneumonia in Carthage, Missouri, on December 16, 1918, during the Spanish influenza epidemic, and was buried in the city's Park Cemetery. Memo from 1st Lt. Louis Dettwiler to Commanding Officer, 128th Machine Gun Battalion, Camp Doniphan, November 7, 1917, Record Group 120, Records of the American Expeditionary Forces, World War I Organization Records, Machine Gun Battalions, 128th Machine Gun Battalion, Box 263, National Archives and Records Administration, College Park, Maryland. (Hereafter NARA) William C. Peters, the company's second lieutenant, was born in Missouri on January 20, 1892. He served as an enlisted man in the Coast Artillery Corps from 1910–12, then enlisted in Company A in 1914. He was soon promoted to sergeant and second lieutenant. Although he initially served as Company A's second lieutenant on the Mexican border, he became the commander of Company F in December 1916 and served with that company until he was mustered out in January 1917. He was commissioned a second and first lieutenant in the Regular Army in June 1917. Peters was promoted to captain (temporary) in August 1917, and permanently in that grade in July 1920. He died in Denver, Colorado, on August 30, 1923. U.S. Adjutant General's Office, *Official Army Register, January 1, 1923* (Washington, D.C.: Government Printing Office, 1923, 741; U.S. Adjutant General's Office, *Official Army Register, January 1, 1924* (Washington, D.C.: Government Printing Office, 1924), 787; *The Service of the Missouri National Guard on the Mexican Border*, 121; HST.

Chapter 2

The Light Guard Prepares

The declaration of war against Germany in April 1917 propelled Missourians into the most eventful period in the state's military history since the Civil War. The United States could not immediately mobilize and transport the gigantic army the Allies needed for service on the Western Front, however. Anticipating that the number of volunteers would be insufficient, the Wilson administration was ready to use conscription, or "selective service," but the first draft registration did not take place until June 5 and the first draft numbers were not selected until July 20. National Guard units needed time to recruit to full strength. In addition, all the required military supplies—arms, equipment, uniforms, trucks, troopships, and aircraft—were in short supply. American soldiers were forced to wait for months until either American factories produced war material or the U.S. government secured supplies from the other Allied powers. Not only were the implements of war needed, but thirty-two training camps had to be built from scratch to accommodate hundreds of thousands of recruits. Consequently, Schrantz's Company A and the other Missouri National Guard units were not ordered into service until the late summer of 1917.

The Carthage men spent those months attempting to fill their ranks and drilling on the city square. Recruits "straggled" into Company A, a few at a time. A number of young men chose not to wait for the National Guard to be called and enlisted in the Regular Army, Navy, or Marine Corps. Others knew that there was no real hurry to enlist, for they would likely be drafted and fulfill their obligation that way.

On August 5, Company A of the 2nd Missouri Infantry officially entered United States service. It was the third time the Carthage Light Guard (though that name was no longer officially used) had gone to war. Although the Light Guard had not faced an enemy during the Spanish-American War in 1898 or on the Mexican border from 1916–17, now the Missourians were set to do battle with a formidable, perhaps unconquerable foe. Finally, on the morning of August 17, 1917, Schrantz and his company, led by color bearers carrying the flags of the United States, England, and France, passed through thousands of enthusiastic well-wishers to the Carthage train station in "one of the largest patriotic demonstrations ever held" in the town.[1] After a flurry of cheers, tears, and farewell kisses, the men were packed into train cars, ready to head to Camp Clark, outside Nevada, Missouri, the mobilization site for the Missouri National Guard.

At Camp Clark, the eager Missouri National Guardsmen, 14,756 in all, were "comfortably sheltered and supplied and actively engaged in carrying out an intensive program of instruction," the Missouri adjutant general reported. They made "remarkable" progress while encamped there, thanks to a spirit of "intense earnestness" and a desire to take advantage of every available moment of training.[2]

After physical examinations and vaccinations were administered, the Missourians were formally mustered into federal service. For many in Company A, it was their first time away from home, but the men were cheered by the arrival of about 500 citizens of Carthage, who traveled by train and automobiles to see their "boys" at Camp Clark and bring them edible delicacies, cigars, and cigarettes.

Schrantz and his company were not destined to remain long at Camp Clark, however. Selected as the advance detachment of the 2nd Missouri Infantry, they were soon back aboard a train and speeding through Kansas and Oklahoma to Camp Doniphan, near Lawton, Oklahoma, the future training camp of the Missouri-Kansas 35th Division. They were tasked with preparing the camp for the arrival of the remainder of the regiment.

1. *Joplin* (MO) *Globe*, August 18, 1917.

2. Adjutant General's Office, State of Missouri, *Report of the Adjutant General of Missouri, January 1, 1917–December 31, 1920* (Jefferson City: Office of the Adjutant General, 1921), 6–7, 10.

The United States entered the World War [on] April 6, 1917, but for some very good reasons it could not start mobilizing an army that day. It had arms and equipment only slightly in excess of those required for the peacetime strength of the Regular Army and National Guard. Even if the million men of whom W.J. Bryan had once spoken had been ready to "spring to arms overnight" there were no arms for them to spring to or clothing for them to wear or tentage under which to sleep.[3] All the wholeheartedness with which the nation plunged into the conflict could not make up for this deficiency. Thus instead of taking the field at the beginning of the war, Company A of Carthage, like other National Guard organizations all over the United States, had to wait long and weary months at home until factories could be diverted to war purposes and begin to turn out the most essential of the articles needed.

With our entry into the war already a week in the background my first duty was to recruit up my unit in an endeavor to build it up to the war strength of 150 men then prescribed for a rifle company. It had been announced that the National Guard would be drafted as organizations into the United States service under the National Defense Act on August 5, 1917, and since this was some months away there seemed ample time. But there were difficulties.[4]

For some reason it had been ordered by the War Department that all enlisted married men, or other men with dependents, be discharged from the National Guard, except for marriages which had occurred after April 6. This was a mandatory thing and the desires of the man had no bearing on it. Always on the return of a military unit from service there is an epidemic of marriages and my own had been no exception. This eliminated a valuable group of men who had had training during the border service. I discharged some, despite their protests, who were shortly thereafter drafted into the National Army despite their dependents,

3. This quote is attributed to William Jennings Bryan, Woodrow Wilson's secretary of state until he resigned in June 1915.

4. In order to ease the burden of mustering nearly 400,000 National Guardsmen, the Guard was called into service in increments. On July 3, President Wilson ordered that the Guard in eleven states be mobilized on July 15, with 19 more states and the District of Columbia on July 25. Further, Wilson ordered that on August 5 the members of the National Guard in every state would be drafted into federal service as individuals. Previously, Guardsmen had entered federal service as part of National Guard units. Michael D. Doubler, *I Am the Guard: A History of the Army National Guard, 1636–2000* (Washington, D.C.: U.S. Government Printing Office, 2001), 171.

and no doubt were badly needed in the new divisions. The order also offered a way out for men who wanted to quit and who could manage to claim dependents other than their wives. I lost some in this classification, none of whom, so far as I can recollect, served later in the war though my memory may be at fault on this. With this stripping-down process complete there were remaining only 42 enlisted men who had served on the border.

For several years the public had been reading of the terrific loss of life on European battlefields and family pressure was put on many of the men to claim dependency even though such claim was not justified and the man desired to go. In most cases the men concerned took care of such situations themselves but a few naturally came to me, the more so since knowledge of military methods were not well known in those days and some relatives thought that the decision on whether or not a man should be discharged rested solely on the captain.

I recall one instance of a rather bellicose lady, an old friend of my family and whose son was a member of my company, who had quite lost her poise about the matter. She came to my home one morning while I was eating breakfast, refused my mother's invitation to enter and asked to speak to me on the front porch. She was a very good woman but on this occasion had worked herself into quite a temper.

"I'll tell you this, Ward Schrantz," she shrilled for all the neighborhood to hear as I stepped out on the porch, "you are not going to take my boy to war!"

But I did. There was another case in which the soldier was much embarrassed by his family's insistence. I explained to his father and mother but a grandfather living down in Oklahoma was not content. He wrote a letter to President Woodrow Wilson saying that he had always voted the Democratic ticket, including the two times the president had run for office, and that I refused to discharge the boy although his parents were dependent on him. This last statement was not true. The father was in ill health and three sons aided in the family's support, neither of the other two married or at that time in the service.

The letter went to one of the secretaries at the White House, was sent over to the War Department, thence to the Adjutant General of Missouri and finally down to me through channels, arriving with an imposing number of endorsements demanding action. I endorsed it back with the explanation that the man did not want a discharge and was not entitled to one under the regulations, the interest of the relatives being concern for his personal safety and not need for his financial assistance. This bounced back quickly from state headquarters with instructions that I should have the man make application for discharge on ground of dependency and express my opinions in an endorsement to that. The soldier flatly refused to sign such application until I explained to him that in view of the endorsement I was going to put on it there was no chance of it going through. And in due time it came back disapproved.

Our recruiting to war strength was also hampered by the fact that while physical standards had been lowered for the Regular Army they were still kept at the old peacetime standards for the National Guard. A number of men turned down by our doctor went down to nearby Joplin and enlisted in the Regular Army. Eventually this was lowered for the National Guard too and I enlisted such of the earlier rejects as were still available. It is only fair to add, somewhat ruefully, that most of this group failed to pass later examinations for overseas service and were assigned to duty in the states or else proved unable to stand up under the rigors of active campaign and were invalided home.

A number of young men enlisted on their claim that they were 18, as they appeared to be, when in fact some were 16 and 17. Since it has always been my opinion, borne out by the pages of history, that a man is old enough to soldier if he is old enough to carry a pack and pull a trigger, I was not inclined to go back of these age claims unless the matter of an underage enlistment was formally called to my attention in which case I had no option but to discharge the man. Most parents did not complain—believing that the boy was big enough to serve and that the country needed his services.

There was one youth who enlisted as 18 who looked as if he might be 19 or more, but his father confided to me that the youth was only 16. However both parents felt that he should serve since there was a need and opportunity and that moreover they were glad that he went into the army [as] he had developed a roving tendency which had led him on two occasions to leave home without notice and steal rides on freight trains to California and back, a thing which had caused them great anxiety. The army might stabilize him, they thought—and in fact it did. He settled down after the war and became a quite solid citizen. His only trouble had been that he had a spirit of adventure which needed an outlet.

A grandmother, however, had quite different ideas about his entry into the armed forces and being a forceful old woman she expressed herself to me quite energetically.

"He is just a boob," she said, "a great big overgrown boob. He'll be the first one killed. The boobs are always the first ones killed—"and she went on to prove that quaint view to her own satisfaction by telling me of boys she had known in that category who went off to the Civil War and were killed in their first battle. Happily for the youth and possibly for me, this lady did not write to the president.

Recruiting a small-town National Guard unit up to war strength of 150 men during the four months which intervened between our entry into the war and the draft of the National Guard into the army was fraught with considerable difficulty. To young men who wanted to volunteer the Regular Army recruiting parties could offer immediate service whereas we could only promise it on August 5, 1917, and thus we lost the restless, the impatient or the unemployed prospect. And indeed, much as I needed the men, I never attempted to enlist anyone who was considering enlistment in the Regular Army, the Navy or the Marine Corps. It was all the same war and I had a certain sympathy for those who did not want to wait around while hostilities were in progress. Had I foreseen the future I might have acted otherwise. So much of the Regular Army was kept at home during this war that many of the impatient ones saw no combat service because [they were] in Regular units. The War Department planned for a long war and wished to feed the Regular Army into it slowly so as not to have its best-trained soldiers killed off in the early stages. The result was that the war ended before most of the Regular formations were engaged—a bitter thing for thousands of fine officers and men and a mistake that was not repeated in the Second World War.

The Selective Service law which Congress wisely had passed operated both for and against our recruiting campaign. It brought into our ranks many men who were not particularly eager to go to war but who preferred to go as volunteers rather than as drafted men, since go they must. It kept from us many other men who would have volunteered because of a feeling that their country needed them except for the Selective Service law which assured them that if they were needed the government would call them.

On Sunday morning, August 5, at which time we donned uniforms for the duration and reported for duty we actually had the allowable three officers and 150 enlisted men present for duty and an additional two men who had been signed up, absent without leave.[5] Being overstrength on paper and called upon to transfer two men to another company which was understrength, I naturally transferred the papers of the two AWOLs. One of these men showed up a few days later, feeling quite badly because he had been transferred. Whether the other ever reported I do not know. Yet of the throng reporting, all but about 30 were in their ordinary citizen's dress, for the government had been entirely unable to fill the requisitions which had been submitted for army garb.

The company as it stood this morning of August 5, was a comparatively youthful one. All officers and noncommissioned officers were well under 30, the oldest being 27. One of the officers and most of the noncommissioned officers were under 25. Four of the corporals were not yet 21. The privates had a wider range in age. Six men were above 30, the oldest being 38 and the others 37, 34, 33, 32 and 30. Most of the rest were between 21 and 25 but 53 of the privates were not yet 21. All, of course, were volunteers and 59 were not within the ages covered by the Selective Service law at that time. All of the officers and noncommissioned officers had served on the Mexican border as had a number of the privates. A few of the other men had had previous military experience of one sort or another but the majority possessed only such military knowledge as they had acquired with the company during the four months of intensive drilling, preceding the call.

No additional equipment had been received at our home station and apparently not at the state mobilization camp and the concentration of the regiment was accordingly delayed, and for

5. The *Carthage Press* reported that due to a lack of uniforms, only about 30 members of the company appeared in regulation dress. For the next several days, the company was given instruction in military courtesy, general orders for sentinels, the reading of the Articles of War, squad, platoon, and company drill and a non-commissioned officer's school. Drill with weapons was hampered by a shortage of rifles. *Carthage* (MO) *Evening Press*, August 6, August 8, 14, 1917.

12 days I conducted a vigorous training program in fundamentals in Carthage, feeding the men in restaurants and letting those who wished go home at night, the remainder—some 40—sleeping in the armory.

It so happened that Mr. Schaefer, proprietor of the restaurant where most of the men ate, was of German birth, and announcement that his eating place would be used caused some lifted eyebrows locally, which perhaps was not strange in a time when fear of spies was widespread and all Germans were looked upon with more or less suspicion. The officers of the company, however, had full confidence in the loyalty of Mr. Schaefer, as indeed did all Carthage people who knew him, and by way of expressing this confidence the company's commander messed at this place with his men.

About 40 men expressed a need or a desire to be quartered at the armory and each night were issued cots and blankets for that purpose. The first day a guard of one non-commissioned officer and three privates was established to enable one sentry to be on duty at all times at the armory, and this was the regular Sunday guard while the organization was in Carthage. On week days the guard consisted of a sergeant, three corporals and nine privates, and during the evening hours a provost patrol was sent through the business district, a normal military precaution to prevent any disorder by military personnel though fortunately there were few if any things which ever required this patrol's attention.

Drills would be held from 8 to 11 o'clock each morning, noncommissioned officers school from 3 to 4 each afternoon, and drill again from 4 until 5. All men would stand retreat at the armory each evening following drill.

There was no indication as yet as to when the company would be called upon to move to Nevada, where the Missouri National Guard was to mobilize as soon as the government was able to supply tents and mess equipment—the four months intervening since the declaration of war not having been time enough for that purpose—but anyhow Company A was now a part of the army.

It was the third time the old Carthage Light Guard—though that name was no longer used officially—had entered the service of the United States. The first was during the Spanish-American War and the second had been during the Mexican border troubles. Both of these previous occasions the Carthaginians had been returned to civil life without engaging in combat. This time it looked as if there might be war enough to go around.

A slow rain was falling on the morning of Monday, August 6, 1917, the first drill day for Company A, Second Missouri Infantry, after its draft into the United States Army the morning before, and the soldiers were given such instruction in the armory as the crowded condition of that building permitted. Advantage of the occasion was also taken to read the Articles of War as required by orders.

The "Articles of War" were the shalts and shalt-nots of the soldier and the paragraphs pertaining to many of the offenses listed concluded with the threat that offenders "may be punished by death or such other punishment as a court-martial may direct." This sounded formidable enough, yet among those who sat and listened that day were several who must have been unimpressed by it for they later deserted, thus rendering themselves liable to this death penalty had a court martial chosen to inflict it.

Subsequent days were not as damp as this first one and daily drills were carried out on the streets. There were only 67 rifles in the company, and platoons alternated in the use of these. Usually at the corner watching the drill was a somewhat pathetic little clump of war brides.

Progress made in instruction of the company was considered satisfactory. The Mexican border training had resulted in a number of men being fully competent to instruct and it was not long until the Carthage soldiers felt that with arms and equipment, and a little target practice, they would be ready to go to the front.

Sometime before the call of Company A into service, the people of Carthage had raised a fund to be used in some suitable way as an expression of appreciation of the company, and gave the guardsmen the option of receiving it for their mess fund, having it spent for a banquet in honor of the company or for silver rings for each member. A check-up of sentiment indicated that the rings were preferred and these were ordered, each embossed with the words, "Company A, Second Missouri, Carthage, Mo." These were presented at a ceremony in the high school [on] Friday night, August 10.

It was at this program at the high school that Carthage formally bade farewell to its National Guard company. The high school auditorium, the largest then in the city, was crowded to capacity and news reports said that enough were unable to get in that had the place been twice as large, it still would have been crowded. The members of the company occupied seats at the front of the auditorium, and the officers, together with former officers, were seated on the rostrum. Members of the Grand Army of the Republic had attended in a body and occupied reserved seats. The Carthage Light Guard band occupied a space at the back of the rostrum and interspersed patriotic music.

Dr. J.D. McCaughtry pronounced the invocation and followed it with the reading of an impressive poem written to answer the pacifist song, "I Didn't Raise My Boy to Be a Soldier." Next Dr. W.G. Clinton spoke feelingly urging the soldiers to come back clean and bring the flag back clean.[6] Allen McReynolds, a former captain of the company, reminded his hearers of the 40 years of history behind that Carthage Light Guard and impressed on the company the honor which was to be theirs in serving in the organization when for the first time it went into battle.[7] Mrs. J.T. Wallace sang, "My Heart is Singing" and "Mother of Mine," accompanied on the piano by Miss Antoinette Francis.[8]

6. James D. McCaughtry was born on December 11, 1863. Before he came to Missouri, McCaughtry served churches in Illinois. He was pastor of the First Presbyterian Church in Carthage for 17 years. He was considered by many Presbyterians to be "one of the outstanding preachers in southwest Missouri" and "a scholar and a man of marked culture." He died in Springfield, Missouri, on June 17, 1936. *Springfield* (MO) *Daily News*, June 18, 1936. Dr. William G. Clinton was born in Warrick County, Indiana, on July 20, 1867. A public school teacher for six years, Clinton was admitted to the Indiana Conference of the Methodist Church in 1892, was transferred to Hyde Park Church in Kansas City in 1912, and to Carthage in the spring of 1914, becoming pastor of the First Methodist Church. He transferred to the Sedalia, Missouri, district in the fall of 1919. *Carthage* (MO) *Evening Press*, January 19, 1950.

7. Allen McReynolds was born in Carthage on November 7, 1877. He graduated from the University of Missouri in 1901, and after graduation served as captain of Company A, 2nd Missouri Infantry for three years. Admitted to the Missouri bar in 1903, McReynolds was active in local affairs and had a successful legal, business, and political career, serving as a Missouri state senator. He died in Carthage on September 29, 1960. *Carthage* (MO) *Evening Press*, September 29, 1960.

8. Lila Oldham Wallace was born in Lexington, Kentucky, on November 26, 1880. She came to Carthage in 1894 when her father became pastor of the First Christian Church there. She married J.T. Wallace in 1903. An "accomplished pianist and singer," Wallace founded the Carthage Choral Society and was its director for years, and was an organist and voice teacher. Wallace died in Carthage on December 20, 1959. *Carthage* (MO) *Evening Press*, December 21, 1950. Eliza Antoinette Francis, the daughter of John R. and Eudora Francis, was born in Missouri on August 4, 1892. She died in Independence, Missouri, on November 23, 1984.

Then Col. W.K. Caffee, active in the initial organization of the Carthage Light Guard in 1876 and for many years its captain and leading spirit, and during the Spanish-American War commander of the Second Missouri Volunteer Infantry in which it served, arose to present the rings.[9] He too recalled the proud history of the Carthage Light Guard and pointed out that although never yet given the opportunity to serve on the battlefield it had always excelled in every competition and had made a reputation worth upholding. He pointed out the value of discipline and cheerful obedience of orders as essentials of fighting efficiency, and he presented the rings—handing them in a package to the company commander—as a reminder of the esteem and good wishes of the community.

The company commander, replying on behalf of his men, expressed the thanks of the organization for the gift and what it signified, and said the company would endeavor to show its appreciation and merit the faith that Carthage reposed in it, by doing all that it could to help contribute to a return of peace through an American victory over the Germans. The band then played the national anthem, Dr. McCaughtry pronounced the benediction and Trumpeter Murl Daugherty sounded taps as the audience filed out.[10]

This was to me a rather welcome opportunity to get my unit organized on an active service basis and in hand before going to camp

9. William King Caffee was born in Newark, Ohio, on June 30, 1856. He came to Carthage in 1868, then attended Shattuck Military Academy in Faribault, Minnesota, where he graduated with honors. He then went into the drug business with his uncle. When the Carthage Light Guard was organized in January 1876, Caffee was a sergeant in the unit. He was promoted to captain about 1880, but the company was disbanded in 1887. When the company was reorganized two years later, Caffee was elected captain, then became the first colonel of the 2nd Missouri Infantry in 1890. He led the regiment during the Spanish-American War and retired from military life shortly afterward. Caffee died in Carthage on March 10, 1923, at the age of sixty-six. At the time of his death, he was the director and treasurer of a local business and a bank director. He was buried in Carthage's Park Cemetery with full military honors, with Schrantz serving as a pallbearer. *Carthage* (MO) *Evening Press*, March 10, 12, 1923.

10. The August 10 ceremony was attended by one of the largest crowds ever seen in Carthage. Allen McReynolds reminded them of the proud associations of the Light Guard, and that they should maintain the unit's good name and carry "the traditions of the company to the firing line" for the first time. Colonel W.K. Caffee urged the men to strictly observe sanitary rules, a lesson learned during the Spanish-American War. Captain Schrantz replied that they hoped to show by their acts that "we appreciate our home community and appreciate their esteem" and would strive to do honor to Carthage, and expected "to accomplish a good deal in this war—all we can as opportunity offers." The *Carthage* (MO) *Evening Press*, August 11, 17, 1917. The citizens of Carthage collected a total of $300 for the rings. *Carthage* (MO) *Evening Press*, July 30, 31, 1917. Schrantz also received a .45 automatic pistol "of the army regulation pattern" presented by E.B. Jacobs, cashier of the First National Bank of Carthage. *Joplin* (MO) *Globe*, August 8, 1917.

but leaving the National Guard companies in their home towns was most distressing to the liquor-sales industry since federal law forbade a saloon to operate within half a mile of an army post and some district attorney had ruled that a National Guard armory used as quarters for a unit on active duty constituted an army barracks. The draft of the National Guard into service thus closed practically all the saloons in all the larger towns of southwest Missouri.[11] The shortage of mess equipment was the final factor delaying move to the state camp—and this was soon solved. Some patriotic citizens of Southwest Missouri—said to have been the saloon men—kindly purchased and presented to the Second Missouri Infantry enough tin plates, tin cups and knives, forks and spoons to equip all personnel with civilian mess gear. Thus outfitted the regiment was ordered assembled at Camp Clark.

It was 9:05 a.m. August 17, 1917, when Company A, Second Missouri Infantry, the Carthage Light Guard of days gone by, swung away from its armory on Fifth Street between Howard and Main bound for the Missouri Pacific station to leave its home city for the World War.

Carthage had turned out in force to bid it farewell and as it marched through the streets it had the best escort that the city could furnish. At the head of the procession were three color-bearers, carrying the flag of the United States flanked by those of England and France. Then followed the Light Guard band, followed in turn by the Carthage home guard. Next came the departing company, three officers and 150 men strong. Behind the soldiers came the city fire truck, then a line of automobiles bearing the Grand Army of the Republic, and finally a long succession of bunting-decorated automobiles of private citizens.

Through densely packed masses of people and flag-bedecked buildings the column moved north on Grant Street to the square, along the east and north sides of the square, west on Third to Garrison—a street named after Capt. Benjamin F. Garrison who in 1876 became the first captain of the Carthage Light Guard—north on Garrison to Vine, thence west to McGregor and so to the Missouri Pacific station and the siding where three empty passenger cars and a baggage coach were waiting.

11. U.S. District Attorney Francis M. Wilson's ruling resulted in the closure of four saloons in Carthage. *Carthage* (MO) *Evening Press*, August 14, 1917.

Company A marching to the Carthage train station to embark for Camp Clark, August 1917 (*Jasper County Records Center*)

"When the procession reached the depot the people simply overflowed the extensive grounds," said the [*Carthage Evening*] *Press* account. "They were banked far back east on Limestone street in throngs, out on the high ground on McGregor street, lined the McGregor street bridge and the High street bridge, and far south along the railroad where the incoming special train was due to pass. . . . While the band played the company formed in line beside its coaches, received brief instructions, and was then placed at ease until time to entrain."

The troop train bearing the Webb City and Joplin contingents had not arrived and for an hour the soldiers talked with mothers and wives, sweethearts and friends, while the band played and the crowd waited. Members of the W.C.T.U. distributed small bags each containing a lunch for a soldier. C.C. Shafer, proprietor of the Mountain Grove Creamery loaded a 15-gallon container full of ice cream into the baggage car.[12] L.H. Dillard passed out ten-cent cigars and packages of cigarettes and smoking tobacco to the members of the company. George Williams, on hand with his

12. W.C.T.U. is the abbreviation for the Women's Christian Temperance Union. Charles Clinton Shafer was born in Franklin, Illinois, on April 2, 1889, died in Kansas City, Missouri, on November 29, 1953, and was buried in Forest Hill Cemetery in Kansas City.

Camp Clark, Nevada, Missouri (*Author's collection*)

motion picture machine, took pictures of the milling crowds as he had of the procession marching to the depot.[13]

Then came the whistle of the incoming troop train. The soldiers in high spirits took their last farewells of those who waited with them. Cheers, tears, farewell kisses, and the men were packed in their cars leaning from the windows. Quickly the Carthage cars were coupled onto the rest. The officers climbed into the officers' coach. "Putt," the canine mascot, barked from the baggage car in sympathy with the general noise. More whistles and the 14-coach heavily loaded train, with hands and hats waving from windows and hats waving and handkerchiefs fluttering in reply, jerked, started and gathered speed and rattled northward across the Spring River viaduct.

Company A was off on the long trail which led eventually to the distant war. When it left, Carthage had probably already contributed more volunteers—including not only this strong unit but all those men who had individually joined the Regular Army, Navy and Marine Corps—than it had all-told to the Spanish-American War and Philippine Insurrection. And the drafted contingents were yet to be called.

That organization reached Nevada at 12:15 and marched to its camping place on the reservation where it found the sites for its tents carefully marked out by the men of the Supply Company.[14]

13. Louis H. Dillard, a "well known Carthage merchant," was born in Illinois on December 10, 1877. He came to Carthage in the early 1900s, first working as a farm manager, then in the grocery business, then purchased a cigar, confectionary, and newsstand on the Carthage square. He died in Carthage on April 24, 1937. *Carthage* (MO) *Evening Press*, April 26, 1937. George Putnam Williams, born in Muncie, Indiana, on December 13, 1893, moved to Carthage with his parents in 1908. They operated the Delphus Theater in Carthage. Williams served in World War I, and died in Wadsworth, Kansas, on February 4, 1955. *Carthage* (MO) *Evening Press*, February 5, 1955.

14. Established on April 28, 1908, about three miles southeast of Nevada, Missouri, Camp Clark was originally 320 acres and named in honor Missouri General Harvey C. Clark, who helped select the location. Betty Sterett, *Scenes from the Past (of Nevada, Missouri)*, revised edition (Nevada, MO: Vernon County Historical Society, 2002), 38–39.

Quickly, too, the Supply Company distributed the tents and despite the newness of most of the men to their tasks, the tents were soon up, and during the afternoon the establishment of camp was completed. The border veterans were frankly glad to be under canvas again, nor did the newer men seem less pleased to be on the road which led to the adventure for which they had enlisted. That evening after darkness fell the general morale of the Carthage company and the regiment as a whole was attested by the singing all over the camp.

In each of the rifle companies of 150 men there were only about 67 rifles. The machine gun company had no guns at all, its four Benet Mercier guns which it had had on the border having been taken away from it and sent east to help equip with machine guns of some sort the 1st American Division, which went overseas in June and July. All of the field officers had been in the regiment for many years, including the period of its border service, and the colonel and lieutenant colonel had served with it during the Spanish-American War, though in lower grades. There were a number of new captains in the regiment, the result of resignations following the return from the border, but most of them had considerable military service of some sort. There was a high esprit du corps in the regiment and on the whole the Second Missouri, save for the matter of equipment, was probably considerably better fitted for war service than the average National Guard regiment.

The 2nd Missouri Infantry was commanded by Col. William A. Raupp of Pierce City, with Lt. Col. Paul Tucker of Lamar as second-in-command. The first battalion was commanded by Maj. Westley Halliburton of Carthage, the second by Maj. T.H. Loy of Aurora, and the third by Maj. Elmer Trowbridge of Carthage. The regiment was composed of the following companies: Headquarters Company, Pierce City; the Supply Company and Machine Gun Company, Nevada; Company A, Carthage; Company B, Butler; Company C, Lamar; Company D, West Plains; Company E, Sarcoxie; Company F, Clinton; Company G and the Sanitary Detachment, Joplin; Company I, Webb City; Company K, Springfield; Company L, Jefferson City, and Company M, Aurora. The total strength of the regiment was 2,002 men.

Now followed on a somewhat larger scale the rather tedious and boresome process of being physically examined again and formally received into the army of the United States, similar to the procedure the previous year when called for duty on the Mexican border.[15]

For the accepted ones, new ordeals waited, specifically the vaccinations against small-pox and the inoculations against typhoid. In the Spanish[-American] War, typhoid had played havoc with the American army, as a year or so later it did with the British army during the Boer War, but now a preventive to that dread disease had been developed and each man who aspired to serve his country in battle had to have the serum injected into his left arm as an assurance that he would live to get to the field. No one liked it but it was a part of the war—as it is of military life today—and there was no choice.

The next day, all formalities having been completed, Company A was formally mustered in at 2:30 in the afternoon.

This formality had no more than been completed when an order was received from the headquarters of the Central Department at Chicago that certain Missouri organizations, including Company A, "will proceed from present station to camp Doniphan, Fort Sill, Okla., each detachment commander reporting on arrival thereat to the camp quartermaster for duty in laying out camps, pitching tents and performing other necessary work in advance of arrival of other troops."

15. Schrantz noted that it was a curious coincidence that seven men were rejected for physical problems on both prior occasions when Company A had been mustered into service (1898 and 1916). Sgt. Guy Roos, who "expected to be reassigned to it for the war," was one of those rejected because of his eyesight. Roos joined Company A, 2nd Missouri Infantry in July 1907. By 1912 he was a second lieutenant, but resigned the following year, only to reenlist a few months later. He was promoted to sergeant and first sergeant in 1914, and served in that capacity with the company on the Mexican border. In December 1916 he was furloughed to the reserves. *The Service of the Missouri National Guard on the Mexican Border*, 121; *Carthage* (MO) *Evening Press*, August 21, 1917.

Chapter 3

Camp Doniphan

The next stop on Schrantz's journey to war was Camp Doniphan, located about five miles outside Lawton, Oklahoma. The sprawling 2,000-acre camp was established on July 18, 1917, to accommodate the National Guard units destined to make up the 35th Division. Construction began on July 23, and eventually 1,267 buildings supported an extensive tent camp. Doniphan's population rose steadily, from more than 11,000 troops in September 1917, to nearly 23,000 the following month, to 26,789 that December.[1]

"Our camp is built in the shape of a huge horse shoe with the open end facing toward the east," wrote one Missourian. "Mountains surround us on all sides and make very pretty scenery when the air is clear enough to see anything." The sight of a huge army camp rising from the prairie was impressive, and the accompanying roar of artillery from a nearby range, and army airplanes, "like big buzzards flying above our heads," filled the new soldiers with wonder.[2]

As the 2nd Missouri Infantry's advance detachment, Schrantz and his soldiers spent the next few weeks engaged in guard, drill, and fatigue duty until their Missouri comrades arrived on September 27.

1. U.S. Army Center of Military History, *Order of Battle of the United States Land Forces in the World War*, 3 vols. (Washington, D.C.: Office of Military History, 1988), vol. 3, pt. 2, 928–929.

2. *The Advertiser-Courier* (Hermann, MO), October 10 and 24, 1917.

The conscientious Captain Schrantz soon began sending requisition letters to army quartermasters with long lists of equipment his men needed. His lists included cots, ponchos, blankets (each man had only one), tent pins, rifles, cartridge belts, canteens, entrenching shovels and wire cutters, along with envelopes, pens, typewriter ribbons, scrubbing brushes, large spoons and paring knives.[3]

The training regimen began as soon as the remainder of the Missourians reached Doniphan. The camp was "a stern old schoolmaster," in the words of one early historian. Battle-tested French and British instructors arrived to share their expertise in "the bayonet, the hand grenade and the gas mask."[4] Close order drill, the manual of arms, semaphore signaling, scouting, patrolling, trench digging, and guard duty also filled the day. Missouri soldier Ray E. Neighbours believed that killing was their trade, and they were "learning their trade rapidly, at the rifle-range and hurling themselves at the dummies used in bayonet drill, learning how to wrestle, box and all that pertains to getting the other man before he gets you."[5] In addition, some daily addresses by the company commander or other designated officer contained useful practical information, while others were clearly part of the government's efforts to convince the new soldiers of the righteousness of their cause.

Lengthy hikes and daily physical exercises hardened the bodies of the new warriors. A correspondent writing to the Hayti, Missouri, newspaper told his readers that it was "as easy for us to step off twelve to fifteen miles as it was for us to walk that many blocks at home." "Every man in the company now is a man," he explained, "and the boys who came with us are also men. Everyone's muscles are as hard as a boilermaker's and we will show those Huns some 'tuff' times."[6] Athletic games such as football, basketball, jumping, races, and boxing also helped improve physical fitness.

In addition to the daily training, Captain Schrantz reported on November 1 that he was conducting a "tactical school" for his officers, non-commissioned officers, and "selected privates" each weeknight from 7 to 8:30 p.m. Although the course of study closely followed the day to day work on the drill field, Schrantz also included

3. Memos from Commanding Officer, Company A, 128th Machine Gun Battalion, to Camp Quartermaster and Camp Ordnance Officer, Camp Doniphan, August 24, 28, 31, September 4, 10, 1917, Record Group 120, Records of the American Expeditionary Forces, World War I Organization Records, Machine Gun Battalions, 128th Machine Gun Battalion, Box 264, NARA.

4. Charles B. Hoyt, *Heroes of the Argonne: An Authentic History of the Thirty-Fifth Division* (Kansas City: Franklin Hudson Publishing Company, 1919), 23–24.

5. *Mexico Missouri Message*, January 17, 1918.

6. *The Hayti* (MO) *Herald*, December 13, 1917.

target designation, trench construction, guard duty, theoretical use of machine guns, "and other kindred subjects." On New Year's Day, 1918, he informed his superior, Major Westley Halliburton, that his company tactical school was continuing, with training in map reading, animal care, and the use of machine guns on outposts and with advance and rear guards. By the end of the month, Schrantz was able to report that instruction in the different classes of machine gun fire, machine gun reconnaissance, indirect fire, and other topics, combined with the use of two actual machine guns and the "heightened interest" of the men, had resulted in "more satisfactory progress" in January than any previous month.[7]

Such training proved invaluable for soldiers preparing for combat in France, but more specialized training was far less intensive. Although Company A had been redesignated as a machine gun company (Company A, 128th Machine Gun Battalion) everything—from training manuals to machine gun carts to the guns themselves—was in short supply. The Carthage men were able to drill with mules and carts, sit through lectures about the workings of the guns, and actually examine some obsolete weapons, but it would not be until just before the Missourians shipped out for France that modern machine guns finally arrived at Camp Doniphan.

But Camp Doniphan was not all drill and classroom instruction. The well-paid soldiers could easily go to nearby Lawton. The city furnished many exotic sights, including "Indians on the street all day; the Indians [sic] squaw carry their papoose on their backs as they did years ago," according to one Missouri soldier.[8] Even those who remained in camp enjoyed some of the comforts of home, thanks to the citizens of Carthage. A group of patriotic women in the town gathered and shipped hundreds of magazines each week to the Carthage men, who distributed them to the mess hall and tents. The townspeople also collected cigarettes and smoking tobacco for the boys, and provided Christmas boxes and even an Edison phonograph. Some lucky soldiers received visits from friends and loved ones. Others spent their time relating their camp experiences to those at home through frequent correspondence. By December 1917,

7. Memo from Commanding Officer, Company A, to Commanding Officer, 128th Machine Gun Battalion, Camp Doniphan, November 1, 1917, Record Group 120, Records of the American Expeditionary Forces, World War I Organization Records, Machine Gun Battalions, 128th Machine Gun Battalion, Box 265, NARA; Memo from Commanding Officer, Company A, to Commanding Officer, 128th Machine Gun Battalion, Camp Doniphan, January 1, 31, 1918, Record Group 120, Records of the American Expeditionary Forces, World War I Organization Records, Machine Gun Battalions, 128th Machine Gun Battalion, Box 264, NARA.

8. *The Hayti* (MO) *Herald*, December 13, 1917.

Company A member William Stapanski, home on a five-day leave, was able to tell his parents that "nothing beats army life."[9]

Despite the best efforts of the civilians to make their men comfortable, Doniphan was not the most hospitable climate for training soldiers. Missouri soldier Edward Seyer lamented that "here we have to sit in a tent like gipsies [*sic*] and have a candle for a light."[10] Lieutenant Warren S. Perry of the 129th Machine Gun Battalion wrote home that the wind and dust at Doniphan was "almost indescribable." "It seems to me," he continued, "as though the wind is blowing constantly and at such a rate that the dust and sand moves in clouds," and was worse than dry, drifting snow. On the other hand, Perry noted, since one didn't perspire, you became "dry dirty," so that when you got so much sand and dirt "on your hide," "the rest just rolls off."[11]

By the end of the year, cold temperatures added to the misery.[12] "A Soldier Boy" vividly described his "quandary" to those at home. If anyone moved three feet away from their tent stove, he explained, they were liable to freeze to death, while if a soldier moved to within two feet of the stove they were "apt to get burnt up." The men were required to keep moving about, however, in order to "keep from being frozen to the ground."[13] Worse, Sibley stoves easily set fire to canvas tents. The day after Christmas, Captain Schrantz reported that although all of his men had overcoats, none had a pair of wool socks or woolen underwear.[14]

9. *The Monett* (MO) *Times*, December 7, 1917.

10. *Scott County Democrat* (Benton, MO), November 29, 1917.

11. *The Monett* (MO) *Times*, October 26, 1917.

12. Frequent windstorms, a "peculiar feature" of the area, lasted from 12 to 24 hours and subjected the area to clouds of dust so thick that it was often difficult to see an approaching vehicle a short distance away. The Army's Surgeon General noted that the temperature fell to 15 degrees on October 30, to 9 degrees on November 30 and close to zero on December 6. Soldiers arrived in camp in cotton uniforms, with wool uniforms not issued until "considerable severe weather had been experienced." The weather in November and December was described as "unusually severe." The troops were quartered in large pyramidal tents, heated by Sibley stoves, with 9 men to a tent, while a number of organizations had 12 to a tent. Measles and German measles made up most of the more than 2,300 diseases treated at the camp from September to December 1917, although an epidemic of pneumonia reached its height with 110 cases in January 1918. U.S. War Department, *Annual Reports, 1918,* 3 vols. (Washington, D.C.: U.S. Government Printing Office, 1919), I: 421–423; Albert S. Bowen, *The Medical Department of the United States Army in the World War*, 14 vols. (Washington, D.C.: U.S. Government Printing Office, 1928), IV: 173–175. Other sources reported sandstorms every afternoon and sometimes in the forenoon so severe that an object could not be distinguished fifty feet away. *Report of the Adjutant General of Missouri, January 1, 1917–December 31, 1920*, 10.

13. *Mexico* (MO) *Weekly Ledger*, December 20, 1917.

14. Memo from Commanding Officer of Company A to Commanding Officer, 128th Machine Gun Battalion, Camp Doniphan, December 26, 1917, Record Group 120, Records of the American Expeditionary Forces, World War I Organization Records, Machine Gun Battalions, 128th Machine Gun Battalion, Box 263, NARA.

Even with the miserable weather conditions in southwest Oklahoma, the time passed quickly at Doniphan, and the Carthage soldiers observed the six-month anniversary of their entry into service on February 5, 1918. Although they intended to hold a special dinner and ceremony to mark the occasion, a far more solemn event took place. The previous December, a measles epidemic reached its peak in the camp. Private Eugene Ring, a New Jersey man and one of the early enlistees in the company, fell victim to the disease and was admitted to the hospital, where he contracted pneumonia, then diphtheria, and died on February 3. He was interred at the Fort Sill Cemetery, his flag-covered casket escorted to the grave by the regimental band and comrades from his company.

Despite the depressing effect Ring's death had on company morale, Schrantz and his men were no doubt cheered when the oft-repeated rumors of movement orders were finally confirmed. An advance detachment of officers and men from all organizations of the 35th Division was ordered to move overseas to attend service schools in France. The remainder of the division would soon follow. On March 20, 1918, the advance detachment of the 128th Machine Gun Battalion (Captain Schrantz, two first lieutenants, two second lieutenants and twelve sergeants) shook hands with their envious comrades and left Doniphan to begin the journey to Europe.

Happily the Camp Clark experience was not to last long for Company A. Camp Doniphan, Okla., on the Fort Sill reservation was already under construction as a training camp for the 35th Division which was to be formed by the Missouri and Kansas National Guard and one company of each regiment was to go there in advance as cantonment guard. My own was selected and on August 23 clambered onto a troop train which Company L, Fourth Missouri infantry, from Mound City, was also boarding, and soon was rattling away to the southward at a rather surprising rate of speed and a relatively clear track. The railways were cooperating wholeheartedly in the war.[15]

15. A committee of five men, known as the Railroads' War Board, was established just after war was declared to coordinate the efforts of American railroads to support the war effort. The Troop Movement Force of the Board was tasked with insuring the smooth operation of troop trains. Because of the Board's lack of authority and other problems, the government assumed control of all railroads in late December 1917, the members of the Board resigned, and the functions of the Troop Movement Force were eventually assumed by the more powerful United States Railroad Administration. Ross H. McLean, "Troop Movements on the American Railroads During the Great War," *The American Historical Review* 26 (April 1921): 464–488. The members of Company A considered it an honor to be selected

Camp Doniphan, near Lawton, Oklahoma (*Author's collection*)

When the members of Company A, Second Missouri Infantry, which on August 24, 1917, had reached Camp Doniphan, near Fort Sill, Okla., looked about them on the prairie at the skeleton for the vast camp which was to be there when the 35th Division was finally assembled, they realized that a division must be a good-sized force. The camp, as outlined by the mess halls and bath houses being constructed by a rapidly-working crew of civilian carpenters, was to be in an angular irregular sort of horse shoe; the north side—just west of the new post at Fort Sill—to be a mile long; the west side, three quarters of a mile long, and the south side, a mile from the north side, to be a mile and a quarter in length.

Camp Doniphan at first sight looked somewhat vague and empty. Off to the east were the buildings of Fort Sill but here were warehouses by the railroad, and all over the prairie carpenters were working frantically erecting mess halls. This seemed to be a land of wide open spaces and nowhere much to go, and the only homelike place about it—homelike from a military angle—was the camp of the First Oklahoma regiment on the hill, mobilized here waiting orders to go south to Texas where, as later events showed, it was to form part of the 36th National Guard Division.

The only orders received here were to go over the hill beyond the First Oklahoma somewhere and find a place to settle down for the time being. It developed later that food and supplies could be had on proper requisition and so the Carthage soldiers, after their

as the regiment's advance detail. *Carthage* (MO) *Evening Press*, August 23, 1917. Named for Col. Alexander W. Doniphan, a Missouri volunteer officer in the Mexican-American War, Camp Doniphan was constructed southwest of Fort Sill near Lawton, Oklahoma. Col. W.S. Nye, *Carbine and Lance: The Story of Old Fort Sill* (Norman: University of Oklahoma Press, 1943), 323–24.

commander had conferred with the captain of the Fourth Missouri unit who had accompanied them, hiked over the hill and billeted themselves in some newly constructed mess halls, and soon were quite comfortable.

It was all very nice—and was still very nice when we assembled in a compact group a few days later with only an occasional guard or fatigue to interrupt training schedules which company commanders drew up for themselves. [16]

The men enjoyed this phase of the Camp Doniphan life.

There was picturesque country to wander over on Sundays, there were jackrabbits in the open treeless plains between the camp and the hills a short distance to the north of us which afforded sport for soldiers and company mascots alike in the evening after mess and without much danger to the rabbits, and beyond the hills, at the foot of 300 foot Medicine Bluffs was Medicine Creek full of fish.[17] If there was any post regulation against fishing we were not informed of it with the result that huge catches augmented the company messes. There was also opportunity to get acquainted with the officers of other regiments, an opportunity of some value, I found, since cooperation on the front in France the following year seemed easier with officers whom one knew already.

16. There was very little for the advance detachment to do to prepare the camp for the arrival of the rest of the regiment. The Carthage company spent one morning cleaning up the ground around five large warehouses and unloading cars of freight. *Carthage* (MO) *Evening Press*, September 6, 1917.

17. Jack rabbit hunting became an elaborate affair. The men formed a long irregular skirmish line and moved across the prairie, with company mascots and men chasing the rabbits. Company A's mascots, "Putt" and "Bat," took part in the fun, and the men who did not chase the rabbits watched the sport through field glasses. Fishing proved a popular pastime as well. On one occasion, 14 members of the company caught 38 pounds of fish in one hour. *Carthage* (MO) *Evening Press*, August 29, September 5, 1917.

Troops fishing at Camp Doniphan (*Jasper County Records Center*)

The vicinity had been used as a firing range for the artillery and we had not been there long until one of my men brought me with great pride a dud shell he had found near camp. He immediately took it back and buried it deep where he found it and I assembled my company for a lecture on dud shells. It was the next day, I think, just after noon that two young fellow townsmen of mine who had enlisted in a Kansas City artillery battery which had just arrived that morning, came to call on me. One was telling me enthusiastically about artillery projectiles when there was a sudden explosion in the kitchen of his own battery, a cloud of rising blue-black smoke, and the tinkle of falling fragments of singing steel which had torn holes through the roof and sides of the building.

"That's one of them now," he concluded with a shocked expression.

It was indeed. And there was one cook dead and another wounded.[18]

18. As Schrantz describes, a Missouri soldier found a shrapnel shell on the military reservation, and thinking it a dud, brought it to the camp of Battery A, 2nd Missouri Field Artillery. An officer took it, and also believing it was harmless, took it into the battery's kitchen. The shell was then placed between the kitchen stove and a wooden partition to keep the latter from catching fire. On the afternoon of August 25, 1917, the shell became heated and exploded, killing cook James Kelley and wounding four others. One of the men was so badly injured that surgeons were forced to amputate his leg. *Kansas City* (MO) *Star*, August 26, 1917; *Kansas City* (MO) *Times*, August 27, August 28, August 29, 1917.

The newspaper accounts of the little tragedy said that by accident the kitchen range had been set over an unexploded shell buried in the ground but serving a short time later on the court martial of the battery's mess officer, I learned firsthand the facts. The lieutenants of the battery had served in it as enlisted men on the Mexican border and had learned about shrapnel but nothing of high explosive. Shrapnel, as is well known, was a projectile which contained in its forward end a large number of lead balls packed in a smoke-producing matrix. In the back of the projectile was a charge of explosive connected with the time fuse on the nose by a tube. At the time set on the fuse, theoretically when the projectile was about 40 feet from its target, the fuse fired this charge, blowing the balls out shotgun fashion in what was supposed to be a deadly manner. These officers knew that after the firing that such cases as had not cracked, and fuses on which the threads were still intact, could be picked up and screwed together to form a harmless memento.

One young officer of the battery picked up a 4.7 shell near the First Oklahoma Infantry camp.[19] It was a new type to him but was hollow at the base and taking a stick and poking it up the orifice he was able to scrape out only dirt and assumed it harmless. He carried it to his own camp and set it down by the kitchen. The mess officer, setting up the company field range, did not have stovepipe enough to keep it more than a short distance clear of the wall. The wall began to scorch and he ordered a griddle iron to be placed against it for protection. There was still a few inches exposed. He directed a soldier to place "that old shell case" in the gap. The meal was finished, the men ate and departed and the officers were eating in the mess hall when the shell exploded. The mess officer was brought before a court martial composed part of Regular officers and part of National Guard of which Colonel (later Brigadier General) Sherwood L. Cheney was president.[20]

19. Possibly 2nd Lt. James M. Pendergast of Battery A, 2nd Missouri Field Artillery, a Kansas City native and close friend of artillery captain and future president Harry S. Truman.

20. Sherwood Alfred Cheney, born on August 24, 1873, graduated from West Point in 1897. He served in Cuba during the Spanish-American War and the Philippine-American War as an engineer, then returned to the United States and performed General Staff duties. After service on the Mexican border, he assumed command of the 110th Engineers in France in 1918, and was promoted to brigadier general the following year. Awarded the Distinguished Service Medal for his service in World War I, Cheney was a member of the Paris peace commission, and was named chief military aide to President Calvin Coolidge in 1925. He retired from the army in 1937 and died on March 13, 1949. *Assembly*, Volume IX, No. 2, July 1950, 61–62.

In view of the officer's entire lack of instruction on the matter of projectiles other than shrapnel and his apparent character and intelligence and potential value to the government he was let off with a nominal punishment—forfeiture of two-thirds of his pay for three months and confinement to camp for the same period, and to a reprimand. Brigadier General Berry, acting division commander at the time this sentence was published Oct. 5, 1917, concluded the order announcing it with these words: "The sentence, although deemed inadequate, is approved and will be duly executed. This ignorant officer has wasted the life of a soldier placed under his command. Further reprimand is unnecessary."

I have always felt that if General Berry had heard the evidence, the reprimand might not have been so savage.[21] And from what I heard of the unfortunate officer's later career I believe the opinion the court martial had as to his future value was justified. Certainly he was one of the officers sent overseas in the advance school detail of the division the following March, a position for which officers were chosen rather carefully. The officer who had brought the dud shell into camp was never tried, for reasons naturally not explained to the court martial since that body had to do only with those brought before it.

A few days later—September 1—the Carthage guardsmen saw another general who visited the company at its daily drill and watched it for 10 or 15 minutes. It was Gen. Wm. M. Wright, U.S. Army, the commander of the 35th Division. At this visit he was

21. Lucien Grant Berry, born in New York on November 29, 1863, graduated from West Point in 1886 and was commissioned a second lieutenant in the artillery. He rose steadily through the ranks, to first lieutenant in 1900, major in 1907, lieutenant colonel in 1911 and colonel in 1913. After serving as an instructor at the Military Academy, Berry served in the Spanish-American War and the Philippine-American War. He led the 4th U.S. Field Artillery during Pershing's "Punitive Expedition" in Mexico. Commissioned a brigadier general in the National Army in August 1917, Berry commanded the 35th Division from September-December 1917, then led the 60th Artillery Brigade during the St. Mihiel Offensive and was acting chief of artillery of the 35th Division during the Meuse-Argonne Offensive. Berry returned to his Regular Army rank of colonel in 1919 and retired in 1921. He died on December 31, 1937, and was buried in Arlington National Cemetery. *The New York Times*, January 1, 1938; U.S. Adjutant General's Office, *Official Army Register, January 1, 1922* (Washington, D.C.: Government Printing Office, 1922), 1204. One officer, years after the war, recalled Berry's "walrus mustache," "barking voice and his relentless hunt for somebody who had failed to button blouse or overcoat properly." *The Kansas City* (MO) *Star*, July 31, 1938. Kansas Capt. Frank Bonney believed Berry to be "a typical example of the old time 'hard boiled' school," who passed on to his subordinates the theory that "discipline was best instilled by fear," and that an officer who was "thoroughly hated by his subordinates was on the high road to success." Frank E. Bonney, "Operations of the 35th Division in the First Phase of the Meuse Argonne," Advanced Officers' Course, 1922–1923, The Infantry School, Fort Benning, Georgia, 2.

still wearing the single star of a brigadier general but on another visit a few days later he wore the double stars of a major general. An individual company normally would not rate so much personal attention from generals but only the advance organizations were yet on the ground and since all of the dignitaries of the division were keen and eager to form an estimate of the quality of troops they were to command, not only the incoming generals but most of the senior members of the division staff came out frequently during drill to observe the training.

My first meeting with him I have occasion to remember with burning ears.[22]

My company was having squad drill on the plain north of camp one day, the corporals giving commands to their squads, the sergeants watching the corporals, the platoon commanders watching their platoons and the company commander—myself—observing all. I was zealous enough about it too, except when the general arrived. Some airplanes rose from a nearby field and began looping the loop and doing other stunt flying—a new thing to us in that day. Airplanes were not as common in 1917 as they have since become and the arrival of a squadron near the camp aroused considerable interest. Daily these pilots were in the air, practicing their loops and nose dives and other maneuvers used in air combat. I had been speaking to my first sergeant about something and together we stood staring at the planes. Suddenly the sergeant broke off the conversation in an awed voice:

"Captain," he said, "Here comes the general."

The general was indeed coming, striding across the field with fire in his eye.

22. William Mason Wright, a career army officer, was born in Newark, New Jersey, on September 24, 1863, and entered West Point in 1882 but left a short time later. Commissioned an infantry second lieutenant in the U.S. Army in 1885, Wright was promoted to first lieutenant in 1892. After participating in the Santiago Campaign in Cuba during the Spanish-American War, Wright was promoted to captain. He took part in Philippine-American War, then served on the General Staff and was advanced to major. Commissioned a lieutenant colonel in 1913, Wright commanded the 19th U.S. Infantry during the 1914 occupation of the Mexican port city of Veracruz. Other promotions followed quickly, first to colonel in 1916, then to brigadier and major general in 1917. He led the 35th Division to France in the spring of 1918, then assumed command of the 89th Division that September, just before the St. Mihiel Offensive, and led that division with success through the Meuse-Argonne Offensive. Following the Armistice, he led the First Corps during the occupation of Germany, and retired in 1922 as a major general. The year before his death on August 16, 1943, Wright was advanced to the rank of lieutenant general. He was buried at Arlington National Cemetery. *The New York Times*, August 18, 1943; Robert H. Ferrell, ed., *Meuse-Argonne Diary: A Division Commander in World War I* (Columbia: University of Missouri Press, 2004), 3–4.

I advanced to meet him and saluted. "Who was that private with whom you are talking?" he demanded furiously. "That was not a private, sir," I answered, "It was my first sergeant." "Were you talking about the drill?" he further queried. "Not just then, sir," I admitted. "We were speaking about the airplanes." Whereupon he read me a doubtless well-deserved few sentence lecture on keeping my mind on the job. "This is wartime, captain," he said, "not playtime." "Yes, sir," I replied, and saluted as he turned away, apparently in some surprise that I did not attempt to argue with him. I was amused, rather than humiliated, by this encounter. Plainly the general thought he had caught some National Guard captain hob-nobbing with some crony of his home town in the ranks. He was a bit taken aback when he found it was my first sergeant, and he was obviously surprised that I knew how to take a reprimand in the approved military manner of the day.

On subsequent occasions when I met General Wright he did me the honor to remember me and was most pleasant. I suspect it had not been an accident that a day or two later Colonel (later Brigadier General) Robert McCleave, his chief of staff, had strolled unobtrusively up to my company when it was engaged in boxing exercise. He probably took back a good report for he told the men of the company that if they put as much spirit in fighting as they did in the boxing exercise that he had no doubt as to their performance.[23]

I believe General Wright to have been a great soldier, though the opportunities for a man like him were not as extensive in the First World War as the Second. He commanded the 35th until it was in the Vosges mountains, then became a corps commander in that quiet mountain sector, later getting assigned to the 89th Division and commanding it during the active operations.

23. Robert McCleave was born in Fort Union, New Mexico, on September 9, 1874, and served as an enlisted man in the 1st U.S. Infantry from 1894 to 1898. Commissioned a second lieutenant of artillery in 1898, McCleave soon transferred back to the infantry, rose rapidly through the ranks, and was a major by 1916. In 1917 he was promoted to lieutenant colonel and the following year to colonel in the National Army. Following World War I, he was promoted to colonel and brigadier general in the Regular Army before retiring in 1933. During World War I, McCleave served as G-3 (training and operations) of the American First Army during the Chateau-Thierry, St. Mihiel and Meuse-Argonne operations (July–October 1918), and later served as chief of staff of the 3rd Division, for which he was awarded the Distinguished Service Medal. He died on October 27, 1961. U.S. Adjutant General's Office, *Official Army Register January 1, 1934* (Washington, D.C.: Government Printing Office, 1934), 893; U.S. Adjutant General's Office, *American Decorations* (Washington, D.C.: Government Printing Office, 1927), 736.

The first guard had come August 31 when Second Lieut. Frank L. Snyder and 26 men went on duty at the quartermaster warehouse for 24 hours.[24] This was followed a few days later by a cantonment guard which took the captain as officer of the day, First Lieut. Louis E. Dettwiler as officer of the guard, and 85 enlisted men. The north side of the huge Camp Doniphan horseshoe, took one sergeant, four corporals and 42 privates; the west side one sergeant, three corporals and 12 privates, the south side one sergeant, three corporals and 18 privates.

From this time on the tours of guard duty followed each other in rapid succession with an occasional day of unloading hay or other similar fatigue. Then the buildings at the remount station east of the old post were added to the guard detail and also the hospital buildings being constructed near the new post. Horses were now furnished to the officer of the day and the officer of the guard—and there was plenty of need for them. To make the round of all the sentries necessitated a 16-mile ride.

The company was fairly comfortable, settled in three mess halls, and other advance detachments were similarly situated—Missouri and Kansas organizations being interspersed together—but on the same day of the fatigue at the quartermaster warehouses there came Brig. Gen. Arthur B. Donnelly of the Missouri National Guard to take charge of the Missouri detachments and ordered their concentration in a single area under canvas.[25] Accordingly the companies

24. Frank LaRue Snyder was born in Carthage on April 11, 1895, and attended school there. He joined Company A, 2nd Missouri Infantry as a private in 1913, was promoted to corporal and sergeant, and served with the company on the Mexican border. He was furloughed to the reserves in December 1916. Commissioned a second lieutenant to rank from August 1917, Snyder was promoted to first lieutenant in April 1918. He served overseas from March 30, 1918 to April 24, 1919. In civilian life, he worked as a ticket clerk for the railroad and in a savings association, and died on May 25, 1963. *Carthage* (MO) *Evening Press*, May 27, 1963; *The Service of the Missouri National Guard on the Mexican Border*, 122; Missouri Secretary of State, State Archives, Soldiers' Records, War of 1812–World War I, www.sos.mo.gov/archives/soldiers; HST.

25. Arthur Barrett Donnelly was born in St. Louis on May 31, 1875. He enlisted as a private in Company F, 1st Missouri Infantry in 1892, served in the company as a first lieutenant during the Spanish-American War, and was promoted to captain in 1901. He became the regiment's major in 1909, its lieutenant colonel in 1913 and colonel in 1914. Donnelly commanded the 1st Missouri Infantry on the Mexican border and was named adjutant general of Missouri in January 1917. Hoping to see action in Europe, Donnelly resigned the Adjutant General's post and resumed command of the 1st Missouri Infantry. Described as "one of the best known citizens of the State of Missouri" and a "big manufacturer in St. Louis," Donnelly seemed destined for greatness after his promotion to brigadier general in August 1917 and command of the 69th Infantry Brigade. In April 1918, after he had arrived at Camp Mills, New York, he was accused of drinking, allowing officers under his command to do so, gambling with the junior officers of his brigade in his quarters and permitting those

and batteries moved down to the point indicated, pitched tents and made themselves at home.

"The dust in the new location is horrible," wrote one Carthage soldier—but "Camp Doniphan" and "dust" were to become more or less synonymous during the coming months. The wagons cut down through the prairie sod on the roads and the soil pulverized into dust which was carried by the winds in great gusts into the tents.

Most of the soldiers had never seen artillery fire, even in maneuvers—perhaps not half a dozen in the company had seen it firing live ammunition—and the work of the batteries attached to the artillery school of fire was a spectacle which attracted considerable attention. Student officers of the school took turns in directing the fire of these batteries, and the staring Missouri infantrymen in their spare time thus became familiar with the thunder of the guns, the screech of the shells through the air and the burst of high explosive shells in the target areas or the little puffs of smoke from bursting shrapnel and the clouds of dust whipped from the ground by the shrapnel balls. Naturally this was all witnessed from the sidelines or from near the firing point. Months were yet to elapse before the soldiers were to observe artillery at the receiving end of the line.

When General Donnelly took command he took command, so to speak, and regulated the daily schedules of the detachments under his charge in minute detail, issuing a long list of instructions and sanitary regulations which Lieut. Dettwiler facetiously termed "rules for moral and spiritual conduct." Moreover he believed in seeing that they were carried out and the Company A cooks and mess sergeant, like those of the other organizations, became accustomed to occasional visits from him in their kitchens. But the Donnelly regimen did no harm and had several positive benefits, one being that he made arrangements for the

officers to gamble at other times. Charged with "conduct unbecoming an officer," Donnelly refused to resign, and a court martial was ordered. Donnelly then resigned "for the good of the service" shortly after the court convened, an action supposedly taken with the permission of the court and on the advice of his friends. The "heart-broken" former brigadier then appeared at Camp Meade and was commissioned a major in the 11th Division, where he compiled an excellent record, and also served as major of the 72nd U.S. Infantry until his discharge. He was killed on July 29, 1919, in an automobile accident. *The Morning Herald* (Hagerstown, MD), July 31, 1919; *Report of the Adjutant General of Missouri, January 1, 1917–December 31, 1920*, 100; *St. Louis Post-Dispatch*, May 10, 1918, August 2, 1919; *Service of the Missouri National Guard on the Mexican Border*, 3.

officers to attend the night lectures being given at the school of fire at the old post at Fort Sill.

Down at nearby Lawton at this time the townspeople were making busy preparations for the coming of the division, listing vacant rooms which might be rented by persons brought there incidental to the camp; and business houses of all kinds were stocking up for the coming of the thousands of troops soon expected. All this did not interest the Carthage guardsmen so much as the Indians. Lawton was something of an Indian center, the more so since there happened to be a carnival in town about this time, and the streets were full of members of the red race.

"Many of the bucks are clad in nondescript civilian clothing, all dirty and tattered, and wear black or white felt hats," wrote one Carthage man. "Their hair is worn in two long plaits tightly bound with bright colored strips of cloth and hangs down in front of their shoulders. The squaws wear bright-colored shawls and dresses, mostly red, purple or green or of patterns in which all three mingle. For footwear some have shoes, some beaded moccasins, and others boots that appear to be made of dressed buckskin."

Occasionally there was a variation from routine. Such an incident was that of the evening of September 3 when after supper a group of Company A men led by the two buglers and an impromptu "wash-pan band" serenaded the rest of the Missouri detachments with a crude rendition of the "Houn' Dawg" tune of the Second Missouri.[26] The marchers first visited the artillery and then the rest of the organizations. Time was when that belligerent tune in a Missouri artillery camp would have caused a riot but this time the artillerymen greeted the fighting song of their ancient enemies with cheers and immediately organized a counter-procession with the trumpeters in the lead sounding that march to which soldiers everywhere had fitted the words, "Gee, I'm glad that I found the army."

Then also there was a pay day with the company commander acting as paymaster, at the door of his tent. This was for the

26. The 2nd Missouri Infantry became known as the "Houn' Dog Regiment" because of their adoption of the song "They Gotta Quit Kickin' My Dawg Aroun'" before their deployment to the Texas-Mexico border in the summer of 1916. According to one reporter, the song was played "from the Mississippi to the Rio Grande," and was "part of the soul of the regiment." *St. Louis Post-Dispatch*, May 1, 1919. The tune was published in sheet music form in 1912, with music by Cy Perkins and lyrics by Webb M. Oungst.

period August 5 to September 1 and the total, not including the officers, was $3,918.89. Private soldiers were now being paid $30 a month, just double what they had drawn on the Mexican border a year before.

Far from a convenient place at which magazines and reading matter could be purchased, the Carthage soldiers for a time felt a distinct lack along this line, but to their aid came the Carthage unit of the Women's Committee of National Defense of which Mrs. Walter MacDonald was chairman and Mrs. E.J. Burch, secretary.[27] This organization of patriotic women had early taken an interest in Company A and learning of the shortage of reading matter undertook the collection of magazines to send to the camp. A committee consisting of Miss Armilda McReynolds, Mrs. George Porter, Mrs. W. R. Heathcoatt, Mrs. J.H. Millard, Mrs. W.E. Foster and Miss Neil Butchers supervised the collection and saw that they reached the Chamber of Commerce rooms in the courthouse in time for weekly shipments.[28] Hundreds of these magazines were shipped every week to the Carthage men at Camp Doniphan and upon arrival were placed in the mess hall and there divided between the various tents. The noncommissioned officer in each tent took charge of the magazines and when one tent was through with its group it would exchange with another. Thus the magazines passed from hand to hand until they were worn out. The regular arrival of these magazines did much to maintain the morale of the organization during the training days at Camp Doniphan and to make life there as pleasant as circumstances permitted.

The women of Carthage also, under the leadership of a committee headed by Mrs. Lloyd Cowgill, made enough small pillows of a size recommended by the government as suitable for shipment to soldiers to supply each member of Company A with one, a thoughtful act which contributed much to the soldiers' comfort.[29] The government had of course furnished no pillows and until the arrival of these the men had used a roll of their extra clothing for that purpose.

27. Mary E. Macdonald (?-?) and Louise W. Burch (1867–1961).

28. Armilda H. McReynolds (1881–1954), Veda J. Porter (1878–1956), Julia E. Foster (1860–1944), Nellie S. Butchers (1869–1963), Jessie V. Dobson Millard (1862–1938), and Minnie M. Hethcoatt (1885–1968).

29. Nellie Porter Cowgill (1880–1951).

Another way in which Carthage expressed its appreciation of its National Guard company was the shipment of tobacco. Newspaper reports state that this idea originated with Mrs. Ed Lanyon.[30] Barrels were placed in several of the leading tobacco stores and customers who felt inclined to do so, purchased extra packages of smoking tobacco or cigarettes and dropped them into the barrels. The contents were collected in the due course of time and sent to Camp Doniphan where they were appreciatively received.

The following extracts from a letter written by Sergeant Norval R. Hopwood under date of September 20 and published in the [*Carthage Evening*] *Press* a few days later gives some idea of the routine and life at Camp Doniphan during this period:

"We draw a guard about every three days now. The officer of the day and his trusty steed are on the go almost continually visiting the different guards which are scattered out all over the reservation.

"For a day's duty we begin by shaking out at 5:45, five minutes calisthenics, then mess, and if we don't go on fatigue at 7, there's close order drill from 7:30 to 11:30, beginning with the school of the soldier and the squad, then platoon formations, and ending with a brisk company drill.

"After mess at 12 there is nothing to do until fatigue call at 1, when the company turns out to police (clean-up) the camp. Afternoon drill commences at 1:30 with field work and extended order until 4. Then there isn't much to do but policing up one's self, clothing and equipment, read, write, get on a detail, or play.

"Mess again at 5:15, retreat at 6, then if you present a favorable appearance to the first sergeant, you may get a pass to visit Lawton.

"To get to town one tries the street car; if you can't find a rail to hold onto, there's the shuttle train or auto line. Right around pay day the auto is most popular at 40 cents one way, and on other days the street car or shuttle train at ten and fifteen cents respectively.

"Camp Doniphan consists of a series of camp areas forming a great squared circle, the artillery to be on one side and the infantry on the other, division headquarters at one end, railway station, constructionists' camps and the new barracks at the other.

30. Grace Black Lanyon (1876–1965).

The barracks are at present occupied by the Fourteenth Field Artillery, part of the Sixth and several detachments of regulars of other branches of the service. The Fifth and Eighth F.[ield] A.[rtillery] are also in camp here and the guns are always roaring on the artillery range out to the west of camp, but we are getting used to it now, and also to the airplanes, several of which are constantly maneuvering over camp, performing breath-taking stunts that grow more and more common to us each day until now one scarcely lifts an eye to view their aerial stunts. We have about all we can do minding our own business.

"One very sad affair, however, happened last week when one of the new student aviators fell to his death from a height of probably 1,000 feet. He lost control somehow and the machine fell to the ground, burning, the aviator beneath it. Our company was at drill at the time and the accident happened in plain view of nearly all of us.

"Of the Kansas and Missouri guardsmen here now, there are detachments of one company or more from each regiment. On one side of us is L Company of the Fourth Missouri and on the other side is one of the Kansas machine gun companies. The machine gunners are perfectly acceptable neighbors and so is L Company if it would only get rid of its phonograph. We can sleep pretty good from about 1 a.m. to about 3. I think they work it by shifts.

"Sergeant Willard Brown has been trying to induce someone to 'just go get it, that's all—I'll do the rest. Oh, if I only had my hands on it.'[31]

"Of the company, Privates John S. Matchael and Dewey Frost have gone home on furlough, being called away by the serious illness of relatives there . . . Corporals Loyd [*sic*] and Lyle E. Stuckey are both still busy collecting souvenirs and are at present hunting for

31. Norval Raymond Hopwood, born in Rogers, Arkansas, on November 19, 1896, enlisted in Company A, 2nd Missouri Infantry as a private in June 1916. He served with the company on the Mexican border 1916–17 and was promoted to corporal. He served overseas with the 128th from April 25, 1918, to February 28, 1919. *The Service of the Missouri National Guard on the Mexican Border,* 126. He is believed to have died in Decatur, Georgia, on April 20, 1967. Missouri Secretary of State, State Archives, Soldiers' Records, War of 1812-World War I, www.sos.mo.gov/archives/soldiers. Willard Brown was born about 1892. He served as a corporal and sergeant with Company A on the border from 1916–1917. He was promoted to sergeant in December 1917, and served overseas with the 128th from April 25, 1918, to April 24, 1919. He died on July 2, 1930, in Denver, Colorado. Missouri Secretary of State, State Archives, Soldiers' Records, War of 1812–World War I, www.sos.mo.gov/archives/soldiers.

some kind of accommodations to care for an ancient cannon, some shrapnel shells and part of an old Indian blockhouse . . ."[32]

Naturally being at Camp Doniphan on advance detail for my regiment I was anxious to find where the Second Missouri's camp was to be and to see what I could do about getting it in order. I could not understand why I could not get this information at division headquarters. The camp was being laid out in the old triangular division formation—three infantry brigades of three regiments each and an artillery brigade of the same number of regiments. Mess halls and bathhouses were being erected, the sleeping quarters of officers and men to be in tents.[33] We had heard nothing of any impending change in organization.

Toward the middle of September a quartermaster captain at division headquarters answered my query with, "my yes, I can tell you" and showed me a plat on which had been marked at one place "Second Missouri infantry (128th, 129th and 130th Machine Gun Battalions and 110th Trench Mortar Battery)."

I pondered this as I strolled over to look at the site. The old regiment was to be broken up. Here was a bombshell indeed for the people at Camp Clark. Mentally I began phrasing the letter I must write to the colonel that night. Happily it was taken out of my hands. That evening at the quarters of Brig. Gen. Arthur Donnelly, National Guard, who had come down to take command of the advance detachments of Missouri troops, I met Major Westley Halliburton,

32. John Serman Matchael was born in Chamois, Osage County, Missouri, on September 24, 1897, and served as a private with the 2nd Missouri Infantry on the Mexican border 1916–17. He served overseas with the 128th from April 25, 1918, to April 24, 1919. He died on November 14, 1921, and was buried in Park Cemetery in Carthage. Matchael held the rank of wagoner in Company A, "driving a motor car in France, and went through the fighting without an injury." *The Service of the Missouri National Guard on the Mexican Border*, 126; Missouri Secretary of State, State Archives, Soldiers' Records, War of 1812–World War I, www.sos.mo.gov/archives/soldiers. *Joplin* (MO) *Globe*, November 15, 1921. Lloyd J. Stuckey was born in Diamond, Missouri, on January 24, 1899. He served with Company A on the Mexican border from 1916 to 1917, and overseas with the 128th from April 25, 1918, to April 24, 1919. He died on November 23, 1980, and was buried in Benton Harbor, Michigan. *The Service of the Missouri National Guard on the Mexican Border*, 128; *The Herald-Palladium* (St. Joseph, MI), November 24, 1980; Missouri Secretary of State, State Archives, Soldiers' Records, War of 1812–World War I, www.sos.mo.gov/archives/soldiers. George Dewey Frost was born on August 30, 1899. He served overseas with the 128th from April 25, 1918, to April 24, 1919. He died on February 4, 1986, and was buried in Riverside, California. Missouri Secretary of State, State Archives, Soldiers' Records, War of 1812–World War I, www.sos.mo.gov/archives/soldiers.

33. The men were apparently pleased with living in tents, for according to an unidentified member of Company A, "in the eyes of most of the men who have had any experience, a life under canvas, even in the winter, has many advantages over an existence in cantonments, such as were expected." *Carthage* (MO) *Evening Press*, September 6, 1917.

my battalion commander, who was attending the infantry school of arms then at Fort Sill. I told him what I had learned. "This calls for a telegram," he said and hurried off to Lawton.[34]

In Camp Clark this created consternation. Queries to congressmen developed the facts. All divisions were to be made square divisions—two infantry brigades of two regiments each and the artillery brigade of three regiments. The Second Missouri was to be divided as the plat which I had seen showed. All other infantry regiments were to be paired, each pair to make one new regiment. It was not the fault of the officers and men of our company that we became machine gunners. Being thus about as ignorant of machine guns as we could well be, we were not anxious to be machine gunners and we were not a bit enthusiastic about the old regiment being divided. For many years we had served under our veteran colonel, W.A. Raupp, in our own state; during the border trouble he had commanded us while we patrolled the Rio Grande in the vicinity of Laredo, Texas, and we had hoped to serve under him in battle in France.[35]

All infantry letter companies continued to be rifle companies as before and each regiment had one machine gun company. Each infantry brigade, under this first plan, was to have a three-company machine gun battalion and in addition there was to be

34. Westley Halliburton was born on November 22, 1879, in Carthage, Missouri, the son of a prominent Democratic attorney. Halliburton was admitted to the bar about 1904 and formed a partnership with his father. He joined the 2nd Missouri Infantry as brevet second lieutenant and battalion adjutant in 1900 and rose to the rank of major by 1910. He served in that capacity with the regiment on the Mexican border. He served overseas with the 128th from April 25, 1918, to April 24, 1919. Following World War I he helped reorganize the National Guard and served as lieutenant colonel of the 203rd Coast Artillery Regiment. He died in Carthage on November 2, 1948, and was buried in the city's Park Cemetery. *The Service of the Missouri National Guard on the Mexican Border*, 107; *Carthage* (MO) *Evening Press*, November 2, 1948; Missouri Secretary of State, State Archives, Soldiers' Records, War of 1812-World War I, www.sos.mo.gov/archives/soldiers.

35. In the reorganization, the 1st Battalion and Machine Gun Company of the 2nd Missouri Infantry formed the 128th Machine Gun Battalion, the 2nd Battalion formed the 129th Machine Gun Battalion, and the 3rd Battalion formed the 130th Machine Gun Battalion. The regiment's Headquarters and Supply companies formed the 110th Trench Mortar Battery, while the Band became the 311th Cavalry. The 128th was assigned as the division's machine gun battalion, while the 129th was attached to the 69th Infantry Brigade and the 130th to the 70th Brigade. As for the remainder of the 35th Division, the 1st and 2nd Kansas Infantry regiments were combined to form the 137th U.S. Infantry; the 1st and 5th Missouri formed the 138th, the 3rd Kansas and 4th Missouri formed the 139th, and the 3rd and 6th Missouri formed the 140th. The 1st Missouri Field Artillery became the 128th Field Artillery, the 2nd Missouri Artillery became the 129th, and the 1st Kansas Artillery became the 130th. The Missouri and Kansas Engineer battalions became the 110th Engineers, the Kansas Signal Battalion became the 110th Field Signal Battalion, and the Kansas Cavalry formed the Division Headquarters Troop and Military Police.

a four-company machine gun battalion directly under division control—all companies animal-drawn. A few months later this was changed to make the divisional machine gun battalion a two company motorized one and the brigade battalions four companies each—animal drawn.

Near the end of September the remainder of the troops from Camp Clark came down, morale depressed because of the coming changes, and on October 1 the new plan was put into effect. [36]

My company became Company A, 128th Machine Gun Battalion, the divisional organization, and whatever the old regiment suffered by the change our own company lot was better than those of units which had to merge. I had one officer and seven private soldiers transferred to me and that was all so far as the reorganization went. Later I received a number of men from the Selective Service Act and two officers from the first officers' training camp at American Lake, Wash., bringing the company strength up to six officers and 172 enlisted men.[37]

As to the wisdom of the War Department in going to the cumbersome square divisions, I have not ventured to pass, even mentally. I believe, however, that the form was about obsolete at the time we adopted it, the French already having passed to a form similar so far as infantry units were concerned to the triangular division

36. Following the war, the Missouri Adjutant General bitterly reported that none of the Missouri regimental or brigade commanders or the state authorities were consulted about the consolidation order, and that the order not only rendered half of the Missouri National Guard officers and NCOs supernumerary, but also wiped out "state sentiment and traditions" and destroyed "the esprit de corps of many organizations which had been in the service more than a quarter of a century," greatly discouraging and disheartening the Guardsmen. The Missouri press, the state's delegation in Congress, and its governor all protested the decision, to no avail. Missouri Adjutant General, *Report of the Adjutant General of Missouri, January 1, 1917–December 31, 1920,* 7-9. Apparently not everyone was as upset at the 2nd Missouri's demise, however. Sgt. Norval R. Hopwood wrote that the men were "very proud" of the fact that the company was attached to division headquarters, "because it is an honor of considerable importance," and participated in a big dinner and "family reunion" to celebrate the passing of the "Hound Dawg" regiment, with a splendid menu enjoyed by all present. A few days later, he noted that the regiment had not been "torn up," and had lost its identity in fact "but not in fancy. The spirit of the Hound Dawg still lives." *Carthage* (MO) *Evening Press*, October 9, 20, 1917. Walter Weber of the 129th Machine Gun Battalion recalled that although the members of the 2nd Missouri were bitter at first about the reorganization, they "became adjusted to the new order of things" and were thankful that the regiment was formed into four units, rather than being merged with another regiment. Walter W. Weber, *History of the 129th Machine Gun Battalion, 35th Division, A.E.F.* (Privately printed, 1920?), 8–9. Further information on the conversion of National Guard units and their redesignation may be found in Doubler, *I Am the Guard*, 172–73.

37. Schrantz refers to Lieutenants Fred Krueger and Bryan Mudgett, from California and New Mexico respectively, who attended the Presidio (California) and American Lake (Washington) training camps. *Carthage* (MO) *Evening Press*, October 20, 1917.

we adopted many years later. At the time I questioned nothing. The War Department had decided and the War Department was all wise so far as I was concerned.

The Second Missouri Infantry, organized in October, 1890, with Col. W.K. Caffee of Carthage as its colonel, officially passed out of existence at Camp Doniphan, Okla., September 30, 1917, at midnight, after 27 years of existence which included service in the Spanish-American War and on the Mexican border. Company A of Carthage, still to remain Company A but now of the 128th Machine Gun Battalion, observed the passing of the old regiment with a turkey dinner, at which there were present in addition to the officers and men of the company a group of guests including the little Lawton colony of Carthage wives, and a number of visiting relatives besides.

Although the Second Missouri died in name that night it did not die in spirit. The units which had composed it remained camped adjacent to each other at Camp Doniphan, performed a joint guard as if they had continued a regiment, and otherwise preserved the old contacts. Even after they went overseas they had a community of interest, all in their acquaintance and the battalions in their machine gunnery, and after the war the three battalions, returning to the United States marched together as a unit—but this end of the war was far away. This was the beginning of it and there was an ocean to cross and recross and an ordeal of blood and fire to endure before the remnants of the old regiment would march triumphantly through Southwest Missouri cities.

Probably it had not been difficult for officers in the War Department at Washington to figure out that certain infantry organizations at Camp Doniphan, Okla., in the late summer of 1917, should become machine gun units with six officers, 172 enlisted men and 12 guns per company, and to issue orders to that effect, but giving the companies machine guns with which to train was a different thing. The government had no guns to issue although the nation had been in the war almost six months, and, as it later developed, there would be no guns for a long time yet. Thus Company A, 128th Machine Gun Battalion, the Carthage organization, found itself obliged to turn in the 67 rifles in its possession but it received nothing in lieu thereof, a fact which was more than a little handicap in training. Probably more than half of the men in the company had never even seen a machine gun and the only officer with machine gun training was the newly assigned Lieutenant Edwin Samuels who had served on the border as a private soldier in a machine gun company equipped with the already-obsolete Benet-Mercier guns.[38] The lot of the Carthaginians was no worse than others. There were, in fact, few trained machine gun officers in the American army and what few there were, to judge from their writings which were being published at this time, knew little about how to use the weapons save as individual guns. Everyone did their best to progress but without equipment and without trained instructors our best was not very much.

Yet there must be training and Company A plodded ahead through the long drill hours scheduled, making the most of what means were at its disposal. Of course there were the intricacies of close order drill to be mastered—these exercises, because of their supposed disciplinary value, having been held in high esteem in the American army since the days of the Revolution when Baron von Steuben made soldiers out of Gen. Washington's ragged Continentals—and then too there was a marching ability to be developed. Semaphore signaling, estimation of distances, writing of messages, scouting and patrolling—all these were possibilities which were exploited to the full. Then daily were addresses by the company commander or some designated officer on some pertinent subject prescribed by higher headquarters—"Personal Hygiene and Care of the Feet," "Orders and Duties of Sentinels," "Military Courtesy," "Articles of War," and finally one on "Why We Are at War."

"As if it made any difference to us why we are at war," grunted the old timers with a fine contempt for the high-motive propaganda of the government. "We are American soldiers and the nation is in a position where it has to fight. That is all that concerns us."

38. Edwin Atkinson Samuel was born in Nevada, Missouri, on April 5, 1896. He joined the Machine Gun Company of the 2nd Missouri Infantry as a private in June 1916, and served with that unit on the Mexican border until early 1917. Commissioned a second lieutenant in May 1917, he served overseas from April 25, 1918, to July 24, 1919, and was wounded in action. Samuel died in California on January 29, 1980. *The Service of the Missouri National Guard on the Mexican Border*, 120; Missouri Secretary of State, State Archives, Soldiers' Records, War of 1812–World War I, www.sos.mo.gov/archives/soldiers; Memo from 2nd Lt. Edwin Samuel to Commanding Officer, 128th Machine Gun Battalion, Camp Doniphan, November 7, 1917, Record Group 120, Records of the American Expeditionary Forces, World War I Organization Records, Machine Gun Battalions, 128th Machine Gun Battalion, Box 263, NARA; HST.

Of most value, during this period, was probably the hikes and the daily physical exercises which hardened muscles and built up physique. The marches were generally to the northwest over Artillery Hill, past Apache Ridge, over Medicine Creek then up the Medicine Park road with White Wolf Hill rising on the right and Monument Hill, on top of which was buried the old Apache chief Geronimo, looming on the left. It was a wild and picturesque-appearing region whose primitiveness was accentuated occasionally by deer trotting unfrightened from bits of woodlands to heads of gulleys. Every practice march at Fort Sill was something of an incursion into the old Southwest, here preserved intact by the taboos which hedge a military reservation.

New types of drill made their appearance also about this time—games meant to develop alertness as well as muscles, boxing, [and] jiujitsu wrestling[,] supposed to be of possible value in rough and tumble fights in the trenches, instruction in the art of disarming men armed with knives, clubs or bayonets.

Along about this time the men of the 35th Division began to wear chinstraps by division order, someone in authority having acquired the idea that a strap worn on the point of the chin gave an air of smartness. A foot soldier does not need a chin strap to keep his hat in place even in a high wind, a strap worn behind the head doing that duty, but the order called for chin straps and so they made their appearance, the soldiers of the division, including the Carthaginians, soon being marked, when uncovered, by a white line from in front of the ears to the point of the chin—the less-tanned strip which the chin strap prevented from being burned to the deep brown of the rest of the face.[39]

Sunshine, dust storms, occasional northers, wind and continual drill occupied the guardsmen the rest of October and early November—and the worst of the drill was that there was no machine gun equipment and every man in the organization knew that because of this lack the company could not be trained in the things in which training was most vital. Occasionally there were visits by some notable, American or foreign, and on one occasion Senator Champ Clark spoke to the Missouri men assembled near

39. Because of this order, the division's Missouri members became known as the "chin strap" Missourians. Weber, *History of the 129th Machine Gun Battalion*, 13. One reporter noted that the guardsmen "as a rule do not fancy the 'monkey straps,' as they term them." *St. Louis Post-Dispatch*, September 28, 1917.

division headquarters, but as usual a high wind was blowing and his words could not carry as far as the Carthage soldiers.[40] The Liberty Loan drive was in progress in the division and on "Liberty Loan Day," October 24, Company A subscribed $2,900, to be paid in installments deducted from the soldiers' pay. Then too there was talk of a forthcoming government insurance plan.[41]

"It only costs 69 cents a month for a thousand," wrote Hobart Havens in a letter home. "The most any man can take is $10,000. If the soldier gets killed his beneficiary gets the money and if he does not he gets the money himself in installments just like a pension," the latter part of which remark seems to indicate that the plan was not being made any too clear to the soldiers.[42]

November 1917 blew down on Camp Doniphan, Okla., in clouds of dust and a cold gale which set the sea of tents dancing madly and tugging at their ten thousands of tent ropes; the horses and mules on their still unsheltered picket lines over in the artillery camp turned backs on the bitter wind and waited with bowed heads for the weather man to relent; the cooks muttered imprecations in their dust-filled kitchens as Oklahoma sand and soil from the unfenced somewheres beyond the north side officers' row billowed through every crevice and into the pans of food, but perhaps the cooks did not grumble so loudly as their non-culinary comrades who bore their heaped mess tins to the dirt-covered tables, gritted food and sand together between chattering teeth and then hurried back from the cheerless mess halls to the shelter of their tents again; at dark 27,000 men sought between blankets a warmth unavailable elsewhere and at dawn rose again to the noise of struggling tentage and whistling wind with an unpleasant feeling that war was an unpleasant pastime and that in due time the Germans must be punished plenty for dragging men out into a land of sand and cold where pitiless buglers blew raucous notes to stir men from cozy dreams to chill reality.

40. James Beauchamp (Champ) Clark (1850–1921) served in the U.S. House of Representatives from 1893 to 1894, was defeated for reelection, but returned to the House in 1897 and served continuously until 1920, when he was once again defeated for reelection. He served as Speaker of the House from 1911 to 1919.

41. A total of four Liberty Loan drives were held during World War I in order to sell war bonds to finance the war, and a "Victory Loan" drive was held after the Armistice. The Second Liberty Loan referenced by Schrantz began on October 1, 1917, and concluded on November 15, 1917, and authorized $3.8 billion in bonds at 3 percent interest.

42. War Risk Insurance provided a payment of up to $10,000 for death or permanent disability in the line of duty. The $10,000 coverage cost the soldier $6.60 per month, and was deducted from his pay.

Then the wind died and the Oklahoma sun beamed down as though it thought August had returned, but the trees over in the valley of Medicine Creek and on Apache Ridge and Rumbough Hill north of division headquarters, knowing better than the sun what the future had in store, began to blush at the thought of soon losing their protecting foliage and exposing their bare limbs to the gaze of the ribald soldiery. Fall had come, and the 35th Division, including Company A, 128th Machine Gun Battalion—the one-time Carthage Light Guard—continued its training for future service overseas. Back in Carthage rumors circulated about that the division was about to move, but down at Camp Doniphan where there was not one overcoat for every three men, and no arms, equipment or animals for the machine gun organizations, there was a well-founded pessimism. Some day there might be a chance to travel aboard at government expense but not just yet.

Meanwhile there was work to be done—hikes around towering Signal Mountain four miles west of the camp, trench digging in a pass beyond, schools to attend, overnight camps in shelter tents and experience in individual cooking, and a multitude of other things which were training of a sort to fill in the gap until machine guns might be secured.

Then too came the advance guard of the gas schools and lectures which were soon to figure so prominently in the training. Capt. Ward L. Schrantz, Lieut. Edwin Samuels and Sergeants Willard Brown and James A. Hines were the first to learn the half-suffocating misery of a gas mask and to master the knack of getting into one in six seconds, finishing the course with an introduction to tear gas and by spending ten masked minutes in a gas house filled with a slightly diluted mixture of the deadly chlorine. About the same time Lieut. Frank L. Snyder was going to a series of lectures at division headquarters given by a French machine gun officer and was passing on each evening to the noncommissioned officers the information thus gained. Corporal Paul Havens too was going to a school for stable sergeants, and a number of other men were also receiving special training.[43]

43. William Paul Havens was born on February 18, 1894, in Carthage. He served on the Mexican border with Company A from 1916 to 1917. He served overseas with the 128th from April 25, 1918, to April 24, 1919. During World War II, Havens served with the U.S. Army Transportation Corps as a cargo security officer on cargo ships. He died on November 18, 1955, and was buried in Park Cemetery in Carthage. *Carthage* (MO)

In early November the machine gunners began to learn something of the drill of a machine gun company. Heretofore no information on what this drill was to be had been available, and training had been in ordinary infantry drill. But the machine gun drill regulations for the whole United States Army were being prepared at the old post at Fort Sill by a board which used the Machine Gun Company of the 139th Infantry to experiment with the different formations.

First this company in its work at the old post had used little, hand-made wooden carts, the length of which was the same as that of a mule and real machine gun cart. Later mules and French carts had been furnished for the purpose.

Each machine gun company was to have 12 guns. A squad operated one gun; two made a section, two sections a platoon and three platoons a company. For each squad there were two carts, each drawn by a single mule. One cart carried the gun and tripod; the second carried ammunition. The 139th Machine Gun Company had no guns but did have the mules and empty carts.

On the forenoon of November 13 the officers of the 128th Machine Gun Battalion were taken in a truck to the west side of the Camp Doniphan horseshoe—the camp of the machine gun battalions was on the north side—and there witnessed a company drill by the 139th machine gunners. That afternoon the officers again returned, bringing with them from each company one sergeant, two corporals and 22 privates—a complete section—and these together with a platoon of the 139th made up a composite company which drilled with the mules and animals under the command of the 128th's officers, the four captains and the various lieutenants taking turns. "The men took to the work with an enthusiasm which was certainly encouraging," wrote a Company A officer, "and all of us were proud of the way that they drilled." This drill was twice repeated the following week with different men and thus half of each company received this training. Other machine gun units of the division were also training with this company.

A part of the discarded dummy carts of the 139th were obtained by the 128th Battalion and these were solemnly dragged around

---

Evening Press, November 18, 1955; *The Service of the Missouri National Guard on the Mexican Border*, 122; Missouri Secretary of State, State Archives, Soldiers' Records, War of 1812-World War I, www.sos.mo.gov/archives/soldiers.

the drills grounds as the men practiced the various evolutions—a spectacle which must have caused wonder and which certainly brought grins to the faces of the passers-by. When we first began to use the carts, officers of other units frequently rode up in amazement and wonderingly enquired [*sic*] what kind of an outfit we were and what we were doing. As for the Carthage guardsmen they smiled ruefully themselves as they recalled that they had once grinned at the wooden guns of the Carthage home guards and had facetiously termed the members of that organization "broom-stickers." They wondered what the home guards would have called them now.

Capt. (later Brigadier General) Julian S. Hatcher, 1st Lt. Glenn P. Wilhelm, and 1st Lt. (later Brigadier General) Harry J. Maloney, had published commercially a book on machine gunnery and this was our only text book aside for some ordnance manuals dealing with nomenclature and functioning.[44]

As to the tactical handling of the guns our army apparently knew only the rudiments and apparently nothing whatever of the massed use of guns such as the new organization implied. I purchased every work on machine gunnery available—there were but few—and learned what I could. After a lapse of some months I found in a Lawton book store a brand new book on machine guns and their use written by a Marine Corps officer. I bore it back to my tent at Camp Doniphan in triumph and settled down to the acquisition of worthwhile knowledge. But the officer who had written it knew even less of machine gunnery than I had already learned. After this I quit the books in despair and tried to turn to common sense instead of instruction. Unhappily it was not until after the war that I came across a copy of Colonel John H. Parker's "Gatling Guns at Santiago" written while he was a lieutenant. Colonel Parker knew more about machine guns and their potentialities in 1898 than the rest of the Regular Army apparently knew in 1917.[45]

44. A reference to Julian S. Hatcher, Glenn P. Wilhelm, and Harry J. Malony's book *Machine Guns*, published in Menasha, Wisconsin, by George Banta Publishing Company in 1917.

45. John H. Parker's *History of the Gatling Gun Detachment, Fifth Army Corps, at Santiago* was published by Hudson-Kimberly Publishing Company of Kansas City in 1898. At the Battle of San Juan Heights, Cuba, in July 1898, Parker and his Gatling guns provided valuable fire support for the American attack on the Spanish entrenchments. Parker retired as a brigadier general following World War I.

Aside from the tables of organization there was no material concerning the new machine gun organizations furnished us and even in our formations it was necessary to use our own judgment.

In the rifle company of that day the men were organized in height from right to left, an obviously unsuitable method for a machine gun unit since there would be heavy carrying to do and all gun squads should be of equal physical strength. I borrowed an artillery drill regulations and devised a formation for my own company based on that and the probable common sense requirements. I showed it to my battalion commander and he made it uniform for the battalion. When the official regulations finally appeared they were almost the same—the board presumably having approached the problem in about the same way that I did it as an individual. Information on machine gun company drill with carts and animals came a little more directly. One of the regimental machine gun companies had been working out at the Infantry School of Arms at Fort Sill under the direction of the board devising the drill. This company, probably at the division commander's direction, gave demonstrations for us using hand drawn home-made wooden carts drawn by men. We made such carts too for ourselves. And my mess sergeant hailing from our own home town knew a stenographer who worked for the board. Through him and her we obtained a carbon copy of the recommended plan and without betraying the source of our detailed information were actually familiar with the drill long before the War Department had approved it—much less had it printed.[46]

In time we got mules—just mules and nothing else—and led them daily by their halters through the drill with imaginary carts—much to their bewilderment. Then in time we received old French carts and harness. This enabled us to break our mules and train them, as well as ourselves.

The animals needed training too. French carts and Missouri mules made an inharmonious combination at first and for some weeks there was no circus in the world that could have compared

46. The Model 1917 machine gun cart carried the machine gun (usually the Vickers, Browning, and Colt machine guns), a spare barrel and cleaning rod, tripod and tool box, and 7 ammunition boxes. The Model 1917 ammunition cart had racks to hold up to 14 boxes of ammunition. Bruce N. Canfield, *U.S. Infantry Weapons of the First World War* (Lincoln, RI: Andrew Mowbray Publishers, 2000), 218–22.

with us. A mule would dubiously eye the cart chosen for him and flatly refuse to get between the shafts. It took much coaxing, cursing and expostulation before he could be hooked up and started off. Then in a panic at the strange vehicle he was drawing he would dash off at a wild run to the picket line to the dire peril of all bystanders and with the driver and squad hanging onto the reins and all projecting parts of the cart, trying to stay its progress.

But in time all was well and since riding horses had been furnished for officers and certain enlisted men we thought we made a smart enough showing. But gradually the mules lost their fear of the carts and route marching was taken up—first on the roads, then cross country, up ravines, along thickly timbered hillsides and similar difficult terrain, simulating what we imagined battle conditions might be. All of this made life more interesting for while we were experts at simulation, having had to simulate equipment and everything else for some months, it is obvious that we could simulate to better advantage if we had something to simulate with. We had simulated until we were sick of the word "simulate" and I trust that enough of the old simulating army has survived the war to see that in future wars it will not be necessary for an American soldier to simulate for months equipment that he should have the day that his training starts.[47]

As for weapons we were in worse shape—there being no machine guns for the American army as yet.[48]

Our first instruction [was] with a borrowed Benet Mercier—the obsolete air-cooled gun I had seen fired so often at Texas City. The first introduction to a machine gun was a verbal explanation of the Benet-Mercier by Lieut. H.J. Beagles of Company C, who had attended the infantry school of arms at Fort Sill and now, by direction of Major Westley Halliburton, had borrowed one of these guns somewhere and was lecturing to the different companies of

47. Schrantz reported that a full complement of horses and riding mules were drawn on November 24, 1917, and on December 14 twenty-four draft mules per company were received. Sixty machine gun carts and appropriate harness were issued to the battalion on February 6, 1918. Missouri Adjutant General, *Report of the Adjutant General of Missouri, January 1, 1917–December 31, 1920,* 95. Major Halliburton noted that "nearly every mule drill was enlivened by a stubborn contest" between mule and man, which "furnished many good laughs and very few injuries." Unbeknownst to the major, unruly mules were often swapped with more pleasant beasts during visits to the poorly guarded stables of other organizations in the camp. Westley Halliburton Manuscript, Jasper County Record Center.

48. In late 1917, Maj. Gen. William Wright reported a shortage of 234 machine guns at Camp Doniphan. *The Outlook*, January 9, 1918.

the 128th concerning it.[49] The Benet was a weird-appearing portable air-cooled weapon, adopted by the army in 1909, and said to be a good light weapon in the hands of experts and with perfect ammunition. However the Regular Army in time of peace had not been able to fire it without a more or less constant succession of stoppages and malfunctions, so it was hardly to be assumed that it would do well in time of war. Still it was a machine gun and though it was well known that it would not be used, Lieut. Beagles' listeners drank in his words with enthusiasm. There was no opportunity for anyone to shoot the gun.

Next the division secured somewhere four American Maxims, Model 1904, an excellent gun, albeit heavy, and with these a division school was started. This was a real gun, albeit heavy, meant to be separated into various loads and carried on pack mules. The American government had only a few of these but the 35th Division had managed to borrow four from the Fort Sill school. The instructors in this school were graduates of the Infantry School of Arms at Fort Sill and it is a safe guess that there was never a group of students more anxious to learn than those that took up the study of the Maxim under their tutelage. The officers of the companies were able to fire these, as well as to assemble and disassemble them, in division machine gun school; and several nights one of the guns was borrowed and placed in the Company A mess hall where its operation was explained to the noncommissioned officers and others.

These guns were important chiefly as interest-maintainers, though the Maxim was almost identical in its operation to the German Maxim and its study was, in effect, instruction in the use of an enemy weapon. The theoretical side of machine gunnery taught at the school was along lines that were not near so useful as was the mechanical teaching. Indirect fire was emphasized and since this could be worked out after a fashion on paper and without guns, every officer and non

49. Harry Jay Beagles was born in Nevada, Missouri, on August 21, 1889. He served as a private and sergeant with the Machine Gun Company of the 2nd Missouri Infantry on the Mexican border from 1916 to 1917. Commissioned a first lieutenant in April 1917, Beagles attended the School of Musketry at Fort Sill from April to June 1917, then he initially served with Company D, 128th Machine Gun Battalion. He was transferred to Company D, 129th Machine Gun Battalion in March 1918, served overseas from May 3, 1918, to April 27, 1919, and was slightly wounded during the Meuse-Argonne Offensive on September 27, 1918. He died on March 25, 1942, in Great Falls, Montana, and was buried in the Montana State Veterans Cemetery in Helena. *The Great Falls* (MT) *Tribune*, March 26, 1942; *The Service of the Missouri National Guard on the Mexican Border*, 118; Missouri Secretary of State, State Archives, Soldiers' Records, War of 1812–World War I, www.sos.mo.gov/archives/soldiers; HST.

commissioned officer of machine gun units in the division was soon, in company schools and in leisure time, struggling with problems of this type. Of course what should have come first in the training of the orgnizations was practical work with the gun including much direct fire at varying ranges but, while starting in on theoretical work was much like going to college without ever having been through high school, the mental exercise was excellent. Many of the methods used were found to be impractical in war but the study of them prepared the mind to quickly grasp truly useful instruction later. Almost a year and a half after this time I conducted a division machine gun school in France and I found that the organizations best informed on barrage methods and practical indirect machine gunnery were those who had worked the hardest on the old original theories in the States.

Then eventually two obsolescent Colt machine guns per company were issued—a gas operated, air cooled gun and this gave an opportunity for training the men in machine gun firing.[50]

50. Schrantz noted that "a few selected officers and non-commissioned officers received some training with the four American Maxims, model 1904, in possession of the Division Machine Gun School." Two Colt machine guns were issued to the company on January 4, 1918, and "some time later" a few officers and non-commissioned officers received training on Vickers guns in the possession of the division school. Missouri Adjutant General, *Report of the Adjutant General of Missouri, January 1, 1917–December 31, 1920,* 95. Maj.Westley Halliburton, the 128th Battalion's commander, noted that "hardly an officer in the battalion was without a mashed finger acquired in learning the mechanical operation" of the Maxims. Even if ammunition had been available, the barrel was so worn that "it could not have fired with any accuracy." Despite the fact that ammunition was available for the Colt guns, and a crude range prepared near camp, the gun's recoil fanned so much sand into the mechanism that it jammed, forcing the company mechanics to disassemble, clean and reassemble the weapon so that it could be ready to fire another 50 to 100 rounds. Westley Halliburton Manuscript, Jasper County Record Center. The Model 1909 Benet-Mercie Machine Rifle was a gas-operated, air-cooled weapon that weighed approximately 30 pounds, and was chambered for the U.S. .30-06 cartridge, fired from 30-round metal strips. Manufactured by the Colt Company and the government's Springfield Armory, the Benet-Mercie was capable of firing about 400 rounds per minute. The gun was used in Gen. John J. Pershing's "Punitive Expedition" in Mexico in 1916–1917 and went to France with the first American troops in 1917, but because of its complexity and tendency to break critical parts and fail under dirty field conditions, it was soon relegated to a training role, and U.S. troops carried more reliable machine guns in combat. The Model 1904 Maxim, a heavy machine gun designed by American Hiram Stevens Maxim and produced by Colt, was a water cooled weapon chambered for the U.S. 30-06 cartridge. The gun itself weighed 74.5 pounds with a full water jacket, and the tripod weighed about 78 pounds. The Maxim could fire 450 rounds per minute. The Model 1904 was also used in training but not in combat. The Model 1914 Colt machine gun weighed 35 pounds, with a 56-pound tripod. The Colt fired between 400 and 450 U.S. 30-06 rounds per minute. Like the other machine guns mentioned by Schrantz, the Colt was not used in combat and was relegated to a training role. Canfield, *U.S. Infantry Weapons of the First World War*, 165–83. At least some members of the company were excited by the appearance of the obsolete Colts, however. An unidentified Carthage man wrote that the guns "made life seem considerably brighter, for we have been longing for real honest-to-goodness machine guns for many a day," and although they would be issued other machine guns, for now "we are enjoying what we have." *Carthage* (MO) *Evening Press*, January 10, 1918.

No instructions came with the guns but early the next morning they were opened and all day Saturday the men of the company worked with the weapons, learning how they operated and why. Until noon Sunday, too, the guns were kept busy, and then there arrived an order from division headquarters that the weapons would not be unboxed but would remain untouched until Monday evening when an officer of the Ordnance Department would unpack and demonstrate them. This belated order caused some mirth. The officers and men of Company A would have been somewhat less than human had they waited five months for machine guns and then, when at last two arrived, waited from Friday evening until Sunday noon before they even opened the boxes. The ordnance officer arrived Monday evening as scheduled and found that not only was there no unpacking to do but that the group he was to address was already possessed of a working knowledge of the gun.

The Colt was an air-cooled, gas operated gun, one of the early inventions of Dr. J.[ohn] M. Browning whose name was later given to the Browning machine gun. The Colt had been used in the Philippines and in Latin-American wars with considerable success and had been utilized by the Canadians and to some degree by the Russians at the beginning of the World War but it was much less efficient than modern guns and was issued now only for training purposes, later to be replaced by some less antiquated weapon. Thirty-fifth Division machine gunners had already been prejudiced against the Colt from hearsay evidence about its unreliability but in Company A at least it was enthusiastically welcomed as a real machine gun at last and the only real regret was that there had not been 12 instead of two. From this time until the guns were finally taken up they were constantly in use, different sections of the company taking turns in their use. They were supposed to fire at the rate of about 600 shots per minute but our experience with them after they were in use awhile was that it was not always certain that they would fire at all. At first there was considerable firing but the firing steadily decreased as the guns grew less and less reliable and it was not long until half of those in the division were incapable of being fired.

A short time before the division moved to a port of embarkation early in 1918, and after I had left in advance, a few Vickers were also loaned for training purposes.

Looking back it seems that we trained as well as we could under the circumstances. There was a flock of foreign instructors around the division but so far as I recall there were no machine gun instructors—at least none prior to the time I left. I attended one excellent tactical lecture on machine guns in trench warfare on the Western Front delivered by a British officer and looked forward with great anticipations to a scheduled lecture by Colonel F.D.? [*sic*] Applin, famous machine gunner of the British Army. Only, to our deep regret, Colonel Applin did not talk about machine guns. He told us of the fine discipline of the British Army and how far we had to go before we could be as good.

"Of course you can hold a line," he said scornfully. "Anybody can hold a line. Even the Portuguese can hold a line." I thought of that some time later when the March 21 German offensive hit and neither the Portuguese or the British were able to hold their line due to circumstances which Colonel Applin had not foreseen. The British are a great fighting people but in that winter of 1917–1918 they still had a good deal to learn about the fighting ability of some of their friends. We were neither pleased nor instructed by the address of the great Colonel Applin—we machine gunners felt quite cheated.[51]

Looking back, the greatest shortcoming in instruction at Camp Doniphan seems to me to have been the lack of division maneuvers. So far as I know, none were ever held. I think I am correct in saying that the first time the 35th Division maneuvered as a complete unit in World War I was in battle in France.[52]

51. Reginald Vincent Kempenfelt Applin, born on April 11, 1869, was educated at Newton College and Sherborne, and in his early twenties served as a cadet in the Chartered Company's service in North Borneo. After eight years he resigned his appointment, but fought in the Boer War with the 6th Lancashire Fusiliers. After serving with the Machine Gun Corps on the Western Front, Applin was sent to America to lecture on machine gun tactics. He was awarded the Distinguished Service Order (DSO) and Order of the British Empire (OBE). Following World War I Applin commanded the 14th King's Hussars and served as a member of Parliament from 1924 to 1929 and again from 1931 to 1935. In the latter year he emigrated to South Africa, and died in Natal on April 5, 1957. *The* (London) *Times*, April 11, 1957. Two of Applin's lectures ("Lecture on Machine Guns and their Tactical Employment" and "Lecture on the Machine Guns at the Battle of Messines," both delivered at the Army War College in Washington, D.C., in November 1917) appeared in U.S. War Department, Office of the Adjutant General, *Machine Gun Notes No. 2, From British Sources*, edited at the Army War College in February 1918.

52. On December 1, 1917, Schrantz reported to battalion commander Halliburton on his company's training progress. He informed the major that a company tactical school had been conducted for the past month, attended by all officers and non-commissioned officers and selected first class privates. Each evening that day's drill and the one scheduled for the following day were discussed. Because a lack of equipment had forced the company to drill

Frequent Carthage visitors came to the camp at Fort Sill—generally parents of the men in the company—and these returning brought news of the company's welfare. Letters from the camp in the paper were few, the authorities discouraging any writing for publication and even banning the taking of photographs unless submitted to divisional headquarters for censorship. Returning from the camp in early November, Mrs. J.J. Daugherty, mother of Corporal Murl Daugherty, reported, according to the *Press*, "that aside from the dust everything is fine at the camp. The boys are pleased at the excellent food they are given." Two weeks later Mrs. C.E. Edwards, mother of Sergeant Charles Edwards, and Mrs. Tom Glass, mother of John Glass, gave a similar report, Mrs. Glass being quoted by a *Press* reporter as saying: "The boys have floored their tents and have stoves and plenty of blankets. Food is good and plentiful. Water is very low as there have been only two rains in ten months but a new 24-inch main is being installed which will give plenty of water. There is no hot water in the bath houses so the boys find a bath a pretty chilly proposition. The men are not yet supplied with woolen uniforms or overcoats and will be glad when they get them. They appreciate the Press next to a letter from home."

Speaking of Corporal Daugherty and the *Press*, the corporal laid himself open to some good natured jibes for the next year or so through a letter which he wrote to a Carthage friend and which appeared in print. Daugherty had just told of being made

---

"largely as an unarmed infantry company," the entire time was not occupied in discussing the daily drill, but the company discussed "machine gun work" focused on "timely" discussions. The evening before the company was sent out to work in the trenches, for instance, the men discussed trench design and construction. Later evenings were devoted to the location and construction of machine gun emplacements, use of machine guns in trench warfare, the relief of trenches, etc. Likewise, drills in outpost work and advance guard were supplemented by discussions about the machine gun's role in these training events. December 1, 1917, Memo from Captain Ward L. Schrantz, C.O., Company A, 128th Machine Gun Bn. to C.O. 128th Machine Gun Battalion, Record Group 120, Records of the American Expeditionary Forces, World War I, Entry NM-91 1256, Organization Records, Machine Gun Battalions, Box 264, 128th Machine Gun Battalion, Co. A – DOC. FILE 1-1203, NARA. At the end of January 1918, Schrantz reported that the company tactical school had continued meeting, using the appendix of the Machine Gun Firing Manual as a guide. Schrantz sought to find training that had been incomplete or "not thoroughly assimilated." The topics discussed in these evening sessions included the classes of machine gun fire, indirect fire, patrolling, map reading, and "kindred subjects." These exercises were intended to "increase the military vocabulary" of those attending. January 31, 1918, Memo from Capt. Ward L. Schrantz, C.O., Co. A, 128th Mach. Gun. Bn. to Commanding Officer 128th Mach. Gun. Bn., Record Group 120, Records of the American Expeditionary Forces, World War I, Entry NM-91 1256, Organization Records, Machine Gun Battalions, Box 264, 128th Machine Gun Battalion, Co. A – DOC. FILE 1-1203, NARA.

company signal corporal and added, "In all probability I will be mounted." During the rest of the service in Oklahoma and during a year of hikes in France, the corporal, plodding along on foot with his comrades, was very likely to hear someone somewhere remark sotto voco, "In all probability I will be mounted."

Thanksgiving Day in the Company A camp was observed in a fitting manner with turkey the principal feature of the menu. There were a number of visitors including twelve ladies—mothers or wives of soldiers.

December, 1917, opened in Camp Doniphan with rumors that the 35th Division was about to move overseas. These reports were eagerly discussed by the men of Company A, 128th Machine Gun Battalion, in the mess hall at meal times, in the tents at night, on the drill field during rest periods, and everywhere else men were congregated and had an opportunity to talk, and doubtless they were brought back to Carthage as fast as dozens of personal letters could bring them and were little less earnestly discussed around the firesides in those homes which had contributed men to Company A.

At the officers mess of the 128th Machine Gun Battalion at Camp Doniphan, the rumors were analyzed, dissected, weighed and believed—and a little more information was available here than elsewhere. A series of more or less confidential division memoranda had started out with the words, "When this division moves overseas," and there was much gossip as to when this long-hoped-for event might be and how the move would be accomplished. Information was that the organizations would be embarked from one port and the animals from another, and 1st Lieut. Louis E. Dettwiler of Carthage had been tentatively designated by Major Westley Halliburton as the officer to command the detail which would take the animals of the 128th to France. Interest was at a high pitch.

But the days rolled on and nothing new developed. Hopes which had been soaring fell again. Evidently the time had not yet come.

The weather again furnished the principal topic of conversation. On December 6 Company A was able to secure overcoats, and it was not too soon. The next day the wind shifted to the north and increased to gale intensity, whipping a mixture of dust and snow

Ward Schrantz's locket (*Memorial Hall, Carthage, MO*)

horizontally across the camp while men shivered around their small tent stoves and canvas hammered ceaselessly on the wooden tent frames. The temperature fell far below freezing. Tents have some advantages for abodes during winter training but they are not so good when 90-mile gales drive Arctic atmosphere into every open place. But back in Carthage the people were shivering too. There was a snow between 20 and 24 inches in depth and the temperature dropped to six below zero. It was the first big storm of an unusually cold winter.

But the cold could not interfere with military training long. There would be winter in France also, but that would not stop the war. Daily some organization hiked to the trenches in Berry Pass beyond Signal Mountain. In Europe trench warfare had been in progress for years and the little flock of foreign officers who had descended on every American camp was emphasizing training in the construction of trenches and the development of "trench sense."

Ward Schrantz's "dog tag" (*Memorial Hall, Carthage, MO*)

Then the division commander, Maj. Gen. William Wright, returned from France where he had been on a tour of observation and brought back with him a new store of energy. The training from now on would be for open warfare. It must be carried on with increased energy. "Mistakes made on the battlefield are paid for in human blood." The personality of the commander, fresh from the scene of war and from interview with General Pershing, impressed itself instantly on the whole division.

During his absence, Brig. Gen. Lucien G. Berry, commander of the artillery brigade, had been in command, and naturally had devoted his attention as far as training went, chiefly to the artillery. Moreover he was believed to be antagonistic toward the senior officers of the National Guard and for one reason or another had relieved a number from command. Others were afraid of him and lived in fear. The return of Gen. Wright not only was a healthful influence on the drill field but it lifted considerably the cloud of apprehension which had hung like a pall over the quarters of most officers above the grade of captain.

Many of my men were married to home-town girls while at Camp Doniphan—most of them probably being marriages that would have occurred had the men remained at home. There being no U.S.O. in those days and no social contacts in Lawton, so far as I know, the brides were all Carthage, Mo., girls who, with or without relatives, came down to the Oklahoma camp to marry their boyfriends while there was still time. So far as I recall the marriages turned out to be reasonably happy ones, but all the same I thought it most unwise for a man to get married on the eve of a campaign. But with normal human inconsistency, since we stayed at Camp Doniphan for a long time, I went against the advice I had given to others. Miss Delphia Hoover of Carthage and I were married February 23, 1918, at Lawton. Three weeks later I started for France. I have never regretted marrying on the eve of a campaign.[53]

Christmas Eve was celebrated in [the] Company A mess hall with a general jollification with all officers and men present. The Carthage Red Cross through the co-operation of Carthage citizens had sent down Christmas boxes for all members of the company and for former members who had been transferred from other units and these were distributed and opened at this time. Then at 5 o'clock that afternoon an Edison phonograph of the type known as the Army and Navy Model, being suitable for shipment in box form, had been received. It too was the gift of Carthage citizens, having been purchased by subscribers to a list circulated by Harry Ulmer and others.[54] It was a pleasant Christmas Eve for Company A. "You may be sure that it seems

53. Delphia Hoover, valedictorian of the Carthage High School class of 1915, was "well and favorably known in Carthage," and was teaching school near Carthage when she married Schrantz. *The Carthage* (MO) *Evening Press*, February 25, 1918. As early as December 1917, one newspaper noted "an epidemic of marrying" among the National Guard troops, despite the best efforts of Gen. Lucien Berry to deny furloughs to men who wished to leave camp to marry. *Kansas City* (MO) *Star*, December 11, 1917.

54. Harry Dewey Ulmer was born on August 15, 1890, in Greenville, Illinois. In 1916, Ulmer's father purchased an undertaking company in Carthage, and his son came to the city to work with his father. He died on December 1, 1943, in Carthage, Missouri. Ulmer was inducted into the army in June 1918 and served in the Quartermaster Corps as an embalmer on American troop transports, making numerous trips across the Atlantic. *Carthage* (MO) *Evening Press*, December 2, 1943.

good to a soldier to be remembered by the people of his home town," wrote the company commander in thanking the donors of the Carthage gifts.

"I have eaten so much that I am in misery," confided Private Harry Palmer in a letter written Christmas night to his parents.[55] "We have 37 boxes in this squad. Your box is sitting here untouched. I am just so full I can't eat any more and the rest of the boys are in the same fix. But we will renew the attack on the eats tomorrow. Last night we had a big time. We decorated the mess hall with fir tree and mistletoe and green paper. I guess the Carthage people must have sent $50 or $75 worth of candy, nuts and cookies, and we popped a lot of corn here. The phonograph that [the] Carthage people sent us is fine. We sure are playing it. The captain came over and had a good time with us, also the lieutenants. We received a sack of tobacco and a cigar last night. This morning we received our Red Cross box. They had tobacco, peanut candy, handkerchief, tablet, envelopes, raisins and a pipe. Then we had some dinner. Major Halliburton sent over a cigar for every man in the company. Last night we had a letter from General Wright wishing us a merry Christmas and a happy new year and thanking us for hard work we had done and for what we would do."

But not all Company A men were present on these occasions. Measles had been spreading in the 35th Division camp for about two months and although Company A had been immune for a time after the outbreak, Christmas found it with six men in hospital as a result of an epidemic and a dozen more in quarantine. Another case in the company developed a few days later and the tent mates of the man went to the isolation camp. In all there were 1,434 cases in the division during the winter—965 cases developing in December—with 46 deaths. The epidemic of measles, it was reported as New Year's Day neared, was the reason the division had not been moved eastward.

On January 11 winter showed its teeth in the worst storm of the year. "A roaring blizzard, the real prairie kind and by far the worst I have ever seen," wrote an officer. "The storm raged all

55. Harry H. Palmer, born in Russellville, Indiana, on March 5, 1899. He served overseas with the 128th from April 25, 1918, to April 24, 1919. He died in Dallas, Texas, on July 1, 1956. *Dallas Morning News*, July 2, 1956; Missouri Secretary of State, State Archives, Soldiers' Records, War of 1812–World War I, www.sos.mo.gov/archives/soldiers.

night and the cold was intense. Snow drifted badly into all of the tents and when I went to bed there was a drift 5 ½ inches deep inside my door and extending half way across the floor, even piling up defiantly around the legs of the stove. I had laid my slicker over my desk and there was an inch of snow on that. The blizzard abated along about daylight. During the night the drift on my floor had increased to 8 ½ inches and there was a little conical mound four inches deep on my bed near the foot. It was intensely cold all day."

It was a cold wave which engulfed the whole Middle West. Two nights later in Carthage the temperature was down to 16 below zero.

February 5, 1918, marked the end of Company A's first six months in the field during the World War and it had been intended to observe this with a special dinner and a little celebration, but instead there was a different kind of observance—a slow marching column with a band playing a dead march, three crashing volleys and a bugler sounding taps in mid-afternoon.

Private Eugene Ring, who had been working on a farm near Knights Station when the war broke out, although his home was in Cresskill, N.J., had been among the early ones to enlist in Company A. When the measles epidemic broke out at Camp Doniphan he went to the hospital with the disease. Next still in the hospital, he took pneumonia, then diphtheria, and died of the latter disease the evening of February 3. Presumably this succession of diseases was a result of the overcrowded condition of the Fort Sill hospital.[56]

Private Ring was buried in the Fort Sill cemetery on the afternoon of February 5, a typical soldier's funeral with the men of his company the only mourners present. Because of the nature of

56. Schrantz received an inquiry about Eugene Ring from Rose Phillips of Cresskill, New Jersey, dated December 28, 1917. She told of "sickness at his home, from worry, about not hearing from him." Schrantz responded that Ring was in the hospital but was much better, and he would send word to Ring "that his people are worried by his silence." On February 6, 1918, Schrantz wrote a condolence letter to Ring's grandfather, stating that Ring was an "excellent soldier" and "universally liked," and that his death was "deeply regretted" by everyone in Company A. In addition, he noted that Ring had "died for and in the defense of his country" as if he had died on a battlefield in Europe. "You have our sincerest sympathy in your bereavement—a bereavement which is also ours." Letter from Rose Phillips to 35th Division, December 28, 1917; Memo from Commanding Officer, Company A, 128th Machine Gun Battalion, to Miss Rose Phillips, January 4, 1918; Memo from Commanding Officer, Company A, 128th Machine Gun Battalion, to D.T. Atwood, February 6, 1918, Record Group 120, Records of the American Expeditionary Forces, World War I Organization Records, Machine Gun Battalions, 128th Machine Gun Battalion, Box 264, NARA.

the disease only the company commander was permitted to view the body. Services were at the grave.

The band of the old Second Missouri led the procession which moved to its solemn music from the post hospital to the graveyard. After the band marched the firing squad with borrowed rifles, then walked the chaplain of the 110th Engineers, next followed the flag-covered casket on a light truck, and finally a platoon of Company A under the company commander. By the grave under the trees of the cemetery the chaplain read a few verses of scripture and offered a prayer. The firing squad fired three volleys over the casket and a Company A musician sounded taps. That was all. Leaving the scene, the band, in accordance with army regulations, played a spirited march. Private Ring had made his sacrifice and the war was over for him.

I had been a member of an "advance school detachment" for some months, a group to precede the division overseas and receive additional training in the A.E.F. So far as the machine gun units were concerned this included a captain from each battalion and a lieutenant and three sergeants from each company. With me from my company was Lieutenant Frank L. Snyder, with whom I had served as an enlisted man on the border in 1916. Sergeant Fred Clark, who like myself had served both at Texas City in the Regular Army and later on the border with the National Guard, Sergeant Edwin W. Wiggins who later was to fall in action, and Sergeant (later Lieutenant) James A. Hines.[57]

On March 20 we finally got underway and were on the troop train crossing New Jersey and nearing New York when newspapers were brought aboard with news of the great German offensive of March 21 and of a German long range gun firing on Paris which was miles beyond any known artillery range from the front. Our artillery officers with us on the train went into a huddle and emerged hooting at the idea. It was impossible, they emphatically agreed, for a gun to be constructed that would fire that far. They had yet to learn that in war the supposedly impossible is frequently accomplished.

57. Fred R. Clark joined Company A in June 1916 and was quickly promoted to sergeant. He served with Company A on the Mexican border from 1916 to 1917. James A. Hines joined Company A in July 1914, as a private, and likewise served with the company on the Mexican border. *The Service of the Missouri National Guard on the Mexican Border*, 122, 126.

USS *George Washington* (*Jasper County Records Center*)

Quickly the train was shunted up northward to Camp Merritt in whose half-finished buildings the detachment was quartered for the time being. It may be mentioned incidentally that in the outskirts of Camp Merritt in Tenafly, N.J., on the route one took to the Fort Lee ferry and New York City, sat a house on which was a placard, "D.T. Atwood, architect," and in the window hung a service flag with a bit of black crepe pasted over the star—the gold star to denote a soldier deceased had not yet come into general use. It was the home of Private Eugene Ring of Company A who had died at Camp Doniphan the month before, and D.T. Atwood was his grandfather and his next-of-kin.

After some days at Camp Merritt, at Tenafly, N.J., we were moved down to the former Hamburg-America Line dock in Hoboken on March 29 and embarked on the *George Washington*, one of the German liners which had been interned in American ports, seized by our government on the outbreak of the war, and operated as navy transports.[58]

58. Camp Merritt, named for Civil and Spanish-American War Maj. Gen. Wesley Merritt, was located 15 miles northwest of Jersey City, New Jersey. The *George Washington*, a German passenger liner, was converted into a transport and commissioned in September 1917. The ship sailed for Europe for the first time as a troopship in December 1917 and made eighteen round-trip voyages over the next two years. Dictionary of American Naval Fighting Ships (http://www.history.navy.mil/danfs/g4/george_washington-ii.htm), accessed May 10, 2011.

This was already a famous ship because of her peacetime voyages. She had been built in 1908 by the A.G. Vulcan Co., of Stettin, Germany, was 722 feet in length and 78 feet in the beam, and had a gross tonnage of around 24,000. She was to carry about 100,000 troops during this war and later was to take President Woodrow Wilson to France to attend the Versailles Conference. At that time she was a two funnel coal-burner, capable of only about 11 knots. In World War II she was again placed in service after complete modernization and the installation of oil-burning engines which gave her a speed of around 16 knots and I sailed in convoy with her on her maiden second war voyage early in 1943.

Going aboard her that March 29, 1918, I was assigned to a stateroom with Major (later Colonel) W.L. Gist; Captain (later Brigadier General) George A. Wark, and Captain (later Lieutenant Colonel) Paul A. Frey. Wark had belonged to the Kansas National Guard, the rest of us were Missourians.[59]

59. Dr. William Lucien Gist, born near Fort Leavenworth, Kansas, on August 9, 1881, enlisted in the U.S. Army for the Spanish-American War at age 17, and also saw service in the Philippines. He began studying medicine when he returned and graduated from the University Medical College in Kansas City in 1906. He joined the Missouri National Guard as a first lieutenant of the Medical Corps in 1912, and was promoted to captain and assigned to Ambulance Company Number 1 later that year. He served with that unit on the Mexican border. In World War I Gist was promoted to major, and during World War II served as medical director of the Selective Service in Missouri. He died on January 25, 1956. *Kansas City* (MO) *Star*, January 25, 1956; *The Service of the Missouri National Guard on the Mexican Border*, 480. George H. Wark was born near Liberty, Kansas, on December 19, 1878. He graduated from the University of Kansas in 1903 and established a law practice in Caney, Kansas. A first lieutenant in the Kansas National Guard, Wark organized Company D, 3rd Kansas Infantry and became its captain in May 1917. The company became Company D, 139th Infantry, but Wark was transferred to command of Company B, 129th Machine Gun Battalion. Wark was cited in division orders for his "coolness, disregard of danger and ability to command" on the morning of September 26, 1918, when he reformed a line of scattered units, instilled in them "his own fighting spirit," and led them into the town of Cheppy. Following the war, Wark rose through the ranks of the Kansas National Guard and was promoted to brigadier general in 1933. When the 35th Division was mobilized for service in late 1940, Wark was given command of the division's artillery brigade, but was released from federal service due to disability before World War II began and returned to his law practice. Wark died on September 21, 1974, and was buried in Caney, Kansas. *Springfield* (MO) *Republican*, December 5, 1918. His published diary of part of his voyage overseas may be found in the *Independence* (KS) *Daily Reporter*, May 4, 1918. Paul Alphonso Frey was born in Paris, Illinois, on May 23, 1883. He enlisted in and was honorably discharged from two companies of the 2nd Missouri several times from 1903 to 1907, then enlisted in Company K in 1908. He became captain in 1911 and led the company on the Mexican border. When the company became Company B, 130th Machine Gun Battalion, Frey continued in command, serving overseas from March 30, 1918, to April 28, 1919, and was seriously wounded in the head by shrapnel on September 29, 1918. Following the war he remained in the Missouri National Guard and retired as a lieutenant colonel. He died on January 4, 1967, and was buried in Hazelwood Cemetery, Springfield, Missouri. *The Service of the Missouri National Guard on the Mexican Border*, 183; Missouri Secretary of State, State Archives, Soldiers' Records, War of 1812–World War I, www.sos.mo.gov/archives/soldiers.

It was a nice stateroom, originally built for two, and I was impressed. In the bathroom I looked with pleasant anticipations at the various faucets, labelled in German, for cold fresh water and hot fresh water, and cold and hot saltwater. I turned the hot fresh water faucet for a shave but what I drew was cold saltwater. That was all any of the faucets yielded. The Germans had disabled the condensing apparatus. All the fresh water we had on the voyage was brought in daily in a small can by the room steward.

That day and the next we lounged on the deck, staring at the North River and the ships, camouflaged in weird World War I fashion, that passed by. Among them was the great *Leviathan*—the former German *Vaterland*— which was fast enough that she ran alone instead of in convoy.[60]

At dusk, March 30 we cast off, proceeded down the river and into the bay, past the brightly-lighted Statue of Liberty, out through the narrows and to sea. Daylight of the next day—Easter Sunday—showed us steaming along behind the cruiser *Frederick* with the *Abraham Lincoln*, the *Antigone*, the *St. Louis* and a smaller ship said to have been a former United Fruit Lines vessel which none of the navy personnel with whom I talked could identify. Later two more transports—the *Susquehanna* and *De Kalb*—appeared and we zig-zagged our way toward Europe.[61]

60. "Dazzle" painting or camouflage used patches of black or color paint to deceive German U-Boat commanders as to a ship's course, range, and speed. *Vaterland* was built as German's largest passenger liner. Launched in 1913, the ship was seized when the United States entered World War I and commissioned in July 1917. Renamed *Leviathan* that September, the 58,000-ton ship completed ten round-trip voyages to Europe before the end of the war. Dictionary of American Naval Fighting Ships (http://www.history.navy.mil/danfs/l5/leviathan.htm), accessed May 10, 2011.

61. *President Lincoln*, originally a German liner, was built in 1907 and seized when the United States entered the war. Commissioned a troop transport in July 1917, *President Lincoln* made four successful round-trip voyages to Europe. The ship reached France on a fifth voyage in May 1918, but while returning to America was attacked and sunk on May 31 by the German submarine U-90, 600 miles off the French coast, with a loss of 3 officers and 23 enlisted men killed and 1 taken prisoner. (http://www.history.navy.mil/danfs/p11/president_lincoln.htm), accessed May 10, 2011; U.S. Navy Department, *American Ship Casualties of the World War* (Washington, D.C.: U.S. Government Printing Office, 1923), 1. Unknown to the Carthage men, Harry M. Bouser, formerly of Carthage and once a sergeant in Company A, was a member of the *George Washington*'s crew. Bouser spent 19 hours on a life raft before being picked up by rescuing destroyers. Harry Michael Bouser had left Carthage in 1913 and opened a greenhouse in Portland, Oregon. He sold the business and enlisted in the U.S. Navy on April 19, 1917. Bouser joined the crew of the *President Lincoln* on September 1, 1917, and made all five of the ship's trips to Europe. Discharged on July 2, 1919, he died on November 14, 1940, and was buried in Paradise Cemetery, Jasper, Missouri. *Carthage* (MO) *Evening Press*, June 1, 1918, July 2, 1918.

Antigone (originally the German liner *Neckar*) was launched in 1900. Seized when the United States entered the war, the ship was converted for use as a troop transport, renamed and commissioned in September 1917. *Antigone* made eight round-trip voyages

The cruiser was the only escort vessel in the early part of the voyage, the danger of submarines in the western or middle Atlantic being deemed slight. All of our guns were loaded and fully manned at all times, a glimpse of a periscope or the wake of a torpedo being the only way the presence of a submarine could be detected. The life jackets issued were fore-and-aft contrivances commonly referred to as "Ostermoors."

to Europe before war's end. Dictionary of American Naval Fighting Ships (http://www.history.navy.mil/danfs/a9/antigone-i.htm), accessed May 10, 2011; *St. Louis*, a passenger liner, was launched in Philadelphia in 1894. Commissioned as an auxiliary cruiser, the ship saw action in the Spanish-American War. Decommissioned, the ship returned to service as a liner until commissioned as the *Louisville* in April 1918 and made several trips to Europe during the war as a troop transport (http://www.history.navy.mil/danfs/s17/st_louis-iii.htm), accessed May 10, 2011; the *Susquehanna*, originally the German liner *Rhein*, was built in 1899 and was seized when the United States entered the war. Commissioned as a transport in September 1917, *Susquehanna* made eight trips to Europe before the Armistice (http://www.history.navy.mil/danfs/s20/susquehanna-ii.htm), accessed May 10, 2011. *DeKalb*, originally the *Prinz Eitel Friedrich*, was launched in 1901. Seized by the United States in 1917, the ship was commissioned as the troop transport *DeKalb* in May 1917. *DeKalb* was part of the convoy carrying the first American troops to France, and made eleven voyages to Europe before the war's end (http://www.history.navy.mil/danfs/d2/dekalb.htm), accessed May 10, 2011.

Chapter 4

The Captain Sails to France

The *George Washington* began its third trip to France on March 30, 1918, the day before Easter. In addition to the 35th Division men, the ship carried the 23rd Engineers, Labor Battalion 308, several truck and repair units, and a number of "casuals." The religious services on Easter Sunday were well attended, with thousands of those on board honoring "Him whose Resurrection Day was celebrated."

Early in the voyage, the ship's newspaper paid tribute to Schrantz and the 136 men of the 35th Division who were aboard. The editors noted that these men "from the stock-yards, cities and farms of the Middle West" were members of a division that "is bound to make its name in this war." The soldiers of the advance detachment were on their way to service schools in France for "final polishing off of metal even now well burnished." They were hardened by the rough winter at Camp Doniphan, the editors claimed, and their "morale is above question." "We are as proud to carry over a bunch of men like these," the paper concluded, "as Emperor William will be displeased at meeting them."[1]

Entertainment in the form of band concerts, boxing bouts, wrestling matches, lectures and vaudeville performances and

1. Edwin T. Pollock and Paul F. Bloomhardt, The *Hatchet of the United States Ship "George Washington"* (New York: J.J. Little & Ives Co., 1919), 31–37.

visits to the extensive ship's library helped pass the time on the *George Washington.*

By the time the ship landed at Brest, France, on April 13, the Western Front was in turmoil. On the morning of March 21, 1918, three German armies struck the ill-prepared and outnumbered British on either side of St. Quentin, France, and the Somme River. The Germans in Operation "Michael" inflicted more than 38,000 casualties on the British on the first day alone, and by the time their advance was finally halted on April 5 they had advanced nearly forty miles. They were unable to push the British back to the English Channel, however, and the cost was enormous. German casualties numbered 240,000, while the British and French lost 250,000. The next offensive, Operation "Georgette," began against the British in Flanders on April 9. The Germans gained ground, prompting British commander Sir Douglas Haig to order every position held to the last man. British and French troops halted the offensive on April 30, inflicting about 85,000 casualties. The Allies continued to hold the city of Ypres, but at a cost of more than 100,000 killed, wounded, or captured.

Despite their failure to achieve a major breakthrough, the Germans were far from finished. With only 434,000 American troops in France by the time "Georgette" was halted, there was still an opportunity for the German Army to strike again before fresh divisions such as the 35th could turn the tide.

This being my first sea voyage everything was new and novel to me, but on the whole—on that first voyage—I was disappointed with the sea. It did not look nearly as pleasant from a ship as it did from the shore, and since the North Atlantic in April is not always smooth I was just enough affected by the motion of the ship to be uncomfortable. However time passed well enough, reading Winston Churchill's "River War" which I found in the ship's library and staring at the other ships in the convoy. Among these was the *Abraham Lincoln*, also a former Hamburg-America liner, which sailed to the port of us. This ship was torpedoed and sunk by the enemy when returning, without troops, from her next voyage. After some days at sea, passenger officers were assigned as additional watchers for submarines. This duty kept me in the open air more and my seasickness touch disappeared.[2]

2. Schrantz was assigned to three watches—8:30 to 9:30 a.m., 4:30 to 5:30 p.m., and 12:30 to 1:30 a.m. *Carthage* (MO) *Evening Press*, May 3, 1918.

There was only one touch of excitement during the voyage. On April 8 there were several cannon shots, followed by the shrilling of the ship's siren which sent all hands hurrying to their abandon-ship stations hastily donning their life-jackets. A gunner at one of our after guns on the port side had mistaken the flash of a porpoise for a periscope and had fired once, and a bow gun of a ship astern of us had fired twice. This episode was recognized in the "Mother-Goose-at-Sea" column in "The Hatchet," the ship's newspaper, as follows:

"Hey diddle diddle, the fish showed his middle,
The cannon began to roar.
The soldier boy laughed to see such sport—
But he put on his Ostermoor."[3]

Approaching the war zone, the cruiser *Frederick* turned back and was replaced by 10 American destroyers which encircled and cruised about the convoy. Life preservers were required to be worn at all times and all persons remain fully clothed. The weather turned stormy and the ships plunged through heavy seas.[4]

On April 13 we sighted land, steamed up the long "Goulet de Brest" and dropped anchor outside the Brest breakwater after a voyage of 3,100 or so nautical miles. We casual officers, at least, were soon landed by lighters. It was the first anniversary of my commission as captain.

The enlisted men of the 35th Division advance school had been formed into provisional companies with an appropriate allotment of officers and all these were quartered at the Pontanezen Barracks some distance outside Brest. The other officers sought quarters where they could in the town and Captain Frey and I shared a room at the Continental Hotel.[5]

Brest being the first European city in which I had been, interested me much and I spent most of my days there roving about it. Of especial interest was the parklike promenade above

3. The poem appeared in the April 9, 1918 (volume 2, number 9) issue of the newspaper. The printed version is slightly different, with the second line reading, "The siren began to roar." Edwin T. Pollock and Paul F. Bloomhardt, *The Hatchet of the United States Ship "George Washington"* (New York: J.J. Little & Ives Co., 1919).

4. Sergeant Ed Wiggins of Company A reported that waves washed over the second deck of the ship. *Carthage* (MO) *Evening Press*, May 3, 1918.

5. A number of American units stayed briefly at Camp Pontanezen, located next to the Napoleonic-era stone barracks buildings, before departing for the front. An extensive history of the camp may be found in The Association of Military Surgeons of the United States, "Camp Pontanezen, Brest, France," *The Military Surgeon* 46, no. 3 (March 1920): 301–13.

the waterfront—Le Cours Dajot. The long, twisting Rue de Siam crowded not only with civilians but men of many nations in many uniforms, as well as Algerian labor groups in their native North Africa habiliments; the walls of the old city and the medieval castle near the port. Once too I visited the Pontanezen barracks to see how my sergeants in the provisional organization were faring out there. They had only one complaint—men at the barracks were not given passes to visit town. There was perhaps ample reason for that. A French admiral with whom Captain Frey had formed an acquaintance said that Brest was the "wickedest city in France," and certainly swarms of prostitutes solicited openly on the main streets and in broad daylight. Many of these women, I was told, had come from Paris, having fled that city as the result of the long-range shelling of the town still in progress. In Brest too I saw my first German soldiers—prisoners of war marching to and from work at the docks or elsewhere, splendid physical specimens almost without exception and with something of an arrogance in bearing even in captivity.

Contracting a sore throat I was placed in an improvised hospital for a time as a diphtheria suspect and remained there for a week or so after my group had gone. During the period I was in hospital there was some sort of disturbance in the city, originating, as I recall it, in some disturbance between Portuguese soldiers and the Algerians but in which the enlisted men of our navy who thronged the streets had somehow become involved. The Algerians looted a number of shops along the Rue de Siam and I believe some were killed by French troops before order was restored. For a time none of the officers of the hospital were permitted to go out except accompanied by armed guards and the nurses were confined to their quarters. All this had eased when I was deemed convalescent but the Algerians were going about their work under armed guard and American naval personnel were still being denied shore leave.

Traveling by French civilian train to Tours, thence by American military train to Chaumont, then by local train to Chatillon-sur-Seine in the Department Cote d'Or, I rejoined my group then quartered in the old Cordelier Barracks in that town, a 13th century monastery which later had been used as a barracks by the troops of Napoleon.[6]

6. As Schrantz notes, the cordeliers convent and church were constructed in the 1230s and 1240s, and were sold during the French Revolution. The three-sided structure, although modified several times, still stands in the town.

Chatillon Sur Seine (*Jasper County Records Center*)

The 35th Division machine gunners, on arriving at Chatillon, had first been formed into classes to study the Hotchkiss machine gun, [the] French regulation weapon with which American troops then in Europe was equipped. While on the way to France we had permitted ourselves to hope that upon arriving at the school we would find as instructors American officers of war experience. In the United States we had been given a number of lectures by foreign officers and, while we had appreciated their instruction, it was a tiny bit humiliating to reflect that there were no American officers who [could] give the same kind of information that these men could. But now our troops had been on the line for some time and many of our machine gun officers, we reflected, had been able to get some experience in battle with the enemy and, having had this, would certainly be substituted for the Allied officers that naturally had to be used at first. But our hopes were [in] vain for there was not a single American officer of experience in the European War at the school.

At the conclusion of the second [officers'] training camp in the United States a large number of newly commissioned second lieutenants had been sent overseas, detailed to attend various schools and those that made the best grades were retained as instructors. Hence the men who were doing most of the teaching were men who had had more school experience than the students but who had had no war experience at all. This was probably inevitable at first but it was continued a little too long until finally, six months or more after the time of which I am writing, there was presented the spectacle of men who had been in no kind of action—excellent instructors but without battle experience—telling men who had fought at Chateau Thierry and on the Vesle how to use machine guns in battle. Many of these instructors were unable to get to the front during the entire war. One who was on duty at Chatillon at the time I was there joined our own division some time after the signing of the Armistice, he having been just relieved from the school.[7] As result of the spring defeats on the British front, however, it had been decided to send the 35th Division to the British area, armed with British weapons, and just before my arrival, the class had been shifted to the Vickers machine gun with a British captain named Sharp in charge. This captain was an excellent and a likeable instructor as well as being the type of man to whose instructions we were most inclined to listen. He had commanded a machine gun company throughout the war until wounds received in action at Cambrai had unfitted him for further service in the field. He had the idea, as did many British at the time, that the American organizations were to be broken up and assigned as individuals to the British Army. He endeavored to teach British soldier psychology, along with machine gunnery, to his officer-students and a common expression with him was: "When you get in command of our Tommies . . ." He was an excellent instructor and a practical soldier besides, having served in a British machine gun unit until disabled by wounds a year before.

7. The French Model 1914 Hotchkiss air-cooled machine gun was the standard heavy gun used by the French Army during this period, and the most common machine gun used by the A.E.F. The Hotchkiss weighed more than 54 pounds and required a 54-pound tripod, but was capable of firing about 400 8mm rounds per minute, contained in 24 or 30 round metal feed strips. Canfield, *U.S. Infantry Weapons of the First World War*, 200–9. "The men had much to say in praise of the French Hotchkiss machine gun," one newspaper reported after speaking with members of the 35th Division. "'You can shoot her till the durned barrel melts off,'" one gunner said, "'and then screw another'n on, an' there you are. She works the best when she's a dull red.'" *St. Louis Post-Dispatch*, May 2, 1919. In a letter to his wife, Schrantz detailed the hectic training schedule, with reveille at 6:30 and breakfast at 7. At 8:10 the group marched to the study room, where classes were held until just before noon, with lunch at 12:15. The men marched back to school at 1:10, with more lectures and work with the machine guns until 5:30 p.m. After a brief break to visit town from 5:30 to six, the group enjoyed dinner at 6, then went back to the study room at 6:50. At nine the company marched back to quarters and worked on notebooks until 10 or 11 p.m. *Carthage* (MO) *Evening Press*, June 4, 1918.

He knew what we needed to know, and there were excellent British manuals to fill the void which had never been filled from our own army sources. And visiting British machine gun officers lectured in detail and with apparent complete frankness on the machine gun lessons of the British defeats in March and April.[8]

Captain Sharp, in his instructional talks, included somewhat apologetically the regulation jokes which seemed to be a part of the course. These were in the form of normal questions with facetious answers. The instructor asked: "Where does the bullet leave the gun?" The official answer was not the obvious "at the muzzle" but "on the tripod." In machine gun parlance a "runaway gun" was one in which the weapon continued firing after pressure on the trigger was released. The way to stop a runaway gun was to twist the belt, thus preventing more cartridges from entering the feed block. But the official facetious answer to the query as to the immediate action to take in case of a runaway gun was: "Send the tripod after it. It has three legs while you have only two."

Our genial instructor deserved a better finale of his service with us than was actually his. The school closed with a demonstration of all infantry weapons, selected students or instructors performing in turn for their group. Captain Sharp elected to be himself one of the two gunners to demonstrate the Vickers machine gun, choosing as assistant Lieut. Monta Moore of the 130th Machine Gun Battalion, one of our own group. It was a good choice. Lt. Moore had been in some Central American wars—with Lee Christmas in Nicaragua if my memory is correct—and had had some practical gunnery experience.[9]

8. On the morning of March 21, 1918, the Germans launched the "Michael" Offensive. The German 17th Army struck the British Third Army, while the German Second and Eighteenth Armies attacked the British Fifth Army, forcing them to retreat some 40 miles. A combination of British and French reinforcements and German logistical problems halted the drive on April 5. Casualties numbered nearly 240,000 for the Germans and more than 250,000 for the British and French. On April 9, the German "Georgette" operation began further north, and the British First and Second Armies likewise were forced back from the Armentieres area with significant casualties. As with "Michael," failed German logistics and a stiffened Allied defense forced the German offensive to sputter to a halt on April 27. Again, losses were high—86,000 for the Germans, 112,000 for the British and French.

9. Soldier of fortune Leon W. "Lee" Christmas was born in Louisiana in 1863. He began his colorful military career in 1897 when he joined a revolutionary movement in Honduras. Although that effort failed, Christmas joined the anti-government force of Manuel Bonilla in 1903. Named a brigadier general, he helped Bonilla assume the presidency, but in 1906, when Nicaraguan army and anti-government revolutionaries invaded Honduras, the Bonilla regime fell. Christmas plotted with Bonilla to return to power. Although their

When the group of observers had assembled behind the two guns, Captain Sharp, with probably pardonable national pride, announced: "You will now see, gentlemen, what an English machine gunner can do with his own weapon."

The two guns began firing. Lieutenant Moore gave a beautiful exhibition, his chattering weapon running without interruption through the whole schedule of fixed fire, distributed fire, searching fire, diagonal traverse and swinging traverse. The unfortunate Captain Sharp had stoppage after stoppage, correcting each one promptly only to run into another, and accompanying his embarrassed efforts with explanatory oaths at "this damned American ammunition." Another English officer, a Captain Fay from British General Headquarters, came around from time to time to deliver lectures on the lessons in the machine gun line that were to be learned from the recent enemy offensives. He discussed the Allied reverses and the machine gun shortcomings with the outmost [*sic*] frankness and as a result his lectures were among the most valuable features of the course.

With us at the school were the advance detachments of the 3rd and 5th American Divisions, both of which continued the Hotchkiss course throughout. They were going to the American or French front and we of the 35th were quite elated that while the Regular divisions were going to a quiet sector, we were scheduled for what was at the time a very active one. Happily for our state of complacency we could not foresee that the course of war would throw them into serious action long before ourselves. A Captain Rainey, who commanded the Machine Gun Company, 7th U.S. Infantry,

---

effort failed in 1910, Christmas and Bonilla entered the country again the following year and returned Bonilla to the presidency. Christmas served as commander of the Honduran army, but after Bonilla's death in 1913, Christmas returned to the United States. Suffering from anemia, he died on January 21, 1924. *The Washington Post*, January 22, 1924. Monta J. Moore, a native of Kerwin, Kansas (some sources state Cameron, Texas) and resident of Los Angeles, California, was born on August 14, 1888. He enlisted in Company C, 2nd Texas Infantry in 1905, was commissioned a first lieutenant in 1909, and served until 1911. He attended the Officers' Training Camp in San Francisco from May to August 1917, then was commissioned a second lieutenant in the Officers' Reserve Corps. Assigned to Company D, 128th Machine Gun Battalion in February 1918, he was transferred to the 130th Machine Gun Battalion the following month. Moore wrote home on October 4, 1918, that his leg had been broken on September 29, "not a very serious wound," but in the "dandy battle" his clothing was pierced five times by bullets. He died on October 3, 1958, in Pauma Valley, California. *The Cameron* (TX) *Herald*, October 31, 1918, October 9, 1958; Memo from 2nd Lt. Monta J. Moore to Commanding Officer, 128th Machine Gun Battalion, Camp Doniphan, November 7, 1917, Record Group 120, Records of the American Expeditionary Forces, World War I Organization Records, Machine Gun Battalions, 128th Machine Gun Battalion, Box 263, NARA; HST.

messed next to me and who commanded our 35th Division machine gun officers in a brief daily close order drill, was killed in action on the Marne before my own guns ever fired a shot in battle.[10]

The closing of the school was accompanied by one disappointment for line officers. We had all expected a tour of observation in the trenches with the French before returning to our units. Only field officers were sent, however, but perhaps it was just as well for some of us that we did not go. An infantry major of my acquaintance who did get to make the visit received from the French a Croix de Guerre and from the Germans a machine gun bullet which smashed some bones and sent him back out of the war home and eventually onto the emergency officers retired list.[11]

While we were at the school, our division had come overseas, my own battalion travelling to Liverpool by a British transport, thence to a rest camp at Romsey, then through Southampton and over the channel to Le Havre, thereafter to the village of Sept Meules near Eu in the department of Seine Inferieure. Our return thereto was by the edge of Paris which we passed in the dusk as the balloon barrage was going up, then to Dieppe which we had full opportunity to explore between trains, then to Eu at which division headquarters was located.

No instructions were given to me when I reported at division headquarters other than information as to where my battalion was located, but while strolling about the town I met an acquaintance who expressed surprise that I was going to the battalion.

10. Jo Hunt Reaney was born in Osage, Iowa, on October 17, 1891, and graduated from the United States Military Academy in 1915. Commissioned in the infantry, Rainey served in Texas and Arizona before World War I, then was stationed at Fort Sill from October 1917 to January 1918. Assigned to the 7th U.S. Infantry, Rainey went to France in April 1918 and was promoted to major (temporary) that June. The popular Captain Reaney was killed during a German bombardment on the morning of July 15, 1918, at the Marne river village of Gland, a few kilometers east of Chateau Thierry. Frederic V. Hemenway, *History of the Third Division, United States Army, in the World War, for the Period December 1, 1917 to January 1, 1919* (Cologne, Germany: M. Dumont Schauberg, 1919), 92–93. *Fiftieth Annual Report of the Association of Graduates of the United States Military Academy, at West Point, New York, June 10th, 1919* (Saginaw, MI: Seemann & Peters, 1919), 53–55; Col. Wirt Robinson, ed., *Biographical Register of the Officers and Graduates of the U.S. Military Academy at West Point, New York, Supplement, Volume VI-B, 1910–1920* (Saginaw, MI: Seemann & Peters, 1920), 1763.

11. An extract from reports detailing the performance of Company A men at the Machine Gun School (April 29–May 25, 1918) noted that Captain Schrantz achieved an "excellent" grade, and "has a through [thorough] and comprehensive knowledge of mechanical and theoretical side of gun." Sergeant Edwin Wiggins was "fitted for instructor at Corps School [and] Recommended as instructor in the Vickers Machine Gun." Memo, Headquarters, 128th Machine Gun Battalion, July 10, 1918, Record Group 120, Records of the American Expeditionary Forces, World War I Organization Records, Machine Gun Battalions, 128th Machine Gun Battalion, Box 266, NARA.

He had heard, he said, that another captain was in command of my company and that I was to be assigned as a machine gun instructor. It was a dark and gloomy period until I reached Sept Meules and found that no one there had heard of orders detaching me, and that while a new captain was in command of my company he would be shifted to another and I returned to it.

The 128th Machine Gun Battalion by this time was only a two-company one, due to a change in tables of organization some time before I left the states which raised the two brigade machine gun battalions from three companies each to four each (animal drawn) while the divisional battalion was reduced to two companies supposed to be motorized.[12]

I found it, however, completely equipped with British horse transport, limbered wagons for each section and some spare ones for ammunition and supplies, complete with a British transport detachment commanded by a pleasant young British lieutenant named Gradwell. And I found, to my pleasure, that there was a horse for me.[13]

Of more importance was the fact that my company had been completely equipped with British Vickers machine guns, .303 caliber, and all necessary fire control equipment. There were 16 machine guns to the company, one for each of the 12 squads and four in reserve. Only our detachment returning from school had received anything like adequate instruction in the Vickers gun and we set to work at once to impart what knowledge we had to the others and to start range firing.

The distant thud of artillery to the eastward and the general military situation indicated the need for haste. The March 21 German offensive on the Somme and the April 7 offensive on the Lys had made deep penetrations in the British front and had resulted in the severe mauling of many British divisions. The day that our school detachment had reached Dieppe the enemy had smashed through the Allied line on the Aisne and now was headed for the Marne through a broken field.

12. In November 1917, the divisional machine gun battalion (in this case the 128th) was reduced to two companies, while the brigade machine gun battalions consisted of four companies. The divisional machine gun companies were motorized in order to quickly cover large distances, while brigade and regimental machine gun units received animals. George T. Raach, *A Withering Fire: American Machine Gun Battalions in World War I* (Bradenton, FL: BookLocker.com, 2015), 18–19. Raach's excellent study covers all aspects of machine gun units in the American Expeditionary Forces.

13. This officer could not be identified.

Our 35th Division was associated with the remnants of the 30th British Division and for the moment was a part of the British XIX corps. The 30th had been on the front line when the March 21 offensive had hit and had been badly cut to pieces. What was left of it had then become involved in the Lys operation and suffered still further. Lieutenant Gradwell told me he was the only officer left of his battalion and he had survived solely because he was in charge of the transport. There were daily expectations that we would move up to battle, and there were, of course, rumors that a new German offensive against the British front was impending.

As a captain I had been allowed to bring 250 pounds of baggage to France and the officially "required" articles took that full poundage enclosed in two trunk lockers and a bedding roll. But the war had broken out of the trenches. Orders were to strip down to 80 pounds. Trunk lockers were to be sent to Calais—in fact they wound up somewhere else—and were to be secured later. The way things were going it looked to me as if the Germans might be in Calais before long and I had small hope of seeing my property again. This was Spring, but Winter would come in time and I placed my long heavy overcoat in my bedding roll, a wise precaution as it turned out as the foot-lockers were returned only after the end of hostilities. I gave my cot, one foot-locker and miscellaneous articles to the housewife in whose home I was billeted and turned in one for storage or capture as the case might be.

Chapter 5

The Light Guard Goes to War

While Captain Schrantz made his way overseas with the battalion's advance detachment, the other men of Company A and the 35th Division asked, "How long before we go?"[1] The answer came in mid-April, when the remainder of the division boarded trains and slowly traveled from Camp Doniphan to Jersey City, New Jersey.

Battalion commander Major Halliburton clearly stated what he expected of his men in his general orders. The movement of the battalion was to be made "under strict military discipline, and will be a reflection of the eight months training of the officers and men." Yelling from train windows, a "sure sign of a recruit soldier," and behavior "not tolerated in trained troops," was strictly prohibited, as was throwing notes or addresses from the train. Every soldier was ordered, "at all times," to "preserve the honor of his uniform, the high standard of the 35th Division and of the 128th Machine Gun Battalion."[2]

"The Big Boys from Out West" awaited a transport ship to France at the unpleasant Camp Mills (Garden City, New York), occupying

1. Weber, *History of the 129th Machine Gun Battalion*, 13.

2. General Orders No. 8, Headquarters, 128th Machine Gun Battalion, Camp Doniphan, OK, April 10, 1918, Record Group 120, Records of the American Expeditionary Forces, World War I Organization Records, Machine Gun Battalions, 128th Machine Gun Battalion, Box 266, NARA.

tents erected in an old cornfield awash in shoe-top deep mud.[3] Mercifully, after only a few days of preparation, the company left the camp on April 24 and boarded the British liner *Caronia*. On April 25, the *Caronia* began its voyage to Europe, passing "it seemed to me, thousands of ships as we were putting out to sea," reported Floy Gibbs of the 128th's Sanitary Detachment.[4] Doubtless many agreed with Walter Weber of the 129th Machine Gun Battalion, who wondered "When are we coming back?"[5]

Unlike the relatively spacious stateroom that Schrantz enjoyed aboard the *George Washington*, his men were placed in cramped and uncomfortable accommodations. A Missourian in the 139th Infantry wrote home that he slept in a hammock like a sailor, swinging from the ceiling above "oil cloth covered tables with benches." The hammocks were "as thick as they can hang, side by side—the ceiling is a mass of white hammocks." Eventually, soldiers "got used to the thing, and you sleep as soundly as 'babe in the crib.'"[6]

Despite a U-Boat scare, the *Caronia* arrived safely in Liverpool, England, on May 7. Company A disembarked and moved by train to Camp Woodley, a rest camp located between Southampton and Winchester. On May 15, the 128th Battalion traveled to Southampton. Crammed on board the steamer *LaFrance*, they crossed the Channel and were unloaded at LeHavre, France, the next day. There, in a perfect example of army bureaucracy at work, the men were ordered to remove and abandon all the extra clothing they had been issued at Camp Doniphan, an attempt, they believed, to equip the poorly supplied divisions that had preceded them to France. On May 18, the Missourians left LeHavre in passenger cars for an eighty-mile trip to the area of France occupied by the British Fourth Army. When they detrained at Eu, they were met by a Scottish bagpipe band, led by a giant drum major wearing a leopard skin over his uniform coat. After a brief stay in a British rest camp, they marched to Sept Meules, about twenty miles from Abbeville and eight miles from the English Channel, and were issued British Vickers machine guns. For the first time in its forty-two-year history, the old Carthage Light Guard could hear the rumble of enemy guns.

Once the battalion was settled in Sept Meules, Major Halliburton issued strict orders regarding the behavior of his troops. Billeting

3. *The Chanute* (KS) *Daily Tribune*, May 28, 1918.
4. *The Houston* (MO) *Herald*, January 30, 1919.
5. Weber, *History of the 129th Machine Gun Battalion*, 15.
6. *The Holt County Sentinel* (Oregon, MO), July 12, 1918.

in a French town called for the "highest type of military courtesy and the most stringent military discipline." Trespassing on private property was prohibited. The men were required to appear in proper uniform when outside their quarters, and be "punctilious" in dress and saluting. Liquor sales to both officers and enlisted men were prohibited, and the enlisted men "will not attempt any infringement" of that order.[7]

The Western Front was thrown into disorder again on May 27, the day before Captain Schrantz returned from the machine gun school to resume command of his company. Seventeen German divisions moved through the darkness that morning in Operation Blücher and crushed the French line along the Chemin des Dames, roughly between Soissons and Rheims. Crossing the Aisne River, they soon captured thousands of Frenchmen and a large amount of French supplies at Soissons and drove on toward the Marne River. The panicked French government made preparations to abandon Paris. The American 2nd and 3rd Divisions left their training areas and rushed to halt the Germans. The 2nd Division took position northwest of Chateau-Thierry, across the road to Paris, stopped the enemy advance, and counterattacked. The U.S. 3rd Division held the Germans along the Marne at Chateau-Thierry. Despite these impressive American achievements, the Germans were weakened but still full of fight.

Although still in training, the men of the 35th Division found themselves perilously close to the front during their first weeks in France. "These were parlous days in the great war," remembered correspondent Clair Kenamore. The city of Eu, where the division was initially stationed, was only thirty-eight miles from the advancing Germans, and the 35th had been attached to the British Army to defend the English Channel ports. Although the division "came mighty near to getting into the war," the German threat was contained by other American and Allied forces.[8]

On the way to France at last. There was a real thrill to that thought as Company A, 128th Machine Gun Battalion, swung its 172 army packs on its 172 pairs of olive drab shoulders down at Camp Doniphan, Okla., in the late forenoon of

7. General Orders No. 8, 128th Machine Gun Battalion, Sept Meules, France, May 20, 1918, Record Group 120, Records of the American Expeditionary Forces, World War I Organization Records, Machine Gun Battalions, 128th Machine Gun Battalion, Box 266, NARA.

8. Clair Kenamore, *From Vauquois Hill to Exermont: A History of the Thirty-Fifth Division of the United States Army* (St. Louis: Guard Publishing Co., 1919), 30, 35.

April 17, 1918, executed "squads right" and swung in column for the last time out of the company street its members had known for so long, and so with the rest of the battalion marched down to the railway yards and waiting cars. "Goodby, Camp Doniphan!"

Cheers, wisecracks, banter, as the 16-coach troop train carrying the 128th Machine Gun Battalion pulled out of the already half-deserted camp; men peering from windows to get their last glimpse of the wind-whipped surroundings they had known as home for eight strenuous months; a settling down in the tourist sleepers with three men to a section, a stacking up of packs and a swinging of campaign hats by sweat-blackened chin straps on convenient hooks, an unbuttoning of blouses, a chatter of speculation as to route, streaks of cigarette smoke as men relaxed and lighted up, a few voices raised in song—the 128th was on the move. Back at Lawton a little group of damp-eyed wives were packing their belongings to catch the next passenger train which would carry them back to Carthage, Mo.

At El Reno, Okla., that evening the soldiers detrained for brief setting up exercises and a short march, then back on the train again and northward on the Rock Island Railway as the shadows fell. The next forenoon, exercise was taken at Kansas City, Kans., and the train rolled on across the state to Eldon, Mo., where there was another stop for the same purpose. In contrast to the journey from Nevada, Mo., to Camp Doniphan the previous summer, this was not a fast trip. "We were traveling on freight train schedule and local freight at that," wrote David H. Havens. "In fact our train was sidetracked for all regular passenger trains and fast freights."[9]

This slowness was a surprise to the soldiers who knew how badly men were needed overseas and had expected to be rushed through at top speed. The answer, of course, was that troop trains were moving all over the United States and it was necessary to keep regular traffic moving too. The dates that ships would be available were known and the troops were started eastward early

9. David H. Havens was born in Carthage on August 30, 1896. He served on the Mexican border as a corporal with Company A 1916–17, and overseas with the 128th from April 25, 1918 to April 24, 1919. He died on December 9, 1965, and was buried in Portage, Michigan. *The Service of the Missouri National Guard on the Mexican Border*, 122; Missouri Secretary of State, State Archives, Soldiers' Records, War of 1812–World War I, www.sos.mo.gov/archives/soldiers.

enough to reach the port of embarkation on time even though traveling leisurely.

Newspapers did not publish reports of troop movements in those days, the press of the nation having imposed on itself a voluntary censorship to prevent transmitting information of military value to the enemy, but somehow or other news of the movements leaked out and St. Louis had heard the report that the 128th was coming through. Now St. Louis had probably never heard of the 128th Machine Gun Battalion and to it there was only one 128th in the world, and that was the 128th Field Artillery which, save for one Kansas City battery, was a St. Louis regiment. When word was passed about that the 128th was coming through, the multitudinous friends and relatives of that regiment turned out to bid "their boys" a fitting welcome. Swallowing their disappointment when they found their mistake, they extended to the Carthage, Nevada and Butler machine gunners the welcome—or a part of the welcome—they had intended for St. Louis' own, and passed out among them the lunches, cakes and other eatables meant for the artillerymen. The 128th Field Artillery, it may be added, had not left Camp Doniphan, and when it did move did not go through St. Louis.

At St. Louis the machine gunners were switched over to the Wabash Railway, exercising once that day at Peru, Ind., and again in late afternoon at Huntington, Ind., at which place the train changed railways again, now traveling on the Erie. Meals were taken on the train, there being a Pullman kitchen car, the colored cooks of which had relieved the company cooks of their normal duties.

The next morning the soldiers exercised in Salamanca, a town of northwestern New York, where they stared and were stared at, and marched through streets where service flags in many windows reminded them that this community like their own and all others had sent its young men to follow the flag. Then down through the mountains of western New York and northern Pennsylvania, greeted by crowds at every station and exchanging banter with the friendly feminine portion thereof. There was exercise again in Susquehanna, some distance beyond which town two engines were required to pull the train up a grade. The next morning, Sunday April 21, the train rolled down to the docks at Jersey City, N.J.

The train had run into a drizzling rain the night before and while that had ceased here, there was a blanket of damp fog.

Detraining at Jersey City the Missourians found themselves in front of a ferry landing and were quickly marched onto a ferry boat. Here was a ship of a sort at least, which, however humble its station, offered a thrill to a good many men who had never seen a ferry boat or smelled salt water. There was a wait here while the baggage was being transferred from the train to the boat, a wait spent by most of the Company A men in trying in vain to see through the fog so as to get a glimpse of the New York sky line, giving this up to glance at the advertisements with which the ferry boat was plastered, one of the principal ones of which featured Al Jolson who at that time was appearing at the Winter Garden Theater in "Sinbad the Sailor."[10] Finally the baggage was transferred, and the *Chautauqua*—for that was the name the ferry boat bore—cast off and plowed its way around the point of Manhattan and Battery Park and up the East River to Long Island City. Here the boat docked and the machine gun battalion marched ashore, unloaded its baggage and entrained on a waiting train of the Long Island Railway which moved up Long Island to Garden City where the organization again unloaded, finishing up with a short march through a drizzling rain to Camp Mills, arriving there about noon.

Camp Mills did not make a particularly favorable impression. "Our camp was pitched in a corn field and the mud was shoe-top deep," wrote Corporal Earl Eastin to his father in a letter published some time later.[11] "We camped in low and muddy ground," says a notation by Major Halliburton, the battalion commander. A statement by David H. Havens is more explicit:

"During our short stay at Camp Mills I was never able to see the whole extent of the camp," he wrote, "but whatever it was it was too small to accommodate the influx of troops at that time. The quarters assigned to us consisted of a row of pyramidal tents pitched on what had been a cornfield the season before. They had

10. Al Jolson (1886–1950) began performing at the Winter Garden in 1911. By the time he appeared in the successful musical *Sinbad* he was one of the most popular and well-paid singers and actors in New York.

11. Carl M. Eastin was born in Carthage on January 1, 1897. He served overseas with the 128th from April 25, 1918, to April 24, 1919. Gassed in France, he was in failing health until his death on February 13, 1954. *Carthage* (MO) *Evening Press*, February 15, 1954; Missouri Secretary of State, State Archives, Soldiers' Records, War of 1812–World War I, www.sos.mo.gov/archives/soldiers.

not been ditched and the rain of the night before and what was falling at the time ran down the furrows right through the tents. Each tent contained six cots and a bale of straw when we arrived. We, in the tent to which I was assigned, debated whether to use the straw in our ticks or spread it on the ground, and finally decided we would be better off to spread it on the ground and sleep on the cots without ticks."

In this camp the 128th Machine Gun Battalion was issued steel helmets and a .45-caliber Smith and Wesson revolver for each man, a weapon firing the same cartridge as the Colt automatic pistol. The pistol was the regulation weapon but the government had an inadequate supply of them as yet and hence furnished the revolvers instead to be used until such day as the pistols had been manufactured in sufficient quantity to supply the needs.

Several days were spent at Camp Mills in final inspections and making up passenger lists preparatory to the journey overseas. Over in Europe, the newspapers said, another great German drive was impending, and the heaviest fighting in which Americans had yet participated had just occurred at Seichprey in the Toul sector where the German had staged a large scale raid against the 26th (New England National Guard) Division, a division of particular interest to the Carthaginians because into it had gone the old 1st New Hampshire and 2d Maine regiments with which the Missouri troops had served at Laredo, Tex., during the 1916 border troubles.[12]

On April 24, 1918, at 4 a.m. the 128th Machine Gun Battalion, including Company A of Carthage, marched out of muddy Camp Mills, and to the railway at Garden City, Long Island. It was an early start but for once the soldiers arose early without feeling aggrieved at any bugler, and before the hour of starting every pack had been rolled and sleep had been banished from eager eyes. This day was to see the 128th on a transport, destination Europe.

The few days at Camp Mills had not been without anxieties. On the train coming east from Camp Doniphan, Private Alvin Bays had become ill, spent the rest of the trip in his berth and went to

12. Early on the morning of April 20, 1918, approximately 3,000 German troops struck a section of the front held by members of 26th (Yankee) Division. After fierce fighting, the town of Seicheprey was captured but the Germans began a fighting withdrawal about mid-morning. The Americans suffered 80 killed, 195 wounded, 216 gassed, and about 190 taken prisoner in this first major battle between German forces and the A.E.F.

an army hospital on arrival at the camp. Soon word drifted back that his illness had been diagnosed as diphtheria, and to this camp rumor added the addition that the machine gun battalion might be quarantined and not sent overseas with the division. Now events had proved this prediction false and the machine gunners were on their way. Hard luck for Bays, that diphtheria business, but it would not have helped him for the rest to have stayed on Long Island. Now they were leaving and in the due course of time Private Bays rejoined the organization in France.[13]

The Long Island train quickly took the battalion to the East River and a ferry boat—the "*Hempstead*" by name—and, loaded on this, the soldiers were soon catching a fine view of the New York skyline as they were borne around the tip of Manhattan Island and up North River to a Hoboken dock at which rested a huge British liner, the *Caronia*. Off the ferry boat, and onto the dock, crowded with troops, the machine gunners marched, halting alongside the 320th Machine Gun Battalion of the 82nd Division. Here the column waited while Major Westley Halliburton, checking up on details, arranged to secure quarters for his officers on the boat, that matter having been overlooked by some curious oversight by the authorities who had arranged for the troop accommodations.

The 320th Machine Gun Battalion was rifle armed and in conversation with its members it developed that they were draft troops from the Atlantic seaboard, some of whom had been in uniform only a short time. When they learned that their chin-strapped neighbors were Missourians and had spent over eight months training in Oklahoma, they at once conceived them to be a "wild and woolly" lot, a flattering opinion to which the men of the 128th henceforth tried to live up.

In time the 128th was put in motion again, but instead of climbing the gangplank up which a row of officers were passing, its members were surprised to find themselves marching up from the dock level through a door opened in the hull of the ship. As the column passed into the vessel each man's name was checked off on the company roster and he was handed a card

13. Alvin Bays, born on September 6, 1889, in Lockwood, Missouri, was promoted to wagoner in Company A in July 1918. He served overseas from May 6, 1918, to April 24, 1919. He died on October 20, 1970, and was buried in Tulsa, Oklahoma. Missouri Secretary of State, State Archives, Soldiers' Records, War of 1812-World War I, www.sos.mo.gov/archives/soldiers.

showing the number of his compartment, his mess number and hammock number.

The compartment in which Company A was quartered was about 40 feet long and ran the full width of the ship. There was a main aisle down the middle and on each side were rows of mess tables with a number on each and a notation of the number of men it would accommodate. Above the tables were hooks from which the hammocks were to be suspended and against the wall were the hammock racks. The soldiers were to find that each hammock contained a blanket and that each night they would sleep suspended above the tables where they ate during the day. There was room for two companies in this compartment but for some reason Company B, 128th Machine Gun Battalion, had been placed in a compartment ahead, while Company A, 320th Machine Gun Battalion, was placed in with Company A, of the 128th, the 82nd Division men occupying the starboard (right) side of the compartment and the Carthage company the port (left). The headquarters of the 128th was in a small compartment back of Company A. The officers of the Missouri battalion were quartered in state rooms up above somewhere and First Sergeant George A. Snyder also rated a separate room, so that active charge of the men in the compartment was exercised by the senior duty sergeant, Willard Brown.[14]

Now entered the Y.M.C.A. with cards bearing the statement, "The ship on which I sailed has arrived safely overseas."[15] One of these was given to each soldier, to be signed and later collected and held at New York until the *Caronia* had reached her destination when they would be forwarded to the person addressed.

When the *Caronia* had been loaded the men were permitted to ascend to the main deck to stare again at New York Harbor and the shipping therein, particularly the weirdly camouflaged ocean-going vessels. For some reason the *Caronia* was not so decorated, perhaps because she had been carrying troops from Australia and the British East Indian colonies through the Suez Canal to French ports on the Mediterranean. Members of the crew told enquiring

14. George Allen Snyder was born in Carthage on April 19, 1892. He served as a corporal and sergeant with Company A on the border from 1916-1917. He served overseas from April 25, 1918, to April 24, 1919. He died on April 12, 1956, in St. Joseph, Missouri. Missouri Secretary of State, State Archives, Soldiers' Records, War of 1812-World War I, www.sos.mo.gov/archives/soldiers.

15. Young Men's Christian Association.

Carthage men that the ship had not been in her home port of Liverpool for 18 months. In the same slip with the *Caronia* was the Cunard liner *Mauretania*, a swift ship said to have been the fastest liner afloat. She travelled alone instead of in convoy. Although loaded already, apparently, this ship was still in the dock when the *Caronia* left but was tied up in Liverpool empty when the *Caronia* arrived in that port.

All day the Missourians lounged about the *Caronia*, but did not expect to start until night, it being generally understand that that was the time troop ships generally sailed, and when they slung their hammocks above their tables and climbed into them that night, they fully expected to find the ship at sea by morning, but morning came and there was still no motion, and soon the men were again on deck. About 10 a.m. some tugs puffed up; the *Caronia* cast off the lines securing her to the dock, and as the tugs prepared to make fast to the ship the soldiers were ordered below out of sight, where they remained as the ship moved out down the harbor.

Down below, the soldiers, anxious to get their last glimpse of land, crowded thickly about the few ten inch port-holes, but the Missourians were particularly anxious to get a glimpse of the Statue of Liberty and this would be on the west side of the ship—the 320th Machine Gunners' side. Thus there was an invasion of the 82nd Division territory but the Eastern men, either because they were used to the coast scenery or because they did not want to argue the point with this Oklahoma-bronzed crowd, yielded possession of their points of vantage for the moment and many of the Carthage men caught their first and only glimpse of the famous statue in this manner. Glimpses from the port holes also showed that some airplanes and blimps were escorting the ship down the bay, and these stayed about until Long Island dropped from sight in the rear. They were just disappearing back toward New York when the soldiers were permitted to come on deck.

The 128th Machine Gun Battalion was on its way at last across the ocean. The next day—April 26—back in Carthage there was staged a great "Liberty parade," the largest parade, the *Press* said, ever held in the city.

When the *Caronia* put to sea on April 25, 1918, carrying, among other organizations, Company A, 128th Machine Gun Battalion, she ran alone, but that night others joined her and when the solders awoke in the morning, the ship was part of a convoy guarded by a British cruiser. The British flag fluttered on each of these oddly camouflaged ships, the urgent need for troops overseas having caused the British government to put all available shipping at the disposal of the United States for getting infantry and machine gun units aboard. All the transports mounted some light cannon, manned by British naval crews.

Careful instructions were given the soldiers as to what to do in case the ship were torpedoed. All men were to move quickly and orderly to abandon ship stations assigned to them, some being detailed to slide down ropes into life boats after the seamen had lowered the life boats into the water—no one except the designated seamen were to enter the boats before they were lowered—and others were to stand at designated sections of the rail, ready to leap overboard and get hold of life-rafts to be tossed overside at that point. There was to be no smoking or lighting of matches on deck at night; all port holes were to be kept closed; no trash or debris of any kind was to be thrown overboard for fear that it might give information to lurking enemy submarines. In case the ship were torpedoed, it would probably list badly to one side, the men were told, but there should be no undue alarm because of that. Almost always in such cases the boat would right itself before it went down.

The first few days at sea the weather was pleasant, then the ocean grew somewhat rougher. As the ship rolled, the water washed well above the port holes of the compartment in which the Carthage men were quartered. Susceptible stomachs reacted to this kind of treatment.

Estel Ziler, writing home later, said:

"If you want to know how we slept coming over, just take a bedsheet and tie it at both ends and stretch it on the ceiling. Then have someone swing it as hard as they can as you are trying to get in. Just after you have managed to go to sleep, get up and feed the fishes for awhile and keep the process up all night."[16]

16. Estel Corban Ziler was born in Maple Grove, Jasper County, Missouri, on February 18, 1895, and was raised in Carthage. He joined Company A in July 1917 and was made mechanic in November 1917. He served overseas with the 128th from April 25, 1918, to April 24, 1919. He died on October 18, 1958, and was buried in Park Cemetery in Carthage. *Carthage* (MO) *Evening Press*, October 20, 1958; Missouri Secretary of State, State Archives, Soldiers' Records, War of 1812-World War I, www.sos.mo.gov/archives/soldiers; HST.

The meals aboard consisted largely, it seemed to the soldiers, of boiled foods. There was boiled mutton, boiled rabbit, boiled potatoes and boiled rice—with the boiled Australian rabbit, not always free from fur, recurring with distressing frequency. A supply of pans and vessels was issued to each mess table with a check for each meal. At meal time the noncommissioned officer in charge of the table went with a few men to draw the food from the galley, turning in the check when he did so. In addition to the food mentioned as being obtained at the galley, bread, jam, marmalade and pickles were drawn from what was called the pantry. What was served as coffee did not taste like the beverage so familiar to Americans and even the tea served on the ship could hardly be termed a palatable drink. A ship's canteen sold candies and cakes to those who had money, but it had been a long time since pay day and there were not so many of these. The $30 monthly pay officially credited to each soldier was in fact so encumbered with allotments, insurance payments, Liberty Loan payments and like items that there was not much left, and it did not last long.

The convoy, instead of following the usual ship route to Liverpool, kept well to the north, passing near the vicinity of Newfoundland and, at one time farther to the east, reached approximately the same latitude as lower Greenland. The weather at this time was cool enough to be uncomfortable.

There were no bathing facilities on the ship for the troops, and men were required to remain fully dressed at all times. The high officers of the 82nd Division headquarters, contemplating this situation, decided the men should have daily baths, and arranged for this with the ship's officers. This was good news for the men until they experienced one. They were led in shivering naked groups into a compartment where ice-cold sea-water was doused on them from a hose. The pandemonium caused by this treatment led the bathing program to be abandoned after Company A had undergone the ordeal just once.[17]

17. The incident led to a formal protest by the acting commander of Company A, who complained that his men took "real" baths on every possible occasion, and the "splashing" they endured was not a proper bath, as it included no soap. In addition, the practice was very dangerous to their health, as the sudden jolt of cold seawater had caused a number of men to catch "hard colds," and several were seasick. Memo from Commanding Office, Company A, to Commanding Officer, H.M.S. *Caronia,* April 28, 1918, Record Group 120, Records of the American Expeditionary Forces, World War I Organization Records, Machine Gun Battalions, 128th Machine Gun Battalion, Box 266, NARA.

Always there was talk of the submarine and there was a constant scrutinizing of the heaving water for sight of a possible periscope, nor was the apprehension without reason.[18] The submarines were taking a heavy toll of merchant ships, and already one loaded American transport, carrying men of the 32nd U.S. Division, had been sent down with a loss of 200 lives on the very path the *Caronia* and her sister ships were now taking. Some of the bravest and most resourceful officers in the German Navy were commanding the submarines which were doing their best to bar the American army from Europe.[19]

On May 5 there appeared some rocky crags or islands far to the right of the convoy and the seamen of the *Caronia* told the soldiers that that was the rocky coast of northern Ireland. The next day there was distant rocky coast in view to the left, and this it seemed was northern Scotland. The convoy had entered the Irish Sea, a favorite hunting ground of the enemy submarines, and life preservers were worn at all times now. A flock of English destroyers and submarine chasers had now appeared from somewhere, relieved the cruiser, and darted about, alert to any sign of danger.

On May 6 as the convoy zig-zagged down the Irish Sea, and while part of the men of the Carthage company were on deck and part below, a heavy explosion shook the *Caronia* violently. "She's 'it," yelled a British steward, who chanced to be in the Company A compartment, and the soldiers below poured out on deck to their abandon-ship stations.

But she had not been hit. Men on deck had seen water shoot high from a depth bomb dropped by a destroyer, and this was the initial shock felt. A second depth bomb had caused another shock and a cannon on one vessel had fired at the flash of the enemy periscope.

18. Keeping watch for submarines was so important that one member of Company A, Pvt. Harley H. Hammons, was accused of sleeping at his post on April 26, 1918, his second day at sea, and was tried by general court martial three days later. Although sentenced to a dishonorable discharge and eight years confinement, the reviewing authority reduced that sentence to six months. Captain Schrantz asked for a remission of his sentence, arguing that Hammons was an excellent soldier before and after the incident, and that it was the opinion of both his comrades and officers that he was extremely sea sick. Memo from Commanding Officer, Company A, 128th Machine Gun Battalion, to Commanding General, 35th Division, July 25, 1918, Record Group 120, Records of the American Expeditionary Forces, World War I Organization Records, Machine Gun Battalions, 128th Machine Gun Battalion, Box 264, NARA.

19. On February 5, 1918, the SS *Tuscania* was torpedoed off Northern Ireland by the German UB-77. The ship carried several aero squadrons, detachments of the 32nd Division, and other units. A total of 210 men were lost in the sinking.

Word spread about after the landing that an enemy submarine had been destroyed but the Carthage men never learned for sure whether these first shots they had heard fired in earnest during the World War had done any damage or not. Figures collected since the war from Allied, neutral and German sources show that during this month of May, 1918, 108 allied and 18 neutral ships were torpedoed, and 17 German submarines sunk.

On May 6 also the 128th was saddened by a death in the battalion. A private of Company B had been slightly wounded a few days earlier by the accidentally discharged revolver of a comrade. The wound had somehow become infected and this day he died, being buried a few days later on British soil.[20]

On the morning of May 7 when the soldiers woke there was a strange stillness evident. At first the reason for this was not clear, then it was realized that the ship's engines had stopped. The *Caronia* had reached port. As soon as possible the men were on deck to get their first look at England—but there was nothing to see. A dense fog enshrouded everything and one could not even glimpse the water when he looked overside, but it was evident that the boat was in some sort of harbor for many whistles and clanging of bells could be heard as various kinds of crafts crept about, hidden by the fog.

About ten o'clock the fog lifted. The *Caronia* lay in the River Mersey, which appeared very dirty after days of clean sea, and a multitude of gulls were wheeling around. Several tugs came out and fastened onto the ship and moved her into one of the labyrinth of docks at Bootle, a northern suburb of Liverpool. All this took time, and there was more delay at the dock, so that it was near evening when the men of the 128th Machine Gun Battalion shouldered their packs and moved ashore.

Four days later, back in Carthage, Mo., the anxiety of the families which had contributed men to Company A was relieved by a little barrage of post cards postmarked at New York and bearing these welcome words: "The ship on which I sailed has arrived safely overseas."

Having debarked at Bootle, a suburb of Liverpool, England, May 7, 1918, the 128th Machine Gun Battalion, including Company A

20. Pvt. Thomas A. Price, born in Spokane, Washington, served as a private in the Machine Gun Company of the 2nd Missouri Infantry on the Mexican border 1916–17, and died on May 6, 1918. He was buried in Brookwood American Cemetery in Woking, England. *The Service of the Missouri National Guard on the Mexican Border*, 120.

128th Machine Gun Battalion flag (*Missouri State Museum, Missouri State Parks*)

of Carthage, glad to feel solid earth underfoot again—even if the earth was in the shape of cobble stones slimy with mud—marched northeastward in the gathering shadows through streets lined with welcoming English people, to a railway station at another suburb, Walton-on-the-hill, some three or four miles distant.

Published extracts from letters the Carthage soldiers wrote home indicate that they were much impressed by the reception.

"The people here are nice and acted as if they were glad to see us. They waved the stars and stripes and cheered us as though they had never see U.S. soldiers before," commented Lyle E. Stuckey.[21]

"When we landed and marched through the streets the people fairly fell on our necks," wrote Sergeant Norval R. Hopwood. "All along the line of march they would run out carrying pots of hot tea and fill up our canteens. In some places we were so crowded we

21. Lyle E. Stuckey was probably born in Diamond, Missouri, on June 14, 1900. He served as a private with Company A on the Mexican border from 1916 to 1917. He served overseas with the 128th from April 25, 1918, to April 24, 1919. He died in February 21, 1986, and was buried in San Bernardino, California. *The Service of the Missouri National Guard on the Mexican Border*, 128; Missouri Secretary of State, State Archives, Soldiers' Records, War of 1812–World War I, www.sos.mo.gov/archives/soldiers.

had to halt and get straightened out again. The little kids wanted buttons for souvenirs, or American pennies. . . "

The lack of men between the ages of 16 and 40 was rather conspicuous in the crowds in Liverpool, mute evidence of the city's contribution to the war, and another reminder of nearness to the conflict, was a hospital, the sidewalks in front of which were lined with convalescent English soldiers, many in wheel chairs or on crutches, waiting to greet the Americans and wish them luck.

It was about dark when the 128th Battalion loaded on second class coaches at Walton-on-the hill, eight or ten men with packs facing each other in each of the small side-entrance compartments, and soon the train was working its way out of Liverpool and speeding southward through the night, unlighted as a precaution against attack by German air raiders. Unlighted too were the towns and villages through which the train passed, for all England in those days lay under the fear of aerial bombs. The coaches in which the Carthage men rode were cold and uncomfortable, but morning—it became light about 4 o'clock—revealed a beautiful park-like region of well-trimmed hedge rows, moss-grown stone walls, green fields, gardens, small stone cottages usually with roofs of red tile but occasionally of thatch, and now and then a huge, grey-stone mansion or castle. There was a pause at Oxford with a glimpse of green campus and grey-stone, ivy-grown buildings, then on toward London, with the soldiers watching the mile posts which told the distance to the metropolis. "London 20 miles," the signs said, then 16, 12, 10, 8; then came an enormous railway yard with miles of switches, hundreds of box cars, numerous idle engines, with the troop train rounding a wide curve and the next sign post said "London 12 miles," and the Missourians knew they were not to see the great city. Not so long later the train was rolling through historic Hampshire, finally stopping at a station where a huge sign said: "Romsey—Famous for its Fine Old Ales."

Here, between Southampton and Winchester, the battalion detrained and marched a short distance to a rest camp known as Camp Woodley.[22] Here, quartered in large tents, the soldiers

22. Walter Weber of the 129th Machine Gun Battalion noted facetiously that "we were never able to determine" why these were called "rest camps." Weber, *History of the 129th Machine Gun Battalion*, 16.

settled down to rest after their sea voyage and to grumble at the quarantine.

This quarantine was an unscheduled event on which no one had counted. Mumps and diphtheria had broken out among members of the 139th Infantry on the *Caronia* and so now the machine gunner shipmates of the doughboys found themselves forbidden to leave camp save in formed bodies, marching under the command of an officer.

Here at Romsey the soldiers made their first acquaintance with English rations, and were particularly displeased with the idea of tea for breakfast, yet those letters home which found their way into print seem to show that they were much interested in England and enjoying themselves.

"Prettiest country round about I ever saw," wrote Sergeant Hopwood. "Everything absolutely clean and spotless. Beautiful forests, glades and pastures thick with spring flowers. No dust and no mud."

"Here in England everything is green and the houses certainly are peculiar," commented Private Leaford J. Akin. "All the fences are hedge and the largest field I have seen is not over ten acres."[23]

"We have good beds and pretty good chow, so what else could a fellow wish for?" asked Lyle E. Stuckey. "Everything here is old-fashioned. They look as though they were 50 years behind the times."

"Everybody from eight to 80 rides bicycles here," commented James D. Mort.

"Good quarters and plenty to eat," averred Bugler Clint Thomas.

Apparently the English ration was not so meager but what the soldiers were managing to get along with it very well, and then too the $500 mess fund furnished by Carthage people before Company A sailed enabled Mess Sergeant Clint A. Miles to add somewhat to the menu despite the general food shortage in England.

On May 15 the battalion was on the move again, entraining at Romsey and rolling down to Southampton where it embarked on a small channel steamer known as *LaFrance*, with Company A furnishing the ship's guard. Back home the relatives of the

23. Leaford J. Akin was born on November 8, 1898, in Barry County, Missouri, and served overseas with the 128th from April 25, 1918, to April 24, 1919. He died on July 21, 1926, in a powder mill explosion. He was buried in Park Cemetery, Carthage. *Carthage (MO) Evening Press*, July 21, 1926; Missouri Secretary of State, State Archives, Soldiers' Records, War of 1812–World War I, www.sos.mo.gov/archives/soldiers.

soldiers had been assured by the post cards they had received a few days before that the company had arrived safely overseas, and so presumed that they had passed the submarine danger, but now in the trip across the Channel the unit again faced the possibility of a German torpedo and immersion in a cold and turbulent sea. In these very waters a week later the transport *Moldavia* carrying part of the Fourth American Division was sent to the bottom and 56 men of the 58th Infantry lost.[24]

But not impossibly the 1,000 American soldiers crowded on the swift but uncomfortable *LaFrance*, a boat practically void of every accommodation, were thinking less of the enemy than of sea-sickness, though as it developed the Channel was not as rough as had been expected. Incidentally, the soldiers were on one of the most famous sea roads of military history. Out of Southampton in August, 1914, had journeyed that initial British Expeditionary Force which was to struggle and die so gallantly while the war was still young, and in the centuries before this, more than one English expedition had followed the same path to France.

Describing conditions on board David H. Havens wrote:

"There was hardly standing room and when tired men began trying to stretch out for a little repose, space in which to lay one's self down was at a premium. There were no lights allowed except those absolutely necessary for the operation of the boat and they were well screened. A tarpaulin, lowered all around to screen in the main deck, restricted the ventilation; and with the packed humanity, conditions were not exceedingly pleasant."

The voyage was uneventful and by daylight May 16 the boat carrying the Missourians had docked at Le Havre at the mouth of the Seine, and soon thereafter the soldiers disembarked on French soil.

"Apparently the French are more accustomed to soldiers than the English," wrote Mack Davis, evidently recalling the welcome at Liverpool, "as we caused not even a ripple on our arrival."[25]

24. The refitted British liner *Moldavia* carried Companies A and B of the 58th U.S. Infantry. The ship was torpedoed by a German submarine on the morning of May 23, 1918, about halfway between Land's End and the Isle of Wright. A total of 56 men were lost, all but one from Company B. Christian A. Bach and Henry Noble Hall, *The Fourth Division: Its Services and Achievements in the World War* (Garden City, NY: Issued by the division [Country Life Press], 1920), 42–45.

25. James Mack Davis, Sr. was born on May 11, 1899, in Carthage. He served with Company A on the Mexican border 1916–17, then served overseas with the 128th from April 25, 1918,

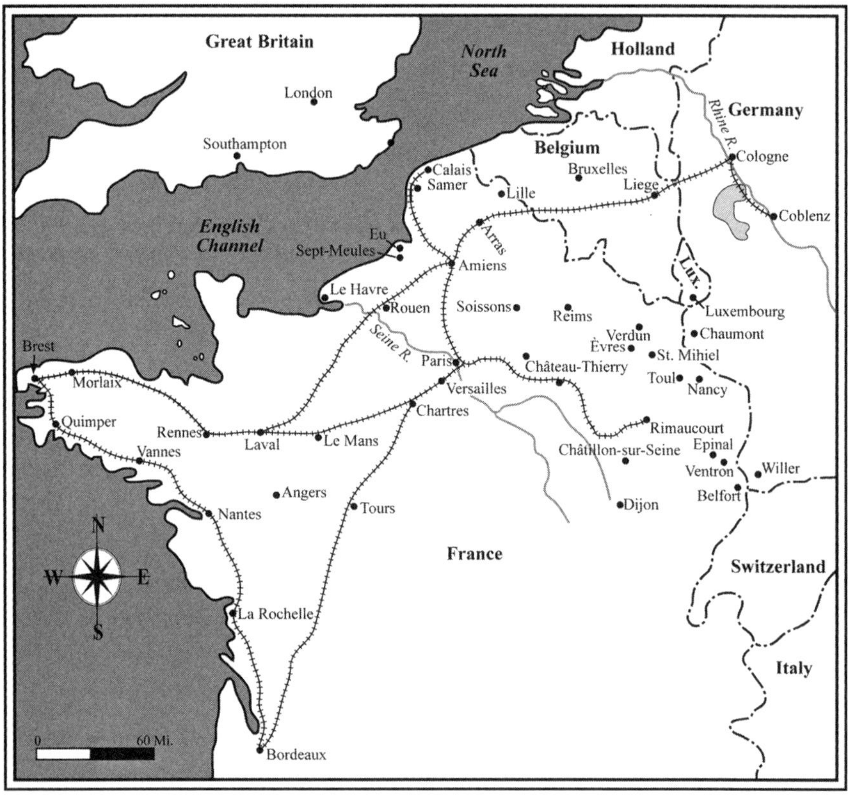

35th Division in Europe

From the water front at Le Havre the 128th Battalion marched to a rest camp—Rest Camp No. 1, Section B—and shortly before noon, the men unslung their packs for a brief breathing spell again. Here the Missourians felt the first result of the German successes in carrying the war over the Allied trench lines and out into the open. Based on the idea of a stabilized trench warfare, the men had been issued considerable extra equipment and clothing which had been carried overseas in blue denim barracks bags. Here orders were issued to turn in this extra equipment and uniform, leaving the soldier only what he could carry in a one-blanket pack, such as was suitable for mobile warfare in the summer time. It was expected that these barrack bags would be

to April 24, 1919. He died on January 24, 1971, and was buried in Park Cemetery. *Joplin* (MO) *Globe*, January 25, 1971; *Carthage* (MO) *Evening Press*, January 25, 1971; Missouri Secretary of State, State Archives, Soldiers' Records, War of 1812–World War I, www.sos.mo.gov/archives/soldiers; *The Service of the Missouri National Guard on the Mexican Border*, 125.

returned later, and many of the optimists put personal belongings in them, never to see them again. Here too gas masks were issued, after a trying march up hill in a blazing sun, and now all that the machine gunners needed to be ready to fight was machine guns—a rather important detail.

As the 128th Machine Gun Battalion, 35th Division, including Company A of Carthage, paused at Le Havre, France, at the mouth of the Seine river, to rest after the trip over the Channel and to strip down for action, the British army in Picardy was preparing to meet another of the terrific German offensives which twice already in that spring of 1918 had so grievously shaken the English front. Here in Le Havre Major Westley Halliburton, the battalion commander, learned that the division, including his battalion, was to be transported by rail some 80 miles to the east and northeast into the area of the Fourth British Army, to be assigned to the British XIX Corps and train with the remnants of the 30th British Division, being available at any moment for service on the front in case the Germans tried to came through the line again.

[On] May 18, at 7:30 p.m., the battalion loaded onto a troop train of third-class passenger coaches, ten men and packs to a compartment and rattled away to the northeastward. This was to be the last time in France that the Carthaginians rode in passenger cars, box cars thereafter being the method of travel by rail, but this night's journey in the packed third-class coaches was made in little more comfort than the subsequent trips, though young soldiers like these headed toward the front were always inclined to take inconveniences lightly.

At 6:45 the next morning the battalion detrained at Eu, a town which the soldiers soon learned was not pronounced as spelled but by some trick of French pronunciation sounded more like an oddly enunciated "Uhr." Here a British first lieutenant, 60 English soldiers and some British horse transport—limbered wagons with a box over each set of wheels—waited, and a certain number of American wagoneers to accompany these were detailed.

"We're motorized," the machine gunners sarcastically told each other with rueful grins as they recalled the motor equipment promised the division machine gun battalion by the American tables of equipment.

The battle-worn British transport men stared blankly and somewhat arrogantly at these broad-hatted, chin-strapped, joke-cracking Yanks and the Americans gazed back interestedly at their war-worn allies whose brass K.O.Y.L.I. insignia, standing, it was ascertained, for "King's Own Yorkshire Light Infantry," apparently showed them to be from one of the 30th's Regular Army battalions, though British military nomenclature was never entirely clear to the Missourians. Then the transport wagons moved off, and the 128th, less the men detailed to the wagons, formed in column and marched out to camp for breakfast—paraded out, in fact—headed by a band of kilted Scotch pipers, probably from the Scots Fusiliers, at the front of which marched an enormous individual beating a bass drum and wearing a gorgeous leopard's skin over his uniform.

Eu was in the French Department of Seine Inferieure but just on its northern boundary and beyond it lay the Department of the Somme. Here also ran the boundary between the old provinces of Picardy and Normandy, the latter on the south, and while the American service in this region was officially classified as service with the British in Picardy, it was really in Normandy that the 128th was stationed, for soon after breakfast it turned its back toward the north, marched up a long hill and continued southward past quaint Norman farms, through the picturesque village of Le Mesnil Reaume, and down a hill past a wood into another valley and so into the typical old-world village of Sept Meules, through which flowed a crystal stream which the map showed to be the Yeres. Here, seven miles south of Eu, the battalion settled down for training.

It was Company A' s first experience in being billeted on the inhabitants after the European custom instead of living in camps. On the front of the masonry walls of each of the houses of the town were marks like this "O 1 H 10 C 2," being the abbreviation for "Officers 1; hommes 10; chevaux 2" which indicated that at this place there was quarters for one officer, a good room in the house; 10 men, in the attic or barnloft; and two horses in the stable. Assignment of officers, men and horses were made in accordance with these marks. The desires of the inhabitants were not consulted; it was the French law that troops be so billeted on the inhabitants, and such quarters were paid for at the rate of a franc a day [for] each officer, five centimes a day for each man, and a suitable sum for each horse. This system, used in France in peace and war for centuries, was especially fitted for the World War, in that villages quickly swallowed up armies which otherwise would often have needed to camp in fields in plain view of any enemy airplane.

A part of Company A was assigned to the second floor of an old mill on the Yeres; others went to barn lofts and attics, and some, the weather being fine, were permitted to pitch their shelter tents under the trees of an orchard near the north part of the town and near the building in which the Company A kitchen had been located.

"My room here would make a nice stall for old Maude," wrote John Glass to his mother.[26]

That night, off to the east, was heard a long-continued dull thudding, a disturbance of atmosphere rather than sound; and vague distant flickers were discernable on the eastern sky. It was the cannonading on the recently established and not-too-secure front east of Amiens. The old Carthage Light Guard after 42 years of existence was at last sleeping within sound of enemy guns.

The 128th Machine Gun Battalion, including Company A of Carthage, had hardly reached the village of Sept Meules, Department of Seine Inferieure, northern France—20 miles southwest of Abbeville, eight miles from the English Channel and 45 or 50 miles from the muttering guns in front of Amiens—when things of organizational importance began to happen.

First it received machine guns. This was in the last half of May, 1918, and although the United States had been in the war over 13 months, machine guns had never been available for this unit until now, and these were British Vickers, caliber .303, beautiful little weapons, 12 to a company, one to each squad. With the guns came a store of accessories, a fixed-base range finder, a supply of field glasses and prismatic compasses, all stamped with the broad arrow of the British War Office. Also there was a little flood of

26. John M. Glass was born on January 22, 1891, in Carthage. His parents owned and operated a cleaning establishment in Carthage, and their son assisted them in the business. He served overseas with the 128th from April 25, 1918, to April 24, 1919. During World War II, he served as a guard at Camp Crowder, Missouri. Glass died on July 18, 1957. He was buried in Park Cemetery, Carthage. *Carthage* (MO) *Evening Press*, July 19, 1957; Missouri Secretary of State, State Archives, Soldiers' Records, War of 1812–World War I, www.sos.mo.gov/archives/soldiers.

booklets of instruction, the contents of which, the printed warning stated, were "not to be communicated to any person not holding an official position in His Majesty's service."

A new great German offensive in Picardy was expected any moment to the east, and if it went through the line as previous offensives had done, there was small doubt that the Missourians would soon be in battle.

On May 27 the Germans launched their long-expected offensive but instead of being in the vicinity of Amiens and aimed at the English Channel, it was down in the Chemin-des-Dames sector and directed toward Paris. The assault broke entirely through the Allied line, crossed the Aisne River the same day and by dusk had destroyed or overrun all opposition, progressed ten miles and was headed south with apparently little between it and the French capital.

That same evening as the Germans streamed southward through the broken Chemin-des-Dames line, a troop train, passing through the northern outskirts of Paris just as dusk was falling and as the balloon barrage which helped protect that city from air attack was being raised, was bearing back to the 35th Division its advance detachment returning from school at Chatillon-sur-Seine and including among others Capt. Ward L. Schrantz , 1st Lieut. Frank L. Snyder, and Sergeants Edwin W. Wiggins, Fred R. Clark and James A. Hines of Company A. This group rejoined their organization at Sept Meules the following evening and Captain Schrantz resumed command of the company.

The new arrivals, fresh from a Vickers machine gun school and knowing the weapon for one of the best machine guns in the world, took up the work of instruction with enthusiasm, and while Lieut. Snyder was ordered a few days later to attend a British gas school at Nouvion, some eight miles north of Abbeville, there still remained the captain and one sergeant-instructor for each platoon.

A machine gunner needs not only to know how to operate his weapon but must have a thorough knowledge of its mechanism. Because during firing it is subjected to a continuous succession of shocks of recoil, various stoppages due to breakage or malfunction are likely to occur just at the time the gun is needed the most. The gunner then must be able to find out quickly what is wrong, and strip the gun and replace broken parts at night or any other time. He must know the entire weapon by feel and be able to take it apart and put it together blind-folded. Nor is it enough for a few selected men to know this. Since there would be losses in battle and the company must continue to function, every man must be a gunner, and hence have a perfect knowledge of the gun. So the Vickers were taken down and put together, and taken down and put together again repeatedly, and each man in the company made progress toward mastery of their mechanism and operation.

The need appeared urgent, too. Although the enemy had attacked to the south, a number of American divisions were being moved toward the break and the 35th expected to be called momentarily, and the harried staff at division headquarters was already worrying about small arms ammunition supply, if the division left the British area. All the machine gunners of the 35th were equipped with the English caliber .303 machine guns, and the rifle organizations upon arrival at Le Havre had exchanged their beloved Springfields for the stubby British Enfields in order that while serving with the British army British ammunition could be used. The artillery of the division was not with the British, there being enough English cannon, and was training near Angers down in Brittany, far from the scene of operations.

June 2 was Sunday, but in view of the emergency, it was just another day of machine gun work. The 128th Machine Gun Battalion must be ready for action. Every hour gained in instruction would be of that much value in case of an early entry into action. All up and down the Yeres Valley the machine gun organizations of the division, most of them from the old Second Missouri, were training with equal energy. And this expectation of immediate service was not based on rumor. On Tuesday, June 4, Col. W.R. McCleave, chief of staff of the 35th Division, visited Sept Meules and said:

"I believe that we shall be in battle by Friday."

Major General William M. Wright, the division commander, also visited Sept Meules during the period to check up on the progress his individual machine gun battalion was making.

Yet if men are to be kept from going stale they can be worked only a certain number of hours every day, even though there is a distant cannonade to spur them on, and Sept Meules had its hours of relaxation. It was a pleasant place and for the most of the machine gunners the stay there is probably a happy memory, marred somewhat by rueful recollections of the British rations—tea, marmalade, dessicated potatoes, tough cured meat, all in what the Americans deemed insufficient quantity. The British normal ration was not so large as an American one and since the English custom at the time was to give only a three-quarter ration to troops behind the line, it will be seen that the Americans were not overfed.

Chapter 6

Promotion and Demotion

A.E.F. commander General Pershing envisioned a three-month training period for each American division after it arrived in France, followed by three or four additional weeks of training. The first phase was the training of small units; the second, training in a quiet sector of the line, and the third, in a training area, correcting any deficiencies and training the division as a whole. Only then would the Americans be ready for combat. In reality, only a handful of divisions came close to finishing Pershing's program. In the case of the 35th Division, the war's frenetic pace dictated that the Missouri and Kansas troops would complete only the first two phases of the regimen (sixty-six days in all), including a brief stint in a "quiet" sector of the Western Front, before being committed to action.[1]

Initially attached to the British Army for this first training phase, Captain Schrantz and his men familiarized themselves with the newly issued Vickers machine guns and tried to grow accustomed to the meager British rations of tough meat and potatoes, tea and marmalade.

Their time with their Anglo allies was brief, however, for on June 6 orders came for Schrantz's company to leave the British

1. Oliver L. Spaulding, Jr., *The Thirty-Fifth Division, 1917–1918* (Washington, D.C.: U.S. Army War College, 1921–22), 23–24.

sector and their Vickers machine guns behind. They marched to the town of Bruchy and boarded a train on June 9, bound for the portion of the front manned by the French Seventh Army.

The Missourians filed off the train near the village of Harol, then marched to Charmois-l'Orqueilleux, where they were warmly received again, the town's residents "quite convinced that an army of 'Franco-Americans' could defeat the world if necessary. There was a high degree of fraternization at every wine shop in the village that evening," Schrantz recalled.

Another march brought them to St. Laurent, where the company found comfortable billets once more, or "campaigning de luxe," as Schrantz described the accommodations. There was relatively little for the men to do in St. Laurent, though, apart from learning the intricacies of the newly issued French Hotchkiss machine guns. As Schrantz noted above, such familiarization was vitally important for their survival, however. With this skill mastered, the Missouri doughboys looked forward to the moment when the guns could actually be used against the enemy.

Such easy and mundane living was destined to end soon, however, as the company was ordered to move closer to the front. In the meantime, Captain Schrantz struggled with army bureaucracy as he tried to determine his actual place in the military hierarchy—whether as a company commander or the division's machine gun officer.

Major General William Wright, our division commander, visited Sept Meules and to my amazement called for me by name and I hurried in from the field. So far as I recall I had not talked to General Wright since the dressing-down he had given me at Camp Doniphan for what he had considered inattention during a drill period.

"You know all about the Vickers machine gun and its use, don't you?" he queried.

"I wouldn't say that, sir," I replied. "I know something about it."

"You received a good report from that school," he answered, "and we count on you as the division machine gun expert."

Somewhat dazed, I expressed gratification, reflecting inwardly that if I was the most expert in the division, the division was indeed in a bad way.

On June 2, Colonel (later Brigadier General) W.R. McCleave, chief of staff of the division visited the village. He also sent for me.

"We count on you to oversee the training of the machine gun units of the division," he stated, "what are you doing now[?]"

"I am training my own company, sir," I answered, "I have received no orders to do anything else."

He reflected a moment.

"That is probably as good as anything," he said. "This is Tuesday and I believe the division will be in battle by Friday. Oversee the training of the companies of this battalion which we count on as the divisional reserve of fire power. See that they not only know how to shoot but that they can bring fire to bear on reverse slopes."

All this personal attention from high places had me puzzled as well as amused. Later the circumstances were to cause me some embarrassment.

Strange as it seemed then, and still seems, an order had been issued or ordered issued the previous day, naming me, a captain, as division machine gun officer while there were three machine gun majors in the division. Presumably division headquarters thought that inasmuch as the division was armed with the Vickers gun that a Vickers man was necessary for that position. I did not receive a copy of that order while in the area. Perhaps there was some days paper work delay and by that time it began to be rumored that we were to be sent out of the British area and the order was never furnished me since a French area at that time meant the Hotchkiss machine gun. Receiving no order I continued to carry on my normal work, deeming it tactful—since the chief of staff had not mentioned the matter to my battalion commander—to confine the supervision of the other company he had directed me to exercise to trading of ideas with my fellow captain and watching his unit work as his and mine functioned side by side.

Sept Meules was a pleasant village in the valley of a stream called the Yeres and I much enjoyed our brief stay there, riding a bit over the country incidental to my unit's training. In the next war—in 1940—the region featured in the news as the Germans overran the country and I wondered, with curiosity unsatisfied as to what happened to Sept Meules.[2]

2. In a letter to his wife, Schrantz shared details about his quarters. He explained that about 30 families lived in the village, where daily life showed no hint of war except for the rumble of artillery. He noted that he was quartered with an old French couple. His room decorations consisted of the family's photographs, a large silver crucifix, various pictures

Our stay there was not to be long. On June 3, five American divisions—the 4th, 28th, 35th, 77th and 82nd Divisions—had been ordered shifted from the British front incidental to the shift of the main danger zone southward, the 35th's orders calling for it to turn in its British weapons and move to the Vosges region.

It was the forenoon of June 6 before the move order had trickled through channels down to the 128th Machine Gun Battalion, nor had we heard any previous rumor of it. We assumed that when we moved it would be toward the front.

That forenoon the 12 guns of my company were busily firing away on a 1000 inch range on a hillside near the camp.[3] First Lieut. Frank L. Snyder who had just returned the day before from the British gas school at Nouvion was telling me about Abbeville through which he had passed. "The German planes are blasting at that place every night," he narrated. Then our attention was attracted by a noisy motor cycle pop-popping up the valley road to Sept Meules. Immediately afterwards a runner from battalion headquarters came out to tell us to come in immediately. We were to turn in our machine guns and move on Neufchatel, clearing Fresnoy-Folny, two hours march to the south, by 1:50. It was now 10 o'clock and we would need to leave the village in an hour and 50 minutes. There followed the usual activity in such cases of rolling packs and bedding rolls. A school detachment which had been at Val du Roi up the valley of the Yeres rejoined breathlessly, and at the time appointed we were on the march—leaving the machine guns in charge of an officer since there as yet were no British authorities to take them.

We marched 15 miles that warm afternoon, lunchless due to the haste of our departure, through Londiniere and up the valley of the river Eaulne to the hamlet of Fesques, near which we pitched shelter tents in the fields for the night. It was the first route march I had made with my unit in France, and the event rather thrilled me. In front as we marched through the countryside was the battalion in column of fours. Behind it came the limbered wagons of both companies. Behind that in a group

of Christ, and a huge bed with canopy and a mattress four feet thick. His conversation with the couple was limited to "bon jour" and "bon soir." The officers' mess was in the priest's home, which was decorated with finely bound books and a number of excellent paintings. *Carthage* (MO) *Evening Press*, June 4, 1918.

3. Approximately 28 yards.

marched the British transport detachment, which our men had relieved.[4]

Lieutenant Gradwell, the British transport officer, and I watched this last detachment as they came in—he with considerable pride since they were finishing in good shape, swinging swagger sticks and singing, though he said most of them had been relegated to the transport because of wounds. Their song had a fine marching lilt to it and was one that I had never heard before, familiar as it has become since:

"Mademoiselle from Armentieres, parley vous,
Mademoiselle from Armentieres, parley vous- - - ."

The next day as we moved southward after a less hurried departure we passed through Neufchatel where the French inhabitants had mustered with great pitchers of cider and numerous glasses to welcome the Americans.

The column could not stop but full glasses were passed out to the marching men which they drank as they walked, handing the empties back to two small boys who had trotted along to receive them. It was a most cheering courtesy.

"They used to do that for us too," commented my British lieutenant somewhat sadly, "When we first came over."

All that day and the next, artillery fire was roaring angrily away far to our left as we marched. Behind me as I marched was a young soldier assigned as a runner, and I heard him muttering distastefully: "Listen to them damn guns; listen to them God damn guns."

This young man was doubtless younger than I knew, for he was rather short and chunky whereas within a year he added about 6 inches to his height. Always an excellent soldier, a wound received in the Meuse-Argonne did not discourage his military leanings and after the war he enlisted in the U.S. Marine Corps, serving with it many years and attaining a commission in World War II. Eventually he was retired as a major when incapacitated by fresh wounds.[5]

4. Schrantz noted that despite the trying conditions, and the fact that stragglers from others units were scattered along the road, only one man from Company A fell out of ranks from fatigue.

5. Schrantz may refer to Lawrence Bert Akin, who was wounded during the Meuse-Argonne Offensive on September 27, 1918, and served for many years in the United States Marine Corps, but attained the rank of captain rather than major. His brother Leaford was a non-commissioned officer in Company A.

That night we camped at a village called Fontaine-en-Bray after a march of only nine or 10 miles, and the following day pounded down the poplar bordered road to the village of Buchy, some 20 miles or so northeast of Rouen and bivouacked, preparatory to entrainment at a railway station to the west about a mile and a half.

There were a number of British hospitals somewhere about and the cluster of wineshops and their vicinity near the railway station that night were filled with Americans, British and Australians, the latter two groups principally convalescents, though part of the British were attached to our own division pending the orders detaching them which came that evening.

A lowered state of discipline was evidenced by the British and Australians, both of which elbowed the British officers rather rudely on the street, and relatively few of the English saluted my British friend Gradwell with whom I had walked to the railway station. One drunken Tommy even stopped him and demanded how long he thought the war would last. The Australians, many of whom were drunk, were the noisiest. A rumor had spread among them that the Australian divisions which had suffered heavy casualties were to be broken up and the men distributed as individual replacements in English divisions and they were quite vociferous in objections to any such arrangement. The British officers circulated through this turbulent mob with unshaken poise, quite admirable under the circumstances I thought. Gradwell made no comment on the English soldiers but in reference to the Australians said: "Good fighters but a wild lot, those fellows. Once they got to firing their revolvers in the streets at Calais—." Our American soldiers wandered about looking at this scene with something like amused amazement, well ordered and behaved.

In Buchy while walking with Major Wesley Halliburton my battalion commander, we encountered Lieutenant Colonel Paul Tucker who had been executive officer of the old Second Missouri before it was broken up and who lately had been acting as division machine gun officer. I explained to him, in response to his query which I had heard frequently from other officers on the march, that I had not gone to Val du Roi to take command of the four regimental machine gun companies which had been training there as a provisional battalion, for the very good reason that I had had no orders to do so. He pulled from his pocket a copy of the order, which I reproduce.[6]

Headquarters 35th Division
American Expeditionary Forces,
1 June 1918
Special Orders
No. 122
Extract

2. Lieut. Col. Paul Tucker, 137th Infantry, is relieved from duty with provisional machine gun battalion and will report to his regimental commander for duty.

3. Capt. Ward L. Schrantz, 128th Machine Gun Battalion, is designated as division machine gun officer. Until further orders he will take station with the provisional machine gun battalion and will exercise general supervision over training of the machine gun battalions in this division.

By Command of Major General Wright
R. McCLEAVE
Colonel, General Staff
Chief of Staff
Official: WM. ELLIS
Major, N. G., U.S.,
Asst. Div. Adjutant

"I am the only Paul Tucker I know of," said the colonel airily, "so I went back to the 137th. You are the only Ward Schrantz I know."

Whatever Major Halliburton felt at this order which assigned one of his own captains—one of his Mexican border sergeants—to supervise the training of his battalion as well as the two other battalions both of which were commanded by majors, he showed no sign of his injured pride. He agreed with me that since the

6. Paul Tucker of Lamar, Missouri, was born on March 1, 1877, and enlisted as a private in Company C, 2nd Missouri Infantry in 1896. He served as the company's quartermaster sergeant in the Spanish-American War, and despite some breaks in service, rose to the rank of lieutenant colonel of the 2nd Missouri Infantry by 1913. He served in that capacity on the Mexican border from 1916 to 17. He began to serve overseas on April 26, 1918, with the 137th Infantry Regiment, and was sent to a hospital because of sickness on the second day of the Meuse-Argonne (September 27, 1918). After the Armistice, he served with the 112th U.S. Infantry and ended his overseas service on April 25, 1919. He died on April 4, 1956, and was buried in Rose Hill Cemetery, Tyler, Texas. *The Service of the Missouri National Guard on the Mexican Border*, 107; Missouri Secretary of State, State Archives, Soldiers' Records, War of 1812-World War I, www.sos.mo.gov/archives/soldiers.

division was on the move that there was nothing I could do about it until we reached the new area. The regimental machine gun companies were all back with their own regiments now.

It was with some amusement that on the evening of June 9 we loaded the British horses and limbered wagons which were our only transport on railway cars. We had expected an order taking them from us before we left the British area, and there was a rumor when we finished loading that such an order had come. If so it never reached us, and we entrained our men and departed about 9 p.m.

Somewhere during the night there was considerable delay, and it was daylight by the time the train passed through Rouen where Joan of Arc was burned at the stake and where, someone said, the heart of Richard Coeur de Leon reposes enshrined in a marble casket; then later the Missourians skirted Paris on the west, passing through Versailles and getting a glance at the old palace of the Bourbon kings and glimpses of white statuary in the glades of the tree-grown palace grounds, then southeastward and eastward through Melun, Troyes and Chaumont, the latter the headquarters of the American Expeditionary Force[s].

It was a beautiful region that the men, clustered around the box car doors saw in passing, rendered more interesting perhaps by glimpses of French soldiers in faded horizon blue at the stations, and enlivened by the waved greetings of French girls at every hamlet or in fields where they were working. At the stops there descended upon the train a swarm of grinning small boys in black smocks, begging for souvenirs or pennies and answering in rapid French the English witticisms of the soldiers, neither understanding what the others were saying. But it was not a comfortable journey, this ride in box cars. “A worse train ride I never had,” commented Mess Sergeant Clint Miles in a letter home published in the *Press*.

In the afternoon of June 11 the battalion detrained at the railway station south of the village of Harol in the Department Vosges about ten miles west of Epinal, then marched south some seven kilometers—between four and five miles—to the village of Charmois, or more completely Charmois-l’Orqueilleux, where it was billeted for the night, quartered in buildings as a rule instead of sleeping in shelter tents as on the march from Sept Meules to Buchy back in the British area.

The Americans were warmly welcomed in Charmois, for the French were elated at the repulse of the Germans by the Americans in the vicinity of Chateau Thierry and to the northwest of that town where fighting was still going on. The German thrust at the Marne had first encountered American resistance when the 7th Machine Gun Battalion, motorized, of the 3rd Division—a divisional battalion like the 128th—had sped ahead of its division in time to join the French defense in and in front of the town of Chateau Thierry [on] May 31, being an important factor in preventing the enemy crossing the Marne here. Farther to the northwest the Second American Division had pushed north past retiring French soldiers and throngs of refugees, encountered the German advance, stopped it and then engaged in that protracted series of conflicts in the vicinity of Bouresches and the Bois de Belleau. Here the Missourians' old associate of Mexican border days, the 9th U.S. Infantry, was hotly engaged and here also a number of Carthage men in the Second and Third American divisions first saw action.[7]

The French government and newspapers had rather played up the American successes in order to boost the French morale, and with considerable success. The good folks in Charmois were enthusiastic about the future, quite convinced that an army "Franco-Americaine" could defeat the world if necessary. There was a high degree of fraternization at every wine shop in the village that evening. Elements of the 137th and 139th Infantry regiments also spent the night in or near Charmois and in the morning there was much to-do when the American officers found that persons unknown, presumably Americans, had looted a citizen's cellar of 20 bottles of wine. Company commanders harangued their companies without discovering the culprits and in the end the cost was met by the government and assessed against the pay of the men.

We marched south some distance, then east, passing through some belts of barbed-wire entanglement which apparently marked the limits of the fortress area of Epinal, to the village of St. Laurent on the Moselle River a few miles above the French city, where we went into billets.

7. Headquarters, the 1st and 2nd Battalions, and Companies L and M of the 9th U.S. Infantry were stationed at Fort Sam Houston and Laredo, Texas, from March 1914 to May 1917. Companies I and K were stationed in Texas until September 1917. U.S. Adjutant General's Office, *Regimental History of the United States Regular Army, Chronological Outline, 1866–1918* (Washington, D.C.: U.S. Government Printing Office, 1918), 8.

The Carthage soldiers seemed to have been pleased with St. Laurent.[8]

"I stay in the cellar of a house and have a bed. Rather a nice place," wrote Cook Albert Weaver. "Our kitchen is just across the road from where we stay. I have seen Spide Stark. He is a sergeant in an auto shop and is doing rear axle work."[9]

Sergeant Paul Havens described Epinal and St. Laurent as being "similar to Carthage and Kendricktown and being just about as far apart," and added: "A custom that exists in the French army is that noncommissioned officers are allowed the privilege of renting rooms, and Sergeant Ernest Ellis and myself have one. We have a dresser, bed, four chairs, a table and electric lights."[10]

This was campaigning de luxe but Sergeant Havens was not the only one. Sergeant Edwin W. Wiggins wrote home as follows:

> "I have a room here with a French family—or rather Sergeant Norval R. Hopwood and I have—and we are fixed up real cozy but I do not know how long it will last . . . I like France better every day and am in the best of health and feeling fine."

8. Some of Schrantz's men were perhaps too pleased with St. Laurent. Privates Joseph Sparks and John F. Sinclair entered the Sport Palace Café in Epinal about 5:45 p.m. on June 21, 1918, ordered two cans of sardines and two quarts of red wine. They refused to pay, then asked a woman working there for "a piece of tail." When she refused, the men chased her through several rooms, caught her, tied her hands with a belt and hit her in the jaw. One of the men had a knife between his teeth. They then went into another room and upset several chairs and a stand, breaking the glass. The men continued their rampage, forcing a lock on a cupboard door, stealing about 40 francs, and broke two bottles of wine and six glasses. Confined in the guard room in St. Laurent, under the charge of the assistant provost marshal, the "somewhat intoxicated" Sinclair and sober Sparks soon picked the lock and escaped. No record could be found of their punishment. Statement by Lt. Gibbes Lykes, 3rd Cavalry, St. Laurent, France, June 22, 1918, Record Group 120, Records of the American Expeditionary Forces, World War I Organization Records, Machine Gun Battalions, 128th Machine Gun Battalion, Box 264, NARA.

9. W. Albert (Al) Weaver was born in Carl Junction, Missouri, on July 16, 1899, and moved to Carthage about 1906. He enlisted on August 3, 1917, was appointed company cook in March 1918, and served overseas from April 25, 1918 to May 31, 1919. He died on December 20, 1920, and was buried in Waco, Jasper County, Missouri. *Joplin* (MO) *News Herald*, December 21, 1920; Missouri Secretary of State, State Archives, Soldiers' Records, War of 1812–World War I, www.sos.mo.gov/archives/soldiers; HST. John Leanord "Spide" Stark was born on February 8, 1889, and died on August 18, 1951. Stark served with the 18th Company, First Air Service Command Mechanics Regiment. He was buried in Fort Leavenworth National Cemetery. *The Joplin* (MO) *Globe*, August 19, 1951.

10. Ernest Essex Ellis was born in Carthage on January 23, 1892. He served with Company A on the Mexican border from 1916 to 1917, and overseas with the 128th from April 25, 1918 to April 24, 1919. He died on October 21, 1964, and was buried in San Diego, California. *The San Diego* (CA) *Union*, October 24, 1964; Missouri Secretary of State, State Archives, Soldiers' Records, War of 1812-World War I, www.sos.mo.gov/archives/soldiers; *The Service of the Missouri National Guard on the Mexican Border*, 123.

Edwin Wiggins (*Memorial Hall, Carthage, MO*)

Mess Sergeant Miles wrote under date of June 14:

"I hope we stay here some time as I sure am located fine. I have a room all to myself with a fine large bed with a feather tick and white sheets and pillow slips. We received our second mail since reaching this side today. I am going to town tomorrow and try to buy some extras to eat. At our last camp I started to buy two cases of peaches and pears like we had in Camp Doniphan but they were $1.32 in our

> money per can, so I didn't buy." But the military menu was not bad, for in a letter written two days later Sergeant Miles said: "For dinner today I gave the men steak with mashed potatoes, cream gravy, green onions and boiled turnips, bread, butter and coffee."

A letter from Private George B. Herron, written about the same time, gives further light on Company A life in St. Laurent.[11]

> "It is raining here now," he said, "it sure does rain a lot in France. I helped two French girls put up hay after drill yesterday and they both wore wooden shoes and had a team of oxen hitched to a wagon. We haven't been paid since we left the states but are looking for it any day. We are getting all we want to eat; and sleep in a good house and our feed is fine."[12]

The division, with units billeted in villages, occupied a considerable area with division headquarters at Arches, a few miles below St. Laurent.

Going to the division adjutant's office at Arches I asked about the order which had been issued concerning me, and if it had been countermanded. Some clerk finally found it and could find no countermanding order. Next I went to the G-3, the divisional plans and training officer, and he looked at it in surprise. He had never known such an order had been issued, he said. Obviously the division had not been very badly upset by my failure to report. G-3 took me to Col. McCleave, the chief of staff, who received us pleasantly, looked at the order, smiled and said, "Oh, yes," smiling again at my explanation of why I had not obeyed it. I suspected that he had intended to countermand it when he learned the division was to leave the Vickers machine gun area and had forgotten to do so. Indeed by this time the division had probably put in a request for a Hotchkiss machine gun officer, however he was not going back on his own order.

11. George B. Herron was born in Joplin, Missouri (some sources state Newton County, Missouri) on August 1, 1894. He served overseas with the 128th from June 12, 1918, to October 23, 1918. He died on December 29, 1968, and was buried in Joplin, Missouri. *Joplin* (MO) *News Herald*, December 30, 1968; Missouri Secretary of State, State Archives, Soldiers' Records, War of 1812–World War I, www.sos.mo.gov/archives/soldiers.

12. Neither Schrantz nor the enlisted men mentioned the memo that Major Halliburton sent to his company commanders on June 14, 1918. The major prohibited cafes from selling anything stronger than light wines and beer, ordered his men to be in their quarters by 9:45, to wear their coats at retreat and afterwards, to shave daily, and to wear their hair short, as "long hair is a woman's pride and a soldier[']s shame." Memo to company commanders, Headquarters, 128th Machine Gun Battalion, June 14, 1918, Record Group 120, Records of the American Expeditionary Forces, World War I Organization Records, Machine Gun Battalions, 128th Machine Gun Battalion, Box 266, NARA.

"You are quite a young man," he commented—I was 27 but that was considered young for a captain in this stage of World War I—"and this is not a boy's job we are giving you. You will remain quartered with your battalion but we will give you a motor cycle with sidecar; you get a driver from your company. I want you to visit every machine gun company in this division, push their training along and keep G-3 informed of their progress."

This was on June 14, and I carried out the order quite zealously—for four days.

Hotchkiss machine guns had been issued to us on our arrival—16 per company, including four to be held in reserve. This Hotchkiss machine gun, model 1914, was the regulation gun of the French army and used by all the early American divisions in France not on the British front. It was a long, gaunt weapon of death—air-cooled, gas-operated, fed with metal strips containing 24 cartridges each, and had an estimated killing range of over 4,000 yards due to its copper, boat- tailed bullets. It was one of the best machine guns in the world in its day and those who used it soon became enthusiastic about it, but it appeared ungainly at first sight to men who had learned to love the trim little Vickers.[13]

"I never knew what a good machine gun the Colt was," I heard one of my sergeants say disconsolately as he first surveyed the Hotchkiss on its tripod, "until I saw this thing."

But the men who had been at the machine gun school at Chatillon-sur-Seine and knew something of the mechanism of the Hotchkiss as well as being familiar with its reputation, were quick to defend it; and as the company began to work with the new instrument of war and learned of its long range, its simplicity of operation and that the metallic strips containing 30 rounds each could be fed to the gun in such quick succession that it could fire as rapidly as the Vickers had consumed the cartridges in its canvas belts of 250, disdain changed to admiration.

13. "The men at first were a little prejudiced against the Hotchkiss," wrote Walter Weber of the 129th Machine Gun Battalion, "but as their familiarity with the weapon increased, they liked it better," and after the Meuse-Argonne Offensive, "they all claimed it was the best gun we ever had." Weber, *The History of the 129th Machine Gun Battalion*, 21. The .303 caliber Vickers Mark I water-cooled machine gun, one of the war's best, weighed 42 pounds with a full water jacket and required a tripod that weighed about 56 pounds. The gun could fire more than 500 rounds per minute. U.S. troops used both the British and American-made versions of the Vickers (the latter designated the U.S. Model 1915, produced by Colt and chambered in .30-06) in training and in combat. Canfield, *U.S. Infantry Weapons of the First World War*, 190-200.

Of the 16 guns only 12 were manned, the remainder being reserve weapons to replace any disabled ones and each of the 12 gun squads beginning from the moment their Hotchkiss was received started work zealously, quickly mastering its mechanism and looking forward to the time it could be fired.

It was urgent that the new gun be learned as quickly as possible since it was expected that the division would move to the front at any time to relieve French troops to move toward the Marne. Indeed some French troops, possibly a reserve division we had relieved, was already moving out on trains passing through St. Laurent. It was necessary that all men be familiarized with its mechanism quickly and be taught to fire it, or otherwise they might be on the front before they had an opportunity.

On visiting the three battalions and each of their companies I found the training being pushed. In the regimental machine guns [*sic*] companies it was less advanced. Two of these regimental companies moved forward within a day or two after I started my tours. In one of the others, the captain—a friend of mine from Camp Doniphan days—had mapped out a week's instruction in mechanism before any firing practice, quite after the British ideas. His lieutenants were secretly fuming with impatience. I speeded him up and explained that while his program would normally be reasonable enough that he might be looking at the enemy within a week. The other regimental machine gun company had done nothing at all with the new guns. Finding the captain at his office I asked him where his company was. It was out having bayonet practice, he said. The rifles which had been issued it were to be turned in and he thought the men should have some more bayonet practice while they still had a chance. I persuaded him that to a machine gun company machine guns were the most important. He stopped bayonet practice and started on the guns. I kept pretty much on the road—a pleasant thing in itself in June—found everyone cooperative, including the majors whatever they thought, and kept the G-3 informed that things were moving along well.

This same day as the soldiers crowded around the still strange guns, there was a cannon shot from a hill to the east across the Moselle River, then another and a third.

Tiny white blotches appeared high in the eastern sky around a speck which, drawing nearer, soon defined itself as an airplane.

Now there were more blotches of smoke, in the center of each as it appeared a tiny flash of angry flame. The roar of the engine of the visitor was quite audible as the machine came on westward, apparently undisturbed by the attention of the anti-aircraft guns.

The machine gunners flattened themselves against the sides of the nearby buildings, in accordance with previous instructions covering such eventualities, so that they might not be visible from above and the village so appear to be empty. Also they watched for some French plane to take the air and assail this impertinent visitor, but the stranger had the sky to himself except for the white puffs of bursting shrapnel interspersed with black splotches caused by exploding shell. He came over near the Moselle River until the black Maltese crosses on his wings were visible, then swerved back to the east and disappeared. It was not until later that the soldiers learned that most of the French pursuit machines were concentrated on more vital fronts and that here the enemy observing planes were usually left for the anti-aircraft artillery to deal with.

This was the first of frequent episodes of this character, occurring perhaps at intervals of several days. Usually the planes passed over the town and on into the interior, and, since what goes up must come down, hot shrapnel balls from the anti-aircraft guns pattered at times on the tile roofs of St. Laurent, and occasionally singing slivers of shell spatted into the earth. This made life more interesting, even though the guns seemed unable to bring the enemy down.[14]

On the evening of the fourth day as I came in late in the 128th Machine Gun Battalion mess after a visit to one of the companies, there was a strange major in the group.

"Captain Schrantz," said Major Halliburton with possibly a touch of malice in his pleasant voice, "I want you to meet Major Hay, our new divisional machine gun officer."

I trust that I took that introduction with as unmoved face as Major Halliburton had taken the original word of my detail as such.

14. Schrantz observed that the engines of German aircraft had a distinctive sound, "very different from an allied engine, and whenever we hear it we are still new enough to want to look at the enemy machine." Schrantz believed that German aerial photographers would develop their photographs, "study them carefully for a few days and then, several days after we are gone, he will come back and bomb the town, like as not killing some women and children, but no soldiers at all. That seems to be the German way." *Carthage* (MO) *Evening Press*, July 16, 1918; August 9, 1918.

"I am glad to have you with us, Major," I said, "and I will turn over the motor-cycle and sidecar I have to you in the morning."

And so I did, together with all the information I had, without ever having seen the order appointing him or relieving me. I never received nor did I ever see a copy of the order.

My successor was Major (later Lieutenant Colonel) Donald D. Hay of the Regular Army. He came to us from some machine gun school in France, as I recall, spent the war with the 35th Division, and after the war was a machine gun instructor at Fort Benning. He had been commissioned in the regular service in 1902 before I was 12 years old and I have no doubt was much better qualified for the position of division machine gun officer than was I.[15]

Perhaps I should have been chagrined at my relief and doubtless would have been had it come later, for then I might have assumed my work had not been satisfactory. Coming this early I felt that it was a thing already arranged before I began my duties. And besides I knew I had done as well in that short time as anyone could. Consequently I did not feel badly and was glad to get back to my company. Naturally my brief elevation did not make me popular with the majors of the machine gun battalions, pleasant as they had been about it, and I suspect that none of them ever really forgave me that brief jolt to their pride.

Among the first things I did when I returned to my company was to take it on the range. Use of a French army rifle range between St. Laurent and Epinal had been secured for certain hours. We waited our turn while a company of French Chasseurs Alpine finished and by the time we were through a French machine gun company was waiting for us.

The Chasseurs Alpine with their dark blue uniforms and berets were of particular interest to the Missourians, for their abilities in a military way had been rather well advertised. Many—or possibly most—of the French soldiers who had come into the service from this Vosges region had been placed in the mountaineer

15. Donald Davie Hay was born in Pennsylvania on October 9, 1881. Appointed a second lieutenant of infantry in 1902, Hay was promoted to colonel in the Regular Army in 1934. He was awarded the Silver Star for his service in World War I. U.S. Adjutant General's Office, *Official Army Register January 1, 1936* (Washington, D.C.: Government Printing Office, 1936), 307. He died on March 23, 1936, and was buried in Arlington National Cemetery.

organizations.[16] Later we shifted to an improvised range of our own west of St. Laurent in the hills and firing was more or less continuous from this time on, mixed with drill and maneuver.

Soon after our arrival [the] British animal-drawn transport was taken from us and a dusty convoy of 30 light Ford gun trucks limped into the village to take its place. The divisional machine gun battalion was to be motorized at last—after a fashion. Whatever had been produced in the United States under war pressure, these vehicles were neither new nor in number or capacity equivalent to those called for by the table of organizations. They were a light model T with a low covered back and had been used during the border troubles by National Guard machine gun companies equipped with Lewis guns. I had seen such vehicles with the Second Florida Infantry at Laredo, and those I now received bore the mark—as I recall it—of a North Carolina organization. With them for the battalion came several motorcycles and 10 ton-and-a-half Garford and G.M.C. trucks. My original allotment of the light cars was 15, but two of these were soon taken away to go to some division headquarters unit.[17]

No additional motor equipment was received by us during the war. This available was sufficient to carry the guns and ammunition and that was about all. Men and their weapons were thus necessarily separated during a march since motor and foot columns could not travel together. Since there was no personnel carriers the mobility of the battalion was no greater than the animal drawn companies of the brigade battalions except when additional trucks could be secured from the division motor pool. Our men composed a satirical little song which they sang as we marched along—"We're Motorized."[18]

16. Schrantz watched his gunners "riddling with their copper, 8-millimeter bullets the silhouette targets which were part of the range equipment—shooting them to pieces while the French range attendants mourned." Company A's Earl Conley thought it "great sport" to fire "500 times a minute" and watch machine gun bullets cut a large tree completely in two. *Fort Scott* (KS) *Tribune and the Fort Scott Monitor*, August 9, 1918.

17. The Garford Motor Truck Company of Lima, Ohio, produced a 1 ½ ton cargo truck. General Motors produced a light delivery truck of one ton or less capacity. According to Maj. Westley Halliburton, the pneumatic-tired G.M.C. trucks were traded to another organization for their hard-tired Garfords, due to the scarcity of tire-repair material and the fact that the battalion's truck complement would be all one model. Westley Halliburton Manuscript, Jasper County Record Center.

18. Schrantz was not impressed with the Ford vehicles, and tried to "trade off for something more suitable. I thought this was a pretty nice war until they took our horses away from us a second time and issued us this dilapidated bunch of automobiles." *Carthage* (MO) *Evening Press*, August 9, 1918.

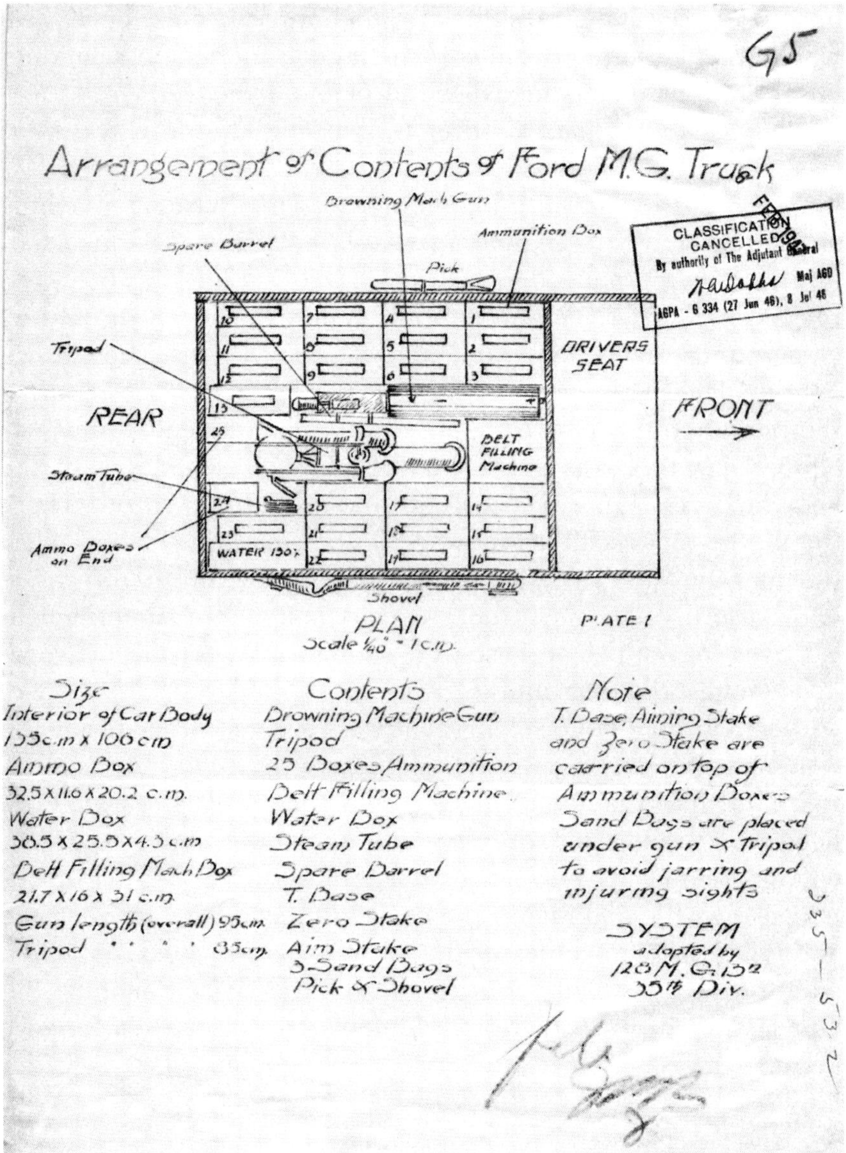

Arrangement of contents of Ford Machine Gun Truck (*National Archives*)

South of St. Laurent was the end of a long ridge, the crest of which stood some 425 feet higher than the level of the village, and the sides of which were cloaked with pines. Up these steep hills and in the quiet woods with occasional open glades, maneuvers were held. Happily there were good gravel roads practically unused now but kept in repair against a possible time when the Epinal defenses would be manned, and these served to help the Fords to get where needed. What with the friendly folk of the village and these majestic woods about which to maneuver, St. Laurent was a pleasant place and the days here were to remain in mind among the happy memories of France.

I was billeted in the home of a middle-aged motherly woman named Madame Flot, who, aided or hampered, by our American army cooks prepared the meals for our officers mess which was served in her dining room. She served with great amusement the canned corn which was a part of her commissary supplies. Corn, she said, was for horses. She had never heard of human beings eating it before. She placed delicious roast beef before us, flavored with wine. She chided us for eating so much. French officers ate little and drank much at their meals, she averred. As for us we ate much and drank nothing. It wasn't seemly. Living with her were two nieces. Jeanne worked in a local camouflage factory. Germaine helped Madame Flot around the house, milked the cows and worked in the hayfield between the house and the Moselle River, an endeavor in which I noticed our soldiers were most anxious to aid.[19]

First Lieutenant Fred D. Hays of Lamar, Mo., also was billeted in the house and he spent a good many evenings in the dining room chatting with the family in our attempted French which amused them much, Hays singing American songs for the girls and they responding with French ones.[20] There was no sentimental inter-

19. Madame Flot was also interested in one of Schrantz's gold teeth, for "in America people had their teeth fixed, which was good; but in France they always pulled them out, which was bad." *Carthage* (MO) *Evening Press,* August 9, 1918. Although Schrantz and his fellow officers enjoyed roast beef, the company's enlisted men also enjoyed roast beef, mashed potatoes, gravy, bread, and coffee. *Fort Scott* (KS) *Tribune and the Fort Scott Monitor*, August 9, 1918.

20. Fred Derth Hays was born on August 3, 1893, in Lamar, Missouri. A roving printer in his youth, Hays returned to Lamar in his teens, attended and graduated from high school. He then enrolled at Drury College in Springfield, Missouri, and worked nights as a linotype operator at the *Springfield* (MO) *Leader* newspaper, but left college to enlist in World War I. Prior to the war, Hays enlisted as a private in Company C, 2nd Missouri Infantry in 1909, and reached the rank of sergeant by 1916. He served in Company C, 2nd Missouri Infantry on the Mexican border 1916–17, and was promoted to first sergeant in July 1916. Commissioned a second lieutenant in Company C, 2nd Missouri, to rank from March 1917, Hays was assigned to Company B, 128th Machine Gun Battalion in February 1918, served overseas from March 28, 1918, to November 3, 1918, but was hospitalized in August 1918 with an ulcer of the duodenum. He returned to Drury following World War I and also attended Washington University in St. Louis. He continued to work as a printer and died in the Missouri State Sanatorium in Mount Vernon on October 13, 1948. He was buried in Lake Cemetery, Lamar, Missouri. *Lamar* (MO) *Democrat*, October 15, 1948; *The Service of the Missouri National Guard on the Mexican Border*, 136; Missouri Secretary of State, State Archives,

est involved so far as I was concerned. They had demanded my marital status on my arrival and finding that I was married no doubt promptly crossed me off the books as a non-prospect. Hays may have rated as a prospect, but that was all so far as I ever saw. I have no doubt that our orderlies and mess attendants paid court but these two young ladies were certainly amply able to hold their own. Sometimes half a dozen officers would be there in an evening. Once or twice some French sergeant or lieutenant came for a hasty visit—these were cousins, it was explained. Madame Flot wept when she found that our men were mostly volunteers. This puzzled us until it was explained. There had been some kind of volunteer company gone to the war from St. Laurent, they said. Now they were all dead—all the eligible young men of the village fallen in battle. War held a sure fate for volunteers, they felt. The madam wept at the thought that soon we and our men too would be killed. In France, they said, after the war each man left would need to have two or three wives. The laws would be changed. Girls must have husbands and there would not be nearly enough men for one apiece. Our lieutenants told the girls that since there might be no husbands for them that they might as well go to war too, and to the young ladies' manifest pleasure indicated their preference between the two to take as orderlies. Then the girls demanded of me which I wanted for an orderly. I said I would have no orderly but Madame Flot. They looked mildly surprised at it, then shrieked with merriment as they figured out the answer for themselves. "She is the best cook," they cried.[21]

Soldiers' Records, War of 1812-World War I, www.sos.mo.gov/archives/soldiers; Memo from 2nd Lt. Fred D. Hays to Commanding Officer, 128th Machine Gun Battalion, Camp Doniphan, November 9, 1917, Record Group 120, Records of the American Expeditionary Forces, World War I Organization Records, Machine Gun Battalions, 128th Machine Gun Battalion, Box 263, NARA; HST.

21. Several members of the company described their living conditions and their relations with French civilians. Sgt. Paul Havens noted that the French had "queer ways and customs," but one French Army custom worked to his benefit: "Noncommissioned officers are allowed the privilege of renting rooms, and Sergeant Ernest Ellis and myself have one. We have a dresser, bed, four chairs, and table and electric lights."

Sgt. Edwin W. Wiggins wrote home that he had "a room here with a French family—or rather Sergeant Norval R. Hopwood and I have—and we are fixed up real cozy but I do not know how long it will last. . .I like France better every day and am in the best of health and feeling fine."

Leaford Akin found the French to be "hospitable." After going to a house and having a friendly old French woman fill his canteen, he decided to try his "French vocabulary" on her. Soon the entire family came outside to teach him French and admire his family photos. He "had a hard time keeping the picture" of his little brother, he wrote. Akin added that the French watched the Americans play ball and tried it themselves, "but they can't get the hang of it." *Carthage* (MO) *Evening Press*, July 18, 1918, August 8, 1918. Earl Conley

In their leisure time, the soldiers strolled about, watched French engineers building practice pontoon bridges across the Moselle River or watched French troop trains, the box cars crowded with men in faded horizon blue and with muzzles of Hotchkiss machine guns mounted for anti-aircraft fire pointing skyward from the flat cars, rattle around the shoulder of the hill back of St. Laurent and disappear to the westward. The advance elements of the 35th U.S. Division were already moving toward the Vosges front as part of the French XXXIII Corps, and reliving French troops for service back in the more active areas.

Toward the end of June rumors began to circulate that we would soon move forward.

Second Lieutenant Ross Dunlap, my company train officer, came to me and said: "Captain, we can't move. These old Fords have had plenty of hard usage before they came to us. Some of the cars had cracked spark plugs and they broke in cleaning. I can get none from division headquarters. They tell me there are no Ford spark plugs in France."[22]

"We must move when ordered whether we can or not," I assured him. "Those cars limped in here under their own power and it is up to you to see that they are able to move out the same way."

He pondered this pronouncement. [23]

---

enthusiastically reported that the French "treat us more like brothers than foreigners," and "are as anxious to learn English as we are for the French." *Fort Scott* (KS) *Tribune and the Fort Scott Monitor*, August 9, 1918.

22. Schrantz recalled that his company's motor transportation required soldier ingenuity: "The 15 Ford gun trucks, model 1916, that Company A, 128th Machine Gun Battalion, received at St. Laurent at the southern edge of Epinal, department Vosges, France, the middle of June, 1918, had not been improved by their two years' service before they came into the hands of the Carthage soldiers, but the mechanical ability of Train Sergeant Thomas E. Clark and his mechanics and wagoners, plus the diplomatic genius which enabled Second Lieut. Ross R. Dunlap, the train officer, to get from the French army the spare parts which the American army did not have, put the vehicles in good running order by the time orders to move toward the front were received." Sadly, Schrantz's men would probably have had no better luck finding spare parts from American sources due to the chaotic method of supplying parts for A.E.F. vehicles. The main American depot for spare parts was located in Verneuil, France, but many boxes arrived there from America without markings, and often the boxes contained a variety of parts that needed to be sorted. Although some parts were then forwarded to depots at Langres and Sampigny, a lack of adequate storage bins meant that parts were stored wherever space could be found. In addition, the A.E.F. needed parts for dozens of different truck models, with an average of 3,500 parts per vehicle, 80 percent of which were unique to a particular make. Matthew G. McCoy, "Grinding Gears: The AEF and Motor Transportation in the First World War," *War in History* 11 (2004): 193–208.

23. Ross Richmond Dunlap was born on May 16, 1884, in Pico, California, and died on October 9, 1970. He attended training at the Presidio in San Francisco from May to August 1917, then enlisted in the 1st Missouri Infantry at Camp Doniphan in September 1917. He served as a sergeant in Company D, 128th Machine Gun Battalion until he attended

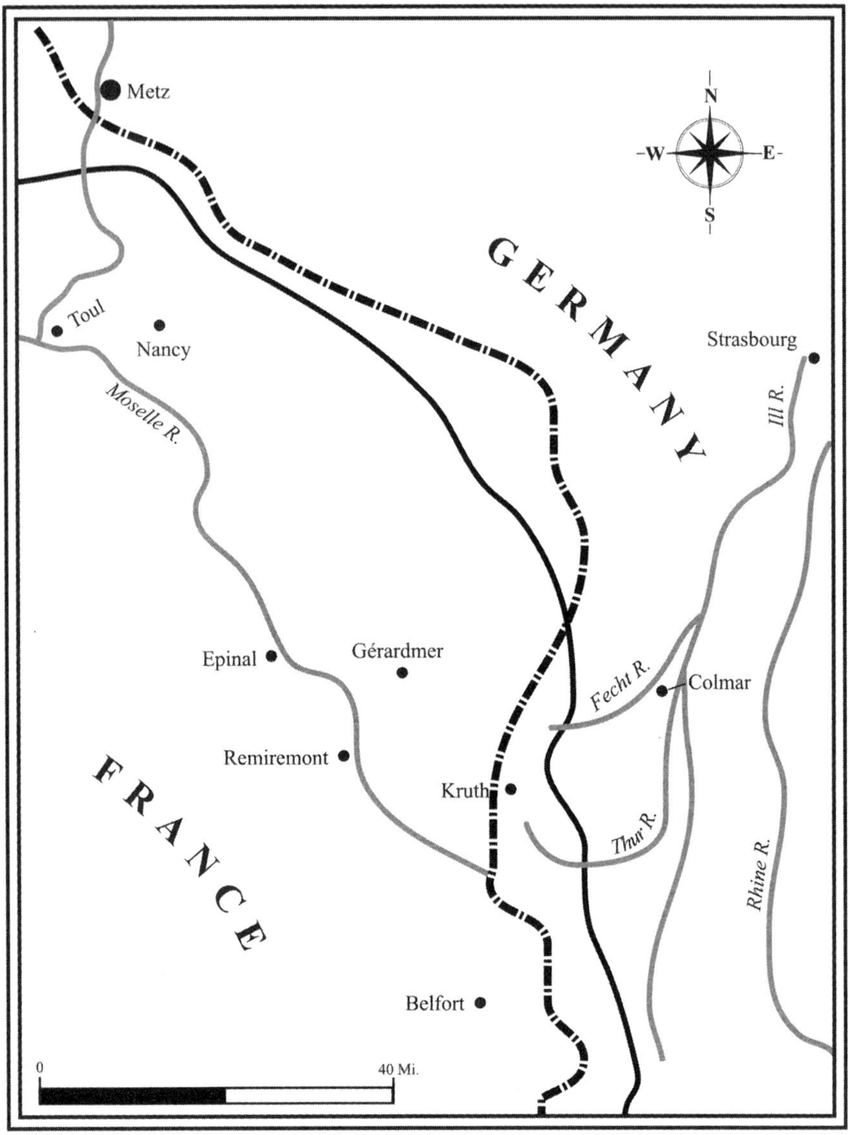

The Vosges Region

"If you will let me take a car and be gone for a few days without asking anything about it," he finally said, "I think I may do something."

Officers Training Camp, then was commissioned a second lieutenant in April 1918 and assigned to Company A, 128th Machine Gun Battalion. Dunlap was buried in San Diego, California. HST.

After checking with the battalion commander I gave the required permission. Two days later he was back with not only an ample supply of spark plugs but with many badly needed spare parts for repairs. He had visited some French motor pool of which he had heard. "These French will give you anything if you will give a receipt for it," he explained. It was so we met our needs until the receipts he had signed began to come in. Then Division headquarters had Major Halliburton on the carpet. "They wanted to court martial somebody," he told me afterwards, "but what they decided to do finally was to take Dunlap away from us and use him themselves. They need someone at division with his ability to get things that everyone says are not available."

Chapter 7

The Vosges Mountains

In keeping with General Pershing's training plan, after the 35th Division spent time receiving instruction behind the front line, the second phase of its training began when the division moved to the Vosges region for service with the French in a quiet sector (this period in the Vosges officially began on June 20, 1918). These areas could indeed be quiet much of the time, with only occasional shellfire, but the peace and quiet would be shattered without warning when one side or the other launched a trench raid or began a heavy round of harassing fire.

The Missourians climbed aboard cars and trucks in St. Laurant and headed for Ventron. The rear echelon of 35th Division headquarters was stationed in the village, and the 128th Machine Gun Battalion was to remain there as part of the division reserve to reinforce any threatened portion of the front.

With the border between French and German Alsace a mere two and a half miles away, French anti-aircraft fire could be heard several times a day, as the gunners tried to bring down roving German aircraft, and that noise, along with the steady "growl" of artillery fire reminded the Carthage men that the real war was close by.

Most of their time was taken up by continued training, including "lugging our rather heavy machine guns up rather steep mountains," as one Carthage man related, which was "excellent practice but . . . not very satisfying."

Despite the intensive training, the 35th Division men did not fail to appreciate the less warlike aspects of the Alsace region. A sergeant major in the 137th Infantry recalled the Vosges Mountains as "one of the most beautiful places I ever saw with all its beautiful evergreen trees and the steep cliffs and beautiful broad green valleys and every few yards a spring can be seen with the most delicious waters, so cool and refreshing."[1]

No matter how picturesque they found the area, the men of Company A still longed to move to the front. Their restless spirits were appeased when orders came for the company to move to Wesserling, the headquarters of the forward echelon of the 35th Division. Arriving there, they were told that the French believed a German attack was imminent, so they were ordered to the village of Willer.

At first, the Carthage men had every reason to believe that they would soon face their trial by fire. Nearby artillery fire provided "a novel and interesting scene," Schrantz wrote, with the both French and German guns in action.

The Missourians were soon disappointed, however, as their training program resumed and the threat of a German attack evaporated. Soon Schrantz and his soldiers were ordered to return to Ventron. "It was a hungry company which clambered from the grimy vehicles, washed the dust of travel from its 172 dirty faces and started telling tall tales of enemy shells," Schrantz recalled. After a hearty meal of roast beef, new potatoes, peas, macaroni and cheese and pears, the Carthage men were "good as new—or almost so." Company cook Albert Weaver reported that his comrades were "crummy" and "had to go and boil up"; in other words, Schrantz noted, "Company A had made the acquaintance of the notorious war cootie" (body lice) in the billets at Willer.

Such typical soldier inconveniences were forgotten by the end of July 1918, however, when orders finally arrived for Schrantz to take his company into the trenches.

It was the forenoon of June 30 when First Sergeant George A. Snyder gave the soldiers the usual final injunctions on the condition in which they must leave their billets; and the final hurry and scurry of breaking camp and telling the friendly townsfolk goodbye followed. Only half motorized, the battalion

1. *Larned* (KS) *Chronoscope*, December 26, 1918.

had been loaned a number of cargo trucks for the move and those men who could not get on the machine gun cars loaded into these. The Company A cars and trucks were soon lined up along the right side of the main street of the long village; Company B, which had been farther away arrived in due time, and about 1 p.m., Major Westley Halliburton, the battalion commander, sounded his whistle and gave the signal for the long column to start.

Passing out through the perimeter of the Epinal forts the road led up the Moselle river, southward through rapidly mounting pine-covered hills to Remiremont, some 15 miles distant, thence to the east and southeast up the valley of the Moselotte as the hills became mountains, past Saulxures and to the village of Ventron in the heart of the Vosges, and two and a half miles from the old Franco-German frontier—the border between French Alsace and German Alsace. The journey of the day had been about 36 miles, including some steep hill climbs, and the recently acquired motor equipment had functioned better than might be expected in view of its vintage and general disability. The infantry-type rolling kitchens, not meant for towing behind trucks, had not fared very well, Company B's being almost disabled and Company A's not much better, but on the whole this first experience in convoy work had been very satisfactory.

Ventron, the new station for the battalion, was a white village in a narrow green valley above which towered still greener mountains, partly wooded but with occasional hayfields and some tiny cottages clinging far up the slopes. The rear echelon of 35th Division headquarters was in the village, the 69th Brigade was going into the trenches on the front far on the other side of the border, the 70th Brigade was in reserve even farther to the rear than Ventron, and the 128th Machine Gun Battalion was to remain at this point as part of the division reserve to reinforce any portion of the front where aid might be required. The 22nd French Division, which the 35th was to relieve by degrees, was still in command of the sector and the region.

To the Carthaginians this location seemed a long way from the war but the nearness of the old international line gave an added interest to life. Then, even before the new comers had settled into their billets, there came the evenly spaced roars of anti-aircraft artillery near at hand and the distant crash of shrapnel bursting high in air; and soon the sky was dotted with smoke puffs as the French cannon kept the German airman high in air, even though they could not bring him down.

There was also other audible evidence that the front was not far away.

"You have read perhaps of the 'growl' of cannon," wrote a Carthage officer the night of arrival at Ventron. "That is just what it sounds like this evening—a steady growl coming through the pass to the east of us."

Anti-aircraft fire by French artillery at German observing planes not only occurred daily but often a number of times a day. First could be heard cannon fire to the east and distant smoke splotches in the sky; nearer guns took up the shooting as the plane came closer, and after it had passed out of range of the Ventron artillery, guns far to the west could be heard taking up the fire. At times the shells seemed to get uncomfortably close, and the planes quickly changed altitude, but as a rule the enemy fliers seemed undisturbed, journeying calmly across the sky with puffs of white smoke spotting the sky behind them and occasionally in front.

The French planes seldom interfered with these visitors but there seem to have been some exceptions in the rule, Private Leaford Akin in a letter written the day after arrival mentioning having witnessed air battles, and adding, "I saw a good one this morning."[2]

One brigade of the 35th Division was now holding trenches over in the mountains of German Alsace. The forward echelon of division headquarters was at Wesserling in the Thur valley across the mountain ridge east of us. The rear echelon of division headquarters was at Ventron. Cornimont, just east of Saulxures and behind us around a shoulder of mountain, was division railhead—the furtherest east point reached by that particular rail line.

Training was promptly resumed at Ventron, and since the valley of the little mountain stream which ran through the village was narrow, the battalion Fords were soon chugging up the angling roads up the mountain sides, bearing the machine gunners to maneuvers in the hills. A target range was found near a little shrine called "The Chapel of Brother Joseph," about a mile and a half

2. Company A's Earl Conley believed that "an air battle is the greatest sport to watch I ever saw. It is worth coming all the way over to see." *Fort Scott* (KS) *Tribune and the Fort Scott Monitor*, August 9, 1918.

Wesserling, 35th Division headquarters, July 15, 1918 (*National Archives*)

south and some 900 feet above the village, and here the first formal shooting with the heavy Smith and Wesson revolvers with which the men of the battalion were still armed was held. Field firing with machine guns at service ranges were also held nearby, and as the soldiers clambered up or slid down the mountains to maneuvers or firing practice, they gorged on the delicious little blue mountain berries which grew everywhere.

Hand grenades too were issued in this village and the first grenade practice was held in trenches on a height at the edge of the village. These were service grenades—dangerous fragmentation bombs. The user pulled a cotter key which held down a lever, then with the lever held down by the fingers, hurled the grenade. When the explosive missile was released by the hand a spiral spring kicked off the grenade lever and the grenade exploded five seconds later. If one dropped a grenade in the trench after pulling the key the unwritten A.E.F. code of ethics specified that he should promptly fall on it, paying for his fumble with his life but protecting his fellows. Grenade tossing thus seemed to be serious business, but the machine gunners entered into it with zest;

the windows of Ventron shook with the shock of the explosions and the crest of "hand grenade hill" was daily crowned with wreaths of white smoke.

July 4 was a holiday. In a letter home written this date Corporal Robert B. Huff said:

> "On the Fourth I could not see the mountain tops for the clouds. All morning I lay in my bed and listened to the clock in the tower of an ancient Catholic church musically strike off the quarter, half and even hours of the day. . .Standing in front of the church one can look up in three directions and see mountains with small patches of ground terraced off and hay growing on them . . . Everyone here, large, small, old or young, wears wooden shoes."[3]

In the afternoon of this day there was a battalion field meet and a program in honor of the Americans, the children singing the French version of the "Star-Spangled Banner."

Back in Carthage this same day, the occasion was celebrated with a monster parade attesting the home town patriotic support of the war. In France in the vicinity of Chateau Thierry and the region northwest thereof several American divisions were still engaged and here on July 5 the first Carthage man killed in action in the war met his end. He was Corporal Earl Casner, a member of the Marine Brigade of the 2nd Division, 22-year-old son of Mr. and Mrs. A.C. Casner.

There was a little spy scare at Ventron. Mysterious lights flashed at night on La Ronde Bruche, a tall hill southeast of the village and looking directly toward the Col d'Odernon, the mountain pass to the east; mysterious thin smoke columns rose from the hills sometimes at evening; curious occasional flashing lights which could be signals were seen from village windows. The first time I was officer of the day I determined to do something about this. I posted men during the day in the pine woods to come down on any smoke columns and hold the persons making them. Across on the hills south of the village as dusk approached I saw smoke columns on the north hill then saw the men I had posted come down out of the woods. I was soon

3. Robert Bernell Huff was born in Saline, Missouri, possibly on May 14, 1895. He died on June 14, 1978, in California. He served overseas with the 128th from April 25, 1918 to April 24, 1919. Missouri Secretary of State, State Archives, Soldiers' Records, War of 1812–World War I, www.sos.mo.gov/archives/soldiers.

with them and found them talking to some small boys and smiling. The smoke "signals" were from fires which were kindled at evening when mosquitoes began to annoy the cattle and were supposed to afford some protection.[4] After it became dark I investigated intermittent lights which apparently started the village phase of the stories. They came from a back window of a wine shop. The room in which the window was unlighted, but an open door lead into a lighted room and men passing back and forth across this doorway gave something of a dot, dash effect seen from a certain angle. Late at night there was an intermittent light far up on the east side of La Ronde Bruche, a hill I knew well as a result of my hill-climbing propensities. I hurried to the guard house to get the sergeant of the guard to accompany me on an investigation patrol. On the way I met First Lieutenant John F. Williams, our battalion adjutant, who was to be a major general and chief of the National Guard Bureau in World War II and for some years before.[5] He suggested that he accompany me instead of the sergeant. Clambering up a circuitous path we finally reached a point above the lights and could hear voices below. Sliding down the steep hill through the pine trees, our pistols in one hand and our flashlights in the other, we cascaded down on two startled French people—an inebriated mountain man and his wife, the latter with a flashlight in her hand and obviously trying to get her drunken mate back to their hut near the summit. That ended the spy scare at Ventron.

This futile spy chase relieved the monotony some, and the daily anti-aircraft bombardments of visiting enemy observation planes gave a tinge of reality to the war, but the soldiers envied their comrades up on the front line. "Most of our time is spent in lugging

4. Earl Conley of Company A told his relatives in Kansas that he thought there were large mosquitoes in the United States, but the "man eaters" in France were more impressive. "They light on you by the dozens," he related, "and all bite at the same time." He vowed to wear his gas mask and winter cap the next time he encountered them. *Fort Scott* (KS) *Tribune and the Fort Scott Monitor*, August 9, 1918.

5. John Francis Williams was born in Pennsylvania on January 7, 1887. He served in the Hospital Corps, 2nd Missouri Infantry 1903–5, then became a first lieutenant and battalion adjutant in the 2nd Missouri Infantry in April 1917. He joined the 128th Machine Gun Battalion as battalion adjutant and supply officer in October 1917. After service in World War I, he became a coast artillery and field artillery officer in the Missouri National Guard, and served on active duty from 1936 to 1940. Williams was promoted to major general and served as chief of the National Guard Bureau from 1940 to 1946, when he retired. He died on May 29, 1953, and was buried in Arlington National Cemetery. *The New York Times*, May 31, 1953; U.S. Adjutant General's Office, *Official Army Register January 1, 1941* (Washington, D.C.: Government Printing Office, 1941), 917; HST.

our rather heavy machine guns up rather steep mountains," wrote one Carthage man under date of July 10. "This is excellent practice but it is not very satisfying."

About 4 o'clock on the afternoon of July 11 while I was maneuvering my company in a wooded valley northeast of the village, a motor-cyclist brought a note from my battalion commander to bring my entire unit in as soon as possible.

The message was dated at 2:45 but the company had not been easy to find in the woods and it was now close to four o'clock. Immediately the shrilling of whistles brought the soldiers and their guns pouring down from their various positions to the vicinity of some ruined huts where the gun trucks had been left and where company headquarters had been established. It was a down hill run all the way back to the village and soon thereafter the Ford train rolled into Ventron, each gun truck clustered with soldiers.

On my arrival he informed me that he had received orders to send one company immediately over into the Thur valley across the old frontier where it was to report to the division chief of staff at Wesserling. He was lending me trucks from the battalion to carry personnel. He stressed the need for haste.

"Commanding Officer, Company A, 128th Machine Gun Battalion:

> Under verbal orders from Chief of Staff, you will move your company, together with all equipment and ammunition, to Wesserling at once. On arrival you will report to the Chief of Staff before unloading.
>
> One ammunition truck and five trucks for the transportation of your men will be placed at your disposal from battalion headquarters, the five trucks to be returned as soon as you can spare them. One sergeant and two privates of the Sanitary Corps had been ordered to accompany you.
>
> (Signed) HALLIBURTON, Major, 128th Machine Gun Bn."

With the necessary instructions I dismissed the company to return to its many billets, scattered over the entire village, and by 5:20 the column of 16 Fords and attached trucks, complete with all of our equipment and ammunition was ready to move.

In accordance with my usual custom, when security measures did not prevent, I gave the full company our destination and such information as I had, concluding by way of general information, with reading an extract from the division daily intelligence report which had just been handed me:

> "Enemy raid at Hilsenfirst at 3 a.m., after artillery preparation, repulsed successfully. Enemy not able to reach our wire. Our casualties are six dead and 20 injured."

Cheering at this little victory, the men streamed back to their trucks and a moment later I led them out of the village. I felt pleased at the time factor. An hour and 20 minutes from time of receiving the word on the training field to time of departure was not bad. In view of the apparent urgent need for us somewhere I would have liked to have done it in less but this could be considered prompt. Later I found that according to the inspectors at the rear echelon of division headquarters who nosed into my empty billets as soon as I departed, it was far too prompt. A scathing letter in due time informed me that they were not at all immaculate and that I should have inspected each of them personally before leaving—a task which probably would have taken an additional hour.

It was a steep climb to the top of the Col du Mont d'Oderon and we paused at the old frontier to fill the radiators of the old model Ts, most of the water having boiled away, then zigzagged down into the Thur valley, thence southward to Wesserling, 15 miles from our starting point.

There was a thrill to the thought that this was Alsace—German soil since 1870—and that the water in the little mountain stream glimpsed near the road ran, not into the Moselle but into the Rhine. The descent from this pass was a sharp one, softened by the steady zig-zags of the road, but in time the zig-zags ceased and the convoy coasted down an angling road on a long slope, crossed a beautiful little valley on each side of which the mountains towered, passed through the outskirts of the town of Kruth and then straight south in the valley along the Thur River, through the villages of Oderen and Felleringen, and so into Wesserling where the convoy with its dust-begrimed soldiers waited while the captain hunted up division headquarters and reported to Col. W.R. McCleave.

Colonel McCleave, division chief of staff, explained the situation to me. Unusual movement of trains and activity of enemy cable systems opposite the front of the 22nd French Division on our right had caused the French to fear that a German attack in the vicinity of Hartmannsweilerkopf was imminent. Lacking reserves the French had asked that an American battalion with machine gun company attached be placed at their disposal to deliver a counter-attack in case, as they expected, the initial enemy attack would make progress. The Second Battalion, 138th Infantry, had been sent down to the villages of Moosch and Willer behind the French positions and I would report to Major Norman B. Comfort, the battalion commander at Moosch.[6] Major Comfort in turn directed me still farther down the valley to Willer. The French were [not] so sure as they had been about the attack, but we should be ready to move out any time we were called upon. Willer[,] nestled among hills, the front line in the direction from which the attack was expected, being three or four miles to the eastward, over the mountain masses which bulked dim in the dusk. A mile and a half below was the partially ruined village of Thann just beyond which, where the Thur River ran out into the Alsatian plains, was the front and that point. As we settled ourselves in the village, a heavy piece of artillery on the hill west of us, fired and sent a projectile over our heads and eastward bound.

It was 8:30, but still daylight, when the company arrived in Willer and parked its cars under shelter of some trees near some frame single story barracks the company was to occupy, and behind which were dugouts, in which the occupants of the buildings could seek shelter from shell fire if necessary.

The officers were quartered in billets some distance away, two of them at the south end of the long Teutonic-appearing village, and command of the camp area was thus left in the very capable hands of First Sergeant George A. Snyder. Mess Sergeant Clint A. Miles and his kitchen force were quickly preparing a hurried evening meal and before long the organization had settled down

6. The son of a St. Louis political and military leader, Norman Comfort was born on March 17, 1888, and educated at Culver Military Academy in Indiana. He enlisted in the 1st Missouri Infantry as a private in 1907, and was promoted to second lieutenant two years later and to captain of the regiment's machine gun company in 1915. He served in that capacity when the regiment was stationed on the Mexican border from June to September 1916. Promoted to major, Comfort was attached to 35th Division headquarters in France and served as a liaison officer between General Peter Traub, the division commander, and the brigade and regimental commanders. After the 138th Infantry's commander was killed on September 29, 1918, Comfort assumed command of the regiment, and was cited in divisional orders for gallantry in action. He served overseas from March 28, 1918, to May 2, 1919. Following the war, Comfort became a member of a realty firm in St. Louis and president of the county real estate board. Comfort died on January 27, 1934, when he accidentally shot himself with a pistol. He was buried at Jefferson Barracks National Cemetery in St. Louis. *St. Louis Post-Dispatch*, January 29, 1934; *The Service of the Missouri National Guard on the Mexican Border*, 14; Missouri Secretary of State, State Archives, Soldiers' Records, War of 1812–World War I, www.sos.mo.gov/archives/soldiers.

Summit of Hartmannsweilerkopf (*Jasper County Records Center*)

Willer (*Jasper County Records Center*)

quite comfortably to wait for whatever might betide. Decidedly Company A was somewhat nearer to the war.

Willer, though within the French artillery lines, was fully inhabited and the German-speaking populace went about their evening affairs in a normal way.

True there were no guns in the village but there seemed to be in the hills on every side of it, and the map showed that the German front line was but little hurt by the war and the[n] four miles east of the Carthage men's quarters in the town. Yet Willer was but little hurt by the war and the inhabitants went about their daily business, each carrying a little French gas mask for use in case of need.

In front of a village café by the river, French soldiers sat at tables and drank undisturbed as guns on the surrounding hills roared into action as night when on—the muzzle flashes stabbing out sharply in the darkness. The German artillery was returning the fire. Shells were exploding not only in the hills to the east but sang over us and burst near the artillery positions on the hills behind. Willer continued to sip its wine. A drunken French soldier poled a boat about in the Thur River adjoining the café and sang alcoholic melodies as the guns roared, in the intervals exchanging witticisms with his comrades on the bank. War in Alsace was probably different in some respects from war anywhere else in the world. Then as night succeeded dusk, the guns gradually lapsed into silence again and peace in the valley seemed restored. We learned that the Germans did not fire at the villages. Nor did the French fire at the villages behind the German lines. We gathered that both France and Germany considered Alsace as their own and wanted to do as little damage as possible—a very nice way to conduct a war, I thought.[7]

But the inhabitants now were plainly apprehensive and with some apparent reason. At the lower end of the village French engineer troops were engaged in feverish activity. Through the green and flourishing potato patches moved the engineers with scythes, cutting broad barren belts; behind them moved others driving down tall stakes, and behind these came still more, unwinding spools of barbed wire and on the posts, across the gardens and orchards, building a broad belt of entanglement to hold the enemy under fire should he approach the lower end of the village. This was taken by the citizenry as ample indication of an impending German attack.

While any major German attack might indeed well include an advance up the Thur valley, which opened into the great Alsatian

7. Schrantz wrote that if a German "wishes to waste his ammunition that way it is perfectly all right with me."

plain only a few miles below, the problem which seemed immediately to concern Company A was squarely to the east over the hills. The masses of the Vosges, piled one on another, rose to the eastward to a height known as Molkenrain which dominated both the Thur valley and the country toward the enemy. Near the foot of a forward shoulder of Molkenrain rose a high but subordinate hill, Hartmannsweilerkopf, three years before the scene of bitter fighting which had left its battered crest between the lines with the Germans on the eastern and the French on the western slopes. Behind the hill stretched the great verdant German-held plain of Alsace.

It was from Hartmannsweilerkopf that the French were expecting an attack. They believed such offensive could carry the French positions on Hartmannsweilerkopf but felt that on the forward shoulder of Molkenrain a strong point known as Camp Pierre could hold out. The enemy attack might work up the wooded ravines on each side of it however, and it was to counter-attack and drive the enemy out of these—or stop them if they had gone beyond—that the Second Battalion, 138th U.S. Infantry and Company A, 128th Machine Gun Battalion, were needed.

In case the attack was launched, the machine gun company was to proceed at once to the neighborhood of the top of Molkenrain to be available for stopping the attack, and the rifle battalion was to follow as soon as possible.

A brief Company A reconnaissance of the road to the front showed that while the 16 Ford gun-trucks of the company carrying two or three men each could climb up the narrow, steep, winding road, that the heavy trucks could not be used, partly because of the steepness of the road and party because the route would be too heavily shelled to permit the use of big trucks packed with men. Most of the company would need to march, but the gun trucks could not be run up into an uncertain situation before the company arrived, and it would not do, either, to have the company arrive in the presence of the enemy without machine guns, so the following plan of action was adopted:

The company headquarters car with the captain, the company range finder, and four runners was to proceed directly to the point of probable need as soon as the call came. The senior lieutenant was to follow with the company, the headquarters group marching in front. Next was to be the first platoon, marching, with its guns on the Ford trucks following in rear; behind it, after an interval, was to come the second platoon in similar order, then the third. This was a painful and unsatisfactory method but the best under the circumstances. Each gun truck, in addition to the gun, carried ten boxes, or 2,880 rounds of ammunition, and each extra platoon car was to carry 20 boxes—5,760 rounds. This would make 51,840 rounds for the company, 17,280 per platoon, 4,320 per gun. Each squad was to carry four offensive and nine defensive hand grenades. One day's rations were to be carried in haversacks. Packs would be left at the camp at Willer, as would also the heavy trucks and surplus equipment.

The day passed without alarm but in the evening the artillery became active. For the Carthage soldiers, for the first time near the front, it was a novel and interesting scene. The flashes of the French cannon were plainly discernible in the dusk both west of the town and east of it as they thundered at the enemy. The German artillery too was in action and while the front line was probably getting the weight of the main bombardment, the French artillery was not neglected.

"The swish of the shells sounded much as they did at artillery practice at Camp Doniphan," wrote one Carthage soldier, "but all of them were directed at battery positions in the hills and none struck the town."

In the morning I went to Moosch to see Major Comfort and to my annoyance found he and his four rifle captains had gone to the front on a reconnaissance without including me in the party. I spent the day in training and in wandering down the valley toward Thann, studying the defense scheme, as outlined by rusty belts of barbed wire, for resisting an enemy attack up the valley.

I was billeted in a tall house, presided over by a English-speaking hostess and having several German-speaking maids. My hostess told me that she had always spoken French and German and was learning English from a Y.M.C.A. man billeted with her.

"Here there is not much danger," she told me in her carefully articulated English when I commented on her nearness to the front. "Of course sometimes comes the obus, and in Thann are 40 civils dead of the gas, but we can go to the celler and we have the masks." The whole valley had a wholesome respect for gas, as well they might. Men and women moving about their daily tasks carried French gas masks of an early type slung over their shoulders and little children going to school were similarly equipped.

"But soon we must go," she amended somewhat sadly later that same day—and indeed she had some reason for being more perturbed about the war. French army engineers had invaded her large potato field south of the house. The vines were growing tall—taller than they did in Missouri I reflected—and the soldiers with scythes were cutting broad diagonal swaths across the field. Then followed others with stakes, and soon a broad belt of new barbed wire had sprung up just below her home.

But she took the situation calmly enough and by way of being courteous enumerated for me the previous occupants of my quarters, apparently having a complete mental roster. There was General this and Colonel that, "dead in the mountains," and Count de somebody and a collection of majors and captains, "dead in the mountains," and there was some officer whose forefather had fought in America with Lafayette, "dead in the mountains." There evidently was no doubt in her mind as to what was going to happen to me soon. Of her sympathies in the war I never asked but while I was with her she was anxious to do all she could to make me comfortable. If the "dead in the mountain" catalog was intended to make me otherwise, it failed in its effect. I had already heard about people being killed during a war. I remember her as a very pleasant, very courteous and very stately woman.

When Major Comfort returned from the trenches that evening I was at Moosch waiting for him. "I forgot I have five captains now instead of four," he told me. "But you can go up in the morning. I know of a French soldier here who speaks English and you can take him along for an interpreter."

So early the next day I chugged up the hill in my headquarters Ford to the French brigade headquarters where I was cordially received and sent down to regimental headquarters where my reception was equally pleasant and shunted on down the hill to the headquarters of the battalion I sought.

Captain Cordon, the battalion commander, eyed me with grave suspicion when he heard my Teutonic name. This deepened when I explained that I commanded the machine gun company with Major Comfort's battalion. "Ah," he commented sharply,

Captain Ward Schrantz in France (*Harry S. Truman Presidential Library and Museum*)

"but Captain Holmes commands Major Comfort's machine gun company."[8] Capt. Cordon had served with the 138th Infantry in the mountains farther north and at that time the regimental machine gun company, of which Holmes was the captain, was attached to the

8. Born in St. Louis, Missouri, on August 10, 1894, John Meston Holmes graduated from Princeton University and the law school at Washington University in St. Louis. He served on the Mexican border with the Machine Gun Company of the 1st Missouri Infantry (June-September 1916) before serving with the 138th Infantry in France. He served overseas from May 2, 1918 to April 29, 1919. Following the war, he practiced law in St. Louis and became the reporter of the Missouri Supreme Court in 1941. He died in Jefferson City, Missouri, on January 4, 1958. *The Service of the Missouri National Guard on the Mexican Border*, 14; *Jefferson City* (MO) *Post-Tribune*, January 6, 1958; Missouri Secretary of State, State Archives, Soldiers' Records, War of 1812–World War I, www.sos.mo.gov/archives/soldiers.

battalion. I explained that an American battalion, unlike the French, did not have an integral machine gun company, these being attached as needed. Finally he decided I was not a German spy after all, and explained to me the situation on the map, then from an observation point nearby pointed it out on the ground.[9]

We stood high on the eastern slope of the central mountain mass between the Thur valley and the Alsatian plane. Below us a shoulder of the mountain ran downward, and beyond the foot of the shoulder rose Hartmannsweilerkopf down toward the summit of which we looked downward. The scene of heavy fighting in 1915 the timber which once had covered it had been chewed away by shell fire until only shattered stumps and churned earth criss-crossed by old trenches remained. To the left and to the right on the approximate line of Hartmannsweilerkopf a zone of stumps and shattered trees indicated the location of the long stabilized front.

In the German positions ahead of us occasional French shells were falling, apparently some battery registering. And off to our left now and then came the crash of an explosion and a little puff of blue-black smoke as some German heavy gun searched out a target or checked its battery's range. Everything else was silent except for an occasional rifle shot.

My first impressions were that it was a pretty peaceful war, and the German trenches looked to be entirely deserted, but all the same I carefully imitated the actions of my guide. When he walked upright, I walked upright; and when he crouched and ran, I too crouched and ran. 'Here it is now nice,' he panted after one of these sprints, 'but when the obus comes it is not near so nice.' I saw four French shells strike in the German trenches, and the enemy was exploding a few himself on the hills to the left, but that was all. Of rifle or machine gun fire there was not any.

The French held the near slope of Hartmannsweilerkopf, Captain Cordon told me, and the Germans the far slope, but the summit itself was between the lines. If the expected German attack

9. Schrantz wrote that the French "are the best and the most courteous of soldiers and have absolute confidence that an army 'Franco-Americane' is bound to be invincible—and so it is." Schrantz believed there were no cases of friction between the French and Americans, and "French and Americans lived in the same dugouts, ate at the same mess, and fought literally side by side in the trenches for several weeks. A closer feeling of brotherhood between allies would not be possible." *Carthage* (MO) *Evening Press*, September 17, 1918.

came, it was believed the French trenches on the near slope would be overrun, the little valley crossed and progress be made up the shoulder as far as Camp Pierre, a concealed strong point below us. Here, it was felt, the enemy could be held, except that he presumably would work up the wooded ravines on each side. The mission of the American battalion would be to counter-attack down these ravines, drive him out and back over the top of Hartmannsweilerkopf again.

Captain Cordon was somewhat depressed but I had heard the reason before I came up. In the French army, as in our own at that time, a French battalion was normally commanded by a major. Cordon, as the senior captain, had been in command for some time but he was 29 years of age whereas the French regulations, I was told, required that a man must be 30 before he could be a major. Therefore he was to be relieved by another captain old enough to be promoted.

I was amused to reflect that this occasion of my first visit to the front was on the 13th of the month. I was born on a 13th, my captain's commission dated from a 13th and I had landed in France on a 13th.

The next day being Bastille Day the French used it as a suitable occasion for a ceremony at Moosch in which certain members of the 138th who had distinguished themselves during a raid on the enemy trenches some time before were decorated with the Croix de Guerre.[10] On the 15th I accompanied Major Comfort and his rifle company captains to the front again. This time we went down the shoulder, and winding through innumerable communication trenches, visited not only Camp Pierre but even the French outpost positions. I noted on this occasion the value of a helmet. I was forever bumping my head on tree trunks which had fallen across the communication trench, or scratching my helmet on barbed wire—the result, of course, of trying to look about instead of watching where I was going.

Neither the Chasseur Alpine captain who had succeeded Cordon as battalion commander, nor his captains that we met, believed that

10. Company H, 138th Infantry carried out a raid on Hilsenfirst on July 6, 1918. Four Americans were killed and eighteen wounded in the raid, while seven Germans were taken prisoner and twenty killed. Nineteen Americans were cited for their participation in the raid. Charles B. Hoyt, *Heroes of the Argonne: An Authentic History of the Thirty-Fifth Division* (Kansas City: Franklin Hudson Publishing Company, 1919), 47–51. Different casualty figures may be found in the *St. Louis Post-Dispatch*, August 5, 1918.

the Germans were going to attack them now—"the instinct of the infantry" I suppose, or perhaps absence of immediate pre-attack signs with which their experience had familiarized them.

"But if they attack, we will not run away," grinned a French captain who had his command post between the foot of Hartmannsweilerkopf on the French-held mountain. "The hill behind us is too steep."

It was steep indeed and on our climb back I was amused at Capt. E.F. Lloyd of one of the rifle companies and a friend of mine from Camp Doniphan days. He was [a] short plump man and at each of our occasional stops to rest muttered angrily as he panted for breath: "Damn the Boche; damn the Boche."[11]

Major Comfort's battalion was from St. Louis where there is a considerable population of German descent and some of his officers spoke German, though none of them spoke French. And though most of the French officers could not speak English, a number of them knew German. So here on this Vosges mountain were allies finding a common tongue in the language of the enemy. Back at the battalion observation post we stared again at the front and the great Alsatian plain beyond the hills. Reading our thoughts, the French captain laughed. "It looks easy, gentlemen," he said, "but it is hard. We have tried it." He pointed out the Black Forest in the extreme blue background and called our attention to a glitter below it which he said was a bend in the Rhine.

Back at Willer the enlisted men waited somewhat impatiently, asking each other discontentedly if this was a war for officers only.

Enemy planes came over perhaps a little more frequently than usual, drawing from the ground the usual anti-aircraft fire which speckled the sky with bursting shrapnel and exploding shell; and Allied planes, headed east, encountered a similar enemy reception within eyesight of the Carthaginians as the fliers approached the front line—but this was little different from normal in the Thur valley.

11. Eugene F. Lloyd was born in Sedalia, Missouri, on October 5, 1881. He enlisted in Company G, 1st Missouri Infantry as a private in 1900. By 1916 he was the captain of Company F, and commanded that company on the Mexican border from June to September 1916. A resident of St. Louis in 1917, Lloyd led Company F, 138th Infantry overseas from May 6, 1918, to April 29, 1919. He died on November 18, 1932, in St. Louis, Missouri. *The Service of the Missouri National Guard on the Mexican Border*, 54; *St. Louis Post-Dispatch*, November 18, 1932; Missouri Secretary of State, State Archives, Soldiers' Records, War of 1812–World War I, www.sos.mo.gov/archives/soldiers.

Back in that evening of July 15 I went down, as was my habit, to use my high school German to buy the Paris newspapers from which I might spell out the course of the war. But that night there were no papers. They had not arrived. There was, of course, the little German-language newspaper published in the valley and carrying only local civilian news, but there were no papers from Paris—either English or French. And the German proprietress who had sold papers in the valley for years had an explanation based on experience. There must be a big offensive somewhere, she said. Always the papers came, she averred, unless there was a big offensive, then they didn't. "Es ist immer so," she concluded.

And she was quite right. That morning the Germans had attacked on the Marne. The signs of an impending offensive in the Vosges which the French had noted and which had brought us to Willer, quite possibly was German deception in cooperation with the great attack in the west.[12]

Undisturbed by the distant major conflict, and with a growing tranquility in the region of Hartmannsweilerkopf and the outlet of the valley of the Thur, the members of the Carthage company of the 128th Machine Gun Battalion, 35th Division, resumed training at Willer within range of the enemy artillery, halting only when enemy observing planes were sighted.

There was no repetition of the bombardment of the evening of July 12, although occasionally enemy shells fell on a hill at the eastern edge of the town, apparently searching for a battery of French 155-millimeter howitzers emplaced in the valley beside it. And on one occasion an enemy dud shell, believed from the angle at which it descended to have been a projectile fired at an Allied airplane, plunged into the edge of the Company A drill field and buried itself deep in the ground. I even had occasion to award a few extra kitchen police to one man who courted disaster by attempting to dig it up to see what it looked like.

On the evening of the 16th the Americans at Moosch and Willer were relieved from duty with the 22nd French Division and on the 17th my company returned to Ventron.

12. On July 15, 1918, the Germans launched an attack on both sides of the city of Reims, named Marneschutz-Reims, their fifth and final offensive of 1918. Both the 3rd and 42nd Divisions opposed the operation. Southwest of Reims, the German Seventh Army crossed the Marne River but was halted by the 3rd Division; the 42nd helped stop the advance of the German First and Third Armies east of Reims. The offensive ended on July 17. Carthage men in the 3rd and 42nd Divisions participated in this battle.

It was a hungry company which clambered from the grimy vehicles, washed the dust of travel from its 172 dirty faces and started telling tall tales of enemy shells to envying members of Company B who had a soldierly discontent at having missed out on the adventure. Mess Sergeant Clint A. Miles and his kitchen force hastened preparations for the noon-day meal, however, and the next day Cook Albert Weaver wrote home:

> "Yesterday noon we had roast beef, new potatoes and peas, macaroni and cheese and pears—so you see we do not want for anything to eat."

And then he added this bit of information:

> "We had quite a joke on a bunch when we came back from the lines. They were 'crummy' so they had to go and boil up. I don't know whether you understand my way of telling it or not."

It was even so. Company A had made the acquaintance of the notorious war cootie, the billets at Willer having been infested with the vermin. Such an experience having been anticipated sooner or later, but was no more pleasant for that fact, but here at Ventron there was an opportunity for cleaning up and boiling up, as Cook Weaver had said, and the situation was soon well in hand again.

Back at Ventron where there was plenty of ground on which to maneuver and few enemy planes to interfere, vigorous training was resumed under dripping skies.[13]

"It has rained every day for five days," wrote Private Vern H. Breckinridge July 24, "but the rain does not bother us with our work. We drill just the same."[14]

13. Major Halliburton continued to impose strict discipline in the battalion. In a memo, he noted the "growing tendency" of the men to leave clothing, mess outfits and equipment "lying around." Property loss through carelessness, he warned, would be charged to the soldier, and conditions indicated a "gross carelessness." Halliburton himself counted two raincoats, four or five coats, and a large number of mess outfits hanging on walls and fences in Ventron. "This Condition must absolutely stop," he concluded. A week later, on July 25, the major chided his men for racing their Fords, and for sleeping on hay stored in barns, and for the "promiscuous" moving around and changing of billets. Memos from Headquarters, 128th Machine Gun Battalion, July 18 and 25, 1918, Record Group 120, Records of the American Expeditionary Forces, World War I Organization Records, Machine Gun Battalions, 128th Machine Gun Battalion, Box 266, NARA.

14. Verne H. Breckenridge was born on February 8, 1900, and died on May 20, 1988. He was buried in Meridian, Idaho. He served overseas with the 128th from April 25, 1918, to April 24, 1919. Missouri Secretary of State, State Archives, Soldiers' Records, War of 1812–World War I, www.sos.mo.gov/archives/soldiers. The War Diaries of the 128th Machine Gun Battalion report that from July 13 to 30, the battalion engaged in 9 days of regular training, 6 days on the machine gun range (including a day with "problems in night firing")

A bit restive at this I wrote a formal letter asking that my officers in turn be allowed to make brief visiting tours with machine gun companies of the division in the line. This seemed such a good idea to Major Halliburton that instead of forwarding my letter he made a similar request for the officers of the battalion and it was authorized.[15]

As a result of this I visited the front July 27 and 28, the days allotted to me, spending the night with Capt. Wm. S. Moore, Co. C, 130th Machine Gun Battalion, the Jefferson City, Mo., unit, near Metzeral in the Fecht valley in Alsace, some 15 miles north of where I had visited the French line during our tour of duty at Willer. The route was over the Col d'Oderon again into Alsace and through Kruth in the Thur valley, then eastward up Wissori Mont to Bussat, the cable head on top of the mountain where Major John F. Constable, 130th Machine Gun Battalion, was stationed. From there guides took me down the back of the mountain to Captain Moore's command post somewhere south of a ruined village named Steinabrück.[16]

---

and 3 days of guard and fatigue duty. War Diaries of 128th Machine Gun Bn., July 13-August 2, 1918, Folder: 128th MG BATL War Diaries 235-33.5, Record Group 120, Records of the American Expeditionary Forces, World War I, Entry NM-91 1241, Records of Combat Divisions, 1917–1919, Box 16, 35th Division, NARA. Each morning from July 22 to 27, the battalion was divided into platoons and assigned to six different training "programs," including pistol practice, gas, gun drill, throwing live grenades, barrage drill, boxing, and "blindfold tests of men." Afternoon drills consisted of "chiefly tactical problems," and three hours of night firing. 1918-07-18 training report, Folder: 128th MG BATL Weekly report—training 235-50.4, Record Group 120, Records of the American Expeditionary Forces, World War I, Entry NM-91 1241, Records of Combat Divisions, 1917-1919, Box 16, 35th Division, NARA.

15. On July 20, 1918, Schrantz wrote a memo to the 35th Division's commander, requesting that he be allowed to visit the trenches, accompanied by 1st. Lt. Charles E. Dunn, the company's reconnaissance officer, and 2nd Lt. Ross Dunlap, the company train lieutenant. He argued that the visit would allow the officers to gain familiarity with the terrain and the trench system, the roads leading to the sector and their suitability for motor transport, and obtain "any other information possible in a machine gun line," "particularly points of value relating to the use of a company of the divisional battalion." July 20, 1918, Memo from Captain Ward L. Schrantz to Commanding General 35th Division re Visit to Front Held by 35th Division [1059] Record Group 120, Records of the American Expeditionary Forces, World War I, Entry NM-91 1256, Organization Records, Machine Gun Battalions, Box 264, 128th Machine Gun Battalion, Co. A – DOC. FILE 1-1203, NARA.

16. John F. Constable was born in Bunker Hill, Illinois, on June 10, 1883. He enlisted in Company H, 3rd Missouri Infantry as a private in 1900, and by 1916 had become captain of Company A of that regiment. Promoted to major that June, he was mustered out of service that September after serving two and a half months on the Mexican border. Constable served as the major of the 140th Infantry while the regiment was in the United States, but served overseas with the 130th Machine Gun Battalion from May 3 to November 24, 1918. Following the war, Constable founded the Constable-Hodgins Printing Company in 1923. He died in Kansas City, Missouri, on February 14, 1944, when he fell down an elevator shaft. *The Kansas City* (MO) *Star*, February 14, 1944; *The Service of the Missouri National Guard on the Mexican Border*, 206, 220; Missouri Secretary of State, State Archives, Soldiers' Records, War of 1812–World War I, www.sos.mo.gov/archives/soldiers.

It was a quiet period even for this quiet front. Metzeral [was] a ruined village nestled at the foot of mountains. East of it was a ridge surmounted by a knob at the north end known as the Kiosque. This was held by our troops as an outpost, except for the extreme east end which was occupied by German wire. The German outpost trenches were just over the eastern slope so close that hand grenades could be tossed back and forth. Above the Kiosque rose enemy-held heights with the result that rifle grenades came into it from time to time from above. It was the hot spot of this sector. In the valley the front line was just north of Metzeral, our forces holding Braunkopf and Altmatt Kopf, the heights on the west side of the Fecht, but with German trenches climbing a short way up their slopes. North of Metzeral in the valley north of where the Fecht turned east was the enemy-held village of Mühlbach.

Accompanied by officers of Company C, I dutifully visited all the machine gun posts of the company, part of which were in the ruins of Metzeral itself and most on the high ground west of the Fecht south of the town. And that Saturday night I spent until midnight or so in a gun position at Geisbodle on a projecting slope southwest of the town, watching the rising flares which kept the area

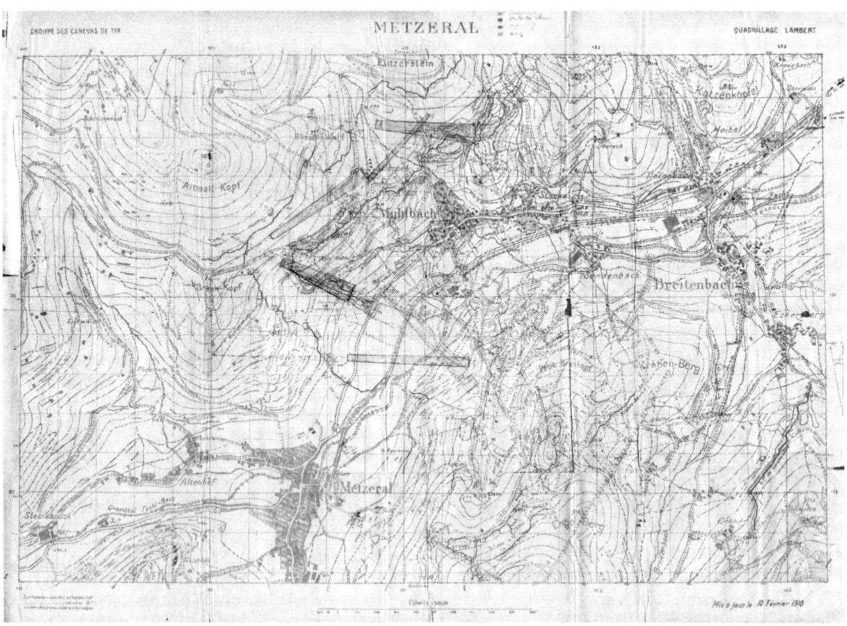

Schrantz's map of positions in the Vosges Mountains (*Jasper County Records Center*)

Ruins of Metzeral (*Jasper County Records Center*)

illuminated and speculated with my companions on the possible meaning of an occasional colored rocket from within the enemy lines. There also was the sound of a quiet front at night–brief sputters of enemy machine gun fire or the rattle of our own automatic rifles, sporadic rifle shots, the occasional crash of grenades, and now and then the sound of a shell going overhead and exploding somewhere in the rear.

The next morning, I aspired to visit Kiosque hurriedly before it came time to depart. Lieutenant Curtle Gates volunteered to show me.[17] We crossed the valley through the trenches, amused at the tiny burros which the French still scattered through the sector used to carry food through the large communication trenches, and finally reached the ridge and started climbing it. But Lieutenant Gates did not know the way and we wandered upward toward the top until we saw the trenches through which we were moving were no longer used—yet interesting with old French bayonets, and other signs of fighting a year or two old. Then we saw that from Mühlbach any enemy observer, looking

17. Curtle C. Gates, born on May 17, 1894, near Ash Grove, Missouri, later moved to Springfield, Missouri. He served overseas with Company B, 130th Machine Gun Battalion from May 3, 1918, to February 28, 1919. Gates was wounded in the Argonne. During World War II, then-Captain Gates first served as provost marshal of the prisoner-of-war facility at Camp Clark, Missouri, then was sent to Europe and served in Normandy as the commander of a military police unit. He died in France on September 18, 1945, and was reinterred in the Springfield, Missouri, National Cemetery in May 1948. *Springfield* (MO) *Leader and Press*, May 26, 1948; Missouri Secretary of State, State Archives, Soldiers' Records, War of 1812–World War I, www.sos.mo.gov/archives/soldiers.

at long range, could see us toiling up the old trenches. Just short of the summit we took council. Gates said that if we thrust our heads over the hill we most likely would get them shot off. It did seem lonely and isolated up there with an air of there being nothing between us and the enemy, for the trenches evidently had long been unused. We decided that since there was no purpose to be served outside of gratifying curiosity that discretion might indeed be the better part of valor. We retraced our steps and since I did not have enough time remaining to visit the Kiosque went back to the command post. Checking our wanderings on the trench maps we found that we had been up the Mamelon, a part of the ridge which our forces had abandoned because [they were] commanded so completely by the enemy hills above it and we were assured by all present that we did well to keep our heads below the summit—that if we had not we might have stayed on the Mamelon without any further interest in the war.

Three days after my return to Ventron orders were received for the 128th Machine Gun B[attalio]n to relieve machine gun companies in the trenches. Some one had finally decided that the divisional machine gun battalion should have some front line experience.

There was a stir of interest when this word was circulated on July 31.[18]

The 128th Machine Gun Battalion was going to the trenches! That word passed about on July 31, 1918, in the little mountain village of Ventron in the French Vosges sent thrills of eager anticipation through the men who had wearied of waiting in division reserve while others were in the presence of the enemy.

A few officers but no enlisted men of the battalion, had been in the front line and the soldiers probably were beginning to wonder if it was a war for officers only. And the division intelligence report that day told of an affray up front which was read to both

18. The citizens of Carthage believed that the men of Company A would be able to meet any future challenge, because Schrantz "is unusually well versed in military affairs in all of their ramifications and it may be depended upon that the company, composed of the material it is and with Captain Schrantz at its head, will make history in France when it has the opportunity." *Carthage* (MO) *Evening Press*, August 5, 1918. The order was received to proceed to Kruth at 5:20 p.m. on July 31, 1918. War Diaries of 128th Machine Gun Bn., July 13–August 2, 1918, Folder: 128th MG BATL War Diaries 235-33.5, Record Group 120, Records of the American Expeditionary Forces, World War I, Entry NM-91 1241, Records of Combat Divisions, 1917–1919, Box 16, 35th Division, NARA.

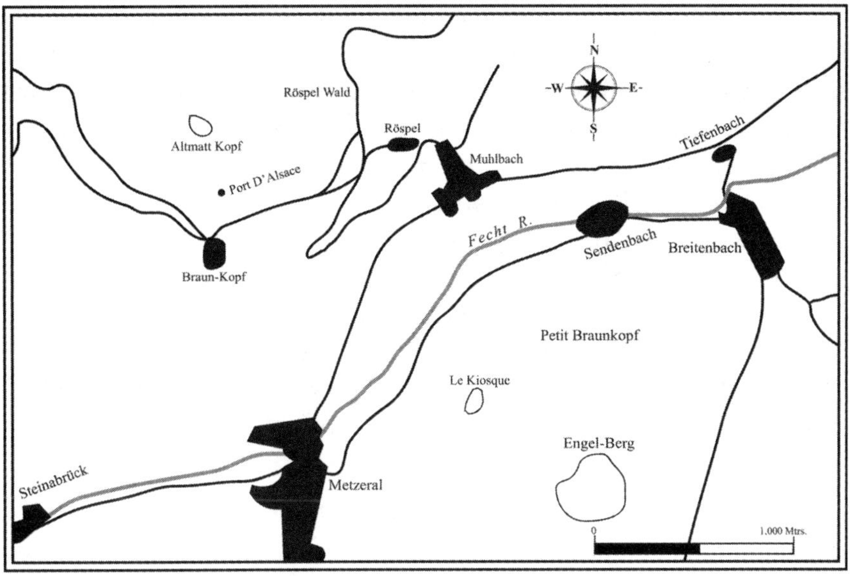

Metzeral

companies at retreat that night to stimulate their interest as well as for their information.

> "At 2355 July 30," read the report, "enemy after a barrage on Hilsenfirst and Epaulette attempted a raid on our trenches at 0030 July 31. Eleven of his men entered our first line trench but were immediately repulsed and retreated, leaving one dead noncommissioned officer in the trench. The enemy secured no identifications. The German unter-offizier killed identified as belonging to 38th Landwehr regiment, 3rd battalion, 12th Company (Prussian). In addition to equipment taken from dead German[s] we have three sacks of hand grenades, two cases Maxim machine gun ammunition, four flame projectors, only one of which has been used, two cases of explosives and a German flag on which is written: 'We fear not France or America. With us it's go again. Regards to Wilson.' Our casualties, two lieutenants and nine men wounded."[19]

19. Sgt. Norval Hopwood wrote on July 23, 1918, that although Company A had not seen action, some of the company's "neighbors" "right next door" had "pulled off some brilliant stuff," with a few men lost, "but that is inevitable." He also proudly explained that German prisoners initially believed the Americans in the area were green troops undergoing training, but when captured proclaimed their enemies to be "shock troops." *Carthage* (MO) *Evening Press*, August 19, 1918.

My company, Company A, was to relieve the Machine Gun Company, 139th Infantry, furnishing the machine gun defense of the frontline immediately north of Metzeral, a sector held by the Third Battalion, 139th Infantry. Thus I was to go to a sector where I was to some extent familiar with the terrain. Company B (Captain J.J. Corey) was to relieve the Machine Gun Company, 140th Infantry, in the vicinity of Hilsenfirst.[20] Company B had drawn the warmer sector, probably as consolation for its disappointment at having been unable to participate in Company A's late jaunt over the line in support of the French in the Thur valley, but the Carthaginians cheered themselves with the fact that there had been rumors of an impending American raid in the Metzeral region.

20. Capt. James J. Corey of Nevada was born on March 25, 1877. He enlisted as a private in Company H, 2nd Missouri Infantry in 1893, served as first sergeant of the company during the Spanish-American War, then was commissioned a captain in 1916. After service with the regiment's Machine Gun Company and Company I as a second lieutenant on the Mexican border 1916–17, Corey was promoted to captain of the Machine Gun Company in April 1917 and served overseas from April 25, 1918, to April 24, 1919, as captain of Company B, 128th Machine Gun Battalion. He died in St. Louis on February 26, 1937. *The Service of the Missouri National Guard on the Mexican Border*, 116; *St. Louis Post-Dispatch*, February 27, 1937; Missouri Secretary of State, State Archives, Soldiers' Records, War of 1812–World War I, www.sos.mo.gov/archives/soldiers; HST.

Chapter 8

To the Front

Once more the men of Company A moved toward the front, but unlike their previous disappointingly brief visit to Willer, this time the Carthage troops actually occupied trenches facing the enemy. Leaving their Ford trucks at Camp Picard near the village of Mittlach, the men hiked forward to relieve the Machine Gun Company of the 139th Infantry and defend a three-quarter mile section of the front line.

Once there, Schrantz and his soldiers were anxious to begin using their Hotchkiss guns; instead they were told that their mission "was one of passive defense only," allowed to open fire only if the enemy attacked. This "live and let live" attitude of the French and Germans in the sector distressed the eager Americans. In the words of one of the 35th Division's historians, the men could see the German trenches nearby, filled with Germans. The doughboys "had trained until training no longer held a beloved spot in their hearts" at Camp Doniphan, sailed across thousands of miles of ocean, and crossed France in order to fight. Now they could not understand why a man would turn down the opportunity to shoot at a German.[1] Fortunately, after a conference with his battalion commander, Schrantz discovered that he was in fact authorized to use his guns to harass the Germans.

1. Hoyt, *Heroes of the Argonne*, 41.

The young captain eagerly embraced this opportunity. Fittingly, on August 5, 1918, the anniversary of their entry into service, the Carthage machine gunners fired their first shots of the war, and the first ever fired at an enemy by the old Carthage Light Guard. The targets of this harassing fire included a German party working on a communications trench, a supply train, and several villages, devoid of civilians but now occupied by the enemy.

Company A was relieved on August 14, their two-week tour of duty in the frontline trenches at an end. Kansas soldier Charles Hoyt correctly noted that the value of the training in the Vosges was measured by the "atmosphere of war" they experienced rather than the actual benefits of training. The Vosges "gave to the Thirty-fifth those conditions under which war must be carried on. Feather beds and waffles for breakfast, they learned, were not a part of it."[2]

After this relatively brief introduction to trench life, Company A was ordered to the village of Gerardmer, where they found far more pleasant quarters in a French Army barracks. There, Captain Schrantz confidently wrote that the company was "ready for service again at the front whenever and wherever needed."

Once clear of the trenches and back in safe billets, battalion commander Major Halliburton made certain that discipline was maintained. He reminded his men on August 14 that they were not allowed to carry weapons when off duty, and on August 24 informed them that a complaint had been made that members of the battalion were "neglectful in saluting and military courtesy." Although the major admitted that he hadn't noticed that his men were "particularly negligent" in this regard, he urged them to salute correctly and rise promptly when an officer approached. "The negligence of any one man in these regards reflects discredit upon the entire organization," he explained to them.[3]

Predictably, the rest at Gerardmer was not to last; the men of Company A and the rest of the 35th Division would be needed again, not to man quiet trenches, but to participate in large-scale American offensives designed to break the stalemate on the Western Front. By late August 1918, Schrantz and his soldiers were on the move to the first such operation—the attempt to eliminate a German salient in the Allied line at the village of St. Mihiel.

2. Hoyt, *Heroes of the Argonne*, 51.

3. Memos, Headquarters, 128th Machine Gun Battalion August 20 and 24, 1918, Record Group 120, Records of the American Expeditionary Forces, World War I Organization Records, Machine Gun Battalions, 128th Machine Gun Battalion, Box 266, NARA.

On the morning of August 1st the battalion formed in Ventron in a long motor column made up of its own vehicles and borrowed trucks, passed the white Christ on a black cross in the center of the village, climbed the long hill to the Col d'Oderon with which Company A was already familiar as a result of its Willer trip, then followed the zig-zag road down the mountain and into the valley of the Thur, bivouacking for the night in a pine wood at the north end of the village.[4]

Two roads led from Kruth to the front, one the route up Drehkopf which I had followed on my reconnaissance trip, and another over a saddle known as the Col du Huss, a route said to be even steeper than the Drehkopf one[,] though of it we knew nothing except that a sign at its entrance said "impassable in case of snow," a fact not particularly pertinent in August even here on what seemed the roof of the world. Corey drew the Drehkopf road, I the Col du Huss, and we were to unite at Mittlach in the Fachtbach valley. The men's packs and miscellaneous paraphernalia went up the cable to Bussat, thence down to Mittlach. The heavy trucks stayed at Kruth. We had to get our light gun trucks over the mountain.

Shortly before dusk the battalion lined up to move forward on foot with gun trucks following. A pistol-armed unit, the officers and most of the men carried steel-shod canes of a type common in the Vosges and quite useful in the trenches there. Normally these were not carried in formation, but this journey was a bit different.

It was somewhat informal, this starting for the front, and Captain Corey whose company had formed on my left—the direction of march—glanced grinning along his company front. Then instead of the expected "squads left" order of the current drill regulations, gave vent to his high spirits by shouting, "Present canes." Then while the battalion laughed, he swung his company into column and stepped off gaily, I following with my own unit. The ways soon separated and I turned my own company to the left up the steep road to the Col du Huss just as the sun was dropping back of the mountain behind us. It was a beautiful evening and the white road

4. According to the battalion's war diaries, the 128th left Ventron about 10 a.m. and moved the 12 kilometers to Kruth by 11:15 a.m. War Diaries of 128th Machine Gun Bn., July 13–August 2, 1918, *Folder: 128th MG BATL War Diaries 235-33.5,* Record Group 120, Records of the American Expeditionary Forces, World War I, Entry NM-91 1241, Records of Combat Divisions, 1917–1919, Box 16, 35th Division, NARA.

could be seen zig-zagging back and forth before us as it climbed the slopes.

It was one of the occasions which suggest a song to the men, one which bursts out spontaneously. I remembered such an occasion in the 22nd Infantry four years before when the column, marching across the causeway to Galveston, Tex., at night and impressed by the brilliant moonlight on the water, broke out in: "I was sailing along, on Moonlight Bay—." Similarly the winding road ahead up this Alsatian mountain suggested a song evidently familiar to the men but then unknown to me. A few men took up a chorus, then apparently all were joining in:

"There's a long, long trail a-winding
Into the land of my dreams."[5]

But the road became steeper and the song dwindled away for the very good reason that all breath was needed for climbing. For hours we struggled up the road through the pine forest. The gun trucks which had left some time after the foot column caught up. It was time too, for at spots they needed help. The Model T Fords just couldn't make it and places it was necessary to set groups of men to add upward pressure on the steepest spots—all this in darkness for the Fords, [which] through the necessities of the situation always moved at night unlighted. At last the company reached the top and was "over the hump." Gravity was now an aid. For the Fords the problem was purely one of peril, with a sharp hill on one side, a drop into nothing on the other and a steep, zig-zagging road down in the black night. To prevent disaster, men walked ahead, marking the sharp curves. Through the pine trees can be seen the rising flares and rockets of the trenches. Reaching the valley of the Fecht-bach, passing up it through Mittlach, we finally came to a locality known as Camp Picard and bivouacked on a boulder-strewn hillside which the men promptly named "the featherbed."[6]

5. Written in 1913 and published in 1914, "There's a Long, Long Trail" was written by Stoddard King and Zo Elliott. The song was enormously popular during World War I. The high spirits of the company came as no surprise to Sgt. Norval Hopwood, who reported that Company A had "organization, discipline, 'esprit de corps,' etc.," and that a committee of Allied officers who inspected the 35th Division believed it was composed of "the best fighting material they had seen in the American forces. I think they meant it, too." *Carthage* (MO) *Evening Press*, August 7, 1918.

6. The battalion's war diaries record that the unit left Kruth at 8 p.m. on August 1 and arrived at Camp Piacardy, a distance of 16 kilometers, at 1:25 a.m. War Diaries of 128th Machine Gun Bn., July 13–August 2, 1918, *Folder: 128th MG BATL War Diaries 235-33.5,* Record Group 120, Records of the American Expeditionary Forces, World War I, Entry NM-91 1241, Records of Combat Divisions, 1917–1919, Box 16, 35th Division, NARA.

It was guides sent by battalion headquarters who had met us as we entered the valley and taken us to the "feather bed," bearing directions from Major Halliburton that we follow them. I had wanted to bivouac in the woods back of Mittlach since the men were very tired and any distance we moved to the south would need to be backtracked the next day to get to our scheduled positions.

At 5:17 a.m., August 2, 1918, the lighter sleepers among the members of Company A, 128th Machine Gun Battalion, stirred restlessly on the rocky Alsatian hillside where they lay, aroused by a series of explosions to the north. The enemy, someone said, was shelling Mittlach; whereupon the raised heads were lowered again to slumber. For men who had marched most of the night, enemy shells falling a quarter of a mile or so away were of only academic interest at such an hour; sleep and rest were more important. Our own position on the hillside to the south could hardly be reached by enemy projectiles. Commanding officers, I reflected, often had a good reason for what they did and Major Halliburton had certainly designated a better place than the one I would have picked.[7]

An hour or so later, gnawing stomachs served as more insistent alarm clocks, and one by one the soldiers unrolled from their blankets, blinked at the pine-clad mountains about them, washed in the water of a little stream which ran down the center of the narrow valley, ate the breakfast which Mess Sergeant Clint A. Miles and the cooks were ready to serve, then returned to the rocky hillside to rest some more against the call for future exertion. The shell explosions had long since ceased and the valley was as quiet as a Sunday afternoon in Missouri.

Camp Picard, for so the place where the company was resting was called, was an area rather than a camp; the few buildings in it being widely scattered to lessen the danger from enemy shell fire. It was entirely concealed from enemy view.

After breakfast I wandered down into Mittlach to look over the situation for through this village my unit must later pass. Mittlach was a somewhat shattered and disheveled Alsatian mountain village, mauled about a bit by shell fire but still inhabited by men,

7. Schrantz related that not only was Camp Picard concealed from enemy view, but "So too was part of the straggling village of Mittlach adjacent to it, but from the north edge of this little shell-shattered town, one looking east could see a tall hill which the map showed to be in the enemy lines."

women and children who long had been living in range of the guns. The Carthage soldiers, remembering the arduous climb over the road from the rear they had traveled the night before, felt that they knew why the Alsatians stayed; then too, some one reflected, the men of many of these families were in the hostile army and the sympathy not unnaturally might be to the eastward down the valleys instead of back across the mountains toward France.

A part of it was hidden from enemy view by a shoulder of a hill but there was a sign suspended over the street—"Take care. The enemy is watching." Beyond this point one could see the pine clad heights east of Metzeral—and could be seen from there, though an isolated individual presumably would attract no attention in a village where civilians moved about. Below this was the village cemetery, swollen now by soldier dead. "Mort pour la France" the French military graves were marked, and, after the French fashion, "he died for his country" marked the graves of the more recent American dead, largely those of the 137th Infantry, 35th Division, which preceded the 139th in the sector.

Soon 1st Lieut. Frank L. Snyder of my company who had gone forward a day early as reconnaissance officer, showed up at Camp Picard with Lieut. Walter A. Wood, commanding the Machine Gun Company of the 139th Infantry which we were to relieve.[8] There were also orders for the relief, though we worked out details on the basis of recommendation of Lieut. Wood. Six of our guns were to go forward by day on French pack mules, since two of them were to go to a reserve position and four to a front line position which could be approached under cover. The other six would go down the Fechtbach valley after dark direct to the positions. The company, less motor section, would move by day through the village and over a mountain to the north, reaching the trenches to be occupied

8. Walter A. Wood of Sedalia was born October 30, 1891, in La Monte, Missouri. Wood joined the Machine Gun Company of the 3rd Missouri Infantry as a private in July 1916 and was soon promoted to sergeant and first sergeant. He served on the Mexican border with the company until the regiment was relieved from federal service that September. Wood served overseas as a first lieutenant in the Machine Gun Company of the 139th U.S. Infantry from March 30, 1918 to May 26, 1919, was wounded in action, and was awarded the Purple Heart Medal. Wood also served in World War II as a first lieutenant in the 757th Military Police Battalion from March 1942 to May 1944. He died in Osage Township, Morgan County, Missouri, on November 4, 1960, and was buried in Sedalia, Missouri. *The Service of the Missouri National Guard on the Mexican Border*, 217; Missouri Secretary of State, State Archives, Soldiers' Records, War of 1812–World War I, www.sos.mo.gov/archives/soldiers.

before the guns came in. The supply section and Fords were to remain at Camp Picard.

I furrowed my brow a bit over the route of the company. In the center of Mittlach and in view of the enemy was a bridge over the Fecht-bach which it would be necessary to cross. Yet Lieut. Wood told me that if we waited until night to start from Camp Picard he could not get his company out before daylight. On a portion of the streets too the unit would be exposed.

As the company was preparing its packs preliminary to falling in for the move shortly after two o'clock, an enemy plane soared over the valley from east to west, drawing the usual shrapnel and high explosive from the anti-aircraft guns, but quickly passed on to the west. Soon thereafter the organization was formed and given final instructions as to the method by which the exposed valley was to be crossed and how the relief would be effected. The plan for the daylight crossing of the exposed stretch was to move in such a way that the enemy artillery observers would not think the target worth wasting shells on; but in case the movement did draw fire, the formation would minimize the danger of losses.

To avoid inviting shell fire there seemed only one way. At 1000 the six guns on the pack mules departed. At 1500 the sergeant range finder—Sergeant Edwin W. Wiggins later killed in the Meuse Argonne—and I led off the move of the marching unit. At irregular intervals of 100 to 150 yards, First Lieutenant Dunn, company executive officer sent the rest of the men in groups of twos and threes, straggling along as if sightseeing. It took considerable time to cross the exposed space but when we reassembled under cover at the foot of the heights to the north there had been no enemy shell fire and I hoped that the hostile observation posts had interpreted the straggling movement as something other than a relief for units in the trenches that night.

This departure was watched somewhat regretfully by the supply and train sections of the company, which were commanded by Second Lieut. Herbert B. Wardin and which included Supply Sergt. Warren A. Ford, Mess Sergt. Clint A. Miles, Train Sergeant Thomas E. Clark and all the company drivers and mechanics, all of whom were to remain at Camp Picard during the tour of duty at the front.[9]

9. Warren Arthur Ford was born on September 30, 1899 (some sources state 1897) and died in San Diego County, California, on July 31, 1980. After serving overseas with Company

The nonchalant stroll of the combat portion of the company in its unusual formation across the view of the German artillery observers, was the Carthage unit's first appearance before the enemy—and the German army did not seem the least bit excited about the event, however important it may have seemed to the men participating. Doubtless the incident was duly recorded in some enemy intelligence report for the day but his guns were silent and in due time the organization had assembled in column of twos in the shelter of a huge hill across the valley where guides from the 139th Infantry Machine Gun Company were waiting.

Up these pine-clad heights—a great hill known as Sillikarkopf—with long gaps between sections and platoons to render a less vulnerable target to artillery, we toiled, finally reaching an elevated little mountain lake by which there was a French artillery camp, then around through the pine woods to the front of the hill where there were some hutments. This was the battalion reserve of the 3d Battalion, 139th Infantry, to which my second platoon (less one section) of my company was to be attached. It was not yet quite dark but it seemed that the guides knew a trench route by which my third platoon, which was to be on the left, could proceed to its sector by day without being exposed.

The third platoon, Lieutenant Samuels, wound its way downward through the woods and out of sight. With the headquarters section, the 1st platoon and one section (Ellis) of the second platoon I waited until dark. Then we too slid downward until we came to a few clustered shelters roofed with logs and earth which [was] the command post of CR (center de resistance) Benoit. Here was battalion headquarters and the stopping place of myself and headquarters section. The gun sections proceeded forward in the direction of the front from which an occasional flare was already

A from April 25, 1918, until April 21, 1919, Ford was commissioned a second lieutenant and continued to serve overseas until August 23, 1919. Missouri Secretary of State, State Archives, Soldiers' Records, War of 1812–World War I, www.sos.mo.gov/archives/soldiers. Herbert Bailey Wardin was born in Nevada, Missouri on June 20, 1893. He died on February 15, 1972, and was buried in Kansas City, Missouri. He served overseas as a sergeant with the 128th from April 25, 1918, to July 14, 1918, then was commissioned a second lieutenant and remained overseas with the battalion until April 30, 1919. *The Kansas City* (MO) *Times*, February 16, 1972; Missouri Secretary of State, State Archives, Soldiers' Records, War of 1812–World War I, www.sos.mo.gov/archives/soldiers. Thomas Ellsworth Clark was born in Carthage (some sources state Preston, Missouri) on December 5, 1893, and served overseas with the 128th from April 25, 1918, to April 24, 1919. He died in Bellflower, California, on April 18, 1963. Missouri Secretary of State, State Archives, Soldiers' Records, War of 1812–World War I, www.sos.mo.gov/archives/soldiers.

rising and from which now and then came the sound of a rifle shot, or a burst of machine gun or automatic rifle fire, or the crash of an exploding rifle grenade.

The headquarters section, under the direction of Lieutenant Dunn and guides, was distributed to the various billets available, replacing the headquarters section of the Machine Gun Company, 139th Infantry, which was formed and ready to move out and to the rear.[10]

With First Lt. Wood, commander of that company, I reported to Major William D. Stepp, commanding officer of the 3rd Battalion, 139th Infantry, in one of the shelters. I already knew Major Stepp. He was an old time Missouri National Guardsman and had been on my examining board when I had been commissioned captain in the spring of 1917. He said the usual things and I said the usual things, I hope, then Wood and I returned to his shelter, which now was to be mine, and he explained the defense of the sector and turned over his maps to me.[11]

It was a log building on the forward slope of the hill, roofed with a layer of logs, a layer of rock, another layer of logs and some dirt. It was concealed by the woods but otherwise would have been quite visible to the enemy. In the same building, and separated only by a thin partition, was the battalion aid station.

We waited in this place, or on the road above it, during the hours which were to elapse before we could hope to receive the messages from the forward platoons that the relief was complete.

10. Charles E. Dunn, born in Wisconsin on October 8, 1892, was a resident of Milton, Wisconsin, when he entered the Second Officers' Training Camp at Fort Sheridan, Illinois, in August 1917. Commissioned a first lieutenant that November, Dunn sailed to France and arrived in France in January 1918. He attended various schools before being attached to Company A, 128th Machine Gun Battalion in July 1918. Dunn died in 1945. He was buried in Mountain View Cemetery in Longmont, Colorado. HST; Memo from 2nd Lt. Edwin Samuel to Commanding Officer, 128th Machine Gun Battalion, Camp Doniphan, November 7, 1917, Record Group 120, Records of the American Expeditionary Forces, World War I Organization Records, Machine Gun Battalions, 128th Machine Gun Battalion, Box 263, NARA; HST.

11. William Dale Stepp of Trenton, Missouri, was born on September 12, 1873. He graduated from Trenton High School, attended the University of Missouri and was admitted to the bar in 1895. "Largely instrumental" in organizing Company D, 4th Missouri Infantry, Stepp was commissioned a first lieutenant, was promoted to captain the same year, and to major of the regiment in 1909. He served as the 4th Missouri's major on the Mexican border June 1916–February 1917. He served overseas from March 30, 1918, until he "died a valiant death" on September 28, 1918. *The Service of the Missouri National Guard on the Mexican Border*, 295; *Trenton* (MO) *Daily Republican*, October 31, November 9, 1918; James Everett Ford, *A History of Grundy County* (Trenton, MO: News Publishing Company, 1908), 563; Missouri Secretary of State, State Archives, Soldiers' Records, War of 1812–World War I, www.sos.mo.gov/archives/soldiers.

I listened with some anxiety to the occasional heavy explosions on the hills ahead of us which I knew were enemy medium trench mortar shells—the vaned projectiles known as "flying pigs" because of the screaming-squealing sound they made as they hurtled through the air. It was one of these, I knew, which had killed Lieutenant George A. Silsbarrow, 138th Infantry—an acquaintance of mine in early Camp Doniphan days, and as I recall the first officer of the 35th Division to die in the trenches of the Vosges.[12] The soldiers were winding through broad trenches now on either edge of which above them they could see barbed wire entanglements silhouetted against the sky. Back and forth in an interminable maze the approach trench wandered, up a hill then down again. The occasional bursts of machine gun fire, intermittent rifle shots, and the crash of an exploding grenade now and then, continued, but rather with a routine air, and only once did a lively burst of firing off to the south somewhere indicate a clash of patrols. A smell of lime—the purifier of the trenches—pervaded the air; lights flared occasionally in the sky; one knew that on the black hill masses to the eastward enemy observers were watching.

A normal night, said Wood, and indeed it was much the same as the night I had spent with the 130th Machine Gun Battalion a mile or so to the south some time before.

The machine guns of Company A had already arrived and were quickly set in position, loaded, and laid on their sectors of fire by the outgoing gunners. Instructions were hurriedly passed in low voices. Company A gunners took positions at the guns, finger on trigger; the men of the 139th quickly filed away and Company A sentries closed the wire gates, then stood on the alert.

In each squad the corporal went over his instructions with the men, the most important for the moment dealing with pyrotechnics.

12. George Albert Bilsbarrow of Maplewood, Missouri, was born in Texarkana, Texas, on October 17, 1889. He enlisted in Company D, 1st Missouri Infantry as a private in 1910, became a first lieutenant in the company in 1914, and served on the Mexican border from June to September 1916. Bilsbarrow served with Company L, 138th Infantry overseas from May 3, 1918, until his death on July 16, 1918 (due to wounds received in action). He was the first officer from the former St. Louis Missouri National Guard units to be killed in action, and was described as "one of the most efficient and experienced officers in the regiment." Missouri Secretary of State, State Archives, Soldiers' Records, War of 1812–World War I; *St. Louis Post-Dispatch*, July 23, August 19, 1918; *The Service of the Missouri National Guard on the Mexican Border*, 40; Missouri Secretary of State, State Archives, Soldiers' Records, War of 1812–World War I, www.sos.mo.gov/archives/soldiers.

Several rockets with large white stars coming up from the American front line was the call for the machine gun barrage and the guns must be firing before the sparks from the rockets died out. It was only so that the enemy could be caught before passing the machine gun line of fire. Several caterpillar rockets were the gas alarm. There must be no smoking in the trenches; no talking other than in a low voice[;] no congregating in groups; gas masks would be carried on the breast in the alert position at all times and steel helmets would be worn outside of dug-outs; half an hour before daylight each morning all men would stand-to in their combat positions.[13]

This over, all hands stood curiously on the firestep at the front of the trench and gazed into the night in the direction of the enemy, listened to the rifle shots that now and then punctuated the stillness, and made witticisms about the apparent mildness of the war.

About 2 a.m., perhaps a few minutes before, we received messages from the platoons that the relief had been completed and without casualties.[14] Lieutenant Wood departed and I remained—thinking with a thrill that I now was in command of a machine gun company in the line. I contemplated my quarters—a room with a bunk, a table, a straight chair and an easy chair, looted doubtless from some wrecked cottage and splintered a bit by bullet holes—seven, if I remember rightly, which appeared to have been made by a burst of machine gun fire. Then I removed my shoes and otherwise fully dressed crawled between the blankets.

I was early astir the next morning. PC Benoit where I stood was 800 meters (about 2,600 feet) above sea level according to the map. About three-quarters of a mile to the northeast rose the summit of Altmatt Kopf, about 260 feet higher than Benoit. From the south slope of this, some 540 feet down and about a third of a

13. Floy F. Gibbs of the 128th's Sanitary Detachment wrote home that "there are two things that one holds on to and that is his gas mask and steel helmet. They are your best friends in this war." *The Houston* (MO) *Herald*, January 30, 1919. The battalion's war diary reported that the battalion finished taking over the positions assigned to them at 3 a.m. on August 3, 1918. War Diaries of 128th Machine Gun Bn., July 13–August 2, 1918, Folder: 128th MG BATL War Diaries 235-33.5 Record Group 120, Records of the American Expeditionary Forces, World War I, Entry NM-91 1241, Records of Combat Divisions, 1917–1919, Box 16, 35th Division, NARA.

14. As Schrantz explained in a letter home, "when men are in the trenches, they can be subjected to a heavy bombardment without suffering much loss, but an organization caught by shell fire while coming along the road leading to or from the trenches is much more exposed." *Carthage* (MO) *Evening Press*, December 9, 1918.

mile distant jutted out another hill known as Braunkopf, slightly south of east from where I stood and some 330 feet lower.

On the forward slopes of Braunkopf and Altmatt Kopf my machine gun positions were located. Immediately after breakfast I was going forward to visit them.

Descending some 400 feet or so into a little gully, through which an ice cold stream of water was gushing, I soon was climbing up Braunkopf and moving forward into its trenches. This entire area had been the scene of severe fighting in the past. A few days later, Private Carl Tangner, my orderly, brought me some German cartridges he had picked up by some unburied skeletons of German dead back near Benoit itself. Braunkopf which had been held for a considerable time by the Germans was a maze of shell holes and rusty barbed wire outside the trenches.[15]

As I went forward I passed occasional old German dug-outs, evidently meant to afford protection from fire in the direction of Altmatt Kopf since their entrances were to the south. These openings were wired up—the rest of the time I was in the sector I wondered what one would find if he removed the wire and went in. I found Lieut. Snyder in a shelter back of the crest of Braunkopf and he accompanied me on my rounds.

Between 5:33 and 5:51 o'clock this morning, a 35th Division "summary of intelligence" for this date shows, ten enemy artillery shells fell on Kiosque, followed an hour later by six trench mortar bombs. These may be said to have started the Carthage men's first day in the trenches off with a bang.

The three-quarters of a mile of line which Company A helped hold was defended by seven combat groups of riflemen, and the five machine gun combat groups with two guns in each—each combat group, in addition to the wire along the entire front, being securely wired in itself, both sides and rear. Each of the machine gun combat groups was named.

The right machine gun strongpoint was about 300 yards due south of the crest of Braunkopf and went by the name of

15. Carl Arthur Tangner, born in Carthage, Missouri, on December 28, 1896, was inducted into Company A on April 4, 1917. Appointed a bugler in October 1917, Tangner was promoted to private first class in June 1918. He served overseas with the 128th from April 25, 1918 to April 24, 1919. He died on March 18, 1972, and was buried in Resurrection Memorial Cemetery in Oklahoma City, Oklahoma. Missouri Secretary of State, State Archives, Soldiers' Records, War of 1812–World War I, www.sos.mo.gov/archives/soldiers; HST.

Sampigny. To the southeast one looked down on the ruined village of Metzeral. The two guns at Sampigny were sighted to protect Metzeral against attack from the north. The next section was in a post known as "Braunkopf" in the saddle between the Braunkopf knoll and the south slope of Altmatt Kopf. Its line of fire was to the northeast in front of our barbed wire entanglement. Below both of these positions some forty feet, in the front line trenches, were rifle combat groups.

These rifle unit GCs (groupes de combat), as we called them after the French fashion, ranged from about 200 yards to 450 yards apart, depending on their locations. The front line trench, though continuous, was thus lightly held, much of the rifle strength being held in support to deliver counter attacks if needed. A broad belt of rusty barbed wire protected the front, yet an occasional infiltration by some bold enemy patrol was not unknown.

My machine gun GCs, like those of the riflemen, were for this reason completely wired in for all around defense and were guarded in the main trench by double-gates of barbed wire which were kept closed at night. These two gates at each of the G.C.s were some distance apart. The trench between the two was roofed by chicken wire which was supposed to bounce off any grenades thrown on it. The sentry stood at the inner gate. A person approaching the GC along the trench pulled the end of a long wire which ran to the inner gate where it jangle[d] a tin can. The sentry then opened the inner gate and cautiously went to the outer, opening it if the caller was of the right faction. This elaborate arrangement had been fixed up by the French and was by us taken over.

On this first visit—it being day—the gates were open and there was no delay in getting from one GC to another. The trenches between, as in the GC areas themselves, spoke eloquently of the hard fighting of the past, notably in 1915 when the trenches had been thick with men. Many bodies of dead had been buried in the parapet and were marked—where marked at all—with little tin tricolors or some German marking where there were enemy dead.[16] Even back near company headquarters a half mile or so

16. Schrantz found the hill to be "a maze of trenches, dugouts and tunnels, choked with tangles of wire, blocked with sand bags and infested with rats, cats and other things." The German graves, some of which were marked with a wooden cross, were "usually half defaced by long exposure to the weather." *Carthage* (MO) *Evening Press*, September 17, 1918. Sgt. Charles Edwards of Company A wrote of occupying two dugouts, built by the

to the rear, there were signs of the earlier fighting, and company runners wandering around on an exploring trip came across skeletons of unburied dead whose arms and equipment showed them to be Germans.

Clambering upward for about 250 yards to the next machine gun GC—a change in elevation of about 140 feet—I came to our post known as "Port d'Alsace." It was aptly named as "the door of Alsace" in that it looked directly down the valley of the little Fecht River toward Munster, a valley leading directly into the enemy lines.

All along, of course, I had been studying the position of the enemy so far as I could see it, but here the view was superb.

About a mile to the southeast was the hill known as Le Kiosque the exact summit of which was American held but with an enemy trench so close beneath it that grenades could be thrown from one to the other. Above it to the southeast towered the enemy held hill known as Engel-Berg, while directly to its east and northeast was a smaller elevation called Petit Braunkopf scarred everywhere with enemy trenches. From the foot of the Kiosque and Petit Braunkopf, the south flank of an enemy salient ran directly in the direction of the Port d'Alsace. The apex of this enemy salient was 400 yards from where I stood staring, though almost 300 feet lower. From there it angled back northeast for another mile or so to join the main north-and-south German line north of the valley which was formed by the Fecht running north through Metzeral, then turning east within the salient.

At the neck of the salient was a ruined town named Mühlbach which was assumed to be strongly held by the enemy, though at this time there was no enemy to be seen. There were no rifle GCs in front of Port d'Alsace—there being a gap of 450 yards between them there—so there was nothing but elevation and barbed wire between this position and the enemy.

As I studied the enemy held territory there came the crash of grenades from the Kiosque and looking over I saw fluffy puffs of white smoke opening above it. These were rifle grenades discharged by the Germans from the hills overlooking the place. It was a thing that happened, apparently, every time anyone on the Kiosque exposed themselves in the slightest degree. Occasionally there

---

Germans, "nice and dry and not wet and muddy," although full of rats as big as his pet terrier back home, "cooties," and fleas. *Carthage* (MO) *Evening Press*, September 26, 1918.

came the crack of a bullet in our direction—some sniper apparently. Except for this occasional sign of the enemy one might have thought the whole front uninhabited this sunny day.

Some 500 yards to the northeast, and perhaps 150 feet higher, I found the right combat group of the third platoon (Lt. Samuels). This GC was known as Röspel because [it was] located in what had been a woodland known as Rospelwald. It was now only shattered stumps and dead down timber, all affording some meager cover from view. Here and there in what had been a clearing were red raspberries, once tame but now growing wild and in profusion, loaded with ripe fruit. Four hundred yards or so farther to the northeast, up over a nose and down, I came to our left combat group—Runz—on one side of a little valley, to the left of which were French troops holding a hill known as Klitzerstein.

The wire at this last group was bad and its left seemed to me to be considerably exposed. Sergeant Joseph E. Taylor, in command there, had mounded up a stack of grenades at the exposed end and gleefully explained to me what he was going to do to the enemy if any night he should come over. This post was not bothered while we were there but a long time later I was told by an officer of the 6th Division with whom I swapped recollections of the sector, that it had been raided by the enemy after they relieved the 35th. The wire was repaired as much as possible as soon as we took possession and as the section had grenades enough on hand to fight two or three wars and was extremely anxious to use them, it probably would have been able to take care of itself in any eventuality.[17]

From Runz I retraced my steps to P.C. Benoit, back over Almatt Kopf north of the summit and then through a trench which had a bamboo screen at both sides and overhead—the work, I was told, of French Indo-Chinese troops which had once held the sector.

17. Joseph E. Taylor was born in Tomah, Wisconsin, on May 17, 1895. He came to Carthage in his youth, and was employed in the coffee department of the Platt-Porter Wholesale Grocery. He joined Company A, 2nd Missouri Infantry in June 1916 and served with the company on the Mexican border until January 1917. Promoted from private to corporal in August 1917, and to sergeant in August 1918, Taylor served overseas from April 25, 1918, to April 24, 1919. Taylor died on June 17, 1957, and was buried in Carthage, Missouri. *The Service of the Missouri National Guard on the Mexican Border*, 128; *Carthage* (MO) *Evening Press*, June 18, 1957; Missouri Secretary of State, State Archives, Soldiers' Records, War of 1812-World War I, www.sos.mo.gov/archives/soldiers; HST.

My company now being in the presence of the enemy, though in a quiet sector, I naturally wanted to give the men such war experience training as was available. The guns in the GCs naturally were all laid on their barrage lines and were not to fire unless the enemy attacked—the only kind of an attack anticipated in that region being a night raid. Our ideal was to have the guns firing before the sparks from the rockets from the rifle GCs calling for aid had died out.

But I had two spare guns in addition to those with the reserve section—10 guns in the line, two in reserve and these two spares for replacement should any of the others go wrong.

It seemed to me that if I placed one of these spare guns on Braunkopf, shifting it about on different nights, and another in Rospel Wald that I might do some harassing fire nightly on the enemy communications coming down the valley. Some beautiful annoyance schemes could be worked out.

I interviewed Major Stepp, though with faint hope. Lieutenant Wood had told me that the major would not permit him to engage in harassing fire. But when the major heard what I had in mind he agreed readily. Lieutenant Wood, he told me, had wanted to set up harassing guns near his command post and drop long range machine gun fire on the enemy front lines. He didn't approve of that. The shelters at battalion headquarters were not very strong ones and he did not care to invite enemy artillery fire on them. As for reaching way back in the enemy lines he was for it. But I would need to submit a chart each day showing exactly what I was going to shoot at and from where, and how many rounds I was going to fire, each of the times during the night I planned to do the shooting. This was agreeable enough so far as I was concerned. I would need to do that anyhow in order to follow the pattern I planned, which was to fire bursts at irregular intervals throughout the night on the routes where I believed there would be enemy night use.

I picked villages behind the line, cable-heads and other points likely. The gun on Braunkopf I scheduled to fire to the northeast, the one on Rospel Wald to the southeast, the two guns thus crossing their fire and being able to reach farther up side valleys leading into the main one.

There was no lack of suitable targets, as the valley, flanked by towering hills, was the natural means of enemy communication from the rear. In the area allotted to the first platoon gun were the enemy-occupied semi-ruined villages of Mühlbach, near the front line, and of Tiefenbach and Heibel a half mile or so beyond—and for several days the daily division intelligence report had stated regularly that wheeled transport had been heard entering Mühlbach from the east during the night. The third platoon had even a better prospect. In its area was the village of Sendenbach about three-quarters of a mile from its position, and Breitenbach some distance east of that, with the village of Eckersberg, out of sight even by day but easy to be reached by bullets, just south of that. Then between Breitenbach and Tiefenbach was an old factory building which the intelligence map said, and which nightly noise indicated, was the distribution point of the German cable system by which food and supplies were sent up to the hills. Then close to the front in this area there was a known live target. A new communication trench was reported under construction here, and in the small hours of August 5, according to the intelligence bulletin, "an enemy working party of about 40 men was seen by one of our patrols about 300 yards northeast of Kiosque."

We began the firing on the night of August 5—the first anniversary of our entry into service. Major Stepp included that night, as well as later, a brief notation of my plan in his patrol orders. Here is his extract for that first night: "Two guns of Company A will use some harassing fire on night of August 5–6. Firing to begin about 10 p.m. continuing at irregular intervals until about 2 a.m., firing about 600 rounds. Guns located as follows: One on unused trenches on south slope of Braunkopf, harassing road running west from Tiefenbach for 500 meters, striking crossroads in Tiefenbach, searching and traversing very thinly through a zone about 500 meters long and 300 meters wide, west of Tiefenbach and north of railway. One gun located in unused trenches in Rospel Wald—harassing a zone 500 meters long west of Breitenbach and 300 meters deep, the Breitenbach-Sendenbach road being the northern edge of the zone."[18]

18. Schrantz wrote, "According to the text books, the object of harassing fire is to prevent overland movement by the enemy and to dislocate the maintenance and supply of his front system." The method "consists in fighting [*sic*] out where the enemy is likely to be out in the open at a certain time and then, when that time arrives, shoot up the area where he is supposed to be." "You do not see him," Schrantz added, "because it is usually night when you fire and you do not know whether you hit him or not. However, you know you annoy him a bit and if he retaliates you know you have annoyed him considerable." *Carthage* (MO) *Evening Press*, September 17, 1918.

This system did not promise to be particularly lethal for the enemy but bullets flying about at unexpected hours of the night where bullets were not reasonably to be anticipated could not make anyone happy except the firer. And I was using the long range of the Hotchkiss with its boat-tail bullets to reach sections which probably had been free of bullets with killing velocity for some time. The killing range of the German, British or American machine guns of the day was only about 2500 yards, or maybe meters, but the Hotchkiss killing range was estimated at from 3500 to 4000 meters, and I had charts showing the angle of fall at all ranges. I actually was firing this first night around 2500 meters. Moreover the Tiefenbach-Breitenbach region was one where there was certain to be circulation after nightfall, and the intelligence maps showed a German cablehead just between the two villages.

I stood in one of the crumbling, unused trenches of Braunkopf as the firing started. I had wanted to pull that first trigger myself, and perhaps should have done so, but I was reluctant to deprive the sergeant in charge of that honor, so I let it pass.

At 10 o'clock the Braunkopf gun started chattering and the Rospel Wald gun cut in a moment or two later, the bullets cracking across each other far up the valley. Most thrilling I found it.[19]

These were not only the company's first shots of the war but were the first ever fired in actual battle by the old Carthage Light Guard. Not that this trench warfare was much of a battle, but it was a battle of a sort.

The reaction of the enemy, I must own, was not encouraging. He simply ignored the whole procedure this first night, somewhat to my chagrin since I had expected him to get stirred up about it. But after all there was no particular reasons for the Germans near us to be disturbed. They could hear the noise but we were not shooting at them. Why should they lose any sleep about American

19. Schrantz's ammunition report for August 6, 1918, notes that his platoons fired 1,376 rounds. On August 7, he recorded that they expended 842 rounds. Ammunition Reports, August 3–7, 1918, Record Group 120, Records of the American Expeditionary Forces, World War I, Entry NM-91 1256, Organization Records, Machine Gun Battalions, Box 264, 128th Machine Gun Battalion, Co. A – DOC. FILE 1-1203, NARA. On August 8, he reported his platoons expended 1,824 rounds; on August 9, 1,202 rounds; on August 10, 1,392 rounds; on August 11, 1,153 rounds, August 12, 1,492 rounds, on August 13, 720 rounds; and on August 14, 1,344 rounds. Ammunition Reports, August 8–14, 1918, Record Group 120, Records of the American Expeditionary Forces, World War I Organization Records, Machine Gun Battalions, 128th Machine Gun Battalion, Box 264, NARA.

noise? Moreover by crossing the fire of the guns even their flash was more or less concealed from the direct front, a thing worked out with some care in picking the locations, and in using wet gunny sacks for screening. Consequently the target presented was an area one rather than specific. So the front line enemy this night treated us with cold disdain. Anyhow it was fun.

It must also be admitted that this two-gun war I was trying to start up in the Vosges never did greatly upset the course of combat in this altitudinous region. The trend of history probably was in no whit changed. But it was not a thing that the enemy would let pass completely unnoticed. Someone back in [the] rear knew bullets were falling where they weren't wanted—knew that someone was breaking the rules in this region where live-and-let-live had been the custom for some years before the Americans came in. So the front line apparently received the word to reply in kind.[20]

This first night's firing was the beginning of a co-ordinated harassing fire which continued the rest of the time Company A remained in the region. By way of retaliation, German machine guns each evening at dusk fired westward up the valley of the Fecht-bach in the American lines, doing exactly the same in this valley as the Company A men were in the valley of the Fecht to the east. Then also whenever the two Carthage guns started firing, a German machine gun opened fire on Braunkopf, the fire being directed with some accuracy now at the old emplacement which had been used by the harassing gun the first night. However the Carthage men never fired two nights in succession from the same point, and this machine gun return did no damage; neither did the Germans show much alertness in trying to find a target, contenting themselves nightly with kicking up the dirt around the spot at which the Carthaginians had started their shooting. The gun in Roespel Wald the German machine gunners completely ignored, and the soldiers over there rarely heard the crack of enemy bullets, though hostile trench mortar bombs fell there occasionally.

20. Schrantz and the other men of Company A were not unique in their eagerness to see action after spending months in training in the United States and France. One historian compared the arrival of Americans at the front to "a sudden burst of noisy roisterers into the truce of a family fireside." Robert B. Bruce, *A Fraternity of Arms: America and France in the Great War* (Lawrence: University Press of Kansas, 2003), 139–40. Also see Richard S. Faulkner, *The School of Hard Knocks: Combat Leadership in the American Expeditionary Forces* (College Station: Texas A&M University Press, 2012), 158–59.

Occasionally enemy artillery during the night rather lazily tried to find our gun in the Rospel Wald. I had instructed that between the times of firing, the gun would be dismounted and taken back into the trench.

Long after the war one of the men in that section told me an incident that occurred. The men were changed nightly on the harassing gun so as to give everyone a little experience of shooting at the enemy. This man—Private Lawrence Akin—was new that night and after a time or two tired of helping take down the gun.

"Why not leave it up here?" he suggested to Sergeant Carl Cain who was in charge. "We must put it up to shoot again in a half hour. Why not let it set?"[21]

"Take it down," replied Cain, and the men did.

No sooner was the gun in the bottom of the trench than came the shrilling of an approaching shell which exploded where the gun had been sitting just a moment before.

As the screaming of the fragments died away and the clods pattered down, the men heard Cain's voice again:

"You see what I mean?"

The war was picking up in a small way.[22]

Company A was now firmly settled in the routine of the trenches. Food, work, harassing fire, stand-to and guard, became the events of importance in the semi-subterranean life in the weathered trenches decorated with grave markers of French and German dead. As for the food there were three meals a day though in many organizations two meals a day was the rule. The ability to have three was due to the fact that the company

21. Lawrence Akin, born in Barry County, Missouri, on April 29, 1901, served overseas with Company A from April 25, 1918 to April 24, 1919, and was severely wounded on September 27, 1918. Following the war, he enlisted in the U.S. Marine Corps and attained the rank of captain. He died on December 28, 1972, in Riverside, California. Missouri Secretary of State, State Archives, Soldiers' Records, War of 1812-World War I, www.sos.mo.gov/archives/soldiers. Carl J. Cain, born in Arkansas on May 8, 1896, served with Company A on the Mexican border from 1916-17, then served overseas from April 25, 1918 to April 24, 1919. He worked as a printer in Springfield, Missouri, after the war and died on June 24, 1964. He was buried at the Springfield National Cemetery in Springfield, Missouri. *Springfield* (MO) *Leader-Press*, June 25, 1964; *The Service of the Missouri National Guard on the Mexican Border*, 125; Missouri Secretary of State, State Archives, Soldiers' Records, War of 1812-World War I, www.sos.mo.gov/archives/soldiers.

22. Earl "Scrub" Conley had a similar experience. A German fired at him but missed, so Conley brazenly climbed the parapet and "thumbed his nose in all directions." About 25 or 30 German machine gun shots followed, so Conley wisely climbed down. A sniper fired three times at Conley's comrade Carroll Baker, with the shots passing overhead. A trench mortar battery also opened up and he "happened to be in the way," but a "Good old dug-out" saved him. *Fort Scott* (KS) *Tribune and the Fort Scott Monitor*, September 27, 1918.

was maintaining five kitchens, two just in rear of the front lines, one at company headquarters, one with the reserve section at Camp Munier and the fifth back with the company motor train at Camp Picard. The only difficulty about supply was in the front line trenches, but the kitchens were near enough to the front that the food could be regularly carried forward in marmite cans to the combat groups. All of the kitchens burned charcoal instead of wood, endeavoring by the absence of smoke to conceal their location from the enemy.

The regular nightly work was on trench repair, varied in Corporal Taylor's section on the extreme left by putting out some additional barbed wire. All men took their turns at guard and at the regular guns, and the men for the harassing fire guns were picked by roster so that in due time all had taken their turns at the firing. The "stand-to" was the waiting in readiness each morning for a period before dawn until some time afterward.

By day the trenches were somnolent under the August sun, and the hours were devoted to sleep by those who needed it, and to a visiting of positions and checking of guns by company officers. By day too the soldiers familiarized themselves with the trench network, and a few men at a time visited neighboring combat squads.

At night this world came to life behind the wire gates of the combat groups. The machine guns—Hotchkiss, Maxim and St. Etienne—raised their voices, grenades and trench mortar projectiles crashed, flares rose, rifle shots were more frequent, and at times in an apparent exuberance of spirit someone down in the valley would empty a revolver. Despite the many old graves and the few fresh ones, the spirit at night in the Vosges at such periods was apparently not unlike that of an American Fourth of July.

An American trench mortar squad back of my Braunkopf position saw no reason why my machine guns should have all the fun. It began to lob over trench mortar projectiles from time to time during the night. I was in the Braunkopf GC the night they started and was quite startled by the sudden swoosh behind me where I didn't know there was anything. This drew some return trench mortar fire.

Back even with the battalion command post and half a mile or so south of it were two French machine guns "of position." They were

St. Etiennes which were regulation in the French Army in 1914 but which had been succeeded by the Hotchkiss in 1915. They were beautiful guns but of considerable complexity compared to the Hotchkiss. The French had a few of them stuck around in the mountains manned by crews which remained with them whoever was in the sector.[23]

On the evening of August 9 as the German gun began firing up the Fecht-bach valley, the two St. Etiennes suddenly cut in, firing some 200 rounds.

The German guns, unlike the American ones, used the same firing point each time, but because Braunkopf was lower and barren, and with no covered machine gun positions except the battle emplacements from which it was forbidden to fire save in case of an enemy attack, the Carthage guns did not reply. The French St. Etienne "guns of position," 1000 meters to the rear and well covered, had no similar limitations, and apparently had carefully figured out the German position, had measured the range from the map, and were waiting, finger on trigger. On the fourth evening of the Germans' shooting, the Maxim began its usual pop-pop-pop but had not fired more than 20 rounds when the angry rat-tat-tat of the St. Etiennes cut in, firing about 200 rounds. The German gun ceased fire abruptly at the beginning of the French blasts and for the next five evenings there was no enemy shooting from this position. Watching this incident with professional interest from the trenches on Braunkopf, Sergeant Willard Brown of the right section of Company A tucked it away in his memory and a couple of months later in another trench sector, as will be related in due time, silenced another German machine gun in the identical way.

The Germans did no more firing from that position that night, though the next evening both these guns and the French ones fired at intervals—stopping in time, however, to get to bed at a decent period—and this continued until I started a new innovation which I will later relate.

In the meanwhile I was irritated a little by daily reports of the sound of wheeled traffic entering Mühlbach at night from the east.

23. Designed as an improvement of the Hotchkiss gun, the Model 1907 Saint Etienne air-cooled machine gun was found to be inadequate for front-line use because mud often clogged the complicated operating mechanism. The gun saw limited use by American troops during the war as a training weapon. Canfield, *U.S. Infantry Weapons of the First World War*, 209–11.

This was closer than I had been firing to our own lines and rifle unit Chauchats—automatic rifles—had fire[d] at the sound a number of times in vain.

One evening a gun was laid by day on a bit of camouflaged road from which this sound seemed at night to emanate. When the sergeant in charge heard the sound that evening he fired a burst into the place and then distributed fire up and down the road.

According to the men on the forward slope of Altmatt Kopf, there was some shouting at the first burst and the noise of teams whipped to a gallop. Then this noise abruptly stopped after some of the succeeding bursts. I hoped that this was true, and the gun crew and others believed it most happily. In any event if the enemy came down in wagons to Mühlbach at night after that they did so more quietly as I recall no more reports of the sound being heard.[24]

During this period I prowled the trenches by day and carefully and long studied the enemy trenches through my binoculars to see what I could see. Nocturnal activities were well enough but we circulated about in our trenches by day, ration parties came and went, and all sorts of other things like that. Something the same must be going on in the enemy lines, even though his positions from our point of view appeared untenanted.

Running down the north slope of enemy-held Petit Braunkopf was what we came to call the "Y" trench because in shape it was like an invented "Y," one arm of which was the front hostile fire trench, as shown on the map and one a communications trench running directly north to the valley south of Mühlbach. Our position in Rospel Wald looked right into these trenches and presumably for that reason the tops of them had been covered with camouflage. Like most things up in this region, this camouflage had fallen into disrepair here and there.

Studying this trench for a prolonged period from the down timber which was all the shells had left of Rospel Wald, I saw now and then men in the enemy trench pass by these open places. The trenches were evidently used. They were in fact the

24. Schrantz believed that this was a German wagon train, located about 1,200 meters from the machine gun. One strip (24 rounds) was fired at the wagons. When the German drivers whipped the train into a gallop, the machine gun was aimed at a point in front of it, where it was sure to pass. When the noise reached that area, five more strips were unloaded. The noise then ceased. *Carthage* (MO) *Evening Press*, September 17, 1918.

obvious way for people to get from the hill down into the valley. And while we could see into them only here and there because of the camouflage our bullets could strike into them anywhere. As for firing positions, the down timber of Rospel Wald offered numerous concealed ones, and firing through a wet gunny sack suspended in front of the gun, as we did at night, would conceal the flash from the hostile hills. And not only the "Y" trench could be annoyed but we could comb out the enemy woods on the hills a bit. Accordingly I submitted to Major Stepp on August 8 the following formal request:

> "1. Permission is requested to install a 'gun of opportunity' in the woods on the eastern slope of Altmatt Kopf beginning on the morning of August 9. This gun is the same one used for harassing fire in Rospel Wald at night. It will work in shell craters and abandoned trenches in the wood, will fire at any target in the enemy lines which may present itself and will from time to time harass likely targets in the enemy lines, particularly the woods on Krahenberg and Engel Berg and the 'Y' trench on Petit Braunkopf.
>
> "2. It is believed that this gun can make the 'Y' trench untenable for the enemy. Short bursts will be fired into it at intervals during the day."

With this I submitted my daily schedule calling for not only the usual night firing but the daylight firing as well. The daylight schedule was as follows, the word "strips" referring to the metallic strips of 30 rounds each with which this type of machine gun was fed.

"9:30 a.m.	3 strips rapid traversing edge of Engelberg woods.
	3 strips traversing Krahenberg wood
10:30	4 strips searching 'Y' trench, bursts of 10.
11:15	2 strips searching 'Y' trench, bursts of 10.
12:00	4 strips in Krahenberg woods, traverse and search
2:10 p.m.	3 strips traversing Engelberg woods
2:20	1 strip searching 'Y' trench—bursts of 5
2:40	same as 2:20
3:05	2 strips 'fanning' Engelberg woods
4:00	1 strip searching 'Y' trench, bursts of 5
4:30	2 strips fanning Engelberg woods.

Note: This gun will also fire on any target that may present itself."

Major Stepp approved this and the next morning the gun went to work.

This was good practice. The men could see what they were trying to hit and could lay the gun with the tangent sight instead of the spirit level or quadrant as in night firing. Good work and most enjoyable for all hands.

But the enemy did not at all like this breach of custom, it would appear. Or it may be that he was just in bad humor that night and felt called on to show his nasty disposition.

Before dark that evening the enemy trench mortar bombs—"flying pigs"—were squealing over and exploding angrily on Altmatt Kopf and these increased after dark. That night for the first time the fire of our harassing guns was interfered with.

Sergeant Fred Clark of the second platoon had brought his section down from reserve to relieve the other 2nd platoon section at Porte d'Alsace—this was done to assure equal training for both—so it was the newcomers who caught the brunt of this unpleasantness. The projectiles kept the squad shifting from one shell hole to another to avoid it, but in time Corporal John Gouty—a gallant soldier who later lost a leg in the Meuse-Argonne—properly felt impelled to cease fire altogether and shelter his men in a dug-out.[25] One of the bombs, or perhaps an artillery projectile, exploded in the trenches of Sergeant Charles Edward's section, doing no damage except shattering some plank revetment.

Angry machine gun fire swept Braunkopf too while my gun there was firing that night but did not interfere.

Either in the "Y" trench or on the hillside above we apparently had touched a sensitive spot. Most gratifying, in view especially of the fact that we had had no casualties.

On the whole I was highly pleased and the next morning my gun in the shattered woodland renewed its wholesome efforts.

But already Major Stepp at his command post was receiving complaints from the angry French.

25. Fred Clark enlisted in Company A, 2nd Missouri Infantry as a private in June 1916, and served with the company on the Mexican border until early 1917. *The Service of the Missouri National Guard on the Mexican Border*, 122. John Charles Gouty, born on November 24, 1891, served overseas with Company A from April 25, 1918, until November 24, 1918, and was severely wounded. He died on May 10, 1957, and was buried in Calvary Cemetery in St. Louis, Missouri. Missouri Secretary of State, State Archives, Soldiers' Records, War of 1812–World War I, www.sos.mo.gov/archives/soldiers.

Our 35th Division artillery had not yet come into the line and we were supported entirely by French guns. They had an observation post up on the top of Altmatt Kopf. The Germans knew where it was, they told Major Stepp—or so I later was told. They could knock it out any time they wished. This day machine gun fire from Rospel Wald by day should cease. That seems to have been the tenor of it. Most, or maybe all of that day's firing was gotten in before I received and relayed to the front Major Stepp's order to stop it. But that was the last time we tickled up the "Y" trench.

By shifting positions to considerably distant from where the firing had been in the day, our Rospel Wald gun got in its schedule very well that night, but some 40 trench mortar or artillery projectiles plastered the front of Altmatt Kopf during the hours of darkness and the machine gun fire on Braunkopf was again heavier—though just as harmless as before. One enemy shell, or mortar maybe, did fall within our GC Braunkopf that night, tearing out some trench revetment but injuring nobody.

A sizeable little war broke out about 11:30 that night a few miles to the south of us [August 10, 1918]. First enemy Maxims, then rising rockets of various colors, and the chatter of Hotchkiss machine guns, and the thunder of both American and German artillery barrages coming down. We supposed it a raid and was interested because our B Company was up there. In point of fact all of Company B's guns actually were blazing away from their battle positions at that time, we later learned. But according to the division intelligence report the next day it was all started by one of the hostile patrols coming over to our wire and opening up with three light machine guns on a rifle company GC. It was lucky if it ever returned home again. But B Company got a great thrill out of the affair and burned up a lot of ammunition.

Five green rockets arched through the air in the zone of tumult—and under the new code of American pyrotechnic signals just promulgated, a green rocket mean poison gas. There had as yet been no gas used in the district since the Americans entered the trenches and the green rocket caused instant alertness all along the front. From Company A's positions, however, the front line was fairly well defined and the rockets were seen to be from within German territory, and hence obviously having no connection with the American gas alarm signal.

The heavy firing continued for almost an hour, then died down. If the Germans planned to raid, as the nature of their fire indicated, the American counter barrage shot the attempt to pieces before it got well started as the intelligence report the next day showed that nowhere in that section had any enemy attempt at advance been noted, though farther north nearer Braunkopf an enemy patrol had taken advantage of the noise to try in vain to penetrate into the American trenches.

This noise to the south stirred up more or less activity all along the line, and the screech and crash of artillery projectiles, and the squeal and explosion of trench mortar bombs, frequently sent the Carthage soldiers crouching below their parapets. The intelligence report the next day estimated that 40 hostile shells struck Altmatt Kopf within an hour and that during the night 150 trench mortar projectiles fell in the general area Altmatt Kopf-Braunkopf-Metzeral.

While the 128th Machine Gun Battalion—the divisional machine gun battalion of the 35th Division—was in the trenches in the Vosges mountains in Alsace in August, 1918, the machine gun companies of the 139th and 140th Infantry regiments were in division reserve back at Ventron, a duty for which companies with animal-drawn vehicles were not entirely suitable on account of the time it would take them to reinforce any threatened point. Therefore the men of the 128th knew that it would not be long until they would be in the rear again, standing by with their motor equipment for any emergency. Thus they tried to absorb on the front all the war atmosphere possible, knowing that their tour in the trenches would be short.

Company A of Carthage on the hills of Braunkopf and Altmatt Kopf continued its nightly harassing fire down the valley of the Fecht up which the Germans brought their supplies to the front. In addition to the fire on the villages of Breitenbach, Sendenbach, Tiefenbach, Eckersberg, Heibel, Unterwida and Oberwida and the roads connecting them, and the woods surrounding them, fire was several times placed on the village of Lutenbach, 3,200 meters distant but well within the killing range of the boat-tailed copper bullets of the Hotchkiss machine guns. This was the longest range at which the Carthage gunners fired during the war.

Members of the 129th Machine Gun Battalion, August 30, 1918 (*National Archives*)

Though daylight firing from Altmatt Kopf—except in the unlikely event of an enemy attack—was now forbidden, Major Stepp gave permission to use a harassing gun by day from Braunkopf. We could not hit the "Y" trench from there and the gun would be a long way from the French artillery observation post.

But Braunkopf was a barren hill and while liberally furrowed with old trenches and pockmarked with shell holes very convenient in night firing, firing by day from any of them would have been distinctly unhealthful. The enemy-held Engelberg looked right down onto the top of Braunkopf at a range of 1700 or 1800 meters. The guns in battle positions were dug in and screened but a gun set up anywhere else to fire would have been visible indeed.

Lieut. Frank L. Snyder in charge of the Braunkopf guns studied hard and prowled long in an effort to find a reasonably safe daylight firing position. No use. Finally he figured that from a certain deep trench on the forward slope he could tunnel out a galley, poke the nose of the gun through the side of the hill and fire from there. This sounded logical, the more so since he had some former miners in his platoon. The tunnel was dug accordingly and the gun set up to fire. But alas for the effort. His ex-miners apparently had had no practice in timbering.

Rat-tat-tat-tat, rat-tat-tat-tat, rat-tat-tat-tat, the gun started out bravely—and then silence prevailed and kept on prevailing in that spot. The hole had caved in. Snyder, deeply chagrined, pulled out his men and gun, dirty but undamaged. Some lively moments followed while the sputtering and disgusted machine gun men and their hardly-warm gun were rescued from their dangerous predicament. The work of rescue was successfully accomplished, however, and if the Germans saw the commotion they at least did not render the situation any worse by shooting at it. He forthwith began to plot and soon began to delve on a new tunnel which would be properly timbered, but we were relieved from the sector before it was completed.

But the night firing went on, and there were plenty of other activities by day.

Lieut. Dunn, my executive and I, took turns in touring the trenches and staying overnight in forward positions. Trenches and shelters were improved where practicable. I had emplacements constructed at a suitable position northeast of PC Benoit for my reserve section at Camp Munier to use if an attack should submerge the front line and the Germans come around to the back side of Altmatt Kopf.

And on one lone occasion I tried my hand at sniping.

The men in Porte d'Alsace GC had discovered what appeared to be an enemy observation post near the foot of Petit Braunkopf. There was an aperture which showed daylight behind it at times. At other times it would be partially blocked out by what appeared a man's head and shoulders. Sergeant Fred Clark, the section chief was telling me about it one day as we went along the trench from Porte d'Alsace toward GC Rospel.

I stood on the fire step and studied the place with my glasses. Sure enough, the place seemed to be as described. Sergeant Clark was carrying a French carbine he had picked up somewhere.

"You watch the place with the glasses while I see if I can make him duck," I said.

He handed me the carbine and took my binoculars. I sighted the weapon hopefully and pulled the trigger.

"He heard the bullet. He's ducked," said the sergeant.

But I was gazing with chagrin at the little cloud of dust drifting from the front part of the parapet from where I had fired. The carbine was short and the muzzle did not reach across it. The muzzle blast of the piece had raised a little dust cloud to show exactly from where the shot had been fired.

"Let's go down a couple of trench bays and see what happens," I told the grinning sergeant.

We did so and watched the opposite hill. Almost immediately there came the crack of a bullet somewhere across the region of the place from which we had fired, and then the sound of a shot from the direction of the enemy. The enemy sniper fired several more times in lazy fashion at the spot where the little dust cloud had been and then doubtless returned to his siesta.

One platoon of Company I, 1st Lieut. Gilfoyle[,] held the Kiosque and both the lieutenant and Capt. Alexander M. Ellet, the Chillicothe, Mo., man who commanded the company, were worried.[26] Not only was there a frequent heaving of hand grenades and the annoyance of rifle grenades there, as previously mentioned, but they thought that they heard the sound of a mine gallery being driven beneath them. I had talked to both of them about it—but there was nothing a machine gunner could do.

New earth appearing one morning in enemy territory showed that the Germans had started work at night on a communication trench near the front line despite the American machine gun bullets which passed over the position nightly directed at more

26. Matthew Guilfoyle, born in Kansas on October 27, 1893, became a first lieutenant in the 3rd Kansas Infantry in July 1917. Appointed a first lieutenant in the 139th Infantry that October, Guilfoyle led his platoon of Company I "with spirit and determination" against German machine gun nests near Charpentry at the start of the Meuse-Argonne Offensive. He subsequently assumed command of the company and led it in the capture of Charpentry. On September 29, when all officers senior to him had become casualties, Guilfoyle assumed command of the battalion. Promoted to captain in October 1918, he was honorably discharged in May 1919. He died in Abilene, Kansas, on October 22, 1955. Clair Kenamore, *The Story of the 139th Infantry* (St. Louis: Guard Publishing Co., 1920), 50; Kansas Adjutant General's Office, *Roster and Directory of the Commissioned Officers of the Kansas National Guard* (Topeka: Kansas State Printing Plant, 1919), 44. Alexander Morris Ellett was born on September 9, 1886. He was commissioned captain of Company F, 4th Missouri Infantry in 1915 and led the company on the Mexican border from June 1916 to February 1917. He commanded Company I, 139th U.S. infantry in France (overseas beginning April 25, 1918) and at the time of his death had done "excellent work in rounding the company into shape." He died on August 7, 1918, and was buried in the Meuse-Argonne Cemetery at Romagne, France. Clair Kenamore, *The Story of the 139th Infantry*, 19; *The Service of the Missouri National Guard on the Mexican Border*, 372; Missouri Secretary of State, State Archives, Soldiers' Records, War of 1812-World War I, www.sos.mo.gov/archives/soldiers.

distant points. I figured out [a] position for a gun which would enfilade it.

The night after this new earth was noticed, the Roespel Wald gun fired for a time on its usual distant targets, then switched onto the fresh trench. The gun crew asserted that following the burst there was some shrilling of whistles in the vicinity of the point of bullet-strike and deducted therefrom that they had scored. Their comrades lifted their eyebrows, however at the assumption that a whistle blast necessarily implied any German casualties, and the matter rested there. I hoped they were right. In any event the Germans stopped digging at that point and no fresh earth was seen there afterwards.

One day Captain Ellet had been conferring with Major Stepp about it and later had started back to his company position. He had been on Kiosque a short time before and instead of a canteen in the canteen cover on his belt he carried a number of grenades—one or more of the "citron" variety, an old-style French type which was plentiful in the Vosges trenches.[27] This lemon-shaped missile did not have a lever and pin like the later types but instead had a sort of screw protruding from its neck. It was started to fusing and spitting fire by striking this screw on a rock or helmet. It was thrown in the four or five seconds which elapsed from that until the time it was thrown [*sic:* exploded]. The screw was protected against being accidentally driven in by a cylindrical tin cap.

I was in my shelter on the hillside at this time and heard an explosion a short distance below. A shell burst, I thought, and paid no attention. Then someone came running and calling for Lieut. Rhode, the battalion surgeon, who was next to me. The call was repeated urgently.[28]

"Keep your shirt on. I'm coming," replied the man of medicine getting into some clothes, and then finished his dressing en route when he realized that the voice was that of Major Stepp himself. But no one had been injured by a shell blast as we expected.

27. Probably the French Model C.F. (Citron Foug) grenade, a cast iron grenade with a metal primer. Adrien Gay, *Grenade Warfare* (Atlanta, GA: E.W. Allen & Co., 1918), 59–60.

28. Paul C. Rohde was a first lieutenant in the 139th Infantry's Sanitary Detachment. He was born in Michigan on June 7, 1886, graduated from Wayne State University Medical School in 1915, and was promoted to captain by the end of World War I. He died in Detroit, Michigan, on September 16, 1972. *Detroit Free Press*, September 17, 1972; Kenamore, *The Story of the 139th Infantry*, 152.

Going down the steep hill Captain Ellet had slipped on a muddy spot, sat down or fell on his canteen cover, drove in the tin cap of a citron grenade and the missile had exploded. He died on his way to Mittlach in an ambulance.

Two nights later there was another accident with a grenade, this time back up Sillikarkopf at Camp Munier where Co. M, 139th Infantry—along with my second platoon (less one section)—was stationed. In one of the rifle company's shelters, for M was a rifle company in World War I, someone accidentally pulled a pin from a grenade and dropped it. Six men were wounded, one fatally according to my notes. The injured were brought down to Lieut. Rhode at his aid station from which I was separated only by a thin wall. He had more help than he could use. I could only listen and suffer mentally as his patients suffered physically.

The sound of German digging underneath the American position on the hill Kiosque had by now stirred such fear of a possible mine explosion, that the French artillery was persuaded to take a hand. The concern of Major Stepp about his platoon on the Kiosque finally brought about an arrangement with the French artillery to react against the German aggression in the form of digging underneath that knoll. One evening I learned that the next noon that Company I platoon there would be withdrawn and at 2:30 p.m. the French artillery would smite the German trenches thereon in and thereabouts in wrath, possibly dropping a shell or two in the American trenches by accident since the lines were so close together. It behooved the embattled defenders of the grenade-pestered hill, therefore, to be well back down the slope when the fireworks started.

I, and most everybody else who could spare the time, had binoculars—or at least eyes—glued on the Kiosque as the hour approached. Not being familiar with the ways of artillery I expected the calm afternoon to be broken suddenly by a terrific concentration of gun fire. Not so.

A shell exploded in a trench over the crest of the hill where the Germans were presumed to be. Then a slow steady series. The French were making a slow and deliberate artillery practice of it. The shooting continued unexcitedly during the afternoon. Occasionally a shell fell within the American position. Most of them went over and burst behind. And the communication trench leading down from Petit Braunkopf and up to the German side of the Kiosque was thoroughly searched. No German guns replied. It seemed that the enemy artillerymen knew their side had been breaking the rules this time and so had no cause to become angry about the matter. This display of artillery work was very interesting to the machine gunners, but not particularly helpful to the riflemen inasmuch as the German digging under the hill was promptly resumed and was still in progress when Company A left the sector. Yet so far as I know no mine was ever exploded there, and if it had been done while the 35th Division was in the line I would have heard.[29]

Along toward evening the fire subsided and by that time there must have been a good deal of work for trench repair parties to do, and, I was told, as the artillery ceased at the appointed time the Company I men climbed back up to the top of their knoll again through the trenches before some German should come nosing over. And I have no doubt that they tossed over a few grenades to remind the enemy that they were there.

As for the war, it had eased up a bit after we ceased annoying the "Y" trench by day. The enemy reaction that had stirred up caused the French commanders to direct the two French St. Etienne machine guns to stop their harassing fire. No longer did their bullets crack above Braunkopf in the twilight.

29. Schrantz recounted his company's attempt to counter German tunneling efforts: "Daylight firing from Altmatt Kopf had been forbidden on account of the protests of the French observation stations on that hill but permission had been given to use daylight fire from bare and battered, enemy-overlooked Braunkopf—if a safe place from which to fire could be obtained. This was not easy, for the only covered machine guns emplacements on the hill were the battle emplacements, which were not to reveal their location by fire except in case of enemy attack. However a company of men containing a good many southwest Missouri miners was not to be daunted by this situation, and under the supervision of Sergeant Willard Brown a tunneling project was started from a forward trench. The plan was to tunnel downward and outward until emerging from the hill, then thrust the nose of the gun through the opening so made and thus fire from a safe and concealed position.

"Work on the tunnel was pressed vigorously, the dirt being carried away from the scene of excavation and scattered so as not to betray the fact that new work was in progress. Finally the emplacement was ready, and the nose of the Hotchkiss was thrust out the hole, aimed at the selected target and the gunner pressed the trigger."

When the vibration of the firing gun caused the emplacement to cave in, "some lively moments followed while the sputtering and disgusted machine gun men and their hardly-warm gun were rescued from their dangerous predicament. The work of rescue was successfully accomplished, however, and if the Germans saw the commotion they at least did not render the situation any worse by shooting at it. Work on a new gallery was started at once by Sergeant Brown but the company was relieved before this second attempt was completed."

And the Germans, after the French-German custom of 1918 in the mountains, ceased in turn their evening firing up the Frecht-bach.[30]

Up to this time—or during the period my company was in the line—the 70th Infantry Brigade of the 35th Division was holding what was known as the Fecht sector, the left [of] which was at Rospel Wald, and the 69th Brigade, which had been in the Fecht sector earlier, was back in reserve somewhere. Then on August 14 the 69th Brigade came into the Gerardmer sector to the left of the Fecht sector, thus doubling the division front. This involved the moving of division headquarters from Ventron to the town of Gerardmer and since both brigades were now in the trenches it necessitated the return of the division machine gun battalion to the reserve and to division headquarters control.

So it was that on August 12 there came an order for the machine gun companies of the 139th and 140th Infantry regiments to return from Ventron to their old trenches, the former relieving my company in the Benoit sector and the latter Captain Corey's company in the Hilsenfirst region.

The relief was made in the same manner as when we had entered the trenches. On the night of August 14 the machine guns of the regimental company came up the valley by pack mule as before. The reserve section at Camp Munier was relieved at dusk and went back over the hill to Camp Picard. Soon after dark Lieut. Wood and his men came sliding down the hill to PC Benoit and Wood and I waited in the command post until word would come that the relief was complete.

By the very nature of things it was an anxious time. If the enemy knew a relief was being made he might shell the communication trenches and cause us trouble—casualties perhaps. Men in position, lying quiet or sheltered in dug-outs, were usually not in great danger during a light bombardment. While moving through the communication trenches likely to be heavily shelled, they were

30. First Lieutenant William O. Jackson of the 128th Machine Gun Battalion inspected Braunkopf on the night of August 10 and 11th. Jackson reported that the trenches and dugouts were in poor condition due to long use, but that the men were constantly at work repairing the sector and had made many improvements. During the day, two men were on watch at each machine gun emplacement, and from dark to daylight the entire crew was "standing to." 8–11 memo regarding inspection, Folder: 128th MG BATL G-3 Inspection 235-37, Record Group 120, Records of the American Expeditionary Forces, World War I, Entry NM-91 1241, Records of Combat Divisions, 1917–1919, Box 16, 35th Division, NARA.

more vulnerable, and therefore a relief always carried with it a certain amount of anxiety.

The night at first was a calm one, just the usual fireworks and sporadic firing at the front but without the usual chatter of my harassing guns. Maybe this would be a giveaway. For once I wanted the enemy to be peaceful—quite peaceful.

Then enemy shells began to drop off to the right somewhere—too far to the right to injure my men. Then about 11 o'clock shells started exploding forward and to the left. They sounded fairly close in, though we could see no flash of explosions, and both Wood and I feared that they might be falling in the communication trenches our third platoons would be traveling. This shelling in that region continued for a couple of hours or so.

Some time after 1 o'clock came a message from Lieut. Snyder saying that the relief of the 1st platoon and of the section of the second at Porte d'Alsace was completed at 12:12. Fine. These men were now on their way up the Fecht-Bach toward Mittlach. But what of Lieut. Samuels and the third platoon. It was about that one I was worrying. About a half hour later came a message from Samuels. Relief completed at 12:12. The shelling, the runner said, had been off to the left farther. No casualties. I breathed a deep sigh of relief. Good work.

I bade good night to Lieutenant Wood and with my headquarters section slid forward down the slippery path to the valley back of Braunkopf, then down this to the Fecht-Bach valley, then up this valley on what was called the ration route. Some machine guns of Company C, 130th Machine Gun Battalion, were chattering away in harassing fire from Geisbodle south of Metzeral. An occasional crack of bullets from the German lines passed high over our heads occasionally.

On our left, in some pine woods, we passed a military cemetery in which some shells had apparently fallen, for the odor of decaying flesh was strong. Then through the shattered village of Steinabrück, then Mittlach and so to Camp Picard some time before dawn. There I unrolled my bedding roll—returned by pack mule—among the rocks of "the feather bed" and went to sleep thankfully.[31]

31. Sgt. Norval Hopwood remarked that no matter how serious the situation or how tired the men were, "somebody always has some humorous remark to make. Imagine a worn and tired company after a hard day's travel, and a 'snooping' Yank, who finds himself a big soft mattress to sleep on and then puts rocks in it, 'just to make it feel natural.'" *Carthage* (MO) *Evening Press*, August 7, 1918.

When I awoke it was broad day and in the flat part of the valley, a bit away from the rocky hillside, the cooks were serving breakfast as candidates appeared, the sleepers being left to rouse of their own accord.

Breakfast to a soldier is an important thing at any time—but the morning gathering for mess of Company A, 128th Machine Gun Battalion, at Camp Picard, south of Mittlach, Alsace, August 15, 1918, was more than just a breakfast. It was a reunion as well, since most of the sections of the company had been separated from each other for two weeks while in the trenches, and had come back to this central point at varying times during the hours of darkness the night preceding.

It was an enjoyable breakfast that for me, despite the brevity of the sleep which had preceded it. The company officers had all assembled and it was nice to have them together again, and the tongues of the men were clacking merrily and busily as they exchanged reminiscences, and doubtless tall tales, of their adventures and doings while they had been separated. Even the rear echelon which remained at Camp Picard had stories to tell of shellings of Mittlach and the Camp Picard region or of adventures on their road to and from the trenches on the ration route. Then too most of the men who had been stationed at Camp Picard had at some time managed to get into the trenches on some pretext or other, so the men of the gun sections did not have the field entirely to themselves.

There was talk too of battalion headquarters near the brigade command post on the hill—or mountain—to the front, where Major Halliburton and his staff had experienced more than one lively shelling by the hostile artillery. And before long there was news of B Company too. Like A company it had finished its tour of duty without casualties but—a less pleasant note—the Machine Gun Company, 140th Infantry, had had a couple of men killed on the road upon the hill the night before as it moved toward the trenches to relieve Company B. Our own route that night, I knew, would lie over that same road, for orders called for us to move to Kruth by way of Bussat and the Drehkopf instead of over the mountain west of us by the Col de Huss route by means of which we had entered the sector.

That day the men's packs and officers baggage were sent up by cable to Bussat at the top of the hill, there to be continued on by the same route down to the cable station at Holsplatz at the foot of the slope near Kruth.

To get to the rear this time we first would go forward, up—and a long way up—to Bussat over a road where shell fire was not at all uncommon. The marching portion of the company was to start in late afternoon and the Ford gun trucks at dark.

As the shadows grew long, but even before the sun had dropped behind the Forêt de Herrenberg which cloaked the huge hill which towered to the west of us, I started off at the head of the marching section with the company strung out behind. The march was in column of twos with great gaps between sections and still greater ones between platoons to lessen the danger of losses by shell fire should there chance to be any. Once, soon after the climb started and while the valley behind us was already in shadow though the sun still shone on the tops of the hills above, there came the drone of an airplane engine. I halted the column and it shrunk to the trees at the side of the road while the distant machine, the tiny Maltese crosses visible on its wings in the upper sunlight, kept a straight course westward while our anti-aircraft guns placed futile blotches of shrapnel smoke about it.

Then the march was resumed, the column climbing upward with straining lungs, zig-zagging back and forth on the white road toward the summit while the darkness climbed up the side of the mountains. Halts were frequent but it was a rather weary organization that finally reached the hilltops and turned southward on the road along the crest, in darkness now, and soon after the column of gun trucks had struggled by us.

The crest of the ridge over which we were now passing was the principal danger stretch as it was a favorite target of enemy guns. The road first passed by some well-sheltered command posts then out on an open prairie with barbed-wire entanglements to the left of the route. It was here, we understood, that the men of the 140th had been killed. However it was a peaceful stretch for us, there being no enemy fire and the only persons seen being a few military pedestrians and once a drunken American soldier riding along [on] horseback, muttering and waving his pistol.

Then we were on the downhill slope of Drehkopf headed westward on the zig-zagging route. Half way down in the deep pine woods there was a welcome stop at a Red Cross station where hot chocolate was served.

Although such incidents were rather well advertised in the papers back home, they were something new for the Carthage soldiers and the kind invitation was accepted with alacrity.

And in due time we reached the bottom of the hill, sorted out the packs at Holzplatz [*sic*] and then to the woods north of Kruth where we had been before and where Company B was already slumbering—a wholesome occupation and which we quickly joined. It was already August 16 by a considerable margin.

In the morning the talk was both of the experiences of the past and the new station to which the battalion was to move. The 35th Division in addition to the Fecht sub-sector which it already held, was to take over the Gerardmer sub-sector which adjoined the Fecht sub-sector on the north. As a result division headquarters were being moved to the city of Gerardmer and there the 128th Machine Gun Battalion was to go also. That afternoon the marching portion of the 128th Machine Gun Battalion loaded into trucks on a street in Kruth and these trucks followed the guns trucks and other motor vehicles belonging to the 128th northward from the town.

The route led up the valley of the Thur, past several villages as the woods and hills closed in on the stream, then northwestward in wide zig-zags up a mountain and across the old frontier into France through a pass marked on the map as the Col de Bramont, then down again. Behind the streams had all flowed ultimately into the Rhine. Those seen now were headed in the other direction toward the Moselle. Down into a little French valley running into the valley of the Moselotte, the column rolled, then up this stream to the northeast, next jogged sharply to the northwest across another great ridge at the Col de la Grosse Pierre, thence downward and northward on a well traveled road at the foot of which a large blue lake soon gleamed.

The road now veered to the eastward around the hill near the shore of the lake. Garish houses appeared, all the earmarks of a resort town, then the route led into a solid-built little French city. This was Gerardmer, named, one discovered later, from Gerard of Alsace, first duke of Lorraine, who in the 11th century built a tower on this lake.

While Gerardmer in the French Vosges was not much of a city as cities go, it having only about 4,000 people in the town proper and some 12,000 in the commune, it was more of a city than any in which Company A, 128th Machine Gun Battalion had been stationed for some months, and for a time town life was something of a novelty.

Here there was even a picture show, and one Carthage soldier wrote home that he had seen "Quo Vadis," adding that it was "the very same picture except for the titles that was shown at the Shotoall theater at home three years or so ago." Then there was a bathing beach at the lake at the western edge of the town, and the stores in the business district were large enough that the machine gunners could stock up on many long needed articles not obtainable in villages.[32]

In the main street of the town of about 4,000 people the main truck column halted, the men scrambled out, formed in column and were marched to the south up a paved street ending in huge, steel-barred gates now swinging wide. On either side of the base of the arch which supported them were French sentries in horizon blue, their long bayonets glittering on their rifles. Above the entrance was the sign "Caserne Kleber." The 128th was to be billeted in old French peacetime military barracks. Inside the gates of the post the street widened out into large courts about which sat many large barracks.

Having seen my company into huge barnlike rooms on the second floor of brick barracks, I was taken to my own quarters in town which the billeting officer had selected for me. "In town" is not strictly correct, for although the houses were more or less continuous, a mile-stone at a road-crossing a short distance east of the one in which I was lodged bore this inscription: "Gerardmer, 1 kilometre." This was a bit far from my unit but with a town full of headquarters of one kind or another the billeting officer could not have done much better.

As for the billet itself, it was all heart could desire. There was a nice ground-floor bedroom with entrance to the street, after a few feet of fenced front yard. A nice old couple lived there with a six

32. Carroll Baker of Company A reported to his sister on August 28, 1918, that a large Y.M.C.A. facility there sold "shockolat" (cocoa), and with the large lake to swim in, he was "feeling as fine as a split frog hair." *Fort Scott* (KS) *Tribune and the Fort Scott Monitor*, September 27, 1918.

or seven-year-old granddaughter with a shy manner, sores on her face and the name of Yvonne. We became good friends and when I left I presented her with a set of captain's bars. Her father—the old couple's son—was off in the French Army somewhere. A not unusual tragedy of war occurred while I was here. One day I found the old woman in tears. They had just received official word that he was "missing in action."

Gerardmer was a pleasant place, with a park suitable for limited instruction at the head of the lake, while there was abundant training room on steep, pine-covered hills all about the town. A lovely spot this and quite suitable for training in mountain warfare, though we hoped and expected soon to move to a more active sphere of operations and leave the mountains, beautiful as they were, behind us.

Yet it was not as far from the fighting front as the general tranquility of the town might indicate.

The first morning the Carthage soldiers were in town—August 17, 1918,—there was the distant thunder of a furious cannonade off to the northeast where some 18 or 20 miles away the 6th U.S. Infantry of the 5th American Division was wresting the village of Frapelle, east of St. Die, from the enemy. Then too, a still grimmer note of the front was a French military hospital down by

Gerardmer (*Jasper County Records Center*)

the park which fronted the lake shore, and from which artillery caissons sometimes as often as several times a day bore troop-escorted caskets covered with the tri-color of France."

In these early days of Company A's stay at Gerardmer the enemy air service was fairly active, sometimes as many as four or five enemy observing planes being over every day. Anti-aircraft guns speckled the sky about them with shrapnel and usually kept the machines well up in the air, while in the park, by the railway yards, and at various other places about the town, French machine gunners stood alert by posts on which were mounted Hotchkiss guns for anti-aircraft fire, waiting ready in case the hostile craft should come within machine gun range.

That all the German visits from the air were not equally harmless was attested by an occasional ruined building and by houses scarred by flying fragments of jagged steel from aerial bombs. The barracks in which the Carthage soldiers, along with many other troops, were quartered would seem to have been a logical target for air attack though there were no signs that they had been made such. A possible explanation of this might be that one building in the barracks was the post hospital and that behind this, worked on the ground in stone and brick was a huge red cross. Presumably the French meant this to protect only the one building but a German aviator would probably interpret it as meaning that the entire barracks was used as a hospital. If this were, as the Carthage soldiers believed, a misuse of the symbol of the Geneva Convention, it was one which was on the conscience of the French and not the American army; and indeed it might have been unseemly for the Americans to complain very loudly about any artifice which might be daily protecting their lives.

From time to time we could hear the thunder of artillery to the northeast of us, and we heard a great deal of talk about how thin the lines were up there. The enemy, it was said, could come through any time he wanted to concentrate force enough there and pay the price of forcing the trench lines.

On the night of August 20 there was an air raid alarm in Gerardmer. About 11 p.m. there came a hum of German airplanes, and such of the soldiers as were asleep were speedily wakened by the roar of the anti-aircraft artillery and the rat-tat-tat of the anti-aircraft machine guns. In the barracks there was little to do save to stay under cover and out of sight, but in the town the citizenry was taking to the cellars and bomb proofs with a clatter of wooden shoes on stairways and a wailing [of] frightened children which might have led anyone to think that the ground forces of the enemy were on the town. However disturbing air raids were to the populace in general they were still new to the Americans and still interesting to the French small boys, with the result that all over the town adult America and juvenile male France were out-of-doors staring skyward as the German planes darted down and dropped flares about the railway station, while searchlight beams stabbed the sky, and while the cannon and machine guns made noisy protests against the hostile visit. No bombs were dropped, the object of the expedition apparently having been to see if troop movements were in progress. About 4 p.m. [a.m.] the next morning the whole performance was repeated and with no more serious results.

After this the Germans seemed less interested in Gerardmer and at times there would be two days together without sight of an enemy plane.

This led me to an experience of pseudo-excitement one night which amused me at the time and remains clearly in my memory.

On that occasion I was awakened from a sound slumber by the old French woman rushing into my room and shrieking at me.

"Les Boches, les boches," she shrilled, "Viennent les Allemands," or better French to the same effect.

There meanwhile was a tremendous clatter on the stair, and the crying of children, as the citizenry from the floor above, wearing wooden shoes, raced down to ground level. And above the sound of frightened feminine voices came the crash of artillery in action somewhere not too far away. "Merci beaucoup," I told the old woman most heartily as I blinked about. Nothing like having a word of warning. Would be bad indeed to be caught asleep. She disappeared and as I struggled into my clothes, still probably only three-fourths awake, there came the familiar rat-tat-tat of Hotchkiss machine gun fire.

The enemy has broken through just like they said, I reflected. But nothing except cavalry could have gotten this far. I listened for the sound of horses' hoofs in the street. Fully dressed, I belted on my pistol, slung my gas mask, tied it at alert position and started for the door.

I would try the front first and if the street was clear would join my company by the most direct route. If the German horsemen came before I got out the front door, I would duck out the back and go down the railway track, shooting my way through if necessary.

In the meanwhile the old woman stuck her head into the room again, shouting about the Boches and wanting me to follow her. I shook my head. I was going to try the street first. If that way was blocked, time enough to get away out the back and down toward the town.

But just as I reached the door I had a thought for the first time, then a conviction.

Enemy planes!

I tossed my pistol and gas mask on the bed in disgust and went out the front door, joining a French small boy in staring up at the sky.

The old lady had been trying to get me to go to some shelter in rear or in the basement somewhere. They had had airplanes before. I had seen the deep scars on the front of the building from where a bomb had burst in the street.

This time there had been no bombs. The planes had circled over the railway yards and dropped flares, then, having had a good look, departed under machine gun and anti-aircraft gun fire.

Rather sheepishly—quite sheepishly in fact—I turned back to my room when the firing had subsided.

The old lady met me there.

"Pas de peu de boches?" she demanded.

"Pas de peu de avion," I replied.

She shook her head wonderingly and departed.

Soon I was asleep again, thinking as I dozed away of the battle I had imagined and missed. Mighty fine of the old woman though to keep trying to drag me to safety instead of getting into safety herself.

During the time we were at Gerardmer, the regulation cal. 45 automatic pistols were issued to the unit, replacing the .45 cal. revolvers which had been issued to it before leaving the States. There being an abundance of ammunition there was a good deal of pistol practice here with the automatic—first at a sand-pit below the Gerardmer lake and later at a French range nearer to town.[33] For the rest there was such other training as we could do, and wandering, on foot or by Ford, over the surrounding hills, including up the road toward the Col de la Schlucht which was the mountain pass leading to the front—a route along which there was a beautiful chain of smaller lakes.

Then too, despite handicaps, there was an occasional trip outside the town in the Fords and heavier trucks for a maneuver, and once a jaunt of some distance eastward up toward the lofty Col du Schlucht which led through the mountains toward the recently occupied 35th Division front. This latter trip was a visit to a delousing station, though as yet the much advertised cooties had gotten no great hold in the Carthage company, but the lowly purpose of the visit did not detract from the beauty of the scenery, marked particularly by the chain of silver lakes upon which one looked down from the heights.

By the latter part of August the dullness was relieved by rumors of a move "in the right direction," letters home said; and a reminder that fall was at hand was given by a period of cool and somewhat rainy weather during which the clouds came half-way down the hills above the town. Then the move rumors increased, and as new American troops made their appearance in the town these changed to certainty.

Headquarters of the 6th U.S. Division moved into the town including a machine gun unit with American cal. 30 Vickers machine guns. This created a stir of interest. It was the first American machine gun organization we had seen armed with American weapons.

Some troops of the 151st French Division were in town too and I stood at the east end of the place one day watching a battalion of French Indo-Chinese soldiers marching toward the front. Instead of the horizon blue uniform of most of the French forces, or the dark blue of the Chasseurs Alpine, with which we had long been familiar,

33. Though the Model 1911 .45 automatic pistol was the U.S. Army's standard handgun in 1917, only about 75,000 were available when the war began. Production of the automatic was increased, but the government also contracted for and issued large quantities of the Model 1917 .45 ACP caliber six-shot, double-action revolver, produced by Smith and Wesson and Colt, to fill the need for handguns until sufficient numbers of automatics could be produced. Smith and Wesson produced more than 166,000 of these pistols, while Colt manufactured more than 151,000. Eventually more than 643,000 automatic pistols were manufactured and gradually replaced the revolvers at the front. Canfield, *U.S. Infantry Weapons of the First World War*, 45–52, 55–60.

these men wore the mustard-colored uniforms and helmets of the French Colonials.[34]

The men were small in size and with oval, feminine-appearing Mongolian faces. In addition to their regulation weapons, some of them wore huge bolo-like knives on their right hips. The officers were French and in a number of cases towered almost head and shoulders above their Asiatic soldiers. Neat and trim-appearing soldiery, these Indo-Chinese, but I stood on the leeward side of them and as they passed there was an over-powering odor of unwashed human bodies. I much regret that I was never able to see these troops in action.[35]

At 7:30 a.m. Sept. 2, 1918, the 128th Machine Gun battalion rolled out of Gerardmer, northward bound, for a staging area prior to entrainment.[36] Of the town I always retained the most pleasant memories—of the friendly children who greeted me each morning as I went down to the barracks, of the kindly old lady and her husband in whose home I was billeted and of their grand-daughter, the shy and tiny Yvonne, her little face disfigured by sores, who was a friend of mine. I hoped as I left that someday her missing-in-action daddy might return to her.

Our motor column, and the borrowed trucks for the non-motorized portion of the battalion, journeyed 18 miles north and west that morning through wooded hills and rapidly decreasing altitude to the twin villages of Le Paire and Taintrux. My company was to be billeted in Le Paire, B in Taintrux.

Our reception in Le Paire was an uncordial one, the only instance of the kind I encountered in France in that war. The reason I do not know.

Troops moving into the billets assigned them were greeted sullenly at best, and in some cases their invasions of the sacred barn-lofts allotted them for sleeping quarters were met with shrilling protests and frenzied weeping by the elder feminine

34. In his newspaper account, Schrantz refers to these men as members of the 131st Division.

35. Some 50,000 soldiers were recruited from Indochina for service in the French Army. Richard S. Fogarty, *Race and War in France: Colonial Subjects in the French Army, 1914–1918* (Baltimore: The Johns Hopkins University Press, 2008), 27.

36. Secret Field Orders No. 28, issued to the 128th Machine Gun Battalion on August 31, 1918, directed the battalion to march to Corcieux, and that "strict attention will be given to march discipline and to the measures to be taken against aerial observation. Not more than one platoon will march together, with from 50 to 100 yards between groups." Field order 8-31-18, Folder: 128th M.G. Batl. Field Orders 235-32.1 Record Group 120, Records of the American Expeditionary Forces, World War I, Entry NM-91 1241, Records of Combat Divisions, 1917–1919, Box 16, 35th Division, NARA.

part of the population. Company A's meager command of French was not sufficient to find the cause of its unexpected unpopularity, nor could much information be secured from the French town major who was in charge of the billeting. His explanation was that the inhabitants were "German sympathizers" did not sound convincing, but he stilled the civilian protests by shrieking louder than they and threatening the objectors with the laws of France.

We had no sooner detrucked and the men moved off to their billets than one of the sergeants sent for me. His section had been assigned to the loft of a village barn. An old woman had stopped them at the door and was shrieking violent French at them and weeping alternately. I sent for the French town major who had assigned them there.

The machine gunners surmised, as the most likely thing, that this hostility must have been caused by some previous misbehavior on the part of some other American unit in the village; another possible factor was the obvious fear of the inhabitants that the stationing of troops in the village would invite bombing by German planes, for new objections were voiced when Company A mounted three machine guns at suitable points around the village, ready for anti-aircraft defense; and the harshness with which the French town major had shouted down objections also indicated that perhaps a lack of tact on his part might have been a contributing factor. Whatever the cause of the unfriendly reception, the popular sentiment toward the Missourians thawed noticeably during their brief stay here and within 24 hours had become almost normally friendly.

Evidently we did not turn out nearly as bad as expected.

Le Paire was about ten miles from the front which the 5th U.S. Division had stirred up by the capture of Frapelle on August 17 and where now the 92nd U.S. Division (Colored) which had succeeded the 5th in the sector was feeling the German resentment. Shattered timber on hilltops visible from Le Paire showed the results of earlier fighting, and frequent German planes in the air showed the present interest of the enemy in the zone. It was the presence of these observing planes, some of which had probably seen the daylight movement of troops into the village, that had caused the mounting of the three machine guns for defense.

To the east was the usual intermittent thud of guns, marking the front. Occasionally there came over an enemy observation plane, flying high amid splotches of bursting anti-aircraft projectiles, and never low enough to be within range of the machine guns we had hidden hither and yon in the orchards, much to the distaste of the villagers.

Soon we would leave the Vosges behind us. We were, in fact, only two days at Le Paire before moving to an entraining point.[37]

On the whole I was reasonably well satisfied with our experience in the mountains considering the fact that we were a division headquarters unit and supposed to be a reserve of fire power. I would indeed have been glad to have spent more time in the trenches and to have had more combat experience there—such as affording covering fire for a raid—but at least the company had been in the trenches, practically every man had taken a turn at fire on the harassing guns, and all had been under enemy fire. That was something.[38]

And they were a good outfit with high morale. I was proud of them.

37. Maj. Westley Halliburton described the difficult move from the two villages in a letter to his mother: "It was some job to lead 10 motor trucks and 34 Fords across 120 kilometers of unknown country, at night and without lights. . . . An exact routing is given in ordering such movements . . . but punctures and accidents always have part of the cars out of action and my repair cars and mechanics had an awful job." It took the battalion 14 hours to reach their destination, due to halts and efforts to locate portions of the column that became lost going through the "maze" of individual French cities. To make matters worse, when the column ran through forests, the overlapping tops of the trees made it "not dark," but "solid black." By the use of "bad French, an automobile map and the first real fluent job of cussing I've done in France," the column made it through, with a broken wheel, bent axle and two punctured radiators. *Carthage* (MO) *Evening Press*, October 3, 1918.

38. Major Halliburton summarized the 128th Machine Gun Battalion's close calls in the Vosges: "Some of the boys have nothing but luck to thank for their inability to wear the wound chevron. I had one machine gun buried by two successive shells and five direct hits were made on the trenches in which the gun crew took shelter, but the boys had no worse experience than being knocked down by the concussions, a few nosebleeds and a little scratch or so from flying gravel. . . . I found three shrapnel holes in the wall alongside of my orderly's bed. . . . Anyway, he was lucky, for we picked a lot of shrapnel bullets out of the walls of the kitchen, dining room and little bed room in that house." *Carthage* (MO) *Evening Press*, September 7, 1918.

Chapter 9

St. Mihiel

Schrantz and his fellow soldiers gained some experience on the frontline in the Vosges, but the short and relatively uneventful time in the trenches had not been what many of the men had expected. Comparing his stay at the front to his time on the Mexican border in 1916, Sergeant Charles Edwards complained that "If all the fronts are as tame as that one was this is not a much harder war than the 'bloody' Mexican campaign." The only enemies they had encountered were rats the size of terriers, cooties and fleas. Edwards and his comrades would soon realize, with tragic results, that some areas of the Western Front were far more lethal than the Vosges Mountains, with more talented opponents than rodents and insects.[1]

Even more detrimental, the 35th's training at Camp Doniphan and in France, along with the period in the "quiet" sector in the Vosges, was largely inapplicable to the campaigns they were ordered to join in the fall of 1918. War correspondent Clair Kenamore perceptively wrote in his history of the 35th that nearly all of the division's training had been for trench warfare, not open warfare, modes of fighting which were "unlike as night and day." Trench warfare, Kenamore believed, consisted of no

1. *Carthage* (MO) *Evening Press*, September 26, 1918.

Charles Edwards (*Memorial Hall, Carthage, MO*)

maneuver or movement, and "seldom seeing the foe." Troops were required to man listening posts, maintain fields of barbed wire, and fight and raid at night. Open warfare, on the other hand, "is a war of movement with the field constantly changing," in which men tried to keep in sight of each other and in touch with the enemy, fighting continued both day and night, the rifle, machine guns and artillery were extensively used, and there was no "burrowing in the ground," except for foxholes. The battlefield was won or lost "above ground and out in the open."[2]

2. Kenamore, *From Vauquois Hill to Exermont,* 74-75.

As Schrantz's men watched the enemy in the Vosges Mountains, the American First Army came into existence on August 10, 1918. At the end of the month, First Army assumed control of the St. Mihiel sector, southeast of Verdun. There, a German salient that extended 16 miles into the Allied line had been in place since 1914. On September 2, Pershing and Allied commander-in-chief Marshal Ferdinand Foch agreed on a plan to give the First Army an opportunity to see action by eliminating the salient.

At 1 a.m. on September 12, some 3,000 Allied guns began bombarding the area. Four hours later, an overwhelming force of doughboys and Frenchmen moved against two sides of the salient and smashed the withdrawing Germans. A mere thirty-six hours later, practically every American objective had been met, and the fighting concluded on September 16. The Americans suffered about 8,500 casualties but took more than 15,000 German prisoners. For the first time in the war, an operation planned, organized, and commanded by the Americans had been conducted, and under Pershing's independent command, the First Army had scored a victory.

Several experienced American divisions took part in the operation, but the green 35th Division was held in reserve and saw no action. On the night of September 11–12, the 128th Machine Gun Battalion moved into the Forêt de Haye. There Schrantz and his men anxiously waited for news, disappointed that they would not be called to assist in this major American effort.

Their disappointment was merely temporary. A mere ten days later, after having moved to a new sector of the line some sixty miles away, the 128th would finally see combat in the largest American operation of the war.

The division was entraining at Corcieux, a railway station four miles south of Le Paire and the departure of that portion of the 128th which was to travel by train was set for the early hours of September 4, and the destination of the trip was said to be Nancy or the nearby St. Nicholas du Port. The train on which Company A travelled was to go first, the train bearing Company B was to follow a few hours later, and the motorized portion of the battalion under the personal command of Major Westley Halliburton was to start late the next afternoon and journey overland.

At 12:10 a.m. September 4 the non-motorized portion of Company A, 128th Machine Gun Battalion, left Le Paire in the

Corcioux [*sic*] staging area west of St. Die and in battalion trucks was conveyed to a railway station north of Corcioux. The motorized section of the battalion was to move overland starting at 4 p.m. that afternoon.

At the railway I found only a part of the French box cars to which my company was allotted. There was one short. Finally I found the other. It was already loaded with a French liaison detachment of some sort—full of bicycles and sleeping French soldiers. No one in authority was about except someone having to do with the railway and he told me that there was another car, probably the one intended for the French, in which railway personnel was sleeping and that it would be available at 4 a.m. There seemed nothing to do but wait but as a result I became involved in an unhappy episode, which I cannot well but relate.

I had the platoon commanders load that portion of the company for which there was cars and their commanders then departed for a passenger car, set apart for officers at the end of the train, to get such snooze as was possible under its crowded condition. The remaining detachment lay down in the yards to get such rest as it could.

At 2:10 a.m. I was talking to a sergeant, 110th Field Signal Battalion, who was enquiring some directions, I apparently being the only officer awake at that unseasonable hour, when a man from the Headquarters Troop came up and told me a tale of trouble.

In a car on No. 3 train, he said, there was a soldier flourishing a pistol and the men there were afraid that he would kill someone.

This didn't sound like a pleasant job, the more so since that was not even my train, but there was no other officer about so I went to the car accompanied by the man and the field signal sergeant.

There was a man standing in the door of the box car and he, it seemed, had been flourishing the pistol. I told him to step down and he did. He appeared quite normal as I questioned him, very soldierly in fact.

He gave me his name and rank, said he was not drunk and had not been drinking, and that there was nothing wrong with him—all these in response to questions.

"Where is your gun," I asked him.

"In the car, sir," he replied.

"Let's get it," I said.

We stepped up into the door of the car which was full of packs and recumbent men, apparently asleep but probably not under the circumstances.

"Where is it?" I asked.

"With my pack, sir," he said and pointed.

I started to reach for it but unhappily a thought struck me. He might think I was afraid to have him get it and give it to me. There was no reason I should be. I was standing at his right and could grab his arm if he tried to shoot me, as I thought possible.

"Get it and give it to me," I said.

He bent over, reached—and instantly shot himself through the head.

The pistol had apparently being laying on the pack and with the safety off.

He slumped forward on his face, his right hand still clutching the gun. The signal sergeant removed the weapon from his hand. Some of my own men were looking in the door and I had him carried outside.

Most surprisingly he still seemed alive, clutching at his head. The signal sergeant placed a first aid compress over the gaping hole in one eyebrow and I believe another, someone handed him, over the exit hole.

His outfit was in a nearby village and with it the battalion surgeon. And he had a truck. We loaded the man therein with two men in behind with him and took him there.

The surgeon was a Lieutenant Greenberg whom I chanced to know.[3]

He looked at the man silently.

"What do you expect me to do with him?" he asked, gazing at the wound he had uncovered. "He's wounded and he's alive and you're a doctor," I said, "What you do is up to you and not to me."

So I departed, leaving him gazing at the unfortunate man who he knew it was beyond his power to aid. He told me later that the soldier died a few moments after I left.[4]

3. Charles Greenberg was born in Massachusetts on December 23, 1888, and served overseas from May 1918 to April 1919, initially with the 137th Infantry and later with the 129th Machine Gun Battalion.

4. Likely this was John David Ramsey from Osage County, Kansas, a private first class in the 35th Division Headquarters. Ramsey, born in 1889, was buried in Osage City, Kansas.

I expected endless paperwork about this tragedy but in fact all I did was to write a letter the next day and handed it to his captain, the letter telling him the circumstances and giving names of witnesses. At the same time I turned over the pistol. He handled any paperwork there may have been in connection with the case as I never heard anything more about it officially. The captain said that the man had been brooding about an invention and had wanted to talk to him about it, but had been told to wait until the move was over. Evidently he had become mentally unbalanced.

As for me I reflected regretfully that if I had reached for that gun myself—if I had not had the fear of being thought afraid—the poor fellow might have continued to live. But it had not occurred to me that he might shoot himself. I had thought only of the possibility that he might try to shoot me.

Back at the railway yards the additional car was available by 4 a.m. and it was with relief that I finally saw my men jammed into it and went back to the officers['] car. Soon the train was rattling away, first to the west, then to the northwest down the Mortagne valley. My principal recollection of the journey is that twice the train stopped for some time because German airplanes were out. The French had counted on having our machine guns for anti aircraft protection and had been quite distressed when they found that our guns were moving by motor. A minor recollection is of a French lieutenant or captain—probably the one whose men were in the car intended for mine—being very happy that we were on the way to the Nancy area. That city, it seemed, was a "petite Paris" and he was looking forward to it with great gusto.

It was about noon when we detrained in Luneville and waited about for orders. I stared about with some interest at this city which I understood had been in German possession in 1914 for a time. One of the lieutenants had been using his eyes to better purpose for he had seen a couple of young French women observing us from a nearby house, engaged them in conversation forthwith, and reported that they had agreed to make coffee and an omelette for us—most welcome news. We stepped in through a window into a home of some evident wealth, and the young women, with manifest amusement, prepared and served us a hasty meal. We paid the normal charge for such food, then stepped back out of the window to the street, and so to duty, leaving the pair in laughter behind us.

It struck me at the time that the two had been highly entertained at the request to fix us some food and regarded it as a great lark. Lark or not, the refreshment was most welcome.

Here there was a two-hour wait, then orders were received to march to the village of Rosieres-aux-Salines some 12 miles to the westward.

The Allied planes seemed in full control of the air and so in broad daylight the company marched out, crossed the Muerthe River and followed the road which winds in a great half circle down the picturesque south bank of that stream. Here were signs of war in the form of shattered buildings and loop-holed walls, relics of the fighting in 1914 when the crest of the German invasion had reached this vicinity. The sleepless night before was telling on the endurance of the column and when after a couple of hours march, a motorcycle messenger flashed down the poplar-bordered highway with word that German planes were out and that all troops should rest under cover of woods until dusk, the opportunity for a little repose was welcome.

Company A at this time was in the vicinity of Blainville-sur-l'Eau, and the Muerthe River had here swung close to the orchard in which the unit took shelter. The opportunity for a bath was too good to be passed up, so while some of the soldiers slumbered, the rest wended their way to the stream, climbed over and through the belts of barbed wire entanglement along the shore, and refreshed themselves in that historic stream which at this point had played a vital part in stopping the German rush of four years before, following the rout of a part of the French army to the northward across the frontier.

At evening the march was resumed, and about 10 p.m. the weary column stumbled into the outskirts of Rosieres-aux-Salines, and flung itself down to rest, part in an orchard bivouac and part in a convenient barn loft. A little later Company B passed by and found quarters in the town.

While the marching portion of the company slumbered more or less uncomfortably here, Major Halliburton was leading the motor train of 10 cargo trucks and 34 Ford gun trucks, all of them unlighted, in their jaunt of some 80 miles on unknown roads on a rainy and pitch dark night. Following the routing given by high authority he had left Le Paire and Taintrux about 4 o'clock that afternoon moving by Brouvelieures and Rambervillers, thence off to the northeast to Barracat near the front, then down the Muerthe to Luneville. It was an arduous trip, with one casualty—a motor cycle rider who was bruised up when he crashed into a bridge abutment at Luneville—and several times parts of the convoy became lost and had to be rounded up by motorcycle, but in the early morning the cars rattled through Rosieres-aux-Seines, and left word with a few wakeful ones there that the marching part of the battalion should wait until trucks came for them; then on over the hill into the Moselle valley and so to the village of Mereville-sur-Moselle, six miles southwest of Nancy, where the new station was to be. At noon the cargo trucks were back in Rosieres, picked up the organizations there and by 3:30 that afternoon of September 5 all were comfortably housed in the ill-smelling billets of Mereville.

Great events were impending in France in early September, 1918, but of these the 128th Machine Gun Battalion stationed at Mereville-sur-Moselle six miles southwest of Nancy had no knowledge other than that the American army was on the move and the general situation indicated that the purpose was to be an offensive somewhere.

Mereville was a venerable appearing agricultural village on low hills rising from the west bank of the Moselle River and despite the inhabitants' penchant for accumulating barnyard manure beside their front doors pending a convenient time to haul it to the fields, they were a friendly and hospitable people, and of the town the Carthage soldiers were to retain happy memories, its odors notwithstanding.

And here for the first time since Camp Doniphan days the machine gunners were to meet their old neighbors of the Oklahoma camp, the men of the 110th Trench Mortar Battery. This organization, commanded by Capt. Fred W. Manchester, one time of Carthage and a member of Company A during the Spanish-American War, was a part of the artillery brigade which had been detached from the 35th Division from the time it left Camp Doniphan until a week or so before it moved out of the Vosges, and here around Mereville it was hopefully practicing setting up its 6-inch mortars against the day when it would be lobbing its huge projectiles over onto the enemy somewhere. Lieut. Clyde A.

Narramore of the battery, once of Company A, was not with it at the moment, being absent at a trench mortar school.[5]

Company A set up three guns here, mounted for anti-aircraft fire, and Company B set up three more, for the sector was quite obviously the most active in the way of aviation of any which the organizations had yet seen. Many of the villages bore marks of hostile bombs, and planes in combat were frequently seen darting about in the clouds.

In fact, though this too was not entirely clear to the machine gunners at the time, a battle for the mastery of the air was in progress in all this section; the Americans seeking absolute control as a preliminary to their coming operation, and the Germans contesting it bitterly. Most of the days were overcast, or with broken clouds, and it was hard to realize that the operators of the tiny planes playing hide-and-seek in the cloud banks above were engaged in the serious matter of trying to kill without being killed, or that the thin streaks of smoke occasionally flashing from one toward the other were tracer bullets marking the stream of fire. Yet the occasional plane which was brought down somewhere in the vicinity was a reminder that it was a grave matter for those engaged in it, and on September 7 scores of the Carthage soldiers watched a combat between three Allied and two German planes which ended in one French plane and both the German ones crashing to earth.

Yet despite all this air combat I personally never saw a plane shot down, though I watched until my neck was sore and weary

5. Born in Big Rock, Scott County, Iowa, on September 15, 1874, Fred Welcome Manchester served as a sergeant in Company A, 2nd Missouri Infantry during the Spanish-American War. Mustered out at war's end, Manchester reenlisted in the 2nd Missouri in 1901, and despite some breaks in service, was a first lieutenant and battalion adjutant by the time the regiment went to the Mexican border in June 1916. He transferred to the 4th Missouri Infantry in December 1916 and was mustered out the following February. After serving overseas from May 19, 1918, until April 30, 1919, and commanding the 110th Trench Mortar Battery in France, Manchester served as assistant adjutant general of Missouri and executive officer of the Missouri National Guard until he retired in 1938. He died on May 27, 1961, and was buried in Mount Hope Cemetery, Webb City, Missouri. *The Joplin* (MO) *Globe*, May 28, 1961; *The Service of the Missouri National Guard on the Mexican Border,* 108; Missouri Secretary of State, State Archives, Soldiers' Records, War of 1812–World War I, www.sos.mo.gov/archives/soldiers. Clyde Alvin Narramore was born on October 6, 1891, in Carthage. He enlisted in Company A, 2nd Missouri Infantry in 1908 and was regimental sergeant major by June 1916. Promoted to second lieutenant in December 1916, while on the Mexican border, Narramore was mustered out with the regiment in January 1917. He served as a first lieutenant with the 110th Trench Mortar Battery overseas from May 19, 1918, to April 20, 1919. He died on October 29, 1971, and was buried in Park Cemetery in Carthage. *The Service of the Missouri National Guard on the Mexican Border,* 108; *Carthage* (MO) *Evening Press*, October 30, 1971; Missouri Secretary of State, State Archives, Soldiers' Records, War of 1812–World War I, www.sos.mo.gov/archives/soldiers.

from tilting my head backward to stare into the sky. But there were planes shot down which incidents others of our organization, more fortunate than myself, occasionally witnessed. One German plane crashed not far east of our village, though on the other side of the Moselle river, and one of our lieutenants, who chanced along about that time, unloaded the machine guns in the wrecked craft.

There were other signs of a big impending Allied offensive too. At days the roads were generally empty but at night they were crowded with artillery, men and trucks moving toward the north. Since the main road ran east of the Moselle and we were on a side road, this was, to us, just something that we knew was happening on the other side of the river.

The days of the 128th at Mereville were not many but they were pleasant ones, marked by a minimum of training, partly because troop formations in the open were not advisable under the circumstances and partly because orders to move forward at night might come any day. The soldiers rested up from their more or less sleepless two-day trip from Corcieux, and wandered about the village and its environs, staring at the canal boats passing through the locks in the canal just across the Moselle River bridge, speculated on the British air squadron and the Chinese laborers working about it at Frolois two miles to the southwest, and commented on the miscellaneous collection of antique firearms and sabres in the mayor's office—which was also battalion headquarters—reminders of 1914 when it was expected that the Germans would occupy the town and the mayor had collected all weapons of any sort to turn over in hope of averting the unhappy fate which befell so many French villages that year. But, since the weapons survived our passing, I presume they stayed there until the end of the war and were then restored to their rightful owners.

Or perhaps I wandered northwest of Mereville through the wood marked on the map as the Moulin Bois to a point overlooking Pont St. Vincent through which I one day saw a column of troops moving in broad day.

At 8 o'clock [on] the evening of September 11 the marching portion of our battalion moved out of Mereville bound for a point in the Forêt de Haye twenty-five kilometers away just south of the town of Liverdun northwest of Nancy. Major Halliburton and the train of motor cars were due to leave Mereville about midnight and expected to reach the camping place in the woods slightly before the marching column did. The army order for the St. Mihiel offensive had been issued four days before but of this Company A knew nothing—not even the company officers having aught other than guesses on which to base an estimate of the future.

It was raining when we started and continued through the night. Our entire division was moving north and perhaps other divisions were doing the same and when we reached the village of Messein two kilometers north of Mereville we ran onto another column of marching troops, moving all that night behind them. Every cross roads villages was disgorging its quota of men and vehicles to join the mass. The road was evidently jammed with traffic its entire length and, for some reason I do not know, the flow of troops forward was anything but steady. Wagons, automobiles, men, were all crowded together and moved forward at a snail's pace. We would march five minutes then halt ten, then march ten and halt five, then march fifteen and be forced to halt half an hour. It took thirteen hours for our battalion to make the twenty-five kilometers, a distance we would normally have covered in six.

The route followed the Moselle River to the northwest; and through alternate rain and drizzle which soaked through the none-too-waterproof army raincoats, the Carthage soldiers moved forward in their place in the snail-like column.

Throughout the night there had been more or less noise of gunfire from the lines to the north, much the same as we had heard nightly during our sojourn in Mereville. It didn't interest us unduly. Just the routine of the front. The real war couldn't start until we arrived—or so we thought.

But as we halted by the massive church in slumbering Maron the gunfire to the north suddenly increased to an angry thudding. "Some one is going over up there," commented the soldiers to each other with the sageness of men who had heard the accompaniments of trench raids and thought they knew the sounds of the front. Here the battalion motor train, in personal charge of Major Halliburton, caught up after fighting its way along the road somehow, and began to pass.

Soon the thud-thud-thudding of artillery merged into an almost continuous roar and the sky all along the north and northwest was constantly lighted up by flashes of light, somewhat like the continual flickering of lightning that is sometimes seen along the horizon on a stormy night. We realized then that this barrage was preparatory to a large attack.

This was no raid, it could be only the prelude to a great attack; and if the residents of Maron had been awake and could have spoken a language the Americans could have understood, they could have told them that though they had lived within the sound of the guns for four long years they had never heard anything as heavy as that before. For that matter neither had anyone else, for that tremendous roar to the northward was the greatest artillery concentration in the history of all war. Within four hours a million shells were to fall in the St. Mihiel salient, making it an inferno of crashing explosions and screaming steel fragments. And 600,000 American soldiers were either up there on the front ready to attack, or like the men of the 35th Division were straining forward to positions in reserve.

"They are going over without us," commented the men of the 128th to each other in dismay, for the veriest novice at war could no longer misunderstand the significance of that portentous noise in the flashing north.

Of course we had known for a month or more that there was a big offensive coming somewhere soon and that our division was to participate in it. This move northward we had of course taken as a preliminary to the great attack but, being ignorant of the details, the most of us took it for granted that we would be in at the jump-off and therefore supposed that the assault would not be for several days yet. In fact we were in the army reserve and at this moment the troops all along the St. Mihiel salient were waiting for the hour to go over in the first great all-American offensive of the war.

But now the column was in motion again and through the dripping avenues in the black obscurities of the Forêt de Haye it toiled painfully, marching a few minutes and halting many as some obstruction far to the front stopped the flow of the endless column. Motor vehicles, horse transport and foot soldiers all were held to this same interrupted snail's pace. Toward daybreak as we moved through the Forêt de Haye the bombardment was intense and we knew that the attack was about ready to start.

Dawn found the roads still jammed, but full day coming on seemed to increase the speed of the flow, as various groups broke out of the column to find their ways to the bivouac areas. Finally the 128th reached the center of the forest and the hub from which all roads therein radiated.

Being caught on the road by daylight was anything but desirable but there was no helping it in this case. By the time we reached Five Trenches, which are not five trenches at all but five roads crossing each other in the center of the wood, it was broad day. Here there was a halt to allow a long regiment of horse-drawn artillery to pass, then from the east headed west came a short string of military trucks bearing French families—men, women, children—refugees, one guessed, from villages on which the enemy artillery had been expected to retaliate. Now the crossing was open and beyond it an open road of black mud down which the organization stepped as blithely as mud permits but with a keen eye on the breaking clouds.

German aeroplanes came over a time or two and we would not have been surprised at a bombing but we split our column to each side of the road and moved on unmolested under cover of the trees to our camping place, a rocky hillside, where we put up shelter tents.

It was now 8:45 a.m. The 16-mile march started at 8 p.m. had taken 12 hours and 45 minutes to complete. Off to the north the bombardment was continuing though with diminishing intensity. By now the infantry attack up there had been under way for three hours.

When Company A bivouacked in the Forêt de Haye, just south of Liverdun, France, and 12 miles from the front at 8:45 a.m. September 12, 1918, the tremendous thunder of the initial barrage of the St. Mihiel offensive had long since faded away but as the Carthage soldiers ate their breakfast and then climbed wearily into their shelter tents for a little sleep after their 13 hours of marching, there was still the steady roar of the rolling barrage in progress.

Then Company A slept while explosions rocked the woods to the west. "Enemy air bombs," said someone, but no one saw enemy planes. Soon overhead there roared groups of Allied planes with occasionally stuttering machine guns. Sleepy eyes blinked at them, then closed once more. It was hard luck being in reserve while a great offensive was in progress but doubtless it was better to be in reserve than not to be in the operation at all—and reserves were meant to be used some time.

Meanwhile up on the front American divisions were plodding forward in a confused but highly successful advance. Pivoting on the 90th Division, the 5th and 2nd Division[s] of the I Corps almost directly north of Liverdun were advancing; next on the left was the 89th Division, then the veteran 42nd or Rainbow, then the experienced 1st, all taking part in the big parade; and while the nose of the salient was pressed slightly by French Colonials the 26th U.S. Division was battering in from the northwest flank.

Back in the dripping Forêt de Haye the soldiers stirred about during the afternoon, camouflaged with branches such shelter tents as were exposed to view in openings of the trees, and listened to the more or less steady stream of rumors which dribbled back of the great advance. On the morning of the 13th these became more authentic; mimeographed intelligence bulletins of the First Army told the story of the great advance and of the capture of thousands of prisoners, and later that day came an eyewitness of part of the field in the person of Otto Kaselack, a member of Company A who was on detached service as orderly for Lt. Col. D.D. Hay, division machine gun officer.[6] Col. Hay in the side-car of a motorcycle driven by Kaselack had visited the front and in the muddy road at the foot of the Company A bivouac, Kaselack was now telling with excited laughter of the throngs of prisoners he had seen; and he proudly displayed an enemy helmet he had picked up on part of the conquered ground.

Major Westley Halliburton, my battalion commander, was chuckling over something he had witnessed and heard just after the march had ended. Some men from one of the brigade machine [gun] battalion companies had been bringing some mules to a little stream just beyond the road to water. A weary mule in drinking had been leaning over on the weary man who led it.

"Lay off of me, you SOB," the major had heard the man tell the animal, "I'm just as tired as you are."

6. Otto Edward Kaselack was born on April 10, 1896, in Hunneywell, Oklahoma. He served with Company A on the Mexican border as a private and private first class from 1916 to 1917, and overseas with Company A from April 25, 1918, to April 24, 1919. He died in California on June 10, 1995. *The Service of the Missouri National Guard on the Mexican Border*, 126; Missouri Secretary of State, State Archives, Soldiers' Records, War of 1812–World War I, www.sos.mo.gov/archives/soldiers.

Otto Kaselack and Carl Cain, 128th Machine Gun Battalion (*Author's collection*)

An afternoon of rest and a pleasant evening meal. Tomorrow, I thought, we may be in battle but this is wonderful—and it was. Few things so wonderful as rest to the weary.

And seated on the hillside I thumbed through an American magazine someone had sent. One article dealt with [the] thoughts of a soldier of [on] the eve of battle. I read them with some distaste. How silly of one man to write what, according to him, other men feel. My own feelings were far from the ones expressed in the article yet this likely was the eve of battle for us as I saw it, I believing that the reserve might soon be committed.

The next morning in company with Major Halliburton and Captain Corey I visited the headquarters of Brig. Gen. C.[I.] Martin[,] commander of the 70th Infantry Brigade. General Martin was a Kansas National Guard officer and in Philippine Insurrection days had been a captain in the 20th Kansas under Gen. (then Colonel) Frederick Funston. Major Halliburton knew him but I met him that day for the first time—a very courteous man who showed us the situation map which members of his staff were keeping up from the reports that were coming in from the front—through [though] from what source he obtained them I do not recall. I liked General Martin and appreciated the opportunity to hear about the war.

Evidently the reserve divisions were unlikely to be needed just yet and that afternoon—with whom or why I do not recall—I went into Liverdun where division headquarters was located. My principal recollection of the visit was seeing a detachment of the 2nd Cavalry Regiment there—the first cavalrymen I had seen in France.

Still no call came for the 35th Division, and indeed matters had gone so well everywhere in the field that the entire salient was reduced without a need for any of the American divisions held in reserve. In a three-days operation 600 square kilometers of French soil was recovered and 16,000 prisoners and 443 enemy cannon captured at a cost of about 13,700 casualties.

That fight, we understood, had been pretty much of a walkaway for our troops. It hadn't been, but that was what we thought and even when I first visited that battlefield two months later I was surprised to see American rifles and equipment still strewn about the field, evidence enough that there had been a battle there and not a parade, even if one did not note the occasional clusters of American graves.

We heard the news with joy but with considerable chagrin that our own division had not been placed among the assaulting organizations. I often think yet of what differences it would have made in our operations in the Argonne if we had had the experience of St. Mihiel.

The sun finally shone on September 15 and the battle was either so calm or distant that for awhile in the afternoon not even the sound of cannon could be heard. Only in the skies was there audible evidence of the war. Squadrons of Allied planes roared over at intervals and only now and then did an enemy flier appear usually hurrying along with a popping of machine guns at his heels. The Allied superiority of the air was being maintained. Major Halliburton in a letter later published in the *Press* wrote home that he went into Liverdun that afternoon.

> "The town proper is situated on a tongue of high land surrounded on three sides by a river or deep valley from which the hill rises very precipitously," he said. "There is an old castle on the end of the hill, and an old stone arch and heavy wooden gates at the edge of the town. There are also the usual crooked twisting streets with every house set in at a different angle from the rest, and all appear very old. I saw more pretty women there in half an hour than I have heretofore seen in France. It is a very curious old town and I would like to have time to investigate it."

Chapter 10

To the Meuse-Argonne Offensive

Although held in reserve at St. Mihiel, the men of the Carthage Light Guard were destined to play a pivotal role in a much larger and more important operation.[1]

The Meuse-Argonne Offensive (so named because the American First Army advanced through the area between the Aisne and Meuse Rivers, including the Argonne Forest) was the bloodiest battle in American history to that time, with more than 120,000 U.S. casualties. The goal was the critical Carignan-Sedan-Mezieres rail line. If the Americans could advance 53 kilometers and cut that

1. The best modern account of the 35th Division's role in the Meuse-Argonne is Robert H. Ferrell's *Collapse at Meuse-Argonne: The Failure of the Missouri-Kansas Division* (Columbia: University of Missouri Press, 2004). Several outstanding accounts of the Meuse-Argonne Offensive have appeared in recent years, including Mitchell Yockelson's *Forty-Seven Days: How Pershing's Warriors Came of Age to Defeat the German Army in World War I*, published by the New American Library (2016), Ferrell's *America's Deadliest Battle: Meuse-Argonne, 1918*, published the University Press of Kansas (2007), Edward G. Lengel's *To Conquer Hell: The Meuse-Argonne, 1918*, published by Henry Holt and Company (2008), and Douglas V. Mastriano's *Thunder in the Argonne: A New History of America's Greatest Battle*, published by The University Press of Kentucky (2018). For a concise account of the 35th's role in the offensive, with an excellent map, see American Battle Monuments Commission, *35th Division Summary of Operations in the World War* (Washington, D.C: U.S. Government Printing Office, 1944). Valuable articles tracing the movements of the division's machine gun companies are Lt. Col. Donald D. Hay's "Machine Guns, 35th Division, Meuse-Argonne Operation, Sept. 26–Oct. 1, 1918," *Infantry Journal* 40 (May–June 1933): 193–206, and Schrantz's own "Initial Machine-Gun Barrage, 35th Division, Meuse-Argonne Offensive *Infantry Journal* 16 (November 1919): 367–71.

vital lifeline, they would end the flow of supplies to the Germany Army west and northwest of Sedan and greatly hamper the enemy's ability to escape. In order to succeed, however, General Pershing's doughboys would first need to overcome four major German defensive lines, named for Wagnerian witches—the Hagan, Giselher, Kriemhilde, and the Freya Stellung.[2] Nine American divisions organized into three army corps were committed to the initial stages of the operation. American success depended on surprising the German forces in the region, overwhelming them with superior numbers, and moving quickly toward their objectives before enemy reinforcements could arrive.

The Germans were well prepared to meet the Americans. Since occupying the region in 1914, they had carefully constructed a formidable array of defenses, bolstered by natural features. "The country . . . is very rugged, being traversed by many streams, gulleys and arroyos . . . forming a series of ridges and spurs admirably adapted to strong defenses," 35th Division signal officer Major Hans Olson recalled. "Within this area," he continued, "every foot of ground had been prepared by the enemy with a very elaborate system of defensive works, everything that German ingenuity, skill, material and the experience of four years of war experience could provide had been injected into the defenses of this position." High ground to the east and west dominated much of the "defile" through which the 35th would attack, a perfect platform to place artillery pieces to shower the attackers with shrapnel and high explosives. In addition, thick barbed wire, machine gun emplacements, and concrete dugouts littered the area.[3] "The boches [*sic*] have an immense number of machine guns with which they are experts," Sidney Houston of the 128th Machine Gun Battalion wrote after the campaign. "Their craftiness in keeping hidden was almost uncanny and most of the time we were going against an unseen, but far from unfelt, enemy." Even worse, "they are great artillerymen and their aerial liaison is almost perfect."[4]

2. Allied commander in chief Marshal Ferdinand Foch envisioned the Meuse-Argonne as merely one in a series of Allied offensives launched in late September. In cooperation with the American effort, the French Fourth Army advanced on the west side of the Argonne Forest. In addition, the British First and Third Armies attacked between Lens and Peronne, toward Cambrai on September 27; the Belgian Army, British Second Army and the French Seventh and Thirty-fourth Corps (combined on October 19 with the French Thirtieth Corps to form the French Sixth Army) moved toward Ghent, between the English Channel and Lys River on September 28; and the French First Army and British Fourth Army advanced on the St. Quentin Canal on the 29th.

3. Hans O. Olson, "Operations of the 35th Division in First Phase Meuse Argonne 1918," Advanced Officer's Course, 1925–1926, The Infantry School, Fort Benning, Georgia, 7–8.

4. *The Kansas City* (MO) *Star*, November 3, 1918.

The Missouri and Kansas soldiers of the 35th Division were assigned to Major General Hunter Liggett's First Corps.[5] Their immediate task was to advance through the Aire River valley, neutralize German opposition, and outflank the German positions in the Argonne Forest. Although they were destined to face some of the toughest German opposition in the region, the men of the 35th were among the least prepared troops in the First Army, having spent only a few weeks in trenches facing the Germans in the relatively quiet Vosges Mountains. In addition, just days before the assault was scheduled to begin, both of the division's brigade commanders and the officers leading three of the 35th's four infantry regiments were replaced, along with the division's chief of staff. On the eve of the largest U.S. offensive of the World War I, many officers and enlisted men were forced to adjust to an entirely new command structure and unfamiliar commanders. Other shortcomings plagued the division as well. The doughboys were extremely fatigued, having been almost constantly on the move since early September; and communications equipment, including telephone wire, radios, flares and aerial signaling panels were either faulty or missing.

Simply moving half a million American troops into position was a herculean effort. On September 18, the 128th Machine Gun Battalion left the Forêt de Haye and moved by truck to the village of Belval, then on the night of September 20–21, to Camp Ribilleau. Finally, on the night of September 24–25, Schrantz and his soldiers rolled through Neuvilly into the Forêt de Hesse and from there into the trenches and their barrage positions for the upcoming assault—an operation one Missourian labeled a "Homeric struggle."[6]

With September 15, the St. Mihiel operation officially closed, although the enemy artillery was pounding viciously at the new front lines, and the reserve divisions were ordered westward for a fresh operation planned between the Meuse River and the Argonne Forest. The 35th Division received its orders this day and at evening the artillery was in motion. Throughout the 16th and 17th the woods thinned out and on September 18 the turn of the 128th Machine Gun Battalion came.[7]

5. The 77th, 28th and 35th Divisions of the First Corps were ordered to make the initial assault on September 26, with the 92nd Division serving as corps reserve and the 82nd Division as army reserve.

6. Weber, *History of the 129th Machine Gun Battalion*, 36.

7. Earl Conley wrote home that the mud was a foot deep, and the men went down the road slipping, sliding and hollering "like so many frogs and ducks." Conley and two other men built a "bush house," a waterproof hut out of shelter tents, and did some "haying" by

Once or twice enemy planes bombed the timber but never near where my own organization was lying, and the forest was too far from the front to ever come under the fire of the enemy guns.

During the forenoon, the camp in the woods was broken up in mud and rain and the battalion moved to the northwest corner of the forest. Here about 1:30 p.m. the marching portion of the companies entrucked in a French truck train and a few minutes later the entire battalion was rolling southeastward up the Moselle valley toward Toul. Though it was broad day the roads were jammed with military transport of one kind or another, all headed west; but Allied planes, soaring overhead, were doing an effective job of keeping the sky clear of enemy aircraft. Particularly were they in evidence late in the afternoon as the clouds cleared away.

The great move by truck was one of the most marvelous things I saw in the war.[8] As far as one could look the road was full of camions loaded with soldiers, yet the mass moved forward with hardly a pause to the destinations of its various portions, a wonderful tribute to the French officers who were in charge of the operation. Under anything except the most expert management a movement of this character would have been an awful mess, with delays and interminable waits of all sorts but this one was smooth and methodical, despite the fact that a number of divisions were in motion.

Up the Moselle River to Toul the column rolled, thence across the river and straight west on the "Route Nationale" heading into one of the most beautiful sunsets the soldiers had seen in France. Then darkness came on and with it alternate rain and moonlight and an endless rolling through silent cities, and later an occasional ruined village to show that at some time or other this region had been touched by the war. From westward the route shifted to northwestward, the roads always full of the transport of many divisions, all trying to get to cover before the light of another day.

---

filling it with leaves, making a comfortable temporary lodging for the three men to sit in. *Fort Scott* (KS) *Daily Tribune and Fort Scott Daily Monitor*, October 28, 1918.

8. Company A's Earl Conley disagreed with Schrantz's assessment. He related to his mother that the 12-hour truck ride was grueling, and "for once I was tired of riding," with 18 men crammed into a truck "about the size of a Ford." *Fort Scott* (KS) *Daily Tribune and Fort Scott Daily Monitor*, October 28, 1918. According to one estimate, some 428,635 troops were moved by truck an average of 77 kilometers for the Meuse-Argonne Offensive, along with 42,233 tons of supplies (81 percent ammunition). G.R. Young, "The Operation of Motor Trucks in War," *The Military Engineer* 13 (1921): 174.

About daylight the French truck train stopped in the village of Charmontois l'Abbe and the weary machine gunners descended into the wet and cheerless streets. This it seemed was not the destination of the 128th, but it was as far as the trucks would go. Forming in the streets the column moved to the west part of the town, thence southward a mile and a half on a poplar-bordered road along which the battalion motor vehicles had already preceded it, and so to the village of Belval, some five or six miles south of the southern edge of the Argonne Forest and some eight or nine miles west of the Aire River.[9]

It was 6 a.m. September 19, and by 7 a.m. the company was snugly established in its billets with all equipment and transport stowed away out of sight of prowling enemy planes.

I was amused when I went to mine and was met with the not unnatural enquiry from the lady of the house as to how long I would be there. Of course I did not know and in reply I used what became with me later a set answer to that question and which I imagined, quite erroneously, doubtless, made a rhyme in French—"Aujourd'hui, pas parti; cet nuit, je ne se pas." (Today we do not depart; tonight, I do not know). It actually did rhyme, after a fashion, the way I pronounced French and this quite uninformative reply to the usual query came to give me somewhat childish glee each time I paraded it.

Then breakfast and bed, and later a little stirring about in the afternoon. The question then, was, would the battalion move that night again or would it rest? The answer came that it would rest, and so the soldiers made up in repose that night what they had lost during their week or so on the rocky hillside in the Forêt de Haye.

At 8 p.m., September 20, 1918, Company A, 128th Machine Gun Battalion found itself again marching toward the sound of the guns.

At dusk the non-motorized portions of the two companies of the divisional machine gun battalion, 35th Division, had formed in the street in the village of Belval some five or six miles south

9. Major Halliburton reported that his battalion with truck column moved at 3 p.m. on September 18 and arrived at Belval at 7 a.m. September 19, 1918. September 21, 1918, Memo from Commanding Officer 128th M.G. Bn, Major Westley Halliburton, to G-3, 35th Division re Change of Station, Folder: 128th M.G. Batl. Location of Troops 235-32.2, Record Group 120, Records of the American Expeditionary Forces, World War I, Entry NM-91 1241, Records of Combat Divisions, 1917–1919, Box 16, 35th Division, NARA.

of the southern and friendly, part of the Argonne Forest, swung across the bridge over the little stream at the outskirts of the village, and stepped out blithely on the poplar-lined road toward the twin villages of Charmontois-l'Abbe and Charmontois-le-Roi some distance to the north, hoping for an open road ahead for this night's march. Back in Belval the motor train of the battalion waited, scheduled to follow some hours later.

The road was indeed clear the mile and a half to Charmontois-l'Abbe but here rifle units were encountered forming in the street, and as these were passed by, the head of the column ran into the tail of the 130th Machine Gun Battalion—the old Webb City, Springfield, Jefferson City and West Plains National Guard units—which just then was leaving the town, the machine gun carts drawn by hand for lack of the mules which were being driven overland from the St. Mihiel vicinity but which had not yet arrived. Other troops too were ahead of the 130th and for another mile and a half the column moved slowly, crossing in the darkness an insignificant little stream which was the famous Aisne River in its infancy. Now the column was entering the village of Senard, and here by the church the 130th Machine Gun Battalion turned to the north, whereas the march order for the 128th called for a turn to the east.

Turning to the right at the church despite the frantic expostulations of the French military policeman on traffic duty there who was sure that the unit was taking the wrong route, the Carthage men, followed by the Nevada-Butler company stepped out cheerily on a clear road. It was an ideal night for marching, cool and with bright moonlight, so this was a pleasant hike, this move forward toward the furnace of battle. Smoking was forbidden, for fear the flash of matches might render futile the elaborate precautions which were being taken everywhere to insure secrecy, and save for the moon there was no light except the occasional quick gleam of flashlights as the two captains of the battalion bent over a map at some cross-roads to ascertain the route.

In the darkened streets of Triaucourt the road turned northeastward, over the hill to Foucaucourt, thence northward to Waly and beyond. The cannon were louder now and all along the northern skyline were the lights of rising flares and of colored rockets. It constituted one of the most beautiful sights of the war and there was no need to tell the machine gunners what it meant. This was a nervous front, one far more active than the old Vosges. By now other columns had been encountered on the road, but all were pushing northward without delay and halts were few. This bit of woods through which the machine gunners were moving as they crossed a hill two miles north of Waly was the southeastern corner of the Argonne Forest, and now across the hill and in a valley they were moving northward along the west bank of the Aire River.

This march with the arching rockets illuminating the northern skyline was not devoid of interest, and the soldiers marched with the buoyancy with which troops of high morale are wont to move to battle.[10] Froidos and Rarecourt were left to the right in the obscurity of the valley, and soon, some two miles southeast of Clermont-en-Argonne, the column turned to the left and up a road to the west as the battalion motor train passed by. This clump of buildings ahead was Grange-le-Compte, where division headquarters were to be located, some one said, and the battalion was to be billeted in the woods beyond. The main road and all the side roads here were filled with men and cannon struggling forward to sheltered positions in the woods; and indeed there was real need to get out of sight before dawn. The occasional roar of artillery well to the north was varied here by the louder, sharper crashes nearer at hand—heavy projectiles from the enemy's long range artillery, exploding a mile or so distant.

The woodland camp at which the battalion halted was known as Camp Ribilleau, but the hutments in the 128th area from which some French troops were just moving were not sufficient for all.[11]

10. Earl Conley of Company A was not as confident as his commanding officer about the possibility of the unit seeing combat, or that there would be casualties. He wrote to his mother that "I guess that some of us will get our names in the casualties, for they say that it is real hot and lively up there now. But maybe we won't get to go up. We hardly ever do when there is a good time in sight, and if we do, it may be like it was before when we were up, we never lost a man." Nevertheless, Conley admitted that it would be "pretty nice now to be in a quiet little town where I could hear a rooster crow, or a church-bell ring, instead of having a big gun talking its fool head off in my ears all the time." *Fort Scott* (KS) *Daily Tribune and Fort Scott Daily Monitor*, October 28, 1918.

11. Major Halliburton reported that the marching portion of the 128th left Belval at "20 hours" September 20, and arrived at Camp Ribolleau at 2:30 on September 21. The truck train left Belval at 10 p.m. on September 20 and arrived at the camp at 2 a.m. on September 21. September 21, 1918 Memo from Commanding Officer 128th M.G. Bn, Major Westley Halliburton, to G-3, 35th Division re Change of Station, Folder: 128th M.G. Batl. Location of Troops 235-32.2, Record Group 120, Records of the American Expeditionary Forces, World War I, Entry NM-91 1241, Records of Combat Divisions, 1917–1919, Box 16, 35th Division, NARA.

Part of Company A entered hutments, part pitched shelter tents, and part stopped by a hutment concerning which a controversy between the battalion surgeon and the captain of Company A developed.

The surgeon—a first lieutenant—and I were not on the same cordial relations that each of us were with the other officers of the battalion. The chill between us had started, if I remember correctly, back at Camp Doniphan during a time when there was an epidemic of colds. He had directed some change in the cot arrangements in my company tents so that the men's heads would be farther apart and I resented the fact that he had given the instructions directly to the tents concerned instead of through me. I did not like the idea of having one man's feet in another man's face anyhow.

Then on the march in France after I had rejoined the battalion I noted that on reaching billets or bivouacs he seemed interested in his own comfort first and that of his men second. This did not appear to disturb his men in the slightest degree, and I believe that he was quite popular with them, but I considered it unofficerlike. To me it was one of the military fundamentals that a good officer looked after his men first and himself second. I do not recall, even if I ever knew, what was the basis of his unfavorable opinion of me but in any event the feeling of polite aversion was mutual. During the Meuse-Argonne operation now so close upon us, he did wonderful work in my estimation and my opinion of him was completely changed. I either did better than he had expected of me—which probably hadn't been much—or there was a reflection of my own changed sentiments for after that we were good friends. But "polite aversion" was still mutual this dawn in the woods west of Grange-le-Comte and oddly enough our difference arose over an effort by him to look after his men's comfort, however little I thought he had done so in the past.

As I stopped the platoons to which reference is made near the hutment Lieut. Tenney, the surgeon, appeared and said that I could not have it; that he wanted it for a hospital. I informed him, rather peremptorily perhaps, that I saw it first, that he had no need of a hospital in those quite safe woods, and perhaps I added either by word or implication the thought that he wanted the place so his men could sleep cozy on bunks while mine slept on the ground. He went away somewhat unhappily.

Directing the platoon leader to move his men into the billet, I checked on my other platoons to see that they were getting settled where they could rest and, it being full daylight now, thought of checking up on my own accommodations wherever and whatever they might be. Then the sergeant of the platoon which had entered the disputed billet came up to me and said: "Could the captain come with me? I want to show him something."

I went to the building with him. The men were inside in the center aisle between the two-tiered bunks, their packs drawn close to their feet. Warned by their experience at Willer back in the Vosges in July, the soldiers had started their occupancy by examining their bunks—and found their worst fears confirmed. The sergeant showed me that the crevices in the bunks were swarming with vermin—very repulsive looking lice those.

"Move your platoon out and pitch shelter tents," I told him. "The ground is many times better than this place."

"Lieutenant, I have thought better of the matter of that hutment," I told him. "You might need it for a hospital at that. I have told the platoon sergeant to pitch shelter tents and the building is now empty if you want it."

He thanked me most appreciatively and a moment later was leading his medical detachment happily toward the structure—His men looked quite pleased too.

But a short time later I saw Lieutenant Tenney shepherding his men away from the building again and gloomily pointing out a place for them to pitch their pup tents.[12]

This combined camp and bivouac west of the Grange-le-Comte farm where division headquarters was located was not an uncomfortable place, as I recall it—at least not for me.

Major Westley Halliburton[,] my battalion commander would have been uncomfortable any place at that time, I remember. Somewhere he had acquired scabies and was the more miserable perhaps because it was on his back, where he could scratch only

12. Edwin Roy Tenney, born in Bloomington, Illinois, on April 9, 1874, graduated from high school in Kansas City in 1893 and from University Medical College in 1897. He served as a contract surgeon in the Philippines from 1900 to 1903, and was commissioned a first lieutenant in the Kansas National Guard in 1916. After attending the Medical Officers Training Course at Fort Riley, Kansas, from June to August 1917, Tenney commanded the Ambulance Company, 139th U.S. Infantry from August 1917 to February 1918, then became surgeon of the 128th Machine Gun Battalion. He died in Honolulu, Hawaii, on May 10, 1930. HST; *Honolulu* (HI) *Star-Bulletin*, May 10, 1930.

with difficulty, that things were the worst. We occupied adjoining rooms in the same hutment and one of my memories of the place is Major Halliburton, stripped to the waist, and with his orderly, curiously enough nicknamed "Scrubby" Hier, working on his back with water, soap and a scrubbing brush.

Hier, whose Christian name was "Issac"—and spelled just that way—had been known to me in boyhood.[13] He had a "tough boy" reputation then and he still had it years later when he applied for enlistment in my company in Carthage. He had never run afoul of the law, not seriously anyhow, so I had enlisted him readily enough. He had been a good enough soldier too, something of a wit in a minor way, and at Camp Doniphan on one or two occasions I remember that after I had admonished about some inattention at drill or something, I was much amused when First Sergeant George Snyder repeated to me later some good natured wise-crack he had overheard the man had made about it afterwards. I always suspected that Hier remembered me as a mild small boy of the neighborhood where he had the reputation of being a tough one and so got a quiet chuckle out of my being his captain and holding him to the paths of rectitude with admonishment or some minor company punishment.

Major Halliburton rather liked Hier's reputation and his devil-may-care attitude and had early secured him as an orderly at which time he was transferred to the headquarters detachment and was no longer under my command. There was once that he came near getting into serious trouble and over this I had an argument with the major and as a result Hier had not even been tried.

He had been gambling with some of my men in one of my billets and some trouble arose between him and one of my men. Hier, I had been informed by all of those present, flew into a rage and secured his pistol, my man, also angry and doubtless fearful of Hier's reputation brought in from civil life, also went after his. The men present immediately were on them and disarmed them but in my mind the offense was plenty serious and I thought both should be court martialed, though I deemed Hier the most at fault since I was informed that he drew first.

13. Isaac E. Hier, born in Taney County, Missouri on October 26, 1887, joined Company A in June 1917. He served overseas from April 1918 to April 1919. He died on March 29, 1942 and is buried in Oak Hill Cemetery in Carthage. *Joplin* (MO) *Globe*, April 1, 1942.

The major, however, accepted Hier's story and insisted that I prefer charges against my man. He would not hear to any charges being preferred against Hier however so I told him to prefer them himself and I would reply with charges against Hier or, if he preferred, I would prefer them against both—which is what I should have done, of course. But he was determined that Hier was the innocent party and so we squabbled and neither of us preferred charges against anyone for what might have been a quite serious incident.

But here in the woods everything was peaceful and harmonious and the trusty Hier treated the major's scabies as best he might and I felt sorry for the major and for Hier both.

For several days the company remained comfortably in this section of the Argonne Forest while preparations for the impending attack in which they were to take part went forward. Messengers came and went in the woods. Huge guns from army artillery organizations strained forward through the mud to get into their initial firing positions. Some rifle organizations moved forward at night to relieve the 73d French Division in the Grange le Compte sector of which the 35th U.S. Division was assuming command, though keeping French battalions in the front line in contact with the enemy to prevent the Germans from finding out that Americans were going in. Senior American officers, including Major Westley Halliburton of the 128th, went forward to the front line where, attired in French overcoats and wearing French helmets, they studied the terrain.

Artillery to the north remained active, and at intervals during the day and night there came the crash of exploding shells a mile or less north of the edge of the woods wherein the Carthage men were encamped. Occasionally the column of smoke rising from the shell burst could be noted, but usually these were over the hill out of sight, and none ever fell near the camp. The enemy long-range guns were shelling Clermont-en-Argonne and the road which ran through it, and the soldiers believed that the closer projectiles were "overs," intended for the town or road. Be that as it may, the noise was a reminder that the enemy was alert, and over at Grange-le-Compte the concussions of the bursts frequently rattled the glass in the old buildings as the various staffs worked on plans for the 35th's part in the great attack.

Heavy guns moving to positions in the woods, roads jammed with motor and animal traffic and columns of marching men, truck loads of shells wallowing through the mud, extreme activity everywhere indicated to the most unobserving that another great attack was in preparation and that this time the 35th Division was to be a part of it.

Major Halliburton had been given a set of the sector—maps on the scale of 1/10000. Then Captain Corey and I were given sets. We pieced them together in Major Halliburton's room and pondered them.

Our sector, from which we correctly assumed we would attack, was bounded on the right by Vauquois Hill, inclusive, and on the left by the enemy-held village of Boureuilles exclusive.

Vauquois was a height which dominated most of the surrounding country since it had a view for miles. It was reputedly extremely strong. Though we did not know it at the time it had been a bone of contention between the French and German forces since the Germans had recoiled thus far after the enemy withdrawal at the time of the battle of the Marne. Since 1915 the line had been stabilized with the Germans on the summit but the French holding the south slope below some mine craters where the village of Vauquois had once stood. A tough front this to attack, as evidenced not only by the hill but by the mazes of enemy trenches shown on the maps.

There was trouble in high places of the division at this time of which we heard rumors or reports but in a disinterested way—we not being particularly concerned since we were division headquarters troops. The division of the day, it will be recalled, was basically one of two infantry brigades of two infantry regiments each, supported by a brigade of three regiments of artillery. On Sept. 21, Brig. Gen. Nathaniel F. McClure, a Regular officer, was relieved of command of the 69th Brigade and succeeded by newly-arrived Col. Louis M. Nuttman. The same day Brig. Gen. Charles I. Martin, a National Guardsman, was relieved of command of the 70th Brigade and was succeeded by Col. Kirby Walker, 139th Infantry.[14] There were some changes in regimental

14. Nathaniel Fish McClure was born in Crittenden, Kentucky, on July 21, 1865. He graduated from West Point in 1887 as a cavalry officer and served in the southwestern United States and with Pershing in the Punitive Expedition. Promoted to brigadier general (National Army) in February 1918, McClure commanded Base Section No. 5 in Brest,

commanders too. These, occurring on the eve of battle, were later credited with being to considerable degree responsible for confusion which occurred during the battle. Obviously changes at such a time were far from good but I have never learned what the division commander considered as justification for them. Both brigade commanders stood high in the estimation of the division, so far as I know.

But this did not worry people like captains of the division machine gun battalion. We were thinking about our own jobs and not that of the commanding general.

At this time I had the privilege of seeing the plan for the operation of the machine guns of the division in the coming attack. Lieut. Col. D.D. Hay, divisional machine gun officer, sent a request to Major Halliburton to send two of his officers to division headquarters to assist in planning the initial machine gun barrage and issuing the organization orders for carrying it into effect. The major sent Lieut. Fred Krueger, the battalion intelligence officer who had just returned from a detail as instructor in the machine gun school at Camiers, and myself.[15]

He was going to the front line on an observation trip and would be gone all day, Colonel Hay informed us on arrival. He had worked out on maps—marked in colored pencil—the estimated position of our infantry front line at various hours after the jump-off of the impending attack. He gave us information as to division boundaries.

France. He took command of the 69th Infantry Brigade, 35th Division in May, commanded the division from June to July 1918, resumed command of the brigade in July, and was relieved of command on September 21, 1918. McClure "took this terrible and unexpected blow with fortitude." He retired in 1929 and died on June 26, 1942. *Assembly* 1, no. 4 (January 1943): 10–11. Charles Irving Martin was born in Ogle County, Illinois, on January 25, 1871. He joined the Kansas National Guard in 1890, served in the Spanish-American War and Philippine War, as adjutant general of Kansas (1909–1917), and commanded the 70th Brigade, 35th Divison from October 1917-September 21, 1918. He retired in 1935 and died on May 8, 1953. *The Leavenworth* (KS) *Times*, May 10, 1953. Kirby Walker was born on January 25, 1867. He graduated from West Point in 1892, and died on January 10, 1960. He commanded the 139th Infantry from June to September 1918, then the 70th Infantry Brigade September 21–October 13, 1918. He retired in 1928.

15. Fred Krueger of Sacramento, California, was a cadet at St. Matthews Military School in Burlingame, California, from 1904 to 1907, then served in the Cadet Corps at the University of California 1908–1910. He attended the Officers Training Camp in San Francisco from May-August 1917, then was commissioned a first lieutenant in the Officers Reserve Corps. He was assigned to Company B of the battalion after his return from duty as an instructor at the British machine gun school at Camiers. Krueger was transferred to the United States as a machine gun instructor in October 1918. Memo from 1st Lt. Fred Krueger to Commanding Officer, 128th Machine Gun Battalion, Camp Doniphan, November 9, 1917, Record Group 120, Records of the American Expeditionary Forces, World War I Organization Records, Machine Gun Battalions, 128th Machine Gun Battalion, Box 263, NARA; HST.

During his absence we would work out the initial machine gun barrage—targets and firing positions of each company, the length of fire on the initial targets, the time of shifts and the length of fire on each subsequent target by each company. He would check our recommendations when he returned that evening.

Here was a task for us of some importance, and we went about it diligently during the day as the explosion of the enemy long-range shells north of us shook and rattled the windows. They seemed much closer than they had before—but perhaps the windows only made them seem so. Krueger was a highly competent officer and a capable and agreeable one with whom to work on such a task.

We started out by studying the enemy positions thoroughly within machine gun range, considering the areas on which we would like to bring fire and then the points from which it could be brought with most effect.

The terrain, the enemy positions and the guns we had available, made it possible to work out what we considered—and which I still consider—an excellent plan.

The 35th Division was to attack on a two kilometre front, the left of the attack moving up the Aire River and the right taking the strongly fortified hill of Vauquois and thence moving north over a long, high ridge known as Rossignol through the towns of Cheppy and Very. The plan of Colonel Hay was to use eight of the machine gun companies of the division—ninety-six guns—in laying down the initial machine gun barrage which would prelude the infantry assault and cover it for a short time. The organizations chosen for this barrage work were the 128th Machine Gun Battalion (two companies), the 130th Machine Gun Battalion (four companies) and the machine gun companies of the 139th and the 140th Infantry Regiments.

The machine gun companies of the 137th and 138th Infantry Regiments and Company A and B of the 129th Machine Gun Battalion were to go forward with the attacking infantry battalions to help the advance as best they might, and the other two companies of the 129th, under the command of Major T.H. Loy, were to occupy Rossignol as soon as it had been captured and cover the attack on the Cheppy positions which it was foreseen would make a strong resistance.[16]

16. Thomas Harkins Loy was born on February 23, 1869, in Elkhart County, Indiana. He enlisted in Company I, 2nd Missouri Infantry as a private in 1905 and became the regiment's

It was decided to place the barrage companies as far forward as possible and cross their fire, that is the companies on the left of the division sector would fire to their right front so as to cover the advance of the troops on the right of the sector, and the companies placed on the right of the sector would fire to their left front so as to cover the advance of the troops on the left. This oblique fire would be more effective against troops in the enemy trenches and would make it harder for the German to locate the guns doing the firing. It was hard to bring much fire against Vauquois Hill without endangering other troops but it was finally decided that the left company would push a platoon of four guns forward to a little knoll known as Hill 202 and rake the most dangerous shoulder of the enemy hill squarely in enfilade.

There was not a great deal we could do about formidable Vauquois Hill. Just west of that height, along its base, the enemy front line trenches ran in a north-northwest direction and we could place a company so that these could be taken in direct enfilade. Company C, 130th Machine Gun Battalion, later handled this fire. Along the west shoulder of the hill the hostile trenches ran upward facing to the south southeast.

This was all we could figure out to do about Vauquois with machine gun fire. We scheduled no fire against it from the east.

I mention this in particular because after the action, Lt. Col. Hay told me that complaint had been made that some of our machine guns, firing on Vauquois Hill from the east, had delayed the attack of the 138th Infantry somewhat. It just couldn't be, I told him, unless some company got clear off its target and even then the fire would come from the south instead of the east.

A good many years later I discussed this matter with Lt. Col. Fred Bottgar who, as a captain, had commanded the assault

---

major in 1916. He served in that capacity with the regiment on the Mexican border from 1916–17. Loy served overseas from May 2, 1918 to April 27, 1919 with the 129th Machine Gun Battalion. He was cited in division orders for making a personal reconnaissance of the town of Cheppy on the morning of September 26, 1918, in the face of intense German machine gun and artillery fire, then skillfully positioning his guns, so that "to him belongs a large share of the credit" for its capture. On September 29, Loy, learning of an enemy counterattack, gathered a force and went to the firing line, which had a "great moral effect" on the men there and allowed them to more easily repel the enemy attack. Loy also served in the Missouri National Guard from 1921 to 1933 and ended his service as a colonel. Loy died on May 6, 1961, and was buried in Aurora, Missouri. *The Service of the Missouri National Guard on the Mexican Border*, 107; *Springfield* (MO) *Republican*, December 5, 1918; Missouri Secretary of State, State Archives, Soldiers' Records, War of 1812–World War I, www.sos.mo.gov/archives/soldiers.

battalion of the 138th that day.[17] He told me that a machine gun company—and not the machine gun company of the 138th Infantry either—had been firing on Vauquois from the east and he could not advance until he had gone up and stopped their fire. That mystified me until I read in the History of the 91st Division (page 21) the following concerning that division's plan of attack:

> "One company of infantry and one machine gun [company] were detailed from the 182nd Brigade as a combat liaison force between the 91st Division and the 35th Division. This liaison force was to neutralize the German machine gun positions on the north slope of Vauquois hill, covering the left flank of the 182nd Brigade."[18]

The fire which hampered the 138th's advance was from a machine gun company of the 91st Division trying to protect its division flank. The machine gun plans of the two divisions had not been coordinated. In point of fact I do not think that there would have been time to coordinate them.

Working in division headquarters that day, with maps spread out on tables and assisted by Private Otto Kaselack, once of my company and now Colonel Hay's orderly, I met Maj. Gen. Peter Traub, 35th Division commanding general, for the first time.[19] He came in the room[,] shook hands with us and asked what we were doing—which we explained. After he had shaken hands with Krueger and I the general advanced on Kaselack with outstretched hand. Kaselack, believing, and perhaps correctly so, that the general mistook him for an officer was embarrassed. "I'm just Private Kaselack, Colonel Hay's orderly," he said. "And what of that?"

17. Frederick Alexander Bottger was born in Williamsport, Pennsylvania, on April 17, 1887. He enlisted as a private in the 1st Missouri Infantry in 1905. Commissioned a second lieutenant and captain in 1914, Bottger led Company K, 1st Missouri Infantry on the Mexican border from June to September 1916. He served overseas from May 1918 to April 1919, and died on September 22, 1961, in Poplar Bluff, Missouri. *The Service of the Missouri National Guard on the Mexican Border*, 84.

18. 91st Division Publication Committee, The Story of the 91st *Division* (San Francisco: H.S. Crocker Co., Inc., 1919), 21.

19. Peter Edward Traub was born on October 15, 1864, in New York City. He graduated from West Point as a cavalry second lieutenant in 1886, served on the American frontier, in Cuba during the Spanish-American War, and in the Philippines, and rose to colonel by 1916. Promoted to brigadier general (National Army) in 1917, and to major general the following year, Traub led the 35th Division until he took command of the 41st Division from December 1918 to Feburary 1919. Traub was promoted to brigadier general in the Regular Army in 1928, retired the same year, and was promoted to major general (retired) in 1930. He died on September 27, 1956, in Manchester, New Hampshire. U.S. Adjutant General's Office, *Official Army Register, January 1, 1931* (Washington, D.C.: U.S. Government Printing Office, 1931), 922.

laughed the general genially and pumping Kaselack's hand vigorously. "You are good enough to shake hands with, aren't you?"

General Traub's cordial manner impressed me quite favorably. I liked him. He was an old cavalryman and while I later thought that maybe his handling of the division in action was based somewhat on the principles of a cavalry mounted charge, I continued to like him even among the post-battle and later post-war recriminations. I have pleasant recollections of him even yet—partly, doubtless, because of his courtesy to Kaselack.

Lt. Colonel Hay, returning in due course, carefully checked our plans and approved of them. This was the initial barrage fired by these eight machine gun companies (96 guns) the morning of September 26.

The five companies or "groups" on the right were to be the four companies of the 130th Machine Gun Battalion and the machine gun company of the 140th Infantry, all to be under the command of Major John F. Constable of the 130th. The three companies on the left were to be the two companies of the 128th Machine Gun Battalion and the machine gun company of the 139th Infantry, all under the command of Major Halliburton of the 128th.

Of all the machine gun companies engaged in the barrage, the extreme left one had the most difficult and dangerous task. One of its platoons was to be pushed out into a very exposed position and the other two in order to hit the target assigned to them had to fire closer to the heads of our own infantry than any other machine guns. The bullets, if all the fire data was figured accurately, would clear the infantry by a safe margin but a slight inaccuracy might land the shots among our own troops. Having helped figure the barrage I felt considerable responsibility for it and worried some about the task assigned to this left company. Immediately upon my return to camp I asked that my company be given this work, a request that he granted much to my relief. It may be stated right here that in firing this barrage my platoon leaders took extreme care not to fire too low and it is a satisfaction to record that no complaints regarding this shooting ever came to me. After the action one battalion commander stated that he was delayed in the jump-off due to machine guns firing too low but the guns of which he complained were on the other flank and, on paper at least, had an ample clearance.

One of my senior sergeants, Charles S. Edwards, came to me that evening with a tale of woe. Edwards had been a member of the company for four years including the period that it had been on duty along the Mexican border. Now he had received an order directing that he, among others, report at Langres immediately as an instructor in the machine gun school there.

"I have been in the company a long time and I don't want to leave it just as it is going into battle," he told me with tears in his eyes. The captain took the matter to the major. "You have there an A.E.F. order," said the major. "I have transmitted it. I am not going to check up to see if it is obeyed before the battle."

It seemed to me that he was needed more right then in his organization than he was at the school and I told him that unless we heard otherwise from higher authority that the order could wait until after the coming battle was over. Four days later he was dead but I am sure that in the intervening time he had done more for his country than he could ever have done in a machine gun school and I know that if he had the choice to make again that he would take the battle.[20]

At dusk, September 24, 1918, the marching portion of the 128th Machine Gun Battalion formed at Camp Ribilleau west of Grange-le-Compte for the move to the front line to make preparations for its part in the great American attack set for the early morning of September 26.

While the helmeted and pistol-armed figures, each with a gas mask in the alert position on his chest and with light pack containing two days' emergency rations on his back, are waiting to march, it may be in order to glance at the three general types of projectiles with which the six miles they were to traverse were intermittently scourged. First was high explosive shells of various calibres which burst on impact with the ground, hurling jagged fragments of steel in all directions. Next was gas shell—a projectile containing,

20. Edwards, a 24-year-old member of Company A, was born in Nevada, Missouri, in 1894 and moved to Carthage with his parents in 1909. He enlisted in Company A in 1914, was promoted to corporal in 1916, and served in that capacity on the Mexican border from 1916–17. He was stricken with spinal meningitis while at Camp Doniphan, but recovered sufficiently to travel with the company to Europe, and served overseas from April 25, 1918, until his death. In civilian life he was a stone cutter and marble polisher. *Carthage (MO) Evening Press*, October 28, 1918; *The Service of the Missouri National Guard on the Mexican Border*, 122; Missouri Secretary of State, State Archives, Soldiers' Records, War of 1812–World War I, www.sos.mo.gov/archives/soldiers.

in liquid form, one of the several forms of poisonous gas and carrying an explosive charge only strong enough to burst the steel envelope and let the poisonous liquid escape and vaporize into gas. Third was shrapnel—hollow tubes of steel with a charge of explosive in the rear, a large group of balls about the size of a marble in front and with a time fuse on the nose of the shell connected by a tube with the powder. The projectile exploded in air, the balls being blown forward with a shotgun effect, and, if the burst was at the right height from the ground, sweeping a space about 20 yards wide and 100 yards long with a deadly shower.

Now the column is stepping off, Company B in the lead. Usually on night marches, Company A marched first, but Capt. Jesse Corey of Company B was senior of the two captains and this night, going forward in the danger zone, very properly claimed his prerogative of marching his Nevada-Butler organization in the position of honor, and letting the Carthaginians follow. The motor train is still motionless and will remain so for some time, later coming forward with the expectation of passing the marching column en route and reaching the bivouac area in the Forêt de Hesse in immediate rear of the trenches before the foot column. Blankets were left with the trucks.

From Camp Ribilleau the marching column moved first to Grange-le-Compte, thence north to Auzeville, thence northwestward through the ruins of Clermont-en-Argonne, from whose high hill the enemy stronghold of Vauquois Hill was by day in easy view. This was in the area on which enemy long range guns were wont to play, and of their might the soldiers had testimony on the highway just north of Clermont where engineers were filling in a deep hole obstructing half the road, the result of an enemy heavy shell striking the highway a short time before—probably about the time the machine gunners were leaving the woods. Company A was now marching in a formation suitable for movement in an artillery-swept zone—column of twos with liberal intervals between sections and platoons. Special provisions to guard against gas were taken by distributing the specially-trained gas experts along the company.[21]

21. Despite the dangerous nature of their surroundings, some men found a certain beauty in the scene. Company A truck driver Estel Ziler wrote home that "Of all the pretty rides I ever had this was one of them, as the roads were simply grand and the airplanes to act as convoys or scouts through the air." The scene was soon spoiled, however, for "as we

Ahead of us the enemy artillery was throwing an occasional shell at the roads and the flares going up along the front showed that the outposts were nervous and on the alert. As we neared Neuvilly there came the whine of enemy shells and seven or eight in succession burst off to the right of the road we were traveling. Soon others struck ahead of us and there came a cry of "Gas!", followed by the click of helmets striking the ground as men knocked off their headgear to put on their masks.

The 128th had never yet encountered gas but it had been well trained what to do. Instantly every man had knocked his helmet off forward with his left hand, drawn his gas-mask from its container with his right, and was thrusting his chin into the rubber face piece even while the steel head-gear was banging on the gravel. Masked and rehelmeted the column moved forward again while other projectiles screeched and exploded, mostly to the right. Marching with gas masks is fatiguing and when cautious sniffs by the officers and the gas noncommissioned officers indicated the air was free, masks were ordered removed. A few moments later from other troops again came the cry, "Gas!" Once more the helmets were knocked off; once more the masks donned; and once more, after a few moments, the cautious testing indicated that the only unusual smell was the acrid odor of shell fumes, and so the word was again passed back to remove masks.

By now it was realized that fear of gas had been so ingrained in some of the units that every time a shell burst near, someone thought it was gas. With this understood, the gas alarms in Company A became less frequent and save for an interval now and then the Carthage men moved forward without masks.

At Neuvilly we left the main road, turning off to the northeast. Here there was no gas for the moment at least, though a sentry encountered in front of the church in the center of the town was waiting with rifle poised, ready to fire in the air to give the alarm if [a] gas shell fell near, a circumstance which probably explained some rapid, evenly-spaced rifle shots heard from this direction when the shell fire first started.

In Neuvilly the 128th's Battalion's motor train passed by, and a few moments later the marching portion of the battalion was

---

came nearer the trenches, the roads became bad and some of the machines were stuck." *Carthage* (MO) *Evening Press*, November 18, 1918.

following it up the "Route des Fascines" northeast of Neuvilly. The shell fire close at hand had ceased for the moment but the woods a mile or two to the north, the objective of the march, was the center of a lively enemy bombardment.

The Route des Fascines was a crowded thoroughfare. It was full of marching troops, heavy trucks loaded with ammunition, and horse and motor transport of all kinds. The heavy trucks, struggling through the muddy road, roared loudly, and the enemy would have needed to be deaf to have remained in ignorance that there was movement back there. Soon there again came the scream of shells and explosions near at hand.

Three kilometers from the village we came to a jam in the roads. A French truck loaded with ammunition had slipped off of the muddy route in the woods ahead in such a way as to block the traffic. The gun trucks of the 128th Machine Gun Battalion had reached this place and stopped and the 130th Machine Gun Battalion, men, mules and carts, which was just in front of us, also stopped.

To add to the anxiety the harassing enemy artillery changed from high explosive to shrapnel. Bad business, these things if exploded at the right height and position.

Properly placed, one of these bursts might have killed some dozens of men and animals but instead they burst high, some directly overhead [of] the Carthaginians, and the balls pattered to earth somewhere in the obscurity to the east. Alarming nonetheless. To lessen the likelihood of casualties, Company A was moved off the road some distance to the west and the men instructed to crouch or lie prone. A few days later such instruction would not be needed, but now the apparent tendency was to show contempt for this still-novel danger by remaining upright in pretended indifference.

There were occasional casualties along the road now, probably from slivers of high explosive shell, for the shrapnel bursts were still high, and several times stretchers containing wounded men were borne back by Company A from somewhere forward. Though none of these casualties were in the 128th, some of them apparently occurred near the battalion's motor train. Mechanic Estel C. Ziler, writing home of this incident said: "Two American boys were killed and three wounded." Official figures show that in the few noisy nights in the Grange-le-Compte sector preceding the

Meuse-Argonne offensive, the 35th Division had 16 men killed and 94 wounded.

The captains of Company A and Company B went forward to the battalion's stalled motor train and discussed with Major Halliburton the question of whether it would be better for the foot column to push on around the motor cars and continue to its destination in the woods, still being heavily shelled, or to wait where they were, chancing the shell fire on the road, until the enemy's pounding of the woods slackened somewhat. Each course appearing fraught with equal peril, it was decided to move forward.

The road ahead seemed quieter, as the column moved northward into the Forêt de Hesse, then turned squarely west at a road junction, marching parallel to the front, here about a mile distant.

The enemy was throwing both gas and high explosive into the woods and occasionally a wounded man from some other organization was carried by us. During this stage of the march there were several alarms of gas caused by the column passing through little valleys where the poison fumes had settled. On this muddy route, poisonous gas lurked in every hollow, though the higher ground was clear, and after an initial alarm or two when the head of the column encountered these pockets, masks were worn in the low ground and removed on the high. Finally we reached the place where we were to stop, a spot in the woods 2000 meters behind the front lines. A short time later near a shallow road-cut on a little hill the column halted, broke ranks and the members of Company A lay down in the woods by a reserve machine gun emplacement, hoping to get a little sleep—a hope which was to prove futile. Some American machine gunner had emerged from the obscurity of an inconspicuous emplacement and told me that the men were in the field of fire of his gun in case he had to start shooting. A few moments afterwards the Ford gun trucks came up, the road having been finally cleared by the simple expedient of toppling the loaded French artillery ammunition trucks over in the ditch to get by. Ammunition was important, all realized, but a truck-load or two of it could not be permitted to hold up the war. Our bivouac was about 2,000 meters south of enemy-held Vauquois and a couple of hundred meters north of the hills marked on the map as the Cotes de Forimont.

The 128th Machine Gun Battalion's hope to get some rest in the Forêt de Hesse after its arrival there some time after midnight September 24—the early hours of September 25—did not last long. There had hardly been time even for a nap when the enemy artillery opened up again and the woods resounded with the crashes of exploding shells and the screaming of projectiles overhead.

There may have been trenches somewhere in the wood but that did not do the machine gunners any good. The only ones known to be near Company A were in the gas filled hollow to the east. North of the organization there was a broad belt of barbed wire entanglement, back of the company was another hollow but this seemed to be one of the targets of the hostile guns; to the west along the road were Company B and battalion headquarters, and beyond them other troops.

Along toward morning the enemy's shelling became heavier and heavier, shrapnel and high explosive bursting around us in rapid succession and causing me considerable worry about my men who were scattered around sleeping, or trying to sleep, with nothing in the way of cover from shell fire.[22] Off to the west of us a battery of 75s began to reply to the hostile bombardment and a little later from the front lines came the familiar pop-pop of the enemy Maxims, followed by the rattle of friendly Hotchkiss.[23] The enemy was coming over. Soon the machine gun fire ceased and the hostile artillery slackened but our own artillery which had been wakened into activity fired until daybreak.

The Carthage men had reached the front just in time to set in on a hostile raid. The men of Company A who had laid down in front of the reserve machine gun position were moved away so the gun could fire if the enemy came back far enough, and as many men as there was room for were placed in the ditch along the shallow road cut. The rest still lay in the open woods; there was nothing else to do. This was complete inadequacy on my part, it felt. I felt responsible for their lives but this was about all I could figure to do.

22. Estel Ziler of Company A attempted to describe this shelling in a letter home: "for one who was not there it can hardly be explained what it was like. It was just a dull thud, or lots of dull thuds, all the time, I should say, and then the zing z-z-z whiz-bang. . . . 'Just like a fire cracker?' I should say not. It was thousands of them and the air was aflame with shots. We were on the ground behind rock and trees, under and in machines." *Carthage* (MO) *Evening Press*, November 18, 1918.

23. Schrantz refers to the French 75mm field gun, Model 1897, the standard artillery piece used by the American Expeditionary Forces.

Whatever the soldiers may have thought or felt, they underwent this ordeal with a fine show of indifference, though it was one of the most trying incidents of their service. A few days later every man would have digged [*sic*] a fox hole for shelter but this stage of development had not yet been reached. All lay stretched quietly as if trying to sleep, and even those ordered to move to the shelter of the ditch did so with apparent reluctance, apparently fearing someone might think them afraid.

Enemy shells passed repeatedly through the upper branches of the trees above, shearing off small limbs which fell among the pretended sleepers. Several times, shells exploded in the trees above, apparently detonated by limbs they had struck, yet there were no casualties. In connection with the arrival of each shell the discharge of the German cannon would first be heard, then the growing shriek of the projectile coming through the air, then the noise of passage overhead and the eventual crash of the explosion. Soon the enemy machine gun fire ceased, though a Hotchkiss chattered for a time longer.

Once I had gotten the men into as much security as I knew how, I too laid down behind a tree—scared a bit now since I had nothing to do—and tried to sleep. I wished drowsily the guns would stop—then went to sleep as the fire slackened and I felt there was little further danger of casualties.

Company A had suffered no casualties, a happy circumstance probably explainable by the fact that the location of the French batteries was definitely known to the Germans and these had been the targets for the enemy artillery, those projectiles which had passed directly over the Carthage men or which had exploded in the trees having been intended for the battery in rear.

I recall hearing no shell fragments down about the ground level—perhaps because I was too busy racking my brain trying to figure out some way to avoid casualties.

Several steel fragments of exploded shells were picked up on the road, however, beside the point where a part of the men of the company had crouched, and other steel slivers doubtless had sunk themselves into the earth elsewhere in the area occupied.

Only one man I saw displayed outward evidence of fear—and I pretended not to see him. He was standing behind a tree, quite wisely and according to my instructions, but shaken with great tremors. I passed him without, I hoped, any indication I had noticed, but I resolved to keep an eye on him in the impending battle. I did as well as I could and he did all right.

No one had been hit in B Company or in battalion headquarters. Just beyond Company B the Machine Gun Company, 139th Infantry, had had some mules killed, and in the French battery just west of that there were four men dead. The Meuse-Argonne battle was not to start for 24 hours yet but this period of preliminaries certainly was not any time of peace.

The Germans had raided the front trenches which were still held by the French and had carried off seven prisoners. Thirty-six hours later these prisoners were rescued from a German dug-out by attacking American infantry.

The American plan to leave the French troops in the front until the last minute in an attempt to keep the American concentration secret from the Germans, apparently had proven effective. Though it is frequently said that the Germans were surprised in the Meuse-Argonne operation, this cannot be true of the Germans in the front line. The noise of trucks in the Allied lines must have told them something of what was in progress and the raid was probably to get identifications of the troops which were to make the attack. The securing of prisoners from the French division which had been holding the line for some time may have deceived them.

In any event during the forenoon of September 25 a German plane came over the Forêt de Hesse and showered down little handbills printed in French, starting out with a huge type "Pourquoi" (Why?) and arguing, so near as the Carthage soldiers could puzzle out, that the English were beaten and the Americans couldn't fight, and there was no need of any Frenchman trying now to win the war. They purported to be signed by "a Poilu who does not want to rot in the trenches."

On September 25, 1918, nine American front line divisions, backed up by heavy reserves, were crouching between the Argonne Forest and the Meuse River getting ready to pounce, the following morning, on the enemy in the toughest and most vital sector of the whole Western Front, for a penetration here would menace the German lines of communications in all western France. The 35th Division was to attack on a front of about a mile and a half. The dominating feature in the front line was the hill of

Vauquois, honeycombed with galleries and enormously strong, one of the most formidable places on the Western Front. The attack was to be supported by a heavy American and French artillery concentration scheduled to start at 2:30 a.m., and by the fire of eight machine companies—96 guns—in an initial barrage. The other six machine gun companies of the division were to go forward with the rifle units at the jump-off as forward guns.

From positions in the west part of the sector the 128th Machine Gun Battalion—the Carthage and Nevada-Butler companies—augmented by the Machine Gun Company 139th Infantry (Sedalia, Mo., and Wellington, Kans.) was to rake the eastern portion of the enemy zone. Major Westley Halliburton of Carthage was in command of this group.

After daybreak Major Halliburton, Captain Corey of Company B of the 129th, Lieut. Wood of the Machine Gun Company of the 139th and I visited Buzemont, the hill from which we were to put down our barrage.

Company A was to be the left company of the eight machine gun organizations furnishing the machine gun barrage, and one platoon was to be pushed out to a low height known as Hill 202 in the extreme outpost line and close to the enemy position, in order to place a flanking barrage on the west shoulder of Vauquois Hill.[24]

The French captain in charge of the hill [Buzemont] had a splotch of blood on his left breast where he had been struck by a partially spent splinter of shell the night before but he was hilariously happy because the Germans had taken no prisoners from his company; he was still thrilled by the excitement of the fight; and quite possibly he was a bit exuberant from pinard, the French issue wine, with which he had been celebrating. He shook all of us vigorously by the hand and laughed much at my German name.

24. According to Schrantz's 1919 account, two platoons of the company were ordered to fire on the forward slope of Rossignol Ridge, while a platoon fired from Hill 202 against Vauquois Hill. The latter platoon was to open fire a minute later than the remainder of the guns in order to make sure that the other guns would be firing before the forward four started. "Had these guns fired even a few shots before the other guns began," Schrantz related, "their exposed position might have been given away." Two platoons of the company eventually lifted their fire nearer the summit of the ridge in order to avoid endangering their own infantry. Although only a portion of the reverse slope of the ridge could be reached, any shots that missed the ridge might do "useful work" in the rear. The secondary target of the four guns on Hill 202 was to be Hill 221. Schrantz, "Initial Machine-Gun Barrage, 35th Division, Meuse-Argonne Offensive," *Infantry Journal* 16 (November 1919): 370.

He welcomed the Americans like long-lost brothers but he had some unpleasant news for Company A. Hill 202 was no longer held, despite the map indication that it was. The barbed wire was so bad out there and the place so close to the enemy that the garrison had been withdrawn. The Company A officers looked at each other with lifted eyebrows. It would be necessary to push one platoon out in No-Man's-Land in order to properly support the attack.

Back in the woods after the reconnaissance, the situation was explained by the company commander, first to the sergeants then to the corporals, after which each platoon commander took up with his own platoon the particular part it was to play. The platoon commanders then accompanied me back to the hill to look at the trenches and terrain itself, then back to the woods where Lieut. Dunn had prepared the company fire charts and from which the platoon commanders prepared their own data.

The heavy trucks of the company—the ones containing the kitchens and food—had not arrived and empty stomachs were clamoring to be filled. Each man had two days reserve rations in his haversack but this could not be touched except on command of an officer. Reluctantly the captain gave the word, adding a warning: "We must eat, and the reserve rations are all that we have," he told the soldiers, "so you may start in on them—but eat as lightly as you can. This is supposed to be a supply for two days but it may be a week before we get anything else. Portion it out to yourself accordingly."

At evening, leaving our transport in the woods, we carried our guns up the trenches to Buzemont, thence over the parapet to a little abandoned orchard from which two platoons of my company were to fire. The second platoon under Lieut. E.J. Bourne moved forward to fire the flank barrage on Vauquois from Hill 202.[25]

At dark the front was again lighted by a succession of flares and the hostile artillery began once more its harassing fires on

25. Edgar Joseph Bourne was born in Carterville, Missouri, on November 5, 1893. He enlisted on June 1, 1917 and became a sergeant in the Machine Gun Company, Sixth Missouri Infantry (later 140th Infantry). Commissioned a second lieutenant in April 1918, and assigned to Company B, 128th Machine Gun Battalion, Bourne served overseas beginning on April 25, 1918, and was transferred to Schrantz's Company A in July 1918. He was severely wounded on September 26, 1918, but continued to serve overseas until April 30, 1919. He died in Los Angeles, California, on May 11, 1981. Missouri Secretary of State, State Archives, Soldiers' Records, War of 1812-World War I, www.sos.mo.gov/archives/soldiers; HST. Schrantz noted that Bourne had only "a couple of bombers" placed on his left flank for protection.

2nd Lt. Edward J. Bourne, 128th Machine Gun Battalion (*National Archives*)

the Forêt de Hesse and on the roads leading to it from the rear. Now the men with the gun cars and the men farther away in the mud with the heavy trucks, again heard the scream of shells, the crash of the explosions and the scream of flying fragments, but after having had a day to pick places of shelter they lay comparatively snug and safe, except for the inconvenience of having to put on gas masks occasionally. Up in the line the men were untroubled by the screeching shells for all of the projectiles were aimed at the rear and hurtled nosily but harmlessly overhead.

Fire data had been figured during the day, and now the first platoon, 1st Lieut. Frank L. Snyder commanding, with Sergeant

Paul Havens as platoon sergeant and Sergeants Willard Brown and Ernest Ellis as section leaders; and the third platoon, Second Lieut. Edwin E. Samuels commanding, Sergeant Carl Cain platoon sergeant and Sergeants James A. Amerman and Joseph E. Taylor section leaders, took up their allotted positions in what had once been an old orchard, emplaced their guns on wooden T-bases to give them solidity, marked the direction of fire, then took the guns down again and placed men, weapons and ammunition under cover for protection against the counter-preparation of the enemy artillery which would certainly follow the opening of the American barrage.[26]

The task of the second platoon in getting into position was more trying. Passing through the actual front line it moved out a quarter of a mile through abandoned trenches with nothing in front of it but the enemy, and took position on Hill 202, nearer the German trenches than its own lines. A bomber post was established to the north to afford warning of any approach by a German patrol and in the intervals between flares the positions for the four guns were selected and the firing stakes set out. This would be an unpleasant situation if the Germans, still curious about their front, would raid again but this night it seemed the enemy was remaining inside his own wire.

This stage of the preparations of the second platoon was probably a nerve-wracking one for the platoon commander, Second Lieut. E.J. Bourne, who bore the responsibility, but he had with him four sergeants each of whom was himself fitted to command a platoon. The platoon sergeant was Norval R. Hopwood, capable, eager and alert; one section was commanded by Sergeant Fred R. Clark, calm and competent veteran with a Regular Army as well as National Guard and World War background; the other section was regularly in charge of Sergeant Charles S. Edwards, an expert machine gunner who mocked indifferently at the war, at the enemy and at death. But Edwards, the senior of the three mentioned, was this night detailed to the particular task of assisting Lieut. Bourne,

26. James William Amerman was born in South Fork, Oregon County, Missouri, on May 10, 1898. He died on November 9, 1974, in Manitou Springs, Colorado, and was buried in Park Cemetery in Carthage. He served as a private with Company A on the Mexican border from 1916–17 and overseas from April 25, 1918, to April 24, 1919; *The Service of the Missouri National Guard on the Mexican Border*, 124; Missouri Secretary of State, State Archives, Soldiers' Records, War of 1812–World War I, www.sos.mo.gov/archives/soldiers; *The Carthage* (MO) *Press*, November 11, 1974.

while Sergeant Clinton E. Miles, an experienced soldier of many years National Guard service, and the senior gas noncommissioned officer of the company, was detailed to handle Edward's section.[27] It was a good platoon and I had no doubts about its performance—had no such doubts about any of the platoons in fact.

In the trenches on Buzemont just back of the first and third platoons, company headquarters had been set up and the company command group waited. Back of the hill Major Halliburton had established the battalion command post near a front line dressing station where American army surgeons were busy laying out their equipment, ready for the flood of wounded patients expected soon.

In most ways it was a quiet night for a nervous front. The usual flares and occasional bursts of fire. The enemy had not been shelling the front lines during the night but was throwing plenty of gas, shrapnel and high explosive along the roads and in the rear areas. The spiteful whine of his shells going over continued until 2.30 a.m. when the situation changed.[28]

27. Actually Albert Clinton Miles, born in Clay Center, Nebraska, in 1894 and who died in Seattle, Washington, on January 18, 1960. He served as a private and private first class with Company A on the Mexican border 1916–17, and overseas from April 25, 1918, to April 24, 1919. *The Service of the Missouri National Guard on the Mexican Border*, 126; Missouri Secretary of State, State Archives, Soldiers' Records, War of 1812–World War I, www.sos.mo.gov/archives/soldiers; *Joplin* (MO) *Globe*, January 20, 1960.

28. Estel Ziler of Company A described the tense situation: "It was like waiting for the town clock to strike twelve, when the Fourth of July celebration would be on." *Carthage* (MO) *Evening Press*, November 18, 1918.

Chapter 11

The Meuse-Argonne Offensive: Day 1

The Meuse-Argonne Offensive was preceded by a massive Allied artillery bombardment. More than 2,700 guns roared to life at 2:30 a.m. on September 26, 1918. "It seemed," wrote one eyewitness, "that for a while the lid of Hell had been pushed back a little space." Another described it as "a Niagara of flame, a river of iron."[1] Walter Weber of the 129th Machine Gun Battalion thought it "a perfect inferno of shrieking and bursting shells as if nature herself was in convulsions and seeking out of this chaos to form a new earth." Weber believed that the very hills rocked at their foundations, and "it did not seem that anything wrought by hand of man could withstand this storm of steel."[2] The noise was so intense, recalled a Kansas soldier, "you couldn't hardly hear yourself think." Separate explosions became indistinguishable and melded into "one loud thunder."[3] "There was no more rest for us," 137th Infantry Chaplain William Ernest Sullens told his mother. "What was happening was too wonderful and too exciting."[4]

Three hours later, the Missourians and Kansans stepped off toward the German lines through a heavy fog, soon made more

1. Kenamore, *From Vauquois Hill to Exermont*, 89; Edwards, *From Doniphan to Verdun*, 58.
2. Weber, *History of the 129th Machine Gun Battalion*, 38.
3. *The Hutchison* (KS) *News*, February 7, 1921.
4. *The Springfield* (MO) *Daily Leader*, November 6, 1918.

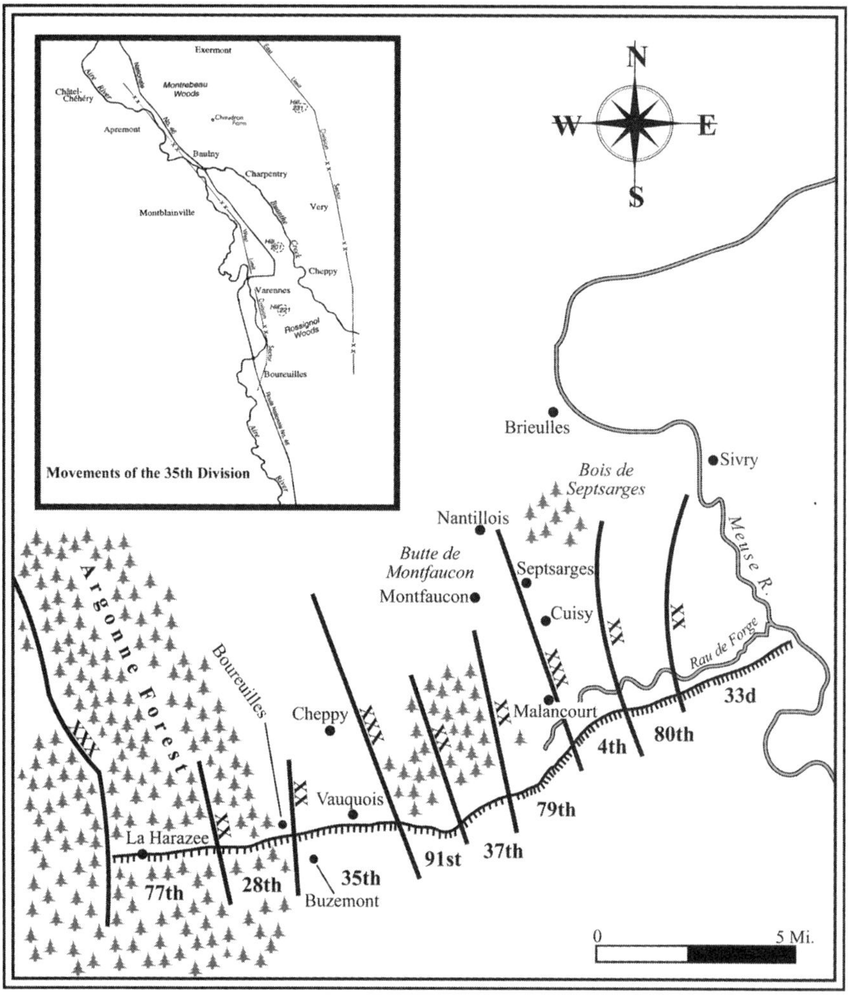

Meuse-Argonne

dense by smoke from the multitude of explosions. "Fog is a help to an attack, in screening you from hostile fire to some extent, but in a difficult country and with troops of short or no battle experience, as here, its advantages were more than cancelled by the added difficulty of holding direction and keeping liaison," observed I Corps commander Major General Hunter Liggett.[5] Once the fog lifted about mid-morning, the Americans were once again easy targets for well positioned machine guns and artillery. In the words of one officer, the early hours of the attack were destined to "'separate the men from the boys.'"[6]

5. *The National Tribune* (Washington, D.C.), July 7, 1927.
6. Kenamore, *The Story of the 139th Infantry*, 40.

The 35th men were expected to cover a division front of about a mile and a half in width at the jumping off point, which gradually widened to twice that distance. The division's 69th Infantry Brigade led the advance, with the 137th Infantry on the left and the 138th Infantry on the right of the sector. In support was the 70th Brigade, the 139th Infantry on the left and the 140th Infantry on the right. Schrantz and most of the men of the 128th Machine Gun Battalion were positioned on Buzemont Hill to provide a machine gun barrage to suppress enemy fire and prevent German reinforcements from moving forward.[7]

The first substantial obstacle the 35th faced was Vauquois Hill, an east-west eminence about a hundred feet high and a thousand feet long. Vauquois was the scene of horrific fighting between the French and Germans earlier in the war, but by late 1918 was only lightly defended. Units of the 35th Division were ordered to bypass the hill on the east and west, while a portion of Schrantz's machine gun company, positioned 800 meters north of Buzemont, enfiladed the German trenches along the southeastern face of Vauqouis. The hill fell easily to a battalion from the division's reserve.

The village of Cheppy, three kilometers north of Vauquois, proved far more difficult. The German position there, consisting of barbed wire, machine gun nests and pillboxes, was located just south of the village on a bluff overlooking Buanthe Creek. Despite their best efforts, the American attack on Cheppy failed. Only the arrival of Lieutenant Colonel George S. Patton and his tanks allowed the infantrymen to finally break the German line about 12:30 p.m. The troops advanced to Very, occupied the town and halted for the day just north of the village.

On the opposite side of the division's sector, the 137th Infantry Regiment's objectives included the villages of Boureuilles and Varennes. The 137th took both, but its drive was stopped just north of Varennes. Colonel Carl Ristine and his 139th Infantry soon arrived on the scene. Ristine, dismayed by the 137th's lack of progress and told that it would be suicidal to advance without artillery support, moved his men forward about 2:45 p.m.,

7. As division machine gun officer Donald D. Hay noted, the 35th's "zone of action" was 2,500 meters in width at the front line, while north of the Cheppy-Varennes line it widened to 4,500-5,000 meters. The division was to be arranged in column of brigades, with regiments side by side, each with one battalion in the front line, one following in support, and one in reserve. The rate of advance from the "line of departure" (500 meters south of a parallel to the German front line) was to be 100 meters in four minutes, up to the Cheppy-Varennes line. Hay, "Machine Guns, 35th Division, Meuse-Argonne Operation, Sept. 26–Oct. 1, 1918," 193.

pressed the attack, and forced the Germans to retreat. By the end of the first day, the 35th Division had advanced a respectable three miles and captured Boureuilles, Vauquois Hill, Cheppy, Varennes and Very. Major Thomas Loy of the 129th Machine Gun Battalion believed that the first day chasing the "Boche" was like "hunting rabbits."[8] Unfortunately for the men of the 35th Division, those "rabbits" would soon be hunting the Americans.

This narrative, perhaps it should be mentioned, is no attempt to describe the Meuse-Argonne Offensive or the participation of the 35th Division therein. It is meant merely to be an account of the experiences of the captain of Company A, 128th Machine Gun Battalion, and since I was this captain the narrative will be liberally sprinkled with "I." There were a million or so other Americans in the battle and each had his own experiences. These just happen to be mine. If failure to paint the big picture makes the battle appear to be mere confusion, it probably is no more confused than were my own impressions at the time.

As the night of September 25, 1918, wore into the small morning hours of September 26, and while the German harassing artillery fire screamed viciously, persistently and interminably over the heads of the Carthage machine gunners on Buzemont, to explode in the woods or on the roads in rear, the front trenches filled up with men of the 137th Infantry, the left assault regiment of the 35th Division. All was now ready for the attack; all minds were set at 2:30 a.m., the hour fixed for the hundreds of American and French cannon closely backing the front from the west side of the Argonne Forest to the east bank of the Meuse River, to open the three-hour barrage which was to prelude the attack.

Shortly before 2:30 there came the noise of a sudden heavy bombardment far to the west. At this thunder of guns all heads turned in that direction. I looked at it surprised. The flashes of light from the muzzle-blasts were from the north to the south; it was the German artillery which had opened fire, not the American. Were the Germans attacking too this night and getting the jump, or had they, like the Allies on the Marne in July, learned of the impending attack and opened fire first? The French captain I had first met the preceding morning stood beside me.

8. Weber, *History of the 129th Machine Gun Battalion*, 51.

"Boche," I said.

"Americaine," he replied laughing and turning to look.

"Boches," he amended in a puzzled tone.

I never did learn the answer to that one. Somewhere to the west the enemy artillery had opened fire first.

No one knew—but now the watches registered 2:30 and the Allied guns all along that great front awoke to action. The opening of the barrage did not come with an instantaneous bark at the exact minute, as the machine gunners had expected. First there was a rather scattered fusillade of cannon shots, quickly thickening to a steady throbbing roar. As far as one could see to the east and the west tongues of flickering fire were darting into the air—but all eyes now were turned forward. "Kaput, les Boches," shouted the merry French captain.

To the front in the enemy position there came a multitude of flashes of bursting shell. Vauquois Hill in particular was an inferno of exploding projectiles. Colored rockets soared everywhere along the German front. A moment later came the crash of the enemy counter-barrage—his "counter-preparation" meant to destroy the attacking troops as they waited the hour of attack or as they moved into their assault positions. The machine gunners were ready for this and crouched under the parapets of their trenches, bowed to the storm.

Buzemont rocked with the impact of enemy projectiles. Fragments of steel sung overhead, though seldom heard in the uproar and an occasional near burst sent showers of clods into the trenches. A regular pandemonium this of screeching shells overhead and explosions close at hand. Most of the German shells pounding Buzemont seemed to be light ones though the Germans apparently were pouring them in as fast as they could work their guns. There was one heavy gun in particular which, judging from the shock, threw a monstrous shell. The first shot from this gun struck somewhat to the front but subsequent ones crawled up the hill until the last one was just back of the trenches on the summit. This was the big gun's last shot, it having apparently been smothered out by our own artillery. Soon there was practically no fire from the enemy while our own shells whizzed over with unvarying regularity, lighting up Vauquois with the flares of tremendous explosions. Good work.

Soon the Allied barrage had fairly well choked off the German counter barrage and the machine gunners emerged from their hiding places, set their guns up on the T-bases previously installed, checked their firing data, and waited their own turn. As yet, the subsequent check showed, no man of the organization had been hit, either in the combat part of the company or with the motor train or supply trucks in the woods. Incessantly the fire from the Allied artillery licked skyward; overhead there was a roof of projectiles traveling northward; in the German lines there was a constant flicker of exploding shells, and those watching knew that in addition the enemy gun positions were being drenched with poison gas. Something bursting above Vauquois was now raining down fire from which rose heavy white smoke—this was white phosphorous, someone said, one of the most fiendish instruments of war.

As 5:25 approached, every officer and every section leader in Company A was studying his watch in hand or on wrist; every gun was laid ready to fire; every gunner's finger was on the trigger; by the left of every gun lay a man with fresh strips of cartridges to follow the first row resting in the brass feed-block of the weapon. Men from the headquarters of the 137th Infantry which had come up during the night as the rifle assault units moved into position [and] thronged the trenches now.

At 5:30 the ninety-six Hotchkiss guns opened up with an amazing rattle, as pretty a sound as ever I heard.[9] The rattle was deafening. By each weapon knelt the corporal, checking its elevation with his bubble-clinometer between the long bursts. It was getting daylight. What appeared to be shells containing liquid fire were bursting over Vauquois and the valleys were totally obscured with fog and clouds of smoke. Leaving Lieut. Dunn, my executive officer—quite serene in the uproar and unmoved of face—at the company command post, I set out to visit the guns, accompanied by Carl Tangner, my orderly, and—if I remember right—by Sergeant Ed Wiggins, the company range-finger.

I visited Snyder's and Samuels' platoons on Buzemont, clambering out of the trenches, of course, to get to them. The uproar was

9. Schrantz recalled that "it was a spectacle as brilliant as a military tournament—the big attack with all calibres of guns hurling a barrage and with smoke bombs filing the sky with flame and smothering the German rockets, also forming a cloud through which our infantry and tanks crossed the enemy line." *Carthage* (MO) *Evening Press*, November 5, 1918.

terrific but the men knew their jobs and the guns were spewing fire in a most workmanlike way. Having taken a look at the platoons on Buzemont, I went forward to Hill 202, moving down a communications trench. Such a cracking of bullets as there was over Bourne's position I had never imagined. The fire of the American machine guns crossed above this point and in addition there was some machine gun fire coming from the enemy, the combination making a most surprising racket. There was the fire from my own two platoons and the two other full companies back on Buzemont. Crossing this fire from the east was the bullets from the 12 guns of Co. A, 130th Machine Gun Battalion, back on La Maize to the east and firing on Boureuilles to the northeast and there was also the crack of German machine guns firing south, though I never heard of where these bullets struck. They must have been clearing Buzemont. The guns on Hill 202 I found blasting away vigorously too with every one excited, workmanlike, and grinning when they looked up. They [there] had been no casualties here. Everything was going fine.

Within a zone less than a mile wide and three-quarters of a mile deep, 96 Hotchkiss machine guns were now firing, theoretically at a rate of 150 shots a minute but in the excitement of the action probably considerably in excess of that.[10] The platoon commanders and platoon sergeants were hovering over their gunners watching to see all was going as it should. Shouting to make themselves heard as I spoke to them or they spoke to their men.

Some of the barrels were beginning to glow with heat and once I saw a flash from a breech from some premature explosion of a cartridge but the gun was firing again in a moment.

Nothing could be seen to the front now except fog and smoke, but the previous careful calculations, and the constant checking of directions by the aiming stakes, and of the elevation by the clinometers, assured the machine gunners that they were on their targets. The first and third platoons were raking the southwest corner of the Bois de Rossignol—wood of the nightingale—1600 meters—almost exactly a mile—distant, enfilading a communications trench known as the Boyau des Houris, peppering the front

10. Schrantz recalled that "there certainly was never a prettier sound than when the rattle of the 96 Hotchkiss guns cut in on the artillery barrage and the guns began to pour their streams of copper into the enemy lines." "Initial Machine-Gun Barrage, 35th Division, Meuse-Argonne Offensive," *Infantry Journal* 16 (November 1919): 370.

of a part of the fire trench called the Tranchee de Gratz, and enfilading a portion of it where following an angle in the wood, it turned north to face the east. A German observation post too, the map had showed, was in the zone, as were also several barracks concealed in the foliage of the woods.

The second platoon out on Hill 202 was nearer its targets. It was enfilading the Tranchee de Brun which faced southeast on a southwest shoulder of Vauquois Hill. The nearest end of this trench was only 650 meters distant; the farthest part which could be reached was 1250 meters and much higher. Fire and elevate, fire and elevate, fire and elevate—this was the work of the gunners; then fire and depress, fire and depress, fire and depress.

Barrels became too hot to touch, the heaps of spent cartridges grew; when a corporal thought one gunner was tired, he had another take his place. Occasionally there was a stoppage or jam, quickly corrected—for it was on such things the machine gunners were long trained. Occasionally some part of the mechanism broke under the succession of rapid shocks caused by the firing, but these parts were almost instantly replaced from the spare parts boxes, and the delay was infinitesimal. The riflemen would be going forward now, but for the machine gunners all that mattered was this firing according to the firing tables furnished. Fire and elevate two mils; fire and tap two mils right; this sort of thing was the whole war for the moment.

Back on Buzemont there was an instant's excitement in the squad of which Private Louis P. Paulson was a member. "Paulson is wounded"—and so he was.[11] No one in the general absorption had noticed any enemy shells burst near, but Paulson was holding a bleeding neck and the blood was very slowly trickling through his fingers. Not serious, apparently; off to the rear with Paulson. Back at the first aid station behind the hill the surgeons were all attention; he was their first patient. The jagged sliver of steel was extracted, the anti-tetanus serum was administered, a tag was scribbled and attached, and Paulson was told to keep on going, one of the first of that long stream of walking wounded to head back that day into the Forêt de Hesse.

After firing 28 minutes, all 12 of the Company A guns switched to their second targets to avoid endangering the advancing riflemen.

11. Louis P. Paulson was born on November 19, 1895, and died on March 30, 1966. He was buried in Hoople, North Dakota.

Members of the 35th Division on the first day of the Meuse-Argonne (*National Archives*)

The first and third platoons were firing into the upper part of the Bois de Rossignol now, on the strong Tranchee de Zurich which topped the summit of the long hill known as Cote 239, a trench 1900 meters distant along which there were numerous artillery observation posts. The second platoon on Hill 202 shifted its four guns to a new line of fire almost at right angles with the first one, now shooting almost due north on the Ouvrage d'Aden on Hill 221[,] 2100 meters distant, a target shared with the West Plains company of the 130th Machine Gun Battalion.

The clatter at the guns prevented the men there hearing anything else but back at the company command post a little away from this noise, there could be heard the occasional stutter of Maxims on and north of Vauquois. The enemy was not yielding without a fight.

After firing 49 minutes the two platoons on Buzemont ceased fire, the calculated advance of the rifle units rending further shooting at their second target dangerous. The platoon down on Hill 202 stayed in action one hour and 17 minutes. At the scheduled rate of fire the eight guns on Buzemont would have fired 58,800 rounds and the four on Hill 202 a total of 46,200 rounds. However the firing, particularly in the excitement of the early stages, had been much faster than scheduled. The Buzemont guns had fired more than 10,000 rounds apiece, and the total ammunition expended by Company A in this barrage could not have been far short of 140,000 rounds.[12]

Back again at my post of command I missed my first sergeant but in about half an hour he showed up carrying a short French carbine which he had acquired in the Vosges. It was after the Armistice before I found out that he had stolen away to go over the top in the initial attack of the infantry and had then come back.

When Company A, 128th Machine Gun Battlaion, finished its participation in the initial machine gun barrage, 35th Division, at the opening of the Meuse-Argonne Offensive [on] the morning of September 26, 1918, there was some uncertainty for a time what to do next, but there was one very obvious and important thing and there was no need to wait for orders to start it. That was the oiling and cleaning of the guns, so they would be ready for use again. All platoons therefore immediately stripped their weapons and busied themselves at this.

Though to ears deafened by the long continued fire of the machine guns this period which followed its cessation seemed comparatively quiet and peaceful, there continued undiminished the thunder of cannon in rear firing the rolling barrage which was preceding the assault. From the front too there came the popping of German Maxims, the rattle of the American Chauchat automatic rifles, intermittent gusts of rifle fire, scattered shots—all the noise of battle somewhere to the northward in a thick fog rendered still thicker by smoke from explosives.

There was also a snorting of tanks and at one time there rose a terrific uproar of Maxim and Hotchkiss guns, a sound apparently caused by one of the tanks waddling through a machine gun nest. As we drew out of our barrage positions, walking on top of the ground by daylight now, streams of prisoners began coming back, most of them seeming cheerful but considerably shaken by the ordeal through which they had just passed. They

12. At 1:30 a.m. on September 26, just four hours before the machine gun barrage began, Major Halliburton sent a message to 35th Division machine gun officer Donald D. Hay, explaining that although he was "in position and ready," his battalion was "very short on ammunition," with 60,000 rounds per company "but nothing more." Hay must have secured more ammunition for the 128th before 5:30 a.m. Hay, "Machine Guns, 35th Division, Meuse-Argonne Operation, Sept. 26–Oct. 1, 1918," 194.

German prisoners captured in the Meuse-Argonne by the 35th Division (*National Archives*)

were in the main sturdy and well clothed and one could not help thinking that they must have been from some of the enemy's best divisions, which in truth they were. They were attended by rifle-armed guards with fixed bayonets, one man to many prisoners. I talked to one of the riflemen guarding them. The man who had about 17 in his charge as I recall, told me excitedly how they had surrendered to him, after he had called upon them in German to do so. He spoke in a voice with a marked Teutonic accent, and vigorously rubbed at this bayonet with his sleeve. I wondered if one might have been slow to yield. The machine gunners gazed at the Germans and the Germans gazed at the machine gunners with curiosity. Someone addressed the passing captives in their own tongue and they replied readily. One of the haggard ones said he had worn a gas mask for almost four hours. No wonder he looked exhausted. Most of these men clung tightly to round tin cans containing their masks; many still wore their helmets though others had tossed them as souvenirs to some of their captors. These prisoners were mainly from the 1st Prussian

Guard Division. Someone said that one of the prisoners who spoke English said that we had over run their front lines but could not get much farther—that we could never take Cheppy and Varennes.

Afterwards—a couple of weeks or so—ammunition was issued to us in ready-filled strips but at this time our ammunition came loose and it was necessary to refill the metallic strips with loaded rounds after they had been emptied. Now the machine gunners were ordered to withdraw behind Buzemont to refill ammunition strips, and they came back lugging their weapons and their rather meager supply of unexpended ammunition.[13] All hands were now set to this task—one of considerable proportions. I repeated to someone something that had amused me. When I had ordered the two platoons on Buzemont back after their firing had been completed, some of the men had asked me if they should pick up their "brass"—the empty cartridge cases—as they had been accustomed to do on the range. While the answer had been in the negative the question had pleased me for some reason.

A few German shells were now exploding a short distance to the north, and the men who had been standing about on top of the trench parapets decided there were safer places. The 139th Infantry was now passing northward to support the 137th, Major William D. Stepp of the Third Battalion, under whose command Company A had been in the Vosges, calling for Lieut. Wood of the Machine Gun Company of the 139th to join him with his organization. It was the last time the Carthage men ever saw Major Stepp. Within a few hours he was killed by machine gun fire some miles to the northward.

Back at Buzemont while we were reloading our machine gun strips we saw more prisoners and before long our own wounded on stretchers began to arrive at the nearby dressing station. All said that the attack was going forward but that there was some fighting. Just behind us a battery of 75s fired away with monotonous regularity.

One of the army motion picture men arrived from somewhere and wanted a picture of a man on a stretcher. Corporal Louis

13. Major Halliburton reported at 9:50 a.m. to division machine gun officer Donald D. Hay that his men were "reloading as far as ammunition permits," but that only one of his men was slightly wounded and the "barrage went according to schedule." Hay, "Machine Guns, 35th Division, Meuse-Argonne Operation, Sept. 26-Oct. 1, 1918," 195.

Hooten of Company A, sound and well, accepted the invitation and stifled his grins long enough to look unhappy for the camera. Twenty-four hours later Hooten with three machine gun bullets through his shoulder could have used that stretcher in real earnest. Sergeant Charles S. Edwards asked me if the 128th Machine Gun Battalion had suffered any casualties. A Company had Paulson slightly wounded I told him. Captain Corey had told me that no one in B Company had been hit.

The sergeant grinned.

"Those S—o—B—'s ought to know, sir," he said. "That they can't kill anyone in this battalion."

Somewhere in a German artillery caisson at that moment was a shell fated two days later to take his life. He was—as it chanced or as it was written—to be the first man in the battalion to die.

Everything seemed calm and peaceful behind this hill as flying fingers shoved cartridges into the metallic strips, for the noise of cannon fire everywhere was now as much a part of the day as the sunshine and blue sky. A regiment of French artillery—the 211th I know now—were behind us engaged in firing their part of the rolling barrage. Most of the batteries were back [at] the edge of the woods. One 75-millimeter cannon nearby was a nuisance, however. Its blast was near enough to be disturbing at every shot and it continued monotonously to blaze away. There was something disquieting about this. It was the first time that most of us had seen the famed '75s in action.

In the sky close beyond the Forêt de Hesse were some captive observation balloons, "sausages," observing for the American artillery. "Look," said someone suddenly, pointing. From each of two of the balloons two men had leaped in suddenly blossoming parachutes. Darting from above there was a tiny plane. One of the balloons burst into flames, the plane swerved and the other great gas bag also was enveloped by blaze. Other balloons in sight were being rapidly lowered. The parachutes were floating to earth but the first falling, burning, writhing gas bag was falling faster. The spectators gasped as it caught in its blazing folds one of the parachutes. Now there were three parachutes descending behind the trees.

By this time the moving picture men could get all the pictures they wanted of real wounded men. Many walking wounded with reddened first aid bandages were in line at the dressing station. Half a dozen bleeding forms on grounded stretchers waited their turns.

At this point the strength of Company A was increased by 24 men from a rifle unit attached for the purpose of carrying ammunition. Two of these were assigned to each gun crew.

Refilling the metal machine gun strips from the great pile of loose cartridges available was a tiresome task, and far too slow for the convenience of the division machine gun officer [Colonel Hay] who wanted the 128th Battalion to rush off with him somewhere at once to join the division reserve [near Mamelon Blanc a couple of kilometers to the northeast], yet machine guns could not shoot without ammunition and refilling the strips was necessary. We hurried the work along as rapidly as we could. The Ford train had come up now out of the woods but the supply trucks were still absent somewhere in the mud with the battalion food. Prisoners were still going by.

At last the cartridge strips were filled, the greater part of the ammunition was loaded into the Fords, and the 128th Battalion was directed by Major Westley Halliburton, in accordance with the instructions of the division machine gun officer, to move a mile or so eastward across the valley to the hill La Maize, carrying its guns and a limited amount of ammunition. It was necessary to push the cars by hand most of the way and the heavy Hotchkiss guns

Vauquois Heights, Missouri State Capitol (*Springfield-Greene County Library*)

had to be carried by the men who were almost exhausted already by their exertions of the previous days and nights. This wasn't an easy walk, due to mud and wire, but both guns and cars finally arrived there, the guns across country, the cars by a roundabout mud trail. But the division reserve wasn't at La Maize. It had moved on somewhere else, and the division machine gun officer, after conference with Major Halliburton, decided the battalion should cross back over the valley to Buzemont and go forward to the west of that hill by way of the village of Boureuilles captured in the first rush. He and Major Halliburton would go ahead in the Ford train. The marching portions of Companies A and B would follow.

Back to Buzemont again, refilling at the spring near the dressing station such canteens as needed it, and then northwestward.

Back at Buzemont on a fairly decent trail the Ford train, less what cars were out of commission and stuck in the mud, moved around the hill and to the front. The division machine gun officer and the major were on the train and left orders with the marching portion of the battalion to join them near the outskirts of Varennes due west of Cheppy. The larger portion of the ammunition was on the cars and all the guns and a few boxes of ammunition per gun were being carried by hand.

The fog had long since lifted and the day was now clear.

It was not often that on a move forward in a dangerous situation the Ford gun trucks of Company A, 128th Machine Gun Battalion, preceded the marching column and it was therefore with some elation at about noon September 26, 1918, the first day of the Meuse-Argonne offensive, that the drivers of the 16 light cars of the company passed the foot portion of the company and, with the rest of the 128th Machine Gun Battalion Fords, followed Major Westley Halliburton around the hill at Buzemont and speeded forward to cross the old trench system and join the division reserve in what had been German territory.

The only road believed to have been built yet over the old trenches was at the village of Boureuilles a mile or so northwest of Buzemont but just as the train reached the vicinity the head of the column of the 129th Field Artillery which was displacing forward passed the crossroads and the Fords had to stop to wait for it to pass—but then the artillery stopped too, for a bridge had been blown up at a ravine just south of the village, and repairs had not yet been completed. Thus the Fords waited south of the artillery, the drivers figuring rather disconsolately, that the footmen would soon come up, pass them and give them the laugh.

About this time the marching column carrying its guns and a few boxes of ammunition—for it had been deemed wise not to separate men and guns at this time—was coming around Buzemont hill.

The battalion was marching in column of twos with Company A, myself at the head, leading. As we came around the hill to the left of Buzemont we met a number of wounded streaming back, most of them with tales of disaster and heavy losses at the front.

The wounded bore vague tales of a check met by the assault units.

"I am the only man left alive out of M Company, 139th Infantry," pessimistically volunteered one haggard individual with bloody blouse as he plodded by.

There were also quite a few prisoners, most of them carrying stretchers with American wounded. Seeing that the country to the front was very open and that we would be exposed to observation from hills probably held by the enemy, I halted the battalion and moved forward around the shoulder to see what I could. Meeting a slightly wounded officer going to the dressing station I asked him if the road was safe for troops. He answered that it evidently was for a train of Ford cars and a column of artillery had just passed up it unmolested. The artillery was still visible but of the Fords I could see nothing.

Going back to the battalion I led it forward but we had not gone far when a shell struck squarely in the road about fifty meters to the front. "The parade's over," croaked a passing wounded man.

"I wonder if that was just an accident," I remarked to Sergeant Edwin W. Wiggins, my company range finder, who was marching beside me. Corroboration came swiftly.

The enemy answered my question before the sergeant had a chance. There was the swift scream of a shell coming squarely in our direction and as we flung ourselves on our faces it struck the ditch at the side of the road about five yards from the sergeant and myself, nearer than that to the company runners who marched behind us, and exploded with a roar, showering us with clods of dirt. The "hit the dirt" instinct saved a fair number of lives that time, including mine. I rose and motioned the company to some trenches which were some distance west of the road—a communication trench running forward. The headquarters section and leading platoons obeyed that order with alacrity and on down the road I saw Lieut. Dunn hurrying the rear of my column in that direction and Captain Corey doing the same with the leading elements of his company. About the same time I could see shells bursting around the artillery column in front of us. Evidently the enemy artillery had just gotten into a position from where they could fire on the road just as our battalion came around the hill.[14]

The question now was what to do next. That certainly wasn't any safe road to travel, even as battlefield safety goes. In view of the vigor with which the enemy was shelling the open over which we must cross I did not particularly desire my aimless wandering around with the entire battalion to find the divisional reserve. Moreover the tales of the wounded coming back worried me somewhat as to the situation to the northeast of us.

The thing to do, it appeared, was to move up the communication trench, a slow process, and one that meant missing any messenger Major Halliburton might send back for me along the road.

I dispatched two runners, Bugler Thomas and Private Mort, both of them resourceful men, forward with a message to the major telling him we had halted for a time but would move on in half an hour up the draw if we did not hear from him.[15] I also asked the runners to find out what they could of the situation at Varennes. There had been no more shells near us but I told the two to use the

14. Division machine gun officer Donald D. Hay recalled that "shells dropped all along the column," but that the artillerymen remained mounted on their horses and caissons, "not a single man dismounting." "I was amazed," he added, "at the amount of fire that fell along this column without inflicting casualties." Hay, "Machine Guns, 35th Division, Meuse-Argonne Operation, Sept. 26–Oct. 1, 1918," 196.

15. Clinton E. Thomas, born in Carthage, Missouri, on August 10, 1897, enlisted in Company A in August 1917. Initially a private first class, Thomas was promoted to corporal in September 1917, reduced to private and became the bugler of Company A in November 1917. Absent without leave from April 1, 1918, until he returned to duty on April 11, Thomas was sentenced by a general court martial to forfeit two-thirds of his pay for three months and perform hard labor for the same period. Thomas continued to have problems with army discipline, eventually forfeiting two-thirds of his pay for three months and paying for damages to a school house in December 1918. He served overseas with Company A from April 25, 1918, to April 24, 1919. He died on May 30, 1954, and was buried in Inglewood, California. Missouri Secretary of State, State Archives, Soldiers' Records, War of 1812-World War I, www.sos.mo.gov/archives/soldiers; HST. James Demell Mort, Sr. was born on March 31, 1899, in Cedarvale, Kansas. A resident of Carthage when the war began, Mort served overseas with the company from April 25, 1918, to April 24, 1919. He died on September 16, 1964, and was buried in Golden Gate National Cemetery in San Bruno, California. *Joplin* (MO) *Globe*, September 18, 1964; Missouri Secretary of State, State Archives, Soldiers' Records, War of 1812–World War I, www.sos.mo.gov/archives/soldiers.

communication trench, however, and they departed. After they had gone I walked to the top of Buzemont to see what I could and discovered the Fords turning around on the road in a hollow about a kilometer to the front and then returning, a number of wounded men sprawled on the low tops of the cars. My two runners missed the Fords entirely and went on to Varennes.

Stopped on the road it [the train] make [made] such an excellent target that the drivers were ordered to leave their cars and take shelter to the west, and here they withstood a lively shelling, some shells bursting among the men as well as the cars on the road, but without inflicting casualties. However it was evident that to remain here was not only useless but would entail the loss of a number of the cars, so the orders were given to return behind Buzemont. Quickly the drivers returned to their machines, turned them about, loaded on the low flat backs of the vehicles the more seriously injured of the wounded struggling to the rear, and then with other wounded men standing on the running boards quickly slipped back up the road and around in the shelter of Buzemont again, dropping the injured at the dressing station there.

Having still been unable to locate the divisional reserve the major ordered us back of Buzemont where we prepared to spend the night. South of the battalion, at the edge of the Forêt de Hesse some colored troops were digging. One wondered idly what the idea was for trenches back here—then the truth dawned. These were not trenches; they were graves.

As to the wisdom of propriety of this return to Buzemont I had no opinion then nor do I have any particular one now. At the time I wasn't even interested. This was the concern of Colonel Hay, who had taken over the direction of the battalion movements and of Major Halliburton. My job was to take my company where I was told.

Had Colonel Hay known the actual situation at the moment, I think he would have had the battalion, other than the motorized portion, move forward in open formation, carrying the guns and some ammunition and then have had the motor column follow as best it could as soon as dusk fell. But he knew nothing of where our front line was, where was division headquarters or where was the headquarters of the reserve he was so anxious for us to join.

Certainly I have no reason to ascribe his course to timidity. At the time the enemy shell fire on our left front was increasing and it seemed to me that it would have been a matter of ordinary precautions to set up a few machine guns on Buzemont while we waited just in case our infantry should be driven back. It would have been no trouble and we might as well do that as just sit, I thought. I mentioned this to Major Halliburton and [he] said it wasn't necessary. Nor was it. In the light of after-knowledge it would even seem a bit silly. But then the situation to the north of us was a complete fog, except for the to-be-expected pessimistic views taken by the walking wounded, and it is always wise to take normal precautions when you have no idea of the exact situation. We waited behind the hill as evening fell. By dark Colonel Hay had still learned nothing, the men he had sent out having not yet returned. I told First Sergeant Allen Hines to have the men find such sheltered places as they could and try to get some sleep. Someone had found a little unoccupied shelter on the south slope of Buzemont and I rolled into one of the berths in this, eventually, and went to sleep—but not for long.[16]

About 11 o'clock my runners came back with the report that they had been to Varennes and found it occupied by men of the 28th Division which was operating on our left and had seen Americans advancing in attack north of that place soon before dark. Here was news we needed and I immediately took the men to Colonel Hay and Major Halliburton. The war was leaving us behind. It was time we were getting somewhere. This renewed Colonel Hay's desire to find the divisional reserve for he was fearful that the advance would get so far forward that we would not be available if required. As we prepared to move—rounding up the sleeping men was something of a task—the men Colonel Hay had sent out returned. The headquarters of the reserve was in a draw east of Hill 221, they said, and Colonel Hay should bring the battalion there. Soon after midnight we were under way.

We moved to Boureuilles over the trail we had started earlier, passed over the German trenches at a point where they had been filled in, then followed a muddy trail northeastward. As we moved forward through the village of Boureuilles which had been taken that morning and thence a little east of north, German machine

16. Little is known about 1st Sgt. James Allen Hines. According to official records, his father lived in Miami, Oklahoma.

guns were firing to the west of us and the flares going up in the woods on the hills west of the Aire indicated that the advance in that region had not been so great as in the valley.

Arrived finally east of Hill 221, we halted in front of a battery of artillery whose gunners were sleeping by their pieces whose muzzles pointed to the northwest. No place to stop that. An artilleryman reminded us immediately that they might need to open fire. We moved on past them and stopped by the woods fringing the hill, close around which woods a tank company or battalion was bivouacked with the tanks partly sheltered from view—had it been day—by the trees.

Colonel Hay departed in the darkness to report and finally found Colonel Hamilton S. Hawkins, division chief of staff, at about the point his runner had indicated.[17]

Soon he returned. We were to go on to Cheppy. The march was therefore continued to the village named, my own company with Colonel Hay at its head being in front, then Captain Corey with Company B and then the Ford train with Major Halliburton in the leading car. As before the marching men carried their guns and a few boxes of ammunition per squad.

The division machine gun officer knew the route too. Some one had coached him quite adequately. With comparatively little trouble we found our way along a hedge north of the woods, past La Timbale, another patch of woods a short distance north of Hill 221, then to a road, and east along it to the easternmost of two roads entering Cheppy from the south, and so into the village.

The air was full of the acrid odor of high explosives as Cheppy was neared; and enemy shells were bursting to the west of the village.

17. Hamilton Smith Hawkins III was born in Fort Buford, North Dakota, on September 25, 1872. He graduated from West Point as a cavalry second lieutenant in 1894, and twice won the Silver Star for gallantry in the Philippine-American War. Appointed a colonel (National Army) in August 1917, Hawkins sailed for France in June 1918. He served as G-3 of the 2nd Division during the St. Mihiel Offensive, then became chief of staff of the 35th Division. Appointed a brigadier general in 1928, he retired in 1936, but was recalled to active duty in 1941 and retired again in 1943. He was awarded a third Silver Star and a meritorious service citation from General Pershing, and was cited by General Traub in General Orders on October 14, 1918, for his "courage and devotion to duty in the face of the enemy" by exposing himself to enemy fire while locating and reorganizing troops of the 35th Division, and assuming command of the 69th Brigade on September 30, 1918. He died on October 19, 1950, and was buried at the United States Military Academy Post Cemetery. *The Macon* (MO) *Republican*, November 22, 1918; *The Morning News* (Wilmington, DE), October 23, 1950. *Assembly* 10, no. 1 (April 1951): 47–48.

As we moved up the route to Cheppy we saw here and there silent forms lying along the road. At one place there were seven or eight in a group and in the darkness as we moved by I could not tell whether they were dead or sleeping. I[t] didn't matter so far as we were concerned and there was no pause. Soon there was no doubt. As we entered the town itself, however, our dead were strewn thick along the right side of the road, lying in a windrow in the gutter. I made no attempt to count the bodies but my impression at the time was that there were about forty along the roadside at this point, apparently having been cut down by enfilade machine gun fire which I thought came from where a little bridge crossed a small stream.

After we had passed some distance beyond the point where the bodies lay thickest the column was halted while Colonel Hay ascertained where we should go. He would get orders and come back.

Habitually on a halt the column fell out to the right of the road—a rule strictly enforced—but on this occasion I couldn't and the men were standing looking curiously down in the half light at the dead. "Fall out to the left of the road and rest," I shouted. "Get away from those bodies."

I walked down the road between the living and the dead and took occasion to comment on what had probably happened. The men had come onto the road from the east and been cut down by enfilade fire from the bridge.

"Some day," I told them, "we will catch the Boches in enfilade with our guns and pile them up like that."

This was all right for morale, for there was an approving murmur, but rather amusingly—under any other circumstances—the enemy artillery seemed to have heard the boast. Just then the German battery which had been firing on the road to the west, switched its fire to our own road.

The head of A Company was where a small trail left the main road and ran down into a little valley and then north. On the left of the main road was low ground falling away to a little stream and, on the right, the ground was somewhat higher than the road. We had been halted here waiting about five or ten minutes when the enemy began to shell the roads around Cheppy.

The first shell struck at the edge of the road about twenty meters in front of where I was standing. One or two others cleared the company by a narrow margin and burst at the edge of a field to the right. Several others struck so near the left edge of the road that had the men not thrown themselves on the ground some of them would have been surely killed by the flying fragments. Explosions to the front and to the rear of us showed that the shells were being impartially distributed. It was only a question of time until we were sure to lose some men if we stayed on the road and to avoid this if possible I moved my company off in the valley to the left toward the stream. I think that Captain Corey in the rear of me did likewise but the Fords had to set on the road and trust to luck. Their platoon commanders directed the hasty movement and soon the road was empty except for the impressive dead lying there indifferently and some runner I retained with me.

Lieut. Dunn strolled up the road to join me. There we waited for Colonel Hay, "hitting the dirt" on the rather frequent occasions when the screech of a shell indicated it was coming straight at us. There was something else that was worrying me. After shelling this road a little while the hostile artillery then vigorously shelled a parallel route to the west across the valley. I thought to myself that if I were in command of the enemy artillerymen doing the firing that I would shell one road, then the other, then the space between the roads. This was not a pleasant reflection but apparently the Germans did not think of it for the only shots that fell in the valley were obviously shorts intended for the roads.

I was most anxious for Colonel Hay to come back so we could get moving.

Monotonously the shells searched up and down the road, far ahead of us, well behind us back where the Fords were, and in our immediate vicinity.

Captain Corey had come up now, as I recall, and it was decided that I should go hunt for Colonel Hay and see if permission could be secured to move on.

I went down from the road and in the direction he had gone and searched about aimlessly at first. As I turned back toward the road an enemy shell screeched down—this fire was coming from the northwest—and burst on the slope just above where I flattened myself.

There was the usual fragments above me, of course, but there was more. A thick cloud of sulphur-smelling smoke rolled down on me.

Gas? I put on my gas mask and then took it off. I had heard of no gas like that and if it was gas I already had it for the smoke cloud had been about me before I put on the mask.

Similar shells were busting about and the valley was filling with smoke. My face burned.

Fearing that this sulphur smoke was some kind of a gas concoction I led the company out of the hollow, forward past some buildings where the headquarters of the 70th Brigade were established and some distance beyond to a quarry which offered shelter from the fire and was out of the sulfur smoke. Just as we came up to the headquarters buildings someone told me that a corporal sleeping in one of them had just had his head blown off by a shell. "Corporal Smith has just had his head blown off in his bed," he burst out to the brigade headquarters officer. "What shall we do with him?"

"What can you do with him?" was the practical reply. "Leave him alone."[18]

"B" Company soon joined us in the quarry and Major Halliburton and the Fords came up and, having a moment's leisure, I washed my face in the little stream to see if I could get rid of the burning, smarting sensation caused by the white smoke from the shell which had burst so near me. After washing, the burning disappeared and aside from a sore throat during the following day I suffered no ill effects from the fumes.

18. Division machine gun officer Donald D. Hay recalled that shortly after he entered the brigade headquarters, then located in a captured German dugout, the enemy began to shell the area. Hay suggested that the major evacuate the rear part of the dugout and move the occupants to the front. Although Hay thought that every man had been moved, a shell struck the rear area, "with a great clatter," killing Cpl. James Smith in his bunk. Hay, "Machine Guns, 35th Division, Meuse-Argonne Operation, Sept. 26–Oct. 1, 1918," 197.

Chapter 12

The Meuse-Argonne Offensive: Day 2

September 27, the second day of the offensive, was far less successful than the opening day as the 35th Division continued to push north and west. On the right side of the division's sector, the 140th Infantry leapfrogged the 138th, according to orders, but was quickly pinned down by German artillery and machine-gun fire. On the left, the 139th was likewise halted after moving only a few hundred meters. "It was a test of morale," wrote division member Charles B. Hoyt. "The damp gloom of the September day; the excitement and strain of the fighting the day before; the lack of food and sleep—all contributed against, and not for, the soldier. The German artillery bit into the ranks at every pace. Fresh gaps opened as the rut-rut-rut of machine guns increased in volume."[1]

Late that afternoon, "the corps and the army demanded an advance," St. Louis *Post-Dispatch* correspondent Clair Kenamore reported. General John Pershing himself was "not satisfied with the division being stopped by machine gun nests here and there" and expected the 35th to continue the attack.[2] At 5:30 p.m., finally aided by sufficient artillery and tank support, the Kansas and Missouri soldiers plunged ahead. The 140th advanced north of Very and ended the attack northeast of Charpentry, while the now

1. Hoyt, *Heroes of the Argonne*, 84.
2. Kenamore, *From Vauquois Hill to Exermont*, 154.

mixed 137th and 139th regiments took Charpentry at 6 p.m. and moved on to Baulny.

Although the division's soldiers could now boast that they had advanced nearly five miles in two days, their units were becoming terribly disorganized and mixed, so that, as correspondent Kenamore noted, "every regiment, in its space, doubtless had elements of every other regiment."[3] The future success of the "Santa Fe" Division hinged on adequate artillery support, preparation time, proper organization, and good communications. All these elements would be in short supply as the offensive ground on.

It was now getting daylight and Colonel Hay and Colonel Carl L. Ristine, the commander of the 139th Infantry, came up to where Major Halliburton, Captain Corey and I were standing.[4] Colonel Hay informed us that the 139th Infantry was to attack at 5:30 and, that since the brigade machine gun companies that would normally be used to support the advance could not be found, that the two companies of the 128th were to act as forward guns with this regiment. The leading battalions of the 139th were several kilometers to the north in front of the enemy town of Charpentry and it was already after five o'clock. It would be a physical impossibility for marching men to reach them by the hour set for the advance but the Fords were too few to be of much assistance and the column started out, Major Halliburton marching with me at the head.

Alas for my reputed ability to get anywhere with a map! Instead of the 1/80000 or 1/50000 hachured maps I had heretofore used

3. Kenamore, *From Vauquois Hill to Exermont*, 160.

4. Carl Lindner Ristine was born on January 14, 1887, in Clay Center, Kansas. He moved to Joplin, Missouri, in 1892 and graduated from the University of Missouri in 1910. He moved to Lexington, Missouri, the same year, established a law practice, and became the football coach at Wentworth Military Academy. Although Ristine was commissioned a first lieutenant in Company G, 4th Missouri Infantry in 1910, he resigned the following year. Commissioned captain of Company A, 6th Missouri Infantry in May 1917, and major of the regiment that July, Ristine also attended and graduated from the Officers Training School at Fort Riley, Kansas. He served overseas from April 24, 1918 to April 24, 1919. Ristine was promoted to lieutenant colonel of the 139th Infantry and led the regiment in the Meuse-Argonne Offensive. His performance led to his promotion to colonel. He left Lexington in 1934 and moved to Washington, D.C., to serve as special assistant to the Attorney General. Recalled to active duty in 1941, Ristine served with the Inspector General's Office and retired in 1949 as a colonel. Ristine died on November 27, 1956, in Liberty, Missouri, and was buried in Arlington National Cemetery. *Lexington* (MO) *Advertiser-News*, November 27, 1956. Correspondent Clair Kenamore described Ristine as "a 'hard-boiled' commander and a man-driver." Kenamore, *From Vauquois Hill to Exermont*, 127; Missouri Secretary of State, State Archives, Soldiers' Records, War of 1812–World War I, www.sos.mo.gov/archives/soldiers.

I now had a stack of 1/10000 maps, each about 30 X 42 inches. Three cornered at this point and the circumstances hardly permitted fitting them together. As they were, I could not make head nor tail of them.

I started out on the road I thought the right one, the battalion following. But after I had gone about a block I saw it was leading to the northeast (it actually was the road to Very) whereas we were to go to the northwest. The guide posts usual in French villages had of course been removed by the enemy. None of the officers I roused from their slumbers knew anything about routes.

Finally Major Halliburton figured it out. He would lead with the Ford train and the rest of us would follow. Turning the cars about he set off [in] the other direction. He crossed Buanthe Creek and went out of Cheppy on the west. In a hollow just out of Cheppy it was deemed unwise to take the transport any further owing to the likelihood of its drawing artillery fire as the country was high and open and it was now broad day.

On a hill just beyond he stopped the train and the companies moved up beside it. The cars would go no farther to the front. We took our full quota of ammunition from the gun trucks and the major led us northwestward to the Route Nationale.

It did not seem a happy situation. The men of both companies were almost exhausted from lack of rest, and the officers were perhaps in even worse shape for they had had less opportunity than had the men to snatch a little sleep during the preceding two days and three nights. Then the attack they were supposed to support was to start at 5:30 and it was 5:30 now, which apparently meant the units would have to join under heavy fire the organizations they were supposed to support.

The battalion was now on French National Highway No. 46 on high ground moving north in view of the misty enemy-held heights of the Argonne west of the Aire River. Company A, marching in column of twos, divided so that there was a file moving in each ditch and the gravel road itself was left clear. Perhaps because of this or perhaps because the visibility was not yet good, the movement did not draw artillery fire. There was cannonading in progress, but in the excitement of moving up, and in the general uncertainty as regarded the situation, it was not clear what artillery was shooting or at what targets. This excitement was an advantage, however, in that it served somewhat to dispel the old fatigue, though the soldiers were wearying anew from the heavy loads they were carrying, the more so since there was enemy trip-wire in the ditches part of the way; and the officers would neither let the men walk in the open road, nor halt the column in this exposed place for rest.

Here and there along the road we saw dead men, some of them Germans[,]more of them Americans—men of the 139th doubtless.

We were now near our destination. At a fork in the road a kilometer and a half south of Charpentry we found Colonel Ristine giving orders to some of his officers. A dead American soldier, his face covered with a raincoat, lay near where they were standing and not far away was a broken down wagon loaded with dead Germans. It would seem that the Germans were trying to haul away their dead the previous day when the horses were killed by an American shell and the bodies abandoned.

Colonel Ristine told me that my company, less one platoon, would be assigned to the Third Battalion of his regiment which had been held up by machine gun fire and barb wire entanglement on a bare hill south of Charpentry. My third platoon was to remain near the road fork as a part of the regimental reserve. Captain Corey's company was to be assigned to the battalion operating on the left of the Third Battalion. A guide was waiting to show me the way.

Deploying into squad columns—each squad in single file and the various squads abreast—so as to present as little target as possible I moved on toward the front. As we moved out we passed, I remember, a wounded German, his face smeared with blood, who stared at us apathetically.

A heavy small-arms fire was in progress to the front and bullets frequently cracked overhead or about.

Suddenly Private Albert L. Spicer of the second squad sat down.[5]

"I'm hit," he remarked, indicating his right leg.

Corporal Leaford Akin, Privates Charles B. Smith and Fred Robinson and others of his squad stopped a moment. The squad at the right glanced curiously over and kept moving; so did the

5. Albert L. Spicer was born on May 30, 1895, in Oak Mills, Kansas, and died on September 8, 1963. He enlisted in Horton, Kansas, on August 5, 1917, and was discharged on May 10, 1919, having served with Company B, 137th Infantry and the 128th Machine Gun Battalion. Spicer was wounded three times by German machine gun bullets, including once in the thigh and once in the hip, while the final and most severe wound was through the stomach. He was buried in Fort Leavenworth, Kansas. *The Leavenworth* (KS) *Times*, September 9, 1963; *The Atchison* (KS) *Daily Globe*, October 10, 1919.

third squad, next on the left. Someone slit the blood-stained leg of Spicer's woolen, olive-drab breeches and bent over the wound. "It was a rifle or machine gun bullet which went through a little above the knee," he said.[6]

Two men lingered to bandage the hurt with a first-aid packet preparatory to letting Spicer start a hobbling progress toward the rear. The squad moved forward again.

The battalion which we were joining was the one to which my company had been attached in the Vosges but Major Stepp had been killed the preceding day and a captain that I did not know was in command.[7] It was from him I learned that Stepp had been killed the day before.

The enemy had so sited his guns as to gain an extremely effective grazing fire over the hill which was absolutely devoid of cover and the advance was made more difficult by a thick belt of unbroken barb wire. As I reported to the battalion commander a gale of machine gun bullets were cracking overhead and some, not so high, were pinging viciously into the barbed wire and ricocheting off with the disagreeable singing noise peculiar to ricochets. A man, probably a headquarters runner, sitting to one side of the captain, suddenly leaned forward on his hands, a long crease on the front of his helmet showing where a bullet had struck slightly at an angle and entered. I remember him only as thus leaning forward—I probably gave him only the one momentary glance as the battalion commander was telling me the situation. What happened to the man or how badly he was hit, I do not know.

The captain said he was held up by wire and the grazing machine gun fire. The enemy had perfect artillery observation over the bare hill and placed shells wherever he wished. But the battalion was to attack and he wished me to give supporting fire as he went forward.

6. Charles B. Smith was born on January 6, 1888, in Medoc, Jasper County, Missouri. He died on December 16, 1958, and was buried in San Bernardino, California. He served overseas with Company A from April 25, 1918, to April 24, 1919. Missouri Secretary of State, State Archives, Soldiers' Records, War of 1812–World War I, www.sos.mo.gov/archives/soldiers. Fred David Robinson was born in Greenfield, Missouri, on February 8, 1888, died on November 3, 1963, and was buried in Dudenville, Missouri. He served overseas with Company A from April 25, 1918, to April 24, 1919. *Carthage* (MO) *Evening Press*, November 5, 1963; Missouri Secretary of State, State Archives, Soldiers' Records, War of 1812–World War I, www.sos.mo.gov/archives/soldiers.

7. Major Stepp was killed when a German bullet struck him in the head about 3 p.m. Kenamore, *The Story of the 139th Infantry*. 23. A soldier incorrectly reported that Stepp was killed by a German shell. *Trenton* (MO) *Daily Republican*, October 31, 1918.

There was no artillery support due to lack of liaison or something at the moment but would be just before he attacked.

I told him I would pick gun positions from which to support the attack when he made it. Unless I could find some less exposed positions than those I then saw, machine guns would not last long so possibly I had better not open fire until he was ready to go forward—something to that effect. He acquiesced in the policy.

A runner came up from the left company as we were talking with a story of heavy casualties and a hopelessly exposed position. The captain cut short his tale of losses and sent him back with a message of cheer—artillery support in two hours and a new attack.

It was evident that the infantrymen could not advance until some artillery fire could be brought to bear on the ruins of Charpentry from which a considerable portion of the heavy fire of the enemy was coming.

A trench mortar and 37-mm gun lieutenant came up and reported as I was studying the front.

"What can you do?" asked the battalion commander.

"I can knock out machine guns if I can get within 500 yards of them," he said.

"There might be such a place down the road," replied the captain. The lieutenant departed.

Leaving a runner with the battalion commander I went back, moved my company up and sent Lieut. Snyder, commander of the first platoon, to the right, and Lieut. Bourne, commander of the second platoon to the left to seek firing positions—telling them the situation first.

I looked for some myself. I could see none that wasn't reasonably sure of being knocked out by artillery the moment fire was opened. Shell fire was falling here and there on the hill and the bullets were still sweeping close to the surface.

In a few moments came First Lieut. Frank L. Snyder of the first platoon from his reconnaissance of the right of the sector.

"I have found a good place for two guns in some shallow trenches east of here over the brow of the hill—but it is big enough only for the two. I am putting Sergeant Brown's section there, but there is no place for Ellis' section. There is no other cover. We could have him set up but we would just get him knocked off." I told him to get them there and open fire. He loped off happily and soon I heard his guns clattering.

These two guns did considerable neutralizing fire against the enemy Maxims during the day and I believe hoped to materially keep down the losses of our troops.

After some time on reconnaissance Lieut. Bourne of the second platoon and his sergeant came back crestfallen. They reported that in their opinion there was no place that a machine gun in the sector assigned to them could be set up and live.

"The only bit of cover is a place right by the road," they said. "While we were there a Stokes mortar went in position at that point and the Germans knocked it out before it could fire. Then a 37 millimeter gun went in and the enemy immediately got a direct hit on it. We will set up our guns if you say so but we probably will not last long enough even to open fire."

That would have been the lieutenant I just heard report, I thought regretfully. There had been a soldier. Now likely he was dead along with his men.

"Shall I set up a section there?" asked Bourne.

"No," I told him. "Not unless I tell you."

I looked some more. There just wasn't any concealment. Better to wait until our fire could do some good in covering the attack than to go into action on a bare hill under the eyes of the enemy artillery and get put out of action before the attack started—or so I thought. Whether or not I was right I still am not sure but at least my decision was in accord with machine gun teaching of the time.

I decided that the rest of the guns I would keep dismounted until the actual moment of attack at which time I would cover the advance as best I might. At this time no American artillery seemed to be firing. I told my men to dig in where they were, the place being a suitable one to set up to repel counterattack.

Back in regimental reserve Lieut. Samuels' platoon was resting and listening, with a somewhat more disinterested air than those on the very front, to the increasing uproar of battle.

At the same time Second Lieut. Herbert B. Wardin in charge of the Company A Ford train, was, together with the officer commanding the Company B Fords, selecting a position to park the vehicles under such concealment as the available trees afforded, at a point on a hillside near a graveyard a short distance east of Varennes.

"Convenient," remarked the Carthage wagoners, referring to the graveyard.

Corporal Louis Hooten of Sergeant Ellis' section had set his squad to digging fox holes for shelter and, having seen them fairly safe, lay down himself. Then the bullets which had missed him while he was standing, scored.

A burst of hostile machine gun fire from the left front sent three bullets into his back just below the left shoulder blade, striking so close together as to go in what seemed to be the one hole. Two of the bullets did not strike a bone and emerged almost as close together as they entered. The third struck a rib, was deflected and made a separate exit some distance from the other two.

Sergeant Ellis bound up two of the wounds with a first aid packet but in the excitement did not see the place where the separate bullet had emerged. He then ordered Hooten to the rear but that worthy objected as strenuously as his rather shaken physical condition permitted. He purposed to stay there on the hill and direct his squad; and a preparatory order from his captain was needed to start him back with the other walking wounded dribbling from the hill. At the busy dressing station in [the] rear someone glanced at the apparently satisfactory dressings and asked if he could walk; then, the answer being in the affirmative, told him to keep on walking. Finally he reached a dressing station at Cheppy and there fainted from loss of blood while waiting his turn for treatment, later being loaded into an ambulance, [and] sent to a hospital. Here in due time he recovered, and eventually rejoined his company.

About the same time Corporal Hooten was hit, Private E. Glenn Havens, a runner on duty back at battalion headquarters and one of the three sons of W.S. Havens serving in Company A, was struck in the right arm by a plunging machine gun bullet. He remained on duty several hours and then he too joined the walking wounded.[8]

8. Louis Edward Hooten, born in Jerome, Missouri, on March 9, 1897, was raised in Carthage and enlisted in Company A, 2nd Missouri Infantry as a private in 1914. He served as a private and private first class with Company A on the Mexican border 1916–17, and overseas with Company A from April 25, 1918 to April 24, 1919. He was severely wounded by three bullets in his left shoulder on September 27, 1918. He died on February 7, 1973, and was buried in Prairie Lawn Cemetery, Wellington, Kansas. *The Service of the Missouri National Guard on the Mexican Border*, 126; *Wellington* (KS) *Daily News*, February 8, 12, 1973; *Joplin* (MO) *Globe*, November 2, 1918; Missouri Secretary of State, State Archives, Soldiers' Records, War of 1812–World War I, www.sos.mo.gov/archives/soldiers. E. Glenn Havens was born in Felicity, Missouri, on October 2, 1898, died in Spokane, Washington,

To the right of us across a hollow, perhaps 1000 or 1100 meters away our troops were attacking, a couple of tanks advancing in the lead. No Germans were visible at first from our position but it was evident that our men were meeting considerable resistance by the way the line swayed back and forth. The enemy were dropping shells with considerable accuracy on our troops, particularly those which were in support and were in squad columns instead of in skirmish formation. Soon a couple of American shells struck in a clump of bushes to the front and numerous Germans swarmed out of the little thicket and raced for the rear over the hill. A number were shot down as they fled. This group did not constitute all of the German defense for a few moments later enemy soldiers began to filter forward across the same hill over which the others had fled. The Prussian Guard did not cede ground easily.

To the northwest of Charpentry, quite a distance from this action, I could see troops in squad column moving southeastward and I thought at the time that the Americans on our extreme left had progressed farther forward and were encircling the enemy positions.

Neither the uniforms nor the shape of the helmets could be distinguished at that distance but the Company A men thought this was part of the 139th Infantry which had encircled the enemy from the west and was taking them in rear. But nothing happened. Too late to bring fire to bear it was realized that these were German troops coming up to support the hostile front line. Subsequent information indicated that this was part of the 5th Prussian Guard Division, probably the 20th Guard Regiment which at this time was being pushed in to thicken the thin line of the 1st Prussian Guard Division, already bolstered by Landwehr troops. The Third Guard Regiment was holding the line in front of the 35th U.S. Division, supported by counter attacks occasionally delivered by the Fourth Guards and now by the 20th Guards also.[9]

---

on June 29, 1982, and was buried in Park Cemetery, Carthage. He served overseas with Company A from April 25, 1918 to April 24, 1919. *Carthage* (MO) *Evening Press*, June 29, 1982; Missouri Secretary of State, State Archives, Soldiers' Records, War of 1812–World War I, www.sos.mo.gov/archives/soldiers.

9. The Germans opposing the 35th at the start of the battle (the 1st Guard and 5th Guard Divisions) were commanded by Prince Fritz, the Kaiser's son. The 1st Guard was withdrawn from the line on the night of September 28–29, and the 5th Guard was relieved by the 52nd Division on the morning of September 29. Conrad H. Lanza, "Supporting an Infantry Division," *The Field Artillery Journal* 23 (September–October 1933): 422–23.

About this time my attention was attracted elsewhere and I do not know how the attack on the east progressed afterwards.

Our infantry battalion was still unable to get forward but off to the left other troops of the 139th had made several advances only to be driven back again. Several tanks came up and waddled down the road into Charpentry from whence there immediately rose a most tremendous din of machine gun fire but the enemy fire was too strong to permit the infantry getting forward and the tanks came waddling back up the road. For some time the enemy had been heavily shelling the hill where we were lying and several of the men of my company were wounded by splinters. One would have thought it impossible for anyone to live on that hill. But men in fox-holes can stand a great deal of shelling so long as they keep down in them. The projectiles exploded as they hit the ground and the splinters thus were propelled at a somewhat upward angle.

I do not recall it myself but since the war one of my men has told me that I had some trouble getting the men to keep down.

"Hell's katoot," he says I admonished them. "How can I keep you men from being killed off if you won't even keep your heads down."

A splinter driven by the back-blast of a shell which exploded close to First Class Private George B. Herron of Sergeant Ellis' section, penetrated that Carthage soldier's helmet, striking him above the right ear. Save for his helmet, he would have been killed. As it was he had a nasty wound, and company stretcher bearers carried him away; eventually he was invalided back to the United States. Soon Private Lilburn F. Stone was severely injured and also was out of the war, never entirely recovering the use of one hand. Private Lawrence Akin inhaled some chlorine gas—the only Company A gas casualty this day—and received a shell splinter in the heel. Privates Lynn H. Berger and Oltman H. Bunger were sent to the rear with shell wounds which kept them in hospitals for a month each.[10]

10. Lilburn F. Stone was born in Marble Hill, Missouri, on April 14, 1890. He served overseas with the 128th Machine Gun Battalion from April 1918 to December 1918, and was 25 percent disabled due to his wound on September 27, 1918. He died on May 23, 1970. Lynn Herald Berger was born on August 11, 1895, in Heartwell, Nebraska, and died on July 6, 1963. He was buried in Minden, Nebraska. Oltman Harry Bunger was born on April 19, 1892, and died on April 24, 1974. He was buried in Hildreth, Nebraska.

Among the early Company A casualties from this furious pounding was Corporal Vertil Gragg of Sergeant Edwards' section, who received a shell splinter in his left shoulder while seeking a gun position.[11] This artillery fire now increased almost to barrage intensity and, fearing that a counterattack was coming, I mounted my guns to meet it. It did not develop, however, though the shelling continued without pause.

While this uproar was at its height and just as the tanks came lumbering back up the road, a number of infantrymen came drifting past the left of our lines at a slow walk under the impression that a retirement had been ordered. These men had advanced in an attack which had just been repelled and as they fell back they continued on past the position from which they had started.

"Why the God damn hell are you running away?" I shouted. This stopped them like a slap in the face. The words revived and jolted their pride. A retirement had been ordered, they said. No retirement had been ordered, I replied. Go back and rejoin your unit.

They all told the retirement story and they all stopped quickly when I hailed them and returned forward. Finally I found what happened. A platoon commander had told his men to fall back behind the barbed wire. Perhaps not all had heard the wire mentioned. Anyhow many had kept going and had been joined by others.

Some sergeant whose name and organization I never learned was very active in helping to turn these stragglers. In justice to the men who took part in this retirement it should be said that they were among those who later that afternoon, helped carry the villages, the next day took Montrebeau woods and the day after that died so gallantly at Exermont.

A month or two before, as a result of some incident at Fismettes, an A.E.F. order had been read to all units. If any one of any rank ordered a withdrawal he was to be shot by anyone of any rank who heard him. In view of the exigencies of battle it perhaps is just as well that this was not taken too literally.

11. Vertil Cloid Gragg was born in Bates County, Missouri, on January 14, 1895, and raised in Carthage. He died on November 17, 1963, and was buried in Webb City, Missouri. He served overseas with the 128th from April 25, 1918, to April 24, 1919. *Carthage* (MO) *Evening Press*, November 19, 1963; Missouri Secretary of State, State Archives, Soldiers' Records, War of 1812–World War I, www.sos.mo.gov/archives/soldiers.

One man, after the sergeant joined me, replied to my heated query by saying, even as he turned back to the front, that Lieutenant So and So had ordered a withdrawal.

"Why didn't you kill him?" asked the sergeant.

The man stared in surprise a moment as he went back to help his lieutenant.

In only one case did men keep going to the rear after I shouted at them. There were two together. At my second shout they turned their heads again and stopped as I laid my hand on my pistol. Then they moved back to the front.

There were several hundred of these drifters all told, I believe and later so reported, thus turned back. Since to head them off required an angling motion toward the rear, I seem some time to have passed by a dressing station where Lieut. Tenney, our battalion surgeon, was working.

"My God, captain," he said later. "I never knew you could swear that way."

I have no recollection of swearing other than as I have indicated but perhaps I did. In any event I never swore directly at a man.

My next older brother Mike had taught me that before I ever put on a uniform. I always admired him and rather took him as a model. Moreover he had been down in Oklahoma and around.

"Never swear at a man regardless of provocation," he had told me. "Swear if you want to. Swear all around his ears. But do not swear directly at him. It hurts his pride."

I had always followed that sage counsel and so I am sure that even in the excitement of battle I did not swear directly at any one.

Doubtless it would have been better if I had not sworn at all. Major J.E. Rieger, who commanded one of the battalions of the 139th and emerged from this battle with the highest credit, was reputed—and even after this battle in which there was much provocation—never to use an oath under any circumstances. It was a thing for which he was much admired in the division.[12]

12. James E. Rieger was born in Peoria, Illinois. A resident of Kirksville, Missouri, Rieger was awarded the Distinguished Service Cross for his actions near Charpentry on September 27, 1918. He was cited for his battalion's capture of Vauquois Hill and the Bois de Rosignel, and for placing himself before his men at Charpentry and leading them to the attack with "such speed and dash" that a large force of the enemy was captured. U.S. Adjutant General's Office, *American Decorations*, 524.

This break on the left seemed to me to indicate a serious situation. I rather felt our left had caved in. I sought Colonel Ristine to report. I couldn't find him but finally found Colonel Hamilton of the 137th Infantry which was in close support.[13]

He didn't like the sound of it either. He gave me an infantry company to take forward to place in a position from where it could offer opposition if the enemy came through. I had the captain move the company forward some distance to where there was a draw and to stop there since this was [would] cover the gap, if any. We suffered some casualties in this move, one shell breaking among the men just as he put them into position.

Finally I found Colonel Ristine. He listened without comment as I told of turning back these men drifting from his regiment. Naturally he wasn't happy about it. The colonel, a man of outstanding courage, had been up trying to command some stalled platoon. Ristine was something of a character. Had he been where he could have stopped that backward movement himself it doubtless would have been a lurid sight worth treasuring in memory.

I now rejoined my unit, after getting lost down the wrong road and wandering across a bare field populated only by bodies of the fallen.

We knew nothing of course as to what had happened to the platoon which was held back in the regimental reserve but later I learned that Lieutenant Samuels had been wounded twice, once in the arm and once in the leg, and had been sent to the rear. Sometime after the battle when he was in a hospital at Bordeaux I received a letter from him in which he apologized for getting put out of action so early in the game. Sgt. Carl Cain had assumed command in his stead.

It seemed unbelievable that so many shells could fall on an area without inflicting greater casualties, but men lying flat on the ground or low in fox holes were almost immune to anything except a direct hit. Yet there were losses.

Up on the hill near the front there was a succession of men hit.

13. Clad Hamilton was born in East Meredith, New York, on May 17, 1867. He graduated from the University of Kansas in 1892 and became a lawyer. Hamilton served as an officer in the 20th Kansas Volunteer Infantry during the Spanish-American War and Philippine-American War. He served as adjutant of the Kansas Brigade on the Mexican border from 1916 to 1917, and was promoted to colonel and took command of the 137th Infantry in April 1918. He died in 1935 and was buried in Topeka, Kansas. *The Kansas City* (MO) *Star*, November 19, 1935.

Second Lieut. Edgar J. Bourne was slightly wounded and severely shaken by shells which burst near him, and the medical officers at the dressing station, after looking him over, sent him to the rear. Sergeant Charles S. Edwards succeeded to command of Bourne's platoon and Sergeant Clint Miles took Edwards' section. Lieut. Dunn told me of other casualties in our own company—wounded only.

In addition to the above there were a number of men bruised by spent fragments of shell or by rocks thrown by explosions and others so slightly wounded that they either did not report to the dressing stations at all or did so only to have the fragments of steel picked out and rejoined their squads. No record was kept of these men and their names are not now available.

Back in the motor train near Cheppy there were no casualties and the men there not only withstood a heavy shelling at their bivouac but several of the drivers carried up trench mortar, 37-millimeter and small arms ammunition on their trucks to those needing it, slipping along noisily but swiftly under the shell-fire, and returning to the rear again loaded with wounded men picked up by the way.

By the evening of the second day of the Meuse-Argonne offensive, the casualty list of Company A, 128th Machine Gun Battalion, held up south of Charpentry with the 139th Infantry, totaled two officers and ten enlisted men, a figure certainly light enough under the circumstances, however much the loss of the injured from the company was regretted.

A much more serious matter so far as the fighting efficiency of the company was concerned was the general exhaustion. This was the evening of September 27, 1918, and since the night of September 23 there had been no opportunity to sleep save for occasional "cat naps" for a few minutes on the battlefield, and the officers had hardly even had a chance for these. Besides this the physical strain of lugging heavy equipment had been wearying on the men, and the nervous strain was not less fatiguing. Already the two days' emergency rations, consumption of which had been started, for lack of any other food, on the morning of September 25, had been made to stretch for three days, and there had been no warm food since the evening meal [on] September 24.

Small wonder then that as the field grew comparatively quiet in the late afternoon and the situation still seemed stabilized, most of the men and even the officers dozed in exhaustion in the fox holes which they had provided themselves on the bullet-swept hill. There had been some talk that artillery support would be available in the evening, but no information of any planned renewal of the attack reached the machine gun company. Doubtless with clear minds this might have been inferred, but there was a company runner at the headquarters of the rifle battalion to bring any orders and so the gunners dozed. Occasionally a hostile shell exploded in the area, sometimes a sniper's bullet cracked across the field, now and then there was a burst of machine gun fire, but these seemed as nothing compared to the uproar of the earlier afternoon.

Along the front there was an uproar of rifle firing, grenade explosions, the chatter of Maxims, the cracking of bullets, but the light was getting too dim for shooting by the machine guns of the attack.

I was pretty well exhausted from my recent exertions, following nights without rest or sleep, and instead of going to the commander of the Third Battalion as I should have done to see if anything was new I sat down in a shell hole to rest a moment—and promptly went to sleep.

Lieut. Dunn woke me.

Shells were shrieking overhead in the direction of the enemy. Hotchkiss machine guns were firing over the hill to the east. There was a hub-bub of firing ahead—Maxims, Chauchats, rifles, the crash of grenades, miscellaneous noises of battle.

The infantry was moving forward, Dunn said. No word of any kind had come from the commander of the 3rd Battalion[,] 139th Infantry with whom we had a runner.

In reference to this it should be said that the 3rd Battalion in this evening attack was in support of the 2nd Battalion and hence the battalion commander probably had seen no need for direct machine gun support of his unit.

But the rifle units were moving forward indeed. I could see nothing of the Third Battalion but other riflemen, presumably of the 137th, were coming up from the south.

I shook the sleep from my eyes with a stinging sense of shortcoming. Our outfits had jumped off and I had not even known that there was going to be an attack.

Lieut. Snyder came up. His section over the edge of the hill had seen our rifle units start forward, had opened fire and continued to fire until their fire had been masked by the advancing troops. That was some thing anyhow.

The question was what I was going to do now.

I told Snyder to take his right section and move around to the right and toward Charpentry, taking on such targets as appeared. With the rest of the company (less the platoon in reserve) I would swing around toward the other flank.

I got my part of the company in motion—most of the men, I suspect, as groggy with sleep as was I.

The leading elements of the 137th were about us now and, loaded down with guns and ammunition, it was evident that we would do well to keep up with them, to say nothing of catching up with the Third Battalion, 139th. And here I was, flundering [*sic*] loose, actually attached to nothing.

For getting lost from this battalion I attempt no excuse. It should never have happened but the fact remains that it did.

The answer to this situation was in all the old books.

Report to the nearest field officer.

"There's brigade headquarters," someone told me. I reported to Col. Louis E. Nuttman, commanding the 69th Brigade.[14]

"Follow my headquarters," he said. "I'll find a job for you pretty soon."

We followed the headquarters group, lugging the guns, ammunition and tripods.

In column of twos, now in the dark, the company moved to the northwest, crossing roads, struggling through barbed wire entanglements occasionally and now and then noting silent forms which attested to the losses of the day. I lost sense of direction in that I did not know just which way we were going. Actually, I figured out later,

14. Louis Meredith Nuttman, born in New Jersey in January 28, 1874, graduated from West Point in 1895. He took part in the fighting around Santiago, Cuba, during the Spanish-American War, helped capture Peking during the Boxer Rebellion, fought in the Philippines, and commanded the 356th U.S. Infantry in France from June 23 to September 20, 1918. He led the Sixty-Ninth Infantry Brigade from September 21 to November 27, 1918. He was awarded the Silver Star with three clusters for heroism in Cuba, the Philippines, China, and France, and the Distinguished Service Medal for his service in World War I. Nuttman retired as a brigadier general at the age of 64 in 1938, the last of his West Point class of 111 graduates to leave the army. He died in San Francisco on November 4, 1978, at the age of 104. *The Washington Post*, February 2, 1938, November 6, 1978; *Assembly*, Vol. 37, No. 3, December 1978, 33.

we veered off to the left. In Charpentry a mine or munition dump blew up with a tremendous explosion that reminded the Carthage soldiers of some of the powder mill tragedies back home.

One's sense of direction became confused but someone ahead knew where he was going; and following brigade headquarters was not hard. A check of the map and ground later showed that the movement was toward the village of Baulny, a mile or so north-west of Charpentry. Finally a highway was encountered—the "Route Nationale" paralleling the Aire River—and this soon dipped into a valley where there was a bridge. Maxim machine guns still sputtered here and there in the darkness—in front, in rear and to the right—and rifle shots and grenades explosions were frequent, but the artillery of both sides seemed to have ceased fire, presumably through ignorance of the location of the front lines.

When we came to the bridge across Buanthe Creek it was deep dusk. Brigade headquarters had passed the bridge and was part way up the hill as we approached the structure.

There was an interval between us and the group with which we were trying to keep up—I had held the pace down as much as possible because the men were so heavily loaded.

A man with a rifle stood at the far end of the bridge.

"The situation seems to be well in hand," I remarked to whoever marched with me—probably Sergeant Wiggins—"someone has posted a sentry on the bridge."

But the man wore a German helmet and handed his rifle to me. It was a slightly wounded German who had come out to surrender. I tossed the rifle to the roadside and passed him back to the rear.

And so, with me at the head of the column and Dunn in his place at the tail to prevent straggling, we came through a portion of a [the] shattered village and halted at the east edge of it.

After a wait of an hour or so here Colonel Nuttman informed me that the remainder of the night would be spent at this point and that I should take a platoon of infantry which he was assigning to me and using this and my six machine guns garrison the town. As yet Col. Nuttman had not oriented himself and he was quite frank about it.

"I do not know for sure what village this is," he remarked, "but I think it is Baulny. I do not know for sure where the enemy is, but I think he is there"—pointing to the north. "I want you to take your six guns and a platoon of riflemen I am sending to you, and organize this town for defense against attack from any direction."

The mission was a logical one and his doubt as to the location of the front was not surprising. German machine guns were firing to the south of us as well as to the north. The front was a sort of conglomeration at the moment. Germans and Americans were somewhat intermingled. When daylight came, some of our men were in the German lines as well as some of the Germans being in ours.

None of those things worried me at the moment. Here I was under competent command and had been given a job to do. I was quite happy about it. I prowled the village and figured out a plan.

The village, consisting of a massive stone church, most of which was still standing, and a large number of shattered stone houses, was rather extensive and it was decided to hold only the upper part. The lower part of the town wouldn't be held. Sergeant Ernest Ellis' section of Sergeant Chas. S. Edwards' platoon was placed near the entrance of the church, one inside the building and one outside, to command the main street downhill toward the west in which direction a Maxim gun was still firing. Sergeant Clint Miles' section of the same platoon was placed in an old trench ready to fire to the north. Sergeant Fred Clark's section was posted in another trench at the southeast part of town to fire in that direction if necessary. The rifle unit was called on to put part of its men in Cossack posts covering the routes of approach and the rest were held in reserve.

Just before day, when there was a little light, I would go down with a squad of riflemen and get that enemy machine gun which was popping away down there somewhere about the south edge of the village. I left instructions to be awakened in time to do that—or earlier if anything showed up.

"Now start digging," I told everyone. "As soon as the enemy finds this village has been taken he will try to blow it off the map."

I reported back to Colonel Nuttman that the place was organized, as directed, for defense against attack from any direction.

The colonel with one of his staff members was in the bottom of a big shell hole using a flashlight to read a message which had just reached him. Whichever one was doing the reading, read aloud.

It was a rather blistering note from General Traub, obviously written in the impression that the brigade headquarters was still far to the south somewhere.

"Baulny has been taken and well mopped up," said the note, and admonished the brigade commander to move up to that point.

Colonel Nuttman appeared neither annoyed nor perturbed at this curt communication. He flashed his light over his map a moment before speaking.

"As near as I can figure out," he said, "we are in Baulny right now. Therefore there is no place to go. We might as well get some sleep."

One good thing about that edge of Baulny was that some of our heavy guns had fired on the region. There were sundry deep shell holes excavated by their blasts.

After a final look around and seeing that our people were pretty well sheltered, Dunn and I descended into one of these holes and tried to sleep.

Just then came down the enemy bombardment—heavy and light.

There were repeated concussions, screaming metal, flying clods and the noise of crashing walls. One enemy gun put another deep shell hole alongside the one in which we were lying. We were half covered by a shower of clods which gleamed with a phosphorescent light in the dark. I suppose that the luminous appearance of this dirt was caused by some of the explosive matter in the enemy shell and, wondering vaguely about it, I dropped off for an hour or so of troubled slumber.

In the meanwhile, Lieut. Frank L. Snyder with Sergeant Willard Brown's section had moved toward Charpentry and not regaining touch with the 139th Infantry attached his group to the 137th Infantry, passed the captured village, then later on the hill north of Charpentry, found and rejoined the Third Battalion, 139th Infantry, which was reorganized there and also met [and] assumed command of Company A's third platoon, Sergeant Carl Cain, which had moved directly from the rear. It had received word from Major Halliburton of the impending attack and had gone forward with headquarters[,] 139th Infantry. That was some thing anyhow.

Here also was met Second Lieut. Hogan, Company B, 128th Machine Gun Battalion, who placed himself and his platoon under

Snyder's command.[15] This group continued on with the 139th until that unit halted, and at the time—probably about midnight—that Captain Schrantz and Lieut. C.E. Dunn were organizing Baulny with the six guns with them and a rifle platoon, Lieut. Snyder was digging in on the hill a mile or more to the east with the other six Company A guns and four guns of Company B. Snyder's section had suffered no losses during the advance though it had had a narrow escape from getting blown up by a couple of mines which the Germans exploded in Charpentry as our troops were advancing.

I didn't worry about Snyder. A most capable officer able to look after himself and his men.

This same night well to the rear the heavy trucks of Company A, including the kitchen force and equipment, moved from the Forêt de Hesse to the Ford train camp between Cheppy and Varennes and Mess Sergeant Robert E. Roach was hoping to be able to find the company the next day and get his comrades some food.[16]

15. Mason Senator Hogan was born on January 13, 1896, died on January 10, 1988, and was buried in West Plains, Missouri. He was commissioned a first lieutenant on April 3, 1918, and served overseas with the 128th from April 25, 1918, to April 30, 1919. Missouri Secretary of State, State Archives, Soldiers' Records, War of 1812–World War I, www.sos.mo.gov/archives/soldiers.

16. Robert E. Roach was born in Crawford County, Missouri, possibly on June 13, 1894. He may have died in Tulsa in April 1983. He served with Company A on the Mexican border from 1916 to 1917, and served overseas with the company from April 25, 1918 to February 28, 1919. *The Service of the Missouri National Guard on the Mexican Border*, 126; Missouri Secretary of State, State Archives, Soldiers' Records, War of 1812–World War I, www.sos.mo.gov/archives/soldiers.

Chapter 13

The Meuse-Argonne Offensive: Day 3

As the third day of the American drive began, maintaining the pace of the advance continued to be a concern, particularly since General Pershing and some of his officers believed that the Germans were actually retreating. Consequently, new assaults were ordered for the morning of September 28. On the right, the 140th Infantry tried to advance but was stopped by heavy and accurate artillery and machine gun fire. Even with the assistance of tanks and elements of the 138th Infantry they failed to achieve a breakthrough, and the bloody slog was finally halted.

On the left, part of the 137th Regiment along with the 139th turned back a German counterattack, then swept forward from Baulny Ridge. Despite being battered as badly as their comrades elsewhere in the sector by a "torrential downpour of enemy machine gun and artillery fire," the Americans were able to move into Montrebeau Wood. There they found the Germans fighting like "the early day American Indian" behind trees and in small ravines. Clusters of German pill boxes were taken only after doughboys crawled toward them in order to effectively use grenades and rifles.[1] With Montrebeau Wood more ore less secure, the Americans dug in for the night. Doubtless no man in the division was surprised when orders were

1. Bonney, "Operations of the 35th Division," 17.

issued late that night to resume the attack the following morning. Now, rather than being arranged as they were on previous days, with two regiments attacking and two in reserve, all of the division's regiments were "on line."

By the end of the third day, the battered 35th men faced practically insurmountable problems. Communications, particularly between division headquarters and subordinate units was poor at best, as runners continued to roam the battlefield in search of elusive command posts and officers; artillery support, critical to eliminating German machine guns and the movement of reinforcements, had been inadequate since the opening barrage on the first day; and the constant series of hurriedly planned, early morning attacks had left no time to reorganize the division. In addition, many officers had been killed or wounded, or were now missing. Fresh German troops had arrived on the scene, and German aircraft directed accurate artillery fire on the American positions. The exhausted doughboys suffered through deteriorating weather, including cold and rain. Despite the difficulties, the men were required to push on. "It would seem that the whole theory of the engagement was attack—advance, without regard to losses," wrote one participant.[2]

Even the wounded could not escape the horror. When a steady rain began to fall that afternoon, water flowed into the captured German trenches north of Baulny, where the 137th Infantry had established an aid station. The men had to be removed from the trenches to avoid drowning, which again exposed them to enemy fire. Other wounded shivered in the cold, mud and rain, waiting to be evacuated from the fighting.

The Missourians and Kansans rapidly approached their breaking point.

Someone woke me up before dawn. Now I would get that machine gun. But when I looked for my rifle platoon, it was gone. A short time before it had received orders from its company commander to rejoin the company—that the battalion was about to attack.

It was half light and an angry rattle of small arms fire to the north and east was rising.

Brigade headquarters had moved during the night, for the pounding Baulny had received from the enemy artillery had caused all troops except its garrison to draw away from it as

2. Ibid., 33.

if it was infested with the plague, but soon the headquarters was found farther to the east. "Report to the 137th Infantry for orders," instructed the brigade commander.

At the headquarters, 137th Infantry, the regimental intelligence officer, Capt. Scott McKenzie, then of Kansas and some years later a resident of Carthage for a while, announced that he was in command of the regiment for the moment. His instructions were to join the Second Battalion.[3]

I went back to the town.

The Germans were counter-attacking—there was a tremendous hub-bub. I moved all guns to the trench at the north of the village. Strong organizations of the enemy in attack formation were seen advancing out of the timber about 1,800 yards to the north.

The guns at Baulny had had a less satisfactory experience, due to the very good reason that other American troops were immediately in front of them and to the right front. Their left along the Aire River was clear however and the men of the flank section saw the front spray of the German attack round the hill. They waited an instant for more to emerge but instead these enemies who had been visible turned and ducked back again before the gunners could pull the trigger.

A mile to the east, 1st Lieut. Frank L. Snyder with the other six guns of Company A and four guns of Company B had a clearer view. Three guns in particular on the exposed right had nothing in front of them but the Germans.

The guns blazed into action. The enemy stopped, then the formation dissolved and the survivors raced back for the shelter of the woods. Then for a time the Hotchkiss blasts were turned on the wood itself, an average of from 150 to 200 rounds per gun being expended. Here was at least some revenge for the windrowed 138th Infantry dead at Cheppy. Most of the six Carthage guns at this point seem to have participated in this firing. The three on the right appear to have fired more. Concerning them Lieut. Snyder's official report says:

"They were, I think, an important factor in breaking up several enemy counter-attacks."

3. Scott McKenzie was born on November 9, 1890, in Eckerte, Indiana, and died on June 21, 1952. He served as a captain in the 137th Infantry. McKenzie was buried in St. Louis, Missouri. *The St. Clair* (MO) *Chronicle*, June 26, 1952.

Before we realized that the enemy attack had been fully stopped, the battalion of the 137th to which we had been attached began to advance. The three sections of my company were scattered along the north edge of Baulny and the infantrymen got started before we did and were somewhat to our right.

My guns were still in defensive positions and it would be some time before the two sections to the left could come up to where I stood on the parapet of the trench where the first section was located. I had mounted the parapet to see, as well as I could, what was going on, and it was from there I noted the 137th start.

There were already some of our troops, probably 139th, on the ridge directly to the north and in action. There seemed no time to lose.

I would lead out, I explained to the headquarters men and the section present in the trench below. The leading section would follow me in squad columns (each of the two squads in single file but the two files abreast). As the other two sections came up, Lieut. Dunn would start them off in turn, following at the rear of the column.

The result was that our sections followed each other at distances of about fifty meters, each section in squad columns abreast of each other with a considerable interval, the men in the squad columns eight or nine paces apart, myself at the front of the whole and Dunn bringing up the rear.

Heavy firing was in progress forward and as I was speaking there came a "phut, phut" of machine gun bullets about my ears. Long range fire this, presumably—for at shorter range bullets crack—and probably overs from fire directed at the hill north of us.

I dropped to one knee at the sound of the bullets but kept on talking. As I went down a weed just in front of one knee bobbed suddenly and several spurts of dirt flew up just beyond.

The men gazed up at me rather amazed as I kept talking but it was only later that I learned why. As I dropped down to my knee, a bullet struck the ground just behind me and threw dirt up over my back.

Seeing dirt kicking both in front of me and back of me, accompanied by my sudden drop to one knee, they thought I had taken some of the bullets through my person, hence were surprised to hear me continue my explanation. I myself would not have thought that one could be in a burst of machine gun bullets and live, but apparently it not only was long range fire but probably from a light machine gun which had a less stable mount than the heavy ones.

But after the dirt kicked I wasn't thinking of these bullets, only of getting forward.

I led ahead and a bit to the right where I saw some tanks rolling across a belt of barbed wire entanglement and opening a path which I quickly followed.

One tank stood squarely on its head in a ditch and a haze of burning oil rose from it. Some man in French uniform was fussing about it as we went by. Off to our right front a few hundred meters away a low flying Allied aeroplane crashed to the ground.

Soon we were down in a swale where the bullets did not reach and leaving the company there I walked forward to the top of the ridge.

A number of machine guns were in action here under Lieut. Wilbur Maring of the Machine Gun Company of the 137th Infantry and he quickly pointed out to me where the enemy line rested.[4]

He had a map in his hand. He showed me where his guns were in position and firing. He showed me the enemy position on the ground and on the map, all in a few brief moments and under a considerable small arms fire.

Maring, who was to have a long career as a citizen soldier ahead of him, has always stood out in my memory because of that incident. So far as I recall he is the only man I saw during the hurly-burley phases of the Meuse-Argonne who knew exactly where he was, exactly where the enemy was and exactly what was going on on his immediate front.

4. Wilbur Fisk Maring was born in Schell City, Missouri, on April 9, 1897 (some sources state 1896), graduated from Carthage High School in 1915 and attended the University of Missouri 1915–17 and 1919–21. He enlisted in the 4th Missouri Infantry and was transferred to officers' training school while at Camp Doniphan in January 1918. When commissioned, he served overseas as a second lieutenant with the Machine Gun Company of the 137th Infantry from April 25 to November 3, 1918. Maring led the company's first platoon, attached to Company E, during the Meuse-Argonne Offensive. Following the Armistice, Maring returned to the United States as a machine gun instructor. Maring also served in the Civilian Conservation Corps in the 1930s, and in World War II and the Korean War, retiring with the rank of colonel. Maring also served two terms in the Missouri House of Representatives. He died in Carthage, Missouri, on December 20, 1970, and was buried in Park Cemetery in Carthage. *Joplin* (MO) *Globe*, December 21, 1970; *Carthage* (MO) *Evening Press*, December 21, 1970; Carl E. Haterius, *Reminiscences of the 137th U.S. Infantry* (Topeka, KS: Crane & Company, 1919), 161; Missouri Secretary of State, State Archives, Soldiers' Records, War of 1812–World War I, www.sos.mo.gov/archives/soldiers.

Our infantrymen were already on the hollow ahead and Maring's guns were engaged in delivering overhead fire. As I looked hastily for a place to put my own guns a burst of enemy machine gun fire depleted one of his gun crews and the gun ceased fire.

I ordered the leading section onto the hill east of Maring, near a concrete observation post of the enemys, but before it could go into action the infantry had pushed so far ahead our fire was masked.

Enemy shells squarely from the west were striking our advancing infantry directly in flank.

We would continue forward in column of sections with each section in squad columns—eight to 10 paces between men in the squad columns, I told Dunn who had come up. He would see that the company got off in that order and with the men in the column so spaced.

I led off and the unit followed as directed.

Still maintaining the same formation as when leaving Baulny my little company followed behind the infantry for a kilometer and a half into Montrebeau Woods. Enemy artillery, squarely on our left flank, fired at the advancing troops from the hills of the Argonne Forest west of the Aire River. The enemy could see the valley bottoms as well as the hill tops from his artillery position. Through the draws and over the rises the enemy guns followed this target.

Shells whose high velocity proclaimed the comparatively short range at which they were fired erupted about the rifle units ahead. The gunners seemed to be laying direct on their targets and their accuracy was uncanny. The infantry in front of us were in squad columns, the men rather close together. Smash—Smash—Smash, the enemy shells followed this battalion as it moved forward. The German gunners could pick up a squad column and hit it squarely in the middle, seemingly almost every time. I saw one entire squad of nine men off to our right front blown down by the blast of one shell. How many of them were killed and how many wounded I have no idea but the entire group which was in single file went down like a bunch of nine pins.

Now the formation which Company A had taken more or less as the result of accident in leaving Baulny was to be a literal life-saver. The organization had moved off in column of sections, each section in squad columns. In other words the first element was company headquarters, each squad in single file, and each, because the exigencies of the situation had plainly dictated it, with a distance of from 6 to 8 paces between men. Behind this came Sergeant Ellis' section, with its two squads abreast but far apart and each in single file with the great intervals. The two remaining sections, one behind the other, followed in similar formation, presenting a shallow and widely dispersed target to the hostile cannon on the flank.

The enemy artillery on those hills, German post-war accounts stated, had been ordered to turn everything they had on the infantry advancing in the valley of the Aire. Major Herman von Giehrl's account says 13 field batteries were so engaged though I doubt if that many were engaged as we crossed the great open space. But the fire was very heavy and it was about a mile and a quarter across that stretch.[5]

The machine gunners felt that all the hits they received in this long heart-breaking passage, lugging their heavy guns, tripods and ammunition boxes, were accidental ones—but at that there were a number of casualties though there is no way now to say just which occurred in this stretch and which later.

Our own formation with wide intervals and considerable distance between men did not make a good artillery target, and that was our salvation as the enemy did not bother to waste shells on us. The rifle units offered a better target than my column and it was at them that the enemy was shooting.

Some other organizations were badly battered however before the woods were reached and the effect of this direct fire from the enemy guns, while our own artillery was apparently silent, was very demoralizing.

I knew that my men were dead weary from carrying heavy tripods, guns and boxes full of ammunition but to stop to rest was out of the question.

Among the slightly wounded was Sergeant Clint A. Miles whose hands and arms were sprayed with numerous fine fragments of steel. An ammunition carrier was hit more seriously beside him, and Miles bandaged this man's hurts before he went back to get the slivers picked from his own wounds at a dressing station. Coming back to rejoin he missed his own company and attached himself to Company A, 130th Machine Gun Battalion (Webb City)

5. Schrantz included excerpts from Major von Giehrl's article in the *Infantry Journal* in an article he penned for the August 21, 1921, issue of the *St. Louis Post-Dispatch*.

and fought with that unit the rest of the day. Miles, never officially reported as wounded, still carries in his hands bits of the steel fragments the doctors did not get. Another man remembered to be among those injured in crossing this zone, was a member of the 128th Machine Gun Battalion medical attachment who had been attached to Company A.

As we approached the southern edge of the woods the ground was littered with German dead, many of them machine gunners who had fought their guns from shallow, open emplacements and now lay sprawled across the weapons which they had served to the last. Other Germans with their hands in the air were passing through our lines to the rear and I noticed several of them smiling nervously. It impressed me that these smiles did not indicate joy at being captured but rather relief at the fact that they had not been killed by our infantry who had just passed them up. The American bayonets had just passed them by and they were still alive and fully appreciative of the fact—whether they lived through their own artillery fire to reach the American rear or not.

As I have stated before, the load that a machine gunner carries into action is a heavy one and my men, already weakened by several days and nights without rest, were almost exhausted when the woods were reached. Moving them into the underbrush some distance from the open I halted to give them a chance to recuperate. We had already lost touch with the battalion to which we were supposed to be attached but this time without any fault of ours. Weighted down with machine guns and ammunition it had been impossible to keep pace with the lightly armed riflemen.

Upon halting the unit I sought the infantry battalion we had been following—one of the 137th, and I think the Second Battalion to which I was properly attached—and found it resting nearby. We would go forward together, the captain commanding it and I agreed, when we had rested.

We rested for a considerable time—overlong, I thought. The war was forward somewhere. We should be pushing through the woods.

I sought the infantry battalion again. It was still where it had stopped. But I could not find its commander. No one knew where he was. Perhaps he was seeking orders from his regimental commander, I do not know. Or perhaps he had laid down to rest somewhere and had gone to sleep as I had done the afternoon before south of Charpentry. That is an easy thing for an exhausted man to do. In any event I could not locate him and the battalion showed no signs of moving.

I returned to my own unit gnawing my nails.

I did not want to be accused of skulking or sitting down doing nothing when an action was in progress. On the other hand a heavy machine gun company could not move through an enemy-held woods alone. Riflemen alone could force a way against opposition through dense brush like that in that long-neglected and overgrown wood. A heavy machine gun company which tried it and ran into enemy rifle units would be easy meat. So I waited with increasing impatience.

Then a new American rifle unit came bursting through the woods on a run, forward bound.

A big lieutenant headed it, flourishing a pistol and shouting to his men: "Come on A Company." His panting men crashed through the thicket after him, their heads bowed so as to catch the scratching branches and briars on their helmets instead of in their faces. I do not know what A Company he commanded, Co. A, 139th Infantry, probably, though it could have been Co. A, 137th Infantry, but it was going somewhere and I wanted to go somewhere and it seemed a good unit to follow.

The brush here was so thick that one could only see a few yards and it was very difficult to traverse. We moved through this jungle in single file, myself in the lead to control the advance and Dunn at the rear to prevent straggling, the men, though staggering with fatigue, plunging gamely head. But again our heavy loads handicapped us.

The lightly armed riflemen quickly disappeared and the machine gunners struggled along in the direction they had taken; but apparently the big lieutenant and his men had veered off somewhere.

I followed on the trail I thought they had taken. Pretty soon we came to a clearing—a clearing in that there were no trees in it though there was low brush everywhere. I could see nothing of the riflemen.

I started across the open space with the column following and perhaps eight or nine men had emerged into visibility behind me and I was in brush and weeds perhaps knee high when there came the cracking of bullets and the pop-pop-pop of a Maxim in the woods on a hill just above the clearing to the north. It seemed to be a light gun and was wobbling about badly, scattering its shots along our entire column.

Dirt kicked in front of me, one man was shot through the shoulder a few paces behind me and still another was wounded near the end of the column—two bullets through the leg. This latter [man] was an infantry ammunition carrier whose name I never learned, this much to my regret for with these two bullets through his leg he struggled on and carried his two boxes of ammunition almost an hour before giving up and going to the rear.

Those of us who were exposed ducked back into the woods and the enemy fire directed at us ceased.

Anyhow the enemy light machine guns were still there. I did not want to go through Montrebeau Woods, under the circumstances, without riflemen.

Heavy machine guns in attack are auxiliary weapons meant to support the attack of riflemen. They are useless in trying to clear a dense wood in which units of both armies are mingled.

From several other points in the woods Maxims were firing and since machine guns not carefully sited beforehand were absolutely useless in this jungle, I decided to take my company back toward the edge of the woods to wait until the infantry had done a little mopping up.

Obviously it would be well to go back and rejoin the battalion of the 137th Infantry.

Turning the column to the rear, I tried to rejoin the rifle battalion which I had abandoned. Either it had moved or I did not go back in the right direction. Later studying the map I decided that I had veered to the southeast on my return jaunt and so missed it.

For an hour or more we rested here, many of the men dropping off to sleep through weariness. A considerable part of the weary men went to sleep as soon as we stopped. Lieut. Dunn and I moved off to the east of the group and endeavored to eat some of our reserve rations—lunch or breakfast or supper of the night before or something. I did not remember when I had last eaten. In the excitement of battle one is apt to forget about things like that, particularly perhaps, if he is an officer with many matters to worry about besides himself.

We were some distance inside the woods and the enemy shell fire was still falling heavily on the open spaces to the south. Then shells began to fall in the woods itself. Some of our tanks had snorted up along the edge of the woods and the flanking artillery on the other side of the Aire had opened up on them, the overs falling among us.

Some one came running up and told me that Sergeant Edwards had been killed.

We hurried down the line and found Edwards dead and Corporal John Gouty and Pfc. Carroll D. Baker severely wounded.[6] Both of the latter two were gray with shock and badly shot up and at the time I deemed them mortally wounded. In point of fact both eventually recovered though Corporal Gouty, a fine soldier, lost a leg. Edwards had placed his men in a shallow ditch for such shelter as was available at the time of the halt, then lay down himself and went to sleep. He was killed by the shell burst while sleeping.

This can perhaps be best described by quoting the official statement made after the battle by Private Alfred Just who was the closest eyewitness.[7] His statement follows:

> "On September 28 some time before noon, my company was in Montrebeau woods[,] halted for a short time. Sergeant Charles S. Edwards was in charge of my section and had placed us in a shallow trench for shelter. He then lay down and went to slept [*sic*], we having been without sleep for several nights. Some tanks approached the edge of the woods, drawing heavy fire to the vicinity. One shell struck among us, killing Sergeant Edwards and severely

6. Carroll D. Baker was born on February 28, 1897. He died on October 24, 1973, and was buried in Mill Springs National Cemetery in Nancy, Kentucky. Corporal John Gouty described what occurred when Edwards was killed and he was wounded: "We were in a comparatively sheltered position and had dropped down for a moment of rest as we had to do whenever we got a chance. Both of us had dosed [*sic*] off in sleep. I feel like it was a pretty close call when the shell which wounded me killed the man next to me." *Carthage* (MO) *Evening Press*, February 24, 1919. First Lieutenant Frank Snyder of Company A described Edwards as "absolutely fearless, not afraid of anything—which was demonstrated by his not even 'digging himself in' for the night, although this would have been useless in this case, for the shell hit very close and probably would have had the same effect had he dug in. He wasn't afraid to die for the cause and for others, if others would be saved thereby." *Carthage* (MO) *Evening Press*, January 8, 1919; *The Service of the Missouri National Guard on the Mexican Border*, 122.

7. Alfred Francis Just, born on August 9, 1894, in Kearney, Nebraska, died on February 6, 1963, and was buried in Kearney. He entered service on October 5, 1917, and was discharged on May 2, 1919.

> wounding Corporal John C. Gouty and First Class Private Carroll D. Baker. The Sergeant was instantly killed while asleep. I was about ten feet from him at the time."

Sergeant Edwards who thus lost his life was 24 years of age and the son of Mr. and Mrs. Charles S. Edwards of Carthage. He had been a member of Company A since 1914 and had been a corporal during the unit's service on the Mexican border in 1916, and a sergeant since the beginning of the World War. Had he lived and the war continued he would soon have been advanced to commissioned rank, the officers of the company believed. A posthumous citation given him in a 35th Division General Order, later repeated in orders issued by General Headquarters, A.E.F., had this to say of him:

> "Commanded his section with extraordinary courage during the operations near Vauquois, Charpentry and Baulny on September 26, 27 and 28, 1918, and during this time set a magnificent example to his section, exposing himself repeatedly to fire until killed in action in Montrebeau woods, September 28."[8]

Corporal Gouty and Private Baker, injured by the same shell which killed Sergeant Edwards were both gravely hurt. Gouty's left leg was badly shot up, and Baker's back and hips were so badly cut by fragments of shell that they looked as if they had been slashed repeatedly with a knife. Both were conscious and uncomplaining.

There is an old battlefield maxim about letting your wounded lie but I was not going to let them lie in these woods where they might not be found. I detailed the men who were applying first aid to get them to the rear somehow, and they did though I do not know just how. It is still some satisfaction to me that right or wrong, none of my men were left lying on the field. If they couldn't walk, someone carried them back.

8. In the letter he wrote in support of the award of the Distinguished Service Cross to Sergeant Edwards, Schrantz noted his "extraordinary heroism" on September 26–28, 1918, beginning with the morning of September 26, when during the initial machine gun barrage his exposed position drew enemy fire on Hill 202. Edwards remained upright on the parapet of the trench, "strolling" from one emplacement to another, directing their fire. During a barrage the following day he refused to take cover but walking along, encouraging his men and watching for a counterattack. That night, and on September 28, he displayed the "same contempt for danger" under enemy fire. Finally, "despite being near to physical exhaustion," Edwards carried two boxes of ammunition in addition to commanding his section. Memo from Commanding Officer, Company A, 128th Machine Gun Battalion, to Commanding General, 35th Division, Record Group 120, Records of the American Expeditionary Forces, World War I Organization Records, Machine Gun Battalions, 128th Machine Gun Battalion, Box 264, NARA.

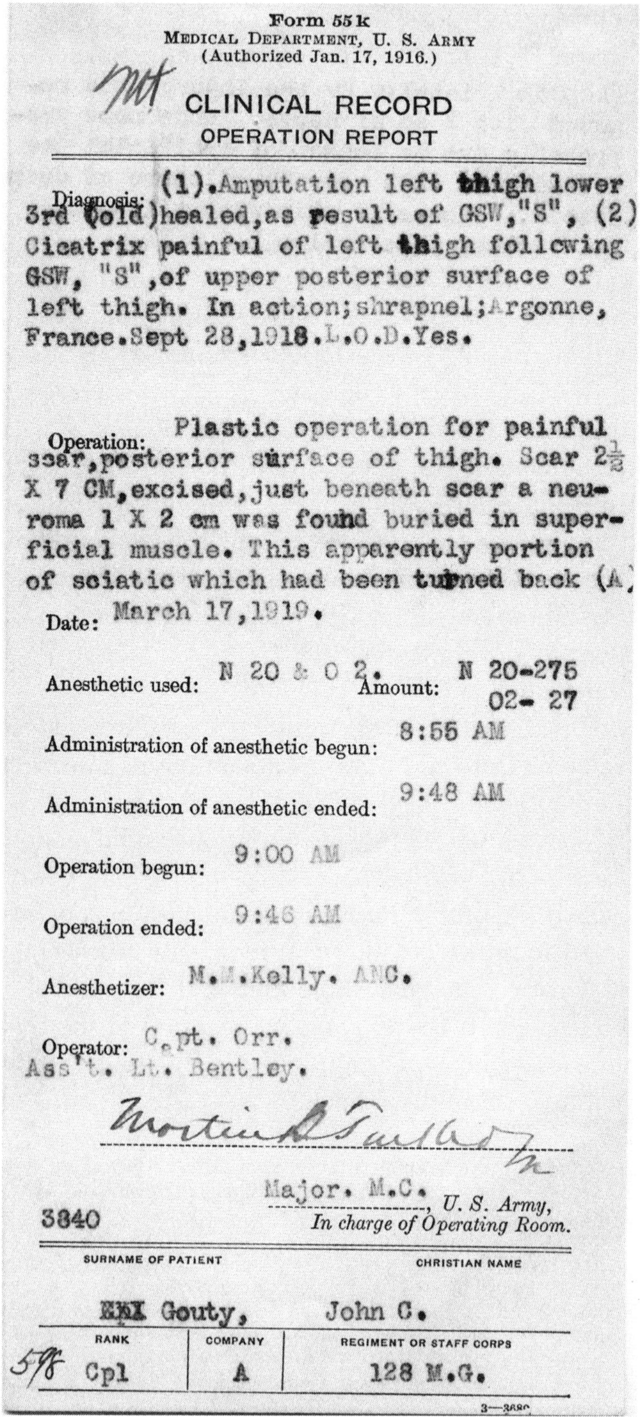

Form 55k
MEDICAL DEPARTMENT, U. S. ARMY
(Authorized Jan. 17, 1916.)

MT

CLINICAL RECORD
OPERATION REPORT

Diagnosis: (1).Amputation left thigh lower 3rd (old)healed,as result of GSW,"S", (2) Cicatrix painful of left thigh following GSW, "S",of upper posterior surface of left thigh. In action;shrapnel;Argonne, France.Sept 28,1918.L.O.D.Yes.

Operation: Plastic operation for painful scar,posterior surface of thigh. Scar 2½ X 7 CM,excised,just beneath scar a neuroma 1 X 2 cm was found buried in superficial muscle. This apparently portion of sciatic which had been turned back (A)

Date: March 17,1919.

Anesthetic used: N 20 & O 2. Amount: N 20-275 02- 27

Administration of anesthetic begun: 8:55 AM

Administration of anesthetic ended: 9:48 AM

Operation begun: 9:00 AM

Operation ended: 9:46 AM

Anesthetizer: M.M.Kelly. ANC.

Operator: Capt. Orr.
Ass't. Lt. Bentley.

Morton [signature]

Major. M.C., *U. S. Army,*
In charge of Operating Room.

3840

SURNAME OF PATIENT	CHRISTIAN NAME
Gouty,	John C.

RANK	COMPANY	REGIMENT OR STAFF CORPS
598 Cpl	A	128 M.G.

3—3880

Operation Report for John C. Gouty (*Author's collection*)

35th Division wounded, Meuse-Argonne, September 29, 1918 (*National Archives*)

There were no stretcher bearers here, and the wounded dotted back on the open ground toward Baulny made certain there would not be for a long time. To let these men lie in Montrebeau woods would have been to let them die. Corporal Mack Davis, the junior gas noncommissioned officer, Bugler Clint Thomas, and two others whose identities are not of record, were left to get them back to a dressing station. This they did, rejoining the next day.

Though exploding shells were still crashing behind us, the small arms fire to the front had virtually ceased. I decided that probably our infantrymen had cleared the woods and it would be safe to go forward now, without riflemen, in an effort to reach the far edge where our guns would have a field of fire.

Leading off I moved north, quickly encountering a ride cut in the brush-grown woods. This was inviting, but I was a machine gunner and knew that the enemy, if he could, would have guns covering such a path. Instead of following it therefore, we crashed along through the brush parallel to it, I stepping out into it from time to time to see if I could see anything.

Avoiding the rides—little straight paths—which criss-crossed the woods we again struggled through the thicket in single file as before. The woods were quiet for the moment and after leaving the vicinity of the southern edge there was neither enemy nor American shell fire at the moment; neither was there sign of American troops. The situation did not look good. In view of the uncertainty of conditions it seemed quite possible that no American troops had yet come through here and that the machine gunners were ahead of their own line—not a pleasant thought in view of the fact that heavy machine guns are only auxiliary weapons in an attack and useless against hostile riflemen in such brush.

Nearing the crest of a rise I became more than a bit concerned about the quietness of the woods and the fact that I could see no sign of American passage—no bodies, no wounded, no equipment or anything, except here and there a few abandoned German grenades.

I begin to worry for fear we had passed through the American line, if there was such thing as a line, and was wandering into enemy territory where a lone machine gun company might fall an easy prey.

It seemed to me that the situation called for an advance guard of some sort, and I became conscious that for some time I had been moving forward with drawn pistol.

First Sergeant James A. Hines was carrying a French carbine he had acquired in the Vosges, and Sgt. Norval R. Hopwood had picked up an infantry rifle. I sent them ahead as an advance guard or point, cautioning them to stay off the ride—advice which probably was unnecessary as they were machine gunners too.

This saved us from casualties, incidentally. By evening there were American dead strung all along these rides—killed by snipers or light machine gunners hidden in trees or perhaps by other German troops. Doubtless we passed beneath some of these tree-ensconced Germans but we were not in the open and by the time they could see us we were probably virtually beneath them and they doubtless had no desire to be brought out of their trees by pistol fire. At the time I did not think of Germans being up trees.

As the two men of the point reached the edge of the wood and peered out, Sergeant Hines signaled back a halt—right arm held upright—and motioned me forward.

Leaving the company stopped, I joined the two.

Here indeed was the enemy.

Not far from the woods, in a little hollow as I recall, was a line of Germans digging trenches, secure in the belief—or perhaps knowledge—that they had covering detachments in the woods.

Was it merely belief or was it knowledge?

I could motion forward a couple of machine guns, have them set up and maybe kill 10 or 12 Germans—and killing Germans was my job.

But if there actually were German covering detachments in the woods anywhere nearby they would swarm down on my detachment through the brush and, since we had no rifle support, perhaps find us easy victims.

It wasn't a chance I was willing to take. I was now certain that we were inside the German lines. I had been convinced for some time that we were the first Americans to come this far through the woods. Had we rifle detachments to guard our flanks it would have been a wonderful opportunity. As it was it would have been risking half a machine gun company and six guns without adequate compensation. I decided we had better get back and find a rifle unit.

Some distance back, just before we had reached the crest of the hill, there had been an opening in the trees and I had seen American bodies in the open space beyond. I would move backward to that point, then to the east to the edge of the woods, and endeavor to find some rifle units.

This was exactly what we did, crashing back alongside the ride as before, then turning sharp to the east and reaching the edge of the woods.

A short distance inside the edge there was a little hollow where a tiny stream trickled and here I had stopped the company, then joined Sergeant Hines and Hopwood at the place the brush and trees ended.

The open ground was sprinkled with American and German dead and wounded but of more interest immediately was two men sitting on a nose several hundred yards northeast of us looking with field glasses to the east. They wore German helmets but a sort of khaki uniform, neither German nor American.

This convinced me more than ever that we were inside the enemy lines though it was plain that Americans had once been here and I forbade Hines and Hopwood to fire at the two for fear of bringing about our undoing from other troops in the brush. Here were dead Americans on the field along with dead and wounded Germans, but no live friendly troops in sight, and there was this evidence the enemy was in possession. Besides this, the garb of the helmeted strangers was odd. It was neither the field-grey of the enemy nor the olive drab of the Americans; instead a yellow khaki such as the Americans had worn years before. Could these be foolish Americans who were wearing enemy helmets with the idea of deceiving German watchers? About this time the two enemies looked around and saw us and drawing their pistols crept quickly over the crest of the hill. In a few moments I saw an American officer about 200 meters away and then I knew that our own lines were still close and that I had been foolish to let the two Germans make their escape. I sent the two sergeants to the hill where we had seen them but they had disappeared as completely as if swallowed up by the earth.

At the time I did not know, and in fact it was long before I learned, that our casualties mixed with German along the wood was the result of fighting at dawn—not of the attack of the day. In the night advance, a spray of our troops had passed this far north. At dawn they were engaged in a close range melee with the enemy. When it was over the enemy still held the edge of the woods. Quite evidently he had moved by day but the two watchers, not knowing of Americans entering it from the south, apparently thought they had friendly territory back of them until they saw me.

A couple of hundred yards to the south I saw an American officer crossing the open space. Sending word to Dunn by Hines to so set up the guns as to prepare the unit for all around defense if necessary, I hurried down and hailed him.

It was Lt. Col. Henry W. Parker, then commanding the 138th Infantry.[9]

9. Henry Wistar Parker, born in Maryland on January 25, 1871, enlisted as a private in the 2nd U.S. Cavalry in 1894. He was commissioned a second lieutenant of cavalry in 1899, a first lieutenant in 1901, and a captain in 1909. Parker served as an officer in both the 21st Kansas Infantry and 12th New York Infantry during the Spanish-American War. He was commissioned a major in the army's Philippine Scouts in 1912. Promoted to lieutenant colonel and assigned to the 138th Infantry, Parker had orders to return to the United States before the battle began, but elected to remain with his regiment, and was killed in action on September 29. U.S. Adjutant General's Office, *Official Army Register for 1916* (Washington, D.C.: U.S. Government Printing Office, 1916), 213; Kenamore, *From Vauquois Hill to Exermont*, 216; *The New York Times*, November 9, 1918.

I explained my circumstances and asked for a mission.

He told me to remain for the moment where I was, holding my position and preventing any German counter-attack coming down the edge of the woods. He was going to send a battalion to attack northward along the edge of the woods and as it came by I would attach my company to it. It was evident that matters were not going as they should from his manner.

"Our orders are to reach this point," he said, laying his finger on his map on some woods southeast of Exermont, "and, by God, we are going to do it. Join the battalion as it comes along."

This was satisfactory and, glad to be under some one's orders again, I sent a runner to report to the colonel and prepared for the advance.

In the thicket west of us, there was considerable small arms fire now—rifles, Chauchats, Maxims. I wondered—and still wonder—how we had been able to reach the north edge of the woods, much less return, without running into a hornet's nest. Certainly there were Germans fighting in the woods now with Americans trying to get forward.

Idle for the moment, the machine gunners did what they could to ease the suffering of American wounded lying about, and, being too hungry to be squeamish, looted the haversacks of the dead Germans. These haversacks each contained untouched food and the canteens at the belts were full, showing these men had just come into action before meeting their death. The food was principally heavy, sweet brown bread, little jars of butter and similar articles. Some of the canteens contained water; some, no less welcome, what appeared to be unsweetened coffee with a dash of whisky. The haversacks of the American dead were also examined but like Company A's own these were pitifully empty.

This portion of the woods was now being heavily shelled by the enemy. Sergeant Ernest Ellis, who had been weakening gradually as a result of enemy gas inhaled earlier in the action, was here sent to the rear, later spending four months in a gas hospital. Corporal Carl M. Eastin succeeded to command of the section.

After about half an hour I became impatient. The battalion which was to attack had not shown up. I decided to go over to a hedge several hundred yards to the southwest and due north of Chaudron farm and see what I could find out. It was to that point my lieutenant colonel [Parker] had gone and that was the region from where the attack was to start.

The open space was scourged with shell fire—directed at I do not know what since only dead and wounded were there—but the hedge itself was something of an inferno of bursting shell. Enemy projectiles were smacking into it from several directions—from the right front (northeast), front, left front, left and left rear. Pretty much of a hot spot and the men there were suffering casualties rather rapidly.

I was met by an old friend—Capt. Paul Frey, Company B, 130th Machine Gun Battalion. He looked at me in amazement, but pleased with something.

"Are you over there in those woods, Schrantz?" he asked. "We have been getting some fire from there. Major Mabry (140th Infantry) has been trying to get me to fire on those woods for half an hour. I wouldn't do it. I told him I knew that there were Americans there."[10]

I found Colonel Parker. He stepped back from a group of field officers with whom he was conferring. One, I believe, was Colonel Nuttman, 69th Brigade commander. Lieut. Col. Parker was earnestly advocating attack. The colonel to whom I had reported was determined to attack but it seemed that he was not the ranking officer and that others thought it best to consolidate the ground already won.

"Stay right where you are," Colonel Parker told me. "We are going to attack and gain the line we were ordered to gain. Join the attacking battalion as it goes forward."

Cheered up by his positive manner I returned to my company, heartily glad that we were in the woods and not along that hedge where shells were dropping with monotonous regularity and men dying fast.

It seems that the troops had become badly disorganized, that the artillery fire that was coming from the left rear, the left, the left front, the front and the right front was causing much worry as well as heavy losses. There was complaint at the lack of artillery support, some complaint that we were already too far ahead of the troops on our right and left and similar talk.

10. Warren Lee Mabrey was born in Cape Girardeau, Missouri, on November 8, 1876. He served in the Sixth Missouri Infantry during the Spanish-American War, and served overseas from March 1918 to August 1919 with the 140th and 138th Infantry regiments. He died on April 2, 1940, in Woodstock, Virginia.

Evidently not every one along the hedge knew the mingled situation in the timber, which perhaps was not strange in view of the fact that enemy machine gun bullets frequently came from that direction.

Passing up along the edge of the wood to find my company, and thinking I had not yet reached the spot, I noted among the American bodies along the edge of the trees one whose leggings were rolled from the top down, a method some of my men used. It [I] thought at first it was that of Sergeant Hines. It wasn't but when I looked at his face I saw it was one of my men, Private Leon S. Palardy, Delaware, O[hio]., Lieut. Dunn's orderly. He had been instantly killed by shell and his body had served in death to carry out the duty to which he had been assigned while alive, that of showing his company commander the location of the company.[11] Private Palardy was 26 years of age, had come to Company A at Camp Doniphan, Okla., March 25, 1918, from Company I, Signal Corps, Fort Leavenworth, Kans., and was the son of Mrs. Dora E. Palardy of Delaware, Ohio. He belonged to the headquarters section of the company, and was Lieut. Dunn's orderly and an excellent soldier.

Sergeant Hines a moment later told me that he had posted Palardy there to keep a lookout and to call to me if I started to pass by the point. This was necessary because the organization was not in the exact edge of the woods but back a little bit in a hollow where there was some protection from shell fire and it would have been easy to have missed the place and gone on by up the edge of the timber.

11. Estel Ziler of Company A recalled that Palardy "was always talking about what he was going to do when he got home." *Carthage* (MO) *Evening Press*, November 18, 1918. Palardy, not a Carthage resident, had been assigned to the company at Camp Doniphan. A company runner, he ran briskly to his assigned spot, but had no sooner reached there than a German shell exploded, killing him instantly. Although the Carthage newspaper reported that he was "annihilated" and no trace of him could be found, Schrantz's report is correct. *Carthage* (MO) *Evening Press*, May 3, 1919. Leon S. Palardy, born in August 1892 in Delaware, Ohio, was living in Cleveland, Ohio, when he joined the Army on March 1, 1918. Palardy went overseas that April, and was killed on September 28, 1918. His remains were returned to the United States in 1921 and he was buried in St. Mary Cemetery, Delaware, Ohio. Adjutant General's Department, State of Ohio, *The Official Roster of Ohio Soldiers, Sailors, and Marines in the World War, 1917-1918*, 23 volumes (Columbus, OH: The F.J. Heer Printing Co., 1926-1929), 13: 12993. Captain Schrantz reported on January 1, 1919, that although men from Company A did not bury Palardy, he saw his grave on a visit to the Argonne, "marked and registered by the Graves Registration Service." Grave Location of Pvt. Pallardy [*sic*], 920200, Leon S. (1192), Record Group 120, Records of the American Expeditionary Forces, World War I, Entry NM-91 1256, Organization Records, Machine Gun Battalions, Box 264, 128th Machine Gun Battalion, Co. A – DOC. FILE 1-1203, NARA.

"I told him to keep back from the edge," he said, "and to keep under cover. But he must have come right out here and sat down under a tree and a shell got him."

On my way back I had noted among the dead the body of a German sprawled across a light Maxim machine gun in such manner that his hip was uppermost and on his belt a canteen. I still had some water in my own canteen, having learned in my early military days never to drink the last of it until more was available, but I unhooked the dead German's canteen and found it full. It actually was not water therein but something that tasted like cold weak coffee with a dash of cognac. It was most helpful under the circumstances, and I had hooked it onto my belt. I had also noted that there was food in the German's haversack. The bread I took from the haversack appeared to be a sort of bran combination but was sweetish and tasted somewhat like molasses.

Since in theory my men's reserve rations would have been used up on September 26, unless they tried to make the two days supplies last four days as I had advised, I now suggested to Hines that he have them look through the German haversacks to see what they could find.[12]

Hines grinned broadly at this example of officer stupidity.

"They did that a long time ago," he said. "They've frisked the haversack of every dead German in reach. They also have gone through the haversacks of all of our dead Americans but those, of course, were empty just like our own."

I returned to the woods, noting our wounded—one poor fellow with his lower jaw shot away but sitting up. One lying down with his eye shot out. I picked up a raincoat and gave it to him the [to] shield his face against the slight rain that was falling. One man, shot through the body, asked me about stretcher bearers. All of our American wounded seemed matter-of-fact and calm. But some German wounded shouted at me beseechingly and waved to call attention to their predicament.

The shells continued to crash into the hill at intervals. German aircraft were flying low above the field. I recalled that I had no anti-aircraft mount attachments (vertical fire brackets) for my tripods.

12. Charles McCune of the 128th Machine Gun Battalion recalled that some of the men found German hardtack, but "a few were afraid to eat it." *The Joplin* (MO) *Herald*, February 21, 1919.

The hubbub of battle in the woods behind us continued—a confusing sound since the firing indicated some of our rifle units had reached the north edge of the woods but others were fighting within them.

Once from the interior of the wood there came some bursts of light Maxim fire directed at us—apparently at the sound of voices since the enemy could not have seen us through the brush, but the declivity in which the men were sheltered prevented casualties. Since our defense gun set up could see any target, and since fire by us into the woods would be more likely to strike Americans and Germans, the bursts were not returned.

The situation at the time seemed to me one of complete confusion and it wasn't far from that. So far as is possible to reconstruct the situation from data later available it was about like this:

Due partly to the situation in which it found itself on the morning of September 28, 1918, and partly to the vigor and promptitude with which it flung itself forward, the 35th Division had by early afternoon driven a deep salient in the enemy line. It was nobly seconded by the 28th Division across the Aire river on its left.

"As was to be expected," writes a German historian of this day's action, "the Americans launched their main attacks on both sides of the valley of the Aire."

But the 28th was held back by the slow progress of the 77th Division in the tangled depths of the Argonne Forest on its left and hence could not keep abreast of the 35th. The 91st Division on the 35th's right was also hacking its way forward gallantly but a bit less impetuously than the 35th, albeit more methodically and in somewhat better order, and it too for the moment was some distance behind.

The natural result of this situation was that the Germans, deeming the forward element of the American army the most dangerous to them, concentrated on it all the artillery within reach. From the right front, from the front, from the left front, from the left flank and even from the left rear the roaring projectiles came to explode in the 35th Division area, preventing reorganization and paralyzing the advance save in Montrebeau Woods where the Missouri and Kansas infantrymen were gradually gaining the upper hand in sporadic and uncoordinated fighting in the tangled thickets.

Intermingled rifle units, mostly of the 137th and 139th Infantry but some of the 138th, had reached the north edge of Montrebeau Woods in places, some accompanied by machine gun units or fragments of them. Other[s] were pushing through the woods. The hedge north of Chaudron farm which I had visited was actually the front line at that point. My own position was a good enough one for my guns to cover its front against counter-attack. Part of the 140th Infantry and part of the 138th were along the hedge. One unit of the 140th had entrenched and was holding Chaudron farm. I actually was on a theoretical part of the front line without knowing it.

I waited longer and became more restive as the firing indicated that more of our people had reached the north edge of the woods. I crossed again to the shell-pounded hedge region. There was no sign of impending activity. I could not find Colonel Parker and someone told me that he had been killed. In fact he was not killed until the following day but under somebody's orders—certainly not his own inclination—was arranging to withdraw the 138th Infantry some distance to a hollow to get it reorganized for the next day, leaving the front to the 140th.

Since I could get no satisfaction there, I decided to make a reconnaissance back through the woods and to the north edge and see if I could find a place there I could fit in.

Accompanied by Pvt. Carl Tangner, my orderly, and one other man whose name I do not recall, I retraced roughly our path of earlier in the day. Again we avoided the ride itself but paralleled it. A good many dead Americans and some dead Germans were strung along it now. There still was shooting here and there all over the woods. It was beginning to get dusk in the trees.

I found riflemen in fox holes at the north edge of the woods. Outside of the blasting enemy shell fire they were all right. And they didn't need machine guns as there was a number with them.

We returned to the company in the hollow. I concluded that we might as well spend the night there.

Just then I saw some officers out in the open space. Walking out to them I found that it was Col. C.E. Delaplane, whom I knew slightly and who was now commanding the 140th, and Major Murray Davis of that regiment, wearing a bandage on his head from a slight wound he had received. It was the first time I recall seeing Major Davis, though I had heard of him, and it was the last time I saw him. He was killed the next day.[13]

13. Murray Davis, born on September 24, 1887, in Burlingame, Kansas, graduated in 1909 from the University of Missouri and became a lawyer in Kansas. He entered the

Colonel Delaplane knew something of the situation. He was going to move forward with his regiment and occupy the nose just north of us but he had sundry machine guns of the 130th Battalion with him—including those of my friend Capt. Frey.

He authorized me to leave the position that Colonel Parker had posted me and to go to the center of Montrebeau Woods where he told me I would find Colonel Hamilton, 137th Infantry, who had charge of the defense of the woods. Colonel Hamilton, he was sure, would have a place for me.

Glad to be acting under competent authority—instead of trying to figure out on my own what to do next—I soon had the company trailing behind me in single file again, thrashing through the dark and dripping woods. Several time[s] the noise of our passage drew light Maxim fire but we suffered no casualties and Colonel Delaplane's instructions had been explicit enough that I found little difficulty in locating Colonel Hamilton's command post.

There I met Maj. Clay C. MacDonald, a fine old St. Joseph, Mo., soldier whom I knew and whose son—though I did not know it then—had been killed September 26 in the storming of Vauquois Hill.[14]

Missouri National Guard as a private in 1913, and rose through the ranks to command Company L, 3rd Missouri Infantry. Promoted to major and named judge advocate general of the 35th Division, Davis led the 3rd Battalion, 140th Infantry during the Meuse-Argonne Offensive. He served overseas from May 3, 1918, until he was killed in action on September 29, 1918. He was awarded the Distinguished Service Cross for "brilliantly" leading his battalion. When wounded, he refused to go to the rear, but had his wound dressed "on the spot" and continued to command his battalion. He was later killed leading his men in an advance. *Kansas City* (MO) *Star*, June 12, 1918; November 7, 1918. U.S. Adjutant General's Department, *American Decorations*, 244; Missouri Secretary of State, State Archives, Soldiers' Records, War of 1812–World War I, www.sos.mo.gov/archives/soldiers.

14. Major Clay C. Macdonald (Schrantz incorrectly capitalized the "D"), born on June 5, 1857 (some sources state May 21, 1857) in Stewartsville, Missouri, joined the Saxton Rifles of the Missouri National Guard as a private in 1879. As major of the 4th Missouri Infantry, he served with the regiment during the Spanish-American War and on the Mexican border in June 1916–February 1917, and was described in the regiment's history as "a tall, elderly man" in 1918. While serving as the 35th Division's mail officer, as "it was assumed he was too old for duty on the battle line," Macdonald learned that his son, 1st. Lt. Donald Macdonald of the 139th Infantry, had been killed in action. The elder Macdonald immediately asked to be assigned to the front lines, and on the night of September 28 found himself in Montrebeau Wood. After leading portions of the 139th Infantry into action, Macdonald took command of a battalion of the 137th Infantry. He was promoted to lieutenant colonel for his actions. He served overseas from May 19, 1918, to April 2, 1919. He died in Kansas City, Missouri, on April 18, 1925, and was buried in St. Joseph, Missouri. *The Service of the Missouri National Guard on the Mexican Border*, 295; Kenamore, *The Story of the 139th Infantry*, 39–40; Missouri Secretary of State, State Archives, Soldiers' Records, War of 1812–World War I, www.sos.mo.gov/archives/soldiers. An emotional account of MacDonald's assignment to the front lines may be found in the *Kansas City* (MO) *Star*, October 27, 1918. Col. Channing Edmonds Delaplane, born in Buckland, Virginia, on July 8, 1871, enlisted as a private in the Signal Corps and fought in Cuba during the Spanish-American War. Commissioned in 1901, Delaplane

Colonel MacDonald had in fact just learned it that day but naturally did not mention it to me.[15]

The situation to the front was obscure, the support troops everywhere had seemed to have halted wherever there was any shelter and the German artillery on the hills of the Argonne squarely to the west was pounding the 35th Division squarely in its left flank on this exposed zone.

The west part of Montrebeau Woods had not been taken, he told me. He needed machine guns covering rides from the occupied portion to the unoccupied portion. He would send guides to show me where.

All day this sniping and machine gun firing had been going on and although a good many of the nests were wiped out I do not think that the wood was ever thoroughly mopped up while it was in our possession.

Soon we had our guns set up covering the rides at the point indicated. I felt happy again mentally, though wet and miserable enough physically doubtless, as I discovered when—everything emplaced, I lay down in the wet leaves and tried to get a little sleep.

On this afternoon while that portion of Company A, 128th Machine Gun Battalion, under Capt. Schrantz was wandering about in the perilous depths of Montrebeau woods, or, later, waiting at its edge under orders to go forward in an advance scheduled to be made by a battalion of the 138th Infantry, the six guns of the company in charge of Lieut. Frank L. Snyder, ensconced in a

---

served in the Philippines, then led troops in San Francisco following the 1906 earthquake. He served as an instructor at Fort Sill, Oklahoma, until World War I. By 1918, Delaplane, a major in the Ordnance Department of the Regular Army, initially served as the ordnance officer of the 35th Division. He was placed in command of the 140th Infantry on September 22, just days before the regiment went into action. He was replaced on October 16, 1918. Delaplane earned the Silver Star and Purple Heart medals for exposing himself to intense enemy fire and leading an attack on the town of Exermont. From 1924 to 1927 he served as chief of the tactical section of the academic department at Fort Benning, Georgia, then commanded infantry and armor units before transferring to the staff of the Hawaiian Department. Delaplane retired from the Army in 1935, moved to Belle Haven, Virginia, for 12 years, then moved to Washington, D.C. He died on April 3, 1956, and was buried in Arlington National Cemetery. Evan Alexander Edwards, *From Doniphan to Verdun: The Official History of the 140th Infantry* (Lawrence, KS: The World Company, 1920), 51, 53, 148; *The Washington Post,* April 5, 1956.

15. Schrantz's recollections of this period differ slightly. In another account, he states that Colonel Delaplane ordered him to take his company to the north edge of the woods. While Schrantz was away reconnoitering that area, Delaplane sent orders to Lieutenant Dunn, commanding the company in Schrantz's absence, that the unit should locate Col. Clad Hamilton. Hamilton ordered Dunn to bring the company to the center of the woods and report to Maj. Clay Macdonald.

ravine with Company B, 129th Machine Gun Battalion south of the woods and not far from Chaudron farm, was enduring the pelting of the German artillery, and suffering mounting casualties.

First Lieut. Frank L. Snyder who had the other half of the combat section of my company under his command that day—the first platoon, less the one section with me, and the entire third platoon—had been having troubles something akin to mine though he did not get so far forward.

He had started forward with the 139th Infantry units to which he had attached himself but since his men were heavily loaded and the rifle units had only their rifles, they quickly moved away from him.

The following are quotations from Lieut. Snyder's official report:

> "The infantry moved too fast for the machine gun units to keep up and I again ordered a rest and the infantry to which I had attached myself was lost. After a short rest I started forward again and advanced as far as the ravine north and east of Baulny, and here another rest was necessary, Private Harmon falling over his tripod onto the ground exhausted. This shows the grit with which all the men were determined to go on to the last. The heavy loads which machine gunners have to carry make it almost impossible for them to keep up."

This advance, though not mentioned in the report, was also under heavy artillery fire which included some gas shell and several casualties were suffered, among others Private J. Barrett of Corporal Charles O. Grissom's squad was severely wounded and left prone on the field for stretcher bearers. He never rejoined.[16] First Class Private Ernest J. Cassady was also injured here. The following formal statement relative to Cassady was made some time later by First Class Private Lloyd J. Stuckey:

> "While we were advancing in the attack of the morning of September 28, Private Cassady was wounded just as he was crossing the wire some distance northeast of Baulny at a

16. According to official records, John Barrett's family lived in Webster County, Nebraska, but no further information could be located. Charles O. Grissom began working for the Missouri Pacific Railroad before World War I. He served overseas with Company A from April 25, 1918, to April 24, 1919. He was active in the 128th's reunion activities after the war. *Carthage* (MO) *Evening Press*, February 28, 1948; Missouri Secretary of State, State Archives, Soldiers' Records, War of 1812–World War I, www.sos.mo.gov/archives/soldiers.

> point near where one of our airplanes had fallen. He was shot through the right knee with a small shell splinter. I had been detailed as stretcher bearer and after some delay got him back to a dressing station, somewhere near Charpentry, I think. He asked me to get him a drink and I was just returning from doing so when a squadron of eight or ten enemy planes, flying low, came over and dropped some bombs. I had almost reached Cassady, being about 25 feet from him, when one bomb hit the dressing station. I escaped by flattening out in a ditch, but Cassady and several others were killed and a number more wounded. This was about 10:30 a.m., as near as I can judge."

Private Cassady was 23 years old, the son of Mrs. Ida M. Cassady of Fort Scott, Kans. He had been born in Nevada, Mo., but had later moved to Fort Scott, enlisted at the outbreak of the World War in the Kansas National Guard and had been transferred to the Carthage company from the 137th Infantry in May while in the British area—a good soldier and one his unit and his comrades much regretted to lose.[17]

Stuckey, it might be mentioned in passing, became an infantry reserve officer after this war and served during World War II and for some years thereafter as a major in the ground section of the air corps. His brother, Lyle Stuckey, also an enlisted man in my company at that time, was first a major and later lieutenant colonel of infantry in World War II.

Coming onto a ravine, which he mentioned as being "north and east of Baulny," and which probably was near Chaudron farm somewhere, he halted to rest in this spot which was to a certain extent sheltered from the heavy enemy artillery fire which was sweeping the area from the Argonne hills west of the Aire.

Corporal Murl Daugherty was hit in the shoulder by a shell fragment and the machine gun of his squad broken. Daugherty

17. Schrantz reported in early 1919 that Cassady's body was "left on the field for the burial parties," and that he "hunted in vain" for his grave on a trip to the Argonne on January 1, 1919. Grave Location of Pvt. Cassady, 1448738, Ernest L (1191), Record Group 120, Records of the American Expeditionary Forces, World War I, Entry NM-91 1256, Organization Records, Machine Gun Battalions, Box 264, 128th Machine Gun Battalion, Co. A – DOC. FILE 1-1203, NARA. As late as 1927, an "investigation" was still being conducted to locate his grave. Company Clerk, "Then and Now," *The American Legion Monthly* 2, no. 3 (March 1927): 74.

remained with his squad, despite his wound, until the next day when he was ordered to the rear.

Some time later Private Charles O. Alkimeyer remarked to his fellows that he was wounded. Private Paul Ford who was nearby stripped or cut away Alkimeyer's raincoat, coat, shirt and undershirt and found that a shell fragment about the size of a man's thumb had buried itself far out of sight in his shoulder. The wound was bound up and Alkimeyer sent to the rear.[18]

Then Private Roy E. Jenkins of Corporal Charles Grissom's squad informed his corporal that he had been injured; and Grissom, investigating, found and bandaged a severe gash on Jenkins' left side near the small of the back—and Jenkins too started his dangerous journey back to a dressing station.[19]

Private D.H Havens, after one shell burst which showered him with dirt, decided that a cigarette would help—but he had none left.

"Got a cigarette, Neely?" he shouted to Pvt. Albert Neely, Gridley, Kans., who was in a shell hole about eight feet from him.

Neely did not reply and Havens investigated. Neely was dead. One shell fragment had passed through his body near the heart and a smaller one through his head. [20]

Among the men nearest this tragedy were Private David H. Havens and Vern Breckinridge, and subsequent to the battle, Private Havens made this formal statement concerning the death:

> "About 1:00 or 2:00 p.m. September 28 my squad was in a reserve position in a little ravine some distance north of Chaudron farm. We were being heavily shelled at intervals, and though we were protected to a certain extent from fire directly to the front, one shell from our left struck among us,

18. Charles O. Alkemeyer was born on December 25, 1895, in Lixville, Missouri, died on May 22, 1991, and was buried in Perryville, Missouri. He served overseas from April 25, 1918, to August 12, 1919 (and with Company A from October 1917 to March 1919). Missouri Secretary of State, State Archives, Soldiers' Records, War of 1812–World War I, www.sos.mo.gov/archives/soldiers. Paul Ford was likely born in Webb City, Missouri, on August 17, 1899, and died in Kirkwood, Missouri, on September 23, 1956. He served overseas with Company A from April 25, 1918 to April 24, 1919. Missouri Secretary of State, State Archives, Soldiers' Records, War of 1812–World War I, www.sos.mo.gov/archives/soldiers.

19. Little is known about Roy Earl Jenkins. Official records list his mother Effie, living in Iola, Kansas.

20. The remains of Ernest Leland Cassady and Albert Neely were never recovered, and their names are engraved on the tablets of the missing at the Meuse-Argonne American Cemetery.

> wounding several men and killing Private Neely, one splinter passing through his body above his heart and another very small fragment penetrating his head above the left ear. He was killed instantly. I was about eight feet from him at the time. We buried him the next morning at this place, marking his grave with a rifle with fixed bayonet stuck in the ground."

Private Neely had been transferred to Company A from the 137th Infantry in the British area May 28, 1918. He was a capable soldier, originally a member of the Kansas National Guard, was 23 years of age and the son of Mrs. Ellen Neely of Gridley, Kans.

Back south of Montrebeau woods, Lieut. Snyder's half of the company remained where it had been most of the day. Restless at the inactivity, the lieutenant had gone forward some time before dusk to near the south edge of Montrebeau woods, met a major of one of the rifle regiments, explained his situation and asked if there was something he could do. The major answered that there was, that he had a place for him and told him to wait there. Lieut. Snyder waited. Dusk came on and changed to dark. Evidently the major had forgotten or couldn't find his way back. Returning to his men, the lieutenant had them try to make themselves comfortable for the night, which they did, disturbed by intermittent gas alarms which caused frequent adjustment of masks.

During this time enemy airplanes in large squadrons were flying low over the battlefield, drawing heavy rifle fire from the ground without any great apparent result. The machine gunners had started in the action with four vertical fire brackets to the company, these to be placed on the infantry tripods to enable the guns to be mounted for anti-aircraft fire, but all of these had been lost somewhere, dropped by wearied soldiers who had all they could do to carry ammunition and who had not been, at the moment, greatly concerned about attack from the air. Now that the brackets were needed there was none at hand, but one gun under Lieut. Snyder's command was fixed after laborious effort in such position that it could fire into the air. As Sergeant Willard Brown was about to take his place at this gun a singing shell fragment from an explosion a considerable distance away hurtled through the air and struck flat on his chest, the slap on the raincoat sounding almost like a pistol shot—but the deadly force of the fragment was gone, and as the spent splinter of steel dropped to the ground, Brown looked quizzically at his lieutenant and without comment, lowered himself to the gun and stared at the sky. A German plane which already had passed over five or six times at a height of only about 150 feet was returning. Laying the point of aim well in front of the German, Brown opened fire and the aviator passed through the sheaf of bullets. That the machine was well riddled, seemed certain, but it did not crash. Instead it quickly gained altitude and quit the fight. From then on this gun fired on other planes which passed over.

Snyder's group remained south of the woods during the night and rejoined the rest of the company the next day under circumstances which will be related later.

In the ravine where he stopped, Lieutenant Snyder found an acquaintance, Capt. George H. Wark, Co. A, 129th Machine Gun Battalion, a Caney, Kans., man who between the wars became a brigadier general in the Kansas National Guard.

Captain Wark's company had suffered considerable losses, including two of his officers killed, and at this time he had with him only one machine gun, his unit having [been] considerably disorganized in the attack. Captain Wark had been with Snyder and I in the advance school detachment of machine gunners who had attended the II Corps machine gun school at Chatillon-sur-Seine and Snyder promptly and properly placed himself under Wark's command.

He spent the remainder of the day at this point, receiving heavy shell fire from which his men sheltered themselves as best they could in fox-holes.

Far to the rear, as distance from front to rear is measured, but not so far back when counted by the range of the active German artillery on the division's left flank, Mess Sergeant Robert Roach and his culinary department had been worrying about the problem of getting food forward to their hungry comrades. The rear echelon of the battalion, including that of my company, was back near a graveyard on the Varennes-Cheppy road this day, and food had come up from the rear.

Early in the morning Sergeant Roach and Private Babcock of the kitchen force, each equipped with two sacks of hardtack and corned beef and piloted by a Ford driver whose identity has since been forgotten, started forward to hunt the company.[21] North of Cheppy a short distance the car stopped by a camouflaged fence while Roach sought to find something about the practicability of using the routes to the north. By the camouflaged fence near the Ford, a part of the carts of the Machine Gun Company, 138th Infantry had halted, some of the drivers leaning on their mules and the mules leaning back, after the fashion of weary men and animals. Some riflemen from somewhere were moving by toward the front.

A sudden concentration of artillery fire on the road brought confusion. By the Company A car a mule was killed by shell fragments which would have killed its driver had its body not intervened. A soldier of another unit was killed a few feet away and a number wounded. All men on the road scattered to the fields for safety. This ended the first attempt of the Company A mess sergeant to get forward, and as soon as the shell fire slackened the Ford car returned to the camp between Cheppy and Varennes. Roach wisely returned to wait until dark.

Neither was this kitchen camp itself immune. Soup was being prepared by the combined kitchens of Companies A and B, when a shell exploded on the hill just above, showering the kitchen and men there with dirt, and hurling clods into the soup. Cooks, kitchen police and drivers hurried for a nearby dug-out, but soon Cook Al Weaver, Private Babcock and others emerged, tasted the soup, found it good despite the dirt, ate thereof and were satisfied.

As soon as darkness fell Sergeant Roach started forward with cans of this soup hoping to find the company.

Many of the drivers of the Company A Ford train were busily engaged in hazardous work all this day, hauling wounded to the rear, and carrying ammunition as far forward as it was possible for cars to go.

Other of our gun trucks were carrying up ammunition for any unit that needed it, as far north as Baulny—Stokes mortar and

21. Guy Babcock was born in Carthage on May 26, 1895. He served with Company A on the Mexican border 1916–1917 and served overseas with Company A from April 25, 1918 to April 24, 1919. Ironically, he died on the 24th anniversary of his enlistment in the company (June 19, 1940), while the company was holding its anniversary celebration at the Carthage armory. *Carthage* (MO) *Evening Press*, June 20, 1940; *The Service of the Missouri National Guard on the Mexican Border*, 124; Missouri Secretary of State, State Archives, Soldiers' Records, War of 1812-World War I, www.sos.mo.gov/archives/soldiers.

37-millimeter among other kinds. Where they had a clear road they could speed through the shelled zones. In my official report I specifically mentioned Wagoners Alvin Bays and Charles McKinney as being active in this work.

But of all this, that wet and miserable night in Montrebeau Woods, I knew nothing.

I knew I needed rest and sleep but, wet and cold and lying in a puddle of water in the saturated leaves, I could get little of either.

The losses of the entire company during the day had been four men killed and 14 members of the company and eight or nine attached ammunition carriers wounded. The members of the company wounded this day and not heretofore mentioned—because of the exact place and time when their injuries were incurred being now unknown—were Privates Ernest O. Capps, David J. Delph, William A. Nichols, Lawrence Siebert, John F. Viles and Harley H. Hammons, all of whom according to the records, were injured by shell fire and Hammons both by shell and gas; and Private Ralph E. Harmon who is listed as having been a gas casualty. Hammons never rejoined but the others eventually came back to the company when their wounds healed, the last being Capps who returned December 28.[22]

The none-too-waterproof raincoats were sodden and everyone was wet and shivering in the chill, late-September night. The carpet of leaves which covered the ground was soaked with water, and even the men whose duties at the guns did not

22. Earnest E. Capps was born in McDonald County, Missouri, on July 25, 1895. He served overseas with Company A from April 25, 1918, to April 24, 1919. He died on October 1, 1968, and was buried in Park Cemetery in Carthage. *Joplin* (MO) *Globe*, October 3, 1968; Missouri Secretary of State, State Archives, Soldiers' Records, War of 1812–World War I, www.sos.mo.gov/archives/soldiers. David Jefferson Delph was born on November 18, 1895, in Reynaldo, Iowa. He died on February 23, 1985, in Red Cloud, Nebraska. Letter from Teresa Young, Webster County (NE) Historical Museum to editor, October 30, 2018; *The Red Cloud* (NE) *Chief*, May 1, 1919. According to official records, William A. Nichols was a resident of Maple, Oklahoma, in 1918. Lawrence George Siebert was born on May 23, 1895 and is believed to have died in St. Louis on December 25, 1982. He served overseas with the 128th from April 25, 1918, to April 24, 1919. *St. Louis Post Dispatch*, April 25, 1919, December 28, 1982; Missouri Secretary of State, State Archives, Soldiers' Records, War of 1812–World War I, www.sos.mo.gov/archives/soldiers. John F. Viles was born in Southwest City, Missouri, on July 30, 1887. He enlisted in Grove, Oklahoma, in September 1917 and was assigned to Company F, 358h U.S. Infantry at Camp Travis, Texas. Transferred to the 35th Division in March 1918, Viles was declared missing in action on September 28, 1918, but was actually slightly wounded and sent to a hospital, He died in Cleora, Oklahoma, in 1964. HST. Harley H. Hammons was born in Mill Grove, Missouri, died in Trenton, Missouri, on August 11, 1984, and was buried in Des Moines, Iowa. *Des Moines Register*, August 14, 1984.

require them to remain awake, were hardly in a position to get much sleep.

That night in Montrebeau woods, cold and shivering and wet through with the steady drizzle of rain, was one of the most miserable that I ever spent in my life and it was with considerable relief some time before daybreak that I heard someone shouting my name as he came down one of the rides.

It was one of the men I had sent back with Gouty and Baker when they were wounded and he had a message from Major Halliburton. It was written at Baulny and stated that the division was to attack at 5.30. The 128th Machine Gun Battalion and the 110th Engineers were to form the divisional reserve and I was instructed to move back and attach my company to the Second Battalion of the engineers.

Chapter 14

The Meuse-Argonne Offensive: Collapse and Withdrawal

Despite issuing yet another attack order, 35th Division commander Maj. Gen. Peter E. Traub recognized that his men were near the point of physical and mental exhaustion by September 29. Early that morning, he accurately noted, "Brigade commanders know little about their brigades and the actual location of the units of their regiments." According to Traub, the division had "lost its punch" because of heavy officer casualties and disorganization. Nevertheless, it appeared that the 35th still seemed capable of achieving some of its goals; at least a portion of the troops were still "game." That morning, the 137th Infantry was ordered to attack on the left, supported by the 139th, while on the right, the 138th Regiment would attack with the 140th in support. A rolling artillery barrage would precede the attack, allowing the infantry to follow closely behind to engage the dazed German survivors.[1] The men were to attack in the general direction of the village of Exermont.

Any advance was destined to be fraught with difficulty. "The division was a division in name only now," concluded the author of the 139th Infantry's history. "Brigade and Division Headquarters had almost ceased to function. The effectives in charge of the direction of the troops were the regimental, battalion and company

1. Kenamore, *From Vauquois Hill to Exermont*, 203-04.

organizations." In effect, the 35th Division was "a number of small units . . . waging little individual wars against a well organized and well directed enemy" who pummeled them with artillery fire from front and flanks and whose disciplined machine gunners worked to outflank the Americans.[2]

Problems developed even before the attack began. Orders to the attacking regiments arrived too late, either only a few minutes before the artillery barrage began or long after it ended. The barrage proceeded as ordered, however, but was of no real use to the attacking regiments.

Despite the lack of artillery support, many of the division's soldiers attempted to carry out the order. Staff officer Major Parker Kalloch led about 125 men forward to a ravine west of Exermont by 6 a.m. Another group of about the same size tried twice to join him, only to be beaten back. A disheartened Kalloch moved back to Montrebeau Woods at 8 a.m.

Two companies of the 139th under Major James Rieger, joined by two more from the 140th, managed to slog forward and reach Exermont about 7 a.m. They even advanced to a ridge 400 meters north of the town, where they dug in. Lieut. Colonel Channing Delaplane led the 3rd Battalion and parts of the other two battalions of the 140th into Exermont at 9 a.m. He was able to move to the northeast of town and dig in as well.

It soon became quite obvious that the beleaguered men outside Exermont were under tremendous pressure and could not hold their positions without reinforcements. Unfortunately for them, their comrades had made little headway and the Germans were already organizing counterattacks.

General Traub, watching the attacks from the north edge of Montrebeau Woods, finally decided that his division had reached its high water mark. "A willing horse had been driven to its death," A.E.F. Colonel Frederick Palmer eloquently wrote.[3] At 11 a.m., Traub sent a message to First Corps headquarters: "Regret to report that this division cannot advance. . . . It is thoroughly disorganized through loss of officers and many casualties. . . . Recommend it be withdrawn for reorganization and be replaced promptly" so that the advance could continue. Under the cover of an artillery barrage, his men were ordered to begin withdrawing from Exermont to Montrebeau Woods beginning at 1 p.m., then to abandon the woods to the enemy and

2. Kenamore, *The Story of the 139th*, 41.

3. Frederick Palmer, *Our Greatest Battle (The Meuse-Argonne)* (New York: Dodd, Mead and Company, 1919), 191.

retire to a line in front of a high ridge northeast of Baulny, where defensive positions had been prepared by the relatively unscathed 110th Engineer Regiment. Entire units, small groups, and even single doughboys found their way back to the ridge. Some organizations remained longer in forward positions at Chaudron Farm and at the southeast edge of Montrebeau Woods to cover the removal of the large number of wounded who had been collected there.

The evening of September 29, 1918 found the exhausted 35th Division "still able and willing to hold its shallow fox holes on the shell-pounded heights," unable to take the offensive but capable of halting any German advance. "Gaunt and unshaven men rubbed weary eyes with grimy hands, glanced at the gray and rain-sodden dawn and looked bleakly at the still grayer faces of men who yesterday had been like them but now had found peace and rest in the midst of the turmoil," Schrantz recalled.

Four days of heavy casualties, fierce enemy opposition and terrible weather conditions had wrecked the 35th Division. On Baulny Ridge, the 128th Machine Gun Battalion and a company of the 130th Machine Gun Battalion, twenty machine guns in all, spent September 30 covering the left half of the division's front line. Although the dire situation improved somewhat, the men were still uneasy. At 10 a.m., when he saw infantrymen withdrawing through his lines and presumably leaving his machine guns unprotected, the exhausted Captain Schrantz sent a desperate message to Lieutenant Colonel Hay, the division machine gun officer: "Machine guns unassisted by infantry are being left to hold enemy. Our best men have already been killed. If the sacrifice is necessary we do not complain, but is it necessary? Only the most immediate action can save the remaining machine guns of the division."[4] Hay inspected Schrantz's position and convinced the Missouri officer that the situation was not as grim as he reported. On the night of September 30, units of the 1st Division, the "Big Red One," moved forward and began to relieve the spent 35th men. The last elements of the 35th left the front line at about 5:45 a.m. on October 1.

"The division looked more like a band of refugees than a military organization" when they withdrew from the front, an eyewitness

4. Edward Payson Rankin, Jr., *The Santa Fe Trail Leads to France: A Narrative of Battle Service of the 110th Engineers (35th Division) in the Meuse-Argonne Offensive* (Kansas City, MO: Dick Richardson Co., 1933), 32. Capt. Arly L. Hedrick of the 110th Engineers thought that Schrantz had received a rumor that the infantry had withdrawn, leaving his machine guns unprotected. It took three hours for Schrantz's message to reach the 35th Division's P.C., then be referred to Colonel T.C. Clarke of the 110th Engineers, then be sent to Captain Hedrick on the left flank of the line for his comments.

noted. "The men were unshaven, dirty and haggard. Their clothing was soiled and torn, their shoes muddy and worn out. . . . Many had grown hoarse from cold or gas, and nearly every one's eyes were red from gas and loss of sleep. A serious dysenteric condition had broken out. Its cause was variously ascribed to the water, to eating canned food continuously, to the lack of hot food for five days." Nevertheless, "It was a sorry band as for looks, but it had played a great part in a great battle."[5]

Understandably, the horrific sights of the bloody field left a profound impression on the men from the cities, small towns and farms of Missouri and Kansas. The battlefield was "a sight no artist can paint nor anyone describe," wrote Jack Williams, a member of Company A of the 128th. "It was a dog fight from the start for every inch had to be fought for. We had two of the Boche crack divisions against us in ideal defenses and they sure hated to give them up." "The ground, of course, was strewn with the debris of battle—dead men and animals," "all kinds of equipments, shattered wagons and big guns, houses crumbled to dust, trees torn down, roads shell-holed and all the ground churned with shells."[6] "I wish I could explain to you how it was, but I can not," reported Estel Ziler of the Carthage company. "The dead Germans were so thick we actually ran over some of them with the machines, and horses and mules were all over the road."[7]

Despite their heavy losses and the fact that they had been withdrawn before victory was won, Schrantz and his comrades could enjoy at least some satisfaction from their role in the fighting in the Meuse-Argonne. They had advanced about twelve kilometers into German-held territory and had held a line ten kilometers forward of the original front line. They had captured at least 751 enlisted men and thirteen officers. Two members of the division were recognized for valor with the Medal of Honor, and eighty-five more with the Distinguished Service Cross. They had finally achieved the status of combat veterans. But that hard-earned distinction had come at enormous cost and had forced them to the limits of their endurance. At least 6,000 members of the division

5. Kenamore, *From Vauquois Hill to Exermont*, 239.

6. *Carthage* (MO) *Evening Press*, November 6, 1918.

7. *Carthage* (MO) *Evening Press*, November 18, 1918. 137th Infantry Chaplain William Ernest Sullens wrote home that the strain on their nerves was terrible, as they watched men falling dead and wounded around them, faced shell and machine gun fire, and realized they might be blown to pieces or struck by a German bullet. Nevertheless, "I would not take anything in the world for the experience I have passed through and I wouldn't pass through it again for anything in the world." *The Springfield* (MO) *Daily Leader*, November 6, 1918.

were dead, wounded, or captured.[8] Nearly half of the division's infantry "was dead on the field or in hospital."[9]

Some of Company A's survivors tried their best to explain their experiences to the civilians back home in Missouri.

"If it had lasted much longer I do not believe I could have stood it," admitted Carthage soldier Otto Grigg. "We were in six days and nights without sleep or shelter. . . . I want to tell you that our little machine gun battalion sure did some good work and any time you go on the line and get back alive, you are lucky; but I am still betting they do not get me. You can not imagine what it is to be under shell and machine gun fire. You think every one is going to get you." Fortunately, with the help of Captain Schrantz and Major Halliburton, "real men and real officers" who "know the game," they had survived.[10]

Dewey Comer assured his mother that "you cannot realize what this war is unless you are over here and see one of these big battles. If hell is any worse—well, I'll take heaven for mine."[11] "I was in that Argonne fight," proclaimed cook Sergeant John Cronk to his father, "and, believe me, your son was lucky to get out alive." Citing one example, Cronk explained that an artilleryman "within ten feet of me" was struck with a piece of shrapnel that went through his helmet "and tore half his head off," just one of many "awful sights."[12] "I have wanted war experience," explained another one of Schrantz's men. "I got it in this show and plenty of it and have emerged a considerably older and somewhat sadder man. Company A functioned perfectly and to the best of my knowledge every man in it acted with as much heroism and disregard of danger as men could possibly ever act. Also, we have acquired some scores to settle—but that is war."

8. There is disagreement about the 35th's losses. Clair Kenamore reported losses of more than 8,000 (960 killed, 6894 wounded, and 169 captured, with those who subsequently died raising the death toll to more than 1,000). Kenamore, *From Vauquois Hill to Exermont*, 240. In his book on the 35th in the Meuse-Argonne, Robert Ferrell's research indicates losses of nearly 7,300 (1,126 killed or died of wounds, 4,877 severely wounded, the remainder slightly wounded). Ferrell, *Collapse at Meuse-Argonne*, 108. In his overview of the entire operation, Ferrell indicates losses of "perhaps 8,000," and cites another source that gives the total as 7,074 (1,204 killed or died of wounds and 5,870 wounded). Ferrell, *America's Deadliest Battle*, 65. The American Battle Monuments Commission's Summary of Operations for the Division indicates 6,006 casualties for this period (904 killed, 226 died of wounds, and 4876 wounded). American Battle Monuments Commission, *Summary of Operations*, 24. The Missouri Adjutant General stated that the 35th suffered 1,530 dead and 6,379 wounded, a total of 7,909. Missouri Adjutant General, *Report of the Adjutant General of Missouri, January 1, 1917–December 31, 1920,* 19. Missouri Gen. Harvey C. Clark reported that the division's losses totaled 7,854. Harvey C. Clark, "Missourians in Service," *The Missouri Historical Review* 14, no. 1 (October 1919): 8.

9. Palmer, *Our Greatest Battle,* 192.

10. *Carthage* (MO) *Evening Press*, November 2, 1918.

11. *Carthage* (MO) *Evening Press*, November 2, 1918.

12. *Carthage* (MO) *Evening Press*, January 3, 1919.

"Please pardon the gloominess of this letter," he continued, "and remember by way of excusing me that Company A is my second love, so to speak, and every man hit is a personal bereavement to me." Although he had a chance to get "bushels" of German Iron Crosses and other souvenirs, "I was a little too near the hereafter myself to care for souvenirs," and superstitiously believed that if he had taken anything other than food and water from the German dead, he might catch bad luck by being struck by one of their shells. "That sounds gloomy, doesn't it. However, I really don't feel that way except when I think of the friends I have lost."[13] Sergeant Norval Hopwood believed that they were grieved to "lose such good men as we did, but at that we got away mighty lucky. In fact, I simply can't understand how it happened."[14] Charles McCune succinctly summarized their experience by writing, "If there is any hell on earth, we, the 35th Division, had it in the Argonne Woods."[15]

Even though they had failed to achieve the optimistic goals the high command had set for them, the men of Company A were proud of their performance and found themselves even more determined to fight until Germany was defeated. Clint Thomas believed that "The Dutch put up an awful resistance and counter-attacked lots of times but did not have any luck with the old Missouri and Kansas boys. We sure did deal them misery."[16] "I certainly was glad to get in this division, for it has made a name that no other body of troops have beaten so far. The one time despised Missouri Guard troops have shown that they can and do deliver the goods as well as the best of troops," Cecil Stemmons boasted to the folks at home. "A once prosperous country now a mass of desolate ruins that defies my description is the result of a nation's desire to rule the world," he added. "I want no peace, regardless of the cost, until Germany is ruined and her power broken forever."[17]

As the soldiers of the "Big Red One" took their places on the line, Schrantz and his men withdrew to the battalion transport camp between Cheppy and Varennes, where the unit rested and reflected. Captain Schrantz was proud of the role his men played in the operation. "However unsatisfactory some of its experience had been, its officers felt that the unit had functioned satisfactorily. Any criticism of it would need to be directed at the officers. Every order had been carried out properly and courageously, and there had been no straggling."

13. *Carthage* (MO) *Evening Press*, November 5, 1918.
14. *Carthage* (MO) *Evening Press*, January 6, 1919.
15. *Joplin* (MO) *News Herald*, February 21, 1919.
16. *Carthage* (MO) *Evening Press*, December 31, 1918.
17. *Carthage* (MO) *Evening Press*, December 4, 1918.

At 4:30 a.m. I was aroused from my misery by someone calling my name.

It was the two men I had detailed the forenoon before to take badly-wounded Corporal Gouty and Private Baker to the rear. They had accomplished that mission somehow and had encountered Major Halliburton.

They brought me a written message from him. The 35th Division was to renew the attack at 5:30. The 110th Engineers and the 128th Machine Gun Battalion would constitute the division reserve. Company A would return to Baulny where it would join the Second Battalion of the 110th.

I was both somewhat surprised and displeased by this order.

The surprise was because of the attack order. The division, insofar as I saw it, was badly disorganized and intermingled—hardly in any shape to make an organized attack. I had rather expected that the days work would to have been to secure the west part of Montrebeau Woods and get the division unscrambled a bit before attacking again. But that was out of my sphere.

The displeasure came from the very obvious fact that to get to Baulny I would need to move back just as the attacking troops were moving forward. That would not look well—though, once back, it would be something to be operating in accordance with a division order instead of wandering about looking for an assignment.

I reported to Major MacDonald, showed him the order and was told by him to return to Baulny in accordance with it.

We moved out, southward bound.

Troops moving northward looked at me curiously. Some lost infantry detachment, plenty disheartened doubtless, tried to join the tail of our column. I shooed it away and told Lieut. Dunn to shoo off any other stragglers of the sort. If there were any other instances like this I did not learn of it.

Just south of the edge of the woods we met an organization from the south coming forward in attack formation.

At its front was a man, considerably older than I, in an enlisted man's raincoat and no rank insignia—by garb an enlisted man.

"Where are you going, captain?" he queried sharply.

It was exactly the question and in exactly the same tone that I might have asked a junior officer had the circumstance been reversed. But except for his age there was no evidence that my questioner was a senior officer or any officer at all. And his question touched my most sensitive point.

"And who the hell are you?" I queried truculently in reply.

He swelled out his chest in affronted dignity.

"I am Colonel Mitchell," he replied impressively.

I expect that even in my wearied and harassed state I grinned at this, because I still smile when I think of it.

"I'm sorry, sir," I said. "I am Captain Schrantz, Company A, 128th Machine Gun Battalion, returning the [to] Baulny under written orders to join the division reserve," and handed him the note I had received.

It was Colonel Americus Mitchell, a fine, 48-year-old Regular Army colonel who just joined the division the day before and assigned to the 139th Infantry.[18] He could only find that part of it south of Montrebeau Woods—two companies, I think—and was leading it forward.

He nodded, pleasantly enough, as he read my orders, and told me to go ahead.

I am inclined to believe that he was pleased and perhaps amused at my indignant reaction to his first question. I perhaps met him casually later when he was in command of the 138th Infantry, but this is the only meeting I recall and it probably was the only one that had any particular reason to be impressed on his memory, but he did me the honor of remembering me.

Many years after the war he met an officer from my town in the military hospital at Hot Springs, Ark., and, learning that my friend was from Carthage, Mo., asked him if he knew me and said some kind words. I was immensely pleased at that, for he was a fine soldier and I was flattered both that he remembered my name and somehow had even learned, and remembered, the town from which I came.

He probably was not accustomed to having captains talk to him like I first did.

18. Americus Mitchell was born in Alabama on December 24, 1870. He graduated from West Point as an infantry second lieutenant in 1895. A major by 1916, Mitchell was promoted to colonel (National Army) in 1917. Mitchell was assigned to the division just before the battle (his orders were dated September 24); he arrived at division headquarters on the afternoon of September 28 and was ordered to take command of the 139th Infantry. Mitchell died on September 1, 1938. U.S. Adjutant General's Office, *Official Army Register, January 1, 1921* (Washington, D.C.: U.S. Government Printing Office, 1922), 716; Kenamore, *From Vauquois Hill to Exermont*, 193–94.

In going into battle without insignia he was following an idea of the time which may even have been a generally unenforced order from somewhere. Naturally if an enemy is close enough he would prefer to shoot at someone with officer's insignia, and, since an officer is commanding something or other, his death, presumably, interferes with some part of the war.

But in the mix-up of battle, with units intermingled, an officer must have insignia of some sort, it seems to me, in order to exert any influence on troops not personally acquainted with him. Certainly I would have had no luck stopping that rearward movement south of Charpentry on the 27th if it had not been evident from my insignia that I was an officer.

I suffered two casualties in leaving the wood. After leaving the woods Corporal Carl Eastin missed Private W.R. Smith of his squad. Smith had been noticed on duty with the gun at 2 a.m. but now he was gone and Corporal Eastin went back to find him. There was no sign of Smith, and the only other persons now in the west part of the woods were some rifle outguards still watching to the west. South of the woods again Corporal Eastin found himself in an enemy artillery concentration of high explosive and gas, and he inhaled some of the gas before he could get into his mask. Gassed, somewhat dazed by the concussion of a shell which burst near him, and with a shell splinter in his right index finger, he wandered back to Baulny and reported to his company commander who sent him on to the rear. Later in a gas hospital Corporal Eastin ran across Private Smith whom he had sought. Smith too was a gas casualty and was never able to rejoin his company.[19] Eastin was returned to duty about six weeks later.

While shelling had resumed, the general visibility was poor and so far as I recall we suffered no casualties on the trip back to Baulny.

We arrived in an exhausted state due to the heavy loads the men were carrying, to previous exertions in the battle and to lack of food. As regards this last I personally had not missed it particularly so far as hunger went—excitement somehow driving hunger

19. William R. Smith was born in Asheville, North Carolina. He served as a private with Company C, 2nd Missouri Infantry on the Mexican border from 1916 to 1917. He served overseas from April 25, 1918, to December 1, 1918. *The Service of the Missouri National Guard on the Mexican Border*, 140; Missouri Secretary of State, State Archives, Soldiers' Records, War of 1812–World War I, www.sos.mo.gov/archives/soldiers.

from the mind—but there can be no question that it was a factor in my own exhaustion as well as that of others.

Major Halliburton, when I reported to him, told me that under the division attack order, the 110th Engineers and the 128th Machine Gun Battalion, were to form the division reserve. Company A would accompany the right battalion, Company B and battalion headquarters the left battalion. He pointed out to me the general direction to take.

Also, he added, the battalion cooks and mess sergeants had brought up hot soup and other food—I could see them as he spoke. He was moving out with Company B—Captain Corey and his men were resting nearby.

I explained the condition of my men. They were exhausted from the long drag back from the woods. They had been without food for some days except what they had taken from the haversacks of the German dead. I must [be] given them an opportunity to rest awhile and eat.

That was up to me, the major indicated. The command of his battalion had in a sense been taken from him by its assignments to other units from time to time. He could not authorize any delay in the execution of the order. I could follow my own judgement and on my own responsibility.

That's all I wanted to know, I told him. I had been doing that for a couple of days. The men would rest and eat. Advantage was also taken of the stop to fill up the canteens, most of which had been long dry.

Major Halliburton himself looked exhausted. I tendered him the German canteen I had and which, I explained to him, contained something that tasted like coffee and cognac. I believed he would like it.

With the stopper out and the canteen almost to his lips, the major paused to ask me where I got it.

"Off the belt of a dead German," I explained.

The major recorked it and handed it back.

"I don't believe I want any," he said.

Later in our period of service he used to comment in jest that I was the only officer of his battalion who did not drink and yet I was the only one who was able to get a drink during the Meuse-Argonne.

Major Halliburton and Captain Corey and Company B (less two absent platoons) moved off to the front. My own men ate, sent their canteens to be filled, and rested. Dunn and I relaxed too after eating, but not for long.

After I deemed that the minimum amount of rest essential had been secured, we started off to the north again, meaning to veer to the east and join the right battalion of the engineers east of Chaudron farm somewhere.

As we passed a little water-course just northeast of Baulny, I found to my surprise that I could not climb out of the ditch. My strength was gone somehow.

"I can't get out of this ditch," I remarked wonderingly.

Two men extended hands and helped me up. I went on but worried a bit. Was I going to be able to make it?

Perhaps this was the result of physical reaction but in a few moments there came excitement to counteract it. I forgot about my extreme weariness and, ignoring it, overcame it somehow. Nor did this weakness which made me unable to climb unassisted from the ditch again return.

Apparently this was an illustration of what reserves the human system has when it is necessary to call upon them. It presumably was what Maj. Gen. Wright back at Camp Doniphan had meant when he wrote in a memorandum: "There is no limit to human endurance." It was the thing to which Maj. Gen. J. Franklin Bell had referred in a talk he made to the 22nd U.S. Infantry at Texas City in April, 1914, when he said that after your first wind, there is a second, and a third, and a fourth—if you just keep on going despite being exhausted.

The excitement this time was when a mounted man rode up from Baulny bringing a message from Major Sammons or someone else there—Major Sammons was with division headquarters at the moment—that airplanes reported there was a great enemy counter-attack coming on our left front and no one apparently there to meet it.[20]

20. This was Capt. Edward C. Sammons, 35th Division inspector. Edward Curf Sammons was born in Portland, Oregon, on August 22, 1891. He left his position as an assistant cashier at a Portland bank and volunteered for service in May 1917. He attended the officers training camp at the Presidio in San Francisco and was commissioned a captain. Promoted to lieutenant colonel on October 10, 1918, Sammons died in Portland on December 2, 1985. *The Oregon Daily Journal (Portland)*, November 10, 1918.

From where we stood it appeared as if the entire left flank of the 35th Division was in the air for the space of a kilometre and a half.

I stopped the company where it was, between the draw and the old German concrete observation post on the ridge north of Baulny and together with Lieutenant Dunn walked to the nose about 500 meters west of where we had stopped—a point also about 500 meters northwest of Baulny itself.

Here we could see the valley of the Aire extending to the northwest.

Seven or 800 meters—between 800 and 900 yards—northwest of us, east of the Aire River and hence in our 35th Division sector—a line of riflemen was deployed on a ridge just east-southeast of L'Esperance farm, watching to the north.

Directly to the west of them across the Aire River the town of Apremont, in the 28th Division sector, was under a terrific enemy shell concentration. It was apparently in the possession of Americans for a heavy German barrage was falling on it. There also was heavy small arms and machine gun fire, though what was most conspicuous to us was the pounding of the German shells.

As we looked the barrage ceased but there was considerable infantry firing and through our glasses we could see men darting about. Then we saw Americans trickling south out of Apremont, slipping back along the base of the river hills to the Vervaux ravine, 1000 meters west-southwest of where we stood. They formed a new defensive front on the nose north of this stream. A few moments later our men seem to have left the town for a fierce American barrage struck the village, half obscuring the place with smoke and with the dust of falling walls. Apparently—obviously it seemed to us—the 28th Division had lost Apremont and its front was due west of Baulny.

While all this was in progress a long line of troops had left the woods well to the southwest of the mouth of the Vervaux ravine and moved eastward. I could not tell whether they were Americans retiring or Germans advancing against our left rear. Dunn and I both, switching between staring at them and at Apremont through our field glasses, tried to distinguish their uniforms and couldn't.

It was too far to make out the uniforms even through the glasses and for a moment I thought that the enemy were cutting off the front of the troops across the Aire. But in a few minutes the men left the shelter of the river bank and moved back to the woods. I fancied that they had been driven out of the woods in the first place and now were returning to the fight and decided that the 28th must be having difficulties with its flank all the way along.

We decided that they probably were Americans because the line was never broken as it would have been had they been Germans retiring after they had come under fire.

But the situation was alarming enough. Here was what seemed a critical situation, with the crucial point the connecting one with the division on the left.

Our 35th Division riflemen on the nose south of L'Esperance were firing now as rapidly as they could work the bolts of their rifles.

It appeared that the left of the 35th Division was wide open—and in point of fact it was.

Our troops had attacked directly north from Montrebeau Woods and parallel positions to the east of them. The 140th Infantry and part of the 139th on the right had advanced a mile or more, passed the Ravine d'Exermont and seized the high ground just north of it. Some of the 138th was west of this, some east, I believe. Elements of the 137th and 139th had taken Exermont and passed on beyond it.

Then the fresh 52nd German Division, plus surviving fragments of the 1st and 5th Prussian Guard Division, had counterattacked, along the trough of the Aire. Part of this may have hit the 28th. At least two regiments of the German 52nd Division struck the exposed flank east of the Aire, and surged in the unoccupied western part of Montrebeau Woods a mile south of our front at Exermont. The 2nd Landwehr Division seems to have retaken Apremont.

The details of this we did not know, of course, but from having been in Montrebeau Woods the night before we knew that the west edge of them had not been secured at the time we left and it was clear that the division had attacked northward leaving this vulnerable gap on the left through which the enemy was counter-attacking.

Dunn and I both estimated the situation the same. It seemed to us that the front of the division was in danger of being encircled—except for the thin line of riflemen we saw and for ourselves.

Study of post-war accounts indicates this view was not far wrong. The only other unit I have heard of as being on the extreme left was a fragment of Company A, 130th Machine Gun Battalion, which had been ordered to advance north along the road north of L'Esperance—was told that other troops had preceded it—and which had run into short range blasts of enemy machine gun and artillery fire when it tried to do so. What was left of it must have been near the road on the left of the riflemen we saw and out of sight under the hill from where we stood. It was pinned down by short range fire at the time and could neither fire nor move.

"This is one of those things mentioned in the books," I said in effect to Dunn. "We are ordered to go way off to the east somewhere. Here is a changed situation from anything foreseen at the time those orders were issued. We are going into action covering this flank. If we have guessed correctly at the situation all will agree that we did the right thing. If we have guessed wrong I probably will be hung. But we must take that chance of hanging."[21]

Of course we did the right thing. A citation which I received after the action—and which was translated into a Silver Star award when this decoration was later created—was based primarily on this decision though other things were mentioned. Moreover Major Halliburton commended me verbally on it as soon as he heard.

Yet my action really called for no brain work or anything else much. Numerous tactical problems published before the war, and which I had studied, visualized situations like this and told what to do—disobey your previous orders and act in accordance with the dictates of common sense.

The company had now come up and the three sections were sited along the hills for fire to the west and northwest but we had not been in position long when the runner whom I had sent forward returned with word that our troops to the north were being withdrawn. I later learned that our units, rather badly mingled as they were, had attacked all along the line and had taken Exermont, suffering heavy losses as they did so. After the town had been held

21. It may be at this moment that Schrantz, north of Baulny, sent a message addressed to "any field officer" and dated 10:15 a.m. on September 29. It simply read, "Enemy threatening left. Infantry urgently needed. Now almost unprotected." September 28, 1918, typed field message from 128th M.G. to Any Field Officer, Folder: 128th M.G. Batl. Field Messages 235-32.16, Record Group 120, Records of the American Expeditionary Forces, World War I, Entry NM-91 1241, Records of Combat Divisions, 1917–1919, Box 16, 35th Division, NARA.

a couple of hours orders were received to abandon it and the whole advance line drew slowly back in accordance with instructions.

Then came word that "the 70th Brigade" was falling back. Actually General Traub had directed the withdrawal of the forward elements of the division as soon as he saw his front had been outflanked.

At this time accident reunited the two sections of Company A. Difficulties of food supply had led someone in one of the infantry regiments to set up an impromptu kitchen in the church in Baulny and issue bread spread with butter and sugar, or with syrup, to all comers, regardless of organization. Lieut. Frank L. Snyder, still without orders south of Montrebeau woods where he had spent the night, heard of this and sent men back to get some of the food for his platoon. These men encountered the rest of Company A and quickly bore orders forward to Snyder to bring his unit. Upon receiving word of the withdrawal I began shifting a portion of my guns to where they could get a field of fire to the north and was worrying about the few available when Lieutenant Snyder came up with his six guns and four of company "B," our battalion, that had attached themselves to him (Snyder also had picked up a stray machine gun squad from one of the regimental machine gun companies and thus actually had six guns of his own). This gave me control of sixteen guns. Some of these I placed northwest of Baulny to flank the hills along the river, others along the ridge north of Baulny to cover the withdrawal which was now in progress and still others at the north edge of Baulny and behind the wire east of the village as a sort of second line.

With these we formed a machine gun defense of the Baulny ridge—its left refused to Baulny itself on the road since the men near L'Esperance had withdrawn.

This was the first occupation of what later was known as the 110th Engineer line in the west part of the sector, the 110th Battalion which had been forward of it falling back and occupying the crest of the ridge along with the machine guns.

This does not mean, however, that I selected what, with some minor variations, became the ultimate 35th Division line. For one thing it was the obvious one and, in addition, some one of the field officers to whom I had talked the day before had told me that this was the line which would be held in case the division was driven back from its forward positions. I do not recall who this was or when but it could only have been at the hedge north of Chaudron farm where there had seemed to be some sort of informal council of war and where some differed from Lt. Col. Parker who wanted to continue the attack. While I had little noted it at the time, it stuck in my memory.

The fragments of rifle units were soon coming back slowly but in some confusion, as was inevitable in view of the disorganization existing. Some rallied on the engineer and machine gun line, others stopped in a swale between Baulny and the hill, but those still in an organized form withdrew under orders, to the general vicinity of Charpentry for reorganization under cover of the engineer defense. Some organizations remained in Chaudron farm and at the southeast edge of Montrebeau woods to cover the removal of wounded who had been collected there in large numbers.

As inevitable in such a movement a fringe of discouraged stragglers seem to have found their way far to the rear with tales of disaster which caused consternation and gave the idea that the front had been broken. The Germans themselves believed this to be the case.

"This attack of the 52nd Division, supported on its left and right by the remainder of the Guards divisions, temporarily but seriously shook the American front until the counterattack was stopped by the bringing up of strong American reserves," wrote Major von Giehrl, the German historian. "The 28th and 35th Divisions bore the brunt of the fighting here and suffered exceedingly heavy losses, partly due to flanking fire from artillery in the Argonne."

In fact the "strong American reserves" to which the writer refers were the reserve elements of the 35th Division itself, principally the 110th Engineers and the already exhausted 128th Machine Gun Battalion. And the troops which fell back behind Baulny did so under orders, as mentioned.

While I was picking gun positions and directing their occupation other elements of the division began coming back under a tremendous pounding of enemy shells. I little noted these, being occupied in my job, but among those returning was Captain Corey with the four guns of Company B under his control.

Corey and I together then coordinated the machine gun defense, insofar as our own guns were concerned, his guns now holding the forward line and my own the village of Baulny and the ridge northeast of it as a reserve line—this because his men were in better condition physically than my own. This doubtless was Corey's idea, he being the senior. He stayed that night on the hill to the north while I endeavored to get some sleep in the village—vain task.

As the division withdrew from Montrebeau woods, the artillery fire of the enemy was shifted back to the Baulny area, and the Carthage company among others began to suffer additional casualties.

Private Frank O. Pierson, sitting in a shell hole with Private David H. Havens, felt a violent blow on the back of his helmet, and that steel head-gear turned violently around, held in place only by the chin strap which Pierson, according to a habit of his own when in combat, wore behind his head. The hand which he raised to the back of his head came away covered with blood. A shell fragment had torn through the steel of the helmet and inflicted a long deep wound in the scalp, which was bleeding profusely. A first-aid dressing was applied and Pierson went back for a month in a hospital. Other casualties followed, some of them resulting from gas shells. Privates Martin Zogg and Charles L. Mertins were among the gas victims and both suffered injuries from shell fragments.[22]

Mertins was able to rejoin after a few days, but Zogg was invalided back to the United States. Private Earl Conley was sent to the rear because of gas and exhaustion, and Private Roy Carlson went back with mustard gas burns which kept him in the hospital two months.[23]

22. Frank Oscar Pierson was born in Fort Scott, Kansas, on January 23, 1892. He died on May 26, 1947, and was buried in the Fort Scott National Cemetery. He enlisted in the Kansas National Guard in 1914, and transferred from Company G, 137th Infantry to the 128th Machine Gun Battalion. His hometown newspaper noted that Pierson was "not consulted" about the transfer, but was "simply moved from one unit to the other." *Fort Scott* (KS) *Daily Tribune and Fort Scott Daily Monitor*, July 15, 1918. Martin Florian Zogg was born on October 1, 1894, in Carterville, Missouri, died on March 16, 1953, and was buried in Paris, Illinois. He joined Company A in August 1917 and was promoted to private first class in October 1917. He served overseas with Company A from April 25, 1918 to February 2, 1919. *The Terre Haute* (IN) *Tribune*, March 17, 1953; Missouri Secretary of State, State Archives, Soldiers' Records, War of 1812–World War I, www.sos.mo.gov/archives/soldiers; HST. Charles Leroy Mertins was born in Carthage on September 9, 1887, and died on February 2, 1969. He served overseas with Company A from April 25, 1918, to April 24, 1919. He was buried in Park Cemetery in Carthage. *Joplin News Herald*, February 3, 1969; Missouri Secretary of State, State Archives, Soldiers' Records, War of 1812–World War I, www.sos.mo.gov/archives/soldiers.

23. Earl Edward Conley was born on May 20, 1897, and died on August 24, 1970. He was buried in Berlin, Maryland. Originally a member of Company G, 137th Infantry,

The situation remained with but little change in the Baulny vicinity for the remainder of the day.

It was a night of wild alarms and confusion, only part of which touched me. My concern again was only my own company. The forward elements of the divison however withdrew under cover of darkness behind this so-called engineer line, parts of the rifle regiments remaining on the new line, others reforming behind it.

Major Halliburton, completely exhausted, had gone back somewhere to rest. Battalion headquarters was in Baulny and with some of the headquarters officers I tried to sleep in a Baulny cellar which afforded protection from the weather but which was partially full of German trench mortar projectiles. We were too tired to worry about that but in retrospect an ammunition dump would seem to have had some perilous aspects as regards a place of abode.

In looking back at the events of September 29 following the enemy counterattack it might be well to glance at extracts from the Intelligence Report of the Third German Army as printed in Jay M. Lee's "The Artilleryman," a history of the 129th Field Artillery, of which, incidentally, Harry S. Truman, later to become president of the United States, was an officer.

"The counter-attack of the 52nd Infantry (division) on the enemy who broke through at Exermont was successful. The two Guard divisions retained contact. For a short time the whole American front between the Aire and the left flank of the army was in retreat. Concentrated artillery fire did great damage among the enemy masses. By quickly bringing up reserves, the enemy, who saw his line yielding, just in time brought the Guard division to a stand east of Apremont and south of Montreabeau . . ."

This last sentence is of interest. The placing of my own machine guns in the gap was of course observed by the enemy and reported since it was wide open to enemy observation from the west. It was interpreted as the entry of reserves into action, which in a sense it was since we were part of the division reserve. The rest of the troops later manning this line came "back" instead of being "brought up." There were no troops, outside of the division, who were in the American line that day or night.

Conley transferred to Company A, 128th in early June 1918. In a letter home, Conley related that his work with the 128th was "more interesting and not so hard as in the infantry." Conley predicted that he would be "making faces at Fritz before long." *Fort Scott* (KS) *Tribune and the Fort Scott Monitor*, August 9, 1918.

Since the enemy interpreted my movement of machine guns into positions covering the gap as the intervention of reserves "just in time" I believe I am justified in thinking that the move was not without its tactical influence on the course of the action as a whole.

The same enemy intelligence report made the evening of September 29 also states:

"At the same time the second line division (apparently 2nd Landwehr) took Apremont."

This was the incident in the 28th Division sector that Dunn and I had witnessed. And the next day the German intelligence report tells of American attacks against Apremont.

This is mentioned because most American reports—including the American Battle Monuments Commission's "35th Division, Summary of Operations in the World War" (1944)—ignores the German recapture of Apremont and says the 35th Division withdrawal left the right flank of the 28th Division exposed.

It was, as I witnessed and is confirmed by the German reports quoted, the other way about. The 28th Division's loss of Apremont and its withdrawal along the Aire to the Ravine de Vervaux directly west of Baulny village, left the 35th Division's flank more exposed than it otherwise would have been.

Until the 28th retook Apremont the following day—afternoon as I recall—our own flank was exposed even on the line to which the withdrawal was made and that was why our defense on the left was refused slightly. It was for this reason that my left machine guns covering the river road were in the trenches just northwest of Baulny instead of 700 meters farther northwest on the next nose.

I have never seen a 28th Division history of that war, nor any 28th Division reports, but I have always assumed that when the 28th Division lost Apremont it did not think it necessary to report the fact since it planned to take it back anyhow. And since it actually did retake it about 24 hours later, it saw no reason to mention the temporary reverse.

Evening of September 29, 1918. The exhausted 35th U.S. Division—worn out by incessant effort, hungry for lack of supplies, disorganized and with units intermingled through four days of battle—lay in the vicinity of Baulny on the east bank of the Aire River, its offensive power almost totally expended but still able and willing to hold its shallow fox holes on the shell-pounded heights. Its casualties had been greater during the preceding four days than those of any other division in the Meuse-Argonne battle; they were greater in fact than any other American division suffered in a similar length of time throughout the war.

The proper use of machine guns was not well understood by many senior officers at that time, due to the fact that our service had not used them to any great extent prior to this war, and Col. T.C. Clarke, commanding the 110th Engineers and now the front line commander, believed that all machine guns available should be distributed along the firing line.[24]

Hostile shell fire fell on Baulny and the region east of it but it was at least known that there were friends in front—but up on the forward line it was a night of wild alarms. Action of enemy patrols caused the fear that a hostile night attack might be imminent and led Col. T.C. Clark[e], commander of the 110th Engineers, who had established his command post at an old enemy concrete observation post on the main line of resistance, to fear that a hostile night attack might be imminent. He felt he needed more machine guns.

Late in the night, perhaps between 10 and 11 o'clock, a runner found me and brought orders to report to Colonel Nuttman, commanding the 69th Brigade. The runner guided me to a Baulny dug-out in which Colonel Nuttman, who was pretty well worn out with exhaustion at that time, and sick besides I have later learned, and a number of other senior officers were installed.

Colonel Nuttman told me to take all of my guns which were in position in or about Baulny and send them up to the firing line. Also I should find Captain Fred Nesbitt, Company A, 130th Machine

24. Thomas Curtis Clarke, born in Philadelphia on December 11, 1873, was said to be the only non-West Point graduate named to command an engineer regiment during World War I. A graduate of the Massachusetts Institute of Technology, Clarke traveled in Europe before World War I and was fluent in both German and French. He joined the New York National Guard in 1895, graduated from the officers' training camp at Plattsburg, New York, and was commissioned as a captain in the engineer reserves in January 1917. Called to active duty in May 1917, Clarke was promoted to lieutenant colonel and assigned to the 110th Engineers. He assumed command of the regiment in July 1918 and was promoted to colonel that September. He commanded the 110th Engineers during the Meuse-Argonne Offensive, served as the 35th Division's engineer officer, and was gassed. He was awarded the French Croix de Guerre for his participation in a trench raid. Clarke died of pneumonia in New York City on May 25, 1921. Rankin, *The Santa Fe Trail Leads to France*, 42; *The New York Times*, May 26, May 27, 1921; "Death of Col. Thomas C. Clarke, E.O.R.C.," *The Military Engineer* 13 (July–August 1921): 342. He was buried in Oak Hill Cemetery, Washington, D.C.

Gun Battalion, who he understood was in Baulny somewhere, and order him to send all his guns up there.[25]

Eight guns of Company B, 128th Machine Gun Battalion, along with some straggler machine gun squads, were already emplaced along that line under the command of Captain Corey, I told him. They were enough to cover that front. Machine guns should be organized in depth to resist any enemy attack and mine were in Baulny and east of it on a support line. Part of them—those on the left—covered the river road and were essential there for the front line's defense.

"No matter about that," said Colonel Nuttman in effect, though pleasantly enough. "Colonel [Clarke] thinks he needs more machine guns and I am going to send up every one I can get. Take them up."

"Yes sir," I told him since I could do nothing else, "but as regards Captain Nesbitt he is senior to me and I am hardly in a position to give him orders."

"You are not giving him your orders but mine," he properly reminded me. "Find him and get him up there." That was that.

I found Captain Nesbitt, an old acquaintance.

"What the ----, ----- hell do they want more machine guns up there?" queried that genial but weary soul, stigmatizing the "they," according to his wont, with many expletives they would not have enjoyed hearing. "If Jesse Corey's guns are up there that is enough. Your guns are emplaced right where they should be. My own men are resting."

However there was no one to whom to appeal. No one knew where the division machine gun officer was—it developed later that he was getting some urgently needed slumber back in Cheppy—and Major Halliburton too was back at his battalion transport camp sleeping the sleep of utter exhaustion after being worn out by the arduous days and nights preceding. The location of the major of the 130th Machine Gun Battalion—Major John F. Constable—was also

25. Frederick H. Nesbitt was born in Mantena, Illinois, on January 5, 1878, and died in Joplin, Missouri on March 12, 1944. A veteran of the Spanish-American War (Company G, 5th Missouri Infantry), he served as captain of Company I, 2nd Missouri Infantry on the Mexican border 1916–17, then commanded Company A, 130th Machine Gun Battalion. He served overseas from May 2, 1918, to April 27, 1919. He was buried in Webb City, Missouri. *Joplin* (MO) *Globe*, March 14, 1944; *The Service of the Missouri National Guard on the Mexican Border*, 175; Missouri Secretary of State, State Archives, Soldiers' Records, War of 1812–World War I, www.sos.mo.gov/archives/soldiers. A tribute to the "popular" company commander may be found in the *Joplin* (MO) *Globe*, March 21, 1944.

unknown though it was learned later that he had gone to the rear, sick and exhausted, to spend the next ten months in a hospital.

Finally we agreed that I should send up four of my 12 guns and he would take up the five he had remaining. Maybe the division machine gun officer would come up in time to save me from the results of not literally obeying orders.

I decided that Cpl. Harry Palmer's section of the second platoon and Cpl. James A. Amerman's section of the third platoon could best be spared.

"I am going to send you up in command," I told Sergeant Edwin W. Wiggins, my company range finder sergeant, "with Sgt. Hopwood (Norval) as platoon sergeant."

A splendid soldier, Wiggins was, and of potential officer material. He grinned happily at the assignment. It was the kind of thing he had been wanting.

Wiggins departed for the front and its hubbub, and I tried again to get some needed rest.

He was killed as he finished putting his guns in position.

Corporal Amerman, as the man nearest to him at the time, later said in his report:

> "On the night of September 29–30 Sergeant Wiggins was in charge of a platoon of four guns sent to the front line on the ridge north of Baulny. He posted my section west of the pill box (former German observation post) during a heavy bombardment and instructed me to tell him when my emplacements were completed. He then went toward the pill box, it being Col. Clarke's P.C., and just as he reached the door the enemy apparently made a direct hit on the building just above the door. Sergeant Wiggins called "Hop"—meaning Sgt. Norval R. Hopwood who was acting platoon sergeant—and fell into the building dead, a very small piece of shell having penetrated his head behind the left ear. This was the only place he was hit. This was about 4 a.m., I think."

Sergeant Wiggins was the son of Mr. and Mrs. T.L. Wiggins of Carthage, was 22 years of age and had been a member of Company A since 1913, serving with it on the Mexican border during the 1916 frontier troubles. Like Sergeant Charles S. Edwards, who fell on the second day of the fight, Wiggins was one of the men who company officers said would eventually have advanced to commissioned rank had he lived. The following is the citation which accompanied the posthumous award to him of the Distinguished Service Cross, for extraordinary heroism in action:

> "Edwin W. Wiggins (Army serial No. 1445247), sergeant, Company A, 128th Machine Gun Battalion. For extraordinary heroism in action near Baulny, France, September 29, 1918. Sergeant Wiggins led a machine gun platoon to a threatened portion of the line under a heavy enemy barrage, encouraging his men and directing the construction of emplacements. He also organized a group of infantrymen who had become separated from their organizations and put them into the line, supervising their entrenchments. This gallant soldier was killed just as this work was completed."[26]

Morning of September 30, 1918, and in the 35th Division area at least the war had grown old. Whatever freshness and glamour there had ever been in battle was long-since gone. Gaunt and unshaven men rubbed weary eyes with grimy hands, glanced at the gray and rain-sodden dawn and looked bleakly at the still grayer faces of men who yesterday had been like them but now had found peace and rest in the midst of the turmoil. "C'est la guerre."

That Gallic philosophy which had aided France to endure four years of war was of no less value to those who repeated it as they helped to fight America's battles on French soil.

26. Edwin Wolfley Wiggins, age 22, was born on May 4, 1896, and raised in Carthage. He was "unusually well known and liked," according to the *Carthage Evening Press*. He was promoted to corporal in June 1917 and to sergeant that August. He served overseas from March 30, 1918, until his death on September 29, 1918. *Carthage* (MO) *Evening Press*, November 1, 1918; *The Service of the Missouri National Guard on the Mexican Border*, 128; Missouri Secretary of State, State Archives, Soldiers' Records, War of 1812–World War I, www.sos.mo.gov/archives/soldiers; HST. According to a friend, Wiggins and his men had not had anything to eat or drink, except what they could find on German bodies, and were tired. Some of them, including Wiggins, dropped off to sleep, when the shelling started and he was killed. Several other Americans were wounded by the same shell. *Carthage* (MO) *Evening Press*, December 31, 1918. Captain Schrantz expressed his "deepest sympathy" to Wiggins's parents, and "the most heartfelt regard at his loss." "Sergeant Wiggins was an excellent soldier," Schrantz continued, "a better one could not be found in any army. His ability, shown both by his long and faithful service and by his courageous conduct in action, would soon have won him commissioned rank. Every man in the company was his friend and every man in the company feels the keenest sorrow at his death—a sorrow mingled with pride at the heroic manner in which he died. And I trust that your sorrow too, will be lessened by the knowledge that no soldier ever died a death more glorious nor in a cause more worthy." His meager personal possessions consisted of a watch, a bill book, and a silver cigarette case. *Carthage* (MO) *Evening Press*, November 26, 1918; December 10, 1918. Schrantz noted in his memoir that Wiggins's D.S.C. was "a richly merited decoration."

Distinguished Service Cross awarded to Edwin Wiggins (*Memorial Hall, Carthage, MO*)

Resignedly and somewhat vengefully the Missouri machine gunners started expectantly to the north, wearily worked the bolts of their weapons to be sure they were still in firing order, and then waited for whatever might betide, while rumors and uncertainties circulated among those from whom they took orders.

Sergeant Hopwood brought me the news [of Wiggins's death]—and some quite disquieting information.

Colonel Clarke had told him, he said, that if it was necessary to abandon the line then held, that the riflemen would fall back first and that the machine guns would stay in position covering their withdrawal, later being withdrawn after the riflemen had established a new line east of Baulny.

This stirred me and I decided that it was high time that the division machine gun officer should be around to have some say about the way the machine guns were being used.

I had not seen him since the morning of September 27 and all this was distinctly in his field. I wrote him a message that I thought would bring him out and sent a runner back toward Cheppy to find him.

While I had not seen Colonel Hay myself he had been running about hither and yon in connection with his work and was getting some much needed slumber at the division command post in Cheppy, where, under normal circumstances, he belonged. What with interdivisional communication non-existent, I thought he should take a look at the situation himself.

The message actually brought him up in the hurry. In an article about the machine guns of the 35th he wrote in the May–June *Infantry Journal* of 1933, he said that he had come up to the front and had talked to me before my message reached him—but that apparently was a lapse of memory. When I saw him the next afternoon the first word he said, with a smile, was:

"Well, captain, I received your S.O.S."

Immediately after writing the message I hurried up front with Hopwood and interviewed Colonel Clarke whom I knew, he having been the commander of the 35th overseas detachment sent across ahead of the division.

His contemplated action, I told him, would likely result in the loss of the machine guns. Due to the heavy burden-bearing involved, the machine gunners could move but slowly. If there was going to be a withdrawal, a fringe of riflemen should cover the pulling back of the guns to a new position.

But he had changed his mind about the possible necessity of any retirement.

"I am not going to withdraw at all," he told me. "I'm going to die right here if necessary." Then he added that if he did find it necessary to retire he would leave a rifle company to cover the MGs withdrawal. This was reassuring. It put all my doubts at rest.

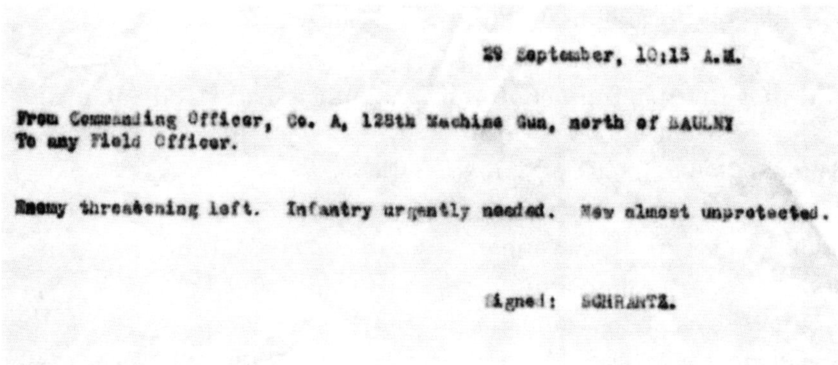

29 September, 10:15 A.M.

From Commanding Officer, Co. A, 128th Machine Gun, north of BAULNY
To any Field Officer.

Enemy threatening left. Infantry urgently needed. Now almost unprotected.

Signed: SCHRANTZ.

Message sent by Captain Schrantz during Meuse-Argonne Offensive (*National Archives*)

It was getting day now.

In the morning the enemy attempted several weak counter attacks from Montrebeau woods but each of them was speedily broken up by furious storm of rifle and machine gun fire from the hill. Our position was constantly shelled and our line being very thick there were quite a few men killed but fortunately for us the enemy was not using shrapnel. The shallow foxholes offered fair protection against anything in the way of high explosive except direct hits but against shrapnel they would have been almost useless.

Movement of men in Montrebeau Woods could be seen occasionally. No one knew for sure whether they were Germans or Americans who had not yet left.

Colonel Clarke—a genial gentleman and a gallant old soldier, but still an engineer suddenly thrown into command of an infantry line—was as uncertain as any of us.

He wrote a message calling for an artillery barrage on the wood, then sent another immediately asking the artillery not to fire, that those might be Americans, then another asking for a barrage, etc.

I mean nothing disparaging to Colonel Clarke by all this. His courage was amply proved that day under my observation and that of everybody else up there. I retain an admiration for him. I merely mean to narrate what occurred and the uncertainty concerning targets. It is a tremendous responsibility to call down fire on what might be friendly troops. I suspect many officers in many wars have faced the same uncertainty.

Captain Corey and I faced it very soon.

It had been thought that Chaudron farm off to the right front had been evacuated the night before, but now stretcher bearers could be seen carrying men out of there and to the south, this being the evacuation of the last of the injured collected at that spot the day before. This caused doubt as to whether or not Americans might still be in Montrebeau Woods. Thus when figures appeared east of the wood darting southward there was at first no firing, and officers studied them through field glasses trying in vain to distinguish the uniforms. Let them come on and show a better target. Colonel Clarke was urging us to fire.

Soon the numbers thickened and there was no doubt that these were enemies. Finally it was clear that they were in attack formation and in the open. Time to open up. A hostile attack against the American line was getting under way. Captain Corey and I gave the word.

The range was 1800 yards. Sergeant Hopwood's platoon of Company A and Lieut. Curtis B. Hostettler's [*sic*] platoon of Company B, 128th Machine Gun Battalion, opened fire, and at the same time some of the guns of Company A, 130th Machine Gun Battalion (Webb City) on the right chattered into action.[27]

The enemy advance stopped abruptly, and most of the men participating in it turned to the right and raced in disorder for the shelter of the timber, those reaching it quickly disappearing therein. The fire was continued for a time on the prone figures—most of them probably having merely sought shelter that way at first, and on the woods into which the fragments of the assaulting unit had disappeared. This attack caused considerable interest on the hill, the riflemen displayed their zeal by opening fire with great gusto though the targets were well beyond effective rifle range. That ended that counterattack.

Colonel Clarke still wanted more machine guns on the hill.

27. Curtis Branson Hostetler was born in Republic, Kansas, on April 28, 1889, and died in Salt Lake City, Utah, on March 20, 1983. He enlisted in the 1st Arizona Infantry in 1914, and served on the Mexican border from 1916 to 1917. He attended the Officers Training Camp at the Presidio in San Francisco from May to August 1917 and was commissioned a second lieutenant. He was attached to Company B, 128th Machine Gun Battalion in October 1917, and was promoted to first lieutenant in March 1918. His hometown newspaper described him as a "real American young man." *Republic County* (KS) *Democrat*, September 25, 1918; HST. One of Hostetler's letters home may be found in the *Republic County* (KS) *Democrat*, November 27, 1918.

I returned to Baulny reluctantly.

In the streets of the town I met Lieut. W.O. Jackson, our battalion supply officer.[28] I mentioned to him the impending destruction of our plan of machine guns organized in depth.

"The general is in that dug-out under the church," he said. "Why don't you tell him?"

"I will," I answered and jumped into the trench he indicated and went under the church.

General Traub was sitting on a bunk looking at the message Colonel Clarke has [had] sent back—probably the conflicting ones in reference to artillery fire written some time before and turned over to him by some artillery officer as showing a gunner's difficulties.

"Colonel Clarke," he commented slowly, "seems to have a first class system of liaison—and not a damn thing else. I wonder what the situation really is up there?"

"I can tell you, sir," I cut in. "I have just come from there."

"And who are you?" he queried.

"Captain Schrantz, sir, Company A, 128th Machine Gun Battalion."

"All right, captain, tell us about it."

I told the situation as it was a few moments before and then launched into my machine-guns-in depth grievance. This time I was talking to an understanding audience. General Traub and his chief of staff knew about how machine guns should be organized.

"Colonel," said General Traub to Col. Hamilton S. Hawkins, the chief of staff. "I think we should place Captain Schrantz in charge of the machine gun situation and let him straighten it out."

He wrote the following note on his field message blank for Colonel Clarke and handed it to me:

"Colonel Clarke:

Turn over machine gun situation to Capt. Schrantz unless you have confided same to some other officer.

Traub"

"I wish," he said to Colonel Hawkins, "that you would accompany Captain Schrantz back to the front line and see what you can

28. William O. Jackson was born on September 22, 1893 (some sources state 1895). A law student from Butler, Missouri, Jackson joined Company B, 2nd Missouri Infantry in April 1917 and was commissioned a second lieutenant to rank from March 1917 and a first lieutenant to rank from July 1917. He died on December 6, 1967. HST.

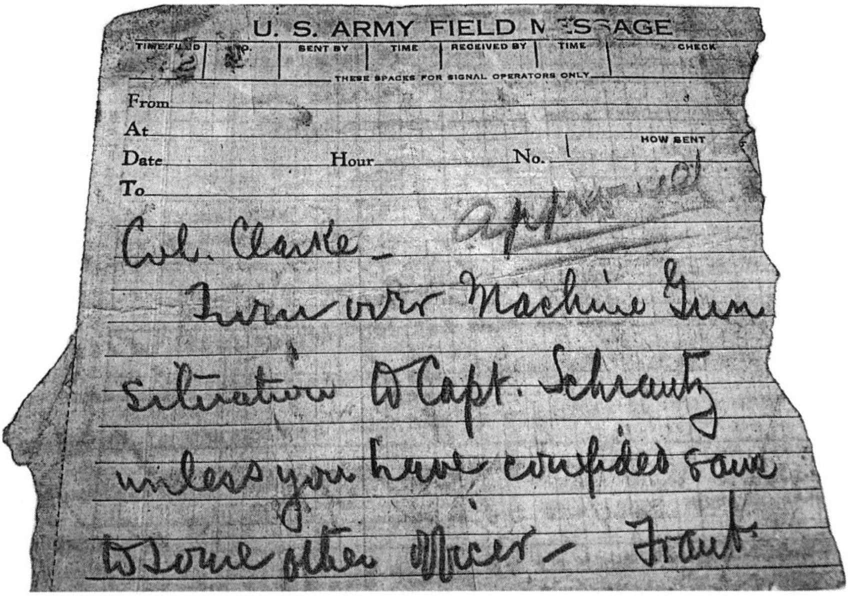
U. S. ARMY FIELD MESSAGE

TIME FILED	NO.	SENT BY	TIME	RECEIVED BY	TIME	CHECK

THESE SPACES FOR SIGNAL OPERATORS ONLY

From

At

Date Hour No. 1 HOW SENT

To

Col. Clarke — approved
Turn over Machine Gun
situation to Capt. Schrantz
unless you have confided same
to some other officer — Traub

Order authorizing Schrantz to organize machine gun defense on Baulny Ridge (*Harry S. Truman Presidential Library and Museum*)

do to straighten out things. Take any steps you think needed. Make sergeants captains in my name if you think necessary."

Colonel Hawkins and I departed for the front.

The dry run between Baulny and the crest held by the front line was jammed with unorganized infantrymen, some wounded some not.

Colonel Hawkins questioned them and finding that there was no organization, divided the unwounded men quickly into small provisional companies, placing the senior sergeant in each group in charge and telling him to organize it with other non-commissioned officers in the group. He told them that he knew they were too tired to go anywhere but that they should line the north side of the ditch and defend it in case the troops on the ridge to the north withdrew.

The sergeants so named started on their work with alacrity. It was clear from expressions that these weary and bewildered men immediately regained confidence.

In fact wherever Colonel Hawkins went that day a feeling of confidence returned. Certainly I had no further worry about the security of the front as I saw order succeeding chaos at a few words from him.

During all this period heavy enemy shell fire was falling on our lines and while I had frequently gone back and forth from the lines to Baulny and had always taken the most direct route, it seemed to me that with the chief of staff following me I should follow the route offering the most shelter. I therefore started to follow the swale which ran northeastward, from the head of which we could jog back behind the crest to the concrete observation post which was Colonel Clarke's P.C.

Colonel Hawkins seemed to sense this immediately.

"Is this the route you always follow?" he queried.

"No sir," I replied. "I have always gone the most direct route before. But this one is safer."

"That's what I thought," he said. "Let's go the way you always go."

So we climbed out of the ditch and went directly to the pill-box.

Colonel Clarke immediately jumped to the conclusion that Colonel Hawkins had come up to relieve him and said he would be very glad indeed to turn things over.

Colonel Hawkins reassured him. He was just looking things over, he said. Post-war reports actually show him as commander of the 69th Brigade that day, Col. Nuttman having gone to the rear sick.

I handed Colonel Clarke the general's note. He wrote the word "approved" on it, started to erase the word when he saw that it was a conditional order, then handed the note to me and said to go ahead.

I left Colonel Hawkins talking to him and proceeded to my task. On the way up I had explained what I wanted to do and he approved the plan—adding that where I withdrew sections from the front line I should give instructions that it be done a man at a time, so that the enemy would not think a retirement had started and so launch a counter-attack.

The task occupied much of the morning, I roving over the west part of the 35th Division sector, followed by a runner at 20 paces so that we would not both be killed by the same shell burst.

A part of Captain Corey's guns, a part of mine (one section) and a part of Captain Nesbitt's, I had withdrawn to a line due east of Baulny. Four guns of the machine gun company of the 137th Infantry, which were back in Charpentry, I had take position on the high ground south of Baulny.

Going back to look for the machine gun company, 138th Infantry, I found it attached to a composite battalion of that regiment which Major Norman B. Comfort had assembled and had brought to the valley southeast of Baulny for counterattack if necessary. Obviously this was the best place for it and I left it there—departing back for the front line myself with some relief since enemy artillery fire was pounding this valley even harder than it was the front.

And I also had a platoon of infantry in position.

In the reorganization of the machine gun positions, parts of all the machine gun companies were moved into support positions, leaving on the front line one gun, 139th Infantry, three guns of Company B, 128th Machine Gun Battalion (one platoon less a gun which had been destroyed during the night), two guns Company A, 128th, three guns Company A, 130th, and one gun, Company D, 130th. The two guns of Company A, 128th, which remained, were those of Corporal James A. Amerman's section, Corporal Palmer's section being withdrawn to the north edge of Baulny between the sections of Sergeant Willard Brown and Sergeant Joseph E. Taylor. Lieut. Frank L. Snyder, who exercised immediate command of the six Baulny guns, sent two men with a salvaged Chauchat automatic rifle to help Capt. Arly L. Hedrick, 110th Engineers, whose company was immediately ahead, to cover a danger spot the machine guns could not reach.[29]

In addition to the 11 remaining guns of my own company, I had placed the seven remaining of Company B (Lieutenant Reardon's platoon of that company was off to the east somewhere and one of Corey's machine guns had been destroyed by a direct hit the night before), one gun of Co. D, 130th Machine Gun Battalion, one gun of the machine gun company 139th Infantry, five guns of Co. A, 130th Machine Gun Battalion and seven guns of the machine gun company, 137th Infanty—this was not counting the eight guns of

29. Arly Luther Hedrick was born in Robinson, Arkansas, on December 25, 1889, and died of meningitis at Brest, France, on March 5, 1919. Hedrick had graduated from Harvard University at the age of 18 in 1908, and completed a two-year engineering course at the University of Wisconsin in 1912. He became a partner in his father's engineering firm in 1916. He had already attained "great success in his profession" when World War I began and he helped recruit a battalion of the 110th Engineers. He served overseas from March 30, 1918, until his death on March 5, 1919. *Kansas City* (MO) *Star*, March 25, 1919; Missouri Secretary of State, State Archives, Soldiers' Records, War of 1812-World War I, www.sos.mo.gov/archives/soldiers.

Trenches on Baulny Ridge (*Author's collection*)

the machine gun company, 138th Infantry, with Major Comfort's battalion.[30]

Lieut. T.C. Bourke, 129th Field Artillery, had gathered up somehow a group of leaderless men he had found wandering somewhere, formed them into a platoon and turned it over to me, saying that someone had told him I was in charge of the defense of Baulny.[31]

I assured him I wasn't, except as regards machine guns, but I had a place where these man would fit and I would be glad to get them. I put them in a trench northwest of Baulny flanking the road and near one of my machine gun sections with the same mission.

In doing all this I was assisted, of course, by all company commanders concerned and by the battalion staff of the 128th Machine Gun Battalion, Major Halliburton not having returned as yet. Lieut. Dunn assumed command of Company A while I was engaged in this work.

30. William Thomas Reardon was born in Kansas City, Missouri, on January 25, 1888. He served overseas with the 128th Machine Gun Battalion from April to December 1918.

31. Thomas C. Bourke was born on April 5, 1893, in Kansas City, Missouri. Bourke served overseas with the 129th Field Artillery from May 1918 to April 1919. He died on September 21, 1977. *Kansas City* (MO) *Star*, September 22, 1977.

From time to time I had seen Colonel Hawkins. He told me that he was not worried any more about the Baulny region but that he did not know what was going on in the right of the division sector and asked me to check over there.

That was the next thing obviously and here I was exhausted again. I was so weary I could hardly get along.

At this time Colonel Hay, the division machine gun officer, showed up smiling with my note.

I told him what I had been doing and about the east half of the sector not having been checked on. He told me to continue on the west half and he would look after the east, and departed forthwith.

Actually things on the east seem to have been better than on the west due in part to the fact that the main enemy threat and pressure had been on the left (west) flank.

The major part of the front line there was in command of Lt. Col. Edward M. Stayton, 110th Engineers, who was a former artilleryman and an old soldier. He apparently had things well in hand. Between the wars he wound up his military career as a major general in the Missouri National Guard. A battalion of the 138th Infantry was east of his position.[32]

Capt. William S. Moore, who had succeeded to the command of the 130th Machine Gun Battalion the day before, either had already organized the machine gun defense of that sector or was put to doing so by Colonel Hay. Or perhaps he only sketched for Col. Hay the location of machine guns already in position there.

Then Major Halliburton, rested and fit for action again, came back to Baulny and I was happy to turn the machine gun situation in the west sector over to him and resume command of Company A.

I have one vivid recollection connected with my showing Major Halliburton about after his return.

We were coming through Baulny from the west when what seemed to me—and I was plenty accustomed to shell fire by that time—a tremendous artillery concentration hit the village.

One shell just in front of us exploded at the base of a standing stone wall, the front of what once had been a building, just in front

32. Edward M. Stayton, born in Independence, Missouri, on September 4, 1874, served overseas with the 110th Engineers from May 1918 to April 1919. He died on March 2, 1954. *The Kansas City Star*, March 2, 1954.

of us. The [it] seemed to pivot on the point of the shell burst and then collapsed in the street.

There were flying stones, flying fragments, billowing smoke and the blast of new explosions everywhere.

I do not know what became of Major Halliburton just then but I dove into the shelter of the embrasure of a concrete machine gun emplacement in the foundation of the church.

The major did all right by himself, wherever he went, for after the uproar quieted down I found him again and we resumed our tour.

I had collected quite a group of unmanned Hotchkiss machine guns while circulating about organizing the machine gun defense. I ran across a number of them abandoned in the field, probably by units which had been so cut down by casualties or exhaustion during the attack of the 28th that they could not carry all they had and necessary ammunition too. I had faced this problem myself in Montrebeau Woods on the afternoon of the 28th and had momentarily considered burying a gun and tripod, marking the place, intending to recover it later. But I had hit on a better solution. Some lost infantrymen had strayed along about that time and asked for a job, so I distributed them as additional carriers and thus kept the gun.

These guns I found on the field on the 30th I had had carried into Baulny and offered them to any outfit that was short. Captain Nesbitt took two, I think, afterwards reporting quite accurately the guns he had lost and stating the number he had received from me—a quite generous thing, I thought, since the fewer guns he had reported lost the fewer explanations he would have had to make.

But, due to preoccupation with other things, I neglected to replace the gun I had had destroyed in my own unit. That chagrined me. My explanation of the lost gun was easy enough and proper—but I could just as well have emerged with 12 guns as 11 since our Ford trucks brought up food that night and I could have sent them back.

The tactical position of the 35th Division—however dubious it might have seemed in the grey dawn of morning—was secure enough by noon as regards defense against any counterattack.

It was properly organized for defense. It had a proper machine gun set-up and the division artillery was giving proper support.

"The coordination between artillery, machine gun and infantry fire has been splendidly maintained and if kept up we can hold this hill till the cows come home," Major O. Hudson of the 110th Engineers had stated in a message written at 10:25 a.m.[33]

The division was not capable of further offensive effort, it is true, for it was still badly intermingled and its members physically exhausted, but it was capable of making a successful defense in place and waiting where it was for relief without any aid in the meanwhile.

But the alarm as to its status the evening before, which probably was greater in high places in the rear than it was on the front, now brought results in the form of reinforcements which might have been useful 24 hours earlier.

From Baulny we could see troops advancing from the south across the hills below Charpentry where we had been pinned down on September 27.

The situation being secure the 35th Division was surprised to see coming from the rear—far back as one looked from Baulny—fresh American troops. Apparently a daylight relief was to be made, the watchers thought. The leading organizations were in heavy squad columns and as they approached Charpentry the Germans concentrated all artillery available on them. They came on doggedly as flames and smoke erupted about them, and casualties were seen to be heavy. The next organization came up in thin lines with great intervals between men and drew little fire. The third drew the same hurricane of death as the first and also suffered severely. By now the leading battalion had emerged from a valley and shown itself on the hill east of Baulny. A tremendous bombardment ensued but the battalion moved up almost to the front line before it halted, thickening the already over-thick 35th Division line.

It was the Second Battalion, 327th Infantry, 82nd Division, apparently sent up from corps reserve. Whether this regiment came into our sector by mistake, as some said, or whether it came in to support our threatened front, its appearance made the enemy abandon any thought of counterattack that he might have had.[34]

33. Orlin Hudson (1880–1948) of Fredonia, Kansas, was actually a captain and battalion commander of the 110th Engineers during the Meuse-Argonne Offensive, but was permanently promoted to major following that campaign. He was awarded the Distinguished Service Cross in 1935 for his actions on Baulny Ridge on September 29–30, 1918. *The Neodesha* (KS) *Daily Sun*, November 8, 1918.

34. The 82nd Division's 327th Infantry Regiment moved forward to the left flank of the 35th Division.

Its forward elements moved right on up past Baulny and to the front line where they lay down intermingled with the engineers and the fragments of infantry units there.

Apparently the intent had been to attack on the east side of the Aire to assist an effort the 28th was to make on the west side, but if so the German bombardment changed the plan and the only way the suffering 327th aided the 28th Division was by drawing on itself and on the 35th Division a mass of artillery fire that otherwise might have been concentrated on the 28th.

Naturally my own company had not escaped without additional casualties during this defensive action north of Baulny on the afternoon of the 29th and forenoon of the 30th. There had been eight or nine of my men wounded, in varying degrees, as I recall, though naturally there had been many killed in the area including some Company B men.

Going forward from Baulny to the front line to check my guns, about 1 or 2 p.m. September 30, I saw a shell burst in Sergeant Fred Clark's section posted behind some barbed wire northeast of the village.

I went over there immediately.

The back-blast of the shell had blown the mangled body of a man forward into the barbed wire and Sergeant Clark and some others were untangling it.

It was Pvt. Agnes Johns, Kenosha, Wis., one of the riflemen serving with us as an ammunition carrier. An enemy projectile had made a direct hit on the fox hole in which he was lying and possibly passed through his body, with the result mentioned.[35]

It seemed necessary to me, for morale's sake, to get the poor fellow's remains out of sight and so told Clark to bury him in the shell-hole, which he did.

35. Contemporary sources provide conflicting information about this individual. According to the 139th Infantry's history, Private Angus G. Johns of Company L was a resident of Wenatchee, Washington, and was killed on September 28, 1918. Kenamore, *The Story of the 139th Infantry*, 93. According to his June 1917 Draft Registration Card, Angus Guy John, born in Gandy, Nebraska, on June 13, 1891, was a farm laborer residing in Epworth, Mountrail County, North Dakota. The American Battle Monuments Commission notes that Angus G. John, a native of North Dakota and a member of the 139th Infantry, was killed on September 30, 1918, and buried in the Meuse-Argonne American Cemetery. Other sources give his unit as Company E. *Roster of the Men and Women who served in the Army or Naval Service (including the Marine Corps) of the United States or its Allies from the State of North Dakota in the World War, 1917–1918 Volume 2 Flagg to Lark,* accessed on Ancestry.com. Stephen Herman Clark was born on January 6, 1898, in Union City, Tennessee, and died on September 30, 1948 in Excelsior Springs, Missouri. He was buried in the Springfield (MO) National Cemetery. *Joplin* (MO) *Globe*, October 1, 1948.

The following New Year's Day, accompanied by Clark, I returned to the field and we placed a wooden cross with his name over his resting place so as to be sure that the graves registration people would find it.

The official statement concerning this made by Sergeant Fred R. Clark is as follows:

> "Agnes Johns was an infantryman carrying ammunition for my section. On September 30 my guns were in the reserve line just back of the wire east of Baulny. We were under shell fire all the time and about 1 or 2 p.m. one shell struck the shell-hole in which Johns was sitting and killed him instantly. He had joined my section the first day of the drive and I do not know where he was from. It was after his death that I found out his name, and I understand that his home is in Kenosha, Wis."[36]

One other casualty was suffered that day, Private Herman Clark, suffering from gas and exhaustion, being sent to the rear by his platoon commander. Except for this the losses of the company this day were light, consisting of several wounded.

Lieut. John F. Williams, the battalion adjutant, (major general and chief of the National Guard Bureau before and during World War II), who had been absent at some school, had just returned and had come forward with Major Halliburton when the latter returned to the front.

That afternoon there was the sound of heavy machine gun fire to the west of us, bursting out all of a sudden. I was working on something at the time by the cellar which had become the battalion PC—probably redrawing my sketch of the machine gun locations—and thought at first that our guns on the slope northwest of the town had opened fire.

"It's across the river in the 28th Division sector," someone told me.

I continued my work.

In a short time Lieutenant Williams came in quite thrilled.

"Those fellows jumped off over there and are attacking that village to the north," he said.

36. Company A documents correct this error and refer to him as John Angus, Company E, 139th Infantry. Missing Report or Details Death & Burial, Headquarters, 35th Division, Statement of Fred. R. Clark, Company A, 128th Machine Gun Battalion, February 15, 1919, Record Group 120, Records of the American Expeditionary Forces, World War I Organization Records, Machine Gun Battalions, 128th Machine Gun Battalion, Box 263, NARA.

Thus it was that I heard of the recapture of Apremont.

As it was the 28th Division, or parts thereof, hopped off in great shape under cover of a lively machine gun barrage and gallantly thrust their way into Apremont again. At least that is what the watching Carthaginians on the east side of the Aire River thought. Officially, it is said, the 28th did not lose Apremont on the 29th and so had no need to retake it on the 30th, this fact, in the opinion of the Company A eyewitnesses, being evidence of the old saying that many things happen in war that never get into the official records.

That night was fairly quiet except for a sporadic bombardment of gas shells. Night of September 30, 1918, brought some diminution in the volume of German shell fire which had been rendering still more ruinous the ruined village of Baulny and sending up fountains of dirt and smoke and flame from exploding shells in the area about it—some lessening in the pounding of high-explosive shell but an increase in the number of gas shells which carried a quieter but more insidious menace.

There had been a few of these all the while.

My company had had some gas casualties during the day as had Company B.

Going to the front line once that day I had met a soldier of Company B, apparently unwounded, coming slowly to the rear.

"Where are you going?" I asked, supposing that Captain Corey had sent him on some errand and thinking that it might have something to do with me.

The man had grinned a bit weakly.

"Look here, captain," he said pointing to his gas mask canister which in those days was worn on the chest, "I've been gassed."

A shell fragment at some time had struck the canister, splitting it wide open. The mask was no protection for him after that.

He did not appear in bad shape when I saw him but he later died in hospital from exposure to the gas which was sending him to the rear.

In the evening gas bombardment, Lieut. Snyder was concerned about some men he had posted, with a salvaged Chauchat rifle, to cover the left flank of the line in the valley.

"There's phosgene down in that hollow on the way there," he said on his return from a visit. "I had to wear my mask all the way through it. I thought I would find all those fellows dead. But they aren't. They're all right."

There was food that evening, as there had been the evening before.

Mess Sergeant Roach brought up soup under cover of darkness and men were relieved a few at a time from the guns to go back and eat.

And some time during the night came word that we were to be relieved by the 1st Infantry Division.

The battalion of the 327th faded back from the lines.

The arrangement of Company A guns remained the same as before. Corporal James A. Amerman's section was on the front line near the German observation post by which Sergeant Edwin W. Wiggins had been killed the night before. The sections commanded by Sergeants Fred R. Clark and Albert C. Miles were on the support line east of Baulny; the sections of Sergeant Willard Brown, Corporal Harry Palmer and Sergeant Joseph E. Taylor, placed from east to west in the order named, held the support line along the north edge of Baulny, and an automatic rifle post of two men was a bit farther forward with Company A, 110th Engineers.

Finally there came shadowy figures moving forward everywhere. It was the 18th U.S. Infantry Regiment of the 1st Division coming forward to take over. They moved forward to the front line and their scouts pushed beyond, rifle and pistol shots telling that the scouts had come into contact with the German outposts or patrols.

The 35th Division rifle units were now pulling back.

Then came the machine gun units belonging or attached to the 18th Infantry and my own company could go.

In order to lessen danger of losses from enemy artillery fire I had each section, under supervision of the platoon commanders, pull back independently from their positions and move direct to the assembly area, designated by division, in the region of Charpentry.

Corporal Amerman's section, still on the front line, would go last of the guns, then company headquarters would follow.

It was time, too, for our men were almost entirely exhausted and while they might have held on indefinitely they certainly were in no shape to renew the offensive. The First Division occupied our old positions until three days later when they moved forward in the great attack of October 4th.

It was near daylight when Amerman's section was relieved.

The 1st Division had had extensive combat experience and consequent heavy losses with the result that there were many new men with it as replacements.

As I stood on the ridge watching Amerman's relief I chanced to be beside the position where one of Capt. Corey's guns had been destroyed by a direct hit.

I heard one 1st Division soldier say in an awed voice: "The captain says that there is a dead man in that hole."

His tone stirred me to something of a grim grin.

"Wait until daylight," I felt like saying though naturally I didn't, "and you will see plenty of dead men about."

We were in truth leaving a good many of our 35th Division dead there. I have no doubt that October 1st was not many hours older before there were 1st Division dead there too.

All about me were only 1st Division men now.

To the best of my knowledge Amerman's section was the last 35th Division unit to leave the front line north of Baulny and, since I followed it, I probably was one of the last of the members of the 35th Division to leave—I and the runner, I forgot whom, who was accompanying me.[37]

I went back to Baulny, picked up the company headquarters section, then moved back to the company rendezvous point.

It was grey daylight when we turned our backs on Baulny. It was day, but with low visibility, when with my company I moved south from Charpentry, the unit in column of twos on the road, with considerable interval between platoons.

For perhaps half a mile south of Charpentry this road was shielded somewhat from enemy observation and fire from the west

37. Thirty-fifth Division commander Maj. Gen. Peter Traub cited Schrantz in General Orders on October 17, 1918, for gallantry in action, for "having received information that the enemy was threatening the left flank of the position, he, without orders, promptly organized for the defense, using machine guns of his own command, certain guns from other companies and turned back into the line a large number of lost infantry. By his hard work and untiring devotion to duty, extending over a period of many hours, aided materially in creating a defensive position." *Carthage* (MO) *Evening Press*, November 13, 1918. Schrantz finally received the Silver Star medal for this citation in 1933. *Joplin* (MO) *News Herald*, January 14, 1933; HST.

or northwest by the hill on the southwest of Buanthe Creek but beyond that the route was fully exposed to either. And by the time we reached that point the morning haze was beginning to lift.

At about the place where we had been pinned down on September 27, I moved the company into the fields well to the east of the road and extended the intervals between men and between sections. We proceeded southward in this manner, the minimum artillery target.

It was just as well.

Already there was an intermittent twinkle of shell bursts visible across the Aire in the 28th Division sector and soon shells were falling also in our own neighborhood along Route Nationale No. 46 which we were now paralleling.

A few of the projectiles exploded about us but we offered little target and these may have been overs intended for the road.

One of our reassembled infantry units had been formed in column of squads—in close order with four men abreast—on the road and in that formation were marching straight down the highway.

I saw one shell strike in the thick of this column.

Men scattered in every direction.

A mounted officer rounded them up as he might have rounded up cattle and, in column of squads again, they marched down the road.

Without casualties my own unit reached its bivouac area near a road junction and at the cemetery by the little narrow-guage station of Batantout a short distance east of Varennes on the Varennes-Cheppy road.

Here was where our train have [*sic*] bivouacked during the period the combat portion of the battalion had been operating farther north.

Breakfast was waiting and we ate a complete meal, free from the strain of battle, for the first time for many a day.

But the battle was still in progress.

A heavy enemy bombardment was still falling on the 28th Division area and ambulances loaded with litter patients came eastward out of Varennes, headed in the direction of Cheppy. Soon there was a solid column of them—every place full. From one I noticed blood dripping as it passed.

Though within shell range yet of the front, I recall no shells falling near us that day.

Here the battalion rested that day and that night, released its ammunition carriers to return to their units, took stock of its condition, and looked back on its experiences. After the breakfast and reunion—the hand-shaking of survivors glad to see each other alive and unwounded—I tried to sleep.

Not much luck. My nerves were still on edge. A captured narrow gauge engine snorted up and down the tracks at the station occasionally. Dozing I thought each time the noise was the screech of shells.

Once an enemy plane came over that day. We expected shells to follow on the congested road junction. They didn't. We were left in peace. Presumably there were too many targets up front to waste ammunition on crowded roads this far back.

There was a deep German dug-out just to the east of which our transport officers knew.

Always we had been cautioned to beware of booby traps. The dug-out, consequently, was suspect.

I saw leaning in one corner a thing which stirred my curiosity.

It was an ordinary German hand grenade—stick-grenade—"potato masher"—but the handle had been sawed off about half-way up and into it a rifle cartridge had been inserted.

I wondered about it but I kept hands off and away from it. I trust others did the same. But I still wonder what the thing was for—whether it was a booby trap or something else.

I slept in that dug-out that night, on the chicken-wire screen of a bunk and in my long-unused bedding roll. And I slept peacefully and well.

My own company losses during our participation in the battle had been five enlisted men and one attached ammunition carrier killed. To this list perhaps should be added the name of Private James A. Morgan of Blew, Okla., who went to the hospital a day or so later as the result of gas and exhaustion and who soon died therein. These losses were severe but might have been heavier.[38]

38. James Atwell Morgan, born on May 18, 1891, died in France on October 28, 1918, and was buried in Durant, Oklahoma. Schrantz wrote a letter to Morgan's father on March 18, 1919, expressing his "heartfelt sympathy" after he learned of his son's death. Schrantz noted that Morgan left for a base hospital on October 6, and probably died of exhaustion and exposure. Schrantz noted that after Morgan's squad leader was wounded,

Two officers and 30 enlisted men of the company were carried on the list that night as wounded and two men were missing. Both of these, it was learned later, had been wounded and evacuated, bringing the wounded list to an aggregate of 34. In addition to the ammunition carrier with me who had been killed, some 12 or 13 of these men had been wounded. The two men of our battalion medical detachment who had been attached to my company for first aid purposes had both been wounded on September 28.

My company losses were about 33 1/3 per cent of the strength of the fighting portion of the unit, in which all of the losses had occurred.

The battalion losses, not counting ammunition carriers, were eight killed in action and one died as a result of wounds, 2 officers and 51 enlisted men wounded.

The division loss was 955 killed in action, 249 died of wounds, 5,870 wounded not mortally.

The battle was over for Company A. However unsatisfactory some of its experiences had been, its officers felt that the unit had functioned satisfactorily. Any criticism of it would need to be directed at the officers. Every order had been carried out properly and courageously, and there had been no straggling.

[The newspaper history of the company noted:]

Concerning the conduct of individuals, Capt. Schrantz in his official report rendered a few days later said:

> "The conduct of the members of the company throughout the five days' battle was without exception so gallant and so meritorious that it is almost impossible to make distinction enough to mention individuals. First Lieut. Charles E. Dunn, the reconnaissance officer and second in command,

---

the young soldier took command of his squad and conducted it with "ability and determination." On those rare occasions during the Meuse-Argonne when the soldiers were allowed an hour or two of sleep, Morgan insisted on staying awake so that his men could rest. Morgan's platoon sergeant informed Captain Schrantz that during the period of enemy counterattacks that he never saw Morgan away from his gun. Whatever the War Department reported as the cause of his death, the real cause was the "work he did in battle" and his death was just as glorious as if he had been killed "in the heat of action." Had he lived, Schrantz explained, he would have been promoted to non-commissioned officer, and there was "not a better or braver soldier in the American Army." He died "in the best of all causes for which men have ever died," and "did his part to make the cause successful." *Durant* (OK) *Weekly News*, April 11, 1919. According to 35th Division machine gun officer Donald D. Hay, Captain Schrantz reported the strength of Company A on October 1 as five officers and 124 enlisted men, with 11 machine guns. Hay, "Machine Guns, 35th Division, Meuse-Argonne Operation, Sept. 26–Oct. 1, 1918," 205.

may properly be mentioned for his fearlessness and devotion to duty; First Lieut. Frank L. Snyder for his absolute indifference to danger and his diligence in seeking opportunity to bring fire to bear on the enemy, particularly on September 27th at Charpentry; First Sergeant James A. Hines showed a fearlessness and ability to command which will be made the subject of a later communication; Sergeants Charles S. Edwards and Edwin W. Wiggins showed unusual bravery and ability until killed in action; Sergeant Carl J. Cain assumed command of his platoon after the wounding of his platoon leader Sept. 27 and ably directed it throughout the battle; Sergeant Norval R. Hopwood showed great bravery all through the action, especially during the night of September 29-30 on the ridge north of Baulny after his platoon leader, Sergeant Wiggins, was killed during a heavy barrage; Corporal Thomas M. Daugherty, wounded by a shell splinter September 28, refused to leave his squad and continued in the action until the next day when he went to a dressing station only on direct order; Private James A. Morgan commanded a squad with great bravery and ability; Privates Herman Clark and Ralph E. Harmon showed unusual gallantry and tenacity, carrying on when almost fainting from exhaustion; Privates Frank H. Jackson, Arthur E. Voorhis and Joe L. Landers, company runners, went repeatedly with messages through the heaviest barrages, Landers especially always volunteering for the most arduous tasks.[39]

"The work performed by the company transport and its drivers is deserving of comment. As fighting limbers the few worn-out Fords in our possession were totally inadequate, yet despite this fact valuable work was performed by them.

39. Ralph E. Harmon of Salina, Kansas. His wound kept him in the hospital for four months, and his parents did not recognize him when he stepped off the train in Salina in May 1919. *The Salina* (KS) *Daily Union*, May 10, 1919. Arthur Ester Voorhis was born in Lebanon, Indiana (some sources state Carthage or Boone County, Missouri), on May 22, 1897, and died on September 6, 1961. He was buried in Gladstone, Missouri. He joined Company A in July 1917, was promoted to private first class in October 1917, and served overseas with Company A from April 25, 1918 until August 3, 1919. *The Kansas City* (MO) *Times*, September 7, 1961; Missouri Secretary of State, State Archives, Soldiers' Records, War of 1812-World War I, www.sos.mo.gov/archives/soldiers; HST. Joe L. (Joseph Ludwig) Landers was born in Carthage, Missouri, on November 8, 1893, and died on July 10, 1949 in Kenosha, Wisconsin. He served overseas from April 1918 to April 1919. *Kenosha* (WI) *Evening News*, July 11, 1949.

> Quantities of machine gun, Stokes mortar and 37-mm ammunition were brought up for any organization needing it; cooked food was brought up as far as possible under heavy shell fire and on each trip loads of wounded were taken to the rear. Wagoners Alvin Bays and Charles E. McKinney are especially mentioned by the transport officer for their fearlessness in this work and for their eagerness to be assigned the most dangerous tasks. Mess Sergeant Robert E. Roach also deserves special mention for his energy and bravery in bringing food under circumstances the most perilous and unfavorable."[40]

The "separate communication" mentioned in reference to First Sergeant Hines recommended him for a battlefield promotion to the grade of second lieutenant. This was not granted but Hines was later commissioned from an A.E.F. officers training camp.

At daylight, October 2, 1918, while cannon were roaring not far to the north, and shells exploding across the Aire River to the west, the marching portion of the 128th Machine Gun Battalion, muddy, gaunt and disheveled in appearance, moved eastward from the cemetery bivouac east of Varennes where the battalion motor train had spent the time during the latter part of the unit's participation in the Meuse-Argonne offensive.

Except for the enemy dug-out not far distant in which I had spent the night, I might not have rested so blissfully.

I led off with A Company behind me, marching in column of twos with considerable intervals between platoons to lessen the danger from possible enemy shell fire. Captain Corey with Company B followed. The battalion train, under Major Halliburton, was to follow separately and by a different route. The vehicles would follow the hard-surfaced but congested roads. The marching column might avoid much of this congestion by traveling part of the distance on the less used trails which I knew.

The route led over the hill toward Cheppy, past newly arrived artillery units of the 1st Division who were digging in the trails of their guns to give them greater range.

40. Charles Edward McKinney was born in Jerseyville, Illinois, about 1898. He served overseas with the Headquarters Train, 35th Division and Company A from April 25, 1918 to April 24, 1919. Missouri Secretary of State, State Archives, Soldiers' Records, War of 1812–World War I, www.sos.mo.gov/archives/soldiers.

The Second Battalion, 129th Field Artillery, 35th Division, was in position along this road, and Battery F, of that battalion, had had two men killed and several wounded, a caisson blown up and 17 animals slain during the hours of darkness which had just ended. The 35th Division gunners were now lounging by their guns, ready for their second day of support for the regular infantry up on the Baulny Hill line. The 35th Division was staying in to support the impending attack by the 1st Division.

I recalled that for some reason the sight of all those dead horses had given me more of a feeling of horror than had all the dead men I had seen. Perhaps my mind had been steeled in advance to dead men and hence had taken them for granted. I just hadn't thought much about horses. Or, possibly with the preoccupation of battle behind, one noticed things like that more now.

Down the hill again into flattened Cheppy the machine gun battalion moved, crossing Buanthe Creek at the bridge where it had crossed five days before and passing south along the road where in the darkness which preceded the dawn of September 27 they had seen so many of the 138th Infantry dead lying. The dead were gone now, and the town was full of men of the rear elements of the 1st Division, going about somewhere apprehensively for fear of a bombardment. But for the time, at least, Cheppy was peaceful enough.

Marching thus near the front in broad day seemed a bit odd, yet the roads were full. Probably all the routes back of the American front were busy and the enemy had other use for his artillery ammunition than to spend it in making these units uncomfortable by that type of fire which does not have observations to render it effective. It was because of the crowded roads elsewhere that the divisional machine gun battalion was moving south by the same route it had come north, and south of Cheppy it moved out on the mud trail which led by Hill 221.

This route, passible enough for foot troops, we had practically to ourselves.

Short rations at the cemetery bivouac had failed to fill the long-empty stomachs of the machine gunners and it so happened that just northeast of Hill 221 was a considerable, neatly-stacked supply of small yellow cans containing corned beef. There was no guard and no witness save a sympathetic-looking lieutenant colonel whose clean clothes indicated he was either from the 1st Division or from some staff. These unguarded yellow cans under the circumstances were as attractive to this hungry horde as a stack of gold would be to a group of desperately poor.

Should I post a guard and so protect the pile from my voracious company—and thus leave all this food for Corey's equally-hungry horde?

Instead of posting a guard I swerved over as we came to the stack, picked up a can and moved on without stopping.

Naturally with this example before them, everyone else did the same. There was a little flurry as the columns passed but no delay and the stack steadily diminished.

The watching colonel still appeared sympathetic and I presume he actually was because I never received any official letters demanding an explanation.

Before the battalion had passed the stack of food had disappeared, and grinning men congratulated each other on their good fortune.

Some time later in the forenoon the column, staring at familiar landmarks, passed through the old German line at Boureuilles, then around the hill at Buzemont from in front of which the initial machine gun barrage had been fired.

Here the column was halted, was told to fall out at the left of the road because of the stream of water at the right, and the men were advised to fill their canteens if they wished, for this water, gushing from a spring, had been used by the French soldiers in the sector before the advance started and the French battalion commander had passed the word on that it was good.

Now a limousine was noticed in front of the dug-out at Buzemont which had been both a headquarters and a dressing station a week earlier, and from the direction of this strode a polished figure who introduced himself with some asperity as Lieut. Col. Peck of General Headquarters.[41]

41. Robert Gray Peck, born in New Jersey on April 10, 1879, enlisted as a private in the 4th Battery, New York Light Artillery in 1898, then enlisted in the Regular Army as an infantry private. He rose through the ranks and was promoted to captain in 1916. Promoted to major (temporary) in 1917 and lieutenant colonel (temporary) the following year, Peck was serving as inspector of the First Army Corps in September 1918. Based on his observations, such as his encounter with Schrantz's men, he submitted a lengthy, critical report of the 35th Division's performance in the Meuse-Argonne. Peck retired as a permanent lieutenant colonel in 1922 and became an industrialist. He retired as president of the Airdor Company in 1945 and died

Thus Company A met the man whose later report on the appearance of the 35th Division as it withdrew from the front included an attack on National Guard divisions in general and caused reverberations which did not cease rumbling until some years had passed.

Col. Peck had hoped to meet one of the two infantry brigades and was somewhat put out when he found that they were traveling on roads farther east and west respectively and that here was only the marching portion of the divisional machine gun battalion. He seemed to be in a highly critical mood.

"Why have you let your men fall out on the left of the road?" he inquired.

The reply was to point out the quite obvious fact that on the left there was the hill on which they could sit, whereas on the right they would need to stand in the water.

"Why are you letting your men drink water not marked as having been tested?" he queried further.

The answer to this was that this water had been said by the French to be good, and that furthermore if the men of this company had confined themselves to water marked as having been tested and found pure that they would have been without for many days, since none of that character had been seen since two days before the battle started.

He wanted to know to which brigade we belonged. I told him we were the division machine gun battalion.

Next he inquired about losses. These as told him included two men missing.

"They will show up," he remarked in a rather unpleasant tone, and they did; both showed up wounded in hospital, which probably was not what the colonel meant.

A quite unpleasant gentleman this.

Capt. James J. Corey of Company B had come up and stood listening. Huge and genial he had evidently tired of this line of conversation.

"For Christ's sake, colonel," he burst in with an expansive grin on the haughty visitor, "give me a cigarette."

---

in Orlando, Florida, on November 12, 1956. He was buried in Arlington National Cemetery. U.S. Adjutant General's Office, *Official Army Register January 1, 1923* (Washington, D.C.: Government Printing Office, 1923), 1129; *Chicago Daily Tribune*, November 13, 1956.

This broke the ice. The colonel produced the cigarettes, asked some normal questions about routes, and as the machine gunners moved on was preparing to sally out in his shining car to hunt the infantry brigades.

At the end of the 10-minute halt we moved on and he maneuvered somehow to intercept the brigades.

Afterwards this officer issued a most caustic report on the 35th Division. It was disheveled in appearance, clothing wasn't neat, many of the men were unshaven—something like that. Moreover he had seen officers talking to enlisted men on apparent terms of comradeship. Poor discipline this, he thought.

"It bears all the marks of a national guard division—which it is," he added.

Naturally when extracts of Peck's caustic report came out, the officers of the 128th were anxious to know just what he had criticized in the battalion. However an officer of the Inspector General's Office of the War Department who later investigated the whole Peck incident assured officers of the battalion that the report contained no mention whatever of the 128th, his specific criticisms being directed principally at the rifle regiments.[42]

The Peck episode created extreme bitterness in the division, but the 128th lost no sleep about it. The organization was disheveled, weary, worn and dirty but this was all incidental to battle, and it felt confident that there was nothing about it with which any officer familiar with combat conditions could find fault.

This report created a tremendous hub-bub in time. It tore open old wounds which the War Department diligently had been trying the [to] heal. It echoed in the halls of Congress. After the war it held up for a time the promotion of all officers of the Regular Army on the list below him because Congress would not confirm him for promotion. It forced—if my recollection is right—his retirement from the army. I have no doubt it had a most adverse effect on post-war appropriations for the Regular Army. It brought a War Department Inspector General's investigation, which involved testimony by every officer to whom he had talked at the time.

42. A scathing assessment of Peck's behavior during the Meuse-Argonne may be found in "Nomination of Maj. Robert G. Peck to be a Lieutenant Colonel, Minority Report," United States Senate, 67th Congress, 1st Session, Report --, Part II.

The I.G. representative told me that what caused the colonel to writhe most—this was before his retirement had been forced—was Captain Corey's testimony that he had come out of the Buzemont dug-out as we came along.

He thus perhaps found my own testimony of some solace. It was my impression that he had been standing in front of the dug-out, but I had paid no particular attention and would hardly have noted had he come from it. He might have stepped into it out of curiosity. There was no shell fire in the area at the time and there was no occasion for him to be concerned about his safety.

On Buzemont that day we of course had no idea of the storm this officer's visit and report would cause. It was just a passing incident remembered only because he apparently had no knowledge of what battle was like.

But at that I was glad that he had not been the lieutenant colonel who had seen us raid that ration dump near Hill 221.

Back into the Forêt de Hesse, following the gravel road where in moving up the men had wormed through the trenches; eastward past the point where the company had endured the trying bombardment in the bivouac the night of September 24; and back southeast on the Route des Fascines to Neuvilly, the machine gunners hiked. Enemy long range guns were dropping shells on this village as the battalion approached, but this ceased before the edge of the town was reached. Those were the last enemy shell-bursts we heard in the battle proper though our service in the trench sector we soon were to occupy was technically counted a second participation in the Meuse-Argonne.

Southeast out of Neuvilly to Aubreville, two miles to the southeast, the battalion moved, meeting here a long column of fresh troops moving up towards the front.

Our men carried only their haversacks on their backs as they had done through the battle. These troops had full packs with their overcoats neatly fastened on top—tremendous loads for men who might soon need all their strength in battle.

The usual line of raillery punctuated the passing of the two, the battle-stained men of the 35th inquiring why the newcomers were taking work away from trucks and the heavily-loaded ones panting back queries as to why the Missourians were marching south when the big noise was to the north.

Beyond Aubreville, on the west side of the Aire, I had a mildly embarrassing experience.

I had regulated the march punctiliously by my watch according to the book and to custom—a 15-minute halt the first hour, a 10-minute halt each subsequent hour.

It was a regular halt period just beyond Aubreville and I lay down, as usual, to rest.

I woke to the voice of First Lieut. Clyde A. Narramore, 110th Trench Mortar Battery, an old friend. This Carthage officer at the moment was hauling ammunition for the 1st Division artillery.

He looked down at me grinning and enquired if I had had a good nap.

My men were grinning too, and everyone else I could see who was awake.

I had slept long past the allotted 10-minutes to the amusement and relief of everybody except my own chagrined self. Narramore, passing on the way to the front with a load of ammunition for someone, rather sympathized with my position and wanted to say hello to me anyhow and so woke me up.

Next the camping place at Auzeville a mile and a half southeast of Clermont, where, after some delay, trucks with the battalion's packs showed up. For the first time in almost two weeks the Company A men this night slept in their shelter tents and under blankets, and with a chance to remove their clothing. The day's march had covered a long 16 miles.

Out of active participation in the Meuse-Argonne offensive, but still in the reserve of the First Army which was carrying on that operation, October 3, 1918, was a day of hard marching for the 128th Machine Gun Battalion, 35th Division, an exertion the more trying because of the still wearied state of the organization from its many days of battle.

To the north, the cannon still thundered steadily, the main roads were busy with supplies and ammunition going forward and empty trucks and loaded ambulances coming back; and overhead, as the battalion left the village of Auzeville in the Aire valley near Clermont-en-Argonne where it spent the night, there was a sputter of machine gun fire and little glinting streaks of tracer machine gun bullets as an American pursuit plane chased a stranger flaunting black Maltese crosses on his wings.

The latter part of the journey this day was in almost a circle, whether because of difficulty of routing or because it was intended to deceive the hostile observation planes which so boldly ran the gauntlet of the front to peer at the American rear areas. South the road ran much as on the trip north in mid-September, back of Froidos, through Waly and to Foucaucourt—familiar-faced masonry villages whose inhabitants stared curiously but apathetically at the mud-stained marchers. At Foucaucourt there was a change of directions and the column followed the poplar-bordered highway a couple of miles west down a valley to the little town of Brizeaux, the soldiers noting idly as they went along the partly-healed scars of the fighting of 1914 which had engulfed this region at the peak of the German invasion. At Brizeaux came the unexpected turn back to the north, up a high road toward the distant guns and past a busy American hospital by the side of which many graves were being dug, others covered up and where numerous wooden crosses were already marking fresh mounds. Here was one of the back eddies of battle—a place from where the "died-of-wounds" joined the "killed-in-action" in whatever Valhalla is reserved for heroes of modern wars.

Next the organization moved between high wooded hills, then panted up a steep road to the ridge village of Beaulieu—a hill which tested the pulling power of the battalion motor transport when it came to make the climb. There was a short halt in the hill-top village, which looked as if the site may have been chosen for defensive purposes in medieval days, while an infantry column toiled by, many of the men carrying German trench caps and other souvenirs of the battle, then down again and to the northeast through the southern part of the Argonne Forest to a level camping place in the Bois de Lavoye, only about five miles from the beginning point of the long circular hike.

Our shelter tents were put up under the trees and for a time I watched still passing columns, including many depleted machine gun units, a mule in some cases drawing two carts, and in other cases carts being pulled by men—a reminder that animals as well as men had suffered in the fighting.

The next morning—October 4—before day and before the weary machine gunners had thought of rolling from their warm blankets under their sodden shelter tents, a loud, angry, insistent thudding from the front, punctuated by frequent louder roars which sounded as if it might be from railway artillery seen near Auzeville, told of a renewed offensive.

In my uncertain knowledge of the general situation I could not be sure who was attacking what. It could only be a renewal of the Allied attack or a mammoth German counterattack—the former I believed.

It was the beginning of the second phase of the Meuse-Argonne operation. This day Montrebeau Woods and the vicinity of Exermont were to be aflame again with battle as the 1st Division entered its hardest fight of the war—but with this the men of the 35th back here in the woods had no great concern except to hope all went well.

Our interest was rather academic at the moment and it was with some relief that I learned we would remain in camp that day instead of continuing our march to the rear. We could use the rest.

The actual reason for our day's rest here, I assume, was that since we were now a part of the First Army reserve it was deemed prudent to hold us thus far forward until it was seen how the renewed battle was going the first day. In any event we rested and scribbled letters and cards letting those back home know that we were still alive. It was to be November 1, however, before the first of these reached Carthage.

Chapter 15

Sommedieue and War's End

The battered Carthage men continued to hike slowly away from the field of battle as fresh A.E.F. divisions prepared to continue the fight. Soon Schrantz led his soldiers into the village of Evres, where they had the opportunity to bathe and rest. The weeks of "of exposure, tinned foods, gas-poisoned water and over-exertion" led to many cases of dysentery. Some who were sent to division hospitals, such as twenty-six-year-old Private James A. Morgan of Company A, died of pneumonia, exposure to gas, exhaustion or other ailments.

Schrantz and his men began to train again, incorporating the lessons they had learned during the recent battle, particularly emphasizing how machine guns could support attacking riflemen.

Battalion commander Major Halliburton sought to restore the order that was in force before the Argonne battle. On October 6, he ordered that "short and snappy" drills would be conducted in order to improve the discipline of the command, and "dawdling over drill" would not be tolerated. The men were ordered to keep themselves clean and tidy, keep their coats buttoned, and pay special attention to saluting and military courtesy.[1] Training consisted of physical drills, boxing, close order drill, first aid, care of equipment, military

1. Memo, Headquarters, 128th Machine Gun Battalion, October 6, 1918, Record Group 120, Records of the American Expeditionary Forces, World War I Organization Records, Machine Gun Battalions, 128th Machine Gun Battalion, Box 266, NARA.

courtesy, platoon and company maneuvers, and even instruction in the German Maxim machine gun.[2] In a magnanimous move, Major Halliburton asked his company commanders to ascertain if any of their men were then under sentence or had charges pending against them. He offered the possibility of clemency for those men who may be entitled "through their action at the front" in the recent fighting.[3]

Newspapers speculated about a possible armistice, but the French townspeople and the doughboys listening to the distant roar of battle remained more than a bit skeptical. "'Finis la guerre,' had been the principal allied joke in Evres," Schrantz recalled. In fact, the war was far from over for the Carthage men. The 35th Division was ordered to relieve the 15th French Colonial Division in the trenches east and southeast of Verdun. Division headquarters was to be located in Sommedieue. The 128th Machine Gun Battalion was initially posted to the division reserve.

The company occupied trenches in the Haudiomont sector on the night of October 24, 1918. Reminders of the war were close at hand. "The country around Verdun is all torn up," reported Kansan Roy H. Smith, and "there isn't a foot of ground that hasn't been moved." Shell holes "big enough to put a house in" could be seen, and trees all shot off "5 or 6 feet from the ground."[4] "The Dutch are not very good neighbors, but they won't allow one to get lonesome," related Logan J. Largen of the 129th Machine Gun Battalion to his sister-in-law on October 25, 1918. When his unit was not in range of machine guns or snipers, Largen wrote, the Germans sniped at them with artillery, "and usually send you one or two for mess, and the boys have named them 'iron rations.'"[5]

Nevertheless, Corporal C.V. Johnson of the 130th Field Artillery wrote to a friend that their sector was "rather quite [*sic*], what we call a 'gentleman['s] war' almost," only firing when "it is really worth the while."[6] Sam H. Pickel of Company A, 128th Machine Gun Battalion believed the sector "seemed like a vacation" compared to the Meuse-Argonne. Pickel and a few men even slipped out of their trenches one night into No Man's Land in order to strip souvenirs from a crashed German plane. When the

2. Memo, Headquarters, 128th Machine Gun Battalion, October 8, 1918, Record Group 120, Records of the American Expeditionary Forces, World War I Organization Records, Machine Gun Battalions, 128th Machine Gun Battalion, Box 266, NARA.

3. Memo, Headquarters, 128th Machine Gun Battalion, October 5, 1918, Record Group 120, Records of the American Expeditionary Forces, World War I Organization Records, Machine Gun Battalions, 128th Machine Gun Battalion, Box 266, NARA.

4. *The Weekly Guard* (Council Grove, KS), December 27, 1918.

5. *The Neosho* (MO) *Times*, December 5, 1918.

6. *The Osage City Free Press* (Osage City, KS), December 5, 1918.

Germans heard them and opened fire with a machine gun, Pickel and his comrades ducked into some shell holes. After about a half hour, when the firing stopped, they slipped back to their own lines. "We acted like fools to go out there," he concluded.[7]

The Carthage men remained here until the early morning of November 6, when the company was relieved. All anticipated a return to "the big show." Instead, as the guns fell silent when the Armistice was declared on November 11, 1918, Company A was not in combat, but in the village of La Vallee, serving as part of the reserve of the American Second Army.

At 11 a.m. that day, when the cease fire went into effect, the band of the 130th Field Artillery, 35th Division assembled in front of regimental headquarters, the band leader raised his baton, and they struck up "The Old Gray Mare," the regimental air. "There were no other formalities," recalled the regimental chaplain. "There was even no cheering. The men stood about in groups, silent and thoughtful for the most part."[8]

Morning of October 5 found the machine gunners hiking south again, part of the route the same as that traversed two days before, then on up the Aire valley to Fleury-sur-Aire, and over the hills southwest to Evres, which a letter home described as "a dirty, disreputable-appearing French village of great age." "There was once a more modern part," the letter said, "but the enemy burned it in the first year of the war."[9] There had apparently been considerable fighting near the place and quite a few wounded were brought into the town. The old women of the village never tired of telling us of the stirring events of those days and how the Germans had behaved while they were in possession.

Captain Corey and I were billeted at a home which had been used for a German hospital and the old woman of the house told us with great glee of the patients that had been stretched on the stone floor of the room in which we slept. The wounded men, laid side by side, filled the entire room, she told us. A German captain had lain in the corner and had died there. The whole floor had been

7. *The Austin* (TX) *American*, December 30, 1918.
8. *The Chanute* (KS) *Daily Tribune*, May 15, 1919.
9. Schrantz reported that his company drilled six hours a day, while the rest of the time he was "making out long-winded reports on our recent operations," and was sure he had used a million sheets of paper. He predicted that the company would soon "be ready to quarrel with the boche [*sic*] again." *Carthage* (MO) *Evening Press*, November 2, 1918.

wet with blood and since it was German blood and the Germans had behaved very badly in the village she was glad.

A few days after our arrival the old lady and her husband called over an elderly woman from across the street who had been outraged by Germans billeted in her house, and introduced her to us.

She had obtained revenge, the woman narrated, by poisoning their food, thus killing nine or 14 of them, I do not remember which. In retaliation her house had been burned but she had escaped by some means not clear to me—my understanding of French being incapable of grasping it. Horrible as her experience must have been at the time, she now was something of a village celebrity and appeared to enjoy it.

"Mauvais les boches," chorused the two women together.[10]

Captain Corey and I were billeted together in a house on the main street in what once had been a kitchen, now a comfortable enough and rather interesting room.

The floor was of stone, a bit chilly on bare feet when one swung them out of bed in the morning, and there was a huge fireplace in the room. On the street side was a stone sink from which a spout protruded through the wall. Since the house was built flush on the street, French fashion, any chance passerby hugging the wall might have found himself dampened in [if] he happened along when water was being emptied in it.

The old French woman who was mistress of this home clattered through our room each morning before we were up, probably going to the kitchen currently used.

"Bon jour, madame," boomed Corey daily, in his great voice, "Finis la guerre."

There was indeed newspaper talk of preliminary negotiations of some kind but this regular morning comment of the big captain was his daily joke with our hostess to get her reaction.

"Finis la guerre," had been the principal Allied joke in Evres. President Wilson had been exchanging notes with the Germans on the subject of peace and the newspapers were speculating on the possible end of the war—but each day the bombardment to the north was as violent as that of the day before, and the

10. Schrantz also reported that "with the horror of her experiences four years behind her," she "appeared not to find her position as such distasteful."

townspeople who had heard the distant thunder of battle for four years were quite as skeptical about the war ending as were the American soldiers who had recently experienced some of the German tenacity in defense. Lack of a common vocabulary limited conversation between the townsfolk and soldiery, and the easy mocking phrase had been bandied about jocularly each morning by way of friendly greeting.

She always broke into a grinning cackle of French, pointing to the north where the guns were thundering violently. Finis la guerre indeed. For four years she had heard that sound. She would believe the war was over when it stopped.

The old lady became a firm friend of ours, dropping through frequently during the day when we were there just to hear Captain Corey's French I think.

He had early learned that the way to get a laugh out of the French was to pronounce French words the way they looked in the book to him—pronouncing them just as they might be pronounced in English. This was his way of cultivating favor with the populace. They would listen to his shouting voice with bewilderment while he patiently roared repetitions of each of his mispronunciations. When they finally understood, and when also, I think, they understood that his slaughtering of their language was deliberate, they would shake with merriment.

There was an opportunity to rest in Evres, bathe and otherwise clean up, but now the results of over-exertion, exposure, and perhaps bad or gas-poisoned water began to make themselves evident. There was an epidemic of sickness. The sick report books were crowded; dysentery, that scourge of armies, pervaded the division; daily the sick went to hospitals, some to die of pneumonia and kindred aliments. Company A lost one man from this aftermath of combat, Private James A. Morgan of Blue, Okla., whose death has previously been mentioned as one directly attributable to the battle.

But in some respects it was a cozy place despite the reaction to battle. I particularly remember with pleasure the officers mess, and the evening spent there before the blazing fireplace—a heavenly sort of spot, filled with geniality and comradeship.

It was a place of training too.

Close order drill was a daily part of it to get the unit back into some semblance of smartness again.

Moreover I had acquired some distinct ideas of how machine guns should be used in battle. All of our pre-battle instruction and the text books on which it had been based, it seemed obvious to me, had overstressed the defensive and in the attack had listed as exceptional the direct support of machine guns during the progress of the attack, and which the infantry needed. It had listed this as exceptional for the very handicaps we had found—the weight of gun, tripod and ammunition and the consequent difficulty of keeping up and the vulnerable target presented by machine guns in close support of infantry. The ordinary use of machine guns in attack, according to these texts we had followed, had been initial barrages such as the one we had fired on September 26, followed by subsequent ones where practicable, and defense against counterattacks. In our experience there had been no opportunity after the initial assault for use of machine gun barrages supporting an attack because information of the attack did not percolate down to the front lines, and perhaps not to the machine gunners at all, until just about the time for the jump off.

It seemed to me that we must study and practice the use of machine guns in close support of rifle units all during the progress of the attack, despite the difficulties involved. And we must think more aggressively and less defensively than we had been.

I preached this doctrine to all and sundry and, with the approval of Major Halliburton and of the division machine gun officer when he came around, concentrated in training on small problems involving the close support of infantry by machine gun sections and platoons.

Inspectors circulated about looking at the men, estimating their fitness to return immediately to battle. During the epidemic of sickness their report could hardly have been favorable, but rest brought recovery and recovery brought a renewal of morale. Youth rebounds quickly, and most of the soldiers were young. Within a week the machine gunners, grimmer than of old as befits men who have looked on their dead, but jaunty nevertheless, were ready to return to the front.

There was one incident at Evres which might have been exciting except that our capacity for getting excited had been fairly well burned out of us for the moment by the super-excitement of battle through which we had gone.

There was a long one-story military barn at the east edge of the village where horses belonging to some French organization were kept securely tied to mangers in care of a French army detachment. The men also slept in the barn or shed and it was full of hay and other feed.

One night this stable caught fire. Our men always said—though I do not know on what grounds—that the French had been drinking and when the place caught fire devoted their efforts to saving a keg of wine and their belongings instead of the horses.

My company was on guard in Evres that evening and when Sgt. William P. Havens and a detachment of the guard—the first Americans to reach the scene—arrived the building was wrapped in flames and the plunging horses were burning to death. Since there was no way to reach and save them Sergeant Havens and his men opened fire with their pistols, killing the suffering animals.

Hurrying up the main street of the village to the blaze I heard the pistol shots from the south of the structure, knew what was happening and looked north of the building quickly to see what might be endangered by bullets which missed their target and passed through the barn.

There were several French soldiers there and, as I looked, one clapped his hand to his leg. I immediately went over and the man told me he was wounded. This was bad. Shooting up our allies might call for some explanations.

A bullet had gone through the inside of the man's breeches leg about half way between the knee and thigh. There was no flow of blood visible and the most effective form of first aid seemed to be to get him to our battalion hospital as soon as possible and let the doctor take whatever steps were necessary.

With his right arm around my neck and his left arm around the neck of a French comrade, the man half-hobbled and was half carried to our dispensary where the medicos bared the flesh to expose the wound, I standing by to see how grave was the injury for which I would need to answer.

The result was a great relief. There was a red welt along the leg where the graze had stung him but the skin was not even broken, hence the absence of blood. His inability to walk had been due to his conviction—and perhaps to mine and that of his French associate—that there was a bullet in the leg. In fact he could walk without even a limp. The only real damage had been the bullet hole through his breeches leg.

After commending the sergeant for killing the horses and not killing any French soldiers—the last of which was an accident—I went to bed and slept most peacefully while no doubt my guard continued to express to each other their very low opinions of the French for saving their wine and clothing instead of the animals entrusted to their charge. I suspect that at the moment the men of the guard would not have felt too badly even if there had been French casualties. It is not pleasant to see horses burning to death.

The repose of the machine gunners at Evres lasted just a week. On the morning of October 11 Captain Corey for the last time boomed his "Finis la guerre, madame," as our hostess came through our room, and she for the last time chattered amused French in reply, pointing to the north from which came the usual thunder of artillery fire. That evening we received orders to move and the next morning before her hour to come through were on the road.

The 35th Division had been assigned to the 33rd French Corps and was scheduled to enter the trenches east and southeast of Verdun.

Those had been genial villagers in Evres but it was pleasant to be facing the sun that morning of October 12, 1918 and leaving the place behind us. Aside from its drabness of appearance it was associated in our minds with our post-battle weariness and depression. Now we were rested and as we strode out up the hill on the road to Beauzee-sur-Aire some four miles or so to the eastward our spirits rose and morale was high. The 128th Machine Gun Battalion was ready to fight again.

Men of the marching column of the machine gun unit breathed deeply with relief and chattered with rising spirits as they swung across the stone bridge over the tiny River La Marque just east of the town and breasted the long slope on the poplar-bordered highway leading toward Beauzee-sur-Aire, over the hill and four miles distant, while back in the battalion motor park at Evres the drivers and machines hummed and whistled in anticipation as they tinkered about their ancient machines waiting for the motorized portion of the battalion to start. Off to the north the thunder of battle was raging anew but attracted little attention aside from facetious remarks about "Finis la guerre." The noise of war had long since become commonplace and was as much a part of the normal day as the routine of the march, the sunshine or the more usual drizzle.

Eastward-bound, headed for the trenches the machine gunners strode up the hill and made their first hourly halt on the crest, noting a heavy column of strange troops detrucking on a road nearby. Conversation with men of these who strolled over showed that they were replacements coming up to fill the gaps in the well-riddled 35th Division.

Some of them strolled over to get acquainted. A lieutenant engaged me in conversation.

"You know, captain," he said after the usual preliminaries about organization, "They tell me that an officer is not permitted to carry his pistol in action."

"The hell he isn't," I snorted. "I carried mine and part of the time I carried [it] in my hand."

He looked at me skeptically.

"Have you people actually been in battle? No kidding? How did it feel?"

As we marched on again he stood staring at the jovial column behind me, obviously wondering if I had lied to him. And I wondered what nit-wit had told him an officer couldn't carry a pistol the only place he needed one and why he had been silly enough to believe it.

Down the hill now into the Aire valley and a short time later the column passed through 1914-scarred Beauzee and crossed the stream which flowed serenely northward, as if quite unconscious that before many miles its waters would be fouled with high explosive and gas and know the taste of human blood.

Eastward now through the day—Amblaincourt, Seraucourt, Rignaucourt. And at Rignaucourt—to my amazement for I was the first in our 128th Machine Gun Battalion column and our motor train had not yet passed us—I saw a copy of the *Carthage* (Mo.) *Evening Press*, the paper I worked on at home, blowing across the road in front of us. It set up an excited chatter in the largely-Carthage column immediately behind me. Some Carthaginian had been that way not long before.

Next appeared Issancourt with a mock airfield and a dummy canvas airplane staked out on the ground to deceive hostile fliers. Now through a wooded hill to the village of Benoite Vaux where roads centered like spokes and about which numerous military hutments clustered, showing it to be an important military center.

At a halt north of Benoite Vaux came a visitor in the person of Lieut. Cecil Stemmons, one-time corporal who had gone from Company A to the first training camp in May 1917, and after various experiences at home and in Europe had now joined the 137th Infantry, 35th Division.[11]

Here also was an old friend coming back to the company. Sergeant George A. Snyder who had been absent since late July at an A.E.F. school rejoined here. Formerly first sergeant, there was now no vacancy for him in that capacity and he was assigned as acting commander, third platoon.

The end of the day's march was near at hand and about a mile and a half farther to the north the battalion, 18 miles of weary road behind it, came to a rest in a hillside camp in the Bois de Pontoux at a spot called "Le Chanois" a mile west of Recourt.

"Comfortable French barracks" one letter home described the quarters, "wooden ones, covered with tar paper. We are waiting for orders."

We stayed at this place not only that night but the next day. Further movement toward the front would be under cover of darkness.

We rested at the Le Chanois camp a mile west of Recourt during the day of Sunday, October 13, 1918, but in late afternoon came the order to move.

As the sun dropped behind the beechwoods the marching portion of the machine gun battalion moved down to the highway and stepped briskly northeastward in the growing dusk. A two and a half mile march carried the column through the villages of Recourt and Villers-sur-Meuse. Here it crossed the stone bridge under which passed the smooth flowing, battle-bound Meuse River;

11. Cecil Ronald Stemmons was born in Avilla, Missouri, on September 17, 1888, died on April 19, 1958, and was buried in Avilla. Although officially listed as having joined Company A in 1913, Stemmons attended the St. Louis World's Fair in 1904 with the company, although under age. He first served with the 356th Infantry before transferring to the 137th. He served overseas from August 30, 1918 to April 23, 1919. *Joplin* (MO) *Globe*, April 20, 1958; Missouri Secretary of State, State Archives, Soldiers' Records, War of 1812–World War I, www.sos.mo.gov/archives/soldiers.

on across the valley and over the canal de l'Est the soldiers moved, thence north on a national highway through Genicourt and after some miles of marching down the valley, the hikers entered the village of Rattentout east of Dieue-sur-Meuse.

Here a certain tenseness, that slight thrill which even old soldiers feel when entering a danger zone, ran through the column.

For a week and a half or so the sound of artillery fire had been just a sound to us but Rattantout was an important supply point. It was shelled by enemy long range guns to the northeast nightly, I had been informed. Our formation since we had started had been the one we used when moving through areas subject to shell fire.

The question was whether we would get through Rattantout before the enemy began his nightly treatment. The place was quiet as we approached and to my relief continued so during our passage.

Just north of this village we left the national highway turning east on the road to Sommedieue and a quarter of a mile or so short of that town we turned right, down to a cluster of partially shattered factory buildings and houses—La Belle Helene, our destination for the night.

Entering the factory buildings, the soldiers spread out their blankets on the floor and spent the rest of the night in sleep.

La Belle Helene, despite its industrial character, was a pretty little place, as indeed a community called "The Beautiful Helen" should be. It was a snug place, this La Belle Helene, it appeared not likely to be a target, and somehow it seemed the snugger when along toward morning I heard the scream of enemy shells far overhead followed by explosions in the direction of Rattantout.

The 35th Division, we knew now, was to relieve the 15th French Colonial Division in the trenches east and southeast of Verdun. Sommedieue was to be division headquarters, Rattantout our rail-head. The 128th Machine Gun Battalion was initially to be in division reserve.

It could be that the 128th Machine Gun Battalion might be left where it was for the time being. After breakfast suitable quarters were found for the company in some of the old factory buildings still standing. The houses were deserted and partially ruined but I found what I thought a very suitable billet for myself in one of the structures. The building had been knocked about a bit but

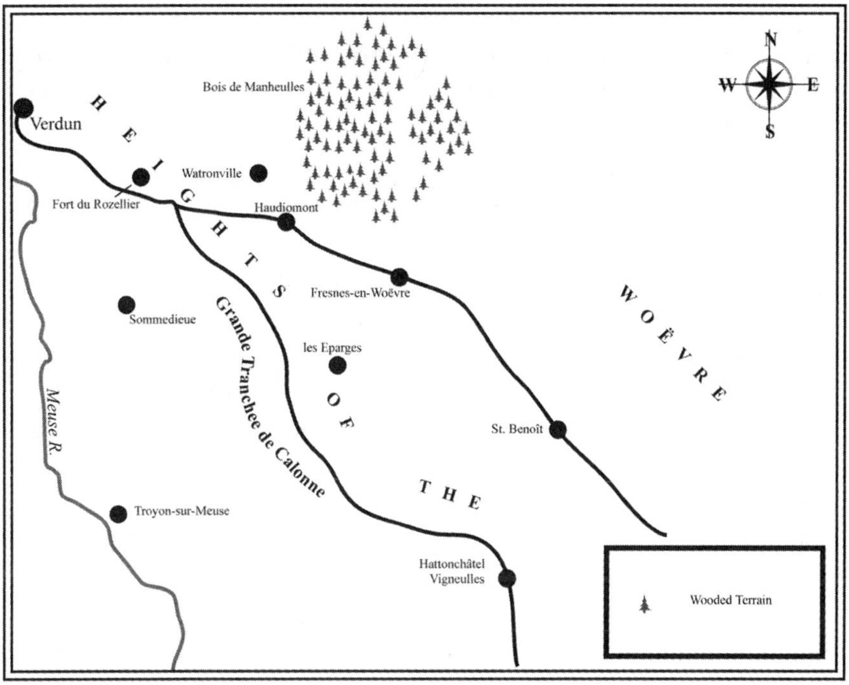

Sommedieue

there was a roof over most of it and the room I selected was good except that the jarring of shells hitting the building somewhere had knocked down the plaster, which remained on the floor. I had this cleaned up during the day and my bedding roll moved in.

Expecting that they might remain here the machine gunners made themselves comfortable and strolled about looking at the surroundings as one does in a new station. One point of interest was some new railway switches which had been installed and camouflaged with green netting. Here, too, under cover in this vicinity, were the heavy American cannon, mounted on railway cars, which fired from these switches. This was another sign of the nearness of the front—were any sign needed.

And here at La Belle Helene came 27 replacements to partially fill the gaps created in Company A by the Argonne battle. These were from the 145th Machine Gun Battalion, 40th Division, one of the A.E.F. replacement divisions, and most of them were trained machine gunners from former National Guard organizations of Colorado, California, Arizona, New Mexico, Nevada and Utah. There were a few comparatively new men from recent drafts. Three of the newcomers were born in Italy, one in Portugal and one, a missionary's son, in Japan. To my relief I found that they were all trained machine gunners from replacement divisions and not newly drafted men with practically no training, such as the infantry were receiving.

"Slowly but surely," a Company A officer wrote back to Carthage, "we are losing our local character."[12]

Late that afternoon my supposition that we might stay at La Belle Helene for a time was shattered by word that we would march on again at dusk. That word passed around Company A, 128th Machine Gun Battalion the late afternoon of October 13, 1918, caused the soldiers to look somewhat ruefully at the preparations they had made for a comfortable night's rest at La Belle Helene, and then to start rolling their packs for the move.

I moved out of my newly cleaned room and hoped someone would get some good from it.

The division was moving into this sector and taking over the trenches which overlooked the plains of the Woevre, a scene of heavy fighting a few years before.

When mess had been served the company formed for departure while the cooks hurriedly cleaned up and loaded the kitchen supplies on the cargo trucks which, together with the gun trucks, were to come up after the foot column had had time to get a good start.

For the new men, as well as for the several old ones who had just rejoined from hospital or school and had not participated in the battle of two weeks before, there was a distinct thrill to this formation in helmets and with gas masks in the alert position on the chest, the more so since they saw the officers before taking charge, pull back and release the slides on their pistols, each thus snapping a cartridge from the magazine into the chamber. Even for the men who so recently had been battle-worn but who were now fresh again, the circumstances quickened spirits.

Our destination was another reserve position west of Fort du Roselier, southeast of Verdun, but our route led well to the east toward the trenches, then angled back. We might come under light

12. Schrantz's unit was not the only one to lose its "local character." By the spring of 1919, the 129th Machine Gun Battalion contained only 52 percent of the men who were with the unit at Camp Doniphan. Weber, *The History of the 129th Machine Gun Battalion*, 58.

artillery fire during the movement so it was in our usual artillery formation—platoons in columns of twos with considerable gaps between sections and platoons—that we marched, and with gas masks tied up in the alert position on our chests.

It was drizzling rain as the column stepped briskly out of La Belle Helene and up the white gravel high road through the darkened village of Sommedieue, a favorite target of the enemy harassing artillery fire. There were no shells falling here, now, however, and the men were soon struggling up the road up the valley beyond. The road base was solid enough but a thin veneer of mud on top made the going so slippery that even the hob-nailed shoes of the soldiers slid from it like from grease. A tough climb, this, though the grade was not extremely steep, and the men had little time to think of the crash of shells which were already audible ahead.

Now there came slipping down the road a stream of French soldiers in twos, and threes and as individuals, the typical Gallic formation—or lack of formation—in coming out of trench sectors in areas subject to artillery fire.

"Finis la guerre," shouted the French jocularly to the passing Americans.

"Finis la guerre," yelled back the Americans in a similar spirit of jocund irony.

And up ahead the shell crashes grew more frequent and the dim light of rising flares were visible through the haze.

This slippery hill, hard for the footmen, was difficult indeed for the motor train and it required all the ingenuity which Major Westley Halliburton had acquired through months of shepherding his dilapidated vehicles over bad roads to finally worm and drag and push his guns and supplies up this high road. Long after the marchers had forgotten this stretch behind them, the drivers and other train personnel were struggling with this hard problem.

The road led some miles eastward to a cross road known as Carrefour de Bernatant, about a mile and a half from the front trenches, then angled back northwestward on a road known as the "Grande Tranchee de Calonne"—the "great trench of Calonne"—apparently reminiscent of some of the age-old military past of the region of Verdun. The noise of the explosions of shells came frequently from the right after the turn was made; but to the relief of the Argonne veterans and the disappointment of those who had missed the experience, none struck near the column.

Another cross road was passed in the rain, and here members of Company B, 129th Machine Gun Battalion, Joplin were recognized in a waiting column of men and mules. The 129th was going into the trenches. As for the 128th, its back was now turned on the trenches and it marched squarely west past places where some batteries of artillery were in position by a wood, and so to Fort Rozelier—mounds of grass-grown earth in the obscurity. Behind the fort the road turned north, angled here and there, flanked by barbed wire; wound through the woods by hutments with other Americans moving in; then southwestward, down into a valley in the timber then eastward again up a muddy trail, and so at last in a dripping wood to a rotting camp which was officially called La Chiffoure. This was the 128th Machine Gun Battalion's position in division reserve. It was four and a quarter miles southeast of the city of Verdun; three and a quarter miles from the front line at its nearest point, and 700 yards northwest of Fort Rozelier.

La Chiffoure was a quiet place at first, so quiet indeed that an officer writing home the first few days there called it "the quietest sector I have seen in France," but a few days later amended this by saying: "Our quiet sector had its quietness rudely shattered last night. The enemy has been nervous and alert for a couple of nights and last night both his and our artillery and machine guns were very active. Only a comparatively small number of shells came back in this area but our own batteries which are located all around us were pounding away most of the night." This was typical of existence at La Chiffoure.

Here I temporarily lost two of my officers, Lieut. Dunn going to the machine gun company, 138th Infantry, of which he took command, and 2nd Lieut. H.B. Wardin accompanying him. This left only Lieutenant Snyder and myself with the combat portion of the company, Lieutenant E. J. Bourne taking Wardin's place with the motor train.

Also I sent four sergeants to an officer training camp from here, one of them, Supply Sergeant Warren Ford, not only so gained a commission but continued as a reservist between the two world wars and served as a lieutenant colonel in the second one.

These departures, plus casualties, called for rather wholesale promotions which were made here.

For ten days the 128th Machine Gun Battalion rested in this snug but wet hollow. Life at La Chifoure was unexciting though.

By day we trained as well as we might in the wet beechwoods. At night outside our shelters we floundered around from one building to another in the pitch blackness for here, as everywhere else near the front, no light could show.

Snyder and I occupied the same ratty dugout and I read of an evening by the light of our candles and he censored mail.

At times he would emit loud chortles, at other times swear to himself but I asked no questions for we most seriously considered censoring of mail as a sacred and confidential task. And it was seldom that he commented.

Only twice did he break confidence, both times bubbling with laughter. One time was a reference to me in a letter.

One young woman at home had been quite solicitous of her brother's welfare, he being a soldier in my company. Five or six times I had received letters from her asking about his safety and in reply I had written her routine notes, as to all anxious relatives, assuring her that he was quite all right and since he was not in the combat section of the company that she need not worry.

Perhaps I had mentioned this to Snyder since it was a little unusual for a sister to be so concerned.

"Listen to this," snickered Snyder one night as he was censoring a letter home by the brother. And he read:

"Tell sister that the captain will not write to her. He is a good man [and] has a good wife. I guess sister's paper is waste."

I was flattered both by the soldier's comment and his implication that the girl had been trying to strike up a mail flirtation with me. I hadn't even suspected that. But I received no more letters from her.

"Listen to what a--- ----liar that W---- is," chortled Snyder on another occasion. "He is writing to his girl and tells her that every time a shell bursts near him while he is writing he will make an 'X.' He has 'X's' all through it and a whole string of them at the end. And there hasn't [been] a shell burst within a quarter of a mile of him for two weeks."

Snyder and I for a brief time had a little local mystery.

During the nights there often would be a loud and strange scratching of some kind up in our roof. It was far noisier than any rat would be and we assumed that it was a wild animal—"varmint" of some sort. Its noise gave us an eerie sort of feeling until we finally solved the mystery. It turned out to be one of the ordinary domestic species of cat but gone wild now—probably born that way, rather in view of how long the war had been in progress—and so gaining its livelihood as it best could, this including going after rats or mice in our dug-out roof.

Though artillery was about us at various places it was seldom active, there being a stringent order about economy of artillery ammunition.

After a nervous preceding night, there was an alarm of some kind on the front the night of October 21–22 and, as I learned later, our 35th Division machine guns on the front near Haudiomont fired a protective barrage. Evidently also, the rifle units had called for artillery support.

The batteries about us suddenly burst into rapid cannonading and there was considerable German return fire though no shells burst in our section of the valley. The German fire gradually died away but shells hurtled over us much of the night as our guns kept pounding away.

Some French soldiers, I learned next morning, had been killed in the village of Belrupt some distance west of us but if there were other casualties I did not hear of them. Certainly there were none near us.

"The leaves of the trees are changing color," wrote home one soldier during this period, "and while the colors are not as brilliant as they are at home—probably due to the continual wet weather—they are nevertheless very pretty. We are in a beech wood and the ground is almost covered with a carpet of beech-nuts. Every wind shakes down a shower of them. Thus even a war like this has its compensating features." Behind us our artillery roared at intervals, sometimes being silent except for an occasional shot, at other times putting down furious barrages that kept the air above our valley ascream with passing shells. The Germans, not to be outdone, replied with vigor but during all this artillery activity not a single shell fell in our camp. Off to the north, day and night, the booming and thudding of cannon told of the "big show" where our troops were pushing back the enemy along the Meuse River.

As dusk fell on October 24, 1918, Company A, 128th Machine Gun Battalion, climbed blithely from the dark valley in which it had spent ten days in division reserve at La Chiffoure and stepped out briskly toward the front.

The machine gunners were under no illusions concerning war, but life gets dull in reserve and the order to move forward to relieve Company A, 129th Machine Gun Battalion (Sarcoxie), in the sector known as C.R. Haudiomont had been received with smiling faces. Now they were on their way.

Company B (Butler and Nevada) was this same night to relieve the Machine Gun Company, 137th Infantry, in the Mont-sous-les-Cotes sector next adjoining Company A on the south. Major Westley Halliburton became acting machine gun officer of the 69th Brigade and was to take post at the brigade command post known as P.C. Toulon, in the woods far to the south, and the motor trains of the battalion were to camp in the same vicinity after they had delivered guns, ammunition and kitchen supplies at the company headquarters.

Once out of the maze of roads around Fort Rozelier, Company A's route lay directly east on Route Nationale No. 3 which would have gone to Metz could one have followed it far enough—but there were some very good reasons that no one on this side of the front lines had gone very far in that direction for over four years and two months. The company officers had already gone up the road as far as one could go, conferred with the officers of the unit to be relieved, and made a reconnaissance of the sector—and now it was the turn of everyone.

Far off to the northwest where the major battle was in progress there was a pounding of gunfire and rising rockets and flares but on the east front where we were heading all seemed quiet except for the rising of routine flares.

Company B, which first accompanied the Carthage company, turned off to the southeast on the road known as the "Grande tranchee de Calonne," and Company A then moved on alone, in column of twos, considerable distance between platoons. This road was subject to frequent lashing by enemy shell fire but now, fortunately, all was quiet.

Distant rifle shots and the crash of grenades and bursts of Maxim and Chauchat fire could be heard from the front occasionally and the flares were brighter as the distance lessened.

There was, of course, no smoking, and conversation was carried on in low tones. Woods loomed on both sides of the road, though to the south there was first a clearing and a little valley. Once someone whispered that the column was passing a battery that the enemy frequently fired upon.

I moved with some trepidation past a battery position I had noted that day, the vicinity of which was liberally pocked with fresh shell holes.

But our guns were silent in the obscurity and the enemy was throwing nothing in that direction as we went by.

Then someone else who knew said the point now being passed was as far as cars could go by day. The hill on the left increased in bulk and the valley on the right deepened. An old quarry on the left evoked more whispered information that the reserve company of the First Battalion, 137th Infantry, to which battalion the company was to be attached, was stationed here. Ahead of this was another quarry on the left, some trucks and Fords clustered along the road, and a huddle of waiting guides. Here the company's guns and ammunition had been unloaded.

Each squad sought its own; the loaded sections formed, and each little queue of men was soon winding in the direction of its own position. Most of the company went toward the south; but the two sections of the first platoon went directly ahead and then into a network of muddy trenches to the left and down a hill.

The kitchen truck was quickly unloaded and the headquarters section went to its various shelters just evacuated by its predecessors.

The motor column slipped back westward in the darkness to take station far to the southwest somewhere near brigade headquarters which was at PC Toulon and which also was to be our battalion headquarters.

Captain Clarence Shaeffer, commander of Co. A, 129th Machine Gun Battalion and I then reported to Maj. John R. O'Connor, a somewhat eccentric Winfield, Kans., character, yet an unusually able and gallant old soldier whom I already knew.[13]

13. Clarence Shaeffer was born in Stevens, Pennsylvania, on August 12, 1894. He enlisted in the Regular Army in El Paso, Texas, and served in various regiments before World War I,

He had come across on the overseas school detail on the USS *George Washington* as had I and had attracted attention on shipboard by the vigor with which he strode constantly round and round the deck, with polished boots and glistening spurs and swinging a riding crop, determined not to soften up physically during the voyage.

And at Brest he had started in vigorously to study French, employing some feminine French teacher whom he escorted about the town for the sole purpose, I feel quite sure, of listening to her French chatter.

In the Meuse-Argonne operation he had displayed outstanding courage and the entire division spoke well of him. He was a voracious student and consequently a well informed tactician and a fighting man besides.

But now he didn't want to fight.

He was there—his battalion—for a rest, he said. It had suffered heavy losses in the late fighting and it probably would have to attack again somewhere soon. He didn't want his machine gunners stirring up trouble and getting people killed. Specifically there would be no harassing fire. The machine guns were not to fire at all in fact unless the rifle units called for protective fire or unless he gave his permission in advance.

That was that. With the grinning Shaeffer I went to the dug-out which had been his and which now was to be Snyder's and mine, since Snyder was second in command and the two of us would need to be stationed at company headquarters so one would always be there while the other was touring the trenches. As for the platoons, each was commanded—and commanded quite capably—by a sergeant.

That dug-out, a neat and trim place with a gas blanket which also served for blackout purposes at the door, was something of an unique place in my experience.

---

then as a second lieutenant in the 91st Division from August to October 1917. He joined the 129th Machine Gun Battalion in October 1917, was promoted to captain, and was discharged in May 1919. He died on April 14, 1965. John Henry O'Connor was born in Kentucky in December 1866. He died on October 4, 1942, and was buried in Winfield, Kansas. He enlisted in the Kansas National Guard as a private in 1885. Discharged in 1891, he entered service again in 1898 with the 21st Kansas Infantry for the Spanish-American War. In 1906, he organized Company H, 2nd Kansas Infantry and became the company's commander. Promoted to major in 1915, he led a battalion of the 2nd Kansas Infantry on the Mexican border in 1916. He commanded the 1st Battalion, 137th Infantry, assumed temporary command of the 137th Infantry September 28–October 9, 1918, then was promoted to lieutenant colonel in February 1919. *The Winfield* (KS) *Courier*, April 3, 1919; *The Winfield* (KS) *Daily Free Press*, November 23, 1921.

Some previous French occupant had completely papered the walls with vivid, artistic and more or less wittily-amorous illustrations from *La Vie Parisienne*, a noted French publication of of its day—and perhaps yet for all I know to the contrary. Even the maps which Shaeffer had pinned on the wall were placed over this bright art work.

Shaeffer's company was originally from Sarcoxie, Mo., but he himself was a former Regular Army sergeant who had gained a lieutenancy at the beginning of the war and just now had received his captaincy. He was a pleasant soul and capable officer and since we had had some background experience in common—I think he had served in some regiment in the old 2nd Division at Texas City when I did—we were already friends.

He explained to us the machine gun protective barrage which was of his own devising.

His predecessor of the French 15th Colonial Division had drawn lines on the map showing the field of fire of each gun but as for the rest Shaeffer had been able to get little out of them, due to language difficulties, concerning the defensive plan.

"Boches, Br-r-r-r-r," with eloquent gestures, was about all the information transmitted. Since the American captain had already assumed that if the enemy started over his guns were to open fire, this was not of particular value.

Consequently he had made his own plan and at the most dangerous part of the front it wasn't good, he said. Certain areas had to be covered by single guns because the extent of front was so great in that platoon area that it could not be covered by sections firing both guns on the same target area—a routine requirement meant to make sure that the front still would be covered if one gun jammed or otherwise had a stoppage.

I worked out my own defensive fires in the ensuing days, altering Shaeffer's in some particular, but I couldn't do anything about the condition he mentioned. There just wasn't enough guns.

The relief of Shaeffer's guns was completed at 23:50—ten minutes before midnight—and as soon as word of this reached our quarry, known as PC Bordeaux, that captain departed and the sector was ours. "Relief completed at 23:50 (11:50 p.m.)" commented the company official report on the movement. "All quiet."

Early the next morning I was out visiting my gun positions.

My own P.C. was in a quarry with that of the headquarters of the First Battalion, 137th Infantry, to which we were attached, 500 meters northwest of Haudiomont. The Haudiomont sector was about three kilometers long and was named for the ruined town of Haudiomont which was in the extreme front line about the middle of the sector. Our lines were at the base of the beech covered hills east of Verdun and the enemy positions were on the great plain which lay to the east.

Here the heights of the Meuse broke away into the flat region to the east known as the Woevre, which day showed to be dotted with white ruins of villages connected with white, tree-bordered ribbons of roads.

"There is something fascinating about this silent plain," one soldier wrote back to Carthage, "with its fallow fields and ruined villages absolutely devoid of signs of life."

It covered a front of about 3,000 meters—around 3,300 yards—measured in a direct line but perhaps about 2 ½ miles the way the line swerved. My northern machine gun section was 200 meters south of Ronvaux and the southern one 1800 meters south of Route Nationale No. 3 where it passed Haudiomont.

Haudiomont had been the north hinge of the Allied drive in the St. Mihiel offensive. North of Haudiomont the Allied and German lines were as they had been since February 1916. But south of the national highway, the 4th U.S. Division had attacked in that September 1918 operation and had taken the town of Manhuelles 2,600 meters east of Haudiomont. The terrain around Manheulles was not suitable for defense and that village was held as an isolated strong point. In theory the Allied territory extended as far north as the highway. Actually the region was a no-man's-land over which strong German patrols roved, as well as an occasional one of our own. The defense of Manheulles itself in a machine gun way was not my problem, it being in Captain Corey's sector.

The enemy held on this flat ground a great wood, known in places as the Bois de Manheulles and in others as the Bois de Massenoue. The Allied line at the north was quite close to this with some 900 yards of barbed-wire and swampy land intervening, but at the south widened away, with a great stretch of open, unoccupied, non-mans-land [no-man's land] between. On the southern part of the sector there was a considerable stretch of unoccupied plain and our guns at the base of the hills would have had to fire at a range of 2000 meters to have even reached the enemy outpost positions.

The enemy held the great woods known as the Bois de Manheulles east of the northern part of our line and 600 to 1,000 distant, and extending to the north of Manheulles itself. The western part of this wood which extended westward in a triangular shape was on flat terrain although 500 or 600 meters east of the edge of it the ground rose in a low hill. This wood was thick and afforded complete cover from view.

Ten Company A machine guns were by now laid on lines to protect the front. Two others in a slightly retired position served as a reserve.

C.R. Haudiomont which the First Battalion, 137th Infantry, Major John R. O'Connor, held with three rifle companies in line and one in reserve, covered a front of two and a half miles, along which the machine guns were posted in pairs.

My northernmost section (Sgt. Leaford Akin) in case of enemy attack needed to cover 600 meters of front with fire direct to the front with a swinging traverse effect. Each gun covered half of the sector. His two weapons were at the base of the hill at a point about three-quarters of a mile north of the ruins of Haudiomont and a few hundred yards south of the shattered village of Ronvaux in the adjoining sector.

This section had an alternate barrage to the northeast to cover the east-northeast front of Ronvaux if the attack were only from that direction. The enemy was 1,000 meters from its gun-muzzles.

The next section (Sgt. R.B. Huff) was located 250 meters north of the national highway partially up the slope of a steep hill marked on the map "Le Grand Mur" (the great wall) and was in a trench known as the Boyau de Mi-Crete. This section had to cover 675 meters, each gun having a sector of its own. This was a much-too-thin barrage but I managed, after some days of study, to supplement it by what I believed would have been a quite effective long-range flanking barrage from the south by another section. These guns were from 700 to 1,000 meters from the edge of the enemy woods but their protective barrage was set to fall a uniform 700 meters in front of their positions.

Sergeant Willard Brown, commander of the first platoon, lived in one of the shallow dugouts with Sergeant Huff and his gunners.

I plodded through deep mud in the Boyau de Ronvaux, through which I reached and returned from the northernmost machine gun section, and there was mud in Le Grand Mur trenches too.

It was not in the mud that I was interested, however. It was lines of fire and emplacements and then how the gun sections were quartered. All these I checked.

I was interested in the enemy-held woods too, now beginning to change color with the advancing season. From the woods, well back, came the occasional pop-pop-pop of an enemy Maxim but at what it was firing I could not tell. No bullets seemed to be striking along our positions. Occasionally there came the crack of an enemy sniper's rifle too as he glimpsed some movement, or thought he did, in our trenches. Off to the north and northwest there was the roar of artillery fire but this front was calm and, at the time, with no firing at all from our side.

To get to the next position to the south I needed to retrace my steps three-quarters of a mile or so, back past the quarry which contained PC Bordeaux, down a hill past a little roadside chapel and shrine, across a dry run known as the Ravin de la Fosse a Greve, to some trenches then forward to the nose of a hill.

Next, as one went on to the south, was the reserve section emplaced on the nose of a hill southwest of company headquarters and a little over a half mile west of Haudiomont. These two guns constituted Sergeant Joseph E. Taylor's part of the third platoon.

By day this section could help protect Haudimont [*sic:* Haudiomont] by overhead fire. If the town fell it could batter its western outskirts. If the enemy advanced either over the hills to the north or against the hill to the south it could swing its guns against him. It had an excellent field of fire. It had a front line defense mission too—long range, indirect fire on the route nationale.

In addition to its own Hotchkiss guns, this section had two French San Etienne machine guns found in the sector.

Half a mile to the southeast of this was the second platoon of the company in emplacements at the edge of a wood, Sergeant Fred R. Clark's section on the north and Sergeant Harry Palmer's section 300 yards farther south. In addition to being in command of his section, Sergeant Clark was in command of this platoon most of the time in the area. The mission of these four guns was to place fire along the National Highway which ran east of Haudiomont; and it is of interest to note as indicating the antiquity of war in this region, that high shots from this barrage would fall on an old Roman road built in the days of the conquest of Gaul.

These guns also had the route nationale as a normal protective line and had alternate protective barrages in front of—east of—Haudimont [*sic*] in case the enemy crossed the road.

Sergeant Clark pointed to the trees in front of his guns and grinned. Here was the explanation of a mystery of which Clark had not heard but with which I was familiar.

In the fire fight on the night of October 21–22 when rifle units along the front had called for both machine gun and artillery support, these guns of course had gone into action.

Captain Shaeffer had told me that some riflemen in trenches in front of and below the machine guns had been wounded by what the infantrymen had thought was our own machine gun fire since they were sheltered from fire from the direction of the enemy. Shaeffer had denied this was possible and had brought Major O'Connor over to show him the amount of clearance that there was—his bullets' line of flight was high above the riflemen's heads. The upshot was that it was decided that there must have been enemy planes overhead during the action and that these had fired down into the trenches.

But here was the explanation written very clearly in the trees. One gun had fired through heavy branches. Some had been shot away and others chewed up. Such branches are quite sufficient to deflect enemy bullets. Unquestionably it was such deflected bullets which had caused the casualties.

Clark knew what happened when bullets were fired through trees like that as well as I knew it and was only waiting my approval to start work on an emplacement a bit to one side where the shots would pass free. Before evening the gun was in its new location.

I think that Captain Shaeffer knew too, after the damage had been done, but his explanation had been sufficient for the rifle battalion commander. Then he perhaps had told me the official decision so I would not innocently betray a fellow machine gunner.

My next section was three-quarters of a mile southeast of this and reached by a winding trench through the valley which passed through the grounds of Murauvaux Chateau, a once-pretentious country establishment now partially in ruins and its grounds furrowed with trenches, yet a rather restful appearing sort of place. At this time my mind was on other things but later, wandering this way, I went through the ruin. Though apparently of reasonably modern construction it was, like most isolated places of this nature, something of a fortress. There even were places which clearly seemed to me to be loop-holes for rifle fire to cover the gates—at least there were holes originally made in the building splayed inward and admirably suited for such purpose.

My final section on the south, commanded by Sergeant George [A.] Snyder was at the opening of a little valley called Fond de la Chavee. At the time this section was scheduled to fire on the route nationale also but I soon changed this—a day or two later—to a long range flanking barrage to thicken the fire in front of the north sector as previously mentioned.

This south section's positions had been sited after the change of lines during the St. Mihiel offensive. It's [*sic*] only cover from view was the leaves which were about to fall. Its cover from fire was meager. There was little cover for the men from the weather. Snyder had a busy time ahead of him and set to it with a will.

The company kitchen was with company headquarters in the old quarry in the center of the section. All food was prepared in the headquarters quarry and because of the length of carry involved it was not possible to serve three times a day so we all only ate twice, once about 9 o'clock and once about 4 p.m., if I remember right, not the most desirable situation gastronomically.

To men who had actively participated in the great battle which was still raging on the Meuse-Argonne front, the service in the stabilized front east of Verdun at the end of October seemed quiet indeed by comparison, yet it was of vital importance for all that. "They also serve who only stand and wait" and it was necessary that someone wait here to repel any German attack which might seek to stop the American advance to the north by striking at its flanks and rear. Though the Carthage soldiers and others on duty in this area considered their work only as occupancy of a defensive sector, the government has since officially credited it as a second participation in the Meuse-Argonne Offensive.

Company A, 128th Machine Gun Battalion, attached to the First Battalion, 137th Infantry, in the vicinity of Haudiomont found life interesting but relatively calm. There was constant work on trenches and dug-outs; there was unceasing vigilance at the guns which must be ready to fire instantaneously day or night; and each morning for an hour before daylight until an hour after, all men in all positions "stood to" ready to repel enemy attack. And when one rested it was in dugouts which generally were little more than wet holes in the earth. In some of these water stood on the floor under and around the rough bunks. For this reason a French sign on one of these in Sergeant Joseph E. Taylor's position reading "Abri B" (Dugout B) had been altered by some wag who added "ains" to the "B," making the sign read "Abri Bains" (Dugout Baths).

Life livened up a little after nightfall.

There were occasional bursts of enemy machine gun fire, several Maxims shooting from the west edge of the Bois de Manheulles. A few hostile shells fell in the area—about ten my daily report said. There was a lively little skirmish of some sort out on the route nationale between our patrols and the German ones—rifle shots, grenades, automatic fire from Maxims or Chauchats.

There was considerable speculation as to the enemy strength in the Bois de Manheulles. It appeared to be the division opinion that the wood was lightly held.[14]

I rather inclined to this view myself.

To me the frequent bursts of enemy machine gun fire, usually at nothing in particular so far as we could tell, seemed possibly to indicate that the shooting was to create an illusion of more strength in the wood than there was.

This seemed the opinion of many others, including division headquarters, but when the intelligence officer of the battalion to

14. In a postwar letter, Maj. Westley Halliburton of the 128th Machine Gun Battalion noted, "It was the general opinion that the Germans were holding their front very lightly and mostly with machine guns." Nightly patrols sent into the German lines with orders to bring back prisoners for interrogation "nearly always returned empty handed." One infantry patrol penetrated several miles into the German lines, hid there all day, and came back the next night and "never saw a German." Letter of Westley Halliburton to American Battle Monuments Commission, Washington, D.C., September 26, 1928, HST.

which we were attached tried to enter the woods one night he was fired upon by three guns sited at the edge of the timber. A few moments later some more guns from a hill back in the wood also opened up on the vicinity of where his patrol had been discovered and he returned to our own lines. He told me afterwards that he thought that there were light machine guns stationed along the edge of the woods and heavy ones further back.

The first night we were in the line there was a patrol fight on the Mannheulles-Haudiomont road in which several men were killed and in which our troops obtained identification of the enemy troops opposite us from the clothing of a dead German.

During the daylight hours in this sector it was often absolutely quiet except for the pounding away of artillery to the north where the American offensive was in progress. This quietness was apt to lead men to become careless. Despite his silence the enemy was over there and watching, a fact that was impressed upon me very emphatically one day.

I was very curious to see what the enemy had in the timber opposite us and as my first sergeant had mentioned that an excellent view of the woods could be had from the hill just north of the quarry, I went up there one evening to see what I could see. Climbing to the top of the hill above Le Grand Mur as the sun dropped into the west—and hence the view to the east was the best of the day—I studied the woods long to see what I could make of them. Outside of impressing the terrain on my mind the effort was of no value—except perhaps in the way of education.

When I arrived at the edge of the timber on the top of the hill I found that I could not get a view of the enemy's very front line from there so I decided to crawl out on the bare hill to a little clump of bushes a foot high and observe from there. I realized that in getting down to the clump I would be exposed on the sky-line with the sun on my back and I certainly would have severely censured any of my men who did a thing so foolish, but all the same I wanted to get the view that could be obtained from that point and decided to take a chance.

I quickly crawled down to the bush and lay with my head behind it, looking over the enemy's territory with my field glasses. But the binoculars I had, a French Army make purchased in Brest and known to our service as "stereo-prismatic field glasses with stadia range finder" had some brass about them, particularly two brass engravings on the inside used in connection with the range-finding (bi-refrigent) prism. Since I used the glass constantly these plates were quite bright. I suspect a sun glint on this brass advertised my position. A bullet cracked some distance north of me.

Bullets are not novelties, even in a quiet trench sector, so I was not particularly disturbed though I wondered vaguely if I might have been spotted. I continued to study the woods.

It was an excellent view and I had lain there fifteen minutes or more when "CRACK," a rifle bullet passed so close to the left side of my head that at the time it seemed to me that there could not have been as much as an inch margin of safety. My bush was no longer a shelter.

It was an excellent shot at a range of more than 1000 meters and if it had been a shade more to the right I would have remained on that hill until someone picked me up. As it was I quickly returned to the timber on top of the hill, so quickly in fact that the sniper only got one more shot at me and it may be that he was firing rapid fire. The second shot went wild but the memory of the first one remains with me vividly enough to make me careful about skylines forever in the future.

This was somewhat instructive as to the care needed in operating outside of trenches in a stabilized sector.

I continued to study the woods from safer points of vantage, comparing them with aerial photographs in my quarters, but I never learned much other than the sector maps showed.

Should it be necessary for me to support an attack against this position I could only site my guns on the hill, I figured, sweep the edge of the timber with fire until the advancing infantry was near it, then lift to the higher ground in the center of the wood where an enemy trench, marked on the map as the Tranchee des Capons, seemed to be his main line of resistance.

On December 11, as previously mentioned, I visited the sector and went over the German positions.

The enemy had first occupied this ground in February 1916 when during the first few days of the Battle of Verdun the French line in the Woevre had been withdrawn to the heights of the Meuse, the hills which we held.

The 81st Division which had relieved us had attacked some days after they had taken over the sector. At the time I visited the place the ground had not been cleaned up since the battle and the whole story of the enemy's scheme of defense and the way it worked out in action was written plainly on the ground.

The Germans had left the spent cartridges of the November 11 fighting at the gun positions. Each position thus was marked by cartridges as well as emplacements, and the direction of fire was indicated both by the bullet-torn brush and by little marker-cards the Germans had set up for each gun.

At the time I revisited the woods I did not yet know that the 81st Division had attacked over the ground.

The whole wood had bristled with machine guns, both light and heavy, but there seemed to have been few more riflemen than were needed for the patrols. The edge of the woods had been used merely as a line of observation to which light machine guns were sent out at night and probably in thick weather. In front of the line of observation, patrols worked with regularity and boldness, as was indicated by the paths leading out into No Man's Land.

The main line of resistance was back in the woods about 300 meters and was held by a considerable number of light and heavy machine guns sited to place interlocking bands of fire through the thicket to their front. So long as the machine guns continued to operate, these interlocking bands of fire made this front entirely impenetrable.

This line was not marked on sector maps except that the belt of barbed wire across its front was shown, this being visible from planes.

Between the line of observation and the line of resistance the underbrush had been permitted to grow up into a dense jungle still further tangled by wire but crisscrossed with rides down which machine guns fired. These rides had also grown up with light brush so the purpose for which they were cut was not at first evident—but there was nothing in them to stop machine gun fire. When the attackers were known to have reached the line of observation all the machine guns began firing down the rides regardless of whether they could see anyone are not. The fire of the guns crossed each other and formed a barrier of flying bullets all across their front, making it impossible for an attacker to get forward while the fire was in progress. On the hills in rear of this main line there were other machine guns sited to fire into the timber in front of them and also out onto No Man's Land with a slightly plunging effect.

Little heaps of empty shells in the German machine gun emplacements showed just what guns had fired and how much. Out in No Man's Land, along the edge of the woods, and to a point about fifty meters inside the woods, rusty rifles, punctured helmets and bloody gas masks told of how the American troops had pushed gallantly across the open and into the woods but had run into the bands of machine gun fire and had been stopped. A line of white stones marked what was evidently the final American line when the Armistice went into effect November 11—and this final line was still some hundreds of meters from the enemy's main line of resistance. Had the war lasted a day or two longer the woods would probably had been taken by being encircled but a more determined pushing of the direct attack would have likely resulted merely in heavier losses.

This equipment was marked 324th Infantry and I judged that regiment had attacked with battalions abreast.

It was well that it stopped there. To have tried to have gone on would have meant only heavier losses because only one German machine gun position that I saw on that line had been knocked out. Some fine courage was shown, and some heavy casualties incurred, I surmised, in order to get that far under the circumstances.[15]

The 81st Division first attacked on November 9 and entered the wood but according to the American Battle Monument's "American Armies and Battlefields in Europe," (1938), did not stay there.

"Only two isolated groups, however, remained in the wood during the night," says that guide book on page 153. "The smaller of these withdrew about 10 a.m. to the road on which the observer is standing (Route Nationale No. 3). The other group, a company, was attacked by the Germans early on the morning of the 10th and about half of its men were captured. The remnants, however, about 40 men, fought their way back to the American position at Haudiomont . . . No attack was made here on November 10 but on the 11th the 81st Division met resistance to its advance in the

15. The 81st Division, including the three attached regiments of artillery from the 35th Division, suffered 982 casualties November 2–11, 1918. American Battle Monuments Commission, *81st Division Summary of Operations in the World War* (Washington, D.C: U.S. Government Printing Office, 1944), 22.

Bois de Manheulles. Its front line was in the wood at the time of the armistice."

It was by such methods that it was finally found how strongly the Germans held the ground in front of us.

But all this was future history—though not far future—when we occupied the sector.

In a sense for us these were pleasant days—the thrill of war without many of its unpleasant features. It was much like the Vosges save that the pleasure of harassing fire was denied us.

Lieut. Snyder and I spent alternate nights at some position in the trenches and by day I roved over the region inspecting gun positions. And in rest intervals Snyder dutifully censoring mail. And once, just once, he broke confidence.

"Just listen to this," he snorted in glee. "Over in Taylor's section some guy has written a clever letter—Ford Nickell, I imagine, since it sounds like him—and six of those fellows have copied it and are sending it out to their girls as their own letter."[16]

He read aloud. It was indeed a clever letter, well-written and humorous, something about living in trenches built before the world was civilized and when men made war upon each other. I would have liked to be able to compose a letter like that myself but I am quite sure that my wife never received one that good.

Except for artillery fire there was not much activity in our immediate sector, our mission apparently being one of almost passive defense.[17]

As the Carthage men in Company A, 128th Machine Gun Battalion, waited by their lean Hotchkiss guns in the region of Haudiomont in late October they listened to an increasing number of enemy projectiles pass overhead and heard the daily thunder of heavy barrages to the north and northwest where their comrades of other divisions were hacking their way forward.

They had more than an academic interest in this fighting. They knew that other Carthage men in the many other organizations

16. John Ford Nickell, born in Carthage on November 10, 1898, died in Tulsa, Oklahoma, on January 16, 1969.

17. Cecil Stemmons of Company A had time to notice that the leaves of the beech trees in the area had turned "a beautiful color," and "the hills are awfully pretty." The nights had turned chilly, so one could "sure sleep well" in a "nice dugout, protected by several feet of solid rock and stout timbers" and a fireplace that "at times smoke like fury." "However, no one minds such a little thing as that," he continued, as "everything around here is very peaceful." *Carthage* (MO) *Evening Press*, December 4, 1918.

were probably involved. In some cases there was a close blood-kinship with these soldiers elsewhere as well as the tie of fellow citizenship in the same town back in the states. As an instance of this was the case of the Davis brothers.

On the morning of October 23 as Corporal Mack Davis of Company A had gone about his normal routine, his brother George A. Davis whom chance had assigned as a replacement to Company B, 102nd Infantry, 26th Division, had plunged forward with his unit in the attack made that day a few miles away north of Verdun and was killed in action in the storming of a wood known as Le Houppy Bois. He was 23 years of age, the son of Mr. and Mrs. John F. Davis of 527 Oak Street, Carthage.[18]

Perhaps the routine of the sector may be described as well any other way by quoting from the daily Company A activity report. The following is that one rendered for the period from 9 a.m. October 2[5] to 9 a.m. October 26:

> "Intermittent enemy machine gun fire during day from well back in Massenoue woods. Some enemy snipers fired occasionally during day. About 6 p.m. about 10 shells fell in the area, most of them well to the rear. Occasional bursts of machine gun fire during the night and a few flares. Our own infantry patrols came in contact with strong enemy patrols somewhere along the Haudioment-Manheulles road. This company spent the day and night in checking barrage lines and working on the trenches which are in bad shape and heavy with mud."

The report for the similar period ending 9 a.m. October 27 narrated this story of continued quiet and steady work:

> "At 3:30 four enemy planes circled our lines, flying low. Intermittent enemy machine gun fire throughout the night. Some shelling by the enemy, none of the projectiles falling in the vicinity of our gun positions. Work on bettering positions being continued as energetically as possible. A new emplacement was built in the third section (Sergeant Fred R. Clark). This was rendered necessary by the fact that fire from the old one passed through trees and brush,

18. Private George A. Davis was born in 1894. He was killed on October 25, 1918, while a member of Company B, 102nd Infantry Regiment, 26th Division. He was buried in the Meuse-Argonne American Cemetery.

> thus deflecting bullets so as to endanger the infantry. The dugout being constructed in the fourth section (Sergeant Harry Palmer) was driven some distance further back into the hill and timbering on it was begun. It is hoped to have this ready for occupancy within three or four days. Emplacements for the sixth section (Sergeant George A. Snyder) are being camouflaged and improved. Those in use there were apparently built after the change of the lines in September and they gave considerable protection from view while the leaves were on the trees but not much now. They gave no cover from the fire at all. Work on the shelter in the first section (Sergeant Robert B. Huff) continued."

The 24-hour period ending at 9 a.m. October 28 showed a little more activity, as the following indicates:

> "Intermittent enemy machine gun fire during the day from Massenoue woods and Bois de Manheulles and some machine gun fire during the night. Several bursts struck in the vicinity of the first section (Sergeant Huff) of this company. At 6:30 p.m. one of our guns at U116.033 (map coordinate showing point north of Haudiomont) fired upon and silenced an enemy machine gun at U210.055 (a point in the Bois de Manheules) nightly from this point and sometimes during the day. He was accurately located and before dark a gun was laid on the place. When he opened up at about 6:30 p.m. our gun fired 50 rounds into his position. There was no further firing by the enemy though some hammering was heard in the neighborhood along toward morning. There was an alarm in the vicinity of our fourth section (Sergeant Palmer) at 7:30 p.m. when an infantry automatic rifle fired at some one the men in the infantry combat group thought was cutting wire. Our men heard nothing but stood to until 8:30 p.m. The usual work on trenches is in progress. Considerable duck-board has been laid, considerable has been done along the line of drainage, work on dugouts is continuing and the emplacements in the sixth section (Sergeant Snyder) have been deepened and approaches dug to them from the main trench."

The silencing of the German machine gun was the work of Sergeant Willard Brown, commander of the first platoon.

But this is getting in advance of our story. The constant firing by the enemy machine guns and the silence of our own was not particularly pleasant even though it was plain why our firing was forbidden. The enemy emboldened by his unhindered performances began firing nightly from the same points—a foolish thing to do. Near a niche in the woods 950 meters in front of our section first north of Haudiomont an enemy gun fired at intervals the night of October 25 and 26. Sergeant Brown in charge of our section referred to was auburn haired and Irish and having definitely located the hostile weapon by the slight flash that no flash arrestor can hide, he pleaded to be allowed to shoot at it.

While understanding Major O'Connor's idea of keeping the sector as quiet as possible, I was not in accord with it. Here was the enemy and in range and I felt that he should be harassed a bit. One objective would be to keep up my company's aggressive spirit and another would be to give battle training of a sort to my replacements. Moreover there was heavy fighting going on in the north and it would seem that we should do something to keep the enemy in our own front occupied—though the decision as to this was obviously one for someone higher in rank and position than myself to determine.

The major seemed to sense my ideas about activity. When I met him, either at the command post or on tours of the trenches, he asked about planned defensive fires and if everything was all right, but when I tried to broach the subject of harassing fire, he always cut the conversation short.

"I haven't time to talk to you," he would conclude and that was that.

But Sergeant Brown reported on the morning of October 27 that on each of the two nights previous an enemy machine gun had fired from the same point at the edge of the Bois de Massenoue, a part of the Bois de Manheulles. He had it definitely located. He could lay a gun on the spot by day—using the map-measured range of 900—meters, and if it opened up again that evening from that place he could certainly choke it off.

Happily I found Major O'Connor in his dugout. I pressed the point concerning that particular gun. It was a chance to kill Germans that shouldn't be passed up. We couldn't miss. This wasn't harassing fire. It was fire for effect against a definitely located target.[19]

The major said he would need to refer the matter to regimental headquarters—it thus appearing that his passive attitude, though he did not say so, was based on orders from above.

He wrote a message asking permission to fire. This was coded and sent into regimental headquarters.

In time came back a reply which also was in code. Decoded it proved to be a query as to why, if the gun had been definitely located, a patrol couldn't be sent out to capture it instead of having a gun shoot at it.

A reply to this was written. The intervening space was a mass of swamp and tangled barbed wire. The place could be raked with bullets without trouble. It would be both a difficult and uncertain venture to send out a patrol to try to capture a gun in the enemy's lines. This was all coded and sent in.

It was well along in the afternoon before the reply came and was decoded. Major O'Connor sent me the following note:

"Permission given to fire—but not too much."

I passed the word along to Brown. He was the more eager to fire because several bursts of machine gun fire had struck during the day near his northern section, that south of Ronvaux.

Sergeant Brown measured the range from the map and before dark laid his gun on the point that he had located the enemy.

At 6:30 p.m. I was sitting writing in my dug-out.

I heard the pop-pop-pop of a Maxim, followed by the sharp rat-tat-tat of a Hotchkiss, about 50 rounds being fired. Later there was another short burst of Hotchkiss fire.

The enemy gun had started to fire again from the place it had used before. At Brown's first shots the enemy machine gun abruptly ceased shooting and we were never fired upon from that point again. Brown had promptly choked it off as promised, Lt. Snyder, if I recall, being there to watch.

When measuring ranges that day Brown had taken the distance to another point from which he had seen a gun firing the night before. After silencing the first gun he swung onto this place and

19. Schrantz indicated that the process was actually a bit more convoluted. He first had to prove to the commander of the infantry battalion to which the company was attached that the German machine gun was at the point he indicated, and that Company A had a fair chance of putting it out of action. *Carthage* (MO) *Evening Press*, December 9, 1918.

waited. Later in the night the Germans opened up and Brown cut him off as he had the first. We never found any evidence as to what damage, if any, was done to the enemy by this latter shooting but in any event the Maxim stopped firing and the place from which it fired was never used again while we were there.

In my daily report I mentioned only one gun. The fire at the unauthorized target had best not be told about, I thought.

On December 11 I was able to visit the spot I had checked on my map as the location of the first enemy gun. There had been a German light machine gun position there with a galvanized iron roof over the place to keep off rain. Several articles of enemy equipment lay about including a gas mask with three bullet-holes through the disk and seven or eight through the carrier can. The galvanized iron was also perforated. Comparing the rust on the disk of the mouldy gas mask with the rust on articles dropped in the November 9–11 actions—of which more later—it was clear that the holes in the gas mask had been made at an earlier time. There is small doubt, I think, that we added slightly to the enemy's casualty list that night.

It was quite futile after that for me to try to talk to the rifle battalion commander about any more shooting at the enemy.

This firing was done from a point near Sergeant Huff's position at a location known as Le Grand Mur north of Haudiomont and the report the next day indicates the enemy may have resented the incident. Extracts of this report, for the 24 hour period ending 9 a.m. October 29, follow: "Enemy machine gun fire at intervals throughout day and night from Bois de Massenoue and Bois de Manheulles against our position near Le Grande Mur. During the afternoon an enemy airplane fired with a machine gun into our trenches north of Haudiomont. Considerable artillery activity by the enemy during the afternoon, most of the shells going over and many of them apparently striking near the battery position west of P.C. Bordeaux (the command post of the infantry battalion and the machine gun company). Usual work on trenches and dugouts. One emplacement was covered at the position near the Fond de la Chavee (Sergeant Taylor). A load of duck-boards and sand bags were delivered to this section during the night." Perhaps it was some training for our replacements too to hear the crack of enemy bullets and see dust kicking on the parapet.

There was patrolling by the rifle units nightly and an occasional clash. The German patrols, I suspect, acted with more boldness than our own and that night there was an alarm at our Bernatant positions when Chauchat riflemen with the rifle unit opened fire with those weapons on what they thought was an enemy patrol at the wire.

During the afternoon of October 29 enemy shells screamed overhead in large numbers, apparently aimed at artillery positions in rear since few seemed to strike in our vicinity.

Then at 10:30 p.m. came a heavy enemy bombardment, directed mainly at the rear areas and at the rifle company in battalion reserve. Mustard gas alternated with high explosive. At company headquarters the officers expected an enemy attack to follow the bombardment but, since they could do nothing else, remained in their quarters waiting for their own machine gun barrage to start. In the gun positions the men were alert, but there was no expectation of attack as the projectiles were all going over, yet the gun crews waited ready by their weapons until the possible danger had passed.

The company report for the period 9 a.m. October 29 to 9 a.m. October 30 took the matter calmly.

> "Usual intermittent machine gun fire from Bois de Manheulles, probably a little less than on previous days and night," it narrated. "Considerable activity of enemy observing planes during day. At 3 p.m. a squadron of six enemy planes passed over our position traveling southeast and flying high. During the afternoon our artillery was registering on enemy woods both with high explosives and shrapnel. Enemy bombardment from 10:30 p.m. to about 3 a.m., most of the shells going in rear of P.C. Bordeaux and apparently many on Manheulles. No shells fell close to our position. Friendly artillery retaliated until about 5 a.m.

Usual work on dug-outs, trenches and emplacements. An anti-avion gun was installed on hill above and about 150 meters in rear of position No. 4 (Sergeant Joseph E. Taylor). The serviceable St. Etienne is being used for this work."

Though no casualties had been suffered by Company A, the rifle battalion to which it had been attached had not escaped so lightly. The reserve company had been making a relief when the quarry in

Anti-aircraft Hotchkiss machine gun, 129th Machine Gun Battalion (*National Archives*)

which it had been located was shelled, and the company returning from the front line thus came back into a gassed area worse, far worse, than the front line. Mustard gas casualties this night, or the next day as the result of the gas holes in the area, totaled over 80 serious enough to cause the victim to be sent back to hospital.

The next morning was calm enough except for the usual apparently aimless chatter of Maxim machine guns and the passing of enemy observation planes which drew heavy anti-aircraft fire, fragments from which descended on us.

It was either on this day or another that as I was wading down the muddy trench from our Ronvaux positions to those on Le Grand Mur I heard a fragment of anti-aircraft shell screaming down noisily. I stopped dead and the great fragment plopped loudly into the mud in the trench just in front of me. Steel helmets are very comforting articles of headgear on such occasions, though if that particular chunk of scrap-iron had lighted on mine it probably would have tested both it and its wearer's skull.

The report for the period from 9 a.m. October 30 to 9 a.m. October 31 contains the daily story of trench routine:

> "Short bursts of enemy machine gun fire during the day and night," it narrated. "Our position near Fond de la Chavee (Sergeant Snyder) swept by long range machine gun fire at 4:30 a.m. Our own artillery was registering on enemy positions during day. Batteries to rear of us were firing over us all night. About 11 p.m. enemy artillery shelled area back of our right and center with high explosive and gas. Three H.E.'s struck near our position in the region of Bernatant (Sergeant Clark's platoon). During the day both our own and enemy aircraft were active, and about 11:30 an enemy airplane dropped a large amount of propaganda printed in French over our positions. At 11:30 p.m. an enemy machine dropped five bombs between Haudiomont and Murauvaux Chateau. A search of our area yesterday failed to show any place where gas shells had fallen during bombardment of the previous night. A considerable number of Yellow Cross (mustard gas) fell on the road about 200 meters back of P.C. Bordeaux and these holes were treated by the infantry. Usual work on trenches, emplacements and dugouts."

The enemy artillery fire was heavy enough and close enough that I thought an enemy attack might be coming over, but there was nothing that I could do about it and I lay drowsily in my bunk—for that was my night to stay at the command post—fully dressed as always except for my shoes—waiting for our machine gun fire to open up before I sallied out to see how events went.

Quite a lively night.

At daybreak I was out to see what casualties, if any, my unit had suffered and I noticed a number of men staring curiously at the gas shell holes on the Route Nationale back of the PC, some to my chagrin, my own. I chased them away and immediately sent out a warning to my own men to avoid the gas area.

My own unit suffered no casualties from this gas attack—and had no occasion to suffer any since none of the shells containing the liquid had struck near our positions.

The reserve company of the rifle battalion suffered heavily however. It had just been relieved from the trenches by another company and came back into this unhappy situation.

The next morning there was a considerable line of men at the dressing station in PC Bordeaux waiting for the doctor to look at them. Despite the fact that the gas holes had been treated with lime and covered up, the line the second morning was longer, some of the men's eyes severely affected. My impression at the time was that between 50 and 60 men of this company had to be evacuated as a result of the enemy's use of this persistent gas. Someone—I forgot who—told me later that the number was near 80.

I also felt at the time that many of the casualties were due to poor gas discipline but not unlikely this was unjust. In retrospect it seems probable to me that the gas had splashed about for some distance and, while men had felt secure after the holes had been treated, the heat of the sun the next day caused the whole area to be dangerous.

The gas bombardment seems to have been on a wide front, nor were all the machine gun companies spared. Farther north, near Watronville, Capt. Mark Springer, commander of Co. D, 130th Machine Gun Battalion, was severely gassed that night along with one of his lieutenants and 11 of his men.[20]

The episode of the airplane bombs perhaps deserves more attention than given it in the daily report. Each of these explosions shook the region and the raid caused some momentary perturbation in Sergeant George A. Snyder's section on the extreme right. The plane was dropping its bombs in a line heading in its direction and the fifth one which exploded near the ruins of the once-pretentious Murauvaux Chateau was only a couple of hundred yards distant. There is said to have been some holding of breath in the section until it was evident that the plane had no more explosive to drop.

The day of October 31 was relatively calm.

> "Some enemy snipers working during day in Massenoue woods," recites the daily report. "Usual machine gun fire in Bois de Massenoue. This fire of the enemy machine guns is not only ineffective but seems vague and at random. Desultory artillery fire during day by both sides. Enemy observing planes up at intervals. About 2 p.m. a hostile machine dropped a large amount of propaganda over our lines but the wind carried it to the southeast and none of it came to earth in this vicinity. A bundle of propaganda

20. Mark Dooley Springer, born in West Plains, Missouri, on October 9, 1883, died on June 15, 1959. He was severely wounded on October 30, 1918.

> apparently dropped some days ago was found about 100 meters north of P.C. Bordeaux. It is printed in English and copies of it are attached hereto. A friendly airplane fired into the Bois de Massenoue with machine gun using tracer bullets at 4:30 p.m."

The propaganda referred to in this report was a small handbill printed on both sides and consisting of extracts of official notes. It was headed, "What Are We Fighting For," and first had an extract of the German note of October 4, 1918, to President Wilson, asking an armistice so that a peace might be concluded on the basis of the terms laid down in the president's message to the American Congress January 8, 1918. Next was the reply of President Wilson dated October 8 asking a clarification of the German note. Then in answer to this was the German reply of October 12 apparently acceding to everything Mr. Wilson asked. The hand bill then concluded with a query in big, black type, "Why Are We Still Fighting?"

Sometimes the leaflets were in French and the subject matter in these cases was considerable different. One of the leaflets purported to be written by "A Poilu who does not want to rot in the trenches." It stated that the French had been trying to defeat the Germans for four years and had never been successful and never could be.

There had been enough ruin and desolation. There had been enough loss of life. It was better to make peace at once and stop the war. Of course the Americans were coming in but they were amateurs at war and could cut no figure. The British had ever thrown the bulk of the fighting on the French. It was time to make peace while the Germans were willing—and so on to the same effect. Sometimes the leaflets were in French on one side and English on the other but the tune was always the same, "Let us stop fighting and have peace."[21] "Enough of death!

21. Hobart Havens of Company A sent a translation of the poster, written in "very poor French," to his parents in Carthage: "They Won't Get Them, The Boches! No, they will not get them! Here we are at the same point where we were last year—stopped in front of their lines. We are done for, the Boches have been too clever for us—ah, the wicked ones! At the beginning we seemed to be doing well, but what are we doing now? The Boches have taken Rheims in spite of us. The Yanks have done what they could, it is true, but it has cost them dear to be novices in a war like this and it will bring them nothing! Instead of the Boches, who we thought we could capture by millions, we have had our country devastated, bridges blown up and towns burned, and after four years we are no better off than we were at first. We were going to have victory over them at the Somme, but the Boches were too much for

Enough of ruin! What good to continue after four years of vain effort?" This was the tenor of the little hand bill. The same day Turkey threw up her hands and accepted an armistice on terms equivalent to surrender. The Austrian Army, crushed on the Piave, was streaming back in confusion and Austria was pleading for an armistice. Even the Germans haggling over a possible armistice was becoming rather frantic and to observers away from the scene of action it was plain that she soon would be forced to terms if the pressure continued.

German planes were frequently overhead and dropped considerable propaganda as well as firing down at our trenches. Our own planes were active against ground targets, at times one swooping down over the Bois de Manheulles almost to the tree-tops, raking it with machine gun fire. This last made an interesting spectacle from our lines and was highly perilous for the flier since naturally heavy fire was drawn from the woods.

Annoyed by the propaganda dropped I had Sergeant Taylor in the position south of the Ravin-de-la-Fosse-a-Greve rig up the serviceable one of the two French St. Etienne machine guns, which he had inherited with his position, to use for anti-aircraft fire.

The planes which strafed our trenches swept down along the hill—over the valley—so low that Taylor could not reach them, but the propaganda planes usually flew higher and over the hill so there would be some hope of striking one of them.

Soon after this gun was installed I was standing out by the Route Nationale in front of PC Bordeaux when I saw an enemy plane zoom over, showering hand bills. I looked toward Taylor's position and listened for his gun to start shooting.

The piece remained silent and the plane disappeared.

In a rage I strode to Taylor's position and made the remarks appropriate to the occasion. The sergeant had not been at the gun himself and the man at the piece had become rattled or something when the enemy plane appeared and it was gone before he collected his wits. The sergeant had just finished scorching him when I arrived.

---

us. They are now well installed in their fine positions and are waiting to receive us—what a joke! This time surprising them will not help us—fogs, tanks or artillery, these boches will hold on. We have had enough of death and ruin. What good is it to continue longer—after four years of vain efforts. We will never get them! Such is the impression of a Poilu, who does not care to rot in the trenches." *Carthage* (MO) *Evening Press*, December 7, 1918.

Determined not to fail again, the sergeant thereafter spent much time at the piece himself.

He thus was waiting and alert when a plane, flying close to the ground and from the direction of the enemy, westward bound, came directly toward his position.

The sergeant opened fire and the plane immediately rose and banked so as to show American markings. Taylor's fire ceased abruptly.

That mistake was humiliation for the zealous sergeant as well as for his captain.

I had run to the road from the quarry as soon as the firing started and knew at once what had happened. Major O'Connor came rushing out too, demanding:

"Why is that machine gun firing?"

I pointed silently to the plane and he grunted and returned to his command post, presumably supposing that it was the plane which fired. Happily for me he did not know that it was my gun which had been shooting at one of our own planes.

Once more I hastened to Taylor's position but this time less in anger than in regret mixed with apprehension. I have always been more kindly disposed toward excess of zeal than to lack of it and I could easily see how the mistake had occurred. I also could see that I probably would have to answer for the error to higher headquarters. My immediate objective was securing statements from the sergeant and the witnesses of his section as to how it occurred so I could submit them as evidence for the defense—that the plane was flying from the direction of the enemy and with no markings visible so it reasonably was supposed that it was a German one.

I secured the written statements but to my pleased surprise I never was called upon to submit them.

Later I learned that battalion headquarters had handled the whole matter for me.

The air corps had indeed complained—I can imagine the pilot's remarks when he landed—but when the complaint came through, Major Halliburton had blandly replied in positive tone without being hampered by any knowledge of the facts.

The lines near Haudiomont were close together, he had written, and the pilot undoubtedly had been fired upon by a German machine gun which he erroneously had believed to have been an American one. That answer seemed sufficient since no more was heard of it. As for Sergeant Taylor, when he finally learned of battalion headquarters' answer, he was so pleased that I was not going to be put in a hot spot by his mistake that he wasn't even angry because battalion headquarters had called him a German.

The tempo of both friendly and hostile artillery fire had been increasing so that we had come to accept it as a matter of course, particularly since few of the enemy shells fell on us.

In my daily written report, in which I meant to include about everything warlike, I made only the most casual mention of it: "Desultory artillery fire by both sides during day (Oct. 31). During the night (Oct. 31–Nov. 1) our artillery was active, and the enemy was fairly so during the early part. Enemy projectiles fell well to the rear."

Each day in the Sommedieue sector east of Verdun in early November, 1918, the Carthage machine gunners near Haudiomont stirred restlessly in their trenches as they heard the constant angry thudding of artillery fire which centered in the northwest; daily they stared across the rain-sodden plain, past ruins, wire entanglement and the wreck of a fallen airplane, to dripping woods where the enemy lurked; constantly there were sentries on the alert; always there was a man at each gun ready to open fire.

Wise-cracks, jokes, anathemas at the mud, anecdotes, speculation concerning the enemy, and a looking forward to the food which came from the company kitchen twice a day—this was the life of the soldier lounging or working in trench or reclining in damp dug-outs. Hostile machine gun fire was a matter of course, though the bullets seldom endangered one; on the eastern skyline a wall of German captive balloons rose each morning to watch until some Allied airmen endangered them by an approach; overhead hostile aircraft soared occasionally amid blotches of American shell-bursts, and the singing fragments from above rained down and spatted in the mud of the trenches or jingled in the barbed wire.

On the early morning of November 1 in a new coordinated attack on the whole active Meuse-Argonne front the American army surged forward. Although so near to this great battle and with the thudding of its cannon constantly in their ears—and indeed forming in a sense a part of the operation—the Carthage machine gun company in the 35th Division helped hold the ground which the great American army was using as a pivot, and had no knowledge that anything greater than the usual day by day fighting was in progress. At 3:30 a.m. on the morning of this November 1 the 35th Division artillery had opened fire in a demonstration to aid the attack to the left by leading the enemy to think it might strike on this front also and in a five hour bombardment some 30,000 shells, about 100 a minute, were fired by the three regiments. The 129th Field Artillery alone fired 10,000 rounds in this affair, Jay Lee's history of that regiment records.

It is a testimony as to the proportions to which the daily artillery firing had grown that the Company A activity report dismissed this bombardment in a few words.

The day of November 1 was one of heavy fog, and in the Company A sector men moving from one position to another avoided the tugging mud of the trenches by clambering on the surface and picking their way through the barbed wire at places where normal exposure above the parapets would mean death.

November 2 both our own and the enemy artillery were firing away at intervals and bursts of enemy machine gun fire swept our positions north of Haudiomont. Several times enemy planes flew low over our trenches but sheltered from Taylor's fire by their lowness and the intervening hills.

> "Usual enemy machine gun fire in the enemy lines during the day and night," recited the daily report for the 24 hour period ending at 9 a.m. November 3. "Several bursts struck in the vicinity of our positions north of Haudiomont. (Sergeant Huff). Both our own and enemy artillery were firing at intervals throughout the period, most of the enemy projectiles going to our right rear. Our section south of Ronvaux (Sergeant Akin) reports that at 3:30 a.m. a new enemy battery, or one which has heretofore been inactive, began firing from somewhere in the woods opposite them. This battery is farther forward than any which have previously fired. It threw ten shells somewhere in our rear area at 3:30 and five more at 5 a.m. Several enemy airplanes flew low over

> our positions during the day. At 11:35 a.m. one dropped a considerable amount of propaganda which fell in C.R. Ronvaux. No copies of this were found in our area."[22]

Aerial activity was increasing.

The enemy was very clearly apprehensive that the offensive would be extended to our front.

Following is the daily Company A report for the 24-hour period ending at 9 a.m. November 4:

> "Increase in enemy machine gun fire in Bois de Massenoue and Bois de Manheulles. Decrease in artillery fire, both allied and enemy. A few gas shells fell somewhere to our left between 7:00 and 8:00 p.m. There was considerable aerial activity during the day. At 11:50 an allied plane flew very low over the Bois de Manheulles, almost to the tree tops, and drew fire from two machine guns and one rifleman. At 3:30 p.m. 32 allied planes passed over our lines flying north. At 4:15 an enemy observation balloon off to our left front was brought down in flames by one of our airplanes. About the same time a French plane flew low over the woods to our front and fired into them with a machine gun using tracer bullets. Usual work on trenches, including the repair of some caved in by the rain."

And there were things going on which were beyond our scope of understanding, such as: "A large fire was observed back of the enemy lines at 9:05 p.m. and searchlights were operating in their back areas most of the night."

And during the early forenoon of November 4 there occurred an enemy incident which salved my injured pride somewhat.

A German plane flew low over the Bois de Manheulles and was fired upon by the German machine guns in the wood. The enemy made mistakes too! Some German machine gun officer probably would have to sweat about that one—unless he could convince his superiors that my guns had done it.

By this time a number of our men who had been wounded, and not too seriously, in the fighting in late September, were trickling back, quite proud of their scars. Lieutenants Dunn and Wardin

22. In a letter home, Cecil Stemmons of Company A described two downed German planes lying in "No Man's Land." One had caught fire in mid-air, he reported, then the pilot had jumped. *Carthage* (MO) *Evening Press*, December 4, 1918.

came back also from the 138th Infantry and resumed their old positions, Lieut. Snyder going back to the first platoon and Lieut. Bourne, relieved by Wardin with the company train, came back forward and took over the second platoon.

There was something fascinating and mentally restful about this peaceful life we were living on a quiet battle front. One floundered through muddy trenches to visit gun positions except in the region of Bernatant where it was normal to use paths in the dripping beechwoods. And I stared daily across the rain-sodden plain, past ruins and rusty belts of ancient barbed wire, to the dark damp woods where the enemy lay hidden. And daily I gazed speculatively at the wreckage of a crashed airplane weathering in the unoccupied ground east of Haudiomont. There was constant study of methods to improve the defensive fires of the machine guns. And daily in our forward company headquarters I personally pecked out typewritten reports of the doings in the 24-hour period ending at 9 a.m.

Yet off to the north the guns were constantly thudding in the active battle and that was, it seemed, where we should be. Moreover it certainly was where we would be going soon. The 35th Division had rested enough.

Soon, I reflected restlessly, I could try out by [my] new ideas of close support of rifle units by machine guns through every phase of the fighting. And soon there might be an opportunity to get revenge on the Germans for the men I had lost in the Argonne and who, I felt had not been adequately revenged at the time. I wanted to see dead Germans piled up in front of my guns as I had seen our own dead of the 138th Infantry windrowed along that road at Cheppy. I had not done as well in that first battle, it seemed to me, as I should have done and could now do. I wanted to shoot at the enemy—and here I was in easy range, with him shooting at my positions occasionally and I was not even permitted to harass him by return fire. Back in the battle there would be an open season again.

I gave no serious thoughts to any impending peace because a considerable part of the hostile army was still undefeated—including that part in front of us—and everywhere he was fighting hard. Now that he was shaken and giving ground on the decisive fronts he certainly would be pressed until his forces were shattered and broken.

On November 5 at 9 a.m. the following report went in:

> "Some sniping from enemy positions during the day and the usual machine gun fire. There was some scattered rifle fire from both his lines and our own during the night, probably about 60 shots. There was a slight increase in the activity of the enemy machine guns and this morning the hill south of Ronvaux was swept by fire, about 25 shots of which struck near our northernmost gun positions (Sergeant Akin). Very little artillery fire from either side during period. Early yesterday morning an enemy plane flew low over our front trenches and dropped a large amount of the usual peace propaganda. This time the matter was printed in English on one side and French on the other. A copy of it is attached. During the early forenoon an enemy plane over the Bois de Manheulles was fired upon by his own machine guns in the woods. At 4:30 p.m. two enemy observation balloons were brought down in flames by our aircraft. During the night the enemy sent up 14 flares in our immediate front. Soon after daybreak the enemy dropped smoke bombs along the edge of the woods held by him opposite our positions, 'as if to cover the withdrawal of his forward guns' states the sergeant (Akin) in charge of the nearest section."

But the war continued. The Allied high command planned a huge offensive in the Metz area and since the 35th Division was scheduled to take part in this its relief from the Sommedieue sector commenced.

Then after I typed my 9 a.m. report that morning I received orders that my company would be relieved that night by Company D, 318th Machine Gun Battalion, 81st Division.

Now we would go some place where firing of machine guns by Americans at Germans was legal and authorized, I thought.

I issued my company order:

> "This company will be relieved tonight by Company D, 318th Machine Gun Battalion. After the relief the company will assemble at the point where the transport is now located.
>
> Guides from Sergeant Snyder's, Palmer's, Clark's and Taylor's sections will be at the crossroads (Carrefour de

> Bernatant) at 7 p.m., will report to Lieut. Smith, 318th Machine Gun Battalion, and will lead the sections he designates to relieve their own. Guides from Sergeant Huff's and Akin's sections will be at the company kitchen (P.C. Bordeaux) at 7 p.m.
>
> The transport officer will have guides (wagoners) at the crossroads (Carrefour de Bernatant) from 8:30 until the relief is completed to guide the returning sections to the proper camp.
>
> The incoming unit will be given all possible information both of our own positions and those of the enemy. Our men will not leave until the guns of the new organization are laid upon their proper barrage lines.
>
> Upon being relieved, Sergeants Snyder's, Palmer's, Clark's and Taylor's sections will move directly back to the assembly point. Their guns will be taken back on the carts of the 318th which will have its transport at the point we now have ours. Sergeants Huff and Akin will move their sections back to the company kitchen and their guns at that point will be loaded on one of our big cars.
>
> One man of each section will remain in the positions until morning. At 7 a.m. they will assemble at the company PC and will report to Sergeant Miles who will conduct them back to the transport location.
>
> As soon as the relief is completed a message will be sent to me at the company PC notifying me of that fact."

Another note sent to Lieut. Herbert Warden, company transport officer, directed that three trucks be sent to the company kitchen as soon after dark as possible and that four guides be used at the Carrefour de Bernatant. Lieut. Frank L. Snyder was to remain in the line with Company D, 318th Machine Gun Battalion, 24 hours after his own company left.

This done I wandered about as usual.

Capt. Russell T. Kerby, commander of the relieving company, rode in soon after dark.[23] He wanted some place in the quarry to

23. Russell Taylor Kerby was born in Brooklyn, New York, on November 15, 1892. He entered a civil engineering degree at Cornell in 1913 and entered active service as an infantry second lieutenant in May 1917 and was promoted to captain that August. Kerby served overseas from July 1918 to June 1919. He died in Summit, New Jersey, on August 25, 1969. *The Ithaca* (NY) *Journal*, August 26, 1969.

stable his horse. He planned to use it to inspect his machine gun positions, he said.

I took him in and explained the situation, pointing out on the map our positions. It wouldn't be practicable, I told him, to use a horse in the trenches. I only half convinced him I think, in view of the extent covered by the southern gun positions, but Lieutenant Snyder was to remain with him 24 hours and I expect their tour of the trenches the next days was convincing enough.

A pleasant officer, Captain Kerby, and I chatted with him in our dug-out plastered with the art of *La Vie Parisienne*, or on the hill above from which we could overlook the front, until in message from the last section to be relieved reached me.

I looked at the hour on the message.

Relief completed at 1:30 a.m.

Then I departed, crossing over Taylor's section and thence southwest over an unused road in a valley marked on the map with the pleasant name of Ravin-de-la Fontaine-St. Robert.

In due time I reached the Carrefour de Bernatant, found guides waiting and proceeded to the bivouac area where I arrived around 4 a.m.

My service in the Sommedieue sector was over.

The last company activity report in the Sommedieue sector, covering the 24-hour period ending a.m. November 6, is as follows:

> "A few snipers on each side fired at intervals during forenoon. Usual machine gun fire in Bois de Massenoue. Enemy artillery fire from 11:00 a.m. to 1:00 p.m., about 25 shots in all. Most of these went to our rear and six fell near Villers-Sous-Bonchamp. At 4:15 p.m. five high explosive shells struck in the vicinity of our position south of Ronvaux, one striking just in front of an emplacement. Airplanes of both sides active during day. A number of flares sent up by the enemy during the night. This company was relieved by Company D, 318th Machine Gun Battalion, during night. The relief was completed in the trenches at 1:30 a.m. and the company assembled at the transport camp near P.C. Toulon, the last section arriving here at 3:30 a.m."

The last enlisted men of Company A to leave the front lines here, the six men who had remained with the incoming sections until morning, reported to Sergeant Clint Miles at P.C. Bordeaux at 7 a.m. the morning of November 6 and were by him conducted to the rear. First Lieut. Frank L. Snyder remained with the captain of Company D, 318th Machine Gun Battalion until after dark November 6 when one of the machine gun trucks of Company A called for him and carried him up to rejoin his company which was then on the move.

When Company A, 128th Machine Gun Battalion was relieved from the trenches in the Sommedieue sector southeast of Verdun in the late hours of November 5 and the early ones of November 6, 1918, it thought with some feeling of superiority that it was going to an active front, back into the "big show," whereas its successors in the trenches here would have the same quiet routine it had had.

In the meanwhile the rest of Company A had spent the day in the vicinity of the 69th Brigade headquarters, the men of the transport which had been stationed there all the time enlarging on the number of artillery projectiles which had struck in the vicinity. This sector, they averred, probably with some accuracy, was one that was more dangerous in the rear areas than in the front trenches. The shells we had heard screaming overhead in CR Haudiomont had gone somewhere and this region had probably received its share.

Only a part of the 35th Division had been relieved the preceding night, the 137th Infantry and Company B of our own battalion, as I recall, staying in until the night of the 6th. Brig. Gen. Louis M. Nuttman, whom I had met as a colonel at Charpentry and Baulny, was still in command at PC Toulon. Major Halliburton was to remain with him as acting brigade machine gun officer until the brigade's relief was complete.

At 2:30 the afternoon of the 6th I received written orders to march my company that night "to Erize la Petite, via Recourt-Heippes-Chaumont."

At 5 p.m. the 128th Machine Gun Battalion, reunited now, left the vicinity of P.C. Toulon with written orders to march to Erize-la-Petite some 30 miles or so distant. This was a big order for one night's march by a foot column but verbal information from good authority said it was expected that trucks would be waiting in Genicourt, in the Meuse valley some 12 or 13 miles distant, to take the marching part of the battalion the rest of the way.

Moving with 100-meter intervals between platoons to lessen the danger of loss from shell fire in the event the enemy should begin a bombardment, Company A wound down the road southwestward through beech-covered hills toward Sommedieue as dusk changed into the darkness of night. Occasional lights flashed from incautiously opened dug-out doors on the hillsides, the newly-arrived division apparently not having fully learned as yet the dangers thus invited, but the enemy artillery remained silent and the machine gunners wound down the road toward Rattentout in peace.

It was a serene enough hike.

At Rattantout a shadowy column of trucks was waiting. These, it developed, were the ones which I had been told might meet me at Genicourt. So much the better that they were up here.

The unit was quickly entrucked, and whisked away westward across the Meuse and out of range of enemy guns. Dieue, Ancemont, Senoncourt, Issoncourt—half-seen places these with buildings veiled in darkness. Then came Chaumont-sur-Aire and just across the river from it the tiny town of Erize-la-Petite. Here the soldiers detrucked, formed up in the darkness, and melted away in little detachments to the billets in loft and barn and abandoned buildings.

The 35th Division (less artillery) was now in First Army reserve.

It was already November 7, and later, after the soldiers had roused from their belated slumbers, they wandered about to stare at the muddy, bedraggled village, undamaged by war, which was their temporary home. Back in their real home town of Carthage, Mo., that evening, the *Press* carried banner heads saying that American troops had reached Sedan and that a revolution had broken out in Germany.

The Carthage men had expected to go back in the active part of the Meuse-Argonne offensive but the enemy was crumbling fast, and on November 8 the 35th Division became a part of the reserve of the Second Army instead of the First. A new great offensive to break through east of Metz had been planned for November 14, and the 35th Division was to be one of the assault divisions in that attack.

On the morning of November 9 there was the roar of a tremendous bombardment from the direction of the front. We did not know it but the 81st Division which had relieved us was attacking that morning, supported by our artillery, its own artillery brigade not being with it. Had someone told me this fact I perhaps would have been skeptical. Far too wide a front, I would have thought, for an attack.

On the morning of November 11 the attack was renewed and the enemy outpost line at the edge of the woods taken, but the Germans who had adroitly worked out a scheme of interlocking bands of machine gun fire through the timber, successfully held their main line of resistance until the Armistice became effective. The 81st Division losses were severe, but to the left and to the right greater gains were made than near Hadiomont [Haudiomont].

One thing that mystified me for some years was the report—repeated in General Pershing's Memoirs and included in the official "Order of Battle—Divisions" (1931)—that on November 9 the 81st had captured Manheulles.

This village east of Haudimont [Haudiomont] had been held by the 35th the night we left the front and so presumably the 81st had it to start with. The Battle Monuments Commission dug into this matter and makes it clear in its guide book that this outpost was already held the morning of November 9. But in truth the village was very isolated and to reach it in strength the 81st probably had to undergo a terrific artillery fire as it advanced from the south.

On November 9 the 128th moved southeastward 12 miles but, wishing to spare his soldiers' strength for the hard days that he believed lay ahead, Major Halliburton avoided any foot-marching this day by having his motor column make two trips, thus carrying the entire unit.

Between the two great wars this method of movement was advocated as something new under the name of "shuttling." It wasn't new. For that matter it wasn't new when Major Halliburton used [it]. It was a common sense method anyone might think of and there are various earlier historical examples.

The road was a poplar-bordered highway, up the tiny Exrule River most of the way, through Erize-le-Grande, Rosnes, Erize-la-Brules, Rument and Erize-St. Dizier. The recurrence of towns of similar names struck the solders' fancy, recalling an old troop train joke. There were as many places named Erize in France, they said, as there were named Derail in the United States.

At Erize-St. Dizier the road left the stream valley, shifted to the east over a hill, then down into another valley and into the village of La Valee [La Vallee] where we were to be billeted.

The southeastward march of the 35th Division had been halted a day or two previously in the St. Mihiel area and the 128th was quartered in the westernmost of the towns occupied by the division. For some days it looked as though an armistice might soon be signed but the likelihood of peace was takely [taken] calmly enough by the army, almost treated as if it was of no importance.

There was war talk as well as peace talk in La Vallee that evening. The place was a bee-hive of activity. Some other division as well as our own was passing through, eastward bound. It was a crossroads village and a military police detachment on duty there had its hands full in regulating traffic.

There was to be a big offensive somewhere, the villagers said. For days long columns of French artillery had been passing through the village moving eastward—other troops too, but it was the great amount of artillery which had impressed the villagers. They had seen much of the passage of armies but they had never seen that amount of artillery before, all on the move at once.

What they had seen, and the movement of which we were a part, was the concentrating of forces for the offensive scheduled for November 14. Twenty French divisions and six American divisions—the 3rd, 4th, 28th, 29th, 35th and 36th—were to participate in a drive east of the Moselle River in the direction of Chateau-Salins with the objective of breaking through east of Metz.

Yet if reliance was to be placed in the newspaper reports, the Germans were about to yield.

But instead of moving again on November 10 as expected our own battalion was directed to stay at La Vallee. There was much talk of an armistice. There was a revolution in Germany. Kaiser Wilhelm had abdicated the previous day and fled to Holland. The stopping of our eastward movement seemed confirmation of newspaper reports that the finish was near.

This was Sunday and I spent it exploring the country about the town, noting particularly the belts of barbed wire entanglement at the eastern bases of the hills. This was far from the front—10 or 12 miles west of the westernmost part of the old St. Mihiel salient—but the French at one time apparently had organized the whole country to some extent so as to be ready in case of a further German advance.

The next morning there was a tremendous cannonading. Later I learned that our forces were attacking everywhere. At the time I thought it sounded as if both the Allied and the German artillery were trying to fire away all of their ammunition before the war could stop.

As I dropped back to my billet after breakfast, the old man in whose home I was quartered asked me if an armistice had been signed. I didn't know. He shook his head rather sadly and pointed toward the sound of the guns.

At 9 a.m. I was on the nose of a hill overlooking the town from the southwest, planning a company maneuver for that afternoon—machine guns supporting infantry in attack.

At that hour I heard the church bell in La Vallee start to ring. The church bells in all other villages began ringing too. I knew the armistice had been signed.

As is well known, French peasants instead of living on their land reside in villages from which they go to and from their work daily. Each village had a church and every bell was ringing without ceasing.

From the hill where I stood the sound was one of indescribable beauty—bells near at hand and bells in the remote distance all blending in a joyful harmony. And behind the sound of the bells was the ceaseless angry roar of artillery fire from east, northeast and north.

All along the front the Americans were attacking, and busy artillerymen were feeding the hungry guns—yet all over the Allied world the bells were ringing.

Then at 11 o'clock the noise of cannon fire ceased. The war was over. The peace had been signed at 5 a.m. to become effective at 11 a.m. The sound of the bells in the church at La Vallee mingled musically with the sound of those in neighboring villages.

It was a strange silence even for me. But it was only a matter of months that I had been hearing artillery fire whereas the villagers of La Vallee had heard it every day for over four years. Its cessation must have seemed stranger to them.

That afternoon I went ahead and held the maneuver which I had worked out during the forenoon.

All day the church bells clanged their joy at the victory after four years of effort and toward evening some small boys paraded the streets singing "Madelon" and the "Marseillaise." They had a brightly polished trumpet which they sounded from time to time. Some of them carried placards showing the military class they would belong to—most or all of them in the 1920s—if they were called up.

In La Vallee these things constituted the celebration of this greatest event of modern history.

There was a holiday air. "It seems almost like Christmas," one of the machine gunners wrote home.

The war was over; the army would soon be going home and that was certainly occasion for rejoicing. Yet there had not been a complete victory. There was merriment in the billets, but with a more somber under-current.

The men of our battalion took the armistice with the same outward indifference that they had learned to take all things. Probably most of them rejoiced inwardly that the war was over. Probably others regretted a little that the opportunity to square old scores with the enemy had passed forever.

Discussion at our officers mess that night of course was on the one topic—peace.

"We had 'em groggy," I insisted, speaking of the war as a whole, "and we ought to have gone ahead and knocked them out."

"Schrantz," replied Major Halliburton, "you are the only man in the world who isn't glad the war is over."

"You're still mad because of the men you had killed," said Captain Corey. "You think you have scores to settle. You want to kill more Germans. But in settling the scores you would get more men killed and that would be still more scores to settle. That kind of thing could go on indefinitely."

Major Halliburton wondered if we should take precautions against any undue celebration by the men. Maybe they might get to firing their pistols in the air or something.

I didn't think it necessary. I believed that too many of them felt as I did. Sergeant Snyder—First Sergeant George A. Snyder, could handle the situation as regarded A Company.

There were great tales told of the delirious celebration of the Armistice in Paris that day and evening—something the same in other French cities. All the women in the crowds kissing everyone in uniform. It seems to have been a great kissing occasion from the stories told.

I only remember one of the stories—one told to me by a nurse I met on a train going to southern France on leave some months later. She had been on duty at a hospital in Paris at the time.

Late in the evening one of the convalescent officers who had been out on the streets all day wandered back in quite unsteady on his feet from the liquid celebration in which he had been imbibing.

He met a nurse as he entered, grabbed her in his arms and suddenly kissed her.

She reacted with a violent slap to his face. In his unsteady condition the blow was too much for his equilibrium.

Seated on the floor, rubbing his cheek where the slap had landed, he looked up at the angry woman in shocked surprise.

"Well," he said slowly. "This is the coldest reception I have received today."

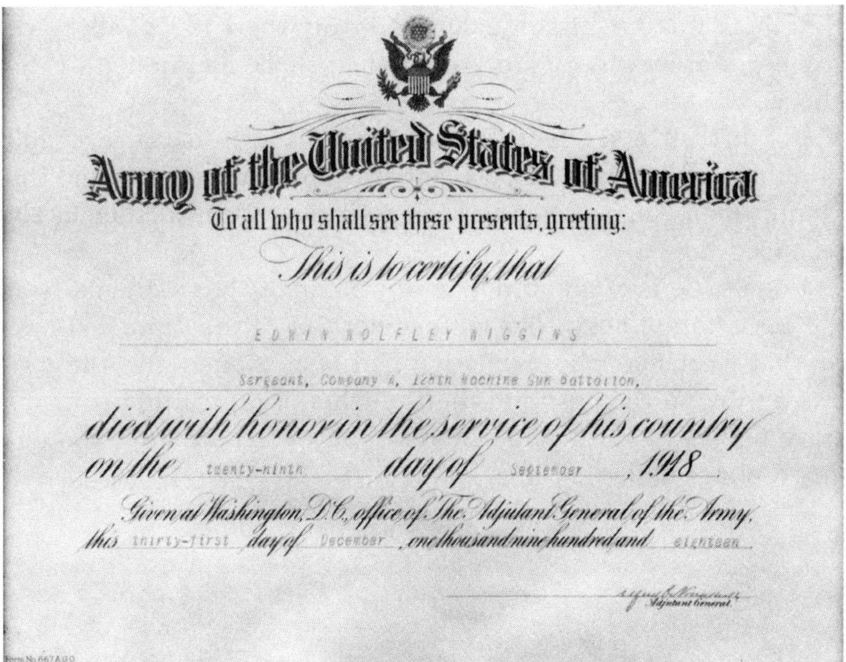

Army of the United States of America

To all who shall see these presents, greeting:

This is to certify that

EDWIN WOLFLEY WIGGINS

Sergeant, Company A, 128th Machine Gun Battalion,

died with honor in the service of his country on the twenty-ninth day of September, 1918.

Given at Washington, D.C., office of The Adjutant General of the Army, this thirty-first day of December, one thousand nine hundred and eighteen

Adjutant General.

Form No. 667 A.G.O.
June 15, 1918

Memorial Certificate for Edwin Wiggins (*Memorial Hall, Carthage, MO*)

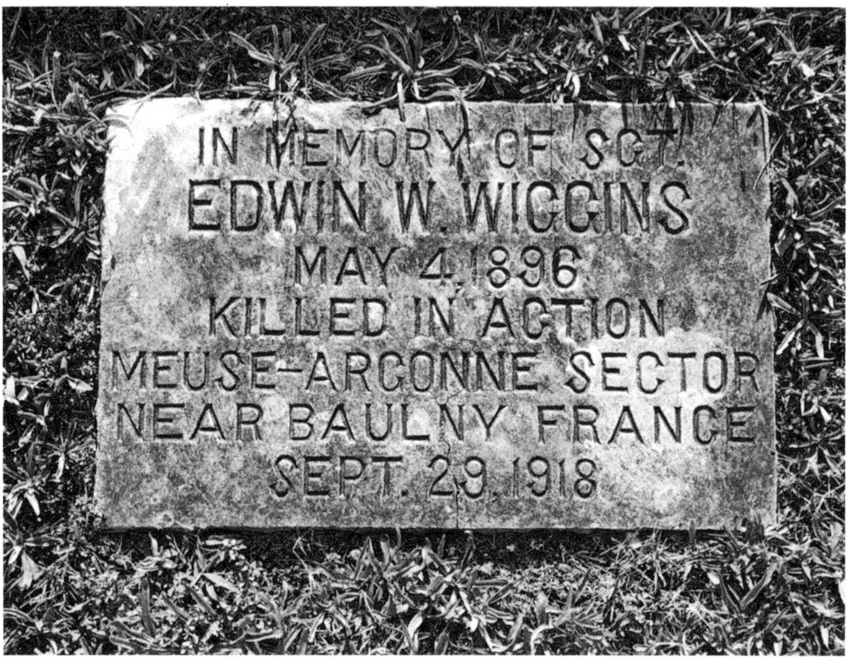

Edwin Wiggins Memorial Marker, Park Cemetery, Carthage (*Author's collection*)

If there was any kissing celebration anywhere in La Vallee—or any celebration of any kind other than those mentioned—I did not see it.

For myself I sat long that night staring into the fire and thinking of Wiggins, Edwards, Pallardy, Cassaday, Neely and the infantryman Angus dead and, by us at least, still inadequately revenged.[24]

I like to believe that others of my company heard the news of the cessation of hostilities with something of the same feelings. Be that as it may the Armistice had been signed and the war was a thing of the past and the thoughts of returning to our far away homes in the United States soon overcame any momentary feelings of depression.

24. According to Lt. Cecil Stemmons, Schrantz felt "very keenly the loss of Edwards, Wiggins and the others and shows it." *Carthage* (MO) *Evening Press*, January 9, 1919.

Chapter 16

Peace

Although the exhausted men of Company A were relieved that the fighting was over, Major Halliburton reminded them that an even more insidious foe than the German Army lurked on the Western Front. Influenza, the dreaded "Spanish Flu," had already killed or incapacitated large numbers in all armies. Halliburton sought to limit the exposure of his men by ordering his soldiers to "sleep as far from your immediate neighbors as possible." Men were to sleep alternately, head to foot, and not "pool" bed coverings when it was cold. They were not to cough or sneeze in each other's faces, use clean handkerchiefs, and not spit indoors (except into a receptacle), or on paths, steps, or in corners. Non-commissioned officers were to keep watch on their men, report any ailments, and see that the men obeyed these orders. Either due to Halliburton's directive, luck, or a combination of both, the 128th Machine Gun Battalion avoided large scale sickness from the "flu."[1]

Although Schrantz and his men wanted to return home as soon as possible, it was simply impossible for the Americans to immediately ship 2,000,000 troops back across the Atlantic. In addition, there was the unlikely possibility that the Germans

1. Memo, Headquarters, 128th Machine Gun Battalion, November 8, 1918, Record Group 120, Records of the American Expeditionary Forces, World War I Organization Records, Machine Gun Battalions, 128th Machine Gun Battalion, Box 266, NARA.

would refuse to negotiate a peace treaty and force the A.E.F. to return to combat operations. Much to the dismay and annoyance of the average doughboy, General Pershing ordered training exercises to begin again to incorporate the lessons learned from the Meuse-Argonne. "Men who had dug in more than once under fire," the historian of the 140th Infantry wrote, "and sometimes with the lid to a mess-kit were taught to dig trenches," while men who had taken machine gun nests without artillery support "were taught how to attack machine guns by men who had never faced them."[2] As the weeks wore on and it became readily apparent that the enemy was not interested in renewing the struggle, soldiers such as the men of Company A became increasingly disgruntled with the training schedule and the fact that they remained in Europe with no clear purpose. (The 35th was not selected as one of the divisions to enter Germany as part of the Army of Occupation.)

The A.E.F. commander-in-chief wisely reduced the amount of training and increased opportunities for troops to visit leave areas at resorts in France and Germany. The A.E.F. offered educational opportunities in the form of a vast school system, ultimately enrolling more than a quarter of a million troops. Classes covered practically every subject, including vocational instruction, and were offered by competent instructors. Athletic events, horse shows and traveling theatrical troupes were organized to help break the monotony. On at least one occasion, the 128th held a drill competition and athletic events, with small prizes.[3]

Major Halliburton made certain that discipline was enforced when it seemed that his bored men were beginning to commit petty theft. On December 5, a memorandum that was read to the battalion noted that complaints had been made by French property owners that soldiers were stealing wood and straw. Any soldiers taking either, or any other private property, would be placed under arrest and tried, Halliburton warned, and the value of the property charged against him. Even more serious, if a man was found in possession of private property, wood, straw or furniture, every man in his billet would be charged. If the offenders could not be found, the entire company or detachment would bear the cost. To help keep the men entertained, the battalion chaplain announced that

2. Edwards, *From Doniphan to Verdun*, 126.

3. Memo, Headquarters, 128th Machine Gun Battalion, March 6, 1919, Record Group 120, Records of the American Expeditionary Forces, World War I Organization Records, Machine Gun Battalions, 128th Machine Gun Battalion, Box 263, NARA.

he was leading a "songfest," with "new marching songs and popular songs," and urged all the men to attend.[4]

One of the most memorable events in the post-Armistice period, and perhaps the most striking display of martial glory experienced by the 128th Machine Gun Battalion, came during a formal review by General Pershing on February 17, 1919. It was a rare opportunity for them to come face to face with their fellow Missourian, the legendary commander who had led the American Expeditionary Forces to victory, and the Prince of Wales.

Detailed orders were issued for the review, instructing the men of the 35th Division to appear with full packs, helmets, gas masks, and fixed bayonets. Officers were to appear in "long coats" with side arms. The men were also ordered to carry "an emergency lunch"—a corned beef sandwich and a canteen of coffee.

On the rainy, dreary day of the review, some units were forced to march 12 or 15 miles to reach the plain where the event was to be held. Unit commanders had to carefully time their departure so as not to block the two roads leading to the site. The adjacent Meuse River was "on a rampage," threatening to overflow its banks and sweep over the plain. Company A's Earl Conley reported that the men "had to wade water and mud over ankle deep in places."

At 12:30 p.m., the troops were ready. A half hour later, several autos could be seen approaching, and Pershing, the Prince of Wales and their respective staffs alighted and mounted waiting horses for the "ride around." The division's line was almost a mile long and 150 yards deep, so it took the dignitaries nearly a half hour to complete their ride. Pershing then dismounted and, accompanied by the Prince of Wales, began walking among the troops for approximately two hours, carefully inspecting each platoon. As Pershing and "H.R.H." reached each battalion, its commander stepped forward and saluted. Pershing returned the salute, shook the commander's hand, and presented the Prince.

As Pershing reached the 128th Machine Gun Battalion, Major Westley Halliburton stepped forward, saluted, and said, "Sir, Major Halliburton, commanding 128th Machine Gun Battalion." "How are you, Major," Pershing replied, as he took Halliburton's hand. "Major, this is His Royal Highness, The Prince of Wales, who is the guest of our army today," he continued. "I sure was fooled about the Prince of Wales," Earl Conley recalled. Expecting

4. Memo, Headquarters, 128th Machine Gun Battalion, December 5, 1918, Record Group 120, Records of the American Expeditionary Forces, World War I Organization Records, Machine Gun Battalions, 128th Machine Gun Battalion, Box 266, NARA.

to see "a great big man with lots of braid and medals on his uniform," Conley saw instead "a little, slim kid, about 17 years old, who looked to be about 5 feet, 6 inches, and I don't think he would weigh more than 120."

The Prince briskly saluted and also shook the major's hand. As the party inspected the troops, who stood rigidly at attention, Halliburton was careful to walk beside Pershing, but not between the general and the men, as he never knew when Pershing would abruptly halt and start "shooting questions" at a soldier.

True to form, Pershing stopped in front of a Company B man. "What did you have for breakfast this morning?" "Oatmeal, sugar, bacon, potatoes, bread, coffee, sir." "Have you got a good cook?" "Yes, sir." "How do you like those shoes?" "They're all right, sir." "Do you use dubbin on them?" "Yes, sir." "Well, they look as though you did, all right," and with that, the general moved on. When Captain Schrantz presented himself, Pershing commented, "I've had my attention called to the excellent work of your company." When Schrantz told the general where the company was from, Pershing replied, "Yes, I've been in Carthage, and it's a very beautiful little city."

Following his inspection, Pershing took position and the entire division was brought to "present arms," then back to "order arms," which the troops executed with precision.

Then came the time for the division to pass in review. The sun broke through the clouds, and as the 35th's colors and standards caught the breeze it became "one of the most inspiring sights imaginable."

Following the review, Pershing and the Prince of Wales addressed the division's officers. The Prince, wearing cheap brown cotton gloves and an ordinary trench coat, appeared quite nervous, and twisted his gloves or pulled at the belt of his coat as he spoke. "We shall always remember you and what you have done for us," he remarked. "God speed and good luck."

Colonel Carl Ristine of the 139th Infantry then called for "three good American cheers" for the Prince, cheers that "shook the hills beyond the Meuse." The startled Prince stood at attention and gave a salute for a full minute. Pershing then saluted, and the division's officers returned his salute and double-timed back to their commands.

Pershing and the Prince then mounted their horses and began to ride back to their autos. On the way they had to jump a wide ditch. Pershing did so beautifully, as did the Prince, but when the latter turned to watch his staff attempt the feat, one of the Prince's staff fell from his horse into the water. His Royal Highness roared with laughter and was joined by a few thousand doughboys who saw the fall. Soon the troops were on their way back to their quarters, singing songs and remarking that the Prince "wasn't a bad fellow." "It sort of makes a fellow feel glad he is one of the boys over here," Earl Conley concluded. "Anyway, I wouldn't have missed it for a lot."[5]

On February 20, 1919, Pershing sent a message to General Thomas B. Dugan, the commander of the 35th Division. Pershing congratulated the division on its record in France, and extended his compliments "upon their excellent appearance" at the review. "It was gratifying," Pershing continued, "to see your troops in such physical shape and to see them so well equipped." What was more gratifying to the commander-in-chief, however, was the "high moral tone" of all ranks. The troops could proudly carry home with them "the gratitude of the allies . . . and the pride of their fellows throughout our forces."[6]

Undoubtedly the men of the 35th appreciated such lofty sentiments, but they also would have agreed with a sergeant in the Machine Gun Company, 140th Infantry, who wrote a far more humble summary of their experience. "I believe I have done my bit," he told his father. "I have walked a million kilos, eaten a million pounds of corn beef[,] slept in a million billets or barns, had a million cooties and still have red in my cheeks."[7]

The war was over—or at least there was an armistice which might or might not mean the same thing. For several days after November 11, 1918, the church bell in the little French village of La Vallee some miles west of St. Mihiel continued to ring in unison with those of other villages, and the men of Company A, 128th Machine Gun Battalion, wondered what was to come next. While waiting to find out, the usual workaday training was resumed in the company and battalion.[8]

5. *Joplin* (MO) *News Herald*, November 18, 1919; *Fort Scott* (KS) *Daily Tribune and Fort Scott Daily Monitor*, March 21, 1919.

6. *Joplin* (MO) *Globe*, April 20, 1919.

7. *Shelbina* (MO) *Democrat*, January 8, 1919.

8. On November 15, 1918, Lt. James J. Corey of the 128th Machine Gun Battalion reported that the battalion would undertake morning drill, consisting of one hour of close and extended order drill, thirty minutes of gas drill, one hour of elementary gun drill, and 30 minutes of physical exercise. Afternoon training would consist of stripping, cleaning, and nomenclature of the guns, and problems for 90 minutes. November 16, 1918, Memo from Capt. James J. Corey, Commanding Officer, 128th Machine Gun Battalion to A.C. of S., G-3, 35th Division re Training, Folder: 128th MG BATL Weekly report – training 235-50.4, Record Group 120, Records of the American Expeditionary Forces, World War I, Entry NM-91 1241, Records of Combat Divisions, 1917–1919, Box 16, 35th Division, NARA.

The Armistice made no difference in our training schedule.

There were several good reasons for this. One was that it was an armistice and not necesssarily peace. For any one of a number of reasons the fighting might be resumed, we thought. Then there was the expectation that we would be ordered into Germany to follow the retiring enemy to the Rhine. We actually were not accorded this honor but we expected it and so warm a rumor circulated for a time that we would go to Luxembourg that I suspect such move must have been considered. If we went into enemy territory there were all sorts of possibilities and we wanted to be as good as could be. Then also an army cannot be left in idleness. Its morale and efficiency sags quickly under such circumstances. Troops must be kept reasonably busy. Habit was a factor too, perhaps. Drill and training was the normal routine of military life anywhere, in peace or in war.

On November 13 the strength of Company A was increased by 37 enlisted men from the 323d Machine Gun Battalion, 83rd Division, one of the A.E.F. replacement divisions which was stationed near Le Mans. Since we were already at approximately our authorized strength of six officers and 172 men to the company this put us considerably overstrength—which didn't matter. They were a good bunch and we were glad to get them.

These new men were from many states, part of them originally having been in the Georgia or Alabama National Guard, 31st Division, and had from there gone to the 83rd.

On November 13 we received an accession of strength, my company getting three additional officers—Second Lieutenants Carl W. Hoffman, Nebraska City, Neb., John J. McMillen, La Jolla,

From November 24 to 30, the battalion's morning training consisted of physical drill, games, and boxing, close order by platoons, gas, nomenclature of the Hotchkiss machine gun, elementary gun drill, and study of the mechanism. Afternoon drill consisted of aiming and sighting, fire control instruments, elementary gun drill, and care and cleaning. November 30, 1918, Memo from Capt. James J. Corey, Commanding Officer, 128th Machine Gun Battalion to G-3, 35th Division re Report of Week 24th–30th November, Folder: 128th MG BATL Weekly report – training 235-50.4, Record Group 120, Records of the American Expeditionary Forces, World War I, Entry NM-91 1241, Records of Combat Divisions, 1917–1919, Box 16, 35th Division, NARA. The training schedule for December 8 to 14 was even more ambitious, with training in machine guns in the attack and platoon maneuvers, safety angle in direct overhead fire, fire orders, military courtesy, barrage drill, rough ground drill and estimating distances, range work, company maneuvers in attack, and patrolling and message writing. Drill Schedule, Dec. 8th to 14th, 1918, with December 14, 1918 Memo from Capt. James J. Corey, Commanding Officer, 128th Machine Gun Battalion to G-3, 35th Division re Report of Training, Week 8th to 14th Dec., Folder: 128th MG BATL Weekly report – training 235-50.4, Record Group 120, Records of the American Expeditionary Forces, World War I, Entry NM-91 1241, Records of Combat Divisions, 1917–1919, Box 16, 35th Division, NARA.

Calif., and William H. Neal, Crawfordsville, Ind., the latter a former officer of the Indiana National Guard.[9]

All the units in the division received similar accessions.

An answer wasn't hard to guess. These presumably were the men who had been scheduled to fill the gaps expected to be created in our numbers by the offensive of November 14. Since fighting had ceased they had been sent up immediately as overstrength because there had been nothing else in particular to do with them. At least so I thought.

There were great expectations of moving toward Germany, a hope that continued for months undeterred by word that only a few of the many divisions of the A.E.F. were to have that privilege. Then there came a flood of orders for intensified training.

"Someone in a considerably elevated position," wrote a Carthage officer, "has decided that the war should close as it began—with a deluge of schools."[10] Whether the idea was to prepare men for the next war or whether it was desired merely to occupy the minds of the troops and to counteract the natural reaction that came with peace I do not know but all of these purposes were served and the winter passed a good deal quicker than it otherwise would have.

On November 15 I obtained permission from Major Halliburton to take a car and go into St. Mihiel to see what I could see in that former German-held town. I spent a quite instructive day studying the German defenses of that place and in the line west of it. It was the machine gun positions which interested me. I found the old enemy emplacements and figured out, as well as I could, the fires which had been planned. This was not too difficult in most places either. Even the range cards were still in some of the old covered machine gun posts.

I missed a distinguished visitor while I was gone.

Lt. Col. Donald D. Hay, the division machine gun officer, had been in La Vallee to see me. Where could he find me, he wanted to know.

9. Carl W. Hoffman of Nebraska City, Nebraska, enlisted in the Nebraska National Guard in 1912. Discharged in 1915, he reenlisted the same year and was commissioned a second lieutenant in the 134th Infantry in October 1917. Hoffman was transferred to the 110th Ammunition Train in December 1918. John J. McMillen enlisted in the New Mexico National Guard in 1903, and rose to the rank of first lieutenant in 1916. He arrived in France in August 1918, and was attached to Company A, 128th Machine Gun Battalion in November 1918. William Herschel Neal was born on August 11, 1894, in Monroe County, Indiana. He died in Bloomington, Indiana, on April 17, 1943. HST.

10. Schrantz was the author of this comment.

Major Halliburton wasn't quite sure of the propriety of his action in letting me go to St. Mihiel on a duty day, this being on a Friday.

"He's out somewhere looking for maneuver places," he told me he told the colonel. "Doggondest fellow you ever see to hunt up maneuver places and figure problems for his company to work out in training."

This flattering but fictitious alibi didn't help any toward keeping me out of the job the colonel had in mind for me.

A system of schools was to be set up in the division, he told the major. One of them was a machine gun school. I was going to run it.

That's the way it was too.

When I reported at Lerouville, then division headquarters, the next day it was Col. Hamilton S. Hawkins, the division chief of staff, who gave me instructions.

I was to have two officers and six sergeants, two of the latter from each of the machine gun battalions, to assist me. We would circulate about the division taking two companies at a time for a week's course. I was to have the complete control of these units during their training time—8 a.m. to 4 p.m. All personnel possible must be present. For instance the battalion or regiment to which they belonged could not take them from me for details or anything else. Where possible the training was to be at the villages where the units were then stationed but if this was not possible in the case of the regimental machine gun companies I should make the necessary recommendations and for the week the companies would be moved to some village where they could be together.

The order covering the school was issued that day.

To assist me I had Lieutenant Dunn of my own company and 1st Lieut. Robert McBride, late adjutant of the 130th Machine Gun Battalion, and the six sergeants, one of whom was Sgt. Fred R. Clark of my own company. All of these, officers and sergeants, were keen soldiers and able machine gunners.

First Lieut. Frank L. Snyder accordingly succeeded to command of Company A. Major Westley Halliburton about this time departed for the A.E.F. machine gun school at Langres, and Capt. James J. Corey of Company B took command of the battalion.

Nor was there any delay in getting started. The next afternoon—Sunday—we descended on Major T.H. Loy, commanding officer of the 129th Machine Gun Battalion, stationed at Chonville, seven kilometers west of Commercy, ready to begin work the next morning.

My good friend Major Loy made us welcome but he obviously lacked enthusiasm. A lot of silliness, he thought, and he probably also felt that he could train his battalion as well as I could and maybe better, which likely was true.

Colonel Hay let me make out my own training plans and schedule without any direction from above except in general terms. So it was that each machine gun unit of the division was that winter treated to a concentrated dose of a combination of what the division machine gun officer and I thought a machine gunner ought to know—Colonel Hay's particular ideas having to do with indirect fire technique, he being a scholarly man, and my own pet ones having to do with closer and better machine gun support of rifle units in attack.

Despite Major Loy's courteously concealed aversion to my barging into his playhouse, he could hardly do other than invite me into his headquarters mess—the 129th not having a battalion officers mess like the 128th and 130th. Instead the headquarters officers had a small mess and the company officers messed in their unit's kitchens, or somewhere, after the men were through.

A quizzical old French lady, assisted by an American sergeant, looked after the headquarters mess and she was much amused at the issue food furnished, at least at those items made from corn. Cornmeal in particular stirred her risibilities. She chuckled about the cornmeal mush—"moosh" she called it—frequently on the menu. Americans were funny. Corn was for horses, not for people.

November 19, found the 128th on the move again, this time merely a shift southward to the unprepossessing village of Domremy-aux-Bois, a name which at first stirred some interest. Someone remembered that Joan of Arc had come from a village by the name of Domremy, but, it developed, that was Domremy-la-Pucelle, some 30 miles or so distant, and this Domremy was just another French town with mud and chickens and cheerless barnlofts. Here Thanksgiving Day was observed with suitable jollity and a home-coming of all former members of the battalion in reach. Concerning the observance at the officers mess, a Carthage officer wrote: "It was quite a dinner and quite an affair. We have a chaplain now and he started off the meal by returning thanks. This took me somewhat aback for to the best of my knowledge it never happened in the battalion before."

The 128th had been rather unfortunate in its chaplains. The first one assigned at Camp Doniphan had died of pneumonia within a few days after joining. The next had been a Catholic by faith, and at that time there were only three or four Catholics in the battalion. A highly educated man and a courteous gentleman, this chaplain was a retiring, reserved churchman, unfitted by training to engage in morale-boosting tasks other than spiritual and Major Halliburton had given him the task of censoring the battalion mail until he was relieved early in the spring. Then there had been no other until the present one arrived after the Armistice. This one—a Chaplain Winters—was a trained army chaplain, a former Y.M.C.A. secretary, and experienced in working with young men.[11] He immediately became one of the most important

11. Timothy A. Murphy, an instructor at the Sacred Heart Mission in Sacred Heart, Oklahoma, became a Knights of Columbus Catholic chaplain at Camp Doniphan. He was commissioned a first lieutenant on February 11, 1918, and made chaplain of the 128th Machine Gun Battalion the following day. He died of lobar pneumonia in the base hospital on the night of February 23, 1918. The 128th Machine Gun Battalion Band played at his solemn requiem mass, and the band and a military escort accompanied the remains to the railroad station. *Emporia* (KS) *Gazette*, February 26, 1918; General Order Number 7, Headquarters, 128th Machine Gun Battalion, Camp Doniphan, OK, February 28, 1918, Record Group 120, Records of the American Expeditionary Forces, World War I Organization Records, Machine Gun Battalions, 128th Machine Gun Battalion, Box 266, NARA. First Lieutenant Joseph Lee Mastaglio, born in New York City on April 11, 1877. He was commissioned a first lieutenant and assigned to the 35th Division in March 1918, but was reassigned to the 16th U.S. Infantry in July 1918. He served overseas from April 1918 to May 1919. He died on July 31, 1959. HST; *The New York Times*, August 1, 1959.

Franklin L. Winter, born in Newark, New Jersey on May 31, 1885, graduated from Colgate University in 1913 and Rochester Theological Seminary in 1915. He served as the pastor of a church in Fowlerville, Michigan, 1915-17, then served as Y.M.C.A. education director at Camp Custer, Michigan, from December 1917–August 1918. He attended Chaplain Training School at Camp Zachary Taylor, Kentucky, from August to September 1918, arrived in France in October 1918, and joined the 128th Machine Gun Battalion as first lieutenant and chaplain the following month. He served with the battalion until May 1919. Winter also received a master of sacred theology from Oberlin. He died on October 27, 1975. *The Evening Star* (Washington, D.C.), November 7, 1975; Rochester Theological Seminary, *General Catalogue, 1850 to 1920* (Rochester, N.Y.: E.R. Andrews Printing Co., 1920), 313; HST. Winter wrote a letter of commendation to the Y.M.C.A., praising the organization for furnishing abundant writing paper, envelopes, books, magazines, hymn books, athletic equipment, etc., between November 1918 and March 1919, and for furnishing him liberal credit for purchasing supplies for the battalion's canteen. The International Committee of Young Men's Christian Association, *Summary of Service, Y.M.C.A. in the Embarkation Center, From December 1918 to July 1919* (Portland, OR: The Arcady Press and Mail Advertising Co., Inc., 1920), 178-79.

men in the battalion, established a reading room, a place to write letters, obtained some books from somewhere, and in addition to holding regular services did much in many ways to render the lot of the soldiers more pleasant through the winter than they would otherwise have been.

While at Chonville—the third day I think—there came in boxes of Browning machine guns which were being issued all over the division to replace the Hotchkiss ones with which we had fought our own particular share of the war.

We had heard of this weapon for a year or so through the newspapers but the only unit we had seen equipped with them was the 81st Division. Some other American units doubtless had them too, but not many. Most of the older divisions had Hotchkiss guns, unless they were on the British front in which case they had .303 Vickers. The 89th Division and some others—the 6th for instance, had cal. 30 Vickers. The Browning in later wars was to prove itself on many battlefields but at this time it was—or so we thought anyhow—the widest publicized and the least-used of all machine guns.

And initially it was greeted with more curiosity than enthusiasm.

It was short and stubby where the Hotchkiss was long and lean. It was water-cooled whereas the Hotchkiss was air-cooled. It was recoil-operated whereas the French weapon to which we were accustomed was gas-operated. It had a killing range of only 2,900 meters or less whereas the Hotchkiss, because of its boat-tailed bullet which balanced well in flight, had a killing range of over 4,000 meters or more.

Men naturally prefer the weapon to which they are accustomed and it was with some regrets that the machine gunners of the 35th saw the French guns go. But the Browning had some mechanical virtues and there was much talk of how much better it was than the Vickers with which the division had been equipped while behind the lines in the British area of northern France. It had been necessary to quarter-turn the rounds in the Vickers belts from time to time or else they would stick so tight that there would be stoppages because the extractor could not pull the cartridge from the belt. In the Browning this didn't happen. The cartridges were pulled from the belt even if they never had been turned. Men came to like the new gun.

Yet the Browning was a beautiful weapon with some mechanical virtues quite as admirable as advertised, and the hills about Domremy were soon echoing to the firing of the guns at targets in a nearby hollow.[12]

Not only in the school but all over the division men were working with and firing the new gun.

We not only taught in the school but we learned. Everywhere we went we encouraged both officers and men to tell of their experiences of the use of machine guns in battle. They all added up to the same thing. To most effectively support rifle units they must be used boldly and well forward—to be used in attack in the role we had been taught in the pre-battle training period was the place of "automatic rifles" such as the Chauchat or Lewis guns.

This recognition of how machine guns could best be used to support attacks was not peculiar to the 35th Division of course. It probably was the same in every division with combat experiences and those which had the more experience probably had learned the lesson in time to be of more use to them than it was to us. But no instructive material to this effect, so far as I know, had ever been issued, so each division had to learn in the school of experience. After the war all this became standard machine gun doctrine.

From December 2 to 7 we were with the 128th. The next week there was no school since there were various changes of station in progress, the principal one which affected the school being the movement of the 130th Machine Gun Battalion to Ville-Issey a town on the Meuse River some four or five kilometers southeast of Commercy, which latter city was now division headquarters. The 128th moved the same week to Vadonville, also on the Meuse, some seven kilometers above Commercy and only a short distance above Lerouville.

This was a larger place, and in the north was silhouetted the distant bulk of the fort of the Camp of the Romans at the tip of the St. Mihiel salient, a hill held by the Germans until the salient had been reduced in early September. Along the canal which bordered

12. The 1917 Browning machine gun, designed by John M. Browning, was the best machine gun of the period. The water-cooled, .30-06 caliber gun was capable of firing about 500 rounds per minute. The Browning weighed more than 34 pounds with a full water jacket, and utilized a 50-pound tripod. Westinghouse, Remington and Colt produced the 1917 Browning. Canfield, *U.S. Infantry Weapons of the First World War*, 211–216.

the east side of the town and between it and the river, barbed wire entanglements told of French preparations to defend Vadonville had the enemy been able to come this far. Many homes in Vadonville had been abandoned by their occupants four years before and these were more comfortable billets for the winter than the lofts of smaller, fully-occupied villages.[13]

Rumors of new moves which never came circulated about every few days. Germany was the favored destination in the reports, though once it was Luxembourg. Then about the middle of December there came a group of men returning from hospital though not entirely fit for duty. This started a story that the division was soon to return to the United States. Then a few days later a large number of horses and mules were issued to the division. This started the rumor that it was to move to North Russia where American troops, along with English and French, were fighting the Bolshevists in the Archangel area. But there was no move—only frequent divisional maneuvers regardless of dripping weather with occasional snows.

A few miles to the north, and across the river, were the old battle lines of the St. Mihiel salient, and a great wasted region on each side. About the trenches lay the debris of years of war, and the melancholy mementoes of major attacks which had failed. Among the skeletons of hundreds of unburied German dead was a litter of rusting weapons and rotting equipment. Nothing had been cleaned up save that those dead easily identified as French had been buried. The whole vast region was now deserted and constituted a souvenir-hunter's paradise, if so ghastly a zone could be designated by that name, and since the Ford gun cars furnished easy transportation to the scenes, there were hours of sightseeing and exploring on this old front.

Christmas Day was as fittingly observed as might be in Vadonville, and Mess Sergeant John Cronk and his helpers had done their best in the way of food. Then there were parcels and letters from home. As for the weather, to quote a letter, it was "trying to snow

13. Capt. James J. Corey of the 128th reported on December 14 that Vadonville was found "in a very filthy condition. Every effort was made to improve this condition." Drill Schedule, Dec. 8th to 14th, 1918, with December 14, 1918 Memo from Capt. James J. Corey, Commanding Officer, 128th Machine Gun Battalion to G-3, 35th Division re Report of Training, Week 8th to 14th Dec., Folder: 128th MG BATL Weekly report – training 235-50.4 Record Group 120, Records of the American Expeditionary Forces, World War I, Entry NM-91 1241, Records of Combat Divisions, 1917-1919, Box 16, 35th Division, NARA.

but with wet splashy attempts that accomplished nothing but to add more water to the already sodden ground."[14]

December 16 to 21 we took Companies B and D, 130th Machine Gun Battalions at Ville-Issey, then suspended to January 9 when we worked with A and C of that battalion, then moved to Sampigny seven kilometers southwest of St. Mihiel where we had the machine gun companies of the 137th and 138th Infantry regiments, then wound up January 20 to 25 inclusive at Girauvoisin, about seven miles northeast of Commercy and an equal distance south of the old battleline of the St. Mihiel salient, where we wound up.

Except for the initial chill at Chonville we were warmly received everywhere. I had indeed had some trepidations as I started the first week at Ville-Issey.

Major Ray E. Powers had been assigned to command of the 130th when it came out of the Sommedieue sector and I had heard much about him.[15] He had come from the rear areas somewhere with a lot of snappy ideas and vigorously set himself to bring the 130th out of what he deemed a slovenly condition. He had quite upset the organization with his spirit of energy and change and had established a rule that every officer and man shave before breakfast. The calls set by division did not permit time for this, so in the 130th it was necessary to get up before reveille in order to get shaved. An officer was stationed at every mess line to inspect the men. No shave, no breakfast. The major himself saw that every officer's chin was smooth and stubbleless at the officers' mess.

Capt. Fred H. Nesbitt of Company A of that battalion was a genial and profane character from the then-mining town of Webb City, Mo. Oaths were an essential part of his ordinary vocabulary, intermingled with chuckles and laughter. When word spread around the division that Major Powers had broken Captain Nesbitt of swearing in conversation while at mess, it was received with amazement. That really was something.

At Ville-Issey the adjutant informed me that my program as regards B and D companies would need to be altered one of the days. Major Powers had something else he wanted to do with one of those

14. John Francis Cronk was born in Springfield, Missouri, on March 22, 1894. He died in Inglewood, California, on August 3, 1980, and was buried in Inglewood. He served overseas with Company A from April 25, 1918, to April 24, 1919. Missouri Secretary of State, State Archives, Soldiers' Records, War of 1812–World War I, www.sos.mo.gov/archives/soldiers.

15. Possibly Ray R. Powers, born in Brooklyn, New York, on November 25, 1884.

companies that day. Not so. My order outranked those of the major, I first explained to the adjutant and then to him, in this particular. It was division headquarters' orders that the companies were mine during training hours. Major Powers said that he had friends at division headquarters—his adjutant and half a dozen other officers had told me that—and that he would see. He hurried up to Commercy and came right back again. His friends had told him that I was right. He was not at all upset by it and gave me all the support he could. Later in the week when we needed something, I forget what, for the school, he remarked that he had friends at division headquarters and hurried right up there. This time his friends seemed to work because he immediately returned with it.

I had anticipated some trouble with commanders of the four infantry regiments. During pre-battle training periods the machine gun companies had been subject to calls for details of various sorts and their technical training had been interfered with. This might happen.

I called on each of the four colonels prior to the time when their companies were due. They were more than cooperative. They were cordial and enthusiastic. The better their units were trained, particularly in giving closer support to rifle units, the better they would like it. They cheerfully acquiesced in the temporary changes of station required for most of the companies—only the 137th, if I remember right, did not need to be moved.

Our machine gun school was only one of many. And the units which were not mixed up in schools were training vigorously on their own. There was little idle time in the 35th Division that winter and I think the same was true of every division in the AEF. Morale, so far as I saw it, was consequently high.

On Sundays and in the intervals of school—such as the moving break mentioned and the Christmas holiday break—I zealously explored the old nearby battlefields, using one of my company Fords for transportation.

One of the first of these was to the southern part of the old St. Mihiel salient. Of the course of battle in the old salient when it was reduced I had only a vague knowledge, but I knew of Seicheprey where the 26th Division had been attacked in April, 1918, and it was there I went by way of Sampigny, Mecrin, Marbotte, and Xivray-Marvoisin.

To my surprise the battlefield had not been cleared up after the September 12 fighting. American rifles—1903 Springfields—and equipments scattered here and there told of casualties in the 1st Division area and the same in the 42nd Division zone of attack farther east. It was not until then that I realized the St. Mihiel operation had really been a battle instead of the grand parade we had pictured. On this and subsequent trips I fairly well covered the whole salient where the Americans had fought—reading the story of the battle fairly well on the ground in fox holes, shell holes and abandoned equipment.

One day, just to see something of the old stabilized trench front, I turned left (north) from Marbotte without having the slightest idea what I would find. What I did discover was the shell-churned battlefields of Ailly and Jaulny woods.

It was a maze of shattered woods, old trenches, shell craters and mine craters, rusting weapons and the skeletons of hundreds of unburied dead, tossed about by shell fire. Apparently the French, following the recovery of the territory, had gone over the field and removed such of the bones as could be identified by their equipment as French, but the bones of the Germans still lay where they had fallen and decayed on top of ground between the lines.

This sounds gruesome in writing but at the time it did not strike me that way. These were just thickly scattered bones, skulls, and weather-hardened shoes containing foot-bones. Fragments of uniforms enabled one to form guesses at nationalities. I regarded them with no more horror, somehow, than students would a skeleton in a class room. Perhaps in a sense I was a student since I was staring to learn—or at least to figure out what happened—rather than out of morbid curiosity.

If the bodies of the French dead were gone, the rusted and broken French weapons remained, mixed with the German relics. It was plain to see that attack and counterattack had swept over this ground. Among the old rifles, both French and German, I noted a number with bolt back and magazine partly inserted in the chamber. The men who had once carried these had been hit just as they were reloading.

These violent combats here had been in 1915, I have since read.

There was an interesting study in grenades in all this ghastly debris. The whole development of them could be traced in the samples still about—jam-tin grenades which were merely cans of explosive with a fuse attached, factory-made hairbrush grenades which were in effect about the same thing except that on one side of a paddle a square tin grenade had been fastened, a fuse protruding from its base; discus grenades, shaped like two saucers placed face to face, and with knobs protruding, the striking of one of which would cause the grenade to explode, and so on up through citrous grenades such as I had known in the Vosges, to the then-modern stick grenades (potato mashers) and egg grenades of the Germans and the OF and F1 grenades of the French.

My interest, in part, was in finding German machine gun positions and tracing as well as I could their systems of fire. To do this it was necessary to cross the old battlefields which had later become no-man's-lands as each side drew back to create a deeper zone between them and their enemies.

One German emplacement I found in Ailly wood on a later trip was something of a gem, I thought, from a machine gun stand point. The two guns were sited to fire a flanking barrage. They were so placed that the trajectory of the bullets approximately followed the curve of the ground making a zone a half mile long or so through which no man could walk while the guns were firing. From the gun positions little of the front could be seen, but in a tree above them was a little chair to which an observer had ascended by means of cleats nailed on to the tree.

I returned to this scene in Ailly and Jaulny woods many times and it became a favorite place for the men of the 128th Machine Gun Battalion to come.

On December 11, as previously mentioned, I returned to CR Haudiomont and explored the German woods which had faced us and also visited Manheulles. The same day I wandered over portions of the battlefields of Verdun—Bras, Talou hill, Cote du Poivre, flattened Beaumont, etc., coming home with a swing into German territory by way of Etain, Fresnes, and back through the old St. Mihiel salient.

On other trips I studied the French plan of defense of woods on the south side of the salient, being particularly struck by one marked Bois-Sans-Nom (wood without a name) on the map and located two kilometers east of Fort de Liouville. Here a great chickenwire fence, 10 or 12 feet tall had been erected, flanked at places by forward-jutting bastions of logs and earth in which machine guns had been sited. The Germans actually never got this far south and there had been no fighting there, but I can imagine that it would have been disconcerting for any infantry to try to push through a woodland and run into this sort of obstacle.

And on January 1 I returned to the Argonne field to find as many as I could of the graves of our company dead.

After the machine gun school had ceased operations, Captain Corey and I made a trip by train to Chateau Thierry to see that battered town and to reconstruct as well as we could from the scenery the methods by which the divisional machine gun battalion of the 3rd U.S. Division had stopped the German advance here in the fighting of June.

Concerning my frequent trips to the old trenches of the St. Mihiel salient, Major Halliburton commented on the possibilities of stepping on a concussion grenade or accidentally kicking the tip of a partially buried dud shell or something.

"Schrantz, you are going to get yourself killed yet," he jested.

The risk in this case was not great of course, if one kept in mind the possibility of enemy booby-traps in dug-outs. However this was the last great war in which this type of exploring unpoliced-up battlefields would be safe. The development and prevalence of land mines in later campaigns would indeed make such activities perilous.

January, 1919, in the Department Meuse, France, was much like a January in Carthage, Mo., U.S.A. There was an occasional rain, occasional snow, occasional sleet, none of which interfered much with military training. The rough hob-nailed shoes of the soldiers splashed daily in the mud or snow about Vadonville and dried nightly by the fire-places in the deserted houses where Company A, 128th Machine Gun Battalion, was billeted.[16] The machine gunners were hard as nails and in better shape for battle than in any time in their unit's history but thoughts were not of war but of when the 35th Division would be ordered back to the United States for discharge—and it was known that that would be soon.

16. Lieutenant Edgar A. Bourne of Company A wrote home in January 1919 that "the war is not so bad." He was quartered in a room with a nice large fireplace, and a real featherbed to sleep on, "instead of wet blankets on the cold ground." He placed pictures of his relatives on the mantel, making it appear "not unlike his room at home." *Joplin* (MO) *Globe*, January 29, 1919.

Hostilities were over but death had declared no armistice and on February 13, Company A lost its last man of the war to that enemy. Private William Wesley James, Richland, Mo., who had joined the company at Camp Doniphan, Okla., with the first Selective Service men in October, 1917, died at Base Hospital 91 at Commercy of pneumonia.[17]

On February 17 came a great day for us.

Gen. John J. Pershing, commander-in-chief of the AEF, accompanied by the Prince of Wales, heir-apparent to the British throne, was to inspect the 35th Division.

The review was held on a plain in the valley of the Meuse near Vignot, on the east side of the river some miles southeast of Vadonville. The entire division was drawn up on the sodden plain, the machine gun units without their vehicles.

The 128th Machine Gun Battalion, like the other units, formed in column of platoons, closed up as much as possible, Company B in front because of the seniority of its captain.

A chill wind, carrying occasional random flakes of snow, whipped the short overcoats of the soldiers around their legs as they waited while the great commander passed through the densely-packed masses of the rifle regiments on the right.

Eventually the reviewing party reached the 128th Machine Gun Battalion.

General Pershing was tall, big, erect and of athletic appearance. The Prince of Wales, then 25 years of age and garbed in the uniform of a British captain, was so slight in build and so youthful in feature that he looked younger than any of the youthful wide-eyed Carthage privates, a few of whom had not yet seen their 19th birthday despite the 18 months of service behind them.

The general was striding rapidly, and the prince and the little group of American and British staff officers panting behind, had a hard time keeping up.

17. Private William W. James, a native of Brumley, Missouri, died of pneumonia at 6 a.m. on February 13, 1919, at Base Hospital 91, Commercy, France, and was buried in the St. Mihiel American Cemetery. He was inducted at Waynesville, Missouri, on October 2, 1917, and assigned to Company A on October 25, 1917. He served overseas from June 4, 1918, until his death. Extracts of Service Records, Record Group 120, Records of the American Expeditionary Forces, World War I, Entry NM-91 1256, Organization Records, Machine Gun Battalions, Box 264, 128th Machine Gun Battalion, Co. A – DOC. FILE 1-1203, NARA; Missouri Secretary of State, State Archives, Soldiers' Records, War of 1812–World War I, www.sos.mo.gov/archives/soldiers.

At the head of the battalion the general shook hands with Major Halliburton and introduced him to the prince. No one below a battalion commander rated a hand shake or an introduction. A captain met the general in front of the right of his leading platoon, announced his rank, name and organization, then walked beside the general—on the side away from the men—as he inspected the unit.

Being a bit shy of great generals I waited with some stage-fright as the AEF commander strode through Company B with Captain Corey at his side.

"Captain Schrantz, Co. A, 128th Machine Gun Battalion," I reported when my turn came as I saluted and fell in beside him, on his right, away from the troops, in accordance with orders and hence directly in front of the Prince of Wales—a rather high-ranking position that I thought afterwards.

"How long have you commanded the company, captain?" the general asked as he strode along.

"Twenty-two months, sir."

"That long? Did you organize it?"

"No sir. It is a very old Missouri National Guard unit." At this the general showed symptoms of increased interest.

"And where is it from?"

"Carthage, Missouri, sir."

"Ah, I have heard of the old Carthage company," he said, then slowed his step slightly and fell silent, looking closely at the second and third platoons which he was then passing, recalling perhaps his days as a small boy in Missouri and later as a young lieutenant in Nebraska when the old Carthage Light Guard had a reputation as a crack unit familiar to most military men in the Middle West, west of the Mississippi River.

He looked at the unit thoughtfully, asked a few questions of some of the men as he passed, and, moved on toward the next organization, the 110th Field Signal Battalion.

He started to inspect this, then abruptly broke off, turned back toward us and called to me.

I returned, and stopped with the usual salute.

"Captain," he said, "I wish you would tell your men that I took a special interest in them, and that I want them to go home feeling a proper pride in themselves and their organization and knowing that everyone over here appreciates all that they have done."

There was a morale builder for any company.

After we had passed in review and after the officers of the division had heard a brief talk from the general and from the Prince of Wales who later was to renounce the British throne and become the Duke of Windsor, the company stepped out quite blithely back toward Vadonville.

A great general had favored us with his attention.

The Company A members, marching back to Vadonville, moved with light steps and high morale. General Pershing had singled them out for special attention—and he had heard of their company.[18]

There had been much granting of leaves both to officers and enlisted men of the division during the winter—the leave area for officers being Nice on the Mediterranean coast near Italy and that of the men Aix-le-Bains.

Lieutenant Dunn and I had had no opportunity to take advantage of this earlier because of being tied up with the division machine gun school, nor had Lieutenant Snyder due to being in command of Company A during our absence.

On February 23 the three of us left on leave for Nice.

I had not been eager to go to Nice for the very reason that it was famed as a resort place and playground for Europe. For some reason I have always been prejudiced against regions which are popular as resorts. I did want to see the southern coast of France and I wanted to visit Carcassone on account of its famous walls. Not a chance. The army apparently wanted its people in the official leave areas so it could keep an eye on them. It was Nice or nothing so I had settled for Nice.

There had been a ban on leaves to visit Paris too. It was presumed to be highly unwholesome for military Americans though there

18. Major Westley Halliburton described the Prince as "a small, frail, rosy-cheeked boy of about 23 and looks about at [*sic*] mature as a 16 or 17-year-old High school boy, and I mean the teacher's pet, not the football player." As Pershing passed by Company A, he asked Captain Schrantz where the company was from. When Schrantz replied, "Carthage, Missouri," the general, who had started to move on to the next company, called Schrantz back and told him he had heard of the Carthage company, "said several things complimentary about their appearance and told the captain to give the company his best wishes for their safe return home." *Carthage* (MO) *Evening Press*, March 12, 1919. Major Halliburton reported that Schrantz "needs some iron bands around his head since that." *Joplin* (MO) *Globe*, March 13, 1919. A more detailed account of the review by a member of the division's military police may be found in the *The Kansas City* (MO) *Star*, March 25, 1919.

seemed to be plenty of them stationed there. All three of us had wanted to see the place, though in my own case my personal prejudice against any spot that was highly popular made my interest largely of a sense-of-duty nature. Obviously a person shouldn't be in France and not see Paris. But the army hadn't figured that way as regards combat troops.

But to get anywhere in France it is necessary to go through Paris. We would stop off 24 hours on our way to Nice for a look, we thought.

But there was a little army of MPs [military police] at the railway station to check our passes and hand us and all other incoming American personnel a little slip reading as follows:

"Take the next train out."

This was morning and the next train to Nice did not leave until evening so we followed the current and formed at the tail of the block-long queue of officers waiting at the office of the American provost marshal to get exemptions from that ruling. About noon our turn at admittance came and our arguments were answered by a smiling, sympathetic and quite firm negative. He was polite and pleasant, that major or whoever it was to whom he [we] talked, but the candy-coated pill was still "Take the next train out."

We took a hasty glance at the Invalides in the meager time left to us and evening found us southward bound on that next train.

Our stay at Nice at the Hotel Westminster on the seafront Promenade des Anglais was a pleasant one and our period on the famed Riviera was made the more interesting by motor trips the Y.M.C.A. conducted to Monte Carlo, Menton, Cannes, Grasse—a perfumery center with a perfume factory on the itinerary—and other spots in the region the sightseers visit.

My preconceived prejudice against the region vanished. It was a spot lovely to behold while we were there, green and entrancing, and I enjoyed it. It occurred even to my contrarywise mind that maybe, after all, when a place was popular there might be some reason for that popularity. I met there a couple of Australian officers, one of them a chaplain—called "padre" of course after the British fashion—and the other a lieutenant whose rank naturally was pronounced "leftenant" aftrer the quaint British custom. They seemed to have like interests as myself and quite as inclined toward trying to see the world on foot so I ran around with them quite a bit, learning considerable about Australia and answering many questions about the States.

Dunn, a single man, by chance met in Nice among the army nurses there a girl from his own home town in Michigan or some place to whom he had once been engaged. He admitted that last but beyond that volunteered nothing and naturally Snyder and I did not attempt to pry into his private love life by questions. They obviously weren't engaged any longer. We met this group of nurses on various trips, or in circulating about Nice, but he never squired his ex-fiancee around anywhere and he talked to her with the same casual friendliness and normal cordiality that he did the other American women, though perhaps with a shade more restraint. She was a very pretty girl and looked at him, I thought, quite imploringly. His reaction was light banter and careful courtesy. Hard-hearted cuss, this lieutenant of mine, I reflected, though he certainly never showed any symptoms that way any other time that I knew him—one of the best-hearted men in the world. Quite obviously this young lady had stamped most painfully on his toes back in Michigan or wherever their home town was.

By March 8, the day our leave expired, we were back in Vadonville again after a few hour peek at Paris between trains.

We were met with chuckles.

Instructions had come down from division to fill out papers for my promotion to the rank of major and that of Dunn to captain.

An essential part of these papers were physical examinations. Lieutenant Martin, the genial battalion surgeon, had examined us in absentia, it appeared, and everything had gone in all filled out and complete a week before.[19]

This was gratifying—both the recommendations and our associates' stretching of several regulations to speed them on their way—but it would be well to wait to see if the eggs hatched before being sure.

So we took the good news calmly and modestly as was befitting in those days.

In World War II, it seemed to me, it was the custom in some quarters to worry more about promotion than the war. And this quite openly—much frankness in the desire for advancement.

19. Melvin Cecil Martin was born on September 24, 1887, in Kendallville, Indiana. He died on Februrary 23, 1961, in Newton, Kansas.

But in World War I, so far as I noted, the old army custom of outward indifference of demeanor toward such things still prevailed. Evidenced anxiety for advancement was not deemed genteel in any rank. One did his job the best he could and if his superiors considered him worthy of promotion and if there chanced to be a vacancy—which there generally wasn't—then action was instituted from above. The one selected was even supposed to be surprised at being singled out, he being assumed to realize that he was among the least worthy of his fellow rankers.

Actually, again in my own narrow range of observation, there was not much promotion in World War I due in part to the shortness of the war, in part to the number of officer replacements available, and in part to the fact that there was fewer table of organization positions in field grade. Battalions, for instance were commanded by majors with no executive at all instead of by a lieutenant colonel with a major to assist him.

Lieutenant colonels were almost as rare as full colonels, the only lieutenant colonel positions being the executive officers of regiments and certain officers on staffs of division or higher.

As for myself, Major Halliburton had told me at the beginning of October that he had recommended me for a battlefield promotion. That indeed had resulted in a citation for which I had not been recommended but I had remained a captain. Nor did I mind. I had hoped to command my company again in battle, and do better than I had the first time, before moving on to a battalion. Now the war was over. Maybe there would be a promotion and maybe there wouldn't be. I didn't lay awake at night about it.

Incidentally the citation I had received in lieu of the battlefield promotion Major Halliburton had recommended turned out in the long run to have been the better of the two since between the two wars such citations were translated into Silver Star decorations. That was a definite asset the rest of my military life—though I think in World War II or the Korean War it might have been only a Bronze Star—whereas a promotion would have meant something only at the time.

While on the subject of decorations it might not be amiss to mention that while authorization of new decorations of lower standing than old ones were presumably meant to reward actions of lesser merit, it has been my opinion that what they usually have actually done was to shove the old ones up a notch.

When the Medal of Honor was the only decoration for valor it often was awarded for things which in World War I would have brought the Distinguished Service Cross, in World War II and in Korea brought only the Silver Star. Similarly—I think without any intent to disparage my own combat decoration—the Silver Stars won in World War I would generally have been Bronze ones in later conflicts.

This has always seemed to me to be a mistake. I think the old World War I level should have been kept in World War II and the lowest decoration—the Bronze Star—given lavishly to all combat soldiers, particularly infantrymen, who did their job well under fire.

In mid-February Company A turned in its machine guns to A.E.F. ordnance officers—indisputable evidence that the 35th Division was soon to return to the United States.

The principal question now was when the division would move to a port of embarkation. Most of the men waited for the day with keen expectancy. Letters from Carthage for weeks had been telling of the return of ex-soldiers who had been discharged. At first these had been the men streaming back from duty in the United States; then casuals from overseas had begun to appear. The constant query in the letters was, "When are you coming home?" A few desired to remain in Europe for a time and discussed the possibilities of transfer.

In early March it was expected that the company was to be sent back home in detachments according to the region from which the men came and at this time the following was posted in the billets and on the company bulletin board:

> "Company A, 128th Machine Gun Bn., Vadonville, Meuse, France,
> March 8, 1919
> Company Order
> No. 3
>
> Within the next few weeks this company may be more or less split up into geographical units preparatory to return to the United States. While the organization is still altogether the company commander wishes to express his appreciation of the work of the members of the company during the war.
>
> In the training period in the States, despite lack of equipment and trained machine gun instructors, you worked

hard and enthusiastically and laid a solid foundation for the extensive machine gun knowledge you acquired later.

Back of the British lines in May and early June, faced with the probability of immediate battle against odds, you learned the British 303 Vickers in an incredibly short time and would have given a good account of yourselves had the enemy elected to thrust toward the seacoast instead of toward Paris.

When shifted to the Vosges and armed with the Hotchkiss you quickly and enthusiastically mastered this gun. In the trenches in Alsace you maintained the best of trench discipline, untiring energy and the most aggressive attitude toward the enemy.

In the Meuse-Argonne battle you handled the most difficult part of one of the best and most important machine gun barrages ever put down by an American division. During the trying days and nights of battle that followed you conducted yourselves with the greatest possible bravery and devotion to duty. Unshaken by losses, without rest or sleep and often without food, the company, through the courage and ability of every man in it, functioned perfectly throughout the battle, each man in his proper place.

In the trench sector in the Woevre near Verdun you displayed the same soldierly qualities as in the Vosges. While the armistice prevented the projected offensive in Lorraine in which you would have participated, your spirit was such that had the battle been fought you could not have failed to exhibit the same heroism and efficiency as in the Argonne.

In the period following the signing of the armistice your discipline was not affected by any reaction of feeling, and when the Hotchkiss gun was taken away and the Browning issued instead you mastered this gun with the same quickness that you had the preceding ones.

Other organizations may have played more spectacular parts in battle and others may have participated in more major operations. That is the fortunes of war. The members of no organization can have behaved themselves with greater gallantry in action or shown more ability in machine gunnery than yourselves.

You can handle any type of machine gun used in modern war and you have taken a worthy part in the winning of the greatest of all wars. You can go back to civilian life well content.

Ward L. Schrantz
Capt., 128th Machine Gun Bn.,
Comdg. Co. A."[20]

Two days after Dunn, Snyder and I returned from Nice, the 128th Machine Gun Battalion departed for western France and the embarkation center at Le Mans. The motorized section of the battalion moved overland, the marching portion by rail.

Part of the division, in fact, had already been in motion when we returned.

The afternoon of March 10 we marched out of Vadonville to Lerouville some miles to the south where we entrained on a troop train which beside ourselves included the 130th Machine Gun Battalion.[21]

For the enlisted men the means of conveyance was the usual "40-men-or-eight-horses" box cars; for the officers third-class coaches whose German "no smoking" and other signs showed them to be enemy rolling stock turned over under the provisions of the Armistice.

It was 6 p.m. that evening when the train pulled out of Lerouville and started its two-days journey across France, slowed up by rail congestion. While this trip was in progress the motorized portion of the battalion was snorting over the French roads overland headed for the same destination

20. Schrantz was not alone in paying tribute to Company A. Lieutenant Cecil R. Stemmons of the 137th U.S. Infantry wrote home that "From what I hear of the boys, Carthage may well be proud of Company A. The way they fought left nothing to be desired. One thing, the boys are lucky in having Ward Schrantz for a company commander, for he certainly is good and does his best for the interest of the boys." *Carthage* (MO) *Evening Press*, January 9, 1919. Mechanic Otto Grigg called Captain Schrantz and Major Halliburton "real men and real officers and all know the game." *Carthage* (MO) *Evening Press*, November 2, 1918.

21. Before they left Vadonville, the men of Company A spent two days (March 3–4) performing road repair work in addition to their regular duties. They left the village at 1 p.m. on March 10, 1919, marched one kilometer and reached Lerouville at 1:30 p.m., and boarded the train at 4 p.m. The train departed at 5 p.m. War Diaries of 128th Machine Gun Bn., March 1–31, 1919, Folder: 128th MG BATL War Diaries 235-33.5, Record Group 120, Records of the American Expeditionary Forces, World War I, Entry NM-91 1241, Records of Combat Divisions, 1917–1919, Box 16, 35th Division, NARA.

The route led by Gondrecourt, Troyes, Bourges and Tours and in the officers' cars at least—and I believe in the men's—the trip was a merry one. The officers of the 130th were a genial lot, as were our own, and what with staring at the scenery, chatting vigorously and betting on church steeples the trip remains in my memory as a short one.

This rather childish yet amusing church steeple game had been evolved by Major Halliburton in the spring on the train journey from the British area to the Epinal region. Two officers sitting on opposite sides of the car with a handful of "clackers," French 10-centime pieces the size of an English penny—would watch for the steeples. The one on the right would collect a clacker for each appearing on his side; the same with the one on the left. Since villages in France are many and since each had its church steeple it kept people bobbing back and forth to verify their opponents' claims before paying off and so made the time pass quickly. As a form of gambling it was inexpensive and had the merit of keeping all participants watching the scenery which was well worth observing.

It was 2 a.m. March 13 when we reached the Le Mans area and detrained, resting in a camp of pyramidal tents and then in the afternoon loading into trucks and moving to the villages assigned as billets. The 128th went to the neat and cozy little village of Tresson, 18 miles southeast of Le Mans, a trim little place with dignified buildings of stone and brick and steep, black slate roofs, quite different for some reason from the villages to which we had been accustomed.[22] One letter home described it as "a newer and cleaner village than any we have yet been in in France."[23]

One incident there, perhaps a bit indelicate to relate, sticks in my memory. Troops had not been stationed there previously and it was necessary to arrange the necessary sanitary facilities by digging

22. The battalion's War Diary noted that the battalion arrived at the Forwarding Camp near LeMans at 3 a.m. on March 13, detrained and marched the two kilometers to camp. At 2:30 p.m., the battalion moved by truck train the 30 kilometers to Tresson, arriving at 4:30 p.m. War Diaries of 128th Machine Gun Bn., March 1–31, 1919, Folder: 128th MG BATL War Diaries 235-33.5, Record Group 120, Records of the American Expeditionary Forces, World War I, Entry NM-91 1241, Records of Combat Divisions, 1917–1919, Box 16, 35th Division, NARA.

23. The dignified appearance of Tresson may have prompted Major Halliburton to issue orders prohibiting the playing of catch, football, or other games in areas that would endanger windows, and warned that all damage to property would be paid for by the offenders. Memo from Commanding Officer, 128th Machine Gun Battalion, March 18[?], 1919, Record Group 120, Records of the American Expeditionary Forces, World War I Organization Records, Machine Gun Battalions, 128th Machine Gun Battalion, Box 263, NARA.

pit latrines in properly secluded places, these being selected by the town major and, for my company, approved by me.

One was just behind an ancient massive church, a narrow plot with the blank church wall on one side and screened by a thick hedge on the other. It had been pointed out by town authorities with the priest's approval. Digging parties set to work.

A short time later Sergeant Willard Brown in charge of the behind-the-church detail sent a man to me to ask if I could come over. I did.

The detail had stopped work and the sergeant was standing by the excavation with a grin on his face. He saluted with his right hand and then showed me a human skull in his left. Two more skulls set by the side of the trench. Other bones could be seen at the bottom of the hole.

Some time in the distant past, too far back for any inhabitant to have any memory of it and the place now entirely unmarked, this had been a burial ground.

"What shall I do, captain—go ahead and finish it?" asked the sergeant to whom human bones were no novelty after prowling over the old battlefields near Ailly woods.

"No indeed!" I replied, very positively, thinking of the bad luck that might follow any such act of folly. "Place those skulls back gently just where you found them and fill the trench back up. We'll find another place."

Chapter 17

Back to "The States"

On March 23, 1919, a "greatly surprised" Ward Schrantz was promoted to major and assigned to command the 130th Machine Gun Battalion in the 35th Division.[1] First Lieutenant Charles E. Dunn was promoted to captain and assumed command of Company A. Dunn led the company to its embarkation port at St. Nazaire. With the threat of U-boat attacks now gone, troop transports sailed rapidly back to the United States. The veterans of Company A ended their uneventful trip at Newport News, Virginia. There, a correspondent noted that many members of the 128th Machine Gun Battalion "bore scars of battle." Battalion commander Major Halliburton was quoted as saying, "It is needless to say how happy we are to get back."[2]

On May 3, the 128th, 129th and 130th Machine Gun Battalions paraded through Joplin past the largest crowd assembled in southwest Missouri to that time, then gathered at a reception in the city's Schifferdecker Park. Organizers assumed that the officers would dine together at an officers' mess and the enlisted men would eat by themselves, in accordance with military discipline. Instead, Major Schrantz, Major Halliburton, and the various captains and lieutenants ate, talked and joked with their men,

1. *Joplin* (MO) *Globe*, April 11, 1919.
2. *The St. Louis* (MO) *Star and Times*, April 25, 1919.

"all on an equal footing." No effort was made to have the men salute or come to attention during the reception. A short time later, they were mustered out of service and returned to civilian life.[3]

Schrantz detailed his return to the United States in his memoirs, while he documented the travels of his old comrades in Company A in the unit history that he wrote for the *Carthage Evening Press*.

Since every move in France in the spring of 1919 was likely to be interpreted by the men involved as a move nearer to the United States, the order for the 128th Machine Gun Battalion to shift from the pleasant village of Tresson on March 22 was received with smiling faces.[4]

Additional motor vehicles were supplied so that the entire movement might be made by truck. Straight north some miles to Bouloire on the Le Mans-Orleans Highway the column rolled, thence westward along this highway a mile more, then northward again, and finally at the end of a trip of some 13 or 14 miles to the village of Soulitre where battalion headquarters and Company B settled down. Company A moved out a muddy road a mile and a half to the west to the muddy grounds of a huge run-down chateau, and in this enormous and once pretentious building spread out its blankets and made itself at home.

La Roche Chateau, for so it was marked on the map, was of uncertain date, but its size, ornateness and general character encouraged the guess that it might have been built in the century or so preceding the French Revolution. There were 101 rooms in the chateau itself, and a number of others over stables that had once had a 50-horse capacity. Broken stone benches here and there about the muddy grounds, and a carved bridge across a little stream, offered materials for the imagination of those who liked to reconstruct mentally this castle in France, now only partly habitable because of the deterioration caused by time and neglect.

3. *Joplin* (MO) *Globe*, May 6, 1919.

4. The battalion moved by truck from Tresson, beginning at 8 a.m. and arriving at Soulitre at 4:30 p.m. on March 22. 1919. While in Soulitre, the commanding general of the 35th Division gave a "short talk" to the battalion on March 27, and the men were inspected for lice and vermin on March 29, with only one man found infected. War Diaries of 128th Machine Gun Bn., March 1–31, 1919, Folder: 128th MG BATL War Diaries 235-33.5, Record Group 120, Records of the American Expeditionary Forces, World War I, Entry NM-91 1241, Records of Combat Divisions, 1917-1919, Box 16, 35th Division, NARA.

128th Machine Gun Battalion, April 25, 1919 (*Author's collection*)

I would have liked to have been billeted there myself and I did spent [spend] such time as I could out there during the brief period I remained company commander.

And here at La Roche Chateau came an invitation for Company A men to join the military police.

The M.P.s were the butts of half of the jokes of the A.E.F. Directing traffic and keeping order in the back areas, the military police had had little opportunity to participate in combat and concerning this fact veterans of the front line were not slow to twit them when the soldier-police carried out their instructions as to what or what not to permit off-duty soldiers to do. A.E.F. regulations were strict, and the enforcers of them were not popular.

"Who won the war?" jibed soldiers passing the military police on duty.

"The military police," loudly chorused their comrades. The hapless guardians of A.E.F. law and order were in a constant state of redness and humiliation from this raillery.

The authorities therefore had begun to recruit the military police from men who had seen battle service, and since the only ones of these they could interest were homeward-bound

soldiers who preferred to stay awhile longer in France, the returning divisions were being canvassed for suitable material. The time-worn who-won-the-war thrust was already losing its point as men with wound chevrons became more common in the M.P. ranks.

Lined up on the south side of the chateau and addressed by a visiting M.P. officer on the subject, the risibilities of the Carthage veterans were smothered but not entirely concealed by habits of discipline, and after ranks had been broken there was much laughter. Who wanted to stay in Europe badly enough to wear the blue brassard of the much-derided military police? Some decided to accept the opportunity.

Here at Soulitre the time-worn and war-worn motor equipment of the 128th Machine Gun Battalion was turned in, and the machine gunners watched the Fords and Garfords rattle away down the road for the last time.

On March 23 I was promoted to major and Dunn to captain. The order said assignment would be "present duties" but obviously that was not to be taken too seriously and I at once turned A Company over to Captain Dunn and became a supernumary major with the 128th.

Needless to say it was with the greatest regret that I left the organization which I had commanded throughout the war and which I knew to be composed of as able and gallant machine gunners as ever served in any army.[5] Now we are all civilians and the business in hand is the business of civil life but it is my hope that in the next war it may be my good fortune to command another organization as good as the old—for if the future may be judged by the past, a "next war" there is always bound to be.

I bought my new majors leaves in Le Mans after a rather protracted [?] haggle with a woman shopkeeper. She insisted that I should not buy gold leaves but instead get new captain bars. My insignia showed I was a captain, therefore captain bars was what I should buy. She met my amused claim that I had been promoted with obvious skepticism. I was too young to be a major, she felt—I was 28—therefore I must still be a captain and it would be wrong for me to buy, or for her to sell to me, the insignia of a major. What I needed, she said, was new captain bars. I remained obdurate, to her disappointment, and finally departed with the leaves, grinning.

Someone obviously had warned her, I reflected, against selling insignia to unauthorized persons and doubtless she also knew that in the French Army one couldn't be advanced beyond the rank of captain until after having attained their 30th birthday. I must be a fraud.

The motherly old lady in Soulitre with whom I was billeted was also surprised and amused that I had become a major. I must have looked singularly unmajorly, I feared. I was just a boy, she said. The battalion already had one commandant, she added between chuckles. How could it use two? What would my job be? I told her that my job consisted only in being her guest—that the American Army considered that hers was too nice a home for a mere captain to be billeted in and that therefore I had been promoted to major.

She was a fine old soul and very solicitous about my welfare.

At this time all personnel returning to the states were being given a shot of some kind—a three-in-one anti-typhoid shot, the

5. The promotion to major came as "a great surprise" to Schrantz. *Carthage* (MO) *Evening Press*, April 10, 1919. The major in command of the 130th Machine Gun Battalion was transferred to an infantry regiment, creating the opportunity for Schrantz to take command. *Carthage* (MO) *Evening Press*, April 10, 1919.

battalion surgeon said. I didn't believe it. Why should the army be inoculated against typhoid when it was homeward bound to the land of safe drinking water. Someone in Washington, I felt, overestimated the temptations to which combat troops were exposed in France or their susceptibility to them and was making everyone take some sort of venereal-curative shot before returning to their native land. Not so, insisted the medico, anti-typhoid. There wasn't any such thing as I talked about.

Whatever it was that his needle put into my veins, the reaction was most unhappy. I was a sick man. My hostess doctored me after her own notions.

She gave me a cup of coffee. When I had drunk half of it she took it away from me and added enough milk to fill the cup. When I had taken half of that, she again took it away from me and added another half cup of milk. This procedure occurred two or three times, by which time I was drinking pure milk.

The next day the reaction has [had] passed, as inoculation reactions do, and I was all right again. She was highly pleased. She had told me that she would restore me to health.

Immediately thereafter I received division orders assigning me to the command of the 130th Machine Gun Battalion, whose headquarters were then at Surfond, a village some distance to the southeast, and I reported there March 28, relieving Major C.H. Fitzgerald, just come to the division who had been in command there four days.[6]

The 130th Machine Gun Battalion consisted of a hq and headquarters detachment, two officers and 42 enlisted; Company A, Capt. Fred H. Nesbitt, 4 officers and 179 enlisted; Company B, Capt. Paul A. Frey, 4 officers and 187 enlisted; Company C, Capt. William S. Moore, 3 officers and 180 enlisted; Company D, Capt. John S. Pearson, 5 officers and 178 enlisted; medical detachment, 1st Lt. Henry S. Rogers, 1 officer and 14 enlisted, and an ordnance detachment of four men. There were six attached lieutenants, attached to various companies for the return to the United States. Altogether there were 19 officers and 784 enlisted, an aggregate of 803.[7]

6. Possibly Clarence H. Fitzgerald, a lieutenant in the 2nd Tennessee Infantry in the Spanish-American War. *Nashville Tennesseean*, January 19, 1919.

7. John S. Pearson, born in Lebanon, Tennessee, on August 26, 1891, served overseas from April 1918 to April 1919. Henry Stanley Rogers graduated from Creighton University

The battalion was all at Surfond except for Company D which was quartered at a village some miles to the south—Volnay, I think.

Under some circumstances my assuming command of the 130th might have been accompanied by a bit of embarrassment. Frey, Moore and Nesbitt were the three senior machine gun captains of the division. The first two had held that rank since 1911, Nesbitt, a Spanish-American War veteran, since 1914. All three had been captains in the Second Missouri Infantry on the Mexican border when I was a sergeant therein. Only Pearson had I outranked as a captain, though he had been a lieutenant on the border.

But there was not the slightest trace of resentment or jealousy indicated by any of them at my promotion or my coming from another battalion to take command of theirs. They welcomed me cordially and whole-heartedly and through the rest of our service gave the same kind of willing cooperation that they would have had I been in command on [all] the while.

Captain Nesbitt was obviously pleased. Although a long time National Guardsman himself his opinion of the Guard was not entirely favorable. He had told me early in the war that I would have done better, instead of accepting a National Guard commission to have gone into the reserve at the time I had considered it, an action which probably would have made me an officer of the 89th Division. My opportunities would have been greater there than in a National Guard division, he thought.

"They've finally given you a promotion," he said to me at Surfond, "but you still should have gone into the 89th. You probably would be a lieutenant colonel there by now."

Had anyone in the battalion other than Nesbitt said that, I might have interpreted as an attempt to be pleasant to a new commanding officer. As it was I was pleased. Nesbitt was no flatterer or handshaker. He said exactly what he thought to anyone of any rank, though to a superior he might couch it in humorous language. He was a product of the southwest Missouri mining field.

Not unlikely my promotion to command the 130th was possibly more or less of an accident, I later found when it came time to make out efficiency reports on my captains and so saw their previous ratings. I had been a bit surprised at the advancement

in Omaha, Nebraska, and was a member of the Kansas National Guard in 1917. He died in 1945. *The Topeka* (KS) *Daily Capital,* July 10, 1917; *The Press Democrat* (Santa Rosa, CA), September 18, 1945.

because we had generally assumed that if a vacancy occurred in the 130th Captain Moore would be moved up to fill it.

Major Powers, who had made out the captains' January 1 efficiency reports, was one of those officers, encountered occasionally in any war, who habitually gave low ratings to everyone. He had given low ones to his four captains, far lower than they deserved. At that time a division commander could make any changes he wished in efficiency reports made in the division. At the time the reports were made out Brig. Gen. Thomas [B.] Dugan commanded the division.[8] He was an old army character known as "Patsy" Dugan. I had heard much of him at Texas City when I was a soldier in the 22nd Infantry and he was a major in the 6th Cavalry. He was a "hell-raiser" of note, according to the stories told.

Once my company was on town guard at Texas City when Dugan was provost marshal. I was a corporal at the time.

"Watch out for Patsy Dugan," the old sergeants told me. "If you meet him he will give you merry hell. It doesn't matter to him whether you are doing things right or wrong. He will tear into you anyhow. Keep out of his way if you can."

Part of my job that night had been to see that order and decorum was maintained in the town open-air theaters in my sector, they always being jammed with soldiers. Approaching one of them during the evening I saw this redoubtable Patsy Dugan on horseback coming from the other direction. Having in mind the sergeants' warnings I did not go ahead and report to him as one normally would do, but instead chose that moment to go into the show to see that was peaceful there. So I missed him and he rode around to the back of the theater where he probably was made happy by finding one of my sentries pausing to look in the stage door. He unloaded on that luckless individual, and doubtless properly so.

Dugan, as division commander, apparently felt that every officer in the division had been rated too high. He seems to have made a general percentage slash in the ratings. The unfortunate captains of the 130th, in view of the lowness with which Powers had already

8. Thomas Buchanan Dugan was born in Baltimore, Maryland, on July 27, 1858. He graduated from West Point in 1882 as a second lieutenant of cavalry, and served in combat in Cuba during the Spanish-American War, then in the Philippines. A colonel by 1915, Dugan served on the Mexican border and was promoted to brigadier general (National Army) in 1917. He commanded the 70th Infantry Brigade from October 13 to December 27, 1918, and the 35th Division from December 29, 1918, to March 1, 1919. He died on April 27, 1940. Kenamore, *From Vauquois Hill to Exermont*, 263–64; *The Baltimore Sun*, April 29, 1940; U.S. Adjutant General's Office, *Official Army Register, December 1, 1918*, 187.

graded them, emerged from this with efficiency ratings so low that they were unqualified for promotion.

I made their final ratings and these were what they should have been but it was too late to do the officers any good. There was no such thing as terminal promotions at the end of World War I.

On April 2 the 130th entrained for St. Nazaire, the port of embarkation, and on arrival at that town were stationed at Camp Guthrie, Montoir, some distance to the east—a rather boresome place, life at which was varied somewhat by some pleasant trips to the country roundabout that the Y.M.C.A. made possible.

Since I had been made captain on April 13, 1917, and had arrived in France on April 13, 1918, I began to wonder if I would leave France on April 13, 1919. Had I remained with the 128th I would have done so but as it was I received orders on April 13 to embark my battalion on April 14, which was done.

The transport which we boarded was the USS *Antigone*, formerly the North German Lloyd Liner *Neckar*, built in 1900. She was of 10,000 tons, 517 feet long, and 13 knots speed. The *Neckar* had sought refuge in Baltimore harbor in 1914 and had been interned there, being taken over by the United States April 6, 1917, when we entered the war. She was commanded on our voyage by Capt. Hugo W. Osterhaus, USN.[9]

Troops aboard were as follows: 129th Machine Gun Battalion (Maj. T.H. Loy) 27 officers, 782 men; 130th Machine Gun Battalion (Maj. Ward L. Schrantz) 25 officers, 783 men; 110th Sanitary Train (Lt. Col. Edmund Moss, M.C.), 40 officers, 896 men; 110th Field Signal Battalion (Capt. Floyd P. Whitmore) 12 officers, 503 men; 137th Infantry detachment 19 men; casuals (mostly convalescent sick and wounded) 76 officers, 10 men, a grand total of 180 officers and 2,993 enlisted men.[10]

9. Hugo Wilson Osterhaus (1878–1972), born in Norfolk, Virginia, was a graduate of the U.S. Naval Academy. He received the Navy Cross for his actions during World War I and retired in 1935. Recalled to active duty shortly before the attack on Pearl Harbor in December 1941, Osterhaus retired for a second time in 1945. *The Washington Post*, September 21, 1972. USS *Antigone* actually had a displacement of 17, 024 tons, a length of 518 feet, and a speed of 14 knots. The ship made eight voyaes to France, carrying more than 16,000 troops. Following the Armistice, *Antigone* brought more than 22,000 troops back from Europe. https://www.history.navy.mil/research/histories/ship-histories/danfs/a/antigone-i.html

10. Edmund Moss was born in Bowling Green, Kentucky, on March 22, 1873. He graduated from the University of Virginia and Tulane Medical School. Moss died in New Orleans, Louisiana, on March 22, 1927. *New Orleans* (LA) *States*, March 22, 1927; *New Orleans Times-Picayune*, March 23, 1927. Floyd P. Whitmore was born in Kansas on November 11, 1891, and is believed to have died in Hopkinsville, Kentucky, on March 7, 1991.

USS *Antigone* (*Harry S. Truman Presidential Library and Museum*)

USS *Antigone* (*National Archives*)

Major Loy was senior line officer and as such was commanding officer of troops since medical officers do not exercise command of anything other than their own units. Loy's adjutant, 1st Lieut. Warren S. Perry, served as ship's adjutant. There was a quartermaster lieutenant permanently assigned to the ship as army personnel officer but his work was with Perry and the unit adjutants and not with me.[11]

It was mid-forenoon or so on April 14 when my unit started up the gang-plank and we were soon stowed away. Since there were convalescent officers aboard and they—as in World War II when I was a transport commander—ranked the best billets, I found myself in rather crowded but quite happy quarters with a bunch of medical majors including Maj. Wm. L. Gist with whom I had been a room mate on the outbound trip on the USS *George Washington* just a year before. By coincidence the two who had shared the stateroom with Gist and I on that outbound voyage were also aboard—Capt. George Wark of Co. A, 129th Machine Gun Battalion, and Capt. Paul Frey of Company B of my own battalion.

The Bay of Biscay is notorious for its roughness at certain seasons of the year and a storm was in progress at this time. In consequence of this, instead of sailing the morning of the 15th, as I presume we otherwise would have done, we lay in St. Nazaire harbor with the ship "buttoned up" until the evening of the 15th without moving.

I didn't mind, being just as willing to wait until the sea went down, and rather enjoying myself anyhow, just visiting around.

About 6 o'clock the evening of the 15th we pulled out into the lock at St. Nazaire sailed about 3 a.m. the morning of the 16th.

The storm may have subsided a bit over what it was the day before but a heavy sea was running and the *Antigone* plunged in a fashion most disconcerting to soldier stomachs. I presume she may have rolled some but it is the plunge that I remember and I recall no trouble in keeping the dishes on the table in the wardroom where we messed as would have been the case had she rolled much.

Major Loy took to his bed and as next senior line officer I made the inspection of the ship with Lt. Com. H.C. Coburn, the ship's executive officer.[12]

The ship was a mess, as might have been expected under the circumstances. All men had been ordered on deck and most of the compartments were empty but they still looked like they had

11. Warren Spencer Perry, born in Boone (some sources state Hamilton County), Iowa, on March 15, 1886, served overseas with the 129th Machine Gun Battalion from May 1918 to April 1919. He died in Monett, Missouri, on May 2, 1952.

12. Harris C. Coburn.

been full of seasick men, and here and there a man, believed by his officers to be too sick to move, lay miserably in his bunk. Coburn grinned quietly as I gave the compartment commanders directions about cleaning up.

Entering a compartment occupied by a part of the 110th Sanitary Train I was aghast. Everyone was still in his standee bunk. I had already felt that the army wasn't showing up so well in the eyes of the navy.

"Captain, why aren't these men on deck?" I asked their medical officer commander.

"I told them to go but they wouldn't go," he replied with a helplessness that I thought at the time was typically "medical officer" but which actually was probably due—it seems in more charitable retrospect—to his own seasickness.

"They'll go when I tell them," I informed him, and raised my voice in tones which sent them scrambling hastily for top-side.

Coburn grinned some more.

It was in the forward and after compartments that I noticed the plunge the most, quite naturally—particularly in the forward ones. The ship would heave up and then the deck would drop away beneath one's feet.

Happily I was too much occupied with the task in hand to get seasick myself. In after-years when sea voyages on crowded troopships were routine I noticed that seasickness usually hit hardest those who had nothing particular to occupy their minds except themselves.

The following morning also I made the inspection with the ship's executive officer and it was clean and in good shape, as indeed it was on the various other days I substituted for Major Loy on this task.

The officers' mess was in a large wardroom with long tables fore and aft, at each of which navy officers and army officers sat together. At our table were three ship's officers and nine of us army ones. There were several vacant army places at breakfast and more at lunch—there being in fact only three or four wearers of the olive drab there. My appetite was unimpaired.

Dinner that night was a wonderful meal—for those who cared for dinner. Before it had progressed far I was the only representative of the ground service still at table. The main dish that evening,

I recall, was turkey and I took on a good supply, topping it off with dessert—ice cream if I remember right. I was feeling quite proud of myself.

Suddenly I felt a woozy feeling in my stomach. To my dismay I realized I was about to get sick. As my companions in blue smiled I rose from the table and hastily dashed for the foyer. I wanted to go out the port door of the foyer for that was leeward, and back in Texas City days when my unit had expected to sail on the since-torpedoed *City of Memphis* for Vera Cruz, we had been lectured extensively about never getting sick to windward while at sea. But the port door was blocked with men. The situation brooked no delay and I bolted for the starboard rail and reached it just in time. Turkey, dessert and everything went overside, the wind blowing it back against the hull of the ship. Happily there were no open lower decks on the *Antigone* and I think all ports were closed because of the seas. I hoped no one else suffered. But all the remainder of the voyage I was humiliated by seeing the remnants of my disgorged meal plastered against the hull whenever I looked over the starboard rail amidships. And somehow I couldn't help looking.

I was back at table the next meal and that one I retained. That turkey dinner is the only meal I have ever lost at sea and I never missed one when it was available. It was some consolation that I had eaten this one and enjoyed it, even if I could not keep it.

The *Antigone* was a happy and well-managed ship and, aside from the episode of sea-sickness mentioned, I do not recall the slightest unpleasantness aboard her.

The weather was pleasant after the first two days and while I recked little of routes, the ship newspaper said that we were following a course about midway between the northern and southern routes.

The war being over, the ship traveled with all lights on at night, and each evening there was a movie on the forward deck and another on the after deck for the men. For such of the officers as cared for pictures—which I didn't particularly—there was one each afternoon in the ward room.

The evening before we made port there was a dinner by the navy officers for the army officers and Captain Osterhaus came down from the bridge to preside on that occasion. Major Loy sat at

130th Machine Gun Battalion, Newport News, Virginia, 1919 (*Harry S. Truman Presidential Library and Museum*)

his right and I at his left and he told of his impressions of the naval battle of Santiago in the Spanish-American War and his personal experiences therein. It was a very pleasant evening.

On April 27 we steamed through Hampton Roads after a voyage of what I suppose to have been about 3,500 nautical miles and debarked at Newport News, Va., marching through the town under an arch under which I understood all returning troops passed and out to Camp Stewart on the east.

Camp Stewart was a smoothly functioning machine. The 130th Machine Gun Battalion was split into 13 geographical detachments so that its members could be demobilized near their homes—groups for Camps Funston, Gordon, Travis, Dodge, Taylor, Dix, Grant, Kearny, Devens, Lewis, Custer, Jackson and Upton.

Under my command to go to Camp Funston, Kans., there remained 12 officers and 436 enlisted men. The 128th Machine Gun Battalion which had arrived at Newport News aboard the U.S. transport *Matsonia* on April 24, and the 129th Machine Gun Battalion, were similarly divided.

On May 1 the three machine gun battalions, or what was left of them, loaded on to trains and rolled westward, Major Halliburton in command of the first train, Major Loy of the second while I had the third.

Through Richmond, Virginia, West Virginia we rolled, eventually through Cincinnati and on May 2 into St. Louis.

Col. W.A. Raupp, commander of the old Second Missouri, at the outbreak of the war, had met us at Newport News.[13] At St. Louis Col. W.K. Caffee, Spanish-American War commander of the old regiment met us, accompanied by ex-Capt. Joe McMillan, his Spanish War adjutant, and I was happy to have these fine old officers, both well known to me since they were fellow townsmen, ride on down into Southwest Missouri on my section with me.

We were scheduled for three parades in as many towns on our way to Camp Funston, St. Louis was the first and we marched through the streets that day in order of rank of majors, the 130th, headed by a quite trim woman's band, bringing up the rear. The city was decorated along the line of march, there being, among other things, streamers bearing the names of towns where the 35th Division had been engaged in battle.[14]

In Springfield the next morning there was another parade, the 130th heading the line of march this time because Company B of my battalion was from Springfield. Company B was placed at the head of the battalion that day.

In Joplin we paraded again that afternoon, meeting many old acquaintances here and I had a brief opportunity to visit

13. William August Raupp, born in Sandusky, Ohio, on November 17, 1868, came to Missouri at the age of two. He enlisted as a drummer boy in the 5th Missouri Infantry in 1886. Discharged the following year, he entered the 2nd Missouri Infantry in 1890 and steadily rose through the ranks. After service in the Spanish-American War as captain of Company E and a battalion commander, he was promoted to major in 1899, lieutenant colonel in 1900 and colonel in 1906. Raupp commanded the 2nd Missouri on the Mexican border 1916–1917. Although he brought the regiment to Camp Doniphan in 1917, he was reassigned to the 56th and 60th Pioneer Infantry and did not serve overseas. Raupp served as adjutant general of Missouri from 1921 to 1925 and as commanding general of the Missouri National Guard until his retirement as a brigadier general in 1932. He died in Pierce City, Missouri, on May 4, 1946. *Joplin* (MO) *Globe*, May 5, 1946; *The Service of the Missouri National Guard on the Mexican Border*, 107; Missouri Secretary of State's Office World War I Military Service Record Database at www.sos.mo.gov/archives/ww1. Raupp appeared before two army efficiency boards. It was not uncommon for National Guard officers to be examined by such boards, removed from their original commands and assigned elsewhere. Such a practice offered Guardsmen like Schrantz even more evidence of a perceived anti-Guard bias on the part of Regular Army officers. *The Butler* (MO) *Weekly Times and The Bates County Record*, February 13, 1919.

14. The *St. Louis Post-Dispatch* reported the "long-limbed" youths towered above the admiring crowds standing on the pavement. The enthusiastic reception surprised the members of the battalion, as the parade was an impromptu affair, organized that morning. The 260 officers and men of the 128th Battalion led the parade, and Major Halliburton pronounced it the finest welcome they had received since arriving back in the United States. Schrantz, then in command of the 130th Machine Gun Battalion, was quoted as saying, "It was the best thing we struck since we left France." *St. Louis Post-Dispatch*, May 2, 1919.

Parade in Joplin for returning machine gun battalions, May 1919 (*Joplin Historical & Mineral Museum*)

Parade in Joplin for returning machine gun battalions, May 1919 (*Joplin Historical & Mineral Museum*)

Parade in Joplin for returning machine gun battalions, May 1919 (*Joplin Historical & Mineral Museum*)

with my wife who with hundreds of others had come down from Carthage.

The next morning—May 4—we reached Camp Funston. I had lost a man during the night. He had fallen somehow from the train and had been run over. The section following mine picked up his body and brought it on into the camp.

The demobilization machinery was geared for smooth, rapid demobilization. All the work I had to do personally was to sign the discharges of the 435 enlisted men I had remaining.

On May 7 we were on our way homewards, the men discharged and the officers given two weeks leave after which they were to report back for discharge.

On May 20, accompanied by Mrs. Schrantz, I returned to the camp and there was separated from the service.

My part in World War I was over.

Many of our National Guard officers came back to civil life with a feeling of resentment which had been aroused over removal of senior National Guard officers during the war, particularly in the early part, and there was considerable recrimination about this or that.

Personally I had no grievance against the Regular Army or anyone else as the result of service.

Happy to be home again, and particularly happy to be reunited with my wife, I still left the army—as was my wont—with some regrets.

However I looked forward to renewed service with one of the civilian components thereof. Colonel Raupp at Newport News had asked me not to take a reserve commission until I saw what the National Guard was going to do and in any event I could get a commission as major in the infantry section of the officers reserve corps for the asking.

Chapter 18

The Return of Company A

On April 1 came move orders—and there was no April fool joke about it. The 128th was to entrain for a port of embarkation.

On April 2 the battalion marched northward to a nearby railroad, found waiting there a string of French box cars and were crowded therein, the officers behind in a third class coach, and soon the equipage was rattling away westward into Brittany, and the next day the battalion detrained at St. Nazaire and went into camp in wooden barracks to the west of that town.

Here there were some days of inspections and re-inspections, but on April 13 the battalion moved into St. Nazaire, climbed the gang-plank of the American transport *Matsonia*, on it slipped out of the concrete-bordered slip of that seaport and out into the estuary of the Loire River down whence, ex-Latin students not too far from their "Gallic Wars," recalled that the soldier-built fleet of Julius Caesar had slipped some thousand years before to destroy the Veneti. And soon the ship was rising and falling on the open sea.[1]

1. *Matsonia*, built in Newport News, Virginia, in 1913, was taken over by the U.S Shipping Board and transferred to the Navy in January 1918 for use as a troop transport.

USS *Matsonia* in St. Nazaire (*Author's collection*)

The Bay of Biscay on which the *Matsonia* was plunging, had a reputation for turbulence which it was doing its best to sustain. A considerable storm was raging, one that kept other shipping in port for the next two days, and in addition to a disconcerting beam-sea roll, the *Matsonia* pitched and bucked in a fore-and-aft direction in a way most distressing to the stomachs of landsmen. This was a great deal to go through with, someone suggested, just for the sake of getting back to the United States again.

But fair weather followed foul, and the *Matsonia* sailed over summer seas. At night all lights blazed in contrast to the darkness of the trip eastward on the English *Caronia* the previous spring, and moving picture shows on deck enlivened the evenings. If the ship menu was not all the soldiers might have liked it was at least both ample and palatable compared to the well-remembered food on the canned-rabbit cursed *Caronia* of pre-battle memory.

On April 24 green land appeared to the westward. America had been re-discovered. Soon the *Matsonia* was passing Cape Henry at the south end of Chesapeake Bay. Then it passed by an old Civil War fort on an island and up historic Hampton Roads, coming to dock at Newport News, Va. Home again. Down the gang plank, and up streets across which a welcoming arch to returning soldiers had been erected, the battalion passed and so to another camp for another necessary pause before continuing westward.

So, after exactly a year of foreign service, Company A returned to the United States.

Newport News, Va., has a rich historical background but to the returning machine gunners of Company A, 128th Machine Gun Battalion, who disembarked there April 24, 1919, it was just a stopping place on the road home. The war was over and the Carthage soldiers were now anxious to be in their home town and in civilian clothes. There was no slackening in discipline, for that was a habit, but with France and the Atlantic Ocean behind, the minds of the men were already divesting themselves of the uniforms which the bodies still wore.

While in camp at Newport News the soldiers were refitted with clothes—of which the government had an ample stock with which

---

Commissioned that March, *Matsonia* completed six trips to Europe before the end of the war, and eight additional trips between the time of the Armistice and August 1919. http://www.history.navy.mil/danfs/m6/matsonia.htm.

USS *Matsonia* at sea (*Author's collection*)

it did not know what to do—and was divided up into detachments to be sent to various posts for muster-out, each man being mustered out as near his home as possible. Capt. Charles E. Dunn was sent in command of a detachment of former replacements to be mustered out at Camp Brady, Mich.—his home being at Nilton, Wis.,—and First Lieut. Frank L. Snyder succeeded to command of Company A which had by now sadly shrunken in size.

On May 1 the three machine gun battalions which had been the old Second Missouri Infantry when the war started, entrained at Newport News, each on a separate troop train, and rolled westward. Here was Richmond, Va., with its vague background of Civil War associations. Now also the fertile region of Virginia, and next the mountains whose name on the map sent the soldiers to singing to the accompaniment of their rocking train, the words of a once-popular song—"In the Blue Ridge Mountains of Virginia, on the Trail of the Lonesome Pine." Later the train was jolting down a valley of Civil War fame at which the machine gunners stared curiously, thinking that at one time it had been something like parts of France they had seen. "Not even a crow could fly across the Shenandoah Valley," some general had said after the hand of devastation had been laid on the region, "without carrying its rations." West Virginia with its mountains and its coal mines followed, then the Ohio River, and eventually Cincinnati.

The night on the troop train was as pleasant as had been the day in traveling comfort. Men whose recent means of transportation by rail had been comfortless French box cars were in a position to appreciate "riding the cushions" and sleeping in the berths of the tourist cars.

From the time the machine gunners had reached America, various communities in Missouri had been endeavoring to get the troops routed through them for parade[s] before going to Camp Funston, Kans., for muster-out.

The first parade was at St. Louis on May 2, the 128th, 129th and 130th Machine Gun Battalions marching in their numerical order which chanced also to be the order of rank of their commanders.

Carthage had tried hard to get a parade of the 128th, but since Springfield and Joplin had wielded more influence in Washington, by virtue of being larger towns, the effort had not succeeded.

At Springfield the 130th Battalion led the line of march, because the Springfield company was in that battalion, and again crowds lined the streets along which roses were tossed under the feet of the marching columns. Here were more Carthage people, including an official delegation headed by W.S. Crane and including Gene Milton, J.D. Carter, Ed Hannum, Roy Reed and Laurence Gray, the last three returned soldiers. Mr. Crane carried the old flag of the Carthage Light Guard.[2]

It was afternoon of May 3 when the three troop trains passed through Carthage en route to Joplin. For miles the Carthage machine gunners had been staring at the landscape for familiar scenes. There were a few persons in Carter's Park to wave as the trains went by, and there was a large group at the Frisco station to shout greetings at hurriedly-glimpsed familiar faces, but the train could not stop and the home town faded behind. Much of Carthage was already in Joplin to cheer the returning troops. After a parade there, a period was allowed at Schifferdecker Park for greetings between soldiers and friends, then the troops were extricated from

2. Walter Silas Crane (1860–1931), Richard Eugene Milton (1876–1953), James D. Carter (1877–1937), Edward A. Hannum (1876–1940), Roy E. Reed (1894?–?), and Laurence H. Gray (1891–1920). The people of the city were proud of "Carthage's Own" company. For nearly two years, they followed Company A's activities closely, and every "wild rumor of disaster" brought a "chill of terror" to the civilians, the *Carthage Evening Press* recalled, while thoughts of Carthage and their loved ones gave the soldiers "added courage to fight and whip the German machine which sought to conquer the world." *Carthage* (MO) *Evening Press*, May 8, 1919.

the crowd and marched to the waiting cars, jolting through the night toward Fort Riley for the muster-out process.[3]

Company A had been mustered out at Fort Riley in January 1917, after its seven months tour of duty on the Mexican border, but now it detrained at Camp Funston some distance to the eastward. What in January, 1917, had been an empty plain was now something of a sea of frame buildings which had first been occupied by the 89th Division and later by the 10th, but which were now waiting empty to receive the returning 35th.

It was the morning of May 4 when the machine gunners reached Camp Funston, and the highly efficient muster-out machinery there started work on them at once. On May 7 each man received his discharge and boarded a train, homeward bound.

In Carthage plans for any parade had been abandoned because of a heavy rain and when the Missouri Pacific train carrying Company A, now consisting of Lieut. Snyder and 69 enlisted men, a group of automobiles were waiting to whisk the men away homeward as soon as their first greetings were over. The train had been due at 6:40 but it was 7:40 before it finally pulled in and the grinning soldiers, looking about at the sea of umbrellas, de-trained at the station which they had left 21 months before, bound for the war.

This was on Thursday. On the following Monday night a reception was held at the armory on Fifth Street for the returning soldiers and this was followed by a dance in the Knights of Pythias Hall on the south side of the square. At the reception there was a short program. Allen McReynolds, who back about 1906 had been a captain of Company A, made a short talk of welcome and the two Carthage majors responded briefly. Mrs. John Bailey sang "There's a Long, Long Trail," and Mrs. Marian Wright Powers, "The Star Spangled Banner."[4]

Refreshments of ice cream and cake were served, and Miss Fagin's orchestra and the Mandolin Club played between numbers on the program. About 1,000 persons were present. It was a very happy occasion. "Finis la guerre."

3. *The Joplin Globe* devoted considerable space to covering the parade, noting that at least 150,000 people cheered the "splendid specimens of physical and intellectual manhood" in the ranks. *The Joplin* (MO) *Globe*, May 4, 1919.

4. Probably Elizabeth Tucker Bailey (1876–1940), and Marian Wright Powers (1880–1969).

When Company A returned to Carthage on May 8, 1919, it had been in the United States service just 21 months and two days. During the war 22 officers and over 300 men had been on its rolls one time or another. It had had five men killed in action, one died as a result of exhaustion in action and two died of disease.[5]

There had been many men lost by transfer and many gained by transfer, and of the company of three officers and 150 men which left Carthage in August, 1917, two had been killed and one died of disease, but only one officer and 69 men came back with the unit. Disabling wounds and sickness had caused the loss of many of the remainder, but numerous others had completed their service in other units as the result of transfers.[6]

Under the law of the time, the National Guardsmen "stood discharged from the National Guard" of the state when drafted into the Army of the United States as a unit on August 5, 1917, and now the officers and men were given a complete severance from service with their discharge from the army. This was different from the time when on the Mexican border in 1916 they served as a part of the Army of the United States "under the call of the president" and had reverted to state control when the emergency ceased.

5. Company A member Norval Hopwood believed that the company's few losses were due to the fine leadership of Capt. Ward Schrantz and Maj. Westley Halliburton. *Carthage* (MO) *Evening Press*, March 20, 1919. Likewise, when Otto Kaselack (likely the last surviving member of Company A) was asked in 1983 about the quality of leadership while he was in the army, he responded, "Excellent & well trained." When asked about the discipline at the time, he answered "strict," as "The officers were Mexican Border experienced [*sic*]." World War I Veterans Survey of Otto Kaselack, U.S. Army Heritage and Education Center, Carlisle, Pennsylvania.

6. According to one document in the 128th Machine Gun Battalion's records, 5 enlisted men were killed by shellfire, 1 officer and 12 enlisted men were severely wounded, 1 officer and 18 enlisted men were slightly wounded, and 2 enlisted men were wounded, degree not determined, for a total of 39 casualties. Casualties, Company A, 128th Machine Gun Battalion, Record Group 120, Records of the American Expeditionary Forces, World War I Organization Records, Machine Gun Battalions, 128th Machine Gun Battalion, Box 263, NARA.

Epilogue

The citizens of Carthage were overjoyed that not only had the majority of the company returned safely, but also that their fellow Missourians had upheld the honor of the community. "Company A covered itself with glory in the American drive on the Argonne sector," wrote the *Carthage* (MO) *Evening Press*.[1] Referring to the 2nd Missouri's "Houn' Dog Regiment" nickname, acquired in 1916, St. Louis correspondent Clair Kenamore reported, "The Houn' Dog again bayed gloriously. They were mighty men of war, these long boys from the Ozarks, and they will not be soon forgot."[2]

Allen McReynolds, a former captain of the Carthage Light Guard, was fully aware of the close ties that existed between the town's military company and its citizens. "For over forty years the community life of Carthage has been enriched by such an institution. . . . It has always played a conspicuous part in community life, and community affairs. For years its home was the social center of the community. On public occasions, at home and aboard, its appearance reflected credit. On its muster rolls have appeared the names of practically every active and purposeful

1. *Carthage* (MO) *Press*, November 2, 1918.
2. Kenamore, *From Vauquois Hill to Exermont*, 248.

man in the community. From its ranks each has carried a definite lesson of discipline and obedience which profited him much in later life."

"Unconsciously supported by its traditions and influence," he continued, "the boys who went from Carthage to France, fought their way through the tangled depths of the Argonne forests, and today bring home the richest heritage yet laid upon its altar. . . . Their duty done, they modestly bring home a record of manly courage, untarnished and unstained. Surely they have a right to expect, and we have a right to hope that the future generations will preserve and carry on the spirit of the old organization in a manner worthy not only of the returning heroes who march today, but of the unforgotten dead whose lives have so nobly sanctified our cause."[3]

"Company A, 'Carthage's Own,' returned home this morning—returned with a record of glorious achievement that will live as long as memory," echoed the *Carthage* (MO) *Evening Press*. "Carthage is proud of your success—proud and jealous of your splendid achievements; Carthage realizes that she owes you much more than she can ever repay—and may the Old Home Town never forget, for one moment, that binding obligation."[4]

The veterans of Company A resumed their former lives as best they could. They couldn't explain the experience of combat to those who remained at home, and many never tried. "The eager, adventure-loving youngsters of 1917 no longer existed; war had seasoned them into manhood; or left a scar from wounds or gas or the blasting of youthful aspirations," reported the *Kansas City Star* on the war's tenth anniversary. "After the cheering and the plaudits died away, the citizen soldiers of the 35th division [*sic*] again took their places back in the old home towns; partly misunderstood, partly victims of envy, partly incapacitated for life by the gallant service they gave to state and nation," the paper continued. "Many of the younger ones went back to school, others returned to the farm, still others hunted for their first job, a small number regained the vocations they had left in 1917."[5]

The 128th Machine Gun Battalion held frequent reunions where the old doughboys could be found "fighting the war over again."[6]

3. *Carthage* (MO) *Evening Press*, May 5, 1919.
4. *Carthage* (MO) *Evening Press*, May 8, 1919.
5. *The Kansas City* (MO) *Star*, July 31, 1938.
6. *Joplin* (MO) *Globe*, August 23, 1927.

But as their numbers dwindled, and the men of Carthage went off to serve in a far more costly war in 1941, the memory of Company A and the sacrifices they endured in the Meuse-Argonne gradually disappeared. Today, no monument or statue stands on the Jasper County courthouse square in Carthage to honor Company A, 128th Machine Gun Battalion, the county's participants in the First World War, or the Carthage Light Guard. But thanks to the literary efforts of their commander, the legacy of a heroic group of Missourians and their role in the Great War has been preserved, ready to be discovered anew by future generations.

Bibliography

Books And Articles

Adjutant General's Department, State of Ohio. *The Official Roster of Ohio Soldiers, Sailors, and Marines in the World War, 1917–1918*. 23 vols. Columbus, OH: The F.J. Heer Printing Co., 1926–1929.

Adjutant General's Office, State of Kansas. *Roster and Directory of the Commissioned Officers of the Kansas National Guard*. Topeka: Kansas State Printing Plant, 1919.

Adjutant General's Office, State of Missouri. *Report of the Adjutant General of Missouri, January 1, 1917–December 31, 1920*. Jefferson City: Office of the Adjutant General, 1921.

Adjutant General's Office, State of Missouri. *The Service of the Missouri National Guard on the Mexican Border*. Jefferson City, MO: Hugh Stephens Co., 1919.

American Battle Monuments Commission. *35th Division Summary of Operations in the World War*. Washington, D.C: U.S. Government Printing Office, 1944.

American Battle Monuments Commission. *81st Division Summary of Operations in the World War*. Washington, D.C: U.S. Government Printing Office, 1944.

Bach, Christian A., and Henry Noble Hall. *The Fourth Division: Its Services and Achievements in the World War*. [Garden City, NY]: Issued by the division [Country Life Press], 1920.

Bowen, Albert S. *The Medical Department of the United States Army in the World War*. 14 vols. Washington, D.C.: U.S. Government Printing Office, 1928.

Braim, Paul F. *The Test of Battle: The American Expeditionary Forces in the Meuse-Argonne Campaign*. Newark: University of Delaware Press, 1987.

Bruce, Robert B. *A Fraternity of Arms: America and France in the Great War*. Lawrence: University Press of Kansas, 2003.

Canfield, Bruce N. *U.S. Infantry Weapons of the First World War*. Lincoln, RI: Andrew Mowbray Publishers, 2000.

Clark, Harvey C. "Missourians in Service." *The Missouri Historical Review* 14, no. 1 (October 1919): 1–15.

Company Clerk. "Then and Now." *The American Legion Monthly* 2, no. 3 (March 1927).

Conard, Howard L., ed. *Encyclopedia of the History of Missouri*. 6 vols. New York: The Southern History Company, 1901.

Doubler, Michael D. *I Am the Guard: A History of the Army National Guard, 1636–2000*. Washington, D.C.: U.S. Government Printing Office, 2001.

Edwards, Evan Alexander. *From Doniphan to Verdun: The Official History of the 140th Infantry*. Lawrence, KS: The World Company, 1920.

Faulkner, Richard S. *The School of Hard Knocks: Combat Leadership in the American Expeditionary Forces*. College Station: Texas A&M University Press, 2012.

Ferrell, Robert H. *America's Deadliest Battle: Meuse-Argonne, 1918*. Lawrence: University Press of Kansas, 2007.

——— *Collapse at Meuse-Argonne: The Failure of the Missouri-Kansas Division*. Columbia: University of Missouri Press, 2004.

——— ed. *Meuse-Argonne Diary: A Division Commander in World War I*. Columbia: University of Missouri Press, 2004.

Fiftieth Annual Report of the Association of Graduates of the United States Military Academy, at West Point, New York, June 10th, 1919. Saginaw, MI: Seemann & Peters, 1919.

Fogarty, Richard S. *Race and War in France: Colonial Subjects in the French Army, 1914–1918*. Baltimore: The Johns Hopkins University Press, 2008.

Ford, James Everett. *A History of Grundy County*. Trenton, MO: News Publishing Company, 1908.

Gay, Adrien. *Grenade Warfare*. Atlanta, GA: E.W. Allen & Co., 1918.

Haterius, Carl E. *Reminiscences of the 137th U.S. Infantry*. Topeka, KS: Crane & Company, 1919.

Hay, Donald D. "Machine Guns, 35th Division, Meuse-Argonne Operation, Sept. 26–Oct. 1, 1918." *Infantry Journal* 40 (1933): 193–206.

Hemenway, Frederic V. *History of the Third Division, United States Army, in the World War, for the Period December 1, 1917 to January 1, 1919*. Cologne, Germany: M. Dumont Schauberg, 1919.

Hoyt, Charles B. *Heroes of the Argonne: An Authentic History of the Thirty-Fifth Division*. Kansas City: Franklin Hudson Publishing Company, 1919.

The International Committee of Young Men's Christian Association. *Summary of Service, Y.M.C.A. in the Embarkation Center, From December 1918 to July 1919*. Portland, OR: The Arcady Press and Mail Advertising Co., Inc., 1920.

Kenamore, Clair. *From Vauquois Hill to Exermont: A History of the Thirty-Fifth Division of the United States Army*. St. Louis: Guard Publishing Co., 1919.

———. *The Story of the 139th Infantry*. St. Louis: Guard Publishing Co., 1920.

Kennedy, David M. *Over Here: The First World War and American Society*. New York: Oxford University Press, 1980.

Lanza, Conrad H. "Supporting an Infantry Division." *The Field Artillery Journal* 23 (September–October 1933): 405–25.

Lengel, Edward G. *To Conquer Hell: The Meuse-Argonne, 1918*. New York: Henry Holt and Company, 2008.

McCoy, Matthew G. "Grinding Gears: The AEF and Motor Transportation in the First World War." *War in History* 11 (2004): 193–208.

McLean, Ross H. "Troop Movements on the American Railroads During the Great War." *The American Historical Review* 26 (1921): 464–488.

No author. "Death of Col. Thomas C. Clarke, E.O.R.C." *The Military Engineer* 13 (July–August 1921): 342.

North Dakota, State of. *Roster of the Men and Women Who Served in the Army or Naval Service (including the Marine Corps) of the United States or Its Allies from the State of North Dakota in the World War, 1917–1918*, accessed at ancestry.com.

Nye, W.S. *Carbine and Lance: The Story of Old Fort Sill*. Norman: University of Oklahoma Press, 1943.

Palmer, Frederick. *Our Greatest Battle (The Meuse-Argonne)*. New York: Dodd, Mead and Company, 1919.

Pollock, Edwin T., and Paul F. Bloomhardt. *The Hatchet of the United States Ship "George Washington."* New York: J.J. Little & Ives Co., 1919.

Raach, George T. *A Withering Fire: American Machine Gun Battalions in World War I*. Bradenton, FL: BookLocker.com, 2015.

Rankin, Edward Payson, Jr. *The Santa Fe Trail Leads to France: A Narrative of Battle Service of the 110th Engineers (35th Division) in the Meuse-Argonne Offensive*. Kansas City, MO: Dick Richardson Co., 1933.

Robinson, Wirt, ed. *Biographical Register of the Officers and Graduates of the U.S. Military Academy at West Point, New York, Supplement, Volume VI-B, 1910–1920.* Saginaw, MI: Seemann & Peters, 1920.

Rochester Theological Seminary. *General Catalogue, 1850 to 1920.* Rochester, N.Y.: E.R. Andrews Printing Co., 1920.

Schrantz, Ward L. "Initial Machine-Gun Barrage, 35th Division, Meuse-Argonne Offensive." *Infantry Journal* 16 (1919): 367–71.

Spaulding, Oliver L., Jr. *The Thirty-Fifth Division, 1917–1918.* Washington, D.C.: U.S. Army War College, 1921–22.

Sterett, Betty. *Scenes from the Past (of Nevada, Missouri).* rev. ed. Nevada, MO: Vernon County Historical Society, 2002.

U.S. Adjutant General's Office. *American Decorations.* Washington, D.C.: Government Printing Office, 1927.

U.S. Adjutant General's Office. *Official Army Register for 1916.* Washington, D.C.: U.S. Government Printing Office, 1916.

U.S. Adjutant General's Office. *Official Army Register, December 1, 1918.* Washington, D.C.: U.S. Government Printing Office, 1918.

U.S. Adjutant General's Office. *Official Army Register for 1921.* Washington, D.C.: U.S. Government Printing Office, 1922.

U.S. Adjutant General's Office. *Official Army Register, January 1, 1922.* Washington, D.C.: Government Printing Office, 1922.

U.S. Adjutant General's Office. *Official Army Register, January 1, 1923.* Washington, D.C.: Government Printing Office, 1923.

U.S. Adjutant General's Office. *Official Army Register, January 1, 1924.* Washington, D.C.: Government Printing Office, 1924.

U.S. Adjutant General's Office. *Official Army Register, January 1, 1931.* Washington, D.C.: U.S. Government Printing Office, 1931.

U.S. Adjutant General's Office. *Official Army Register, January 1, 1934.* Washington, D.C.: Government Printing Office, 1934.

U.S. Adjutant General's Office. *Official Army Register, January 1, 1936.* Washington, D.C.: Government Printing Office, 1936.

U.S. Adjutant General's Office. *Official Army Register, January 1, 1941.* Washington, D.C.: Government Printing Office, 1941.

U.S. Adjutant General's Office. *Regimental History of the United States Regular Army, Chronological Outline, 1866–1918.* Washington, D.C.: U.S. Government Printing Office, 1918.

U.S. Army Center of Military History. *Order of Battle of the United States Land Forces in the World War.* 3 vols. Washington, D.C.: Office of Military History, 1988.

U.S. Government. *The Statutes at Large of the United States of America from December, 1915, to March, 1917.* Vol. 39, Part I. Washington, D.C.: U.S. Government Printing Office, 1917.

U.S. Navy Department. *American Ship Casualties of the World War.* Washington, D.C.: U.S. Government Printing Office, 1923.

U.S. War Department. *Annual Reports, 1918.* Washington, D.C.: U.S. Government Printing Office, 1919.

U.S. War Department. *Histories of Two Hundred and Fifty-One Divisions of the German Army Which Participated in the War (1914–1918).* Washington, D.C.: U.S. Government Printing Office, 1920.

von Giehrl, Herman. "Battle of the Meuse-Argonne." *Infantry Journal* 19 (1921): 131–38.

Weber, Walter W. *History of the 129th Machine Gun Battalion, 35th Division, A.E.F.* N.p., n.d.

Wilhelm, Glenn P. *Machine Gun Fire Control.* Cleveland, OH: Edward C. McKay, 1917.

Williams, Walter. *The State of Missouri: An Autobiography*. Columbia, MO: E.W. Stephens, 1904.

Witwer, Reverend George, and Ananias Clime Witwer. *Witwer Genealogy of America*. N.p., 1909.

Yockelson, Mitchell. *Forty-Seven Days: How Pershing's Warriors Came of Age to Defeat the German Army in World War I*. New York: New American Library, 2016.

Young, G.R. "The Operation of Motor Trucks in War." *The Military Engineer* 13 (1921): 99–103, 157–74.

Newspapers

The Advertiser-Courier (Hermann, MO)

The Atchison (KS) *Daily Globe*

The Austin (TX) *American*

The Butler (MO) Weekly Times and The Bates County Record

The Cameron (TX) *Herald*

Carthage (MO) *Evening Press*

The Chanute (KS) *Daily Tribune*

Chicago Daily Tribune

Dallas (TX) *Morning News*

Des Moines Register

Detroit Free Press

Durant (OK) *Weekly News*

Emporia (KS) *Gazette*

The Evening Star (Washington, D.C.)

Fort Scott (KS) *Tribune and the Fort Scott Monitor*

The Great Falls (MT) *Tribune*

The Hayti (MO) *Herald*

The Herald-Palladium (St. Joseph, MI)

The Holt County Sentinel (Oregon, MO)
Honolulu (HI) *Star-Bulletin*
The Houston (MO) *Herald*
The Hutchison (KS) *News*
The Ithaca (NY) *Journal*
Jefferson City (MO) *Post-Tribune*
The Joplin (MO) *Globe*
Joplin (MO) *News Herald*
Kansas City (MO) *Star*
Kansas City (MO) *Times*
Kenosha (WI) *Evening News*
Lamar (MO) *Democrat*
Larned (KS) *Chronoscope*
The Leavenworth (KS) *Times*
Lexington (MO) *Advertiser-News*
The Macon (MO) *Republican*
Mexico Missouri Message
Mexico (MO) *Weekly Ledger*
The Monett (MO) *Times*
The Morning Herald (Hagerstown, MD)
The Morning News (Wilmington, DE)
Nashville Tennesseean
The National Tribune (Washington, D.C.)
The Neodesha (KS) *Daily Sun*
The Neosho (MO) *Times*
The New York Times
The Oregon Daily Journal (Portland)
The Osage City Free Press (Osage City, KS)
The Press Democrat (Santa Rosa, CA)
The Red Cloud (NE) *Chief*
Republic County (KS) *Democrat*
The St. Clair (MO) *Chronicle*
St. Louis Post-Dispatch
The St. Louis (MO) *Star and Times*
The Salina (KS) *Daily Union*
The San Diego (CA) *Union*
Scott County Democrat (Benton, MO)
Shelbina (MO) *Democrat*
Springfield (MO) *Daily News*
Springfield (MO) *Leader and Press*
Springfield (MO) *Leader-Press*
Springfield (MO) *Republican*

The Terre Haute (IN) *Tribune*
The (London) *Times*
The Topeka (KS) Daily Capital
Trenton (MO) *Daily Republican*
The Washington Post
The Weekly Guard (Council Grove, KS)
Wellington (KS) *Daily News*
The Winfield (KS) *Courier*
The Winfield (KS) *Daily Free Press*

Internet Sources

Dictionary of American Naval Fighting Ships (http://www.history.navy.mil/danfs/)

Manuscript Sources

Frank E. Bonney, "Operations of the 35th Division in the First Phase of the Meuse Argonne," Advanced Officers' Course, 1922–1923, The Infantry School, Fort Benning, Georgia (http://www.benning.army.mil/library/content/Virtual/Donovanpapers/wwi/index.htm)

Westley Halliburton Manuscript, Jasper County (MO) Record Center.

Hans O. Olson, "Operations of the 35th Division in First Phase Meuse Argonne 1918," Advanced Officer's Course, 1925–1926, The Infantry School, Fort Benning, Georgia (http://www.benning.army.mil/library/content/Virtual/Donovanpapers/wwi/index.htm)

Record Group 120, Records of the American Expeditionary Forces, World War I, Entry NM-91 1241, Records of Combat Divisions, 1917–1919, Box 16, 35th Division, National Archives and Records Administration, College Park, Maryland.

Record Group 120, Records of the American Expeditionary Forces, World War I, Entry NM-91 1256, Organization Records, Machine Gun Battalions, Boxes 263–266, 128th Machine Gun Battalion, Co. A – DOC. FILE 1-1203, National Archives and Records Administration, College Park, Maryland.

Twelfth Census of the United States, 1900, Population Schedule for Carthage, Marion Township, Jasper County, Missouri, T623, Roll 866.

Thirteenth Census of the United States, 1910, Population Schedule for Carthage, Marion Township, Jasper County, Missouri, T624, Roll 791.

World War I Veterans Surveys, U.S. Army Heritage and Education Center, Carlisle, Pennsylvania.

Index